$\mathcal{F}$amily
Papers

A Rhetoric and Reader for Writers

Family Papers

A Rhetoric and Reader for Writers

Barney Pace
The City University of New York

HarperCollins*CollegePublishers*

For Joanna, Sonia and Gina

■

Acquisitions Editor: Patricia Rossi
Project Coordination, Text and Cover Design: Proof Positive/Farrowlyne
    Associates, Inc.
Cover Photo: *The Cloud,* Jose de Creeft, Collection of WHITNEY MUSEUM OF
    AMERICAN ART, NEW YORK. Photography by Jerry L. Thompson, N.Y.
Production Manager: Kewal Sharma
Compositor: Proof Positive/Farrowlyne Associates, Inc.
Printer and Binder: Malloy Lithographing, Inc.
Cover Printer: Malloy Lithographing, Inc.

For permission to use copyrighted material, grateful acknowledgment is made to the
copyright holders on pp. 515–520, which are hereby made part of this copyright page.

Family Papers: A Rhetoric and Reader for Writers, First Edition
Copyright ©1994 by HarperCollins College Publishers

Library of Congress Cataloging-in-Publication Data
Pace, Barney.
    Family papers: a rhetoric and reader for writers / Barney Pace.
        p.   cm.
    Includes index.
    ISBN 0-06-501222-4 (student edition) — ISBN 0-06-501223-2 (instructor's edition)
    1. English language—Rhetoric.   2. Family—Problems, exercises, etc.
 3. Readers—Family.   4. College readers.   I. Title
 PE1408.P23   1993
 808'.0427—dc20   93-20911
                                                                    CIP

93 94 95 96   9 8 7 6 5 4 3 2 1

$\mathcal{B}$rief Table of Contents

■

*T*able of Contents

■

Chapter 2 ■ Family Portraits   69

Chapter 3 ■ Families Plural: Culture and Family   132

Chapter 4 ■ The Family, Past Tense   210

Chapter 5 ■ Today's Families   288

Chapter 6 ■ The Family and Politics   359

Preface

■

Family Papers is a complete habitat for student writers.

It contains instruction in every aspect of essay writing, many opportunities for formal and informal practice, and the work of writers from quite a few cultures, eras, fields, and types of publications. Their ideas and insights are illuminating and provocative, and their techniques are well worth studying.

The book's organizing theme, the family, is engaging and controversial, and it's broad enough to hold the attention of even the most advanced writing class for a semester. The most fundamental institution of every society, the family, shares a border with politics, ethics, culture, and economics. It's a compass point and a persistent concern in many different kinds of writing. It's in the paper every day. It's in fiction, film, plays, biographies, and autobiographies. It's in the work of sociologists, anthropologists, historians, and other social scientists who spend millions of words a year studying family problems, patterns, and changes. It's on the tongues of politicians, in the sermons of the clergy, in legal briefs and judicial decisions, and on everyone's mind from time to time. Everyone has questions about it and opinions about what's good for it. Everyone has a stake in it; everyone has something to say about it, which makes it a rich source of topics for people who want to become better writers.

The book's readings—its essays, poems, and short stories—and its documents and photographs are grouped in chapters, each of which has its own distinct focus. Chapter 1 is family narratives; Chapter 2, family portraits; Chapter 3, cultural studies; Chapter 4, historical studies; Chapter 5, contemporary trends and problems; Chapter 6, politics and social policy; and Chapter 7, families in short fiction. I also made an effort to include writers who have written for various kinds of publications to raise considerations of audience and purpose and to introduce students to a wide array of conventions—academic, journalistic, and literary.

Each chapter is somewhat self-contained, yet at the same time, each contributes in a cumulative way to the book's design, the point of which is to equip students with a growing fund of ideas, theories, anecdotes, arguments, discussions, and writing experience that they can draw on as they write.

People who write for a living or who write often in the course of their jobs know what they're writing about or learn something about it in the process of getting ready to write. The book's thematic design is an attempt to replicate the situation of a working writer.

Most of the selections are well written; the remainder, like Jonathan Swift's "A Modest Proposal" and Joyce Carol Oates's "Four Summers," are brilliantly written. In other words, there are writing lessons implicit in all of them; I tried to flush those lessons out into the open through the questions that follow each selection and through the discussions of technique in each chapter's "Writing Workshop." Development, proof, patterns of organization, style, metaphor, and tone make up a partial list of the issues a student will encounter. Diction receives attention in two ways. A "Words to Note" section follows each reading. It is simply a list of the reading's key and resonant words and phrases. My hope is that looking at these words a second time will encourage students to remember them and to look up the ones they're not sure of in a dictionary. There is also a word essay in each chapter, called "Word Play," in which I spend a few pages brooding on the origin and evolution of words that are important members of our vocabulary of family. I pay especially close attention to current usage, often comparing a word with its synonyms or cognates in an effort to identify the precise spin we currently put on that word. The point of these essays is that a word is a complicated thing.

The book is ridden with opportunities to write. The discussion and journal topics are rooted in specific readings, documents, or photographs. They furnish simple practice putting words on the page, which everyone who wants to become a better writer must do as much as possible, and the topics are phrased to encourage reflection and critical scrutiny, which should flow, like tributaries, into class discussion and the papers students write.

The paper topics evolve out of each chapter's readings, discussion and journal topics, and the larger questions, themes, approaches, and ideas that hold the chapter together. I have made an effort to mirror the approach most of the writers in any given chapter take in the paper topics; for instance, students are invited to write family portraits in Chapter 2, which is about description, in Chapter 3, the anthropological chapter, students are invited to write a cultural comparison.

Family Papers begins with an introductory chapter, in which I lay out the writing process. I don't believe there is any one best way to write, so instead of blazing the one best path, I describe the strengths and limitations that the various approaches to the different stages of writing possess. Then, in each chapter's "Writing Workshop," I model *a* writing process. In other words, I walk students through one possible approach among many, encouraging students to experiment with various mixes of freewriting, mapping, brainstorming, and outlining until they discover the approach that works best for them. There is also quite a bit of attention paid to revision, an unheralded and strenuous part of the writing process that many inexperienced writers skip or breeze through in five minutes. I attempt to be as specific as possible and urge students to do religiously what professional writers would never dream of not doing—to revise thoroughly.

Family Papers is the result of years of study, teaching, and collaboration with colleagues at the University of Michigan and the City University of New York (CUNY). First, I would thank three of my teachers at Michigan, Cecil Eby, the late Marvin Felheim, and the late David Huntington: each in his own way taught me to look both ways before crossing.

Some of the essays and short stories that appear in this book I worked with under the aegis of a curriculum development project at CUNY, funded by the Ford Foundation. Alison Bernstein, Director of Education and Culture at the Ford Foundation, was generous with her time and encouragement; and the following CUNY colleagues and project members were generous with their insights: Nan Bauer Maglin, John Chaffee, Norah Chase, and Carol Groneman, among others. Zelda Gamson, Director of the Center for the Study of Teaching at the University of Massachusetts at Boston, evaluated the project and served as its all-purpose fairy godmother. She was also kind enough to comment on an outline of *Family Papers*, as were Roberta Matthews and Ed Quinn of CUNY.

I would also like to thank colleagues from around the country who took the time to review the project and offer valuable suggestions: Professor Irene L. Clark, the University of Southern California; Professor Jinny Marting, the University of Akron; Professor Anita Moss, the University of North Carolina at Charlotte; and Professor Mary Sue Ply, Southeastern Louisiana University.

I am indebted to my agent, Thomas Wallace, for finessing the dollars and sense of this project. Patricia A. Rossi, my editor, and, I suspect, the best in the business, made this a better and more useful book with every suggestion.

In fact, my debt to everyone I have mentioned is so profound that I must share with them credit for the book's flaws as well as its virtues. *Salute.*

—Barney Pace

Family Papers

A Rhetoric and Reader for Writers

Notes on the Family
and the
Writing Process

■

Reading maketh a full man, conference a
ready man, and writing an exact man.
—Francis Bacon, *Essays, Of Studies*

The Family Writ Large

In newspapers, magazines, novels, critical studies, new laws, court decisions, and many other places, Americans expend millions of words a year
reflecting on, arguing about, and trying to change the family. *Family Papers* is
an invitation to spend a few thousand on the subject.

Why the family? Because everyone has something to say about it.
Everyone has one, wants one, or is trying to get away from one; everyone has
a fund of family experiences, beliefs, and feelings to draw on.

In fact, it is hard to think of a topic that is richer in experiences, beliefs,
and feelings. *Family* includes but means so much more than the faces you see
at the dinner table or at weddings and reunions. The topic of family is

charged with politics and economics and is shot through with cultural and social values. It is an avenue of approach to the past and to the future of society. As a subject of study and a topic for writing, the family is broad, complex, and important enough that we will not come close to exhausting it in a single semester.

Also, writers are at an advantage when they write about something they know and care about. Most professional writers specialize in a particular subject or area. The more they read, think, and write about their specialties, the broader their frames of reference become and the more they have to say. Knowledge is not the liability for writers that it is for politicians, especially those of the Teflon persuasion. For these reasons, I am asking you to become a family specialist—for the semester, at least. The range of cultures, ideas, opinions, and experiences you will encounter in these pages will enrich, inform, and sharpen your own ideas and opinions about the family, as well as about culture, politics, the individual, and society. You will agree with some of these writers, disagree with others, and learn from all of them. The dialogue that unfolds between you and this book will furnish you with the material, models, motivation, direction, and practice that you need to become a better writer.

Studying how these writers say what they say will pay off, too. There are lessons in every piece about word choice, phrasing, sentence structure, paragraph development, tone, style, overall patterns of development, and unity. As we go along, I will call attention to some of the techniques these writers use and ask you to experiment with them in your own writing.

My aim is to intertwine lessons in learning to write well with an exploration of the family. I want to give you the practice you need to feel more comfortable putting words on paper, to help you develop a writing process, to teach you to learn from the writers you read, and to familiarize you with techniques and patterns for exploring, organizing, and developing your thoughts and feelings so that you will be prepared for whatever kind of writing you choose to do.

🌿 The Writing Process

The *writing process* encompasses all the steps and stages a writer takes a piece of writing through to produce final copy. As a term, the writing process doesn't mean much to most inexperienced writers because they haven't really developed one yet. In fact, novices often get stuck when they write because they collapse too many stages of the writing process into one and try to do too many things at once. They are simultaneously trying to figure out where their sentences, paragraphs, and essays are going, and as their minds jump from one level to another, they get stymied, distracted, stuck. Writing never becomes easy even for writers who have become very good, but breaking a complicated process down into steps makes it more manageable. We'll take a look at the stages that most practiced writers move through, and we'll take some time in each chapter to experiment with various approaches. The point is to develop your own writing process.

The first rule is there is no first rule. There is no one best way to write. Life would be simpler by one if there were, but people and what they write about vary. Temperament, training, and the material a writer is working with all affect the way writers proceed. Brilliant and dismal results have been produced by writers working in every way imaginable.

Complicating matters further, writing is not simply a matter of copying thoughts out of your head onto the paper. It's a creative, associative process: one word, phrase, or sentence often calls up another, and coverage of one point can illuminate or clarify a related point, which is why writers who have made an honest effort know more about their subjects after they have finished writing.

Furthermore, writing, unlike a scientific experiment, is not simply a step-by-step process. It is recursive: the mind circles back and spirals ahead. Even though experienced writers tend to move in steps or stages, they know to leave themselves open to whatever comes to them as they go along. Phrases and finished sentences come to some writers even before they begin to write a first draft, and new ideas, ways to begin, or ways to express a point come to others as they are proofreading and polishing.

However, even though it's not possible to map out the one best way to write, it is helpful to understand the stages of the writing process: prewriting, writing, revising, editing, and proofreading.

Prewriting.   Prewriting encompasses all the various kinds of work writers do—with and without pens—to get a first draft started: reading, interviewing, thinking, talking, freewriting, brainstorming, mapping, outlining, and journal writing. The order and combination of activities varies with writers, topics, and the writing situation. In fact, the only rule that applies to this stage of the writing process is that it is a good idea to do *something* before you start writing a draft.

Reading about something, which is what many professional writers do, is a good place to start, although some writers like to jot down their own thoughts on a topic before they read anything about it. It's simply a matter of temperament and taste; either way, the point is to flesh out your own thoughts and to learn about your topic. When writers read, of course, they gather material, but more importantly, they sharpen their own perspectives by studying someone else's. Taking notes as you read will strengthen your command of the material and make it easier for you to use it when you write. Writing a short summary or response to each piece that you read will help you to see the larger contours of the issue or topic you're pursuing and may suggest a direction to take when you write.

Discussing what you have read is a good next step. Experienced writers do it in newsrooms, with their editors, or with business associates before writing an article, a report, a memo, or a proposal. Explaining your ideas to someone else is one of the best ways to clarify them to yourself. In the classroom, a small group of students working on the same topic is a productive forum. The shared purpose gives the discussion focus and direction, and the ebb and flow of the conversation can make the challenging task of articulating your ideas easier. Again, it's a good idea to take notes as you go along, and as you take notes, remember that whole sentences are always preferable to words and phrases because they give you more to work with when you start writing.

There are three ways at this point to move towards a first draft: freewriting, brainstorming, and outlining. Some writers favor an *outline.* Whether the outline is written in phrases or sentences, it starts with a main point, thesis statement, or key theme, which is followed by a complete list of the supporting points the writer intends to make, usually organized in the order in which they will be made. Some writers also include supporting detail for each point, some don't. All college writing handbooks contain examples of various outline formats. If you haven't used outlines before and want to try one out, consult a writing handbook first.

Though outlines exude confidence and finality, writers who use them often make changes as they write, switching the order of their paragraphs or adjusting the focus, emphasis, or tone of their main point. Departing from the outline is a sign of wisdom, not indecision, because an outline is only a proposal of what you think you will say; it is not a contract. As many writers have pointed out, it is hard to know what you are going to say before you've said it.

Some people, before outlining or writing, first like to *brainstorm,* which entails jotting down every word and phrase that comes to mind. Don't worry about whether you'll cover every idea you put down or whether every word and phrase has something to do with how you intend to approach the subject or topic. The point is to warm up and to get as much raw material onto the page as possible. Some brainstormers then use this material to put together outlines and begin writing, while others write paragraphs about the words and phrases they like best and work on order and unity later. Regardless of which route you take after brainstorming, the object is to find a pattern and a unifying idea in your collage of stray words and phrases. Whether you draw up an outline or move directly to a first draft, what you have come up with is subject to change.

Finally, some writers prefer to freewrite about their topics first. *Freewriting* means putting pen to page and writing nonstop about your topic, even if it means repeating phrases or sentences. While freewriting, a writer should not even think about spelling, punctuation, grammar, or organization: these considerations can derail a writer's train of thought. Also, the purpose of freewriting is not to produce a piece of writing that someone else can read; it is to stick as closely as possible to your thoughts and to use the associative power of language to explore and develop these thoughts. A word, phrase, or image can evoke another; an experience or an example can suggest or clarify an idea.

Freewriters then sift through what they have written for the ideas and phrases they like best and begin the process of developing and translating what only they can understand into a piece of writing that a reader can appreciate. Like brainstormers, some freewriters outline before they write, while others write and then reorganize and work on unity and development.

Journal writing is a rich complement to all of the approaches I have spelled out. A journal can be a simple, undirected, private diary that a student writes in on a regular basis for the sake of practice. Practice is crucial whenever one is learning to do something, whether it's dance, sports, music, or writing. There's no substitute for time in the studio, at the keyboard, on the field, or at the page, typewriter, or computer. It's not that the ideas of a writing class are difficult to grasp, but it is one of the few performance courses most American college students take, if not the only one.

Journals were a rarity on American campuses until the late 1970s and early 1980s. Students in creative writing classes or psychology seminars sometimes kept them, but for most American students, journals were something that professional writers like Virginia Woolf kept. Then came Peter Elbow's *Writing Without Teachers* (which ironically was read mainly by teachers and people who were becoming teachers), Mina Shaughnessy's *Errors and Expectations,* and a number of other books that taught the writing profession a simple but far-reaching lesson: we can help students with the writing process itself, as well as the product of that process—the papers we comment on, correct, and grade. Since then, brainstorming, freewriting, multiple drafts of a paper, peer editing, and journal writing have become standard fare in composition classes. Most writing instructors ask their students to keep some type of journal even though most of these instructors had no experience with journals as students.

Sometimes writing instructors will ask students to react to the reading they're doing for the course, or to respond to questions, claims, issues, and problems that point in the direction of the next formal writing assignment. Often, when instructors comment on journal entries, they overlook matters of punctuation, grammar, and style. They react instead to what students have said by posing questions, commenting critically, adding ideas, examples, and points, or by encouraging students to explain themselves more fully. Instructors who take this approach tend to believe that journals should be a place for the pursuit of ideas—comma splices and all other capital offenses be hanged.

You will find quite a bit of journal fodder in this book. You can react to the book's photographs, documents, essays, short stories, and poems; a strong reaction, positive or negative, tends to be a productive occasion for a journal entry. Furthermore, there are a number of topics in each chapter; you can write informally in your journal about the topics your instructor doesn't assign.

Journal writing is especially worthwhile if your instructor is asking you to come up with your own topics. Journals can also be a rich source of ideas for formal papers. If you think of an idea you want to pursue, whether your instructor has assigned a journal or whether you are keeping one on your own, ask your instructor if you can write about it. Most writing instructors are receptive to student-created or student-tailored topics. As a profession, we believe in independent thought, and most of us are willing to pay more than lip service to that belief.

If you are an inexperienced writer or someone who has not done much writing recently, try experimenting with all these approaches. If you tend to get stuck when you write, try freewriting; it may enable you to circumvent the worries and difficulties that trip you up. There is no one best approach; each is as good as the others. The object is to tailor an approach that suits your temperament and work habits. Remember, the only rule that applies to the prewriting stage of the writing process is that it is a very good idea to do something before you begin your first draft.

There is quite a bit of prewriting built into this book. The readings in each chapter are related to the chapter's paper topics, and the journal and discussion questions are designed to help you engage these topics. For that matter, the various perspectives on the family featured in each chapter—from cultural to historical to sociological to political—complement one another and will have a cumulative effect on your understanding of the book's overall topic of the family. Finally, in the writing workshop sections of each chapter, I have mapped out a variety of prewriting routes to encourage you to try out different approaches. The best way to use this introduction is to read it before you write your first paper, read it again after your instructor returns the first paper, and review it toward the middle of the term.

Writing a First Draft.

Look at the topic you were assigned or thought of, study your notes and outline, brainstorming, or freewriting, and go to work. If it's a fairly short paper, between 300 and 700 words, try to write the whole paper in one sitting. Don't worry about word choice, spelling, grammar, or phrasing at this point. Just put a check or some other mark next to words, phrases, and sentences that need work. Pausing to look things up or to worry about them derails your train of thought, which, un-derailed, will carry you through to the end of the draft. The point when writing a first draft is to get black on white. There will be time later to elaborate, correct, rearrange, change words, tighten, and rephrase.

Of course, some writers are temperamentally incapable of going on until they are satisfied with each sentence and then each paragraph. The prevailing wisdom, which is accurate in this case, is that you make the job harder if you work this way. People who suffer from varying degrees of writer's block often work this way. If I have just described the way you work, writer's block and all, it's a good idea to push yourself to write a complete draft before thinking about revising, especially if the writer's block is so bad that writing is torturous. But if you revise as you go and can work without stalling, keep it up. However, it is still important to study the coverage of rewriting in the next section because all writers must attend to the same concerns regardless of how they write or when they revise.

If you get stuck, going back a paragraph or even to the beginning of the essay and reading aloud is a good way to reimmerse yourself in your thoughts. If you get lost, look at your notes, reread your preceding paragraph, and start again.

As for the contours of the essay, there are too many types of essays and too many ways to write them to provide blueprints here. For now, I will simply say that every writer who has ever written has put the subject on the page, gone into it in some detail, and broken away at the end, providing a summary or some sense of closure while giving the reader something to think about, something to take home.

Rewriting.   After completing a first draft, you have reason to breathe a sigh of relief but not to quit. Professional writers wouldn't think of submitting their first drafts, and neither should you. Why? Because you can always make your work better if you let it sit for a while (at least a day) and then rewrite.

One of the paradoxes of writing is the better you get, the more you will revise. Inexperienced writers tend to feel bound by or limited to their first drafts as if their words set like concrete. As writers become more and more practiced, their standards go up, and through experience they learn more ways to make their writing better. The balance you must learn to strike when revising is between perfecting what is on the page and leaving yourself open to the new ideas, insights, examples, details, sentences, phrasing, and words that come to writers when they rewrite.

Furthermore, it's important to remember that writing isn't just an act of expression; it's also an act of communication. The reader doesn't know what you mean until you say it. You need to put your topic on the page; you need to state your ideas clearly and explain them, fleshing them out and backing them up sometimes with examples, descriptions, statistics, ideas, and quotations from authorities on the subject or whatever other kind of material or evidence you have at your disposal.

Rewriting can be divided into three overlapping concerns: revising, editing, and proofreading. It is best to revise first and then edit and proofread what you have revised, although there is nothing especially sacred about that particular order. It is, however, important to be systematic and thorough; in other words, it is important to study and work on development and sentence and paragraph order throughout the entire draft, to look at and rework phrasing and word choice throughout the entire draft, and to check grammar and punctuation throughout the entire draft. If you don't tend to put much time into rewriting, it's a good idea to try the sequence I map out in the following pages.

Revising.   Get out your first draft and some extra paper. Tell everyone to go away. Then, read the introduction, the first sentence of each paragraph, and the conclusion. This will enable you to see the larger lines of your paper. If you get ideas about reorganizing your paragraphs or about what you left out, make a note, but don't rewrite yet. Next, reread the entire paper. Don't let minor matters get in the way of the big picture. Simply put a check next to words and phrases you want to work on later. For now, concentrate on paragraph development, organization, and order.

Sometimes writers discover that they have taken a second pass at the same topic, repeating themselves in the process, or that they have run a few topics together into one paragraph. The solution is fairly simple: reorganize and, if necessary, cut. After reorganization, it often becomes apparent that further development is needed.

Writers may also find that passages and even whole paragraphs are unnecessary. If it takes you a few paragraphs to get to the point of a short essay, one or two of those paragraphs may be dispensable. Writers frequently build scaffolding that serves a purpose during composition but none at all for readers.

Conversely, writers sometimes find they have included everything but the most important point, example, detail, or episode. It is easier to see what you have and haven't said after you've said it, so it makes sense that writers often realize their omissions when they reach this stage of the writing process. The first draft is a platform, a reviewing stand. Leave yourself open to what you see when you get there.

If you discover the ground shifted as you wrote—the tone growing sharper or milder, or your emphasis changing—decide which tone or emphasis best represents your point of view and revise. Comparing and contrasting the beginning and end is the surest way to detect shifts, and it is those parts of the essay that will need the most attention as you revise.

If you are unsure of the order you have come up with, cut and paste and experiment with different schemes. Consulting your notes and rereading the first sentence of each paragraph will help you to gain the perspective you need to reorganize a paper. Writers, especially inexperienced ones, often order their paragraphs as they thought of them, which may or may not be effective. Again, the reader's needs must be considered. Are there points that provide a context or background for others, and should they go first? Is the organization as effective as it could be? Writers often save their most important points for last, especially when they are trying to persuade.

Now review the introduction. Most writers have to rewrite their introductions since they usually know more about their topics when they finish than they did when they began. Make a list of the main points or themes you cover throughout the paper and check to see that your introduction really introduces them. It should pull them together in a thesis statement, unifying theme, or central problem. You may also wish to compare the introduction with the conclusion since they are both paragraphs that provide overviews and pull the points of the paper together. If you find that you have changed your emphasis in the conclusion, decide which is correct and rewrite accordingly. If you find that your conclusion is simply fuller, borrow from it to build up the introduction. Remember, an introduction should not simply be a record of your first encounter with the topic; it should be a way into your essay. It should orient your readers, giving them a clear idea of the point of the paper and a sense of direction, of the ground you will cover in pursuit of your point. Introductions are not necessarily long, but most of the introductory paragraphs or sections that follow are substantial.

Now you are ready to work on the middle paragraphs. Check to see that the point or idea of each paragraph is clear and well explained. How much is enough? How much is too much? Is it clear? You will need to think about your reader to make those judgments. Don't write up or down to your reader. Your paper isn't a conversation in the cafeteria or a proclamation at the court of King Louis XIV, nor is it a letter to a good friend who knows all about you. Think of your reader as a peer you want to say something to in a fairly formal way. Don't assume your reader knows what you mean until you say it and explain it. If you use an example, make sure that the point of the example is clear and that it really supports the topic of the paragraph. If your example is an anecdote, ask yourself if you have included only as much of the story as you need to illustrate your point. A story is a seductive thing and can easily sidetrack a writer.

Finally, check to see that your transitional words, phrases, and sentences work. Well-worded transitions connect ideas or events and remind the reader of the essay's direction and main point. Transitions are too valuable a resource to be overlooked.

The introduction, transitions, and conclusion hold an essay together and give it a sense of direction and some of its power. Give them the time they deserve.

Editing.   Mies van der Rohe, a twentieth-century architect who designed skyscrapers, once remarked, "God resides in the details." Now it's time for the details, which in writing means word choice and phrasing. In other words, it is time to work on style, about which Mark Twain astutely observed a century ago: "Style is just a matter of getting the right words in the right places."

Read your draft aloud and mark words, phrases, and sentences that don't sound right. Many people find it helpful to read aloud to someone else; having an audience inspires closer scrutiny. Also, you have the benefit of any comments or suggestions the listener makes.

Rephrase awkward phrases and sentences until your ear is satisfied. If you turn up a cliché, end the relationship immediately. Look up words you are not sure of in a good collegiate dictionary, one with synonyms, antonyms, and secondary meanings. You may wish to resort to a thesaurus if you decide you have the wrong word and can't think of the right one. Is the word you have chosen too informal? Too formal? Is it true to the tone of the essay? Can you hear your voice—the voice you have created on the page—in the word? If not, find one that is more apt. Plug each candidate into the sentence, read it aloud, and choose the best fit.

"The difference between the right word and the almost right word is the difference between lightning and a lightning bug." That's Twain again, and again he's on target. Finding the right word is always worth the trouble. If you never change words, you are the most brilliant writer ever to have written, or you are being lazy about word choice.

Word work follows every reading in this book. There is a "Words to Note" section that highlights words and phrases that are a little unusual and especially well used. If you aren't sure of the meaning and feel of any of these words and didn't look it up when you first encountered it, this section will remind you to do so. There are also questions about word choice and levels of usage, intended to direct your attention to the minutia of good writing, which is where the good comes from. The writers know their craft and can teach you quite a bit by example. You can expand and sharpen your own vocabulary by paying close attention to theirs.

Proofreading.   Get your dictionary and your handbook and proofread. Look up the spelling of every word you aren't sure of. In fact, the best way to check for spelling errors is to read your draft backwards. That way, you won't skim over phrases and sentences that you almost know by heart by this point. Instead, you will look at each word as a word.

If you are working on a computer and your word processing program has a good spell-checker, use it, but a spell-checker is no substitute for a good dictionary. You will still need to use a dictionary for help with nuance of meaning and level of usage.

However, if your program has a grammar-checker, don't use it. Grammar-checkers inspire a false sense of confidence, and because they are not capable of considering matters of style, they're inadequate. As you probably know, computers can't consider anything because they can't think. They just do what you and the people who wrote the program you're using tell them to do. Buy one if you can afford it or work on the computers your school makes available. I'm working on one right now. A computer is a good tool, no more, no less. It makes it easier to run off drafts of your work and to experiment with different plans of organization. A computer can also make it easier to revise and polish, but, of course, it won't do those things for you. It will save you time and trouble—that's all. You will still have to exert yourself as much as someone working with a ten-cent pencil if you want your writing to be good.

Next, check the grammar. Pay especially close attention to constructions you tend to have trouble with, checking a handbook if you're not sure of the principle. Some students have chronic problems with participial phrases, others with pronoun agreement, and so on. As the semester progresses, develop a checklist of your weak points. It is more likely that you will catch an error if you are aware of your weaknesses. Eventually, you will become so aware of the problem and so clear on the principle that it will disappear from your writing.

Now, type or rewrite your paper. Check with your instructor about the format, if it hasn't been specified. Most instructors ask students to double-space so there is room between the lines for comments, rephrasing, suggestions, and corrections, but margin requirements vary. If better words and phrasing come to you as you type or rewrite, take them. Again, writing is a recursive process. There is never a wrong time for a good idea, a resonant word, or a tighter phrase. After you finish, proofread the final draft against the original to check for copying errors and kiss it good-bye.

Regardless of the approach you settle on, at some point in your writing process you must be open to the thinking, exploring, pursuing, and associating that putting words, sentences, and paragraphs together entails; and at some point, you must concentrate on sentence and paragraph order, connection, unity, phrasing, grammar, punctuation, and polish.

Chapter 1

ℱamily Stories

∰ Introduction to the Family

The family is on people's minds these days. Preachers, politicians, filmmakers, talk-show hosts and guests, reporters, scholars, feminists, and government officials are busy talking, writing, broadcasting, and arguing about how the family is doing and what it needs to survive.

The news is full of reports of single-parent families, two-career couples, super-moms, surrogate mothers, high divorce rates, high marriage rates, child abuse, and domestic violence, just to name a few of the family issues we hear about daily. Newscasters chronicle the problems and challenges that confront the family on the nightly news, special reports delve into this or that problem, and commentators try to convince us (and themselves) that they know what it all means. "Is the family dying?" American journalists ask us. Some say yes, some say no, some say it's too early to tell, but maybe.

Hollywood has filled the big screen and our TV tubes with dramas, sitcoms, and docudramas about the family. "Roseanne, "thirtysomething," "I'll Fly Away," "Sisters," "Homefront," and "Brooklyn Bridge" are not just shows with families in them; they are about family predicaments and family values. Though many still believe that Father knows best and that the nuclear family with a stay-at-home mom is the only healthy form of family, the single-parent family has been increasingly in front of our faces over the past decade in shows like "Kate and Allie" and "L.A. Law" and in films like *Kramer vs. Kramer* and *Men Don't Leave.* Through the miracle of reruns, even Archie Bunker becomes a single "mother" about once a year, after his wife Edith dies.

The Black family has also gained a greater TV and Hollywood presence over the last ten years. "Good Times" was popular in the 1970s, and "The Cosby Show" commanded top ratings throughout the last half of the 1980s and has found a secure and prominent place for itself in rerun heaven. "Roc" and "Fresh Prince of Bel Air" are popular today. Alice Walker's *The Color Purple* and Richard Wright's *Native Son,* two major works of Black American fiction, have been made into movies that dramatize powerful family strife. There have also been *Mo' Better Blues, Boyz N the Hood,* and *Malcolm X,* to name a few films that feature Black families. Though some critics continue to be unhappy with how the Black family is portrayed, it is being portrayed more frequently.

Finally, a recent spate of shows, movies, and documentaries have explored family crises that had previously been off limits, at least on prime-time TV. Programs like "The Burning Bed" and "Baby M" air problems that are ripping some American families to pieces.

Family crisis dramas, which strive to change attitudes or to get people involved, find an audience that is increasingly receptive because feminists and conservatives have been politicizing the family for the last fifteen years. In 1992, in fact, presidential and vice-presidential candidates competed with one another to see who could chalk up the most sound bites containing the phrase "family values." The family has become a political football, not for the first time, historians tell us.

Though most Americans associate the Women's Movement with agitation for political and economic equality, feminists have also been working on a cluster of family issues, ranging from a national child-care program and reform of the alimony and child-support payment systems to domestic violence, a pro-choice stance on abortion, and guaranteed maternity leaves. Feminists have built shelters for victims of domestic violence, organized rallies to support *Roe v. Wade* (the Supreme Court decision that guarantees a woman's right to have an abortion), elected feminists to political office at almost all levels, and lobbied locally and nationally in support of women's issues. Running throughout the best political, social, and written work on the Women's Movement is a clear sense of the connections between family and work for women. For instance, feminist critics have recently pointed out that since men still earn more than women, since women usually take care of the children after a divorce, and since men don't pay much of the alimony and child support the courts award, women and their dependents are the fastest growing group below the poverty line. They have named this trend "the feminization of poverty." In essence, quite a few feminists argue that social policy and economic arrangements are out of sync with reality and that those to the right of center, who are the strident defenders of the status quo in American politics today, are responsible for much of the suffering families must endure.

Conservatives, on the other hand, believe that reformers, particularly feminist reformers, and government intervention are at the root of the family's troubles. The Reverend Jerry Falwell has been preaching for years that the goals and attitudes of feminists amount to nothing less than an assault on the traditional family, which is the pillar of American society. George Gilder, once an advisor to the Reagan administration and an economist at the conservative Heritage Foundation, reaches the same conclusion in his book *Progress and Poverty*. He believes there is no worker more productive than a man with a wife and children to support. Insofar as the Women's Movement has undermined that "traditional" arrangement, he argues it is responsible for the destruction of many families and for the slipping of the U.S. economy. His ally, former vice-president Dan Quayle, has identified the culprit: the TV character Murphy Brown. Quayle complained that she undermined the importance of fathers and hence the integrity of the family when she had a child out of wedlock as if it were, in his words, "just another life-style choice." If the family is dying, conservatives warn, departing from tradition is killing it.

The family is, however, very much alive in recent American scholarship. Particularly in the social sciences, the study of family has grown in stature over the last generation and is widely regarded as one of the keys to understanding individuals, society, and culture. Anthropologists have demonstrated the way in which culture informs family structures and family values. Social historians have studied the organizing role family has played in the lives of Americans, especially women, the majority of whom have always worked for wages as well as for their families; they have also attempted to measure the impact of the rise of the city and the factory on the family. Sociologists have tended to concentrate on the intersections between the contemporary family and other major social institutions, such as schools, workplaces, and the welfare state.

On the practical level of social policy, judges, lawmakers, and government administrators interpret the family daily, whether they are acting on individual cases at welfare offices or family courts, or enacting legislation at the local, state, or federal level. Sometimes the decisions of family policymakers have been influenced by the works of scholars; sometimes, influence works the other way around. Either way, it is important to scrutinize the connections between scholarship and social policy because the way a problem is analyzed and defined determines how a society will try to solve it.

Arlene and Jerome Skolnick, two prominent sociologists of the family, say that we worry too much about the family, in part, because we have romanticized what the family was like in the past. Working mothers and single-parent families are not new; unfortunately, domestic violence and child abuse are not new either. The family has changed and is changing, but those features and problems have been with us for a while. However, the Skolnicks add that Americans have always worried about the state of the family. If worrying is an indication of how important something is to us, we Americans are family-minded people.

🎴 Word Play: *Family*

In the twentieth century, throughout the English-speaking, industrialized West, the word *family* means the heterosexual, *nuclear* family: Mom, Dad, and the kids. We identify most other types of families by adding modifiers to *family.* We add *extended* when we mean more than just two generations, often living in more than just one household. *Single-parent family* is a near Victorian euphemism that is used to describe a woman who has children without any intention of marrying and who raises the children alone or with the help of a mother, grandmother, or other relative. When American journalists use the expression, many mean a family started by a Black, inner-city teenager who was trying to fill a nameless void in her life with a baby, whether she was or not. *Broken family,* of course, means a family that has been reordered through the legal process of divorce. Its use as a critical term that has the sting of disapproval has faded as divorce has become more widespread, but it is still popular with conservatives who believe that most of society's problems have spun from the downfall of the traditional family. The expression *second family* is in itself neutral, but it is almost always used to describe the second nuclear family of a divorced man who isn't raising the children of his first marriage. There are also *gay families* and *lesbian families,* which have recently been included in the New York City Board of Education's "Children of the Rainbow" curriculum. The furor that former Chancellor Joseph Fernandez encountered when he unveiled this new curriculum in the fall of 1992 demonstrates just how important heterosexuality is to the dominant view of family.

The word *family* (meaning nuclear family) is at the center of the language we use to identify the different types of families; it is also often used as the norm by which other forms of families are found to be deficient, deviant, or less important. At this point in time, *family* has strong moral overtones to it; politicians conjure with it at election time. It is much more loaded, much more evocative than its synonyms *kin* and *relatives,* but *family* has not always been this loaded in just this way.

The English word *family* is a descendant of the Latin word *familia,* which means "a household of slaves, a household." It is possible that the word came to English through an intermediary Romance language. French was the language of the court in England from 1066 through the time of Chaucer in the late fourteenth century. The French word *famille* means "household, fami-ly." The Italian word, *famiglia*, means "family, community." The point is there is no insistence on the nuclear family in any of the possible sources of *family*, and in all three instances, *family's* ancestors imply a place, not just social relationships between parents and children.

For that matter, there is no universal essence that our word *family* might have described. In the West, *family* has taken different forms throughout his-tory: Before the rise of industry and cities, families with many children, some of them into their adult years, living and working in and around the family's dwelling, were much more common because of patterns of land ownership and land-use. Throughout the rest of the world, the predominant family of other cultures has taken different forms. Before European colonization in what is now Nigeria, the prosperous families of the Ibo tribe were polygamous. Each wife and her children had her own house within a walled compound that also contained the husband and father's house. The family owned and worked land jointly. Yams were the staple crop. The family grew and gath-ered other fruits and vegetables, and animals were herded and hunted for meat. The Ibo family was another world.

In other words, *family* did not come to the English language pre-loaded, not as we know it. It is loaded because history—with its shifts, dislocations, social changes, reform movements, and struggles over laws, social norms, and meaning—loaded it. Put more generally, the denotation (the explicit meaning) and the connotation (the aura, feel, or sense) of a word may change, gradually or abruptly, infinitesimally or radically, because words are the property, tools, and weapons of human beings who never stay still for long.

Journal Entry

How have people around you—parents, teachers, religious leaders, and others—used *family* as you grew up and today? What does the word mean to you? Have you or anyone you know well been cut by any of the world's sharp edges?

$\mathcal{R}$eadings

My Mother Never Worked

—Donna Smith-Yackel

Donna Smith-Yackel is a freelance journalist who has chiefly written about women's issues. "My Mother Never Worked," which first appeared in a feminist magazine called *Women: A Journal of Liberation,* is a personal reflection on her mother's life and one of the ways in which American values and social policy devalued her life and work.

"Social Security Office." (The voice answering the telephone sounds very 1 self-assured.)

"I'm calling about . . . I . . . my mother just died . . . I was told to call you and 2 see about a . . . death-benefit check, I think they call it. . . ."

"I see. Was your mother on Social Security? How old was she?" 3

"Yes . . . she was seventy-eight. . . ." 4

"Do you know her number?" 5

"No . . . I, ah . . . don't you have a record? 6

"Certainly. I'll look it up. Her name?" 7

"Smith. Martha Smith. Or maybe she used Martha Ruth Smith. . . . Sometimes 8 she used her maiden name . . . Martha Jerabek Smith."

"If you'd care to hold on, I'll check our records—it'll be a few minutes." 9

"Yes. . . ." 10

Her love letters—to and from Daddy—were in an old box, tied with ribbons 11 and stiff, rigid-with-age leather thongs: 1918 through 1920; hers written on stationery from the general store she had worked in full-time and managed, single-handed, after her graduation from high school in 1913; and his, at first, on YMCA or Soldiers and Sailors Club stationery dispensed to the fighting men of World War I. He wooed her thoroughly and persistently by mail, and though she reciprocated all his feeling for her, she dreaded marriage. . . .

"It's so hard for me to decide when to have my wedding day—that's all I've 12 thought about these last two days. I have told you dozens of times that I won't be afraid of married life, but when it comes down to setting the date and then picturing myself a married woman with half a dozen or more kids to look after, it just makes me sick. . . . I am weeping right now—I hope that some day I can look back and say how foolish I was to dread it all."

They married in February, 1921, and began farming. Their first baby, a daugh- 13 ter, was born in January, 1922, when my mother was 26 years old. The second baby, a son, was born in March, 1923. They were renting farms; my father, besides working his own fields, also was a hired man for two other farmers. They had no capital initially, and had to gain it slowly, working from dawn until midnight every day. My town-bred mother learned to set hens and raise chickens, feed pigs, milk cows, plant and harvest a garden, and can every fruit and vegetable she could scrounge. She carried water nearly a quarter of a mile from the well to fill her wash boilers in order to do her laundry on a scrub board. She learned to shuck grain, feed threshers, shock and husk corn, feed corn pickers. In September, 1925, the third baby came, and in June, 1927, the fourth child—both daughters. In 1930, my parents had enough money to buy their own farm, and that March they moved all their livestock and belongings themselves, 55 miles over rutted, muddy woods.

In the summer of 1930 my mother and her two eldest children reclaimed a 40- 14 acre field from Canadian thistles, by chopping them all out with a hoe. In the other fields, when the oats and flax began to head out, the green and blue of the crops were hidden by the bright yellow of wild mustard. My mother walked the fields day after day, pulling each mustard plant. She raised a new flock of baby chicks— 500—and she spaded up, planted, hoed, and harvested a half-acre garden.

During the next spring their hogs caught cholera and died. No cash that fall.   15

And in the next year the drought hit. My mother and father trudged from the 16 well to the chickens, the well to the calf pasture, the well to the barn, and from the well to the garden. The sun came out hot and bright, endlessly, day after day. The crops shriveled and died. They harvested half the corn, and ground the other half, stalks and all, and fed it to the cattle as fodder. With the price at four cents a bushel for the harvested crop, they couldn't afford to haul it into town. They burned it in the furnace for fuel that winter.

In 1934, in February, when the dust was still so thick in the Minnesota air that 17 my parents couldn't always see from the house to the barn, their fifth child—a fourth daughter—was born. My father hunted rabbits daily, and my mother stewed them, fried them, canned them, and wished out loud that she could taste hamburger once more. In the fall the shotgun brought prairie chickens, ducks, pheasant, and grouse. My mother plucked each bird, carefully reserving the breast feathers for pillows.

In the winter she sewed night after night, endlessly, begging cast-off clothing 18 from relatives, ripping apart coats, dresses, blouses, and trousers to remake them to fit her four daughters and son. Every morning and every evening she milked cows, fed pigs and calves, cared for chickens, picked eggs, cooked meals, washed dishes, scrubbed floors, and tended and loved her children. In the spring she planted a garden once more, dragging pails of water to nourish and sustain the vegetables for the family. In 1936 she lost a baby in her sixth month.

In 1937 her fifth daughter was born. She was 42 years old. In 1939 a second 19
son, and in 1941 her eighth child—and third son.

But the war had come, and prosperity of a sort. The herd of cattle had grown 20
to 30 head; she still milked morning and evening. Her garden was more than a half
acre—the rains had come, and by now the Rural Electricity Administration and
indoor plumbing. Still she sewed—dresses and jackets for the children, housedresses and aprons for herself, weekly patching of jeans, overalls, and denim shirts. She
still made pillows, using the feathers she had plucked, and quilts every year—intricate patterns as well as patchwork, stitched as well as tied—all necessary bedding
for her family. Every scrap of cloth too small to be used in quilts was carefully
saved and painstakingly sewed together in strips to make rugs. She still went out in
the fields to help with the haying whenever there was a threat of rain.

In 1959 my mother's last child graduated from high school. A year later the 21
cows were sold. She still raised chickens and ducks, plucked feathers, made pillows, baked her own bread, and every year made a new quilt—now for a married
child or for a grandchild. And her garden, that huge, undying symbol of sustenance,
was as large and cared for as in all the years before. The canning, and now freezing,
continued.

In 1969, on a June afternoon, mother and father started out for town so that 22
she could buy sugar to make rhubarb jam for a daughter who lived in Texas. The
car crashed into a ditch. She was paralyzed from the waist down.

In 1970, her husband, my father, died. My mother struggled to regain some 23
competence and dignity and order in her life. At the rehabilitation institute, where
they gave her physical therapy and trained her to live usefully in a wheelchair, the
therapist told me: "She did fifteen pushups today—fifteen! She's almost seventy-
five years old! I've never known a woman so strong!"

From her wheelchair she canned pickles, baked bread, ironed clothes, wrote 24
dozens of letters weekly to her friends and her "half dozen or more kids," and made
three patchwork housecoats and one quilt. She made balls and balls of carpet
rags—enough for five rugs. And kept all her love letters.

"I think I've found your mother's records—Martha Ruth Smith; married to 25
Ben F. Smith?"

"Yes, that's right."   26

"Well, I see that she was getting a widow's pension. . . ."   27

"Yes, that's right."   28

"Well, your mother isn't entitled to our $255 death benefit."   29

"Not entitled! But why?"   30

The voice on the telephone explains patiently: 31

"Well, you see—your mother never worked."   32

■ *Questions for . . .* **My Mother Never Worked** by Donna Smith-Yackel

Words to Note

self-assured	thongs	dispensed
wooed	reciprocated	dreaded
scrounge	shock	thistles
flax	spaded	hoed
trudged	shriveled	nourish
sustain	scrubbed	plucked
competence	dignity	

Language

1. Compare *scrounge,* which appears in paragraph 10, with *gather, collect,* and *scrape together.* Look them up in a collegiate dictionary. Now, look at *scrounge* in context. Is it the best choice? Why or why not?
2. Smith-Yackel nonchalantly tosses off *threshed, shucked,* and other words that are part of a farm vocabulary but aren't widely used these days. When can a writer use special language and technical terms?

Style

1. What is the tone of the essay's title? When do you know?
2. Smith-Yackel uses many powerful and vivid verbs to describe the work her mother did. What tone do those verbs convey?

Development and Organization

1. Why does Smith-Yackel sandwich the story of her mother's life into the story of her phone call to the Social Security office? Why not the call first, then her mother's story?
2. Why does she survey her mother's life at a gallop? Why doesn't she dramatize key episodes for the reader?

Discussion and Journal Writing

1. What did Smith-Yackel's mother do for a living? What kinds of work did her job entail?
2. Who supported the children?
3. Why does the clerk at the Social Security office tell her that her mother never worked? What larger point is Smith-Yackel making about the work women do in America?

○○○○○

1500 Slave Descendants at Carolina 'Reunion'

—New York Times

Since there is no by-line for this piece, I have no choice but to regard the *New York Times* as its author. The *Times* was born in New York City in the 1850s to German Jewish immigrants named Salzberger and came of age in the twentieth century as a voice of moderate Northern liberalism. In addition to reporting all the news that's fit to print, the *Times* has long taken an interest in race relations and family stories, and the following piece is both. They also pride themselves in their ability to spot trends on the American horizon; to my knowledge, this pride is an article of belief, not fact.

CRESWELL, N.C., Aug. 30—On the same cypress-shaded plantation where his ancestors arrived in chains 200 summers ago, 80-year-old John Thomas Baum cleared his throat under his white straw hat today and recited the slavery story he had heard as a child. [1]

"He had to run from his master every time he went out," Mr. Baum said of his grandfather's efforts to court the girl he married. [2]

"His master had a big dog that he'd go out and sic on him," the retired farmer suddenly added, straining to remember through the mists of the past. [3]

Mr. Baum, who was born here in Creswell, revived such memories at the elegant site where they began—Somerset Place, once North Carolina's second-largest plantation, now a state park, and today the scene of an extraordinary "family reunion" of hundreds of descendants of 21 slave families who worked the vast rice and corn estate from 1786 through the Emancipation. [4]

Among them today were Clarence Blount, the Democratic leader of the Maryland Senate, and William E. Honeyblue, the Mayor pro tem of Williamston, N.C. There were lawyers and doctors, soldiers and teachers. There were farmers, like Mr. Baum. [5]

Also at Somerset Place today were Josiah Collins 6th, a descendant of the plantation's founder; Alex Haley, the "Roots" author whose slave history inspired the effort that led to today's gathering, and Gov. James G. Martin, who said in a speech that the event focused attention on the descendants themselves, not the slavery and segregation they had suffered. [6]

In 1986, many of those descendants still bear the names their ancestors took from their first owners: Littlejohn, Baum, Collins, Blount, Cabarrus, Palin, Phelps, Reavis. So, first and foremost, today's remarkable gathering provided a rare opportunity to track down relatives and roots. [7]

And it happened just steps away from the cream-colored 1830 Greek Revival plantation house that Somerset slaves once served. [8]

Here, under sunny skies, a crowd of 2,000, three-quarters of them descendants 9
of Somerset slaves, picnicked on lawns canopied by swamp chestnut trees,
hummed along with Negro spirituals, and observed the re-enactment of a slave
wedding.

Yet, despite the joyous mood and the lack of actual reminders of slavery at 10
Somerset, where only a wooden marker indicates the site of the slave quarters,
descendants inevitably reflected on their grim common heritage.

"He said they would hang people there," Mr. Baum recalled of his grandfather 11
as he pointed to a row of sycamore trees. "I don't want to talk about it. It gets to
me."

The heritage Mr. Baum shares with the others here today began with a boat- 12
load of 80 African slaves that an Edenton businessman, Josiah Collins, and two
partners imported in June 1768 to their newly purchased 100,000-acre plot in the
Great Alligator Swamp about 50 miles in from the Atlantic and an equal distance
south of Virginia.

Struck down by malaria in the marshes, victims of back-breaking labor in the 13
untamed fields, Somerset slaves "belonged" to the new estate like so much human
chattel.

'A Shared Recognition'

Modern-day descendants, however, second-, third- and fourth-generation free 14
black Americans arriving by busload today from Florida and Maryland, flying in
from as far away as California, were clearly here by choice.

They belonged to Somerset only in terms of the heart, said the homecoming 15
organizer, Dorothy Spruill Redford, in welcoming remarks.

"From this day forward, there will always be a shared recognition," she told 16
the crowd. "They'll think of the Josiah Collins family, but they'll think of my family too." Somerset plantation, she said, "is a living monument to ordinary folks—to
our toil, our lives, our lineage."

It was Mrs. Redford, a 43-year-old social services supervisor in Portsmouth, 17
Va., whose research into her family tree beginning 10 years ago led to today's
event.

Like many descendants, Mrs. Redford, a native of nearby Columbia, N.C., had 18
never known her connection to Somerset Place. It took her five years of record
searches to discover it. Eventually, her odyssey through faded court records and
plantation inventories shook her to her core with the revelation of history's harsh
realities.

"I believed everything I saw on TV" of slave life, Mrs. Redford said in an 19
interview last week. "That people making love were alone. That there were neat little cabins with flowers on tables. It didn't dawn on me that 15 people could live in
a space 18 feet square."

Families Kept Together

Mrs. Redford's eventual tracing of Somerset's 21 slave families sprang from 20
research into her mother's maiden name, Littlejohn. "In searching through property

books in Chowan County, I found the bill of sale selling or transferring 30 Littlejohn slaves to Josiah Collins" in 1826, she said.

Included were her great-great-grandmother, Elsy, and Elsy's first five chil- 21 dren. Somerset had already bought Elsy's husband, Peter.

That was the family-oriented approach Josiah Collins, the sole owner of the 22 5,800-acre plantation after 1803, favored. Hardly able to control a slave population of intermarrying Africans and Americans that rose to 322 by 1862, Collins repudiated the family breakups of other slave owners in favor of a reward system, literacy and freedom of movement.

Those choices were not humanitarian, Mrs. Redford said; they were "manage- 23 ment techniques."

Other descendants today told family stories indicating plantation life as a time 24 of pain for many.

"The saddest story I was ever told," Clara Owens of Williamston said of her 25 grandmother, Morning Dixon, a house slave, "was how her sister Rebecca was sold. She never saw her again."

Willis Phelps of Norfolk said of his great-grandmother Anne Norman: "I 26 remember her saying right from her own lips that they weren't allowed to pray. They had to go out to the woods and hide."

Not All Sad Stories

But today's homecoming was hardly all sad stories. To the background beat of 27 African drums, descendants ate chitterlings and corn pone and forged new ties with kin never before seen. "Today, I feel as if it were Christmas and I were waking up on Christmas morning," said Willis Phelps. "This is the one time in my life I can say where I started from."

To find the people who met here today Mrs. Redford worked forward from the 28 first plantation inventory she found, for 1803, to the 1880 Federal census, cross-checking through 450 death and marriage records. A major stroke of luck was that the Collins family's records had been donated to the state archives.

She learned that Peter and Elsy lived to old age, giving birth to 11 children by 29 1839. She learned the locations of slave cabins and their numbers of occupants. She delved into a lost era of lavish parties and poetry readings held by Josiah 3d and his wife, Mary.

Most of all, Mrs. Redford said, she learned about herself. 30

"I'm the third generation in my family born free and I learned that I wasn't 31 talking about something ancient" in speaking of slavery, she said. "It makes you think of the monumental accomplishments in two generations."

■ *Questions for . . .* 1500 Slave Descendants at Carolina 'Reunion' from the *New York Times*

Words to Note

cypress	elegant	plantation
vast	emancipation	descendant
hummed	grim	chattel
toil	lineage	core
harsh	forged	era
lavish	odyssey	

Language

1. In paragraph 10, the writer says the lawns were "canopied by swamp chestnut trees." What does *canopy* mean? How can swamp chestnut trees canopy a lawn?
2. Is the vocabulary too difficult for a newspaper story?

Style

1. How does the writer use descriptive writing?
2. Many people think journalism is or should be neutral in tone, but that's seldom the case. What is this reporter's attitude toward the reunion? How do you know?

Development and Organization

1. Why does the writer begin with a couple of paragraphs about just one individual, John Thomas Baum?
2. How does the writer use people's family anecdotes?
3. Why does the reporter quote so many people?
4. What function do the subheadings perform?

Discussion and Journal Writing

1. Why is the word *reunion* in quotation marks in the title? What was ordinary and extraordinary about this reunion? Why do families hold reunions?
2. Why was Alex Haley there?
3. How many people attended the reunion? Where did they come from? How do they make their livings?
4. What was on the reunion menu? How was the day choreographed? What kinds of music played? Why, in particular, did the organizers reenact a slave wedding?
5. This article appeared on the front page of the *New York Times*. Why do you think the *Times* decided the reunion was national news?

ooooo

Halfway to Dick and Jane: A Puerto Rican Pilgrimage

—Jack Agueros

Jack Agueros, a graduate of the New York City public schools and of Brooklyn College, is a New York City administrator. A son of Puerto Rican migrants, Agueros grew up in Spanish Harlem before it was known as Spanish Harlem. He spends most of his time in "Halfway to Dick and Jane: A Puerto Rican Pilgrimage" trying to make sense of his dual heritage.

1   I was born in Harlem in 1934. We lived on 111th Street off Fifth Avenue. It was a block of mainly three-story buildings—with brick fronts, or brownstone, or limestone imitations of brownstone. Our apartment was a three-room first-floor walk-up. It faced north and had three windows on the street, none in back. There was a master bedroom, a living room, a kitchen-dining room, a foyer with a short hall, and a bathroom. In the kitchen there was an air shaft to evacuate cooking odors and grease—we converted it to a chimney for Santa Claus.

2   The kitchen was dominated by a large Victorian china closet, and the built-in wall shelves were lined with oilcloth, trimmed with ruffle, both decorated by brilliant and miniature fruits. Prominent on a wall of the kitchen was a large reproduction of a still life, a harvest table full of produce, framed and under glass. From it, I learned to identify apples, pumpkins, bananas, pears, grapes, and melons, and "peaches without worms." A joke between my mother and me. (A peach we had bought in the city market, under the New Haven's elevated tracks, bore, like the trains above, passengers.)

3   On one shelf of the kitchen, over the stove, there was a lineup of ceramic canisters that carried words like "nutmeg," "ginger," and "basil." I did not know what those words meant and I don't know if my mother did either. "Spices," she would say, and that was that. They were of a yellow color that was not unlike the yellow of the stove. The kitchen was itself painted yellow, I think, very pale. But I am sure of one thing, it was not "Mickey Moused." "Mickey Mousing" was a technique used by house painters to decorate the areas of the walls that were contained by wood molding. Outside the molding they might paint a solid green. Inside the wood mold, the same solid green. Then with a twisted-up rag dipped in a lighter green they would trace random patterns.

4   We never used wallpaper or rugs. Our floors were covered with linoleum in every room. My father painted the apartment every year before Christmas, and in addition, he did all the maintenance, doing his own plastering and plumbing. No sooner would we move into an apartment than my father would repair holes or cracks, and if there were bulges in the plaster, he would break them open and redo the area—sometimes a whole wall. He would immediately modify the bathrooms to

add a shower with separate valves, and usually as a routine matter, he cleaned out all the elbow traps, and changed all the washers on faucets. This was true of the other families in the buildings where I lived. Not a December came without a painting of the apartment.

We had Louis XIV furniture in the living room, reflected in the curved glass   5
door and curved glass sides of the china closet. On the walls of the living room hung two prints that I loved. I would spend hours playing games with my mother based on the pictures, making up stories, etc. One day at Brooklyn College, a slide projector slammed, and I awoke after having dozed off during a dull lecture to see Van Gogh's "The Gleaners" on the screen. I almost cried. Another time I came across the other print in a book. A scene of Venice by Canaletto.

The important pieces of the living room, for me, were a Detrola radio with   6
magic-eye tuning and the nightingale, Keero. The nightingale and the radio went back before my recollection. The bird could not stop singing, and people listened on the sidewalk below and came upstairs offering to buy Keero.

The Detrola, shaped like a Gothic arch with inlaid woodwork, was a great   7
source of entertainment for the family. I memorized all the hit songs sung by Libertad Lamarque and Carlos Gardel. Sundays I listened to the Canary Hour presented by Hartz Mountain Seed Company. Puppy, a white Spitz, was my constant companion. Puppy slept at the foot of my bed from the first day he came to our house till the day he died, when I was eleven or twelve and he was seven or eight.

I am an only child. My parents and I always talked about my becoming a doc-   8
tor. The law and politics were not highly regarded in my house. Lawyers, my mother would explain, had to defend people whether they were guilty or not, while politicians, my father would say, were all crooks. A doctor helped everybody, rich and poor, white and black. If I became a doctor, I could study hay fever and find a cure for it, my godmother would say. Also, I could take care of my parents when they were old. I liked the idea of helping, and for nineteen years my sole ambition was to study medicine.

My house had books, not many, but my parents encouraged me to read. As I   9
became a good reader they bought books for me and never refused me money for their purchase. My father once built a bookcase for me. It was an important moment, for I had always believed that my father was not too happy about my being a bookworm. The atmosphere at home was always warm. We seemed to be a popular family. We entertained frequently, with two standing parties a year—at Christmas and for my birthday. Parties were always large. My father would dismantle the beds and move all the furniture so that the full two rooms could be used for dancing. My mother would cook up a storm, particularly at Christmas. *Pasteles, lechon asado, arroz con gandules,* and a lot of *coquito* to drink (meat-stuffed plantain, roast pork, rice with pigeon peas, and coconut nog). My father always brought in a band. They played without compensation and were guests at the party. They ate and drank and danced while a victrola covered the intermissions. One year my father brought home a whole pig and hung it in the foyer doorway. He and my mother prepared it by rubbing it down with oil, oregano, and garlic. After prepara-

tion, the pig was taken down and carried over to a local bakery where it was cooked and returned home. Parties always went on till daybreak, and in addition to the band, there were always volunteers to sing and declaim poetry.

My mother kept an immaculate household. Bedspreads (chenille seemed to be 10 very in) and lace curtains, washed at home like everything else, were hung up on huge racks with rows of tight nails. The racks were assembled in the living room, and the moisture from the wet bedspreads would fill the apartment. In a sense, that seems to be the lasting image of that period of my life. The house was clean. The neighbors were clean. The streets, with few cars, were clean. The buildings were clean and uncluttered with people on the stoops. The park was clean. The visitors to my house were clean and the relationships that my family had with other Puerto Rican families, and the Italian families that my father had met through baseball and my mother through the garment center, were clean. Second Avenue was clean and most of the apartment windows had awnings. There was always music, there seemed to be no rain, and the snow did not become slush. School was fun, we wrote essays about how grand America was, we put up hunchbacked cats at Halloween, we believed Santa Claus visited everyone. I believed everyone was Catholic. I grew up with dogs, nightingales, my godmother's guitar, rocking chair, cat, guppies, my father's occasional roosters, kept in a cage on the fire escape. Laundry delivered and collected by horse and wagon, fruits and vegetables sold the same way, windowsill refrigeration in winter, iceman and box in summer. The police my friends, likewise the teachers.

In short, the first seven or so years of my life were not too great a variation on 11 Dick and Jane, the school book figures who, if my memory serves me correctly, were blond Anglo-Saxons, not immigrants, not migrants like the Puerto Ricans, and not the children of either immigrants or migrants.

My family moved in 1941 to Lexington Avenue into a larger apartment where 12 I could have my own room. It was a light, sunny, railroad flat on the top floor of a well-kept building. I transferred to a new school, and whereas before my classmates had been mostly black, the new school had few blacks. The classes were made up of Italians, Irish, Jews, and a sprinkling of Puerto Ricans. My block was populated by Jews, Italians, and Puerto Ricans.

And then a whole series of different events began. I went to junior high 13 school. We played in the backyards, where we tore down fences to build fires to cook stolen potatoes. We tore up whole hedges, because the green tender limbs would not burn when they were peeled, and thus made perfect skewers for our stolen "mickies." We played tag in the abandoned buildings, tearing the plaster off the walls, tearing the wire lath off the wooden slats, tearing the wooden slats themselves, good for fires, for kites, for sword fighting. We ran up and down the fire escapes playing tag over and across many rooftops. The war ended and the heavy Puerto Rican migration began. The Irish and the Jews disappeared from the neighborhood. The Italians tried to consolidate east of Third Avenue.

What caused the clean and open world to end? Many things. Into an ancient 14 neighborhood came pouring four to five times more people than it had been designed to hold. Men who came running at the promise of jobs were jobless as the war ended. They were confused. They could not see the economic forces that ruled their lives as they drank beer on the corners, reassuring themselves of good times to come while they were hell-bent toward alcoholism. The sudden surge in numbers caused new resentments, and prejudice was intensified. Some were forced to live in cellars, and were then characterized as cave dwellers. Kids came who were confused by the new surroundings; their Puerto Ricanness forced us against a mirror asking, "If they are Puerto Ricans, what are we?" and thus they confused us. In our confusion we were sometimes pathetically reaching out, sometimes pathologically striking out. Gangs. Drugs. Wine. Smoking. Girls. Dances and slow-drag music. Mambo. Spics, Spooks, and Wops. Territories, brother gangs, and war councils establishing rules for right of way on blocks and avenues and for seating in the local theater. Pegged pants and zip guns. Slang.

Dick and Jane were dead, man. Education collapsed. Every classroom had ten 15 kids who spoke no English. Black, Italian, Puerto Rican relations in the classroom were good, but we all knew we couldn't visit one another's neighborhoods. Sometimes we could not move too freely within our own blocks. On 109th, from the lamp post west, the Latin Aces, and from the lamp post east, the Senecas, the "club" I belonged to. The kids who spoke no English became known as the Marine Tigers, picked up from a popular Spanish song. (The *Marine Tiger* and the *Marine Shark* were two ships that sailed from San Juan to New York and brought over many, many migrants from the island.)

The neighborhood had its boundaries. Third Avenue and east, Italian. Fifth 16 Avenue and west, black. South, there was a hill on 103rd Street known locally as Cooney's Hill. When you got to the top of the hill, something strange happened: America began, because from the hill south was where the "Americans" lived. Dick and Jane were not dead; they were alive and well in a better neighborhood.

When, as a group of Puerto Rican kids, we decided to go swimming to 17 Jefferson Park Pool, we knew we risked a fight and a beating from the Italians. And when we went to La Milagrosa Church in Harlem, we knew we risked a fight and a beating from the blacks. But when we went over Cooney's Hill, we risked dirty looks, disapproving looks, and questions from the police like, "What are you doing in this neighborhood?" and "Why don't you kids go back where you belong?"

Where we belonged! Man, I had written compositions about America. Didn't I 18 belong on the Central Park tennis courts, even if I didn't know how to play? Couldn't I watch Dick play? Weren't these policemen working for me too?

Junior high school was a waste. I can say with 90 per cent accuracy that I 19 learned nothing. The woodshop was used to manufacture stocks for "homemades" after Macy's stopped selling zipguns. We went from classroom to classroom answering "here," and trying to be "good." The math class was generally permitted to go to the gym after roll call. English was still a good class. Partly because of a damn good, tough teacher named Miss Beck, and partly because of the grade-number system (7-1 the smartest seventh grade and 7-12, the dumbest). Books were left in school, there was little or no homework, and the whole thing seemed to be a holding operation until high school. Somehow or other, I passed the entrance exam to Brooklyn Technical High School. But I couldn't cut the mustard, either academically or with the "American" kids. After one semester, I came back to PS 83, waited a semester, and went on to Benjamin Franklin High School.

I still wanted to study medicine and excelled in biology. English was always 20 an interesting subject, and I still enjoyed writing compositions and reading. In the neighborhood it was becoming a problem being categorized as a bookworm and as one who used "Sunday words," or "big words." I dug school, but I wanted to be one of the boys more. I think the boys respected my intelligence, despite their ribbing. Besides which, I belonged to a club with a number of members who were interested in going to college, and so I wasn't so far out.

My introduction to marijuana was in junior high school in 1948. A kid named 21 Dixie from 124th Street brought a pack of joints to school and taught about twelve guys to smoke. He told us we could buy joints at a quarter each or five for a dollar. Bombers, or thicker cigarettes, were thirty-five cents each or three for a dollar. There were a lot of experimenters, but not too many buyers. Actually, among the boys there was a strong taboo on drugs, and the Spanish word *motto* was a term of disparagement. Many clubs would kick out members who were known to use drugs. Heroin was easily available, and in those days came packaged in capsules or "caps" which sold for fifty cents each. Method of use was inhalation through the nose, or "sniffing," or "snorting."

I still remember vividly the first kid I ever saw who was mainlining. Prior to 22 this encounter, I had known of "skin-popping," or subcutaneous injection, but not of mainlining. Most of the sniffers were afraid of skin-popping because they knew of the danger of addiction. They seemed to think that you could not become addicted by sniffling.

I went over to 108th Street and Madison where we played softball on an 23 empty lot. This kid came over who was maybe sixteen or seventeen and asked us if we wanted to buy Horse. He started telling us about shooting up and showed me his arms. He had tracks, big black marks on the inside of his arm from the inner joint of the elbow down to his wrist and then over onto the back of his hand. I was stunned. Then he said, "That's nothing, man. I ain't hooked, and I ain't no junky. I can stop anytime I want to." I believe that he believed what he was saying. Invariably the kids talking about their drug experiences would say over and over, "I ain't hooked. I can stop anytime."

But they didn't stop; and the drug traffic grew greater and more open. Kids 24 were smoking on the corners and on the stoops. Deals were made on the street, and you knew fifteen places within a block radius where you could buy anything you wanted. Cocaine never seemed to catch on although it was readily available. In the beginning, the kids seemed to be able to get the money for stuff easily. As the number of shooters grew and the prices went up, the kids got more desperate and apartment robbing became a real problem.

More of the boys began to leave school. We didn't use the term drop out; 25 rather, a guy would say one day, after forty-three truancies, "I'm quitting school."

And so he would. It was an irony, for what was really happening was that after many years of being rejected, ignored, and shuffled around by the school, the kid wanted to quit. Only you can't quit something you were never a part of, nor can you drop out if you were never in.

Some kids lied about their age and joined the army. Most just hung around. 26 Not drifting to drugs or crime or to work either. They used to talk about going back at night and getting their diploma. I believe that they did not believe they could get their diplomas. They knew that the schools had abandoned them a long time ago— that to get the diploma meant starting all over again and that was impossible. Besides, day or night, it was the same school, the same staff, the same shit. But what do you say when you are powerless to get what you want, and what do you say when the other side has all the cards and writes all the rules? You say, "Tennis is for fags," and "School is for fags."

My mother leads me by the hand and carries a plain brown shopping bag. We 27 enter an immense airplane hangar. Structural steel crisscrosses on the ceiling and walls; large round and square rivets look like buttons or bubbles of air trapped in the girders. There are long metallic counters with people bustling behind them. It smells of C.N. disinfectant. Many people stand on many lines up to these counters; there are many conversations going on simultaneously. The huge space plays tricks with voices and a very eerie combination of sounds results. A white cabbage is rolled down a counter at us. We retaliate by throwing down stamps.

For years I thought that sequence happened in a dream. The rolling cabbage 28 rolled in my head, and little unrelated incidents seemed to bring it to the surface of my mind. I could not understand why I remembered a once-dreamt dream so vividly. I was sixteen when I picked up and read Freud's *The Interpretation of Dreams*. One part I understood immediately and well, sex and symbolism. In no time, I had hung my shingle; Streetcorner Analyst. My friends would tell me their dreams and with the most outrageous sexual explanations we laughed whole evenings away. But the rolling cabbage could not be stopped and neither quack analysis nor serious thought could explain it away. One day I asked my mother if she knew anything about it.

"That was home relief, 1937 or 1938. You were no more than four years old 29 then. Your father had been working at a restaurant and I had a job downtown. I used to take you every morning to Dona Eduvije who cared for you all day. She loved you very much, and she was very clean and neat, but I used to cry on my way to work, wishing I could stay home with my son and bring him up like a proper mother would. But I guess I was fated to be a workhorse. When I was pregnant, I would get on the crowded subway and go to work. I would get on a crowded elevator up. Then down. Then back on the subway. Every day I was afraid that the crowd would hurt me, that I would lose my baby. But I had to work. I worked for the WPA right into my ninth month."

My mother was telling it "like it was," and I sat stupefied, for I could not 30 believe that what she said applied to the time I thought of as open and clean. I had been existing in my life like a small plant in a bell jar, my parents defining my awareness. There were things all around me I could not see.

"When you were born we had been living as boarders. It was hard to find an apartment, even in Harlem. You saw signs that said 'No Renting to Colored or Spanish.' That meant Puerto Ricans. We used to say, 'This is supposed to be such a great country?' But with a new baby we were determined not to be boarders and we took an apartment on 111th Street. Soon after we moved, I lost my job because my factory closed down. Your father was making seven or eight dollars a week in a terrible job in a carpet factory. They used to clean rugs, and your father's hands were always on strong chemicals. You know how funny some of his fingernails are? It was from that factory. He came home one night and he was looking at his fingers, and he started saying that he didn't come to this country to lose his hands. He wanted to hold a bat and play ball and he wanted to work—but he didn't want to lose his hands. So he quit the job and went to a restaurant for less pay. With me out of work, a new apartment and therefore higher rent, we couldn't manage. Your father was furious when I mentioned home relief. He said he would rather starve than go on relief. But I went and filled out the papers and answered all the questions and swallowed my pride when they treated me like an intruder. I used to say to them, 'Find me a job—get my husband a better job—we don't want home relief.' But we had to take it. And all that mess with the stamps in exchange for food. And they used to have weekly 'specials' sort of—but a lot of things were useless—because they were American food. I don't remember if we went once a week or once every two weeks. You were so small I don't know how you remember that place and the long lines. It didn't last long because your father had everybody trying to find him a better job and finally somebody did. Pretty soon I went into the WPA and thank God, we never had to deal with those people again. I don't know how you remember that place, but I wish you didn't. I wish I could forget that home relief thing myself. It was the worst time for your father and me. He still hates it.

(He still hates it and so do many people. The expression, "I'd rather starve than go on welfare" is common in the Puerto Rican community. This characteristic pride is well chronicled throughout Spanish literature. For example, one episode of *Lazarillo del Tormes,* the sixteenth-century picaresque novel, tells of a squire who struts around all day with his shiny sword and pressed cape. At night the squire takes food from the boy, Lazarillo—who has begged or stolen it—explaining that it is not proper for a squire to beg or steal, or even to work! Without Lazarillo to feed him, the squire would probably starve.)

"You don't know how hard it was being married to your father then. He was young and very strong and very active and he wanted to work. Welfare deeply disturbed him, and I was afraid that he would actually get very violent if an investigator came to the house. They had a terrible way with people, like throwing that cabbage, that was the way they gave you everything, the way we used to throw the kitchen slop to the pigs in Puerto Rico. Some giving! Your father was, is, *muy macho,* and I used to worry if anybody says anything or gives him that why-do-you-people-come-here-to-ruin-things look he'll be in jail for thirty years. He almost got arrested once when you were just a baby. We went to a hospital clinic—I don't remember now if it was Sydenham or Harlem Hospital—you had a swelling around your throat—and the doctor told me, 'Put on cold compresses.' I said I did that and it didn't help. The doctor said, 'Then put on hot compresses.' Your father blew up. In his broken English, he asked the doctor to do that to his mother, and then invited him to transfer over to the stable on 104th Street. 'You do better with horses— maybe they don't care what kind of compresses they get.'

"One morning your father tells me, 'I got a new job. I start today driving a 34 truck delivering soft drinks.' That night I ask him about the job—he says, 'I quit— bunch of Mafia—I went to the first four places on my list and each storeowner said, "I didn't order any soda." So I got the idea real fast. The Mafia was going to leave soda in each place and then make the guys buy from them only. As soon as I figured it out, I took the truck back, left it parked where I got it, and didn't even say good-bye.' The restaurant took him back. They liked him. The chef used to give him eggs and meats; it was very important to us. Your father never could keep still (still can't), so he was loved wherever he worked. I feel sorry for people on welfare—forget about the cabbage—I never should have taken you there."

My father and I are walking through East Harlem, south down Lexington from 35 112th toward 110th, in 1952. Saturday in late spring, I am eighteen yeas old, sun brilliant on the streets, people running back and forth on household errands. My father is telling me a story about how back in nineteen thirty something, we were very poor and Con Ed light meters were in every apartment. "The Puerto Ricans, maybe everybody else, would hook up a shunt wire around the meter, specially in the evenings when the use was heavy—that way you didn't pay for all the electric you used. We called it *'pillo'* (thief)."

We arrive at 110th street and all the cart vendors are there peddling plantains, 36 avocados, yams, various subtropical roots. I make a casual remark about how foolish it all seemed, and my father catches that I am looking down on them. "Are they stealing?" he asks. "Are they selling people colored water? Aren't they working honestly? Are they any different from a bank president? Aren't they hung like you and me? They are *machos,* and to be respected. Don't let college go to your head. You think a Ph.D is automatically better than a peddler? Remember where you come from—poor people. I mopped floors for people and I wasn't ashamed, but I never let them look down on me. Don't you look down on anybody."

We walk for a way in silence, I am mortified, but he is not angry. "One day I 37 decide to play a joke on your mother. I come home a little early and knock. When she says 'Who?' I say 'Edison man.' Well, there is this long silence and then a scream. I open the door and run in. Your mother's on a chair, in tears, her right arm black from pinky to elbow. She ran to take the *pillo* out, but in her nervousness she got a very slight shock, the black from the spark. She never has forgiven me. After that, I always thought through my jokes."

We walk some more and he says, "I'll tell you another story. This one on me. 38

I was twenty-five years old and was married to your mother. I took her down to Puerto Rico to meet Papa and Mama. We were sitting in the living room, and I remember it like it happened this morning. The room had rattan furniture very popular in that time. Papa had climbed in rank back to captain and had a new house. The living room had double doors which opened onto a large *balcon.* At the other end of the room you could see the dining table with a beautiful white handmade needlework cloth. We were sitting and talking and I took out a cigarette. I was smoking Chesterfields then. No sooner had I lit up than Papa got up, came over, and smacked me in the face. 'You haven't received my permission to smoke,' he said. Can you imagine how I felt?" So my father dealt with his love for me through lateral actions: building bookcases, and through tales of how he got his wounds, he anointed mine.

What is a migration? What does it happen to? Why are the Eskimos still dark 39 after living in all that snow all these centuries? Why don't they have a word for snow? What things are around me with such high saturation that I have not named them? What is a migration? If you rob my purse, are you really a fool? Can a poor boy really be president? In America? Of anything? If he is not white? Should one man's achievement fulfill one million people? Will you let us come near your new machine: after all, there is no more ditch digging? What is a migration? What does it happen to?

The most closely watched migrants of this world are birds. Birds migrate 40 because they get bored singing in the same place to the same people. And they see that the environment gets hostile. Men move for the same reasons. When a Puerto Rican comes to America, he comes looking for a job. He takes the cold as one of a negative series of givens. The mad hustle, the filthy city, filthy air, filthy housing, sardine transportation, are in the series. He knows life will be tough and dangerous. But he thinks he can make a buck. And in his mind, there is only one tableau: himself retired, owner of his home in Puerto Rico, chickens cackling in the backyard.

It startles me still, though it has been five years since my parents went back to 41 the island. I never believed them. My father, driving around New York City for the Housing Authority, knowing more streets in more boroughs than I do, and my mother, curious in her later years about museums and theaters, and reading my books as fast as I would put them down, then giving me cryptic reviews. Salinger is really silly (*Catcher in the Rye*), but entertaining. That evil man deserved to die (*Moby Dick*). He's too much (Dostoevski in *Crime and Punishment*). I read this when I was a little girl in school (*Hamlet* and *Macbeth*). It's too sad for me (*Cry, the Beloved Country*).

My father, intrigued by the thought of passing the foreman's exam, sitting 42 down with a couple of arithmetic books, and teaching himself at age fifty-five to do work problems and mixture problems and fractions and decimals, and going into the civil service exam and scoring a seventy-four and waiting up one night for me to show me three poems he had written. These two cosmopolites, gladiators without skills or language, battling hostile environments and prejudiced people and systems, had graduated from Harlem to the Bronx, had risen into America's dream-cherished lower middle class, and then put it down for Puerto Rico after thirty plus years.

What is a migration, when it is not just a long visit?   43

I was born in Harlem, and I live downtown. And I am a migrant, for if a 44 migration is anything, it is a state of mind. I have known those Eskimos who lived in America twenty and thirty years and never voted, never attended a community meeting, never filed a complaint against a landlord, never informed the police when they were robbed or swindled, or when their daughters were molested. Never appeared at the State or City Commission on Human Rights, never reported a business fraud, never, in other words, saw the snow.

And I am very much a migrant because I am still not quite at home in 45 America. Always there are hills; on the other side—people inclined to throwing cabbages. I cannot "earn and return"—there is no position for me in my father's tableau.

However, I approach the future with optimism. Fewer Puerto Ricans like 46 Eskimos, a larger number of leaders like myself, trained in the university, tempered in the ghetto, and with a vision of America moving from its unexecuted policy to a society open and clean, accessible to anyone.

Dick and Jane? They, too, were tripped by the society, and in our several 47 ways, we are all still migrating.

■ *Questions for* . . . Halfway to Dick and Jane: A Puerto Rican Pilgrimage by Jack Agueros

Words to Note

pilgrimage	foyer	Victorian
prominent	random	bulges
dismantle	immaculate	migrants
peeled	quick	shingle
anointed	environment	spic
spook	wop	hustle
intrigued	hostile	swindled
molested		

Language

1. Compare *rag* in paragraph 3 with *cloth* or a *piece of material*. Agueros uses *immaculate* in the first sentence of paragraph 10. Look it up. What do its connotations contribute?
2. Generally, Agueros uses standard English, and uses it well, but there are patches of slang and colloquialisms. In your opinion, is Agueros's mix of levels of diction successful?

Style

1. Why does Agueros repeat the word *clean* so many times in the tenth paragraph?
2. There are ethnic slurs, one-word sentences, and slang toward the end of the fourteenth paragraph. Why?

Development and Organization

1. Why does Agueros begin with a description of his family's apartment in paragraph 11?
2. In paragraph 27, Agueros shifts to the present tense to relate a memory of his mother and himself. He does the same thing with his father, beginning with paragraph 35. Why does he shift to the present tense? Is that legal? Why didn't he just work this material into the chronological frame of the essay?
3. Where does the conclusion begin? What does it do for the essay?

Discussion and Journal Writing

1. How does Agueros's father feel about his son's success? His mother?
2. If Agueros is a success and his essay, a success story, what is he complaining about?
3. According to Agueros, when, how, and why did New York's treatment of Puerto Rican migrants change?
4. Decipher the title. How can one go halfway to Dick and Jane?

ooooo

The Man That Was Almost a Man

—Richard Wright

Richard Wright, a major figure in twentieth-century American literature, was one of the first writers to put the Black experience on the page. He grew up in the Deep South in the early part of the century when segregation was still the rule and the law. He fled, as a young man, to points north, mainly Chicago and New York, but his imagination never left the South. Quite a bit of his fiction, as well as his nonfiction, is set in the towns and sharecroppers' fields of a South characterized by the relentless code and hateful ethic of Jim

Crow. In the story that follows, Dave, the main character, searches desperately and foolishly for the room he needs to become a man in a society that is set against the proposition.

Dave struck out across the fields looking homeward through paling light.   1
Whut's the use of talkin wid em niggers in the field? Anyhow, his mother was putting supper on the table. Them niggers can't understan nothing. One of these days he was going to get a gun and practice shooting, then they couldn't talk to him as though he were a little boy. He slowed, looking at the ground. Shucks, Ah ain scareda them even ef they are biggern me! Aw, Ah know whut Ahma do. Ahm going by ol Joe's sto n git that Sears Roebuck catlog n look at them guns. Mebbe Ma will lemme buy one when she gits mah pay from ol man Hawkins. Ahma beg her t gimme some money. Ahm ol ernough to hava gun. Ahm seventeen. Almost a man. He strode, feeling his long loose-jointed limbs. Shucks, a man oughta hava little gun aftah he done worked hard all day.

He came in sight of Joe's store. A yellow lantern glowed on the front porch. He mounted steps and went through the screen door, hearing it bang behind him. There was a strong smell of coal oil and mackerel fish. He felt very confident until he saw fat Joe walk in through the rear door, then his courage began to ooze.

"Howdy, Dave! Whutcha want?"

"How yuh, Mistah Joe? Aw, I don wanna buy nothing. Ah jus wanted t see ef yuhd lemme look at tha catlog erwhile."

"Sure! You wanna see it here?"   5

"Nawsuh. Ah wans t take it home wid me. Ah'll bring it back termorrow when Ah come in from the fiels."

"You plannin on buying something?"

"Yessuh."

"Your ma lettin you have your own money now?"

"Shucks, Mistah Joe. Ahm gittin t be a man like anybody else!"   10

Joe laughed and wiped his greasy white face with a red bandanna.

"Whut you plannin on buyin?"

Dave looked at the floor, scratched his head, scratched his thigh, and smiled. Then he looked up shyly.

"Ah'll tell yuh, Mistah Joe, ef yuh promise yuh won't tell."

"I promise."   15

"Waal, Ahma buy a gun."

"A gun? Whut you want with a gun?"

"Ah wanna keep it."

"You ain't nothing but a boy. You don't need a gun."

"Aw, lemme have the catlog, Mistah Joe. Ah'll bring it back."   20

"But Ma, we needa gun. Pa ain got no gun. We needa gun in the house. Yuh kin never tell whut might happen."

"Now don yuh try to maka fool outta me, boy! Ef we did hava gun, yuh wouldn't have it!"

He laid the catalogue down and slipped his arm around her waist.

"Aw, Ma, Ah done worked hard alla summer n ain ast yuh fer nothin, is Ah, now?"

"Thas whut yuh spose t do!" 25

"But Ma, Ah wans a gun. Yuh kin lemme have two dollahs outta mah money. Please, Ma. I kin give it to Pa . . . Please, Ma! Ah loves yuh, Ma."

When she spoke her voice came soft and low.

"Whut yu wan wida gun, Dave? Yuh don need no gun. Yuh'll git in trouble. N ef yo pa jus thought Ah let yuh have money t buy a gun he'd hava fit."

"Ah'll hide it, Ma. It ain but two dollahs."

"Lawd, chil, whut's wrong wid yuh?" 30

"Ain nothin wrong, Ma. Ahm almos a man now. Ah wans a gun."

"Who gonna sell yuh a gun?"

"Ol Joe at the sto."

"N it don cos but two dollahs?"

"Thas all, Ma. Just two dollahs. Please, Ma." 35

She was stacking the plates away; her hands moved slowly, reflectively. Dave kept an anxious silence. Finally she turned to him.

"Ah'll let yuh git tha gun ef yuh promise me one thing."

"Whut's tha, Ma?"

"Yuh bring it straight back t me, yuh hear? It be fer Pa."

"Yessum! Lemme go now, Ma." 40

She stooped, turned slightly to one side, raised the hem of her dress, rolled down the top of her stocking, and came up with a slender wad of bills.

"Here," she said. "Lawd knows yuh don need no gun. But yer pa does. Yuh bring it right back t me, yuh hear? Ahma put it up. Now ef yuh don, Ahma have yuh pa lick yuh so hard yuh won fergit it."

"Yessum."

He took the money, ran down the steps, and across the yard.

"Dave! Yuuuuuh Daaaaave!" 45

He heard, but he was not going to stop now. "Naw, Lawd!"

The first movement he made the following morning was to reach under his pillow for the gun. In the gray light of dawn he held it loosely, feeling a sense of power. Could kill a man with a gun like this. Kill anybody, black or white. And if he were holding his gun in his hand, nobody could run over him; they would have to respect him. It was a big gun, with a long barrel and a heavy handle. He raised and lowered it in his hand, marveling at its weight.

He had not come straight home with it as his mother had asked; instead he had stayed out in the fields, holding the weapon in his hand, aiming it now and then at some imaginary foe. But he had not fired it; he had been afraid that his father might hear. Also he was not sure he knew how to fire it.

To avoid surrendering the pistol he had not come into the house until he knew that they were all asleep. When his mother had tiptoed to his bedside late that night and demanded the gun, he had first played possum; then he had told her that the gun was hidden outdoors, that he would bring it to her in the morning. Now he lay turning it slowly in his hands. He broke it, took out the cartridges, felt them, and then put them back.

He slid out of bed, got a long strip of old flannel from a trunk, wrapped the 50 gun in it, and tied it to his naked thigh while it was still loaded. He did not go in to breakfast. Even though it was not yet daylight, he started for Jim Hawkins' plantation. Just as the sun was rising he reached the barns where the mules and plows were kept.

"Hey! That you, Dave?"

He turned. Jim Hawkins stood eyeing him suspiciously.

"What're yuh doing here so early?"

"Ah didn't know Ah wuz gittin up so early, Mistah Hawkins. Ah wuz fixin t hitch up ol Jenny n take her t the fiels."

"Good. Since you're so early, how about plowing that stretch down by the 55 woods?"

"Suits me, Mistah Hawkins."

"O.K. Go to it!"

He hitched Jenny to a plow and started across the fields. Hot dog! This was just what he wanted. If he could get down by the woods, he could shoot his gun and nobody would hear. He walked behind the plow, hearing the traces creaking, feeling the gun tied tight to his thigh.

When he reached the woods, he plowed two whole rows before he decided to take out the gun. Finally, he stopped, looked in all directions, then untied the gun and held it in his hand. He turned to the mule and smiled.

"Know whut this is, Jenny? Naw, yuh wouldn know! Yuhs jusa ol mule! 60 Anyhow, this is a gun, n it kin shoot, by Gawd!"

He held the gun at arm's length. Whut t hell, Ahma shoot this thing! He looked at Jenny again.

"Lissen here, Jenny! When Ah pull this ol trigger, Ah don wan yuh t run n acka fool now!"

Jenny stood with head down, her short ears pricked straight. Dave walked off about twenty feet, held the gun far out from him at arm's length, and turned his head. Hell, he told himself, Ah ain afraid. The gun felt loose in his fingers; he waved it wildly for a moment. Then he shut his eyes and tightened his forefinger. Bloom! A report half deafened him and he thought his right hand was torn from his arm. He heard Jenny whinnying and galloping over the field, and he found himself on his knees, squeezing his fingers hard between his legs. His hand was numb; he jammed it into his mouth, trying to warm it, trying to stop the pain. The gun lay at his feet. He did not quite know what had happened. He stood up and stared at the gun as though it were a living thing. He gritted his teeth and kicked the gun. Yuh almos broke mah arm! He turned to look for Jenny; she was far over the fields, tossing her head and kicking wildly.

"Hol on there, ol mule!"

When he caught up with her she stood trembling, walling her big white eyes at 65 him. The plow was far away; the traces had broken. Then Dave stopped short, looking, not believing. Jenny was bleeding. Her left side was red and wet with blood. He went closer. Lawd, have mercy! Wondah did Ah shoot this mule? He grabbed for Jenny's mane. She flinched, snorted, whirled, tossing her head.

"Hol on now! Hol on."

Then he saw the hole in Jenny's side, right between the ribs. It was round, wet, red. A crimson stream streaked down the front leg, flowing fast. Good Gawd! Ah wuzn't shootin at tha mule. He felt panic. He knew he had to stop that blood, or Jenny would bleed to death. He had never seen so much blood in all his life. He chased the mule for half a mile, trying to catch her. Finally she stopped, breathing hard, stumpy tail half arched. He caught her mane and led her back to where the plough and gun lay. Then he stooped and grabbed handfuls of damp black earth and tried to plug the bullet hole. Jenny shuddered, whinnied, and broke from him.

"Hol on! Hol on now!"

He tried to plug it again, but blood came anyhow. His fingers were hot and sticky. He rubbed dirt into his palms, trying to dry them. Then again he attempted to plug the bullet hole, but Jenny shied away, kicking her heels high. He stood helpless. He had to do something. He ran at Jenny; she dodged him. He watched a red stream of blood flow down Jenny's leg and form a bright pool at her feet.

"Jenny . . . Jenny," he called weakly." 70

His lips trembled. She's bleeding t death! He looked in the direction of home, wanting to go back, wanting to get help. But he saw the pistol lying in the damp black clay. He had a queer feeling that if he only did something, this would not be; Jenny would not be there bleeding to death.

When he went to her this time, she did not move. She stood with sleepy, dreamy eyes, and when he touched her she gave a low-pitched whinny and knelt to the ground, her front knees slopping in blood.

"Jenny . . . Jenny . . ." he whispered.

For a long time she held her neck erect; then her head sank, slowly. Her ribs swelled with a mighty heave and she went over.

Dave's stomach felt empty, very empty. He picked up the gun and held it gin- 75 gerly between his thumb and fore-finger. He buried it at the foot of a tree. He took a stick and tried to cover the pool of blood with dirt—but what was the use? There was Jenny lying with her mouth open and her eyes walled and glassy. He could not tell Jim Hawkins that he had shot his mule. But he had to tell something. Yeah, Ah'll tell em Jenny started gittin wil n fell on the joint of the plow. . . . But that would hardly happen to a mule. He walked across the field slowly, head down.

It was sunset. Two of Jim Hawkins' men were over near the edge of the woods digging a hole in which to bury Jenny. Dave was surrounded by a knot of people, all of whom were looking down at the dead mule.

"I don't see how in the world it happened," said Jim Hawkins for the tenth time.

The crowd parted and Dave's mother, father, and small brother pushed into the center.

"Where Dave?" his mother called.

"There he is," said Jim Hawkins.   80

His mother grabbed him.

"Whut happened, Dave? Whut yuh done?"

"Nothin."

"C mon, boy, talk," his father said.

Dave took a deep breath and told the story he knew nobody believed.   85

"Waal," he drawled. "Ah brung ol Jenny down here sos Ah could do mah plowin. Ah plowed bout two rows, just like yuh see." He stopped and pointed at the long rows of upturned earth. "Then somethin musta been wrong wid ol Jenny. She wouldn ack right a-tall. She started snortin n kickin her heels. Ah tried t hol her, but she pulled erway, rearin n goin in. Then when the point of the plow was stickin up in the air, she swung erroun n twisted herself back on it . . . She stuck herself n started t bleed. N fo Ah could do anything, she wuz dead."

"Did you ever hear of anything like that in all your life?" asked Jim Hawkins.

There were white and black standing in the crowd. They murmured. Dave's mother came close to him and looked hard into his face. "Tell the truth, Dave," she said.

"Looks like a bullet hole to me," said one man.

"Dave, whut yuh do wid the gun?" his mother asked.   90

The crowd surged in, looking at him. He jammed his hands into his pockets, shook his head slowly from left to right, and backed away. His eyes were wide and painful.

"Did he hava gun?" asked Jim Hawkins.

"By Gawd, Ah tol yuh tha wuz a gun wound," said a man, slapping his thigh.

His father caught his shoulders and shook him till his teeth rattled.

"Tell whut happened, yuh rascal! Tell whut . . ."   95

Dave looked at Jenny's stiff legs and began to cry.

"Whut yuh do wid tha gun?" his mother asked.

"Whut wuz he doin wida gun?" his father asked.

"Come on and tell the truth," said Hawkins. "Ain't nobody going to hurt you . . ."

His mother crowded close to him.   100

"Did yuh shoot tha mule, Dave?"

Dave cried, seeing blurred white and black faces.

"Ahh ddinn gggo tt sshooot hher . . . Ah ssswear ffo Gawd Ahh ddin. . . . Ah wuz a-tryin t sssee ef the old gggun would sshoot—"

"Where yuh git the gun from?" his father asked.

"Ah got it from Joe, at the sto."   105

"Where yuh git the money?"

"Ma give it t me."

"He kept worryin me, Bob. Ah had t. Ah tol im t bring the gun right back t me . . . It was fer yuh, the gun."

"But how yuh happen to shoot that mule?" asked Jim Hawkins.

"Ah wuzn shootin at the mule, Mistah Hawkins. The gun jumped when Ah 110 pulled the trigger . . . N fo Ah knowed anythin Jenny was there a-bleedin."

Somebody in the crowd laughed. Jim Hawkins walked close to Dave and looked into his face.

"Well, looks like you have bought you a mule, Dave."

"Ah swear fo Gawd, Ah didn go t kill the mule, Mistah Hawkins!"

"But you killed her!"

All the crowd was laughing now. They stood on tiptoe and poked heads over 115 one another's shoulders.

"Well, boy, looks like yuh done bought a dead mule! Hahaha!"

"Ain tha ershame."

"Hohohohoho."

Dave stood, head down, twisting his feet in the dirt.

"Well, you needn't worry about it, Bob," said Jim Hawkins to Dave's father. 120 "Just let the boy keep on working and pay me two dollars a month."

"Whut yuh wan fer yo mule, Mistah Hawkins?"

Jim Hawkins screwed up his eyes.

"Fifty dollars."

"Whut yuh do wid tha gun?" Dave's father demanded.

Dave said nothing. 125

"Yuh wan me t take a tree n beat yuh till yuh talk!"

"Nawsuh!"

"Whut yuh do wid it?"

"Ah threwed it erway."

"Where?" 130

"Ah . . . Ah threwed it in the creek."

"Waal, c mon home. N firs thing in the mawnin git to tha creek n fin tha gun."

"Yessuh."

"Whut yuh pay fer it?"

"Two dollahs." 135

"Take tha gun n git yo money back n carry it t Mistah Hawkins, yuh hear? N don fergit Ahma lam you black bottom good fer this! Now march yosef on home, suh!"

Dave turned and walked slowly. He heard people laughing. Dave glared, his eyes welling with tears. Hot anger bubbled in him. Then he swallowed and stumbled on.

That night Dave did not sleep. He was glad that he had gotten out of killing the mule so easily, but he was hurt. Something hot seemed to turn over inside him each time he remembered how they had laughed. He tossed on his bed, feeling his hard pillow. *N Pa says he's gonna beat me* . . . He remembered other beatings, and his back quivered. *Naw, naw. Ah sho don wan im t beat me tha way no mo. Dam em all! Nobody ever gave him anything. All he did was work. They treat me like a mule, n then they beat me.* He gritted his teeth. *N Ma had t toll on me.*

Well, if he had to, he would take old man Hawkins that two dollars. But that meant selling the gun. And he wanted to keep that gun. Fifty dollars for a dead mule.

He turned over, thinking how he had fired the gun. He had an itch to fire it 140 again. Ef other men kin shoota gun, by Gawd, Ah kin! He was still, listening. Mebbe they all sleepin now. The house was still. He heard the soft breathing of his brother. Yes, now! He would go down and get that gun and see if he could fire it! He eased out of bed and slipped into overalls.

The moon was bright. He ran almost all the way to the edge of the woods. He stumbled over the ground, looking for the spot where he had buried the gun. Yeah, here it is. Like a hungry dog scratching for a bone, he pawed it up. He puffed his black cheeks and blew dirt from the trigger and barrel. He broke it and found four cartridges unshot. He looked around; the fields were filled with silence and moonlight. He clutched the gun stiff and hard in his fingers. But, as soon as he wanted to pull the trigger, he shut his eyes and turned his head. Naw, Ah can't shoot wid mah eyes closed n mah head turned. With effort he held his eyes open; then he squeezed. *Blooooom!* He was stiff, not breathing. The gun was still in his hands. Dammit, he'd done it! He fired again. *Blooooom!* He smiled. *Blooooom! Blooooom! Click, click.* There! It was empty. If anybody could shoot a gun, he could. He put the gun into his hip pocket and started across the fields.

When he reached the top of a ridge he stood straight and proud in the moonlight, looking at Jim Hawkins' big white house, feeling the gun sagging in his pocket. Lawd, ef Ah had just one mo bullet Ah'd take a shot at tha house. Ah'd like t scare ol man Hawkins jusa little . . . Jusa enough t let im know Dave Saunders is a man.

To his left the road curved, running to the tracks of the Illinois Central. He jerked his head, listening. From far off came a faint *hoooof-hooof; hoooof-hoooof; hoooof-hoooof.* . . . He stood rigid. Two dollahs a mont. Les see now . . . Tha means it'll take bout two years. Shucks! Ah'll be dam!

He started down the road, toward the tracks. Yeah, here she comes! He stood 144 beside the track and held himself stiffly. Here she comes, erroun the ben . . . C mon, yuh slow poke! C mon! He had his hand on his gun; something quivered in his stomach. Then the train thundered past, the gray and brown box cars rumbling and clinking. He gripped the gun tightly; then he jerked his hand out of his pocket. Ah betcha Bill wouldn't do it! Ah betcha . . . The cars slid past, steel grinding upon steel. Ahm ridin yuh ternight, so help me Gawd! He was hot all over. He hesitated just a moment; then he grabbed, pulled atop of a car, and lay flat. He felt his pocket; the gun was still there. Ahead the long rails were glinting in the moonlight, stretching away, away to somewhere, somewhere where he could be a man . . .

■ *Questions for . . .* **The Man That Was Almost a Man** by Richard Wright

Words to Note

nigger	bandanna	ooze
sprawled	clattered	thumbed
cornering	jammed	gritted
flinched	crimson	stooped
slipped	quivered	clutched
ridge	jerked	

Language

1. Get out your dictionary and compare *nigger* with *Black, Negro, Afro-American,* and *African-American.* Why didn't Wright use *Negro?*
2. Does the dialect Wright uses in the dialogue enhance the story or make it hard to read?

Style

1. Wright's language is fairly simple and blunt in the story's dialogue, but it's quite descriptive and evocative when the narrator takes over to relate events and describe the story's people and places. Why the shift?
2. Why is the story's dialogue rendered in Southern dialect, Black and White?

Development and Organization

1. Why does Wright divide the story into a sequence of scenes? Wouldn't it have been easier just to tell it straight through?
2. Why does he dramatize so much of the story? Wouldn't it have been more straight forward just to narrate it?
3. Put the story's key theme into your own words.

Discussion and Journal Writing

1. How many people call Dave "boy"? Does the word mean the same thing to each of them?
2. How do his mother and father treat him? What does he owe them? What privileges do they allow him?
3. What do the Black men in the story do for a living?
4. Why does he want a gun? Who else has a gun?
5. Why does he run for the train? What's he running from? What's he running toward?

ooooo

My Papa's Waltz

—Theodore Roethke

Theodore Roethke was a much decorated poet: he won a Pulitzer Prize for *The Waking* (1953), a National Book Award and Bollingen Prize for his collected poems, *Words for the Wind,* and another National Book Award for *The Far Field,* a volume of poetry that was published in 1964, a year after he died. He was born in Saginaw, Michigan, where his father and German-immigrant grand-father kept greenhouses that became the subject of many of his poems. Poem by poem, he constructed a literary world out of the raw material of the family greenhouses and his childhood memo-ries; "My Papa's Waltz" is one of the more distinguished panes of that world.

> The whiskey on your breath 1
> Could make a small boy dizzy,
> But I hung on like death:
> Such waltzing was not easy.
>
> We romped until the pans 5
> Slid from the kitchen shelf;
> My mother's countenance
> Could not unfrown itself.
>
> The hand that held my wrist 9
> Was battered on one knuckle;
> At every step you missed
> My right ear scraped a buckle.
>
> You beat time on my head 13
> With a palm caked hard by dirt,
> Then waltzed me off to bed
> Still clinging to your shirt.

■ *Questions for* . . . **My Papa's Waltz** by Theodore Roethke

Words to Note

dizzy	hung	romped
countenance	unfrown	battered
scraped	buckle	caked
beat	waltzed	clinging.

Language

1. Why does Roethke rely so heavily on descriptive words?
2. Compare *clinging* in the fourth stanza with its synonyms. Has Roethke made the best choice?

Style

1. What is the poem's rhyme scheme? Listen closely as you read it aloud. What's the effect of the rhyme scheme?
2. Study Roethke's phrases and sentences. How do they correspond with his use of lines and stanzas?

Development and Organization

1. Does the title prepare the reader for the poem?
2. Summarize the poem's plot. How are its characters portrayed? What are its themes?
3. How many patterns of organization do you see?

Discussion and Journal Writing

1. How does the speaker of the poem feel about his father? His mother?
2. Is this a happy family? A pathological family?

ooooo

Uncle Harold, Family Liar

—Russell Baker

A satirist, Russell Baker has been scanning the American landscape for over thirty years, cutting the great and pompous down to size and inflating the trivial to levels of epic importance. He is a syndicated columnist whose pieces appeared weekly in the *New York Times'* editorial pages for more than 30 years, where they still appear from time to time when he has something to say. The following piece about Baker's Uncle Harold is from his autobiography *Growing Up.* Though passages of the book are serious and poignant, his treatment of his Uncle Harold is characteristic of his newspaper style. After pages of silliness, an important point or observation falls out of the last laugh into the reader's lap, which is the way any good satirist works.

Uncle Harold was famous for lying.   1

He had once been shot right between the eyes. He told me so himself. It was   2
during World War I. An underaged boy, he had run away from home, enlisted in
the Marine Corps, and been shipped to France, where one of the Kaiser's soldiers
had shot him. Right between the eyes.

It was a miracle it hadn't killed him, and I said so the evening he told me   3
about it. He explained that Marines were so tough they didn't need miracles. I was
now approaching the age of skepticism, and though it was risky business challenging adults, I was tempted to say "Swear on the Bible?" I did not dare go this far,
but I did get a hint of doubt into my voice by repeating his words as a question.

"Right between the eyes?"   4

"Right between the eyes," he said. "See this scar?"   5

He placed a finger on his forehead just above the bridge of his nose. "That's   6
all the mark it left," he said.

"I don't see any scar," I said.   7

"It's probably faded by now," he said. "It's been a long time ago."   8

I said it must have hurt a good bit.   9

"Hurt! You bet it hurt."   10

"What did you do?"   11

"It made me so mad I didn't do a thing but pull out my pistol and kill that   12
German right there on the spot."

At this point Aunt Sister came in from the kitchen with cups of cocoa. "For   13
God's sake, Harold," she said, "quit telling the boy those lies."

People were always telling Harold for God's sake quit telling those lies. His   14
full name was Harold Sharp, and in the family, people said, "That Harold Sharp is
the biggest liar God ever sent down the pike."

Aunt Sister, Ida Rebecca's only daughter, had married him shortly after my   15
mother took Doris and me from Morrisonville. He'd spent sixteen years in the
Marines by then, but at Aunt Sister's insistence he gave up the Marine Corps and
the two of them moved to Baltimore. There they had a small apartment on Hollins
Street overlooking Union Square. Our place was a second-floor apartment on West
Lombard Street just across the square. It was easy for my mother to stroll over to
Aunt Sister's with Doris and me to play Parcheesi or Caroms or Pick-Up-Sticks

with the two of them, but the real pleasure of these visits for me came from listening to Uncle Harold.

It didn't matter that my mother called him "the biggest liar God ever sent 16 down the pike." In spite of his reputation for varnishing a fact, or maybe because of the outrageousness with which he did the varnishing, I found him irresistible. It was his intuitive refusal to spoil a good story by slavish adherence to fact that enchanted me. Though poorly educated, Uncle Harold somehow knew that the possibility of creating art lies not in reporting but in fiction.

He worked at cutting grass and digging graves for a cemetery in West 17 Baltimore. This increased the romantic aura through which I saw him, for I had become fascinated with the Gothic aspects of death since arriving in Baltimore. In Baltimore, disposing of the dead seemed to be a major cultural activity. There were three funeral parlors within a one-block radius of our house, and a steady stream of hearses purred through the neighborhood. I had two other distant relatives from Morrisonville who had migrated to Baltimore, and both of them were also working in cemeteries. In addition, there was a fairly steady flow of corpses through our house on Lombard Street.

Our landlord there, a genial Lithuanian tailor who occupied the first floor, lent 18 out his parlor to a young relative who was an undertaker and sometimes had an overflow at his own establishment. As a result there was often an embalmed body coffined lavishly in the first-floor parlor. Since our apartment could be reached only by passing the landlord's parlor, and since its double doors were always wide open, it seemed to me that instead of finding a home of our own, we had come to rest in a funeral home. Passing in and out of the house, I tried to avert my eyes from the garishly rouged bodies and hold my breath against inhaling the cloying odors of candle wax, tuberoses, and embalming fluid which suffused the hallway.

When Uncle Harold came over for an evening of card playing and found a 19 corpse in the parlor, his imagination came alive. On one such evening I went down to let Aunt Sister and him in the front door. Noting the coffin in our landlord's parlor, Uncle Harold paused, strode into the room, nodded at the mourners, and examined the deceased stranger with professional scrutiny. Upstairs afterwards, playing cards at the dining-room table, Uncle Harold announced that the old gentleman in the coffin downstairs did not look dead to him.

"I could swear I saw one of his eyelids flicker," he said.   20

Nobody paid him any attention.   21

"You can't always be sure they're dead," he said.   22

Nobody was interested except me.   23

"A man I knew was almost buried alive once," he said.   24

"Are you going to play the jack or hold it all night?" my mother asked.   25

"It was during the war," Uncle Harold said. "In France. They were closing the 26 coffin on him when I saw him blink one eye."

The cards passed silently and were shuffled.   27

"I came close to being buried alive myself one time," he said.   28

"For God's sake, Harold, quit telling those lies," Aunt Sister said.   29

"It's the truth, just as sure as I'm sitting here, so help me God," said Uncle 30 Harold. "It happens every day. We dig them up out at the cemetery—to do autopsies, you know—and you can see they fought like the devil to get out after the coffin was closed on them, but it's too late by that time."

Uncle Harold was not a tall man, but the Marines had taught him to carry him- 31 self with a swaggering erect indolence and to measure people with the grave, cool arrogance of authority. Though he now shoveled dirt for a living, he was always immaculately manicured by the time he sat down to supper. In this polished man of the world—suits pressed to razor sharpness, every hair in place, eyes of icy gray self-confidence—I began to detect a hidden boy, in spirit not too different from myself, though with a love for mischief which had been subdued in me by too much melancholy striving to satisfy my mother's notions of manhood.

Admiring him so extravagantly, I was disappointed to find that he detested my 32 hero, Franklin Roosevelt. In Uncle Harold's view, Roosevelt was a deep-dyed villain of the vilest sort. He had data about Roosevelt's shenanigans which newspapers were afraid to publish and occasionally entertained with hair-raising accounts of Rooseveltian deeds that had disgraced the Presidency.

"You know, I suppose, that Roosevelt only took the job for the money," he 33 told me one evening.

"Does it pay a lot?" 34

"Not all that much," he said, "but there are plenty of ways of getting rich once 35 you get in the White House, and Roosevelt's using all of them."

"How?" 36

"He collects money from everybody who wants to get in to see them." 37

"People have to give him money before he'll talk to them?" 38

"They don't give him the money face to face. He's too smart for that," Uncle 39 Harold said.

"Then how does he get it?" 40

"There's a coat rack right outside his door, and he keeps an overcoat hanging 41 on that rack. Before anybody can get in to see him, they've got to put money in the overcoat pocket."

I was shocked, which pleased Uncle Harold. "That's the kind of President 42 you've got," he said.

"Do you know that for sure?" 43

"Everybody knows it." 44

"How do *you* know it?" 45

"A fellow who works at the White House told me how it's done." 46

This was such powerful stuff that as soon as I got home I passed it on to my 47 mother. "Who told you that stuff?" she asked.

"Uncle Harold." 48

She laughed at my gullibility. "Harold Sharp is the biggest liar God ever sent 49 down the pike," she said. "He doesn't know any more about Roosevelt than a hog knows about a holiday."

Through Uncle Harold I first heard of H. L. Mencken. Mencken's house lay 50 just two doors from Uncle Harold's place on Hollins Street. Uncle Harold pointed it out to me one day when we were walking around to the Arundel Ice Cream store for a treat. "You know who lives in that house, don't you?"

Of course I didn't.   51

"H. L. Mencken."   52

Who's H. L. Mencken?   53

"You mean to tell me you never heard of H. L. Mencken? He writes those 54 pieces in the newspaper that make everybody mad," Uncle Harold said.

I understood from Uncle Harold's respectful tone that Mencken must be a 55 great man, though Mencken's house did not look like the house of a great man. It looked very much like every other house in Baltimore. Red brick, white marble steps. "I saw Mencken coming out of his house just the other day," Uncle Harold said.

It's doubtful Uncle Harold had ever read anything by Mencken. Uncle 56 Harold's tastes ran to *Doc Savage* and *The Shadow*. Still, I could see he was proud of living so close to such a great man. It was a measure of how well he had done in life at a time when millions of other men had been broken by the Depression.

He had left home in 1917 for the Marines, an uneducated fifteen-year-old 57 country boy from Taylorstown, a village not far from Morrisonville, just enough schooling to read and do arithmetic, not much to look forward to but a career of farm labor. Maybe in the Marines he even became a hero. He did fight in France and afterwards stayed on in the Marines, shipping around the Caribbean under General Smedley Butler to keep Central America subdued while Yankee corporations pumped out its wealth. For a man with negligible expectations, he had not done badly by 1937 standards. Full-time cemetery labor; a one-bedroom apartment so close to a famous writer.

My first awe of him had softened as I gradually realized his information was 58 not really intended to be information. Gradually I came to see that Uncle Harold was not a liar but a teller of stories and a romantic, and it was Uncle Harold the teller of tales who fascinated me. Though he remained a stern figure, and I never considered sassing him, I saw now that he knew I no longer received his stories with total credulity, but that I was now listening for the pleasure of watching his imagination at play. This change in our relationship seemed to please him.

Over the Parcheesi board one evening he told a story about watching the dead 59 in Haiti get up out of their shrouds and dance the Charleston. Aunt Sister and my mother had the usual response: "For God's sake, Harold, quit telling those lies."

His face was impassive as always when he issued the usual protest—"It's the 60 truth, so help me God"—but I could see with absolute clarity that underneath the impassive mask he was smiling. He saw me studying him, scowled forbiddingly at me for one moment, then winked. That night we came to a silent understanding: We were two romancers whose desire for something more fanciful than the humdrum of southwest Baltimore was beyond the grasp of unimaginative people like Aunt Sister and my mother.

Still, it took me a while to understand what he was up to. He wanted life to be 61 more interesting than it was, but his only gift for making it so lay in a small talent for homespun fictions, and he could not resist trying to make the most of it. Well, there was nothing tragic about his case. Our world in Baltimore hadn't much respect for the poetic impulse. In our world a man spinning a romance was doomed to be dismissed as nothing more than a prodigious liar.

■ *Questions for* . . . Uncle Harold, Family Liar by Russell Baker

Words to Note

underaged	shipped	skepticism
dare	hint	varnishing
aura	garishly rouged	cloying
suffused	strode	nodded
scrutiny	swaggering erect	immaculately manicured
shenanigans	indolence	sassing
stern	credulity	scowled

Language

1. Baker tells us his Uncle Harold had a reputation for "varnishing" a fact. What words could Baker have used instead of *varnishing?*
2. In paragraph 2, Baker tells us his underaged uncle had enlisted in the Marine Corps and been shipped to France to fight in World War I. What's unusual about using *shipped* to describe the transportation of a person? What's the tone of this word?

Style

1. Why didn't Baker incorporate the sentence fragment that concludes the second paragraph into the preceding sentence?
2. How does he use dialogue?

Development and Organization

1. The first sentence is called a *lead* in the newspaper business, which is Baker's business. What does it do for the rest of the piece?
2. After the lead, Baker dramatically renders one of Uncle Harold's lies, then he gives the reader some background information about Harold, then he serves up another lie, and so on. What's the effect of interspersing anecdotes with background information? How would the piece read if he had given us all the background first and then the anecdotes?

Discussion and Journal Writing

1. What sort of man was Uncle Harold?
2. Describe the stages of Baker's awareness of what his Uncle Harold was up to when he told his lies. Why did Baker the boy admire Uncle Harold? Why does Baker the man admire him?
3. What role did Uncle Harold play for Baker when he was a boy? What gift did Uncle Harold give him?
4. Compare Baker's Uncle Harold with a relative who influenced you in a unique way.

ooooo

─────────────── *F*amily Documents One ───────────────

Duties of Young Wives

William A. Alcott, *The Young Wife, or, The Duties of the Wife in the Marriage Relation* (Boston, 1838), pp. 6–13.

Chapter VII. Friendship.

Few real friends. Parents not always true friends to children. Anecdote. Stormy period of life. Necessity of a friend. Arrangement of Providence. Woman sent as the friend of man. Wives the truest friends. Four qualifications for this office. Religion considered. Enemies sometimes friends.

Chapter VIII. Love.

Is it necessary for love to decline after marriage? Internal love increases. Means of increasing it. Doing good to others makes us love them. Anecdotes; the little girl— the deist. Love, a matter within our own control. General rule. Cautions.

Chapter IX. Delicacy and Modesty.

Many forms of immodesty. A quotation. Modesty in matrimony. Unchaste language. Example to the husband. Specimens of bad examples.

Chapter X. Love of Home.

Paul's opinion. Effects of "gadding." Anecdote. Dislike of home. Error in female education. Importance of loving home. A picture drawn by Solomon. Two pictures by Abbott. Effects of loving home on the family. Hints to the reader. The Family Monitor.

Chapter XI. Self-Respect.

A principle. Self-respect should be early cultivated. An anecdote.

Chapter XII. Purity of Character.

Explanation of the term. Impurity of character very common. Case of Lucius and Emilia. Seduction. The consequences. Several hints.

Chapter XIII. Simplicity.

Simplicity a virtue. Very rare. Simplicity of language. Story of Mrs. L. Simplicity of conduct.

Chapter XIV. Neatness.

Great importance of neatness. Want of it. Effects on the husband. Neatness in small matters. Structure of the skin. Necessity of bathing. Effect of neatness on morals. Effect of example. Difficulties considered. How to train a husband to slovenliness. Want of neatness in little things.

Chapter XV. Order and Method.

Order, heaven's first law. Importance to the housekeeper. Book-learning. Prejudices against it. Story of Fidelia. Consequences of disorder.

Chapter XVI. Punctuality.

Punctuality lengthens life—is indispensable. Its influence on others. Various forms of punctuality. Anecdote. Reflections. Case of the farmer. The wife's excuses. Real state of the case. Appeal to those whom it concerns.

Chapter XVII. Early Rising.

The young wife should rise early. Means of forming the habit. Retire early—with a quiet stomach—a quiet mind. Resolve strongly. Early training. Mr. and Mrs. Clifford. Samuel Sidney. Reflections.

Chapter XVIII. Industry.

An ancedote. Motives to industry. Bible examples of this virtue.

Chapter XIX. Domestic Economy.

Economy a word of broad meaning. Much of this chapter anticipated. Servants—their general employment to be regretted. Spirit of the times—illustrated by an anecdote. American nobles. Servants cannot always be dispensed with. Seven reasons for avoiding them, if possible. 1. They are unnecessary. 2. Costly. 3. Break in upon the order of families. 4. Create distinctions in society. 5. Are bad teachers. 6. Practice anti-republican. 7. It is unchristian. Waste of time in cookery. What useful cookery is. Other wasteful practices. Morning calls. General remarks. An anecdote.

Chapter XX. Domestic Reform.

Present state of things. Female ignorant of domestic concerns. A great mistake in education. Nature of the mistake. Cause of the pecuniary distress of our country. Examples of ministers. Change or reform necessary. How it is to be effected. By whom begun. The young wife to begin it. She should begin immediately. One serious difficulty. How to overcome it. Gradual reformation. Rapid progress, ultimately. Book learning. How far books are useful. "The Frugal Housewife." "Bread and Bread-making."

Chapter XXI. Sobriety.

Definition of the term. Something more than temperance. Tea drinking. Effects of tea and coffee. Physiology of their effects. Nervous excitement—compared with intoxication. Proofs of the author's views. Sobriety at feasts. Sobriety in company. Other forms of sobriety.

Chapter XXII. Discretion.

Paul's estimate of the importance of discretion. Opinions of Gisborne. Various forms of indiscretion. Danger of extremes. What true purity is. A word of caution to the indiscreet.

Chapter XXIII. Scolding.

Many kinds of scolds. Internal scolding. Intermittent scolds. Periodical scolding. Other forms of scolding. Hints over the husband's shoulder.

Chapter XXIV. Forbearance.

Perfection not to be expected. Maxim of a philosopher. Spirit of forbearance a pearl of great price. Cases where forbearance is required. Triumphing, "I told you so." Comparisons. Joking. Saying of Salzman.

Chapter XXV. Contentment.

Value of contentment. Why it is especially valuable to the young wife. Duty to her own family and others. Duty to God.

Chapter XXVI. Habits and Manners.

Little things. Setting out in life. Important to set out right. Difficulty with some husbands. How to manage. Eugene and Juliet. General principles.

Chapter XXVII. Dress.

Opinion of Paul. Real objects of dress. Modesty. Dress should regulate our temperature. Frequent change—why useful. General rule. A painful sight. Nature of profuse perspiration, or sweating. Material of dress. Objections to cotton. Fashion of dress. Compression of the lungs—its evils. Sympathies. Moderate indulgence. Hiding defects by dress. Dress of the husband.

Chapter XXVIII. Health.

Purity of the air in our apartments. Purity of clothing—furniture—cellars—drains—wells, &c. Personal cleanliness. Its expense not to be considered. Various modes of exercise. Household labor. Exercise in the open air. Walking. Riding. Health, in our own keeping. The husband's health. General remarks.

Chapter XXIX. Attending the Sick.

Attending the sick should be a part of female education. Objections to this view considered. Reasons why females should be thus trained. Their native qualifications for this office. Their labor cheaper. They have stronger sympathies. Application of the principle to the case of the young wife.

Chapter XXX. Love of Infancy and Childhood.

What the love of childhood is. Frequent want of it. Dr. Gregory's opinion—Mr. Addison's. Great gulf fixed between children and adults. Love of childhood favorable to mental improvement—to the happiness of the wife—to the happiness of her husband—to religious improvement. Example of the Saviour. How to elicit this love, when it is wanting. Remarks on faith. What faith can enable us to accomplish.

Chapter XXXI. Giving Advice.

Advice of females in regard to business. Why it is often undervalued. Objections answered. How far advice is applicable. Advice in manners and morals. Advice in religion.

Chapter XXXII. Self-Government.

Difficulties of self-government. Meaning of the term. Error in education. What is to be done? Motive to be present. Directions how to proceed. Cooperation of the husband. The results happy.

Chapter XXXIII. Intellectual Improvement.

Anecdote of Mrs. H. Course of study after marriage. Much of it excellent. Cooperation of the husband and wife. Nature of education. Difficulties of studying in married life. They may be overcome. Importance of system. Evils of a want of it. Anecdote. Chemistry. Its importance illustrated. Terrible consequences of ignorance in housewifery. Much poisoning in the community. Study of other sciences. Anatomy and physiology. A few books recommended. Collateral topics of study. Knowledge necessary to benevolent effort. Study of the subject of education. Errors. Theory and experience.

Chapter XXXIV. Social Improvement.

Anecdote of Alcibiades. Intention of the Creator. Marriage of course a social state. Morning calls. Evening visits. Excitements. Balls and theatres. Visiting in the afternoon. Social advantages of large families. Visiting by large companies. Topics of conversation. Scandal. Opposition of human nature to the gospel. Reading at social meetings. An important caution.

Chapter XXXV. Moral and Religious Improvement.

Doing good. Many forms of doing good. Philosophy of doing good. Associated effort. How to select societies. Individual charitable effort. The poor. The ignorant. The vicious. The sick. Caution in regard to visiting the sick. Prayer as a means of improvement. Self-examination. Reading. The Bible. Other useful books.

Chapter XXXVI. Moral Influence on the Husband.

Mode of female influence on the husband. Mr. Flint's encomium. Examples of female influence. Wife of Jonathan Edwards—of Sir James Mackintosh. True position of woman in society. Serious error of some modern writers. A caution. Making haste to be rich. A species of mania. Its extent and evils. How the young wife is concerned with it. What she can do to remove it. Agur's prayer—seldom used in modern times. Particular modes of female influence. Office seeking. How to dissuade from it. Exposures to intemperance. Female consistency. Female piety. Its effects on the husband—compared with amiableness and beauty. Apparent objection to the writer's views. Woman's prerogative.

■ *Questions for* . . . Duties of Young Wives by William A. Alcott

Discussion and Journal Writing

1. Is Alcott's book for husbands or wives? How can you tell?
2. How would you update Alcott's book? Which categories would you drop entirely? What ones would you add?
3. Can you think of any stories, fictional or real, that typify expectations today's husbands and wives have of one another? How do those expectations vary from one class, region, or ethnic group to another? Despite the differences, are expectations essentially the same?

○○○○○

Matter of Baby M

Supreme Court of New Jersey, 1988.
109 N.J. 396, 537 A.2d 1227.

WILENTZ, C.J.

I. FACTS

In February 1985, William Stern and Mary Beth Whitehead entered into a surrogacy contract.

* * *

The contract provided that through artificial insemination using Mr. Stern's sperm, Mrs. Whitehead would become pregnant, carry the child to term, bear it, deliver it to the Sterns, and thereafter do whatever was necessary to terminate her maternal rights so that Mrs. Stern could thereafter adopt the child. Mrs. Whitehead's husband, Richard,[1] was also a party to the contract; Mrs. Stern was not. Mr. Whitehead promised to do all acts necessary to rebut the presumption of paternity under the Parentage Act. Although Mrs. Stern was not a party to the surrogacy agreement, the contract gave her sole custody of the child in the event of Mr. Stern's death. Mrs. Stern's status as a nonparty to the surrogate parenting agreement presumably was to avoid the application of the baby-selling statute to this arrangement.

Mr. Stern, on his part, agreed to attempt the artificial insemination and to pay Mrs. Whitehead $10,000 after the child's birth, on its delivery to him. In a separate contract, Mr. Stern agreed to pay $7,500 to the Infertility Center of New York ("ICNY"). The Center's advertising campaigns solicit surrogate mothers and encourage infertile couples to consider surrogacy. ICNY arranged for the surrogacy contract by bringing the parties together, explaining the process to them, furnishing the contractual form, and providing legal counsel.

* * *

Mrs. Whitehead had reached her decision concerning surrogacy before the Sterns, and had actually been involved as a potential surrogate mother with another couple. After numerous unsuccessful artificial inseminations, that effort was abandoned. Thereafter, the Sterns learned of the Infertility Center, the possibilities of surrogacy, and of Mary Beth Whitehead. The two couples met to discuss the surrogacy arrangement and decided to go forward. On February 6, 1985, Mr. Stern and Mr. and Mrs. Whitehead executed the surrogate parenting agreement. After several artificial inseminations over a period of months, Mrs. Whitehead

---

1. Subsequent to the trial court proceedings, Mr. and Mrs. Whitehead were divorced, and soon thereafter Mrs. Whitehead remarried. Nevertheless, in the course of this opinion we will make reference almost exclusively to the facts as they existed at the time of trial, the facts on which the decision we now review was reached. We note moreover that Mr. Whitehead remains a party to this dispute. For these reasons, we continue to refer to appellants as Mr. and Mrs. Whitehead.

became pregnant. The pregnancy was uneventful and on March 27, 1986, Baby M was born.

* * *

Mrs. Whitehead realized, almost from the moment of birth, that she could not part with this child. She had felt a bond with it even during pregnancy. Some indication of the attachment was conveyed to the Sterns at the hospital when they told Mrs. Whitehead what they were going to name the baby. She apparently broke into tears and indicated that she did not know if she could give up the child. She talked about how the baby looked like her other daughter, and made it clear that she was experiencing great difficulty with the decision.

Nonetheless, Mrs. Whitehead was, for the moment, true to her word. Despite powerful inclinations to the contrary, she turned her child over to the Sterns on March 30 at the Whiteheads' home.

* * *

Later in the evening of March 30, Mrs. Whitehead became deeply disturbed, disconsolate, stricken with unbearable sadness. She had to have her child. She could not eat, sleep, or concentrate on anything other than her need for her baby. The next day she went to the Sterns' home and told them how much she was suffering.

The depth of Mrs. Whitehead's despair surprised and frightened the Sterns. She told them that she could not live without her baby, that she must have her, even if only for one week, that thereafter she would surrender her child. The Sterns, concerned that Mrs. Whitehead might indeed commit suicide, not wanting under any circumstances to risk that, and in any event believing that Mrs. Whitehead would keep her word, turned the child over to her.

* * *

The struggle over Baby M began when it became apparent that Mrs. Whitehead could not return the child to Mr. Stern. Due to Mrs. Whitehead's refusal to relinquish the baby, Mr. Stern filed a complaint seeking enforcement of the surrogacy contract. He alleged, accurately, that Mrs. Whitehead had not only refused to comply with the surrogacy contract but had threatened to flee from New Jersey with the child in order to avoid even the possibility of his obtaining custody. The court papers asserted that if Mrs. Whitehead were to be given notice of the application for an order requiring her to relinquish custody, she would, prior to the hearing, leave the state with the baby. And that is precisely what she did. After the order was entered, *ex parte,* the process server, aided by the police, in the presence of the Sterns, entered Mrs. Whitehead's home to execute the order. Mr. Whitehead fled with the child, who had been handed to him through a window while those who came to enforce the order were thrown off balance by a dispute over the child's current name.

The Whiteheads immediately fled to Florida with Baby M. They stayed initially with Mrs. Whitehead's parents, where one of Mrs. Whitehead's children had been living. For the next three months, the Whiteheads and Melissa lived at roughly twenty different hotels, motels, and homes in order to avoid apprehension. From time to time Mrs. Whitehead would call Mr. Stern to discuss the matter; the conversations, recorded by Mr. Stern on advice of counsel, show an escalating dispute about rights, morality, and power, accompanied by threats of Mrs. Whitehead to kill herself, to kill the child, and falsely to accuse Mr. Stern of sexually molesting Mrs. Whitehead's other daughter.

Eventually the Sterns discovered where the Whiteheads were staying, commenced supplementary proceedings in Florida, and obtained an order requiring the Whiteheads to turn over the child. Police in Florida enforced the order, forcibly removing the child from her grandparents' home. She was soon thereafter brought to New Jersey and turned over to the Sterns. The prior order of the court, issued *ex parte*, awarding custody of the child to the Sterns *pendente lite*, was reaffirmed by the trial court after consideration of the certified representations of the parties (both represented by counsel) concerning the unusual sequence of events that had unfolded. Pending final judgment, Mrs. Whitehead was awarded limited visitation with Baby M.

The Sterns' complaint, in addition to seeking possession and ultimately custody of the child, sought enforcement of the surrogacy contract. Pursuant to the contract, it asked that the child be permanently placed in their custody, that Mrs. Whitehead's parental rights be terminated, and that Mrs. Stern be allowed to adopt the child, *i.e.*, that, for all purposes, Melissa become the Sterns' child.

The trial took thirty-two days over a period of more than two months. It included numerous interlocutory appeals and attempted interlocutory appeals. There were twenty-three witnesses to the facts recited above and fifteen expert witnesses, eleven testifying on the issue of custody and four on the subject of Mrs. Stern's multiple sclerosis; the bulk of the testimony was devoted to determining the parenting arrangement most compatible with the child's best interests. Soon after the conclusion of the trial, the trial court announced its opinion from the bench. 217 *N.J.Super.* 313, 525 *A.2d* 1128 (1987). It held that the surrogacy contract was valid; ordered that Mrs. Whitehead's parental rights be terminated and that sole custody of the child be granted to Mr. Stern; and, after hearing brief testimony from Mrs. Stern, immediately entered an order allowing the adoption of Melissa by Mrs. Stern, all in accordance with the surrogacy contract. Pending the outcome of the appeal, we granted a continuation of visitation to Mrs. Whitehead, although slightly more limited than the visitation allowed during the trial.

* * *

(Excerpt of decision.)

■ *Questions for* . . . Matter of Baby M, Supreme Court of New Jersey, 1988.

Discussion and Journal Writing

1. What is a surrogacy contract? Should surrogacy contracts be lawful?
2. The case is shot through with conflicting family values and feelings. What and whose are they?
3. Go to a law library and read the rest of Judge Wilentz's decision. Write about whether you agree or not and why.

$\mathcal{F}$amily Album One

Movie Stills

Giant (1956, Warner Bros.)

Shane (1953, Paramount)

Cat on a Hot Tin Roof (1958, MGM)

■ *Questions for* . . . Movie Stills

Discussion and Journal Writing

1. These stills are from blockbusters about troubled families or families facing a crisis. Does it tell us anything about America's or Hollywood's attitudes toward family that these and so many other families on the silver screen are in trouble?

ooooo

Narrative Writing

A *narrative* is a story that writers tell for different reasons: to entertain, to instruct, to inform, to explore, to record. Unlike expository writing, which moves from one idea to the next and revolves around a thesis, central problem, or unifying idea, narrative writing moves from one event to another and conveys themes through action, characterization, and description. A narrative can take many forms. It may be a short story, a newspaper or magazine story, the minutes of a meeting, a chapter of history, a biographic or autobiographic essay or book, gossip, a letter, a court transcript, a report, or instructions in an operator's manual, just to name a few of the more popular forms.

The narratives in this chapter chronicle the experiences of people in different families in different circumstances and times. In the short story "The Man That Was Almost a Man," Richard Wright dramatizes the plight of Dave, a 15-year-old Black Southerner who is the son of sharecroppers. Hemmed in by Jim Crow racism, the strictness of his parents, and the economic needs of an oppressed family, Dave angrily gropes for a way to come of age, until he gets his hands on a gun. "1500 Slave Descendants Attend Carolina 'Reunion'" is a newspaper story about a reunion of people whose ancestors shared a slave past on a North Carolina plantation. While challenging conventional associations of plantations and the Southern gentry (Scarlett O'Hara and fancy-dress balls in the big house), these descendants reclaimed a proud legacy of struggling and persevering against the inhumanity of slavery. Donna Smith-Yackel, on the occasion of her mother's death, remembers the life of hard work her mother led, raising her eight children on a Midwestern farm in her magazine piece "My Mother Never Worked." She also exposes the sexism of our Social Security system, which will not issue a death-benefit check because it does not recognize a wife's hard work. Jack Agueros's "Halfway to Dick and Jane: A Puerto Rican Pilgrimage" is an autobiographic essay about growing up in East Harlem, the son of Puerto Rican migrants. Agueros writes about the tensions his family experienced trying to fit in while holding on to the culture they brought with them. These stories do not exhaust the varieties of family experience or narrative forms, but they suggest the range and possibilities.

The narrative is probably the oldest form of writing, and it has always been the most popular. Students tend to be more at ease with the narrative form because they have had practice telling, watching, and listening to stories. However, these facts do not make writing a narrative easy. Mastering it takes practice and effort, but it is worth mastering. Not only is the narrative—in all its forms—popular and practical, but a short narrative, called an *anecdote,* can also help a writer make or illustrate a point in an expository essay.

A poorly written narrative usually moves monotonously and colorlessly from one event to the next. There is no sense of development; it's just one thing after the next. The people involved are stereotypically drawn, or they make no impression at all. They are just names. There's no sense of place or purpose. With a bad story, it is hard to tell why the writer wrote it or why you're reading it. Think of Edith Bunker's style: she tells stories in that sing-songy voice that wanders from tangent to tangent. Before long, we want to shout with Archie, "Get to the point, Edith! The point!"

A good story, on the other hand, has a point or a central theme, and all the elements of the story—order, plot, characterization, dialogue, description, and word choice—contribute to it. Most stories begin at the beginning, build to a point or climax, and end with parting reflections on the story's point, or a denouement—that is, the closing action of a story. Donna Smith-Yackel creates a variation on standard narrative order for the sake of her theme. "My Mother Never Worked" begins shortly after her mother's death with a phone call she makes to the Social Security Office to see about a death-benefit check. She is put on hold, and while she waits, she reminisces about her mother's hard, loving life: raising eight children, cooking, farming, making quilts and clothes, and so on. Her mother's life was an epic of hard work, endurance, and love. Then the clerk at Social Security returns and tells Smith-Yackel that her mother does not have a death-benefit check coming because she never worked; Social Security only recognizes her husband's work. The reader shares Smith-Yackel's shock and indignation chiefly because of the way she inserted the story of her mother's life within the story of her conversation with Social Security.

Characterization is as important as narrative order or action because a reader understands or cares about the action of a story while coming to know the people involved. A writer can reveal character through action, dialogue, and direct comments about a character. Furthermore, the way someone says something, as well as what that someone says, provides insight into that person's character. In "The Man That Was Almost a Man," it is through Dave, the story's protagonist, that we feel the choking force of Jim Crow racism. At every turn, he is cuffed by the epithet "boy," and as he scans his surroundings and thinks on the lives of grown Black men of his acquaintance, he sees an eternity of "boyhood." Seeing Black men yoked to plows, working the land of White bosses, he rejects the plow and chooses the gun. There is a brighter future in the gun, he thinks; a gun is loaded with power and respect. Though Wright uses every technique of characterization available to a writer, he reveals Dave's character especially through dialogue and reckless action. As Dave sneaks the gun around and insists again and again that he's almost a man, we feel the full force of the story's theme.

Descriptive detail and good word choice are important to narrative development, too. Well-chosen details can evoke an era or conjure up a place, and it is through word choice that a writer's tone and voice come through most clearly. In paragraph nine of "Halfway to Dick and Jane: A Puerto Rican Pilgrimage," Jack Agueros describes his parents' Christmas gatherings so vividly that you can see the crowd, smell the aromas of the holiday dishes, and hear the music.

> My father would dismantle the beds and move all the furniture so that two full rooms could be used for dancing. My mother would cook up a storm, particularly at Christmas. *Pasteles, lechon asado, arroz con gandules,* and a lot of *coquito* to drink (meat-stuffed plantain, roast pork, rice with pigeon peas, and coconut nog). My father always brought in a band. They played without compensation and were guests at the party. They ate and drank and danced while a victrola covered the intermissions. . . . Parties always went on till daybreak, and in addition to the band, there were always volunteers to sing and declaim poetry.

Of course, Agueros's fondness for his parents and the loving childhood they gave him comes through in his phrasing and wording. Later in the essay, when Agueros writes about the rise of gangs in New York City in the 1940s, he uses slang and choppy phrasing to give his writing the feel of the street.

> In our confusion, we were sometimes pathetically reaching out, sometimes pathologically striking out. Gangs. Drugs. Wine. Smoking. Girls. Dances and slow-drag music. Mambo. Spics, Spooks, and Wops. Territories, brother gangs, and war councils establishing rules for right of way on blocks and avenues and for seating in the local theater. Pegged pants and zip guns. Slang.

Similarly, in "1500 Slave Descendants Attend Carolina 'Reunion,'" the writer sets the stage with a few deft strokes of description: "Here under sunny skies, a crowd of 2000, three-quarters of them descendants of Somerset slaves, picnicked on lawns canopied by swamp chestnut trees, hummed along with Negro spirituals, and observed the re-enactment of a slave wedding." The words *canopied* and *hummed* convey so much about the tone of the gathering.

All kinds of narratives benefit from particularity—a sense of place, characterization, vivid word choice, and descriptive detail. An inexperienced writer's tendency is to assume too much on the part of the reader. Remember that the reader wasn't there; he or she doesn't know what you mean until you say it.

🕉 Writing Workshop

The purpose here is to walk you through a narrative essay, applying what you have read about the writing process and narratives. The approach we take to the following topic will also work with the other topics that appear at the end of each chapter.

The Topic: Family gatherings and what they reveal about family feelings, customs, taboos, traditions, values, and roles.

The Assignment: Write an essay about a reunion, birthday, wedding, funeral, naming ceremony, christening, special holiday meal, or some other family gathering, and assume your essay will be read by someone from a different background. In other words, don't assume that the reader is an insider to your culture who understands how things are done. Explain yourself. Elaborate. As you tell what happened and describe who was there and where it took place, try to prove a point or reveal something special about your family. Develop your account with details and examples. Edit and revise for phrasing and development. Proofread carefully for errors—grammar, punctuation, and spelling.

To begin, brainstorm family gatherings. Take about 15 minutes to make a list of as many gatherings as you can recall: birthdays, anniversaries, religious events, celebrations, holidays, and so on. As you jot down phrases, try to include specific details that will help you remember the event: "Emilio and Rosa's wedding in Bayonne, 1989"; "the party at Aunt Mary's for Cerese's christening in 1990, I think"; "the reunion at Grandma's in Pasadena; it must have been 1986." Take a look at how Jack Agueros writes about the Christmas parties his family used to throw in their apartment in East Harlem— paragraph 12, "Halfway to Dick and Jane: A Puerto Rican Pilgrimage."

Study your list and choose the two family gatherings about which you have the strongest feelings and most vivid memories. It is hard to make a reader care about a subject if you don't. Write each one at the head of separate sheets of paper and go on brainstorming. Try to remember everything you can about those events. Read what you've written and choose the one you like best.

Next, freewrite about that event for ten minutes. Remember, freewriting means that your pen doesn't stop. The point is to gather momentum, to exploit the associative power of words to call up more words. Write down whatever comes to mind, and don't worry about making yourself understood to anyone else. No one but you will read what you freewrite. Wander through your memory of the event, or if you discover a theme or a thread that draws your interest, pursue it.

Now, take another look at the topic, and study your brainstorming and freewriting. Mark phrases and ideas that you like and may want to use. Draft a tentative outline of the points you want to make about the people who were at that gathering, the events you want to write about, and the theme or themes you want to develop. Think of what you are producing as an inventory. If you can, try to state the point of the essay in a sentence.

Before you write a first draft, you may find it helpful to talk to someone else who attended the gathering. Reminiscing may help you to recall details, events, and conversation that you had forgotten. Looking at photos or videos can do the same thing. Take advantage of your resources.

When you've gathered all the information you can, study your outline with an eye to sequence and organization. Do you want to begin with a paragraph or two of background? Do you want to plunge right into the middle of the story and then work your way back to the beginning? Perhaps you want to begin at the end and then jump back to the beginning. Or, you may simply want to begin at the beginning and work background information in as you go along. Though it is a good idea to give some thought to order before you begin your first draft, you can always change your mind and reorder your sentences and paragraphs. So, just think about order at this point, but don't worry about it.

Now, set aside a couple of hours and write a first draft. Try to stay with it from beginning to end; the more immersed you become in the writing process, the richer your writing is likely to be. As you are writing, concentrate on the flow of your sentences and the development of your paragraphs. If you are unsure about the grammar or punctuation or a sentence, mark it. Do the same for a word that isn't exactly the right one. You can come back later and work on those problems, but try not to let them interrupt your train of thought. Let your outline be your guide.

Allow your first draft to sit for a day before you correct and polish it. Look up any words or grammatical principles you are unsure of and revise accordingly. If you have trouble with apostrophes and possession, for instance, review the principles and apply them. If you review the grammatical principles that give you trouble each time you polish a first draft, sooner or later you will master those principles. Also, consider the sentence and paragraph order you have chosen, work on characterization, add or develop descriptive detail, and read your draft aloud to test the phrasing.

Remember your reader as you work. He or she isn't necessarily privy to the particulars of your culture, region, and family, so spell everything out. Write as if your piece were going to appear in a local newspaper or magazine. Writing isn't authentic if it isn't an act of expression, but it's not likely to be effective unless it is also a self-conscious act of communication. Simply put, you are saying something to someone.

Try reading your draft to a classmate or friend. Perhaps your instructor will ask you to do this in class. Often, the act of reading aloud makes writers so self-conscious that they see problems and errors they overlooked before. Furthermore, you can take advantage of your audience's response. Invite your listener to comment on everything from phrasing to characterization. Take notes, especially when your narrative confuses your listener. You may have to rephrase or reorder a passage so that it will have the effect you want.

Review the narratives I have included in this chapter; at this point, you will be especially open to learning from their techniques. If, for instance, you have included a patch or two of dialogue that you are not happy with, study how this chapter's writers do it. If you can't see the personalities of the key people in your descriptions, consult the essays. Make notes about what needs to be done and put your essay through one last draft. By this point, you should be working chiefly on development—description and characterization.

Finally, give your essay a title that expresses its theme and tone. Perhaps studying the titles the writers in this chapter use will help. Then, type your finished essay if you can. If you cannot type, I suggest you learn. With the growing importance of computers, everyone needs to know how to use a keyboard. Furthermore, typing a piece of writing gives the writer one last chance to make revisions, and typed final copy is more satisfying. It looks good. Regardless of whether you type or write, proofread your work carefully for typos or copying errors. Most instructors don't mind if you make final corrections with a pen or correction fluid, but it is a good idea to check with your instructor ahead of time so there are no surprises. Make a photocopy or a file copy on a back-up disk in case the paper is lost, and hand it in.

When you get your paper back, reread it and study your instructor's comments, suggestions, and corrections. If you don't understand a comment, ask your instructor. After all, those comments are there for your benefit. It is a good idea to remind yourself of your strong points and to study your shortcomings so that you will be able to do a better job on the next paper.

 Chapter 2

$\mathcal{F}$amily Portraits

■

🐾 A Gallery of Family Portraits

Paule Marshall's *Brown Girl, Brownstones* is a novel about the Boyces, a family of Barbadian immigrants who settle in Brooklyn. In the first chapter, Selina, the main character, is roaming around the house looking for company, distractions, and trouble. She is 11. It's a beautiful day, but Selina is cooped up in the house because her big sister Ina isn't feeling well and can't take her to the movies with the rest of the neighborhood children. After spatting with Ina, Selina is drawn to an old family photograph:

> She snatched up the family photograph from the buffet and stared at it bitterly in the scant light.
>
> It was her father, mother, Ina and the brother she had never known. The picture of a neat, young family and she did not believe it. The small girl under the drooping bow did not resemble her sister. The young woman in the 1920's dress with a headband around her forehead could not be the mother. This mother had a shy beauty, there was a girlish expectancy in her smile. Then there was the baby on her lap, who stared out at Selina with round blank eyes. His hair capped his head like fur and his tiny fists held tightly onto nothing.

"He's like a girl with all that hair," she muttered contemptuously. He had been frail and dying with a bad heart while she had been stirring to life. She had lain curled in the mother's stomach, waiting for his dying to be complete, she knew, peering through the pores as the box containing his body was lowered into the ground. Then she had come, strong and well-made, to take his place, but they had taken no photographs. . . .

Her father was the only one she believed in the picture. Despite the old-fashioned suit and the spats, it was her father. The angle at which he held the cane, his detached air, the teasing smile proclaimed him. For her, he was the one constant in the flux and unreality of life. The day was suddenly bright with the thought of him upstairs in the sun parlor, and slamming down the photograph she bounded from the room, taking the steps two at a time.

In just a few paragraphs, Marshall puts the Boyce family on the page. During the 1920s, when the photograph that Selina holds was taken, the Boyces were a young family of four. The oldest child, Ina, is quite young: she submits to her mother doing her hair and adorning it with a "drooping bow." The second child, the sickly boy who did not survive, is an infant in her mother's lap. Selina's father, Deighton, is something of a dandy in his white spats and cane. He is confident, verging on cocky; and his young wife, Silla, is girlish. Her expression says the future lies before them.

We see this photo through Selina's eyes, so it's not surprising that we learn more about Selina than about anyone in the photo. In fact, it's Selina's perspective that gives this passage depth and complexity. She is jealous, suspicious, and even a little resentful of the life her family had before she was born. There is an intimation that the family has undergone a fundamental change for the worse: Deighton and Silla Boyce no longer gather their family together, dressed in their Sunday best, to smile for the future. Selina "believes" no one in the photo except her father. She sides with his likeness and runs to find him, suggesting that the Boyce family is troubled and divided. In Marshall's portrait of the Boyces, there are emotions, attitudes, and even an abbreviated family history.

In other words, there are ideas in pictures. There are also perceptions, impressions, and points implicit in descriptions of the way something smells, feels, and sounds. Descriptions are not the things themselves; descriptions are verbal representations of things. They are the things inflected with thought.

The family portraits included in this chapter are about a wide range of families and represent several kinds of writing, such as autobiography, fiction, and history. All the authors, however, deliver impressions that speak to the senses, especially the sense of sight, and they are all trying to say something about the families they describe. The purposes that shape their descriptions vary, but there is always a purpose to effective descriptive writing.

Family descriptions take so many forms. Family court caseworkers fill their files with family profiles and accounts of events that may have some bearing on the cases they handle. In private practice, family therapists do the same to help them treat troubled families. School psychologists often record family dynamics to gain a fuller understanding of the problems students face. Social scientists, especially anthropologists and social historians, tend to categorize and analyze families based on detailed portraits of specific, representative families.

Novelists and writers of biography and autobiography draw especially vivid and emotionally charged family portraits. Think of the work of any major novelist, and the names of the families he or she created will come to mind: Faulkner's Snopeses, Joyce's Daedaluses, Woolf's Ramseys, Thackeray's Crawleys, Tolstoy's Karenins, and so on. Photographers, painters, and filmmakers also produce arresting images of real or imagined families.

Journalists often describe families in trouble. A glance at the metropolitan section of any major newspaper is likely to turn up a story of family violence, abuse, or neglect. Family success stories also turn up in the media, but not as frequently, because journalists usually consider success to be less gripping, less entertaining, less newsworthy.

Insurance adjusters sometimes keep family records; so do some clergy. Government agencies often compile family data: some agencies are interested in the shape and history of specific families; others are interested in an aggregate portrait of families of a certain type, in a certain region, or at a certain income level. Lawyers describe families in courtroom arguments and in legal briefs.

The description of a particular family reflects the specific characteristics of that family, the purpose of the description, and the views, perspective, perceptions, style, and talent of the writer.

All the pieces of writing in this chapter convey highly individualized descriptions of families, as opposed to the clinical or statistical impressions people working at psychiatric hospitals or government agencies produce. Six write about their own families, but the two journalists, Agee and Kotlowitz, the songwriter, Bill Withers, and the novelist, Paule Marshall, are also powerfully attached to the families they write about. They all express complicated ideas and emotions in their family portraits; in the process, they provide us with instances of descriptive writing at its best.

Word Play: *Home*

Home comes to us from the Germanic roots of the English language, unlike *family*, which derives from the Latin and Romance language grafts English began to acquire in the ninth century. *Home* is a descendant of the Old English *ham*, which means "the place where one lies, dwelling." It is a derivative of the Indo-European *kei.*

In traditional societies, *dwelling* is just the right word to describe the homes people lived in and in some cases still live in. The Sioux built tepees, the Eskimo made igloos, and in the Kalahari desert today, the !Kung build huts.

In industrial societies, *homes* are houses and apartments. There are other places where people lie or dwell, but they are not called *homes;* for instance, prisons, army barracks, and mental-health institutions are not *homes.* Neither are the semi-permanent boxes, crates, and makeshift shanties of the homeless.

In contemporary America, *home* is an especially charged word. Single people have *homes,* and millions of families live in apartments; however, *home* evokes an idealized image of complete nuclear families living in houses with yards. The white picket fences of the movies, Norman Rockwell's paintings, and the Dick-and-Jane readers are optional, but a middle-class house occupied by two parents and their children is indispensable to the image the word evokes. There are hyphenated and modified *homes,* like the *foster homes* that orphans and other wards of the state live in or the *second* or *vacation homes* the rich own, but they revolve like satellites around the plain, unmodified word and emphasize its centrality.

What does it tell us about language that the experience of a specific group can color the way we use a word?

In the minds of many Americans, *home* is also a safe haven from the country's larger social forces and ills, despite the fact that experts continuously show us how those forces slip under the doors and through the windows of America's homes. *Home* is that place in a mass society where you have a name and an identity, where your birthday is celebrated. It's the place where you are supposed to matter. As the saying goes, "A man's home is his castle." It's telling that the expression refers to "the man of the house," which is, of course, another expression.

The sanctity of the home is often invoked in speeches and sermons, and it is encoded in our laws to such an extent that, in some cases, we are permitted to harm and even kill intruders into our homes. Campaigning politicians often address the homeowner, especially in national elections. In Thomas Jefferson's time, the noble yeoman who owned his own farm was the model solid citizen, but with the rise of cities and industry, the homeowner took his place. (In America's political imagination, the solid citizen has traditionally been a man.) In fact, the wish to own a nice home for the family is the first idea that occurs to many people when they hear an expression politicians love to conjure with—"the American dream."

Home overlaps in meaning with *household, house, apartment,* and *domicile,* but it is much more resonant than its synonyms. *Home*'s positive connotation is also present in most of the compound words it is part of. Think of *homeland, home port, homestead, homemaker, homecoming,* and *home plate. Homely* and *homespun* are exceptions, but they only prove the rule. At first glance, the recently coined word *homeless* would fit in the same category with *homely* and *homespun.* The homeless lead lives of misery. However, the word has the positive meaning of *home* built into it since the homeless are identified as lacking something Americans find sacred: a home.

Journal Entries

Choose a family word, such as *mother,* look it up in a dictionary that contains word origins, think about how you and others use the word, and write about it. Comparing a word with its synonyms is a good way to place it. Or, ask people what *home* means to them and write about what you discover.

——————————— $\mathcal{R}$eadings ———————————

Photographs of My Parents

—Maxine Hong Kingston

Like Paule Marshall, Maxine Hong Kingston is the daughter of immigrants. She was born in Stockton, California, in 1940 and has made her heritage and the immigrant experience the subject of her work. "Photographs of My Parents" is a passage from *The Warrior Woman: Memories of a Girlhood Among Ghosts* (1975), which won the National Book Critics Circle Award. Through the picture she writes about, she makes a number of rich suggestions about the differences between life in China and America.

Once in a long while, four times so far for me, my mother brings out the metal   1
tube that holds her medical diploma. On the tube are gold circles crossed with seven red lines each—"joy" ideographs in abstract. There are also little flowers that look like gears for a gold machine. According to the scraps of labels with Chinese and American addresses, stamps, and postmarks, the family airmailed the can from Hong Kong in 1950. It got crushed in the middle, and whoever tried to peel the labels off stopped because the red and gold paint came off too, leaving silver scratches that rust. Somebody tried to pry the end off before discovering that the tube pulls apart. When I open it, the smell of China flies out, a thousand-year-old bat flying heavy-headed out of the Chinese caverns where bats are as white as dust, a smell that comes from long ago, far back in the brain. Crates from Canton, Hong Kong, Singapore, and Taiwan have that smell too, only stronger because they are more recently come from the Chinese.

Inside the can are three scrolls, one inside another. The largest says that in the   2
twenty-third year of the National Republic, the To Keung School of Midwifery, where she has had two years of instruction and Hospital Practice, awards its Diploma to my mother, who has shown through oral and written examination her Proficiency in Midwifery, Pediatrics, Gynecology, "Medecine," "Surgary," Therapeutics, Ophthalmology, Bacteriology, Dermatology, Nursing and Bandage. This document has eight stamps on it: one, the school's English and Chinese names embossed together in a circle; one, as the Chinese enumerate, a stork and a big

baby in lavender ink; one, the school's Chinese seal; one, an orangish paper stamp pasted in the border design; one, the red seal of Dr. Wu Pak-liang, M.D., Lyon, Berlin, president and "Ex-assistant étranger à la clinique chirugicale et d'accouchement de l'université de Lyon"; one, the red seal of Dean Woo Yin-kam, M.D., one, my mother's seal, her chop mark larger than the president's and the dean's; and one, the number 1279 on the back. Dean Woo's signature is followed by "(Hackett)." I read in a history book that Hackett Medical College for Women at Canton was founded in the nineteenth century by European women doctors.

The school seal has been pressed over a photograph of my mother at the age   3
of thirty-seven. The diploma gives her age as twenty-seven. She looks younger than I do, her eyebrows are thicker, her lips fuller. Her naturally curly hair is parted on the left, one wavy wisp tendrilling off to the right. She wears a scholar's white gown, and she is not thinking about her appearance. She stares straight ahead as if she could see me and past me to her grandchildren and grandchildren's grandchildren. She has spacy eyes, as all people recently from Asia have. Her eyes do not focus on the camera. My mother is not smiling; Chinese do not smile for photographs. Their faces command relatives in foreign lands—"Send money"—and posterity forever—"Put food in front of this picture." My mother does not understand Chinese-American snapshots. "What are you laughing at?" she asks.

The second scroll is a long narrow photograph of the graduating class with the   4
school officials seated in front. I picked out my mother immediately. Her face is exactly her own, though forty years younger. She is so familiar, I can only tell whether or not she is pretty or happy or smart by comparing her to the other women. For this formal group picture she straightened her hair with oil to make a chinlength bob like the others'. On the other women, strangers, I can recognize a curled lip, a sidelong glance, pinched shoulders. My mother is not soft; the girl with the small nose and dimpled underlip is soft. My mother is not humorous, not like the girl at the end who lifts her mocking chin to pose like Girl Graduate. My mother does not have smiling eyes; the old woman teacher (Dean Woo?) in front crinkles happily, and the one faculty member in the western suit smiles westernly. Most of the graduates are girls whose faces have not yet formed; my mother's face will not change anymore, except to age. She is intelligent, alert, pretty. I can't tell if she's happy.

The graduates seem to have been looking elsewhere when they pinned the   5
rose, zinnia, or chrysanthemum on their precise black dresses. One thin girl wears hers in the middle of her chest. A few have a flower over a left or a right nipple. My mother put hers, a chrysanthemum, below her left breast. Chinese dresses at that time were dartless, cut as if women did not have breasts; these young doctors, unaccustomed to decorations, may have seen their chests as black expanses with no reference points for flowers. Perhaps they couldn't shorten that far gaze that lasts only a few years after a Chinese emigrates. In this picture too my mother's eyes are big with what they held—reaches of oceans beyond China, land beyond oceans. Most emigrants learn the barbarians' directness—how to gather themselves and stare rudely into talking faces as if trying to catch lies. In America my mother has

eyes as strong as boulders, never once skittering off a face, but she has not learned to place decorations and phonograph needles, nor has she stopped seeing land on the other side of the oceans. Now her eyes include the relatives in China, as they once included my father smiling and smiling in his many western outfits, a different one for each photograph that he sent from America.

He and his friends took pictures of one another in bathing suits at Coney   6
Island beach, the salt wind from the Atlantic blowing their hair. He's the one in the middle with his arms about the necks of his buddies. They pose in the cockpit of a biplane, on a motorcycle, and on a lawn beside the "Keep Off the Grass" sign. They are always laughing. My father, white shirt sleeves rolled up, smiles in front of a wall of clean laundry. In the spring he wears a new straw hat, cocked at a Fred Astaire angle. He steps out, dancing down the stairs, one foot forward, one back, a hand in his pocket. He wrote to her about the American custom of stomping on straw hats come fall. "If you want to save your hat for next year," he said, "you have to put it away early, or else when you're riding the subway or walking along Fifth Avenue, any stranger can snatch it off your head and put his foot through it. That's the way they celebrate the change of seasons here." In the winter he wears a gray felt hat with his gray overcoat. He is sitting on a rock in Central Park. In one snapshot he is not smiling; someone took it when he was studying, blurred in the glare of the desk lamp.

There are no snapshots of my mother. In two small portraits, however, there is   7
a black thumbprint on her forehead, as if someone had inked in bangs, as if someone had marked her.

"Mother, did bangs come into fashion after you had the picture taken?" One   8
time she said yes. Another time when I asked, "Why do you have fingerprints on your forehead?" she said, "Your First Uncle did that." I disliked the unsureness in her voice.

The last scroll has columns of Chinese words. The only English is   9
"Department of Health, Canton," imprinted on my mother's face, the same photograph as on the diploma. I keep looking to see whether she was afraid. Year after year my father did not come home or send for her. Their two children had been dead for ten years. If he did not return soon, there would be no more children. ("They were three and two years old, a boy and a girl. They could talk already.") My father did send money regularly, though, and she had nobody to spend it on but herself. She bought good clothes and shoes. Then she decided to use the money for becoming a doctor. She did not leave for Canton immediately after the children died. In China there was time to complete feelings. As my father had done, my mother left the village by ship. There was a sea bird painted on the ship to protect it against shipwreck and winds. She was in luck. The following ship was boarded by river pirates, who kidnapped every passenger, even old ladies. "Sixty dollars for an old lady" was what the bandits used to say. "I sailed alone," she says, "to the capital of the entire province." She took a brown leather suitcase and a seabag stuffed with two quilts.

■ *Questions for . . .* **Photographs of My Parents** by Maxine Hong Kingston

Words to Note

tube	ideographs	gears
scraps	pry	scrolls
embossed	wisp	tendrilling
pinched	dimpled	mocking
crinkles	skittering	blurred
glare	photograph	snapshot

Language

1. Kingston uses two different words to describe the images cameras make: *photographs* and *snapshots.* Look them up. How does Kingston use them? Why does she make the distinction?
2. In the first paragraph, Kingston says someone tried to "pry" the end off the tube that contains the scrolls. Try to come up with a better word.

Style

1. What techniques does Kingston use to describe these family pictures?
2. How does her tone toward each picture come through?

Development and Organization

1. How does Kingston move from the graduation photograph of her mother to the snapshots of her father? Is it an effective transition?
2. Map the piece. Why does it begin and end with Kingston's mother?
3. How does Kingston frame these individual photographs? What holds her descriptions together?

Discussion and Journal Writing

1. According to Kingston, how do the Chinese pose for photographs? How do Americans pose? How does she explain the differences? Which style of posing does she prefer?
2. How does she feel about her heritage? Sentimental? Distant? Objective?
3. In your opinion, why does Kingston recount the occasions or reasons for the photographs of her mother and the snapshots of her father?
4. What do these photographs reveal about Kingston's parents? About Kingston? What does this piece tell us about Kingston's family?

ooooo

The Kitchen: The Great Machine That Set Our Lives Running

—Alfred Kazin

Alfred Kazin is best known as a literary critic. *On Native Ground* (1936), an original study of the themes of alienation that run through American realism, put Kazin on the map. "The Kitchen: The Great Machine That Set Our Lives Running," an excerpt from *A Walker in the City,* is Kazin in an autobiographical key. When Kazin was a boy, the Brownsville section of Brooklyn was a Jewish immigrant enclave.

The last time I saw our kitchen this clearly was one afternoon in London at the end of the war, when I waited out the rain in the entrance to a music store. A radio was playing into the street, and standing there I heard a broadcast of the first Sabbath service from Belsen Concentration Camp. When the liberated Jewish prisoners recited the *Hear O Israel, the Lord Our God, the Lord is One,* I felt myself carried back to the Friday evenings at home, when with the Sabbath at sundown a healing quietness would come over Brownsville. 1

It was the darkness and emptiness of the streets I liked most about Friday evening, as if in preparation for that day of rest and worship which the Jews greet "as a bride"—that day when the very touch of money is prohibited, all work, all travel, all household duties, even to the turning on and off of a light—Jewry had found its way past its tormented heart to some ancient still center of itself. I waited for the streets to go dark on Friday evening as other children waited for the Christmas lights. Even Friday morning after the tests were over glowed in anticipation. When I returned home after three, the warm odor of a coffee cake baking in the oven and the sight of my mother on her hands and knees scrubbing the linoleum on the dining room floor filled me with such tenderness that I could feel my senses reaching out to embrace every single object in our household. One Friday, after a morning in school spent on the voyages of Henry Hudson, I returned with the phrase *Among the discoverers of the New World* singing in my mind as the theme of my own new-found freedom on the Sabbath. 2

My great moment came at six, when my father returned from work, his overalls smelling faintly of turpentine and shellac, white drops of silver paint still gleaming on his chin. Hanging his overcoat in the long dark hall that led into our kitchen, he would leave in one pocket a loosely folded copy of the New York *World;* and then everything that beckoned to me from that other hemisphere of my brain beyond the East River would start up from the smell of fresh newsprint and the sight of the globe on the front page. It was a paper that carried special associations for me with Brooklyn Bridge. They published the *World* under the green dome on Park Row overlooking the bridge; the fresh salt air of New York harbor 3 lingered for me in the smell of paint and damp newsprint in the hall. I felt that my father brought the outside straight into our house with each day's copy of the *World.* The bridge somehow stood for freedom; the *World* for that rangy kindness and fraternalism and ease we found in Heywood Broun. My father would read aloud from "It Seems To Me" with a delighted smile on his face. "A very clear and courageous man!" he would say. "Look how he stands up for our Sacco and Vanzetti! A real social conscience, that man! Practically a Socialist!" Then, taking off his overalls, he would wash up at the kitchen sink, peeling and gnawing the paint off his nails with Gold Dust Washing Powder as I poured it into his hands, smacking his lips and grunting with pleasure as he washed himself clean of the job at last, and making me feel that I was really helping him, that I, too, was contributing to the greatness of the evening and the coming day.

By sundown the streets were empty, the curtains had been drawn, the world 4 put to rights. Even the kitchen walls had been scrubbed and now gleamed in the Sabbath candles. On the long white tablecloth were the "company" dishes, filled for some with *gefillte* fish on lettuce leaves, ringed by red horseradish, sour and half-sour pickles, tomato salad with a light vinegar dressing; for others, with chopped liver in a bed of lettuce leaves and white radishes; the long white *khalleh,* the Sabbath loaf; chicken soup with noodles *and* dumplings; chicken, meat loaf, prunes, and sweet potatoes that had been baked all day into an open pie; compote of prunes and quince, apricots and orange rind; applesauce; a great brown nutcake filled with almonds, the traditional *lekakh;* all surrounded by glasses of port wine, seltzer bottles with their nozzles staring down at us waiting to be pressed; a samovar of Russian tea, *svetouchnee* from the little red box, always served in tall glasses, with lemon slices floating on top. My father and mother sipped it in Russian fashion, through lumps of sugar held between the teeth.

Afterwards we went into the "dining room" and, since we were not particular- 5 ly orthodox, allowed ourselves little pleasures outside the Sabbath rule—an occasional game of Casino at the dining-room table where we never dined; and listening to the victrola. The evening was particularly good for me whenever the unmarried cousin who boarded with us had her two closest friends in after supper.

They were all dressmakers, like my mother; had worked with my mother in 6 the same East Side sweatshops; were all passionately loyal members of the International Ladies Garment Workers Union; and were all unmarried. We were their only family. Despite my mother's frenzied matchmaking, she had never succeeded in pinning a husband down for any of them. As she said, they were all too *particular*—what a calamity for a Jewish woman to remain unmarried! But my cousin and her friends accepted their fate calmly, and prided themselves on their culture and their strong *progressive* interests. They felt they belonged not to the "kitchen world," like my mother, but to the enlightened tradition of the old Russian intelligentsia. Whenever my mother sighed over them, they would smile out of their greater knowledge of the world, and looking at me with a pointed appeal for recognition, would speak of novels they had read in Yiddish and Russian, of *Winesburg, Ohio,* of some article in the *Nation.*

Our cousin and her two friends were of my parents' generation, but I could   7
never believe it—they seemed to enjoy life with such outspokenness. They were
the first grown-up people I had ever met who used the word *love* without embarrassment. *"Libbe! Libbe!"* my mother would explode whenever one of them
protested that she could not, after all, marry a man she did not love. "What is this
love you make such a stew about? You do not like the way he holds his cigarette?
Marry him first and it will all come out right in the end!" It astonished me to realize there was a world in which even unmarried women no longer young were simply individual human beings with lives of their own. *Our* parents, whatever affection might offhandedly be expressed between them, always had the look of being
committed to something deeper than *mere* love. Their marriages were neither happy
nor unhappy; they were arrangements. However they had met—whether in Russia
or in the steerage or, like my parents, in an East Side boarding house—whatever
they still thought of each other, *love* was not a word they used easily. Marriage was
an institution people entered into—for all I could ever tell—only from immigrant
loneliness, a need to be with one's own kind that mechanically resulted in the *family*. The *family* was a whole greater than all the individuals who made it up, yet
made sense only in their untiring solidarity. I was perfectly sure that in my parents'
minds *libbe* was something exotic and not wholly legitimate, reserved for "educated" people like their children, who were the sole end of their existence. My father
and mother worked in a rage to put us above their level; they had married to make
us possible. We were the only conceivable end to all their striving; we were their
America.

In Brownsville tenements the kitchen is always the largest room and the center   8
of the household. As a child I felt that we lived in a kitchen to which four other
rooms were annexed. My mother, a "home" dressmaker, had her workshop in the
kitchen. She told me once that she had begun dressmaking in Poland at thirteen; as
far back as I can remember, she was always making dresses for the local women.
She had an innate sense of design, a quick eye for all the subtleties in the latest
fashions, even when she despised them, and great boldness. For three or four dollars she would study the fashion magazines with a customer, go with the customer
to the remnants store on Belmont Avenue to pick out the material, argue the owner
down—all remnants stores, for some reason, were supposed to be shady, as if the
owners dealt in stolen goods—and then for days would patiently fit and baste and
sew and fit again. Our apartment was always full of women in their housedresses
sitting around the kitchen table waiting for a fitting. My little bedroom next to the
kitchen was the fitting room. The sewing machine, an old nut-brown Singer with
golden scrolls painted along the black arm and engraved along the two tiers of little
drawers massed with needles and thread on each side of the treadle, stood next to
the window and the great coal-black stove which up to my last year in college was
our main source of heat. By December the two outer bedrooms were closed off, and
used to chill bottles of milk and cream, cold borscht and jellied calves' feet.

The kitchen held our lives together. My mother worked in it all day long, we   9
ate in it almost all meals except the Passover *seder,* I did my homework and first

writing at the kitchen table, and in winter I often had a bed made up for me on three kitchen chairs near the stove. On the wall just over the table hung a long horizontal mirror that sloped to a ship's prow at each end and was lined in cherry wood. It took up the whole wall, and drew every object in the kitchen to itself. The walls were a fiercely stippled whitewash, so often rewhitened by my father in slack seasons that the paint looked as if it had been squeezed and cracked into the walls. A large electric bulb hung down the center of the kitchen at the end of a chain that had been hooked into the ceiling; the old gas ring and key still jutted out of the wall like antlers. In the corner next to the toilet was the sink at which we washed, and the square tub in which my mother did our clothes. Above it, tacked to the shelf on which were pleasantly ranged square, blue-bordered white sugar and spice jars, hung calendars from the Public National Bank on Pitkin Avenue and the Minsker Progressive Branch of the Workman's Circle; receipts for the payment of insurance premiums, and household bills on a spindle; two little boxes engraved with Hebrew letters. One of these was for the poor, the other to buy back the Land of Israel. Each spring a bearded little man would suddenly appear in our kitchen, salute us with a hurried Hebrew blessing, empty the boxes (sometimes with a sidelong look of disdain if they were not full), hurriedly bless us again for remembering our less fortunate Jewish brothers and sisters, and so take his departure until the next spring, after vainly trying to persuade my mother to take still another box. We did occasionally remember to drop coins in the boxes, but this was usually only on the dreaded morning of "mid-terms" and final examinations, because my mother thought it would bring me luck. She was extremely superstitious, but embarrassed about it, and always laughed at herself whenever, on the morning of an examination, she counseled me to leave the house on my right foot. "I know it's silly," her smile seemed to say, "but what harm can it do? It may calm God down."

　　The kitchen gave a special character to our lives; my mother's character. All 10 my memories of that kitchen are dominated by the nearness of my mother sitting all day long at her sewing machine, by the clacking of the treadle against the linoleum floor, by the patient twist of her right shoulder as she automatically pushed at the wheel with one hand or lifted the foot to free the needle where it had got stuck in a thick piece of material. The kitchen was her life. Year by year, as I began to take in her fantastic capacity for labor and her anxious zeal, I realized it was ourselves she kept stitched together. I can never remember a time when she was not working. She worked because the law of her life was work, work and anxiety; she worked because she would have found life meaningless without work. She read almost no English; she could read the Yiddish paper, but never felt she had time to. We were always talking of a time when I would teach her how to read, but somehow there was never time. When I awoke in the morning she was already at her machine, or in the great morning crowd of housewives at the grocery getting fresh rolls for breakfast. When I returned from school she was at her machine, or conferring over *McCall's* with some neighborhood woman who had come in pointing hopefully to an illustration—"Mrs. Kazin! Mrs. Kazin! Make me a dress like it shows here in the picture!" When my father came home from work she had somehow mysteriously interrupted herself to make supper for us, and the dishes cleared and washed, was back at her machine. When I went to bed at night, often she was still there, pounding away at the treadle, hunched over the wheel, her hands steering a piece of gauze under the needle with a finesse that always contrasted sharply with her swollen hands and broken nails. Her left hand had been pierced through when as a girl she had worked in the infamous Triangle Shirtwaist Factory on the East Side. A needle had gone straight through the palm, severing a large vein. They had sewn it up for her so clumsily that a tuft of flesh always lay folded over the palm.

The kitchen was the great machine that set our lives running; it whirred down 11 a little only on Saturdays and holy days. From my mother's kitchen I gained my first picture of life as a white, overheated, starkly lit workshop redolent with Jewish cooking, crowded with women in housedresses, strewn with fashion magazines, patterns, dress material, spools of thread—and at whose center, so lashed to her machine that bolts of energy seemed to dance out of her hands and feet as she worked, my mother stamped the treadle hard against the floor, hard, hard, and silently, grimly at war, beat out the first rhythm of the world for me.

■ *Questions for* . . . The Kitchen: The Great Machine That Set Our Lives Running by Alfred Kazin

Words to Note

liberated	rangy	*khalleh*
tenements	annexed	innate
subtleties	boldness	argue
shady	scrolls	engraved
tiers	stippled	squeezed
salute	dreaded	dominated
clacking	treadle	hunched
steering	gauze	swollen
severing	whirred	

Language

1. Which words stand out in Kazin's description of the kitchen walls in paragraph 9?
2. Make a list of the words he uses to describe his mother. What do they tell us about her? Do they reveal enough?
3. There are quite a few metaphors in this piece. Locate and study a few of them. What do they add?

Style

1. Why does Kazin spend so much time describing his mother's sewing machine?

2. What is the pace of this piece? How does Kazin set the pace?
3. Kazin's last sentence is his longest. Read it out loud. Study it. What's unusual about the phrasing? The wording? Why didn't he write a few short sentences?

Development and Organization

1. Do we need to know the bank names of the calendars that hung on the kitchen wall?
2. Does Kazin's description progress according to a discernible plan, or is it a random collection of remembered impressions?

Discussion and Journal Writing

1. What does the sewing machine symbolize?
2. Spell out what you think Kazin means when he says the kitchen held their lives together.
3. Compare Kazin's portrait of his mother with Smith-Yackel's in "My Mother Never Worked." Are they both feminist portraits?
4. What does he mean when he says that he and his siblings were his parents' America?

ooooo

The Way to Rainy Mountain

—N. Scott Momaday

N. Scott Momaday, born in Oklahoma in 1934, is a Kiowa who attended schools on various reservations—Navajo, Apache, and Pueblo. He went to college at the University of New Mexico and earned a Ph.D. at Stanford University in 1960. He is now a professor of English and comparative literature. His heritage and identity are the themes of most of his writing: *House Made of Dawn* (1968), which won a Pulitzer Prize in fiction, and *The Way to Rainy Mountain* (1969), which is a collection of Kiowa folk stories.

A single knoll rises out of the plain in Oklahoma, north and west of the   1
Wichita Range. For my people, the Kiowas, it is an old landmark, and they gave it the name Rainy Mountain. The hardest weather in the world is there. Winter brings blizzards, hot tornadic winds arise in the spring, and in summer the prairie is an anvil's edge. The grass turns brittle and brown, and it cracks beneath your feet.

There are green belts along the rivers and creeks, linear groves of hickory and pecan, willow and witch hazel. At a distance in July or August the steaming foliage seems almost to writhe in fire. Great green and yellow grasshoppers are everywhere in the tall grass, popping up like corn to sting the flesh, and tortoises crawl about on the red earth, going nowhere in the plenty of time. Loneliness is an aspect of the land. All things in the plain are isolate; there is no confusion of objects in the eye, but *one* hill or *one* tree or *one* man. To look upon that landscape in the early morning, with the sun at your back, is to lose the sense of proportion. Your imagination comes to life, and this, you think, is where Creation was begun.

I returned to Rainy Mountain in July. My grandmother had died in the spring, 2 and I wanted to be at her grave. She had lived to be very old and at last infirm. Her only living daughter was with her when she died, and I was told that in death her face was that of a child.

I like to think of her as a child. When she was born, the Kiowas were living 3 the last great moment of their history. For more than a hundred years they had controlled the open range from the Smoky Hill River to the Red, from the headwaters of the Canadian to the fork of the Arkansas and Cimarron. In alliance with the Comanches, they had ruled the whole of the southern Plains. War was their sacred business, and they were among the finest horsemen the world has ever known. But warfare for the Kiowas was preeminently a matter of disposition rather than of survival, and they never understood the grim, unrelenting advance of the U.S. Cavalry. When at last, divided and ill-provisioned, they were driven onto the Staked Plains in the cold rains of autumn, they fell into panic. In Palo Duro Canyon they abandoned their crucial stores to pillage and had nothing then but their lives. In order to save themselves, they surrendered to the soldiers at Fort Sill and were imprisoned in the old stone corral that now stands as a military museum. My grandmother was spared the humiliation of those high gray walls by eight or ten years, but she must have known from birth the affliction of defeat, the dark brooding of old warriors.

Her name was Aho, and she belonged to the last culture to evolve in North 4 America. Her forebears came down from the high country in western Montana nearly three centuries ago. They were a mountain people, a mysterious tribe of hunters whose language has never been positively classified in any major group. In the late seventeenth century they began a long migration to the south and east. It was a journey toward the dawn, and it led to a golden age. Along the way the Kiowas were befriended by the Crows, who gave them the culture and religion of the Plains. They acquired horses, and their ancient nomadic spirit was suddenly free of the ground. They acquired Tai-me, the sacred Sun Dance doll, from that moment the object and symbol of their worship, and so shared in the divinity of the sun. Not least, they acquired the sense of destiny, therefore courage and pride. When they entered upon the southern Plains they had been transformed. No longer were they slaves to the simple necessity of survival; they were a lordly and dangerous society of fighters and thieves, hunters and priests of the sun. According to their origin myth, they entered the world through a hollow log. From one point of view, their migration was the fruit of an old prophecy, for indeed they emerged from a sunless world.

Although my grandmother lived out her long life in the shadow of Rainy 5
Mountain, the immense landscape of the continental interior lay like memory in her
blood. She could tell of the Crows, whom she had never seen, and of the Black
Hills, where she had never been. I wanted to see in reality what she had seen more
perfectly in the mind's eye, and traveled fifteen hundred miles to begin my pilgrimage.

Yellowstone, it seemed to me, was the top of the world, a region of deep lakes 6
and dark timber, canyons and waterfalls. But, beautiful as it is, one might have the
sense of confinement there. The skyline in all directions is close at hand, the high
wall of the woods and deep cleavages of shade. There is a perfect freedom in the
mountains, but it belongs to the eagle and the elk, the badger and the bear. The
Kiowas reckoned their stature by the distance they could see, and they were bent
and blind in the wilderness.

Descending eastward, the highland meadows are a stairway to the plain. In 7
July the inland slope of the Rockies is luxuriant with flax and buckwheat, stonecrop
and larkspur. The earth unfolds and the limit of the land recedes. Clusters of trees,
and animals grazing in the far distance, cause the vision to reach away and wonder
to build upon the mind. The sun follows a longer course in the day, and the sky is
immense beyond all comparison. The great billowing clouds that sail upon it are
shadows that move upon the grain like water, dividing light. Farther down, in the
land of the Crows and Blackfeet, the plain is yellow. Sweet clover takes hold of the
hills and bends upon itself to cover and seal the soil. There the Kiowas paused on
their way; they had come to the place where they must change their lives. The sun
is at home on the plains. Precisely there does it have the certain character of a god.
When the Kiowas came to the land of the Crows, they could see the dark lees of the
hills at dawn across the Bighorn River, the profusion of light on the grain shelves,
the oldest deity ranging after the solstices. Not yet would they veer southward to
the caldron of the land that lay below; they must wean their blood from the northern winter and hold the mountains a while longer in their view. They bore Tai-me
in procession to the east.

A dark mist lay over the Black Hills, and the land was like iron. At the top of 8
a ridge I caught sight of Devil's Tower upthrust against the gray sky as if in the
birth of time the core of the earth had broken through its crust and the motion of the
world was begun. There are things in nature that engender an awful quiet in the
heart of man; Devil's Tower is one of them. Two centuries ago, because they could
not do otherwise, the Kiowas made a legend at the base of the rock. My grandmother said:

Eight children were there at play, seven sisters and their brother. Suddenly the 9
boy was struck dumb; he trembled and began to run upon his hands and feet. His
fingers became claws, and his body was covered with fur. Directly there was a
bear where the boy had been. The sisters were terrified; they ran, and the bear
after them. They came to the stump of a great tree, and the tree spoke to them. It
bade them climb upon it, and as they did so it began to rise into the air. The bear

came to kill them, but they were just beyond its reach. It reared against the tree and scored the bark all around with its claws. The seven sisters were borne into the sky, and they became the stars of the Big Dipper.

From that moment, and so long as the legend lives, the Kiowas have kinsmen 10 in the night sky. Whatever they were in the mountains, they could be no more. However tenuous their well-being, however much they had suffered and would suffer again, they had found a way out of the wilderness.

My grandmother had a reverence for the sun, a holy regard that now is all but 11 gone out of mankind. There was a wariness in her, and an ancient awe. She was a Christian in her later years, but she had come a long way about, and she never forgot her birthright. As a child she had been to the Sun Dances; she had taken part in those annual rites, and by them she had learned the restoration of her people in the presence of Tai-me. She was about seven when the last Kiowa Sun Dance was held in 1887 on the Washita River above Rainy Mountain Creek. The buffalo were gone. In order to consummate the ancient sacrifice—to impale the head of a buffalo bull upon the medicine tree—a delegation of old men journeyed into Texas, there to beg and barter for an animal from the Goodnight herd. She was ten when the Kiowas came together for the last time as a living Sun Dance culture. They could find no buffalo; they had to hang an old hide from the sacred tree. Before the dance could begin, a company of soldiers rode out from Fort Sill under orders to disperse the tribe. Forbidden without cause the essential act of their faith, having seen the wild herds slaughtered and left to rot upon the ground, the Kiowas backed away forever from the medicine tree. That was July 20, 1890, at the great bend of the Washita. My grandmother was there. Without bitterness, and for as long as she lived, she bore a vision of deicide.

Now that I can have her only in memory, I see my grandmother in the several 12 postures that were peculiar to her: standing at the wood stove on a winter morning and turning meat in a great iron skillet; sitting at the south window, bent above her beadwork, and afterwards, when her vision failed, looking down for a long time into the fold of her hands; going out upon a cane, very slowly as she did when the weight of age came upon her; praying. I remember her most often at prayer. She made long, rambling prayers out of suffering and hope, having seen many things. I was never sure that I had the right to hear, so exclusive were they of all mere custom and company. The last time I saw her she prayed standing by the side of her bed at night, naked to the waist, the light of a kerosene lamp moving upon her dark skin. Her long, black hair, always drawn and braided in the day, lay upon her shoulders and against her breasts like a shawl. I do not speak Kiowa, and I never understood her prayers, but there was something inherently sad in the sound, some merest hesitation upon the syllables of sorrow. She began in a high and descending pitch, exhausting her breath to silence; then again and again—and always the same intensity of effort, of something that is, and is not, like urgency in the human voice. Transported so in the dancing light among the shadows of her room, she seemed beyond the reach of time. But that was illusion; I think I knew then that I should not see her again.

Houses are like sentinels in the plain, old keepers of the weather watch. There, 13 in a very little while, wood takes on the appearance of great age. All colors wear soon away in the wind and rain, and then the wood is burned gray and the grain appears and the nails turn red with rust. The windowpanes are black and opaque; you imagine there is nothing within, and indeed there are many ghosts, bones given up to the land. They stand here and there against the sky, and you approach them for a longer time than you expect. They belong in the distance; it is their domain.

Once there was a lot of sound in my grandmother's house, a lot of coming and 14 going, feasting and talk. The summers there were full of excitement and reunion. The Kiowas are a summer people; they abide the cold and keep to themselves, but when the season turns and the land becomes warm and vital they cannot hold still; an old love of going returns upon them. The aged visitors who came to my grandmother's house when I was a child were made of lean and leather, and they bore themselves upright. They wore great black hats and bright ample shirts that shook in the wind. They rubbed fat upon their hair and wound their braids with strips of colored cloth. Some of them painted their faces and carried the scars of old and cherished enmities. They were an old council of warlords, come to remind and be reminded of who they were. Their wives and daughters served them well. The women might indulge themselves; gossip was at once the mark and compensation of their servitude. They made loud and elaborate talk among themselves, full of jest and gesture, fright and false alarm. They went abroad in fringed and flowered shawls, bright beadwork and German silver. They were at home in the kitchen, and they prepared meals that were banquets.

There were frequent prayer meetings, and great nocturnal feasts. When I was a 15 child I played with my cousins outside, where the lamplight fell upon the ground and the singing of the old people rose up around us and carried away into the darkness. There were a lot of good things to eat, a lot of laughter and surprise. And afterwards, when the quiet returned, I lay down with my grandmother and could hear the frogs away by the river and feel the motion of the air.

Now there is a funeral silence in the rooms, the endless wake of some final 16 word. The walls have closed in upon my grandmother's house. When I returned to it in mourning, I saw for the first time in my life how small it was. It was late at night, and there was a white moon, nearly full. I sat for a long time on the stone steps by the kitchen door. From there I could see out across the land; I could see the long row of trees by the creek, the low light upon the rolling plains, and the stars of the Big Dipper. Once I looked at the moon and caught sight of a strange thing. A cricket had perched upon the handrail, only a few inches away from me. My line of vision was such that the creature filled the moon like a fossil. It had gone there, I thought, to live and die, for there, of all places, was its small definition made whole and eternal. A warm wind rose up and purled like the longing within me.

The next morning I awoke at dawn and went out on the dirt road to Rainy 17 Mountain. It was already hot, and the grasshoppers began to fill the air. Still, it was early in the morning, and the birds sang out of the shadows. The long yellow grass on the mountain shone in the bright light and a scissortail hied above the land. There, where it ought to be, at the end of a long and legendary way, was my grandmother's grave. Here and there on the dark stones were ancestral names. Looking back once, I saw the mountain and came away.

■ *Questions for . . .* The Way to Rainy Mountain by N. Scott Momaday

Words to Note

knoll	landmark	blizzards
anvil	brittle	writhe
crawl	proportion	alliance
affliction	brooding	migration
nomadic	myth	pilgrimage
cleavages	luxuriant	solstices
caldron	wean	procession
engender	legend	scored
kinsmen	tenuous	wariness
awe	rites	birthright
disperse	deicide	postures
rambling	urgency	transported
illusion	sentinels	opaque
vital	lean	shook
cherished	indulge	compensation
fringed	banquets	nocturnal
perched	fossil	purled
ancestral		

Language

1. Why does Momaday, in paragraph 7, call the highland meadows a "stairway" to the plain?
2. Is this piece overwritten?

Style

1. Momaday favors short, simple sentences. How does he avoid choppiness?
2. Why does he expend so many words creating vivid images of his people's land?

Development and Organization

1. Momaday pans out from his grandmother to her tribe and its history and back again a few times. How does he keep the reader from getting lost?
2. Why does he repeatedly digress from his grandmother?

1. What do Momaday's accounts of Kiowa history and his descriptions of their land tell us about his grandmother?
2. In paragraph 17, Momaday watched a cricket on the windowsill of his deceased grandmother's house. In Kiowa tradition, he invented a legend. Interpret the legend of the cricket.
3. Why did he visit his grandmother's grave?

ooooo

The House of Gudger

—James Agee

James Agee and the photographer Walker Evans were sent south in the middle of the Great Depression by *Fortune* magazine to do a series of documentary articles and photographs about the conditions of tenant farmers. When they arrived in Alabama, they were overwhelmed by the squalor and misery there. They produced writing and photographs that *Fortune* rejected as too disturbing. Agee and Evans refused to change their work, saying they wouldn't pretty up their subject for the sake of their own advancement and the magazine's circulation. Instead, they collaborated on a book-length study of the lives of these farming families, *Let Us Now Praise Famous Men.* "The House of Gudger," an excerpt from that book, is easily the most detailed and evocative description of a cabin ever written. Henry David Thoreau's celebrated cabin on Walden Pond is a quaint cottage by comparison.

And this hall between, as the open valve of a sea creature, steadfastly flushing 1 the free width of ocean through its infinitesimal existence: and on its either side, the square boxes, the square front walls, raised vertical to the earth, and facing us as two squared prows of barge or wooden wings, shadow beneath their lower edge and at their eaves; and the roof:

And these walls:

Nailed together of boards on beams, the boards facing the weather, into broad 2 cards of wood inlet with windows stopped with shutters: walls, horizontals, of somewhat narrow weatherboarding; the windows bounded by boards of that same

width in a square: the shutters, of wide vertical boards laid edge to edge, not overlapped: each of these boards laid edge to edge, not overlapped: each of these boards
was once of the living flesh of a pine tree; it was cut next the earth, and was taken
between the shrieking of saws into strict ribbons; and now, which was vertical, is
horizontal to the earth, and another is clamped against the length of its outward
edge and its downward clamps another, and these boards, nailed tightly together
upon pine beams, make of their horizontalities a wall: and the sun makes close horizontal parallels along the edges of these weatherboards, of sharp light and shade,
the parallels strengthened here in slight straight-line lapse from level, in the subtle
knife-edged curve of warping loose in another place: another irregular 'pattern' is
made in the endings and piecings-out of boards:

And the roof:

It is of short hand-hewn boards so thick and broad, they are shingles only of a   3
most antique sort: crosswise upon rigid beams, laths have been nailed, not far apart,
and upon these laths, in successive rows of dozens and of hundreds, and here again,
though regularly, with a certain shuffling of erratism against pure symmetry, these
broad thick shingles are laid down overlapping from the peak to the overhung edge
like the plumage of a bird who must meet weather: and not unlike some square and
formalized plumage, as of a holy effigy, they seem, and made in profligate plates of
a valuable metal; for they have never been stained, nor otherwise touched or colored save only by all habits of the sky: nor has any other wood of this house been
otherwise ever touched: so that, wherever the weathers of the year have handled it,
the wood of the whole of this house shines with the noble gentleness of cherished
silver, much as where (yet differently), along the floors, in the pathings of the millions of soft wavelike movements of naked feet, it can be still more melodiously
charmed upon it knots, and is as wood long fondled in a tender sea:

Upon these structures, light: 4

It stands just sufficiently short of vertical that every leaf of shingle, at its   5
edges, and every edge of horizontal plank (blocked, at each center, with squared
verticals) is a most black and cutting ink: and every surface struck by light is thus:
such an intensity and splendor of silver in the silver light, it seems to burn, and
burns and blinds into the eyes almost as snow; yet in none of that burnishment or
blazing whereby detail is lost: each texture in the wood, like those of bone, is distinct in the eye as a razor: each nail-head is distinct: each seam and split; and each
slight warping; each random knot and knothole: and in each board, as lovely a
music as a contour map and unique as a thumbprint, its grain, which was its living
strength, and these wild creeks cut stiff across by saws; and moving nearer, the
close-laid arcs and shadows even of those tearing wheels: and this, more poor and
plain than bone, more naked and noble than sternest Doric, more rich and more
variant than watered silk, is the fabric and stature of a house.

It is put together out of the cheapest available pine lumber, and the least of   6
this is used which shall stretch a skin of one thickness alone against the earth and
air; and this is all done according to one of the three or four simplest, stingiest, and
thus most classical plans contrivable, which are all traditional to that country: and

the work is done by half-skilled, half-paid men under no need to do well, who therefore take such vengeance on the world as they may in a cynical and part willful apathy; and this is what comes of it: Most naïve, most massive symmetry and simpleness. Enough lines, enough off-true, that this symmetry is strongly yet most subtly sprained against its centers, into something more powerful than either full symmetry or deliberate breaking and balancing of 'monotonies' can hope to be. A look of being most earnestly hand-made, as a child's drawing, a thing created out of need, love, patience, and strained skill in the innocence of a race. Nowhere one ounce or inch spent with ornament, not one trace of relief or of disguise: a matchless monotony, and in it a matchless variety: and this again throughout restrained, held rigid: and of all this, nothing which is not intrinsic between the materials of structure, the earth, and the open heaven. The major lines of structure, each horizontal of each board, and edge of shingle, the strictness yet subtle dishevelment of the shingles, the nail-heads, which are driven according to geometric need, yet are not in perfect order, the grain, differing in each foot of each board and in each board from any other, the many knots in this cheap lumber: all these fluencies and irregularities, all these shadows of pattern upon each piece of wood, all these in rectilinear ribbons caught into one squared, angled, and curled music, compounding a chord of four chambers upon a soul and center of clean air: and upon all these masses and edges and chances and flowerings of grain, the changes of colorings of all weathers, and the slow complexions and marchings of pure light.

Or by another saying: 7
'In all this house: 8
'In all of this house not any one inch of lumber being wasted on embellish-   9
ment, or on trim, or on any form of relief, or even on any doubling of walls: it is, rather, as if a hard thin hide of wood has been stretched to its utmost to cover exactly once, or a little less than once, in all six planes the skeletal beams which, with the inside surface of the weatherboarding, are the inside walls; and no touch, as I have said, of any wash or paint, nor, on the floors, any kind of covering, nor, to three of the rooms, any kind of ceiling, but in all places left bare the plain essences of structure; in result all these almost perfect symmetries have their full strength, and every inch of the structure, and every aspect and placement of the building materials, comes inevitably and purely through into full esthetic existence, the one further conditioner, and discriminator between the functions and properties of indoors and out, being the lights and operations of the sky.'

Or by a few further notes: 10
'On symmetry: the house is rudimentary as a child's drawing, and of a bare-   11
ness, cleanness, and sobriety which only Doric architecture, so far as I know, can hope to approach: this exact symmetry is sprung slightly and subtly, here and there, one corner of the house a little off vertical, a course of weatherboarding failing the horizontal between parallels, a window frame not quite square, by lack of skill and by weight and weakness of timber and time; and these slight failures, their tensions sprung against centers and opposals of such rigid and earnest exactitude, set up intensities of relationship far more powerful than full symmetry, or studied dissym-

metry, or use of relief or ornament, can ever be: indeed, the power is of another world and order than theirs, and there is, as I mentioned, a particular quality of a thing hand-made, which by comparison I can best suggest thus: by the grandeur that comes of the effort of one man to hold together upon one instrument, as if he were breaking a wild monster to bridle and riding, one of the larger fugues of Bach, on an organ, as against the slick collaborations and effortless climaxes of the same piece in the manipulations of an orchestra.'

Or again by materials: and by surfaces and substances: the build and shape of 12 walls, roof, window frames, verticals of shutters, opposals and cleavings of mass as I have said, and the surfaces and substances: 'The front porch of oak two-by-twelves so hard they still carry a strong piercing fell of splinters; the four support-ing posts which have the delicate bias and fluences of young trees and whose sur-face is close to that of rubbed ivory; in the musculatures of their stripped knots they have the flayed and expert strength of anatomical studies: and the rest of the house entirely of pine, the cheapest of local building material and of this material one of the cheapest grades: in the surfaces of these boards are three qualities of beauty and they are simultaneous, mutually transparent: one is the streaming killed strength of the grain, infinite, talented, and unrepeatable from inch to inch, the florid genius of nature which is incapable of error: one is the close-set transverse arcs, dozens to the foot, which are the shadows of the savage breathings and eatings of the circular saw; little of this lumber has been planed: one is the tone and quality the weather has given it, which is related one way to bone, another to satin, another to unpol-ished but smooth silver: all these are visible at once, though one or another may be strongly enhanced by degree and direction of light and by degree of humidity: moreover, since the lumber is so cheap, knots are frequent, and here and there among the knots the iron-hard bitter red center is lost, and there is, instead, a knot-hole; the grain near these knots goes into convulsions or ecstasies such as Beethoven's deafness compelled; and with these knots the planes of the house are badged at random, and again moreover, these wild fugues and floods of grain, which are of the free perfect innocence of nature, are sawn and stripped across into rigid ribbons and by rigid lines and boundaries, in the captive perfect innocence of science, so that these are closely collaborated and inter-involved in every surface: and at points strategic to structure: and regimented by need, and attempting their own symmetries, yet not in perfect line (such is the tortured yet again perfect inno-cence of men, caught between the pulls of nature and science), the patternings and constellations of the heads of the driven nails: and all these things, set in the twisted and cradling planet, take the benefit of every light and weather which the sky in their part of the world can bestow, this within its terms being subtly unrepeatable and probably infinite, and are qualified as few different structures can be, to make full use of these gifts. By most brief suggestion: in full symmetry of the sun, the surfaces are dazzling silver, the shadows strong as knives and India ink, yet the grain and all detail clear: in slanted light, all slantings and sharpenings of shadow: in smothered light, the aspect of bone, a relic: at night, the balanced masses, patient in the base world: from rain, out of these hues of argent bone the colors of agate, the whole wall, one fabric and mad zebra of quartered minerals and watered silks:

and in the sheltered yet open hallway, a granite gray and seeming of nearly granitic hardness, the grain dim, the sawmarks very strong; in the strength of these marks and peculiar sobriety of the color, a look as if there has been a slow and exact substitution of calcium throughout all the substance: within the yellows, reds, and peasant golds drawn deep toward gray, yet glowing quietly through it as the clay world glows through summer.'

But enough.   13

The hallway is long courses of weatherboard facing one another in walls six 14 feet apart, featureless excepting two pair of opposite doors, not ceiled, but beneath the empty and high angling of the roof: perhaps because of the blankness of these walls, and their facing closeness relative to their parallel length, there is here an extremely strong sense of the nakedness and narrowness of their presence, and of the broad openness, exposing the free land, at either end. The floor is laid along beams rather wide apart. In all the rear end it yields to the ground under much weight: the last few feet lie solid to the ground, and this is a strong muck in wet weather.

The one static fixture in the hallway is at the rear, just beyond the kitchen 15 door. It is a wooden shelf, waist-high, and on this shelf, a bucket, a dipper, a basin, and usually a bar of soap, and hanging from a nail just above, a towel. The basin is granite-ware, small for a man's hands, with rustmarks in the bottom. The bucket is a regular galvanized two-gallon bucket, a little dented, and smelling and touching a little of a fishy-metallic kind of shine and grease beyond any power of cleaning. It is half full of slowly heating water which was not very cold to begin with: much lower than this, the water tastes a little ticklish and nasty for drinking, though it is still all right for washing. The soap is sometimes strong tan 'kitchen' soap, sometimes a cheap white gelatinous lavender face soap. It stands on the shelf in a china saucer. The dipper again is granite-ware, and again blistered with rust at the bottom. Sometimes it bobs in the bucket; sometimes it lies next the bucket on the shelf. The towel is half a floursack, with the blue and red and black printing still faint on it. Taken clean and dry, it is the pleasantest cloth I know for a towel. Beyond that, it is particularly clammy, clinging, and dirty-feeling.

A few notes of discrimination may be helpful: 16

The towels in such a farmhouse are always floursacks. 'Kitchen' towels are of 17 another world and class of farmer, and 'face' and 'turkish' towels of still another.

By no means all poor farmers use any sort of 'toilet' soap. Some seldom use 18 soap at all. When they use other than kitchen soap, it is of one of about three kinds, all of them of the sort available in five-and-tens and small-town general stores. One is 'lava' or 'oatmeal' soap, whose rough texture is pleasing and convincing of cleanliness to a person who works with his hands. The white soaps smell sharply of lye: again, the odor is cleansing. Or if the soap is more fancy, it is a pink or lemon or purple color, strongly and cheaply scented and giving a big lather. No cheap yet somewhat pleasantly scented soap such as lux is used.

Rather more often than not, the basin and the dipper are plain unenameled tin. 19 I expect, but am not sure, that this is a few cents cheaper. In any case the odor, taste, and shiny, greasy texture soon become strong. The use of enamel ware is a small yet sharp distinction and symptom in 'good taste,' and in 'class,' and in a sort of semi-esthetic awareness, choice and will. The use of gray as against white is still another discriminative. That they bought small sizes, which are a very few cents cheaper, speaks for itself. So does the fact that they have afforded still another basin, not quite big enough for its use, to wash their feet in.

At times, there is also a mirror here, and a comb; but more often these are on   20 the bedroom mantel.

The hall and front porch are a kind of room, and are a good deal used. Mrs.   21 Gudger and her children sit in the porch in empty times of the morning and afternoon: back in the rear of the hall is the evening place to sit, before supper or for a little while just after it. There are few enough chairs that they have to be moved around the house to where they are needed, but ordinarily there is a rockingchair on the porch and a straight chair in the rear of the hall next the bedroom door. This rockingchair is of an inexpensive 'rustic' make: sections of hickory sapling with the bark still on. On the hard and not quite even porch floor the rocking is stony and cobbled, with a little of the sound of an auto crossing a loose wooden bridge. Three of the straight chairs are strong, plain, not yet decrepit hickory-bottoms, which cost a dollar and a half new; there is also a kitchen-type chair with a pierced design in the dark scalloped wood at the head, and the bottom broken through.

When we first knew the Gudgers they had their eating-table in the middle of   22 the hall, for only in the hall is there likely to be any sort of breeze, and the kitchen, where nearly all farm families eat, was so hot that they could at times hardly stand to eat in it. This was only an experiment though, and it was not successful. The hall is too narrow for any comfort in it for a whole family clenched round a table. If it were even two feet wider, it would be much more use to them, but this would not have occurred to those who built it, nor, if it had, would anything have been done about it.

Four rooms make a larger tenant house than is ordinary: many are three; many   23 are two; more are one than four: and three of these rooms are quite spacious, twelve feet square. For various reasons, though, all of which could easily enough have been avoided in the building of the house, only two of these rooms, the kitchen and the rear bedroom, are really habitable. There is no ceiling to either of the front rooms, and the shingles were laid so unskillfully, and are now so multitudinously leaky, that it would be a matter not of repairing but of complete re-laying to make a solid roof. Between the beams at the eaves, along the whole front of the house, and the top of the wall on which the beams rest, there are open gaps. In the front room on the right, several courses of weatherboarding have been omitted between the level of the eaves and the peak of the roof: a hole big enough for a cow to get through. The walls, and shutters, and floors, are not by any means solid: indeed, and beyond and aside from any amount of laborious caulking, they let in light in many dozens of places. There are screens for no windows but one, in the rear bedroom. Because in half the year the fever mosquitoes are thick and these are strong rainstorms, and in the other half it is cold and wet for weeks on end with violent slanted winds and sometimes snow, the right front room is not used to live in at all and the left front room is used only dubiously and irregularly, though the sewing machine is there and it is fully furnished both as a bedroom and as a parlor. The children use it sometimes, and it is given to guests (as it was to us), but storm, mosquitoes and habit force them back into the other room where the whole family sleeps together.

But now I want to take these four rooms one by one, and give at least a certain 24 rough idea of what is in each of them and of what each is 'like,' though I think I should begin this with a few more general remarks.

ODORS

Bareness and space

The Gudgers' house, being young, only eight years old, smells a little dryer 25 and cleaner, and more distinctly of its wood, than an average white tenant house, and it has also a certain odor I have never found in other such houses: aside from these sharp yet slight subtleties, it has the odor or odors which are classical in every thoroughly poor white southern country house, and by which such a house could be identified blindfold in any part of the world, among no matter what other odors. It is compacted of many odors and made into one, which is very thin and light on the air, and more subtle than it can seem in analysis, yet very sharply and constantly noticeable. These are its ingredients. The odor of pine lumber, wide thin cards of it, heated in the sun, in no way doubled or insulated, in closed and darkened air. The odor of woodsmoke, the fuel being again mainly pine, but in part also, hickory, oak, and cedar. The odors of cooking. Among these, most strongly, the odors of fried salt pork and of fried and boiled pork lard, and second, the odor of cooked corn. The odors of sweat in many stages of age and freshness, this sweat being a distillation of pork, lard, corn, woodsmoke, pine, and ammonia. The odors of sleep, of bedding and of breathing, for the ventilation is poor. The odors of all the dirt that in the course of time can accumulate in a quilt and mattress. Odors of staleness from clothes hung or stored away, not washed. I should further describe the odor of corn: in sweat, or on the teeth, and breath, when it is eaten as much as they eat it, it is of a particular sweet stuffy fetor, to which the nearest parallel is the odor of the yellow excrement of a baby. All these odors as I have said are so combined into one that they are all and always present in balance, not at all heavy, yet so searching that all fabrics of bedding and clothes are saturated with them, and so clinging that they stand softly out of the fibers of newly laundered clothes. Some of their components are extremely 'pleasant,' some are 'unpleasant'; their sum total has great nostalgic power. When they are in an old house, darkened, and moist, and sucked into all the wood, and stacked down on top of years of a moldering and old basis of themselves, as at the Ricketts', they are hard to get used to or even hard to bear. At the Woods', they are blowsy and somewhat moist and dirty. At the Gudgers', as I have mentioned, they are younger, lighter, and cleaner-smelling. There, too, is another and special odor, very dry and edged: it is somewhat between

the odor of very old newsprint and of a victorian bedroom in which, after long illness, and many medicines, someone has died and the room has been fumigated, yet
the odor of dark brown medicines, dry-bodied sickness, and staring death, still is
strong in the stained wallpaper and in the mattress.

Bareness and space (and spacing) are so difficult and seem to me of such 26
greatness that I shall not even try to write seriously or fully of them. But a little,
applying mainly to the two bedrooms.

The floors are made of wide planks, between some of which the daylighted 27
earth is visible, and are naked of any kind of paint or cloth or linoleum covering
whatever, and paths have been smoothed on them by bare feet, in a subtly uneven
surface on which the polished knots are particularly beautiful. A perfectly bare
floor of broad boards makes a room seem larger than it can if the floor is covered,
and the furniture too, stands on it in a different and much cleaner sort of relationship. The walls as I have said are skeleton; so is the ceiling in one of these rooms;
the rooms are twelve feet square and are meagerly furnished, and they are so great
and final a whole of bareness and complete simplicity that even the objects on a
crowded shelf seem set far apart from each other, and each to have a particularly
sharp entity of its own. Moreover, all really simple and naïve people[1] incline
strongly toward exact symmetries, and have some sort of instinctive dislike that any
one thing shall touch any other save what it rests on, so that chairs, beds, bureaus,
trunks, vases, trinkets, general odds and ends, are set very plainly and squarely discrete from one another and from walls, at exact centers or as near them as possible,
and this kind of spacing gives each object a full strength it would not otherwise
have, and gives their several relationships, as they stand on shelves or facing, in a
room, the purest power such a relationship can have. This is still more sharply true
with such people as the Gudgers, who still have a little yet earnest wish that everything shall be as pleasant and proper to live with as possible, than with others such
as the Woods and Ricketts, who are disheveled, and wearied out of such hope or
care.

[1]And many of the most complex, and not many between.

■ *Questions for* . . . The House of Gudger by James Agee

Words to Note

weatherboard	angling	muck
dipper	basin	shine
grease	gelatinous	blistered
bobs	rustic	sapling
decrepit	clenched	shingles
eaves	peak	caulking
parlor	odor	distillation
moldering	blowsy	fumigated
knots	trinkets	disheveled

Language

1. In paragraph 9, Agee writes, "The hall is too narrow for any comfort in it for a whole family clenched round a table." What does he mean by *clenched?* Do you like the way he uses the word?
2. Why does he use so many words?

Style

1. Why is the first paragraph just one sentence? Why does Agee use so many long sentences?
2. How does he use sentence fragments?
3. How does he use colons?

Development and Organization

1. What is the logic of the way Agee has organized the piece?
2. Why does he describe the wood so closely in paragraph 2?
3. Why does he include a section on odors?
4. Why the recurrent references to Beethoven and Bach? What do their symphonies and fugues have to do with the Gudger cabin?

Discussion and Journal Writing

1. Why does Agee describe the Gudgers' house without any Gudgers in it?
2. How much is the house itself able to tell us about the lives of the people who live in it? Is this description or biography?
3. How does Agee feel about the Gudgers and their house? How do you know? How does he want the reader to feel?

ooooo

Black Alexandra

—Mark Mathabane

Kaffir, the South African equivalent of the racist epithet *nigger,* is the opening note of Mark Mathabane's *Kaffir Boy.* In that book, Mathabane chronicles his childhood and teenage years in the segregated town of Alexandra. The key theme is the relentless struggle with the laws, forces, and dehumanizing culture of apartheid. Though Mathabane's approach is personal, it is broad and well informed, transforming his story into the story of Black South Africa. The following domestic sketches give a sense of most of the book's hard themes.

1 The Alexandra of my childhood and youth was a shantytown of mostly shacks, a few decent houses, lots of gutters and lots of unpaved, potholed streets with numbers from First to Twenty-third. First Avenue was where Indians—the cream of Alexandra's quarantined society—lived, behind their sell-everything stores and produce stalls, which were the ghetto's main shopping centre. Indians first came to South Africa in 1860, as indentured servants, to work the sugarcane fields of Natal.

2 Second, Third, and Fourth avenues were inhabited mostly by Coloureds, the mulatto race which came into being nine months after white settlers arrived in South Africa in 1652—without women. The rest of Alexandra's streets were filled by black faces, many of them black as coal, full-blooded Africans. Many of these blacks were as poor as church mice. In South Africa there's a saying that to be black is to be at the end of the line when anything of significance is to be had. So these people were considered and treated as the dregs of society, aliens in the land of their birth. Such labelling and treatment made them an angry and embittered lot.

3 The Alexandra of my childhood and youth was one of the oldest shantytowns in the Witwatersrand—the area where black miners toil night and day to tear gold from the bowels of the earth so that the white man of South Africa can enjoy one of the highest standards of living in the world. Many of Alexandra's first settlers came from the tribal reserves, where they could no longer eke out a living, to seek work in the city of gold. Work was plentiful in those days: in mines, factories and white people's homes. As a result these black pioneers stayed, some bought plots of land, established families and called Alexandra home, sweet home. Many shed their tribal cloth and embraced Western culture, a way of life over 350 years of white oppression had deluded them into believing was better than their own. And so it was that in the mid-1950s Alexandra boasted a population of over one hundred thousand blacks, Coloureds and Indians—all squeezed into a space of one square mile.

My parents, a generation or so removed from these earliest settlers of 4 Alexandra, had, too, come from the tribal reserves. My father came from what is now the so-called independent homeland of the Vendas in the northwestern corner of the Transvaal. Venda's specious independence (no other country but South Africa recognizes it) was imposed by the Pretoria regime in 1979, thus at the time making three (Transkei and Bophuthatswana were the other two) the number of these archipelagos of poverty, suffering and corruption where blacks are supposed to exercise their political rights. Since "independence" the Venda people have been under the clutches of the Pretoria-anointed dictator, Patrick Mphephu, who, despite the loss of two elections, continues clinging to power through untempered repression and brutality.

My mother came from Gazankulu, the tribal reserve for the Tsongas in the 5 Northeastern Transvaal. Gazankulu is also being pressured into "independence." My parents met and married in Alexandra. Immediately following marriage they rented a shack in one of the squalid yards of the ghetto. And in that shack I was born, a few months before sixty-nine unarmed black protesters were massacred—many shot in the back as they fled for safety—by South African policemen during a peaceful demonstration against the pass laws in Sharpeville on March 21, 1960. Pass laws regulate the movement of blacks in so-called white South Africa. And it was the pass laws that, in those not so long ago days of my childhood and youth, first awakened me to the realities of life as a Kaffir boy in South Africa. . . .

One night our dingy shack, which had been leaning precipitously on the edge 6 of a *donga,* collapsed. Luckily no one was hurt, but we were forced to move to another one, similarly built. This new shack, like the old one, had two rooms and measured something like fifteen by fifteen feet, and overlooked the same unlit, unpaved, potholed street. It had an interior flaked with old whitewash, a leaky ceiling of rusted zinc propped up by a thin wall of crumbling adobe bricks, two tiny windows made of cardboard and pieces of glass, a creaky, termite-eaten door too low for a person of average height to pass through without bending double, and a floor made of patches of cement and earth. It was similar to the dozen or so shacks strewn irregularly, like lumps on a leper, upon the cracked greenless piece of ground named yard number thirty-five.

In this new shack my brother, George, was weaned. It was amusing to witness 7 my mother do it. The first day she began the process she secretly smeared her breasts with red pepper and then invited my brother to suckle. Unsuspecting, George energetically attacked my mother's breast only to let go of it instantly and start hollering because of the hot pepper. This continued throughout the day whenever he wanted to suckle. Finally, after a few days, he began to dread the sight of my mother's breast, and each time she teased him with it he would turn his face. He was now weaned. My father bought a small white chicken, my mother brewed beer, a few relatives were invited, and a small celebration was held to mark George's passage from infancy to childhood. He was almost two years old. He now had to sleep with Florah and me in the kitchen.

Soon after George was weaned my father began teaching him, as he had been 8
teaching me, tribal ways of life. My father belonged to a loosely knit group of black
families in the neighbourhood to whom tribal traditions were a way of life, and who
sought to bring up their offspring according to its laws. He believed that feeding us
a steady diet of tribal beliefs, values and rituals was one way of ensuring our normal growth, so that in the event of our returning to the tribal reserve, something he
insistently believed would happen soon, we would blend in perfectly. This diet he
administered religiously, seemingly bent on moulding George and me in his image.
At first I had tried to resist the diet, but my father's severe looks frightened me.

A short, gaunt figure, with a smooth, tight, black-as-coal skin, large prominent 9
jaws, thin, uneven lips whose sole function seemed to be the production of sneers, a
broad nose with slightly flaring nostrils, small, bloodshot eyes, which never cried,
small, close-set ears, and a wide, prominent forehead—such were my father's fearsome features.

Born and bred in a tribal reserve and nearly twice my mother's age, my father 10
existed under the illusion, formed as much by a strange innate pride as by a blind-
ness to everything but his own will, that someday all white people would disappear
from South Africa, and black people would revert to their old ways of living. To
prepare for this eventuality, he ruled the house strictly according to tribal law, toler-
ating no deviance, particularly from his children. At the same time that he was
force-feeding us tribalism we were learning other ways of life, modern ways, from
mingling with children whose parents had shed their tribal cloth and embraced
Western culture.

My father's tribal rule had as its fulcrum the constant performing of rituals 11
spanning the range of day-to-day living. There were rituals to protect the house
from evildoers, to ward off starvation, to prevent us from becoming sick, to safe-
guard his job, to keep the police away, to bring us good luck, to make him earn
more money and many others which my young mind could not understand.
Somehow they did not make sense to me; they simply awed, confused, and embarrassed me, and the only reason I participated in them night after night was because
my father made certain that I did, by using, among other things, the whip, and the
threat of the retributive powers of my ancestral spirits, whose favour the rituals
were designed to curry. Along with the rituals, there were also tribal laws governing manners.

One day I intentionally broke one of these laws: I talked while eating. 12

"That's never done in my house," my father screamed at me as he rose from 13
the table where he had been sitting alone, presiding over our meal. I was eating
pap 'n vleis out of the same bowl with George and Florah. We were sitting on the
floor, about the brazier, and my mother was in the bedroom doing something.

"You don't have two mouths to afford you such luxury!" he fumed, advancing 14
threateningly toward me, a cold sneer on his thin-lipped, cankerous mouth. He
seemed ten feet tall.

Terrified, I deserted the *pap 'n vleis* and fled to Mother. 15

"Bring him back here, woman!" my father called through the door as he 16
unbuckled his rawhide belt. "He needs to be taught how to eat properly."

I began bawling, sensing I was about to be whipped.   17

My mother led me into the kitchen and pleaded for me. "He won't do it again. 18
He's only a child, and you know how forgetful children are." At this point George
and Florah stopped eating and watched with petrified eyes. "Don't give me that,"
snarled my father. "He's old enough to remember how to eat properly." He tore me
away from my mother and lashed me. She tried to intervene, but my father shoved
her aside and promised her the same. I never finished my meal; sobbing, I slunk off
to bed, my limbs afire with pain where the rawhide had raised welts. The next day,
as I nursed my wounds, while my father was at work, I told my mother that I hated
him and promised her I would kill him when I grew up.

"Don't say that!" my mother reprimanded me.   19

"I will," I said stoutly, "if he won't leave me alone."   20

"He's your father, you know."   21

"He's not my father."   22

"Shut that bad mouth of yours!" My mother threatened to smack me.   23

"Why does he beat me, then?" I protested. "Other fathers don't beat their chil- 24
dren." My friends always boasted that their fathers never laid a hand on them.

"He's trying to discipline you. He wants you to grow up to be like him."   25

"What! Me! Never!" I shook with indignation. "I'm never going to be like 26
him! Why should I?"

"Well, in the tribes sons grow up to be like their fathers."   27

"But we're not living in the tribes."   28

"But we're still of the tribes."   29

"I'm not," I said. Trying to focus the conversation on rituals, my nemesis, I 30
said, after a thoughtful pause, "Is that why Papa insists that we do rituals?"

"Yes."   31

"But other people don't."   32

"Everybody does rituals, Mr. Mathabane," my mother said. "You just don't 33
notice it because they do theirs differently. Even white people do rituals."

"Why do people do rituals, Mama?"   34

"People do rituals because they were born in the tribes. And in the tribes 35
rituals are done every day. They are a way of life."

"But we don't live in the tribes," I countered. "Papa should stop doing 36
rituals."

My mother laughed. "Well, it's not as simple as that. Your father grew up in 37
the tribes, as you know. He didn't come to the city until he was quite old. It's hard
to stop doing things when you're old. I, too, do rituals because I was raised in the
tribes. Their meaning, child, will become clear as you grow up. Have patience."

But I had no patience with rituals, and I continued hating them.   38

Participation in my father's rituals sometimes led to the most appalling scenes, 39
which invariably made me the laughingstock of my friends, who thought that my
father, in his ritual garb, was the most hilarious thing they had ever seen since
natives in Tarzan movies. Whenever they laughed at me I would feel embarrassed
and would cry. I began seeking ways of distancing myself from my father's rituals.
I found one: I decided I would no longer, in the presence of my friends, speak

Venda, my father's tribal language. I began speaking Zulu, Sotho and Tsonga, the languages of my friends. It worked. I was no longer an object of mockery. My masquerade continued until my father got wind of it.

"My boy," he began. "Who is ruler of this house?"   40

"You are, Papa," I said with a trembling voice.   41

"Whose son are you?"   42

"Yours and Mama's."   43

"Whose?"   44

"Yours."   45

"That's better. Now tell me, which language do I speak?"   46

"Venda."   47

"Which does your mama speak?"   48

"Venda."   49

"Which should you speak?"   50

"Venda."   51

"Then why do I hear you're speaking other tongues; are you a prophet?"   52
Before I could reply he grabbed me and lashed me thoroughly. Afterward he threatened to cut out my tongue if he ever again heard I wasn't speaking Venda. As further punishment, he increased the number of rituals I had to participate in. I hated him more for it.

Toward the end of 1966 my father was temporarily laid off his job as a menial   53 labourer for a white firm in Germiston, a white city an hour's bus ride southeast of Johannesburg. He had been told by his *baas* (boss) that he would be recalled as soon as the reorganization of the firm was complete: it was coming under new ownership. The first few weeks my father stayed at home awaiting the recall. It never came. As weeks slid past, he began making plans to seek another job, thinking that he had been permanently laid off. But first he had to go to BAD (Bantu Affairs Department)* to obtain a permit to do so.

I was out in the streets playing soccer one weekday afternoon when Florah   54 came running up to me, crying. She told me that something terrible had happened at home and I was wanted immediately. When I reached home I found my mother pacing mechanically about the shack, murmuring helplessly, desperately, uncontrollably, clasping and unclasping her hands.

"It cannot be! No it cannot be! Not my husband! Not my husband!" She   55 was saying to herself.

"What happened to Papa, Mama?" I said with fright as I flung myself at her. I   56 thought that maybe he had been killed. For a while my mother did not answer; but finally she controlled her emotions and between sobs told me what had happened. My father had been arrested that morning at the bus stop—for being unemployed.

*Now renamed Department of Cooperation and Development.

A man who had been with him as they waited for the bus to Johannesburg to apply for permits had brought my mother the grim news. The man's story was as follows: as he and my father waited for the bus several police vans suddenly swooped upon the bus stop. People fled in all directions. My father was nabbed as he tried to leap a fence. His pass was scanned and found to contain an out-of-work stamp; he was taken in. His crime, unemployment, was one of the worst a black man could commit.

A few weeks after we had become nominal Christians my mother collected 57 our rent receipts, hers and my father's marriage license and passbooks, and once again began the ritual of going to the superintendent's office to seek a permit to go search for a job in the white world. At the end of each day she would come back home—after having been denied the permit because she lacked this and that document—tired and downcast, and tackle the chores of cooking, cleaning the house, washing and patching our rags and nursing back to health Florah and George who from time to time came down with malnutrition-related diseases. Despite all that, she still found time to tell us stories, teach us tribal songs and pose riddles for us to grapple with, as we all gathered around the smouldering embers of the brazier. When I was younger some of the stories did not seem to have much meaning beyond being entertaining, but now, at six years old, they took on a new life, and I began to see them in a different light, and to understand their various shades of meaning. They made me feel and see and think in a way I had never before done.

My mother said that her stories had been handed down to her from past gener- 58 ations; and that, therefore, she was narrating them not only to entertain us children and to teach us morals, but also that we, in turn, would come to tell our children, and they, their children, and so on through posterity. She was such a mesmerizing storyteller that once she began telling a tale, we children would remain so quiet and so transfixed, like mannequins, our eager and receptive minds under her hypnotic voice, that we would often hear ourselves breathing. Whenever she ended a particular story, saying that it was past our bedtime, we would implore her to tell another one—a request she always heartily granted—until either my father screamed from the bedroom that the candle be snuffed, or we children simply dozed off into faraway worlds, our minds pregnant with fantastic yarns we wished never to forget.

My mother's vast knowledge of folklore, her vivid remembrance of traditions 59 of various tribes of long ago and her uncanny ability to turn mere words into unforgettable pictures, fused night after night to concoct riveting stories.

On some nights, she would tell of chiefs, witch doctors, sages, warriors, sor- 60 cerers, magicians and wild, monstrous beasts. These stories were set in mythical African kingdoms ruled by black people, where no white man had ever set foot. She would recount prodigious deeds of famous African gods, endowed with unlimited magical powers among them the powers of immortality, invincibility and invisibility, powers which they used to fight, relentlessly and valiantly, for justice, peace and harmony among all black tribes of the Valley of a Thousand Hills.

On some nights, she would quaintly and proudly tell legends about great and 61 noble chiefs of her tribe, the Tsongas; chiefs who, along with powerful chivalrous warriors, undertook many daring and perilous missions into the unknown interiors of Africa, and there fought many a brilliant battle against ferocious enemy tribes. When the battles were won, however, instead of subjugating the conquered people as other tribes did, the Tsonga *impis* always allowed the vanquished to continue following their old beliefs, customs and tradition, and to worship their own gods, as long as they pledged to live in peace with, and to pay homage to, their conquerors.

On some nights, she would tell stories about animals. These animals, to whom 62 she gave the complete gamut of human traits—strength, cowardice, love, hate, honesty, wisdom, magnanimity, cunning, treachery, fear and so on—behaved very much like humans, and she would highlight their interactions with human beings. The animals in her stories were always smarter than humans, and capable of making complex moral decisions.

And on some nights she would teach us tribal songs, proverbs and riddles, all 63 of which she encouraged us to commit to memory, saying, "Memory to us black people is like a book that one can read over and over again for an entire lifetime."

There were dance songs, mimic songs and many others, which, she said, black 64 people of long ago sang during harvest seasons, initiation ceremonies, burial ceremonies, witch hunts, auguries, ceremonies welcoming victorious warriors and other festivities and celebrations that formed the daily life of black people. The proverbs intrigued us children, and the riddles baffled us by their seeming unsolvable despite an abundance of clues. Each time my mother divulged the "easy" solutions, and uncamouflaged the pitfalls inherent in such exercises of common sense, I would marvel at her intelligence.

As we had no nursery rhymes nor storybooks, and, besides, as no one in the 65 house knew how to read, my mother's stories served as a kind of library, a golden fountain of knowledge where we children learned about right and wrong, about good and evil.

I learned that virtues are things to be always striven after, embraced and culti- 66 vated, for they are amply rewarded; and that vices were bad things, to be avoided at all cost, for they bring one nothing but trouble and punishment.

I learned that sagacity and quick wits are necessary in avoiding dangerous sit- 67 uations; and that fatuity and shortsightedness make one go around in circles, seemingly unaware of the many opportunities for escape.

I learned that good deeds advance one positively in life, and lead to a greater 68 and fuller development of self; and that bad deeds accomplish the contrary.

I learned that good always invariably triumphs over evil; that having brains is 69 often better than having brawn; and that underdogs in all situations of life need to have unlimited patience, resiliency, stubbornness and unshakable hope in order to triumph in the end.

I learned to prefer peace to war, cleverness to stupidity, love to hate, sensitivi- 70 ty to stoicism, humility to pomposity, reconciliation to hostility, harmony to strife, patience to rashness, gregariousness to misanthropy, creation to annihilation.

■ *Questions for . . .* Black Alexandra by Mark Mathabane

Words to Note

shantytown	shacks	gutters
stalls	mulatto	dregs
aliens	embittered	eke
tribal cloth	untempered	repression
squalid	massacred	creaky
strewn	moulding	gaunt
innate	deviance	fulcrum
rituals	retributive	curry
fumed	bawling	welts
nursed	nemesis	countered
mesmerizing	transfixed	hypnotic
folklore	uncanny	fused
concoct	endowed	gamut
homage	stoicism	strife
misanthropy	annihilation	

Language

1. What are some synonyms for *shack?*
2. What is the level of diction of the word *kaffir?* What is its origin?

Style

1. How does Mathabane use phrasing and sentence structure in paragraps 11, 51, and 52 to underscore meaning?
2. What is the effect of his repetition of *learned* in the last five paragraphs?

Development and Organization

1. How does Mathabane mix narration with dramatization?
2. What does he emphasize in his descriptions of his parents?
3. What aspects of family life does he dwell on? Why?

Discussion and Journal Writing

1. What bearing did the tribal background of Mathabane's parents have on his family life?
2. What is the point of his father's rituals? Why does Mathabane resist them?

3. Why is Mathabane more responsive to his mother's stories?
4. According to Mathabane, how has South African society harmed his family?

ooooo

The Supremacy of Mother-in-Law Rule

—Russell Baker

Russell Baker, whose acquaintance you made in the previous chapter, is still a satirist. In this selection from his book *Growing Up,* he writes about the initial encounters between his mother and his maternal grandmother, Ida Rebecca, who was very much the queen of her family. Nobody gets out alive. The caricatures he sketches give us a glimpse of the inner workings of the Baker family, with an emphasis on power with a very small *p*.

Ep Ahalt's farm looked down across sloping cornfields toward a small village   1
a quarter mile to the south. The village consisted of seven houses and a general store, a few vegetable gardens, a couple of straw ricks, and a scattering of barns, chicken houses, and pigpens. On a summer afternoon the whole place dozed in the sun, under silences broken only by the occasional cluck of a hen, the solitary clack of a closing screen door.

This was the center of the universe in the days of my innocence. Its name,   2
Morrisonville, dated from the early part of the nineteenth century. By the time I came along it could have been appropriately renamed Bakerville, for almost every soul in the community was a member in some degree of the prodigious Baker family, which had settled in the region around 1730.

Why a settlement rose there in the first place is a mystery. The village sat a   3
third of a mile back from the only paved road in the territory, and the sole waterway was a creek so shallow I could wade across it and barely get my feet wet. To get in from the main highway, travelers had to wind through thick stands of brush along a dirt road that could swallow an automobile all the way to the axles in the mud season. When it finally arrived at Morrisonville, this road forked. One branch ambled toward my Uncle Irvey's house, then lurched to avoid hitting the creek and disappeared into a briar patch. The other branch ran smack through the middle of town as though intending to become a real road, but it lost heart after it passed my grandmother's house and meandered off in a lackadaisical path toward the mountain.

This was the same road that ran past the Arlington School to Sam Reever's   4
bootleggery. It came to rest smack against the mountain two miles west of
Morrisonville. My great-grandfather Daniel Baker used to live in a log house back
there. He was a gunsmith who turned to tailoring after the declining need for full-
time gunmakers made the craft unprofitable. Born shortly after the War of 1812, he
could still walk five miles carrying a sack of cornmeal when he was eighty years
old, and he lived to see the arrival of the twentieth century.

His son George moved down to Morrisonville around 1880 and went into   5
blacksmithing. George was short and on the slender side, not the towering, heavily
muscled stereotype of the blacksmith celebrated in Longfellow's poem. His devo-
tion to Christian worship was remarkable. He required a minimum of two church
services each Sunday to keep his soul in sound repair, and after partaking of the
Gospel at morning and afternoon servings he often set out across the fields for a
third helping at dusk if he heard of a church with lamps lit for nocturnal psalming.

Shortly before moving into Morrisonville, he had married Ida Rebecca Brown,   6
the daughter of a local farmer. Ida Rebecca was only nineteen at her marriage, but
she took to power as naturally as George took to toil. George built his blacksmith
shop hard by the stone-and-log house in which Ida Rebecca ruled, and there he pursued a life of piety, toil, and procreation.

He was as vigorous at procreation as he was at churchgoing. In the first year   7
of their marriage, Ida Rebecca produced a son. In the next ten years she produced
nine more, including twin boys. In 1897, after an uncommonly long pause of more
than four years, an eleventh son was born. He was to become my father. They
named him Benjamin.

The line didn't stop there, though. Two years later there was, at last, a daugh-   8
ter; and five years after her, a twelfth son. Thirteen children was not a record for the
neighborhood, nor even very remarkable. One family close by produced children in
such volume that the parents ran out of names and began giving them numbers.
One of their sons, whom I particularly envied for his heroic biceps, was named
Eleven.

How big my father's family might have become eventually is hard to say, for   9
Grandfather George suffered a stroke in 1907 and died at home, at the still fruitful
age of fifty-two. There was a family mystery about his dying words. These, according to Ida Rebecca, were "into midget and out of midget." At least, they sounded
like "into midget and out of midget," though Ida Rebecca never knew if this was
exactly what he was trying to say or, if it was, what he meant by it. Nor did she ask
him. He belonged to the Order of Red Men, one of those lodge brotherhoods common at the turn of the century which cherished secret handshakes and mumbo-
jumbo passwords. Ida Rebecca hesitated to ask him what he meant by "into midget
and out of midget" for fear she might be delving improperly into the sacred mysteries of the lodge.

In the eighteen years between Grandfather George's death and my arrival in   10
Morrisonville, Ida Rebecca established herself as the iron ruler of a sprawling family empire. Her multitude of sons, some of them graying and middle-aged, were celebrated for miles around as good boys who listened to their mother. If one of them

kicked over the traces, there was hell to pay until he fell obediently back into line. In Morrisonville everybody said, "It's her way or no way."

Her sons' wives accepted the supremacy of mother-in-law rule as the price of 11 peace and kept their resentments to themselves. When her boys married the women she approved, their wives were expected to surrender their swords in return for being allowed to keep their husbands for the spring planting. Among them, only my mother refused to bend the knee. It's easy to understand why the two disliked each other instinctively from the first meeting, long before the awkward question of marriage arose. One can readily imagine the scene at that first confrontation:

Ida Rebecca would have been sitting in state in the front porch rocker that 12 served as her throne, waiting for Benny to arrive from Ep Ahalt's with his new girl. Her porch commanded a view fit for an empress. It sat high above the road overlooking Morrisonville's rooftops and behind them the distant rampart of the Blue Ridge Mountains. Arriving visitors had to look up to her, for the road lay three steps below the level of her lawn, and after climbing those steps and passing through the whitewashed picket gate, they had to mount another set of broad stone steps before reaching the presence.

My mother could only have been impressed when she finally attained the top- 13 most level and Ida Rebecca rose to meet her. Seated, Ida Rebecca looked much like any other country woman whose style had been formed in the 1870s. She wore home-sewn gray that enclosed her from neck to wrists to ankles and, if there was the smallest glint of sunshine, a gray bonnet with a wide bill that kept her face buried in shadow. When she stood, though, she projected physical power and moral authority. Fully erect, she was six feet tall and seemed to look down on the world. She certainly looked down on my mother, who was almost a foot shorter.

Under the enveloping gray dress were shoulders square and broad. The hands 14 were big and gnarled. They were hands that could prepare a feast for thirty people, deliver a baby, grow a year's supply of canning vegetables in a summer of garden toil, or butcher a hog, and they had done all these things many times long before my mother was born and many times after. The long jaw under her bonnet was combatively prominent. Her hair was a glistening silvery white. Peering through steel-rimmed spectacles were chilly gray eyes that found little to be amused by. What my mother saw was an overpowering figure accustomed to command.

What Ida Rebecca saw was a frail little creature with her hair cut in the sassy 15 new pageboy bob. A suspicious touch of the city flapper, that haircut. Decent women let their hair grow and tied it in a knot on the back of the head. And skinny little ankles and wrists like twigs that looked as if they'd snap if they had to do any real work. What in the world did Benny see in her? She certainly wasn't pretty. Didn't have enough weight on her to be pretty. Hardly an ounce of flesh anywhere.

Conversation couldn't have improved matters. Ida Rebecca's respect for 16 schoolteachers was slight. Her sons left school when they were big enough to work. By then they could read, write, and do sums and knew who George Washington and Abraham Lincoln were and had learned a little geography. How to find Europe on a map, and Virginia, and China. That was enough. Man was born to work, not to sit around with his nose in a book. She was totally uninterested in the proposition that a man ought to make something of himself. A man's duty was to provide. Provide for his wife, provide for his children. And pay his duty to his mother. Beyond that . . . It's doubtful she ever thought much beyond that.

My mother, always education-proud, wouldn't have hesitated to talk too much 17 and show off her learning. Maybe just to prove her spunk, she mentioned how backward the children around Morrisonville seemed, compared to the youngsters where she came from, for she was appalled by the unworldliness of her students. One day she asked one of them if she had ever been to Frederick over in Maryland. "No indeed, ma'am, and I don't ever expect to," the girl replied. "I once went all the way to Brunswick and just about knocked my brains out *there* looking at all the buildings."

Ida Rebecca had small book learning but highly developed sensitivity, particu- 18 larly when it came to judging outsiders. In Morrisonville outsiders were under suspicion until they proved they could fit comfortably into Morrisonville society. Ida Rebecca must have sensed immediately what her eleventh son failed to: that this book-proud schoolteacher who gave herself airs about her fancy family would never accommodate to Morrisonville.

■ *Questions for* . . . The Supremacy of Mother-in-Law Rule by Russell Baker

Words to Note

sloping	straw ricks	scattering
dozed	clack	prodigious
rose	wade	swallow
forked	ambled	lurched
meandered	lackadaisical	bootleggery
towering	partaking	psalming
procreation	delving	sprawling
empire	supremacy	resentments
confrontation	rocker	throne
rampart	mount	buried
projected	erect	gnarled
bonnet	glistening	peering
spectacles	chilly	frail
sassy pageboy bob	flapper	spunk
loyalties		

Language

1. Baker uses the language of the monarchy to characterize Ida Rebecca's place in her family: *iron ruler, sprawling family empire, supremacy, surrender their swords, bend the knee, throne,* and *presence.* Why? What's the tone of these words and phrases?

2. Look at the words Baker uses in paragraph 3 to describe Morrisonville's roads. Why is he making fun of them?

Style

1. In paragraph 15, Baker tries to imagine how his mother looked to Ida Rebecca. There are four sentence fragments in the course of this short paragraph. Why so many? When is a fragment effective, and when is it a mistake?
2. Baker covers quite a bit of time in just a few pages, but it's not scattered or jumpy. What techniques does he use to carry the reader along?
3. Why are his sentences so short?

Development and Organization

1. How does Baker's description of Morrisonville prepare us for Grandmother Ida Rebecca?
2. What does the story of Grandfather George Baker's last words add to this family portrait?
3. How does Baker characterize his mother? Why does he dwell on the initial confrontation between his grandmother and his mother?

Discussion and Journal Writing

1. What do Morrisonville's roads tell us about the town?
2. Why don't Ida Rebecca and Russell Baker's mother get along? Compare and contrast what each woman stood for.
3. Is Baker's family a matriarchy?

ooooo

Brown Girl, Brownstones

—Paule Marshall

Paule Marshall, the daughter of Barbadian immigrants, grew up on Brooklyn's Fulton Street in what was the Bajan section of Brooklyn in the 1940s and 1950s. After graduating from Brooklyn College, she has spent her life writing and teaching. *Brown Girl, Brownstones,* the source of the following passage, is her first and, in

my opinion, best novel. The ensuing family portrait is electric with
the tensions that seem to be an inevitable part of immigrant family
life in America.

They were very proud of the sun parlor. Not many of the old brownstones had 1
them. It was the one room in the house given over to the sun. Sunlight came
spilling through the glass walls, swayed like a dancer in the air and lay in a yellow
rug on the floor.

Her father was there, stretched dark and limp on a narrow cot like someone
drunk with sun. He had lain there since the mother left, studying a correspondence
course that he had just started, reading the newspapers and letters, listening to the
radio. Selina sat on the floor facing him, waiting, watching his lids move as his
eyes moved under them.

Deighton Boyce's face was like his eyelids—a closed blind over the man
beneath. He was well-hidden behind the high slanted facial bones, flared nose and
thin lips, within the lean taut body, and his dark skin, burnished to a high fine gloss,
completed the mystery.

"How the lady-folks?" he called finally, his eyes reaching over the letter he
was reading. They were a deeper brown than his skin with the sun in their centers.

His tone was the signal that they had stepped into an intimate circle and were 5
joined together in the pause and beat of life. Selina scratched where the elastic of
her sock made ridges in her flesh. "I couldn't go to the movies today because Ina
has her pains. I don't see why I can't go with my girl friend, but Mother says not
without Ina."

"You got to heed yuh mother."

"I know, but I still don't understand why. Ina doesn't look after me."

"Yuh mother know best."

He returned to his letter and she closed her eyes. The sun on her lids created
an orange void inside her and she wanted to remain like this always with the sun on
her eyes and bound with her father in their circle.

"I don know what wunna New York children does find in a movie," he said 10
after a time. "Sitting up in a dark place when the sun shining bright-bright outside."

"There's nothing else to do on Saturday."

"We had Sat'day home too and found plenty to do when we was boys coming
up."

She opened her eyes and there was a halo of bluish orange around his head.
She blinked. "I don't see what you could do that's better than the movies."

"How you mean? You think people din make sport before there was movie?
Come Sat'day, when we was boys coming up, we would get piece of stick and a
lime and a big stone and play cricket. If we had little change in we pocket we
would pick up weself and go up Kensington Field to football . . ."

"What else?" 15

"How you mean? I's a person live in town and always had plenty to do. I not
like yuh mother and the 'mounts of these Bajan that come from down some gully or

up some hill behind God back and ain use to nothing. 'Pon a Sat'day I would walk 'bout town like I was a full-full man. All up Broad Street and Swan Street like I did own the damn place."

"What else?"

"How you mean?"

"Didja play any games?"

"Game? How you mean? Tha's all we did. Rolling the roller and cork-stick- 20 ing . . ."

"What's that?"

"But how many times must I tell you, nuh? It some rough-up something. Throwing a tennis ball hard-hard at each other and you had to move fast, if not it would stun you good . . ."

"What else?"

"Plenty else!" he cried, angered that she remained unimpressed. "We would pick up weself and go sea-bathing all down Christ Church where the rich white people live. Stay in the water all day shooting the waves, mahn, playing cricket on the sand, playing lick-cork . . ." Anticipating her, he lifted his hand. "Don ask, I gon tell you just-now. Lick-cork is just play-fighting in the sea after a cork."

He paused, lifting his head, and the sunlight lanced his eyes. "And when a 25 tourist ship come into Carlisle Bay we would swim out to it and the rich white people from America would throw money in the water just to see we dive for it. Some them would throw a shilling and all. I tell you, those people had so much of money it did turn them foolish." He smiled, his teeth a dry white against his darkness, and abruptly returned to his letter.

Selina closed her eyes again and the orange void tried to see him diving after the coins. But thoughts of the mother intruded. What had she and the others who lived down in the gullies and up on the hills behind God's back done on Saturdays? She could never think of the mother alone. It was always the mother and the others, for they were alike—those watchful, wrathful women whose eyes seared and searched and laid bare, whose tongues lashed the world in unremitting distrust. Each morning they took the train to Flatbush and Sheepshead Bay to scrub floors. The lucky ones had their steady madams while the others wandered those neat blocks or waited on corners—each with her apron and working shoes in a bag under her arm until someone offered her a day's work. Sometimes the white children on their way to school laughed at their blackness and shouted "nigger," but the Barbadian women sucked their teeth, dismissing them. Their only thought was of the "few raw-mout' pennies" at the end of the day which would eventually "buy house."

They returned home with throw-offs: the old clothes which the Jews had given them. Whenever the mother forced her to wear them, Selina spent the day hating the unknown child to whom they belonged. Anger flashed now within the orange depth and it was only her father's voice which restored her.

"Yes, lady-folks, we did make plenty sport when we was boys coming up . . ." he was saying, his eyes pierced with memories.

"What is it like—home?"

"What I must say, nuh? Barbados is poor-poor but sweet enough. That's why I 30 going back."

"When?"

"Soon as I catch my hand here. You see this?" He held up the accounting manual. "This gon do it. I gon breeze through this course 'cause I was always good in figures. I ain even gon bother my head with all this preliminary work they sending now." He tossed aside the manual. "I gon wait till they send the real facts and study them. Then a job making decent money and we gone."

"Taking me?"

"How you mean! And we gon live in style, mahn. No little board and shingle house with a shed roof to cook in. We gon have the best now." He waved the letter he had been reading, then as quickly dropped it, turning suspiciously to the door. "Where yuh sister?"   35

"Downstairs, I think."

"You sure? 'Cause I thought I did hear somebody outside . . . You know how she does sneak 'bout listening to what we say and then lick she mouth to your mother."

"She's supposed to be sick and sleeping."

Reassured, he held up the letter again. "You see this? Don't broadcast it to the Sammy-cow-and-Duppy but my sister that just dead leave me a piece of ground. Now how's that for news?" His teeth flashed in a strong smile. "Now let these bad-minded Bajan here talk my name 'cause I only leasing this house while they buying theirs. One thing I got good land home!"

For a moment she did not understand. From his smile and the way his eyes 40 glowed she knew that it was important. She should have leaped up and pirouetted and joined his happiness. But a strange uneasiness kept her seated with her knees drawn tight against her chest. She asked cautiously, "You mean we're rich?"

"We ain rich but we got land."

"Is it a lot?"

"Two acres almost. I know the piece of ground good. You could throw down I-don-know-what on it and it would grow. An we gon have a house there—just like the white people own. A house to end all house!"

"Are you gonna tell Mother?"

His smile faltered and failed; his eyes closed in a kind of weariness. "How 45 you mean! I got to tell she, nuh."

"Whaddya think she's gonna say?"

"How could I know? Years back I could tell but not any more."

She turned away from the pain darkening his eyes.

"Ah come nuh!" he cried after a long pause. "What I frighten for? It my piece of ground, ain it? And I can do what I please with it. So come, lady-folks, let we celebrate with something from the candy store . . ."

"Hootons!"   50

He brought the coins from his pocket. "I tell you, this Hooton is the one thing you children here have that I wish we did have when we was boys coming up."

She laughed and shoved the coins around in his palm until she found a nickel.

With her hand still in his, she suddenly sat on the bed and, leaning close, whispered, "Look, I know you told me not to tell the Sammy-cow-and-Duppy about the land, but might I tell Beryl since she's my best friend? I'll make her swear and hope to die not to tell anyone . . ."

"Tell she," he said tenderly and closed his fist tight around her hand. "Your mother will know soon and then the world and it wife gon know." He freed her and swiftly she was gone, through the master bedroom, hurtling through the hall, her arms pumping, stopping only on the stoop to pull her socks out of the backs of her sneakers.

Chauncey Street languished in the afternoon heat, and across from it Fulton Park rose in a cool green wall. After the house, Selina loved the park. The thick trees, the grass—shrill-green in the sun—the statue of Robert Fulton and the pavilion where the lovers met and murmured at night formed, for her, the perfect boundary for her world; the park was the fitting buffer between Chauncey Street's gentility and Fulton Street's raucousness.

The sun was always loud on Fulton Street. It hung low and dead to the pave- 55 ment, searing the trolley tracks and store windows, bearing down until the street spun helplessly in an eddy of cars, voices, neon signs and trolleys. Selina responded to the turbulence, rushing and leaping in a dark streak through the crowd. Passing the beauty parlor she saw the new tenant Suggie and turned in.

Suggie Skeete's full-fleshed legs and arms, her languorous pose, all the liquid roundness of her body under the sheer summer dress hinted that love, its rituals and its passion, was her domain. As Selina's shadow slanted across her she looked up, greeting her with a laugh as murmurous as water. "Wha'lah, wha'lah, Selina? But where you always running to with yuh head down like a goat when it ready to butt? Look the clothes in strings like you belong to some string band society. The eyes wild like a tearcat. The hair like it curse comb, damn oil and blast the hairdresser. Come, let Miss Thompson slap the hot comb in it."

"Not me, Miss Suggie. I'd never get my hair done in this heat."

"Well you best put a comb to it before your mother come and put that mouth of hers 'pon you."

"Selina?" A voice hurdled above the tangled voices and the angry clicking of the hot curling tongs inside the shop.

"Yes, Miss Thompson, it's me."   60

A tall drawn woman—a faded brown in color and no longer young—came from behind the partition, whirling a smoking curling tong in one thin hand and flicking perspiration from her face with the other. The soiled nurse's uniform fell straight down her fleshless body, hiding the bones jutting under the skin. Her long lean shadow cut into the sunlight and brought a sudden darkness into the waiting room. Amidst the noise, she and Selina shared a quiet tender smile.

"I'm on my way to the candy store," she said softly. "You want me to bring you a Pepsi?"

"No thanks, honey. Just had one. That damn Pepsi don't do nothing but fill me with gas anyways. What I needs . . ." She thought a moment, her sunken eyes with the circles of age and weariness under them turned toward the sun in the doorway. "What I needs is to be sitting out in the park with them cool breezes blowing over me. That's what I needs. One of them c-o-o-l breezes. Then I'd feel human instead of like some old mule. That's all I needs," she repeated, sighing and turning away, "and it don't cost nothing and don't gimme no gas . . ."

On her way back through the park, Selina heard her name rising in a strident chant behind. Turning, she saw the girls waving their bright movie handbills and recognized her best friend Beryl. She was suddenly jealous of the others for the hours they had spent with her in the dark theater. She gave them a disinterested wave and hurried on.

"You missed the best Tarzan chapter today, Selina," one shouted. "Tarzan was 65 captured and he . . ."

"I'm bored with Tarzan," she cried and wanted to shout that she would be leaving them soon to live in a big house in a sweet land and that they would miss her. She walked faster.

At the park gate Beryl caught up with her. "I knew you'd be mad. I was gonna come and ask your mother if you could go but I knew she'd of said no. And I knew you'd be mad."

Something in Beryl always soothed her and destroyed her anger. Perhaps it was the way Beryl's thick braids rested quietly on her shoulders or the way her tiny breasts nudged her middy blouse. They made Selina shy, those breasts, and ashamed of her own shapelessness. "I'm not mad."

"Yes you are. But I didn't have any fun today without you. And Tarzan *is* boring because he always escapes. Today he . . ."

As she talked Selina watched the shifting pattern of sun and shade on her face. 70 She wished suddenly that her eyes could pierce Beryl's skin and roam inside her. What would Beryl be like inside? Like a small well-lighted room with the furniture neatly arranged around it.

"You're not listening."

"I was too. Look, I gotta give my father these Hootons. You want one?"

"No, it's too hot for chocolate. Can you come out later?"

"Maybe, if you come ask my mother. Oh, do come, I've got something to tell you." She grabbed her arm, remembering, and felt Beryl's warmth rush into her. "Something very, very special. Come later and ask," she shouted, running up the stoop.

She found her father asleep, seduced like her sister and the old woman 75 upstairs by the siren call of the afternoon. He still held the letter, and she slipped it away and placed it on the pillow beside his face. Downstairs she put his share of the candy in the icebox, then went up to the parlor and sat in the window seat behind the curtains. She ate slowly, melting the chocolate between her hands and then carefully licking it up from each palm and finger. As it slipped warmly down, her mind filled with warm thoughts of the secret she would share with Beryl. When she finished she watched a train of ants move along the ledge and wondered whether to kill them and make it rain . . .

She had decided to kill them when she sensed the mother, and her hand paused mid-air. It was strange how Selina always sensed her. Even before she looked up and over to the park she knew that she would see the mother there striding home under the trees.

Silla Boyce brought the theme of winter into the park with her dark dress amid the summer green and the bright-figured house-dresses of the women lounging on the benches there. Not only that, every line of her strong-made body seemed to reprimand the women for their idleness and the park for its senseless summer display. Her lips, set in a permanent protest against life, implied that there was no time for gaiety. And the park, the women, the sun even gave way to her dark force; the flushed summer colors ran together and faded as she passed.

There was something else today in the angle of her head that added to Selina's uneasiness. It was as though the mother knew all that had transpired in the house since morning—her father's idleness, her quarrel with Ina, the news of the land—and was coming to chastise them all. Selina's eyes dropped to the mother's legs, and with drawn breath she sought the meaning in that purposeful stride. Suddenly in one swift pure movement she was in front of the mirror, struggling out of her shorts and tugging at her matted braids.

■ *Questions for* . . . Brown Girl, Brownstones by Paule Marshall

Words to Note

parlor	brownstones	spilling
swayed	cot	slanted
flared	taut	burnished
gloss	ridges	wunna
bright-bright	halo	weself
gully	full-full	void
seared	lashed	distrust
sucked their teeth	hurtling	pumping
tong	jutting	chant
nudged	siren	seduced
sensed	striding	lounging
reprimand	idleness	flushed
uneasiness	transpired	quarrel
chastise	struggling	tugging

Language

1. How does the Barbadian, or *Bajan,* dialect read? Should Marshall have used Standard English?
2. Why does Selina speak differently from her parents?

3. "The sun was always loud on Fulton Street," Marshall writes. How can the sun be loud? How is she using the word?

Style

1. In how many ways does Marshall use color?
2. Study her sentences. How would you describe the rhythm of her prose?

Development and Organization

1. How does Marshall use dialogue?
2. What techniques does she use to develop character?
3. Why does she use Selina to tie this passage together?
4. What do the patterns of contrast that run throughout the passage add?

Discussion and Journal Writing

1. What's wrong with the Boyce family?
2. What does Deighton Boyce's preoccupation with Whites tell us about him? About the world where he grew up in Barbados?
3. Compare and contrast Deighton and Silla Boyce. Which parent does Selina seem to love the most? Why? Which parent does she resemble the most?

ooooo

Bronx Shtetl

—Kate Simon

Kate Simon grew up in a Bronx that only exists today in people's memories, in their family stories, in the archives, and in books like *Bronx Primitive,* the autobiography from which "Bronx Shtetl" is excerpted. Simon grew up in the vicinity of Crotona Park in the 1920s when it was the property of White, blue-collar immigrants whose accents and clothing marked them and who worked in the factories before New York became a city of offices and skyscrapers. Simon's neighborhood and the surrounding ones hadn't yet been redlined by racist real estate interests or burned for insurance premiums. They hadn't been broken up yet by city planners. There were gangsters, trouble, sin, and crime, but the drug plague had yet to descend; kids on their way to buy milk at the corner store were not gunned down in drug crossfires. Simon's borough is the Bronx primeval.

We lived at 2029 Lafontaine, the last house on the west side of the street from 1
178th to 179th, a row of five-story tenements that ended at a hat factory. To the north and solidly, interminably, along the block to 180th there stretched a bitter ugliness of high walls of big stones that held a terminal point and service barns of El trains. (It may be that my recoil from early Renaissance palaces, their pugnacious blocks of stone and fortress grimness, stems from these inimical El walls.) Across from the factory were a garage and the Italian frame houses that lined that side of the street down to 178th Street. At the corner of 178th Street, on our Jewish-German-Polish-Greek-Hungarian-Rumanian side, was Mrs. Katz's candy store. The only other store I knew at first was the grocery run by a plodding elderly couple at te corner of 179th Street and Arthur Avenue, the street to the east. In spite of their lack of English and my frail Yiddish, I eagerly ran errands there to watch their feet slide and pat in their brown felt slippers and to admire the precision with which the old man cut once, twice, into a tub of butter to dig out exactly a quarter pound. And on their side of 179th Street, about midway between Arthur and Lafontaine, there was a big tree, the only street tree in the neighborhood, which showered me, and only me, with a million white blossoms. It was my tree and I watched and touched it as carefully as the Italian grandfathers watched and touched the tomato plants in their backyards.

Our station of the El was Tremont, which was numerically 177th Street, and 2
Main Street. Between dark Third Avenue and its changing grids and slashes of light and Lafontaine, there was Monterey Avenue, on its west side a row of tenements and on its east, running from 178th to 179th, a resplendent, high empty lot, as full of possibilities as a park. It had patches of daisies and buttercups, plumy and scratchy bushes; on its eastern edge and below our fire escapes, seductive glittering objects thrown from Lafontaine windows—a shining knife handle, red glass and blue glass, bits of etched cut glass. Once my brother and I fond a seltzer bottle nozzle and once a Chinese record, a wonderment we played over and over again on the Victrola, until our parents, impatient with the repetition of high thin notes with startling starts and stops, caused it to disappear. There were two ways of getting onto the lot: 178th Street was an easy, gradual slope; 179th Street was jutting rock for a height of two stories. The few girls who managed it were never quite the same again, a little more defiant, a little more impudent.

To the west of Lafontaine was Arthur Avenue, a mixture of Jewish tenements 3
and frame houses in which lived Italian families and a number of Irish. Beyond was Belmont, whose only significance was that it held, at its meeting with Tremont, the

movie house we all trooped to on Saturday after lunch. The other movie house, which offered a combination of films and vaudeville, was a rare pleasure; it cost more and was saved for special occasions, a birthday or a report card that said A for work, A for effort, A for conduct.

This theater for celebrations was also on Tremont, toward the west, not far 4 from Webster Avenue, beyond Bathgate and Washington. Bathgate, moving southward from Tremont toward Claremont Parkway, was the market street where mothers bought yard goods early in the week, as well as dried mushrooms and shoelaces. On Wednesdays they bought chickens and live fish to swim in the bathtub until Friday, when they became gefilte fish. Most women plucked their own chickens. A few aristocrats, like my mother and Mrs. Horowitz (who spoke English perfectly, the only Jewish woman we knew who did), paid a little dark bundle in a dusty red wig ten cents to pluck fast, her hand like the needle of a sewing machine, up down, up down, as a red and black and white garden of feathers spread at her feet. On the next block, Washington, was the public library, and a block north of it, on the corner with Tremont, the barber shop where I went for my Buster Brown haircut. Tremont west of Third also held the delectable five-and-ten, criscrosses of rainbows and pots of gold.

Our suburbs, our summer country homes, our camps, our banks and braes, our 5 America the Beautiful, our fields of gaming and dalliance and voyeurism, were in Crotona Park, whose northern border fronted on Tremont Avenue.

Our apartment, 5B, was a top-floor railroad flat, with most of the rooms strung 6 off a long hall. The first room nearest the outer door was a small bedroom with a large bed in which my brother and I slept, a chair on which we were to put our clothing rather than drop it on the floor, and, shortly after my sister's birth, her crib. From the bed I could see a hallway picture of the explosion of Vesuvius, a red horror of flames and fleeing bodies toward which I felt quite friendly when I was very young, not then knowing what it meant except bright color and lively lines. The next room off the hallway was the bathroom, all our own and a luxurious thing, with a tub, a sink, and a toilet that didn't have to be shared with neighbors. On Wednesday and Thursday nights we watched the big, vigorous carp in the tub, to be killed on Friday (when we were, unfortunately, in school) and chopped, in concert with the chopping that sounded from a dozen other kitchens, for Friday night's meal. The toilet had constantly to be pumped with a plunger to disgorge the inventive matter—spools, apple cores, a hank of wool—my brother threw in to see the water swirl and swallow, which it often didn't. The bathroom was also the torture chamber. It was here, after a long lecture explaining that the act was essential to the improvement of our conduct and we would be grateful for the lesson later on, that the strap was slowly, very slowly, pulled out of the loops on my father's pants while we bent over the lidded toilet bowl to be whipped, my brother much more often than I. He was an adventuresome explorer and breaker, while I was already well practiced in the hypocrisies of being a good girl. Furthermore, there was something shameful, except for extraordinary infractions, in beating a girl; a girl was for slapping rather than whipping.

The next room along the hallway was the kitchen where we chattered, ate,   7
fought over who had more slices of banana in his dish and who was the biggest pig,
the one who ate fast or the one who ate slowly, savoring each delicious bit when
the other had long finished. Here we watched my mother peel, for our pleasure, a
potato or an apple in one long unbroken coil. It was in the kitchen that we learned
to understand Yiddish from my father's accounts of union news read from the
socialist paper, the *Freiheit.* My mother read from the *Jewish Daily Forward* the
heartbreaking stories gathered in the "Bintel Brief" (bundle of letters) that wept of
abandoned wives, of "Greene Cousines," spritely immigrant girls who were hanky-
pankying with the eldest sons of households, set to marry rich girls and become
famous doctors. These stories moved me deeply, as all stories of betrayal and abandonment did, while my mother laughed. We loved to watch her laugh, big tears
rolling down her face as the laughter rocked her plump body back and forth, but I
found her humor chilling, heartless. She told one laughing story that appalled me
for years: there was a man who could neither sit nor stand nor lie down (this with
elaborations of voice and gesture), so he found a solution—he hanged himself.
Another story concerned an old man who had trouble peeing—great effort and pain
contorted her face and body—and consulted a doctor for relief. The doctor asked
the man how old he was. Eighty-three. "Well," said the doctor, "you've peed
enough. Go home, old man." We were constantly told to respect the old; here she
was being amused by a sick old man. It wasn't until I picked up the fatalistic
ironies of Jewish humor that I understood and almost forgave her the cruel jokes.

Beyond the kitchen hallway opened to the "living room," almost always   8
unused because we had few relatives and they visited rarely. We might look at the
things in it but must not touch, except to practice the piano when that inevitable
time came. The room was my mother's art museum, her collection of treasures. In
the china closet a few pieces of cut glass, an etched pitcher, two little china bowls.
On the round oak table a machine-embroidered cloth covered with fat red and pink
roses and thick green stems with thorns; a mighty work I thought it, and so did she,
since she paid the Arab peddler who sold it to her endless weekly quarters for its
ebullience. On a sideboard stood my favorite piece—a marble bowl on whose rim
rested two or three pigeons (a copy of a famous Roman mosaic repeated in many
materials throughout the centuries). The pigeons could be lifted off and set back
into little holes in the rim, a loving, absorbing game and a rare privilege never at all
permitted my brother. He could not resist inventive variations on any theme, would
try to place the pigeons where there were no holes and they would certainly crash,
and he would get a beating and—just better not. It was in such circumstances that
our parents used an odd phrase for both of us: "They have to know from where the
feet grow," an amused reference to our curiosity, a phrase that my mind moved
from feet to knees to genitals, where the ancient phrase with its sexual connotations
probably found its origins. Not for the first or the last time I wondered why words
and suggestions allowed grown-ups were forbidden children. There was no answer,
it was just another example of "walking on eggs," words I found felicitous to
describe our delicately balanced lives.

The end room was my parents' bedroom with its big bed, chests of drawers, 9 and my mother's talented sewing machine. Her feet rocking the treadle that said in metal letters "Singer," her hand smoothing the material taut as the needle chased her fingers, the turning, turning spool of thread feeling the jumping needle were a stunning show. Equally remarkable were the narrow long drawers, three on each side of the machine. You pulled a knob and out came long open boxes full of papers of shining, meticulously spaced pins, empty spools to string as trains, full spools that spilled baby rainbows, bits of silke and matte cotton to mix and match in myriad combinations, the dull with the shiny, the yellow with the blue, the white with the red, the square with the round; endless. Whether it was because of the dignity of the parental bed or the multitude of treasures in the sewing machine, it was in this room that my brother and I played most peacably, most happily, a room I still see, rain softly streaming down its windows, when I hear Mozart quartets. That end room was also the room of the fire escape. The balconies that jut out of modern apartment houses are empty stages, staring and lifeless compared with the old fire escape and its dynamic design of zigzag stairs and the teasing charm of potential danger when the metal stairs were wet with icy rain. Our fire escapes were densely inhabited by mops, short lines of washed socks, geranium plants, boxes of seltzer bottles, and occasional dramatic scenes. Skinny Molly, whose mother had an explosive temper, could escape by running down the fire-escape stairs where her fat mother couldn't follow, forcing her to expend her rage by threatening, "Wait till your father gets home, you crazy thing!" The fire escape was our viewing balcony down on the eventful lot we shared with Monterey Avenue, and it became our minute bedroom on hot nights when we slept folded on each other tight as petals on a bud, closed from the perilous stairs by a high board.

My family arrived on Lafontaine the summer before I was six and ready to be 10 enrolled in the first grade, my brother in kindergarten. As I had learned to do in European trains and stations, in inns, on the vastness of the ship *Susquehanna* when I was an immigrant four-year-old, I studied every landmark, every turning of our new surroundings.

On the day we registered for school, P.S. 58 on Washington Avenue at 176th 11 Street, my mother pointed out each turn, the number of blocks to the left or right and here we were at the big red building, the school, across from the little white building, the library. On the first day of school we went unaccompanied—hold his hand, don't talk to strange men. He complained that I was squeezing his hand and I probably was, tense and worried, avidly searching for the places I had marked out on our route: first to Tremont Avenue and right to the cake store, cross Third Avenue under the El, pass the butcher's with the pigs' feet in the window, cross Tremont at the bicycle shop to the barber's pole, continue on to the white library, and cross Washington Avenue to the school. It was a long walk, and I reached the school confused and exhausted, with just enough presence of mind to thrust the papers my mother had given me at the first teacher I saw, who led us to our respective rooms. We made the trip three more times that day, home for lunch and back and home again at three, and I was so bloated with triumph on the last journey that

I varied the turns and crossings while my brother pulled in the directions he had memorized, as frightened as I had been that morning. With no memory of the feeling and no sympathy, I pulled him along, calling him a crybaby.

Except for those journeys, all that remains of P.S. 58 is a Mrs. Henkel, a   12 brown old lady addicted to Spencerian handwriting. She pushed our hands around and around on the ridged, worn desks, grinding dust into our skin so that a number of us developed abscesses. Somehow the practice stopped; we were never told why. Certainly it could not have been complaints from our awed mothers, to whom schools were sacred citadels, except maybe English-speaking Mrs. Horowitz, who navigated comfortably in alien worlds.

As the street, the shops, the people became more familiar, there were rules to   13 learn, accumulated gradually and hardened into immutability like big pink patches always England in geography books, like Italy always the shape of a boot. Rumanian ladies used rouge and laughed a lot and ran around too much. Hungarian men were stuck-up and played cards late into the night and all day on Sunday. Bad girls who didn't go to school and who hid with tough boys were invariably the daughters of Polish janitors. Saturday night thumping and crashg and loud Victrola records came exclusively from Irish houses. The Jews stuck together, the Neapolitans and Sicilians stuck together, altogether apart from the northern Italians. Yet, in spite of momentary flare-ups, a mutter of anti-Semitism, "savage" thrown at a Sicilian, they clung to one another, arranging and rearranging the symbiotic couplings of the poor and uncomprehending in confrontations with the enemy, the outsider who spoke English without an accent. Except for a few entertaining, itinerant drunks, unaccented English was the alarm for the wary silence and the alert poise of the hunted. Not that it was a troublesome block. Most of the inhabitants were inert with timidity, but some of them had had and all of them had heard fearsome stories of brushes with truant officers, visiting nurses, people from naturalization offices, *Them* of the bewildering powers, and uncomfortably close. The Bronx County Building was stuffed with policemen, judges, immigration officials, women who looked like nurses or assistant principals. This confident, inimical enclave that spoke fast English and ate peanut butter sandwiches on white bread sat at our edge of Crotona Park, dourly in our line of vision almost everywhere we went. We children couldn't imagine them in ordinary tenements or frame houses, like ours, so we pushed them all into cold cubicles in the big-bellied building, like sides of beef in a huge butcher's icebox.

■ *Questions for* . . . Bronx Shtetl by Kate Simon

Words to Note

tenements	plodding	slide
pat	felt	precision
showered	grids	slashes
patches	nozzle	defiant
impudent	bundle	delectable
crisscrosses	strung	luxurious
disgorged	hank	swirl
torture	strap	infractions
slapping	whipping	chattered
coil	Yiddish	betrayal
abandonment	fatalistic	ironies
etched	embroidered	mosaic
rim	connotations	felicitous
matte	myriad	zigzag
perilous	balcony	bloated
awed	citadels	couplings
symbiotic	wary	alert
poise	inert	timidity
brushes	enclave	cubicles

Language

1. Who is the "little dark bundle in a dusty red wig" that the neighborhood aristocrats paid to pluck their chickens?
2. How can a sewing machine be *talented?*

Style

1. A single *our* in paragraph 5 would have sufficed. Why does Simon repeat the word so many times?
2. What is the tone of the piece? How does she convey the tone?

Development and Organization

1. Why does Simon move from the neighborhood to her family's apartment and back to the neighborhood again?
2. How does she organize her description of the apartment? Can you think of any other approaches that would have worked?
3. What is she trying to tell the reader in her description of each room?

Discussion and Journal Writing

1. How much do we learn about Simon's family from her description of the apartment and neighborhood?
2. Why was unaccented English an alarm for Simon's family and their neighbors?
3. Compare Simon's and Kazin's kitchens. Which description do you like better? Why?

ooooo

*F*amily Document Two

Grandma's Hands

—Bill Withers

Grandma's hands clapped in church on Sunday morning,
Grandma's hands played a tambourine so well.
Grandma's hands used to issue out a warning.
She say, "Scottie, why you run so fast?
Might fall on a piece of glass,
Might be snakes there in that grass."
Grandma's hands, they keep calling my name.

Grandma's hands soothed the look of unwed mothers,
Grandma's hands used to ache sometimes and swell.
Grandma's hands, Lord, they really come in handy,
She say, "Bobby, why you whip that boy?
He didn't throw no apple core. What you want to whip him for?"
Grandma's hands, they keep calling my name.

Grandma's hands soothed the look of unwed mothers,
Grandma's hands used to ache, well, they really came in handy.
She say, "Bobby, why you whip that boy?
Why you want to whip him for? He didn't throw no apple core."
But I don't have Grandma anymore;
When I get to heaven, I'll look for Grandma's hands.
They keep on calling my name,
Yeah, yeah-ah, keep on calling,
They keep on calling my name.
Yeah-ah, I can't look back,
Can't look back, but I still remember
Things that mean so much to me
About the way I am and how I came to be.
Yeah-ah, say yeah-ah, I need, I need, I need,

I feel more like everyday I need to say,
Everyday I need to say,
Everyday I need to say,
I feel like that because of Grandma's hands,
I feel like, I feel like that because of Grandma's hands.
I'm the way I am because of Grandma's hands,
Touching me and moulding me and shaping me and holding me.

Reprinted with permission. (Los Angeles, CA: Interior Records)

■ *Questions for* . . . **Grandma's Hands** by Bill Withers

Discussion and Journal Writing

1. Withers's lyrics tell about his entire grandmother, but "Grandma's hands" is the song's refrain and title. What effect does the tight focus he maintains on her hands have on the reader?
2. What do we learn about Grandma? Does Withers mean for her to be typical? Symbolic? Is it possible to interpret the song as Withers tribute to the strength of the Black family?
3. Some take exception to *unwed mothers,* an expression Withers uses twice. Why?
4. Translate the song into Standard English. What happened?

ooooo

$\mathcal{F}$amily Album Two

Black Family, Civil War Period

Five Generations of an Enslaved Black Family, All Born on J. J. Smith's Plantation in Beaufort, South Carolina, circa 1863. *(Library of Congress)*

■ *Questions for . . .* Black Family, Civil War Period

Discussion and Journal Writing

1. Herbert Gutman, in his book, *The Black Family in Slavery and Freedom,* says this photograph is visual proof that the Black family wasn't torn apart by slavery. What does it tell us about this particular family that five generations assembled for the camera?

ooooo

🎴 Descriptive Writing

All writers develop their ideas or risk being misunderstood or dismissed. With descriptive writing, development means detail. A piece of descriptive writing is successful when the selection, presentation, and arrangement of detail advance the purpose of the writer. Handling detail is especially crucial when a writer is trying to convey a personal or subjective impression, but detail is also important in objective description. In a biology textbook, for instance, DNA is described: the nucleic acids are the details, the biologist presents and defines their properties, and the double helix is the arrangement of nucleic acids.

Selecting detail requires judgment. Though most writers employ a number of connected details, describing something or someone isn't simply a matter of taking inventory. Too much can be too much. You can bury a reader in insignificant detail. Similarly, a writer can fail to provide enough detail for the reader's imagination to go on. The question, then, is how much is enough, and the answer is that it all depends on what the writer is trying to do. But, as a general rule of thumb, good writers favor brush strokes that are particular and vivid in and of themselves but suggest so much more of the picture. Alfred Kazin, for instance, in "The Kitchen: The Great Machine That Set Our Lives Running," tells us about his mother's Singer sewing machine, the coal-black stove, the "fiercely stippled," whitewashed walls, a naked bulb hanging over the table, a spice shelf with a calendar from the Minsker Progressive Branch of the Workman's Circle, a spindle of household bills, and two little connection boxes, lettered in Hebrew, for less fortunate Jewish brothers and sisters; thus, we not only see but understand and have a feel for the room in which he did most of his growing up.

Of course, the details writers select are inseparable from how they present them, but I'm making this somewhat artificial distinction to emphasize the importance of word choice. This chapter's "Words to Note" sections make the point: These writers favor words that are concrete, expressive, and evocative—words that speak to the senses as well as the mind. Maxine Hong

Kingston says that her mother, in a graduation picture taken in China before she came to America, has "spacy" eyes, which do not "focus" on the camera. Chinese people, Kingston explains, do not smile for photographs; their faces "command" relatives who have emigrated to send money. Her mother's naturally curly hair is parted on the left, a "wisp tendrilling off to the right." After her mother came to America, Kingston says later, she learned the "barbarians' directness," her eyes never "skittering" off a face. It's through the arresting words Kingston chooses that she measures the geographical and cultural distance her mother has traveled; it's through her words that she invites us into her rather intent meditation on her mother's life.

The language of these pieces approaches the language of poetry: it's musical, it's rich in connotation, and it's figurative. In Momaday's essay about his grandmother and her tribe, the Kiowas, the language is especially metaphoric. The highland meadows, through which the Kiowas trekked, are a "stairway" to the plain. The sky there is immense; "great billowing clouds . . . . sail" upon it. The houses of the Kiowas are "sentinels in the plain." The prairie in the summer is "an anvil's edge," the grasshoppers in the grass "popping up like corn to sting the flesh." When a writer uses a metaphor or a simile to compare one thing to another, he or she expresses an attitude or feeling. Here, Momaday's nature metaphors express the bond his grandmother and her tribe have with the land. The land is their chronicle and their scriptures; it is a vital part of who they are.

The arrangement of detail can also be important. In most cases, writers arrange detail in patterns, which are meant to approximate perception: this is how it sounds, from beginning to end; this is how it feels, moving from one point to another; or, this is how it looks, starting from one side of a room and moving through it to another. However, in good writing, the details add up— the effect is cumulative—and beneath the perceptual surface there is a deeper logic that comes from a writer's purpose. At first glance, Kingston seems to be paging casually through her family album: there's one of her mother, a few of her father, and two more of her mother. However, the tone is lighter, almost dismissive when she moves to the images of her father. The situations that produced these pictures are different, which she distills in the distinction she makes between the photographs of her mother and the snapshots of her father. The few notes of family history she sounds serve to secure the reader's sympathies for her mother. There is nothing casual or accidental about the way she has arranged these images from her family album. She begins and ends the piece with her mother because it is really about her mother. The different poses her father strikes in each snapshot and his hats, outfits, and frivolousness set her mother's dignity and seriousness of purpose in high relief.

Kate Simon and James Agee take us on house tours. Simon, after giving us a quick sense of the old neighborhood, leads us, room by room, through the top-floor railroad flat she grew up in. There is nothing static about her description. She tells us so much about what happened in each room and what it felt like to be in those rooms as a child that we realize her family, not the apartment, is the true subject of this piece and, at a deeper level, her feelings about her family.

The passage from Agee's *Let Us Now Praise Famous Men,* his book-length diatribe about the lives of Southern sharecropping families during the Great Depression, is a play on the kind of piece Simon wrote. No one's home at the house of Gudger. Agee gives us the smell and feel of the bucket and dipper they drink from, of the granite-ware basin in which they wash their hands, and of the flour sack they dry themselves with, but we see no Gudgers drinking or washing. Their absence gives the passage an eerie, poignant feel. They are present only by implication; they are silently couched between the lines. Their muteness and invisibility underscore the desolate lives they lead. Agee acquaints us with them through understatement, leading us through room after deserted room. The wood itself, which is beautiful despite its unplanned cheapness, despite the frequent knots and knotholes and the "shadows of the savage breathings and eatings of the circular saw," stands for the Gudgers, who, as sharecroppers, occupy the ladder's lowest rung in a hard region during hard times.

✂ Writing Workshop

The Topic: An important relative

The Assignment: Write a sketch of a relative you like, respect, or are simply intrigued by. The point is to enable the reader to see and understand the person you write about.

Get together with a small group and open your notebook. Present your relative to the group, describing that person's appearance, expressions, style, values, beliefs, virtues, shortcomings, ticks, favorite sayings, and so on. Does this relative have a special role in your family, like Russell Baker's Uncle Harold, the family liar? Is he or she the family peacemaker? The one people take their problems to? The one who won't let family secrets be and is always causing scenes? The clown? The scapegoat? The gossip? The bully?

Take notes as you talk, as the members of your group ask questions and you answer them. Presenting your subject verbally should help you to gain some distance from a person you are, by definition, close to.

If possible, bring a photo of your relative to class. Write a paragraph or two describing the person and read it to the members of your group before you show them the picture. Then ask them to tell you what you left out. Or, you could ask a member of your group to look at the photo before you present it and write a paragraph describing the person. That person's impressions might open your eyes a little wider.

Next, study your notes and brainstorm. What features and details do you want to stress? Are there family anecdotes you should bring in? Who is this person? What do you want to say about him or her?

Review what you have and freewrite for about 15 minutes; afterwards, let it sit for at least a few hours. Then, read your notes and your freewriting, underlining words, phrases, and ideas you think you can use. Write down what you think the main idea, theme, or impression will be, and try to make a list of the items, details, points, and anecdotes you will cover in the order you think you will write about them. In other words, draw up a rough outline. You may, for instance, want to begin with a fairly brief anecdote that puts your subject on the page. Then, perhaps, you'll write a paragraph describing the person or a paragraph describing that person's role in your family. There's no one way to approach this topic, nor is there any one set of items that every writer will cover.

Write a first draft. If you get stuck, go back and reread a couple of this chapter's descriptive essays. Perhaps you'll see an approach that helps. Reading someone else's words will often break the spell. Proofread and polish your draft and give it to your instructor. Include notes, if requested.

When your sketch is returned, study your instructor's comments, read your draft out loud to yourself or to someone whose opinion you value, and rewrite. Review the section on rewriting in the Introduction if you want to be reminded of what should be scrutinized and possibly reworked.

Does the beginning work? Is the organization right? Do you need to add more material? More detail? More explanation? Do the words you've chosen and the phrases you've made say just what you want to say? Check a thesaurus. Try other ways of phrasing sentences that don't read the way you want them to. Read the different versions aloud to test them. Is your relative on the page and not just in your head?

Let this second draft sit for a while, then proofread it for grammar, punctuation, spelling, capitalization, word choice, and phrasing. If you tend to make quite a few little slips, you need to put more time and effort into proofreading.

Type a final draft, proofread for typos, turn it in, and take a break.

Additional Writing Exercises

- Describe a place (a room, a house, a neighborhood, a town) that is important to your family. Why and how it is important should be clear in the way you write.
- Take a photograph from your family album of relatives at a family event you did not attend and describe the people in the photo. Try to capture their expressions and convey their personalities.
- Write a description of your immediate family for a time capsule that will be opened by your great-grandchildren in the year 2054. What should you say about each person? How should you mix public facts with personal impressions? Try to limit yourself to a paragraph or two per person.

Chapter 3

$\mathcal{F}$amilies Plural: Culture and Family

■

✵ Culture, a Key to Understanding Family

Is it natural for a 9- or 10-year-old girl to take a grown man for a husband and have him live with and provide for her and her family for a few years before the marriage is consummated sexually? There are cultures and societies that would find this arrangement bizarre and perhaps even illegal, but among the !Kung, a tribe of hunters and gatherers who live in Africa's Kalahari Desert, it is called a *trial marriage* and is quite common.

Is it natural for parents to work all day in exchange for money while others take care of their children in exchange for less money? For a man to marry his brother's widow?

Is it natural for a child to expect that people whom her wealthy, busy parents employ will wake her up, feed her, take her to and from school, play with her, teach her, bathe her, and love her? For parents to raise their children on the streets or in crowded and filthy shelters because they lack resources in an affluent society?

Is it natural to expect everyone in your community, neighborhood, or village to make wedding robes for you and your spouse by hand from raw cotton? For female kin who live in several different households to share meals, supplies, blankets, and child care just so they can get by?

Most of us grow up with such a keen sense of what a family should be, even if our families fall short of the mark, that we have a hard time imagining or understanding anything different; however, common sense and a little reading tell us that families aren't and haven't been the same the world over. The shapes families take and the values they hold have been different from one historical period to another, are different from culture to culture, and are somewhat different even from class to class within a society. An appreciation of these differences, which can be confusing and bewildering at first, leads to a deeper understanding of one's own family.

Explorers and missionaries were the West's first cultural chroniclers: Marco Polo, Christopher Columbus, and Fathers Bartolomé de Las Casas, and La Salle brought back, amongst other things, impressions of other ways of life. They were followed by waves of military officers, trading company executives, and colonizing officials who put their knowledge and the knowledge of the explorers and missionaries to imperial use. A ragtag band of intellectuals, writers, and painters also followed but put their perceptions to a less profitable use. Herman Melville, Denis Diderot, Joseph Conrad, and Paul Gaugin, to name a few, drew pictures of Asia, Africa, and the South Seas that explicitly or implicitly compared life there with life in Europe and America. In asking who these new people were, these "others," they asked who they and their countrymen were: their answers were often critical of European and American social and familial customs and values, undermining the presumption of the West's superiority.

The twentieth-century record of the family worldwide has been made chiefly by journalists—print, broadcast, and photojournalists—and anthropologists. It's hard to generalize about the work of journalists since it has been colored by their individual interests, temperaments, beliefs, and prejudices. Three observations, however, are possible: trains, planes, and cars have enabled journalists to take their pens and cameras to almost every square inch of the planet; their work is superficial because of limited time and space; and their reports, articles, and photographs are generally influenced by the editorial policies of the papers, magazines, or networks that employ them. After all, most of them work for mainstream media that produce mainstream views.

Anthropologists have produced a rich body of family, group, and community studies since anthropology emerged as a distinct social science discipline in the early twentieth century. They have written about marital customs among the Trobriand Islanders, the rites of passage of the BaMbuti, a Pygmy tribe, the community festivals of the Balinese, the life of Puerto Rican sugar cane workers, and a religious/economic symbol system used by Native American tin miners in Bolivia, just to name a few studies. As a group, anthropologists have tried hard not to project their values on the lives of others. Whether or not they succeed in avoiding the pitfalls of ethnocentrism is a matter of debate each time a new study is published, which is a sign of the field's vitality. Clifford Geertz, an eminent American anthropologist, argues in *The Interpretation of Cultures* that anthropologists should restrict themselves to "thick descriptions" of their subjects: instead of theorizing about human behavior, the politics of culture, and the politics of scholarship, anthropologists should, Geertz believes, devote themselves to rich, multilayered descriptions of their subjects.

Few anthropologists, however, have taken Geertz's advice. Most of them write in-depth analyses and critiques; and, like the previously mentioned intellectuals, writers, and artists of the eighteenth and nineteenth centuries, they tend to compare their own cultures with the cultures they study and are often quite critical of their own cultures' presumptions. As a group, anthropologists have been accused more than once of Western Civ. bashing.

For our purposes, there are three key points to stress. First, despite the common features families share, they are different from one culture to the next, which means there is no one best family. Second, it's important to examine the assumptions that writers make about their subjects and the situations that produce pieces of writing, just as it's important to examine your own assumptions when you write. Third, the comparative approach that many anthropologists use is a powerful tool. Comparing one subject with another is one of the fundamental approaches human beings have devised for making sense of the social and physical world. The comparative approach, which is important in all fields, is also a powerful writing strategy: it is a way of generating, organizing, and clarifying ideas.

Bohannan, Kluckhohn, Mintz, Shostak, and Stack—the majority of the writers in this chapter—are anthropologists. With the exception of Kluckhohn, whose essay on culture is more general, these writers gathered material firsthand. Anthropologists believe in what they call *participant observation,* which means living with the people you intend to write about in an effort to see their lives as they do. The poet Robert Hayden recollects a weekly ritual in "Those Winter Sundays" with such power that we can see into the family he is writing about. Helen Sekaquaptewa writes an account of Hopi life that is somewhere between autobiography and cultural reportage, and Sallie Bingham's "Southern Princess" is from her autobiography *Passion and Prejudice.* It's impossible in a single chapter to include something about every major cultural group; nonetheless, this chapter's collection of evocative, well-written readings do suggest a wide world of family experience.

Word Play: *Kin*

Kin, a synonym of *family* and *relatives,* comes from the Old English *cynn,* which in turn derives from the Indo-European root *gen,* meaning "to produce." *Gen* is also the source of the Latin word *generes,* which is the root of *generate* and *generations.*

In contemporary American English, *kin* is rarely used. It was, however, more common in the past, and it still has some currency in Southern dialects. *Kin* is a key word and a vital principle in the feud between the Grangerfords and the Shepherdsons in Mark Twain's *Huckleberry Finn,* not to mention the legendary feud between the Hatfields and the McCoys. And *kinfolk* can be found in the theme song of the TV sitcom "The Beverly Hillbillies." In fact, Americans and anyone who watches American movies and TV regularly recognize *kin* as a verbal mainstay of stereotypic hillbilly talk. "Who's your kin?" "What kin are you?" That's *kin* with a twang, which on the silver screen is verbal make-up.

Outside of Hollywood and the South, however, *kin* is the property of anthropologists. They have husked the word of its folksy overtones, compounded it with other words, and invested the whole family of *kin* words with the authority of science. Anthropologists draw charts of *kin groups,* diagramming all possible permutations. They analyze the functions of *kin-based households,* including the participation of *fictive kin,* individuals who are not related by blood or marriage but are part of the family anyhow; and they hypothesize and attempt to trace the lines of *kin networks,* which may encompass a number of households.

Kin and its compounds are just a small part of anthropology's extensive vocabulary. Anthropologists study family patterns that are *patrifocal* and *matrifocal,* which are Latinate coinages for "father-centered" and "mother-centered," respectively. They differentiate between *consanguineous* bonds and *conjugal* bonds, which is Latinate terminology for being related "by blood" and related "by marriage," respectively. They distinguish *polygynous polygamy* from *polyandrous polygamy;* here the source is classical Greek, *polyandros,* meaning "having many husbands" and *polygynos,* meaning "having many wives." (*Gyno,* meaning "woman," is at the root of two words feminist critics have popularized: *gynophobic,* meaning "one who fears women" and *misogynist,* meaning "one who hates women.") The term for the studies anthropologists write also comes from classical Greek: *ethnographies,* which comes from *ethnos,* meaning "race, people, or cultural group" and *graphien,* meaning "to write." The name of the field itself stems from the Greek *anthropos,* which means "man" or, originally, "one with a bearded face," plus *logos,* which means "word," but also has the broader meaning of "thought or reckoning."

It's no wonder that some anthropologists, especially the mediocre ones who don't have anything new to say and don't know how to say it, sound abstract and vaguely foreign to most ears: like most academic disciplines, anthropology has spawned its own polyglot patois, which presents the layperson with a problem and a question. The problem is reading it; the question, could it be written in plain English? In other words, is the language of anthropology a specialized vocabulary that specialists need to convey their distinct insights into human behavior, or is it jargon?

The problem of reading anthropology is more or less severe from one writer to another. Sidney Mintz's introduction to the life and village of Don Taso, a Puerto Rican sugar cane worker, reads like a novel: his sentences are beautifully paced and his language is simple and vivid. On the other hand, Carol Stack, who is generally a good writer and always a good thinker, loses the reader from time to time in thickets of abstraction and odd terminology.

Those who make the case for a specialized vocabulary argue that there is no simple way to express complicated ideas. Furthermore, even the terminology of previous generation of scholars in the same field is no longer useful because it is an inextricable part of a dated approach. The assumption throughout the social sciences and the humanities is that if one is to be original, the questions one asks, the methods one uses to explore those questions, and at least some of the terminology must be original. Adam naming the animals in the Garden of Eden is invoked: there is power in naming because names can define and codify reality. In academia, there is a premium placed on coinage, regardless of the difficulty or obscurity of the word or phrase coined.

The American economist Thorstein Veblen, a cutting critic of human pretensions, argues in *The Theory of the Leisure Class* that academic vocabularies are the language of groups of professionals who are subconsciously insecure about their status and authority and who use jargon to entrench themselves and to mystify the populace. Scholarship in any field, then, is the work of a semi-isolated group of insecure professionals who are interested not only in communicating but also in veiling their meaning. Think of how an economist sounds, Marxist or Keynesian; a sociologist on the topic of alienation; or a literary critic who has been influenced by deconstructionism's theorists. Academics like to try on new words the way people try on new clothes. It is ironic that they often complain about how distant they are from the rest of society, yet the way they write and talk partially accounts for that distance.

There are serious arguments on either side of issue, and there's no easy way to tell at a glance whether scholarly writing is jargon-ridden or written thoughtfully in the language of a specialist. Unfortunately, good thinkers are not necessarily good writers; you will encounter inept writers whose ideas are well worth your time. I can only offer a rule of thumb and some advice. Writers who use jargon are usually poor writers in other ways: phrasing is indirect and off balance, verbs are often passive, clichés abound, ideas are out of focus and sometimes contradictory, explanations further muddy the water, examples don't suit the points they are meant to support, and the thread of the argument is hard to follow because of disorganization.

Keep your eyes and your dictionaries open when you read, especially if it is a field you're not familiar with. Don't be intimidated or put off by long, unfamiliar words. Look them up. Question authority.

Journal Entry

How has *primitive* been used by social scientists to describe the cultures and family customs of others? How is it used today? Has its meaning or use changed in the last 30 years? Is there anyone on campus you could interview to help with this project? A librarian? An anthropologist?

$\mathcal{R}$eadings

The Concept of Culture

—Clyde Kluckhohn

Clyde Kluckhohn became interested in anthropology when he went to New Mexico in the early 1920s to recover from an illness and was enchanted by Navaho life and culture. After studying the discipline at Princeton and Oxford Universities, he taught anthropology at Harvard University and wrote, among other books, Mirror for Man, a meditation on the nature of culture with a small *c* and the source of the following essay.

Why do the Chinese dislike milk and milk products? Why would the Japanese [1] die willingly in a Banzai charge that seemed senseless to Americans? Why do some nations trace descent through the father, others through the mother, still others through both parents? Not because different peoples have different instincts, not because they were destined by God or Fate to different habits, not because the weather is different in China and Japan and the United States. Sometimes shrewd common sense has an answer that is close to that of the anthropologist: "because they were brought up that way." By "culture" anthropology means the total life way of a people, the social legacy the individual acquires from his group. Or culture can be regarded as that part of the environment that is the creation of man.

This technical term has a wider meaning than the "culture" of history and lit- [2] erature. A humble cooking pot is as much a cultural product as is a Beethoven sonata. In ordinary speech a man of culture is a man who can speak languages other than his own, who is familiar with history, literature, philosophy, or the fine arts. In some cliques that definition is still narrower. The cultured person is one who can talk about James Joyce, Scarlatti, and Picasso. To the anthropologist, however, to be human is to be cultured. There is culture in general, and then there are the specific cultures such as Russian, American, British, Hottentot, Inca. The general abstract notion serves to remind us that we cannot explain acts solely in terms of the biological properties of the people concerned, their individual past experience, and the immediate situation. The past experience of other men in the form of culture enters into almost every event. Each specific culture constitutes a kind of blueprint for all of life's activities.

One of the interesting things about human beings is that they try to understand themselves and their own behavior. While this has been particularly true of Europeans in recent times, there is no group which has not developed a scheme or schemes to explain man's actions. To the insistent human query "why?" the most exciting illumination anthropology has to offer is that of the concept of culture. Its explanatory importance is comparable to categories such as evolution in biology, gravity in physics, disease in medicine. A good deal of human behavior can be understood, and indeed predicted, if we know a people's design for living. Many acts are neither accidental nor due to personal peculiarities nor caused by supernatural forces nor simply mysterious. Even those of us who pride ourselves on our individualism follow most of the time a pattern not of our own making. We brush our teeth on arising. We put on pants—not a loincloth or a grass skirt. We eat three meals a day—not four or five or two. We sleep in a bed—not in a hammock or on a sheep pelt. I do not have to know the individual and his life history to be able to predict these and countless other regularities, including many in the thinking process, of all Americans who are not incarcerated in jails or hospitals for the insane.

To the American woman a system of plural wives seems "instinctively" abhorrent. She cannot understand how any woman can fail to be jealous and uncomfortable if she must share her husband with other women. She feels it "unnatural" to accept such a situation. On the other hand, a Koryak woman of Siberia, for example, would find it hard to understand how a woman could be so selfish and so undesirous of feminine companionship in the home as to wish to restrict her husband to one mate.

Some years ago I met in New York City a young man who did not speak a word of English and was obviously bewildered by American ways. By "blood" he was as American as you or I, for his parents had gone from Indiana to China as missionaries. Orphaned in infancy, he was reared by a Chinese family in a remote village. All who met him found him more Chinese than American. The facts of his blue eyes and light hair were less impressive than a Chinese style of gait, Chinese arm and hand movements, Chinese facial expression, and Chinese modes of thought. The biological heritage was American, but the cultural training had been Chinese. He returned to China.

Another example of another kind: I once knew a trader's wife in Arizona who took a somewhat devilish interest in producing a cultural reaction. Guests who came her way were often served delicious sandwiches filled with a meat that seemed to be neither chicken nor tuna fish yet was reminiscent of both. To queries she gave no reply until each had eaten his fill. She then explained that what they had eaten was not chicken, not tuna fish, but the rich, white flesh of freshly killed rattlesnakes. The response was instantaneous—vomiting, often violent vomiting. A biological process is caught in a cultural web.

A highly intelligent teacher with a long and successful experience in public schools in Chicago was finishing her first year in an Indian school. When asked how her Navaho pupils compared in intelligence with Chicago youngsters, she replied, "Well, I just don't know. Sometimes the Indians seen just as bright. At other times they just act like dumb animals. The other night we had a dance in the high school. I saw a boy who is one of the best students in my English class standing off by himself. So I took him over to a pretty girl and told them to dance. But they just stood there with their heads down. They wouldn't even say anything." I inquired if she knew whether or not they were members of the same clan. "What difference would that make?"

"How would you feel about getting into bed with your brother?" The teacher   8 walked off in a huff, but, actually, the two cases were quite comparable in principle. To the Indian the type of bodily contact involved in our social dancing has a directly sexual connotation. The incest taboos between members of the same clan are as severe as between true brothers and sisters. The shame of the Indians at the suggestion that a clan brother and sister should dance and the indignation of the white teacher at the idea that she should share a bed with an adult brother represent equally nonrational responses, culturally standardized unreason.

All this does not mean that there is no such thing as raw human nature. The   9 very fact that certain of the same institutions are found in all known societies indicates that at bottom all human beings are very much alike. The files of the Cross-Cultural Survey at Yale University are organized according to categories such as "marriage ceremonies," "life crisis rites," "incest taboos." At least seventy-five of these categories are represented in every single one of the hundreds of cultures analyzed. This is hardly surprising. The members of all human groups have about the same biological equipment. All men undergo the same poignant life experiences such as birth, helplessness, illness, old age, and death. The biological potentialities of the species are the blocks with which cultures are built. Some patterns of every culture crystallize around focuses provided by the inevitables of biology: the difference between the sexes, the presence of persons of different ages, the varying physical strength and skill of individuals. The facts of nature also limit culture forms. No culture provides patterns for jumping over trees or for eating iron ore.

■ *Questions for* . . . The Concept of Culture by Clyde Kluckhohn

Words to Note

instincts	habits	shrewd
anthropologist	culture	clique
bewildered	gait	remote
reared	queries	biological process
cultural web	huff	incest taboos
clan	shame	life crisis rites
poignant	inevitable	

Language

1. At the end of the second paragraph, Kluckhohn uses the metaphor *blue-print* for *culture*. What exactly is a *blueprint?* According to this metaphor, what is *culture?* Is it a helpful metaphor? Why or why not?
2. Kluckhohn says the American who was orphaned in infancy and raised by a Chinese family in a remote village has a "Chinese style of gait." What does he mean? How is *gait* different from *walk* or *stride?* Did he choose the best word?

Style

1. Why does Kluckhohn put *culture* in quotation marks in the first two para-graphs and *blood* in quotations marks in the fifth paragraph? Would those sentences read differently if the quotation marks were deleted?
2. How would the beginning of paragraph 8 be different if he had translated his question about the teacher sleeping with her brother into indirect address?

Development and Organization

1. What would be left if you deleted Kluckhohn's examples? Would his essay be easier or harder to understand? Why?
2. Map the essay. What sort of transitional words, phrases, and techniques does Kluckhohn use to direct the reader?

Discussion and Journal Writing

1. Spell out what you think Kluckhohn means when he says "a humble cook-ing pot is as much a cultural product as is a Beethoven sonata." Listen to a sonata, look at a cooking pot. Write about what you see and hear. Do you agree with Kluckhohn?
2. Compare the concept of culture with the concepts of evolution, gravity, and disease. Use a collegiate dictionary if you're not sure of the definitions and significance of these concepts. Do you agree or disagree with Kluckhohn about the parallel importance of these concepts?
3. According to Kluckhohn, what is the relationship between biology and cul-ture? Culture and the "facts of nature"? Culture and individualism?
4. What are your family's taboos? Are these taboos cultural, or are they mat-ters of your particular family's preferences? How were you made aware of these taboos? How are they enforced?

○○○○○

Shakespeare in the Bush

—Laura Bohannan

Laura Bohannan, like Clyde Kluckhohn, is an American who went abroad to Oxford University to study the study of culture. She became a professor of anthropology at the University of Illinois in Chicago and did field work with the Tiv, a Nigerian tribe. In "Shakespeare in the Bush," Tiv elders correct Prince Hamlet's behavior and the young Bohannan corrects her assumptions about cultural universals.

Just before I left Oxford for the Tiv in West Africa, conversation turned to the 1
season at Stratford. "You Americans," said a friend, "often have difficulty with Shakespeare. He was, after all, a very English poet, and one can easily misinterpret the universal by misunderstanding the particular."

I protested that human nature is pretty much the same the whole world over; at 2
least the general plot and motivation of the greater tragedies would always be clear—everywhere—although some details of custom might have to be explained and difficulties of translation might produce other slight changes. To end an argument we could not conclude, my friend gave me a copy of Hamlet to study in the African bush: it would, he hope, lift my mind above its primitive surroundings, and possibly I might, by prolonged meditation, achieve the grace of correct interpretation.

It was my second field trip to that African tribe, and I thought myself ready to 3
live in one of its remote sections—an area difficult to cross even on foot. I eventually settled on the hillock of a very knowledgeable old man, the head of a homestead of some hundred and forty people, all of whom were either his close relatives or their wives and children. Like the other elders of the vicinity, the old man spent most of his time performing ceremonies seldom seen these days in the more accessible parts of the tribe. I was delighted. Soon there would be three months of enforced isolation and leisure, between the harvest that takes place just before the rising of the swamps and the clearing of new farms when the water goes down. Then, I thought, they would have even more time to perform ceremonies and explain them to me.

I was quite mistaken. Most of the ceremonies demanded the presence of elders 4
from several homesteads. As the swamps rose, the old men found it too difficult to walk from one homestead to the next, and the ceremonies gradually ceased. As the swamps rose even higher, all activities but one came to an end. The women brewed beer from maize and millet. Men, women, and children sat on their hillocks and drank it.

People began to drink at dawn. By midmorning the whole homestead was 5
singing, dancing, and drumming. When it rained, people had to sit inside their huts:
there they drank and sang or they drank and told stories. In any case, by noon or
before, I either had to join the party or retire to my own hut and my books. "One
does not discuss serious matters when there is beer. Come, drink with us." Since I
lacked their capacity for the thick native beer, I spent more and more time with
Hamlet. Before the end of the second month, grace descended on me. I was quite
sure that Hamlet had only one possible interpretation, and that one universally
obvious.

Early one morning, in the hope of having some serious talk before the beer 6
party, I used to call on the old man at his reception hut—a circle of posts supporting a thatched roof above a low mud wall to keep out wind and rain. One day I
crawled through the low doorway and found most of the men of the homestead sitting huddled in their ragged cloths on stools, low plank beds, and reclining chairs,
warming themselves against the chill of the rain around a smoky fire. In the center
were three pots of beer. The party had started.

The old man greeted me cordially. "Sit down and drink." I accepted a large 7
calabash full of beer, poured some into a small drinking gourd, and tossed it down.
Then I poured some more into the same gourd for the man second in seniority to
my host before I handed my calabash over to a young man for further distribution.
Important people shouldn't ladle beer themselves.

"It is better like this," the old man said, looking at me approvingly and pluck- 8
ing at the thatch that had caught in my hair. "You should sit and drink with us more
often. Your servants tell me that when you are not with us, you sit inside your hut
looking at a paper."

The old man was acquainted with four kinds of "papers": tax receipts, bride 9
price receipts, court fee receipts, and letters. The messenger who brought him letters from the chief used them mainly as a badge of office, for he always knew what
was in them and told the old man. Personal letters for the few who had relatives in
the government or mission stations were kept until someone went to a large market
where there was a letter writer and reader. Since my arrival, letters were brought to
me to be read. A few men also brought me bride price receipts, privately, with
requests to change the figures to a higher sum. I found moral arguments were of no
avail, since in-laws are fair game, and the technical hazards of forgery difficult to
explain to illiterate people. I did not wish them to think me silly enough to look at
any such papers for days on end, and I hastily explained that my "paper" was one
of the "things of long ago" of my country.

"Ah," said the old man. "Tell us." 10

I protested that I was not a storyteller. Storytelling is a skilled art among them; 11
their standards are high, and the audiences critical—and vocal in their criticism. I
protested in vain. This morning they wanted to hear a story while they drank. They
threatened to tell me no more stories until I told them one of mine. Finally, the old
man promised that no one would criticize my style "for we know you are struggling
with our language." "But," put in one of the elders, "you must explain what we do

not understand, as we do when we tell you our stories." Realizing that here was my chance to prove Hamlet universally intelligible, I agreed.

The old man handed me some more beer to help me on with my storytelling. 12 Men filled their long wooden pipes and knocked coals from the fire to place in the pipe bowls; then puffing contentedly, they sat back to listen. I began in the proper style,

"Not yesterday, not yesterday, but long ago, a thing occurred. One night three men were keeping watch outside the homestead of the great chief, when suddenly they saw the former chief approach them."

"Why was he no longer their chief?"   13

"He was dead," I explained. "That is why they were troubled and afraid when 14 they saw him."

"Impossible," began one of the elders, handing his pipe on to his neighbor, 15 who interrupted, "Of course it wasn't the dead chief. It was an omen sent by a witch. Go on."

Slightly shaken, I continued. "One of these three was a man who knew 16 things"—the closest translation for scholar, but unfortunately it also meant witch. The second elder looked triumphantly at the first. "So he spoke to the dead chief saying, 'Tell us what we must do so you may rest in your grave,' but the dead chief did not answer. He vanished, and they could see him no more. Then the man who knew things—his name was Horatio—said this event was the affair of the dead chief's son, Hamlet."

There was a general shaking of heads around the circle. "Had the dead chief 17 no living brothers? Or was this son the chief?"

"No," I replied. "That is, he had one living brother who became the chief 18 when the elder brother died."

The old men muttered: such omens were matters for chiefs and elders, not for 19 youngsters; no good could come of going behind a chief's back; clearly Horatio was not a man who knew things.

"Yes, he was," I insisted, shooing a chicken away from my beer. "In our coun- 20 try the son is next to the father. The dead chief's younger brother had become the great chief. He had also married his elder brother's widow only about a month after the funeral."

"He did well," the old man beamed and announced to the others, "I told you 21 that if we knew more about Europeans, we would find they really were very like us. In our country also," he added to me, "the younger brother marries the elder brother's widow and becomes the father of his children. Now, if your uncle, who married your widowed mother, is your father's full brother, then he will be a real father to you. Did Hamlet's father and uncle have one mother?"

His question barely penetrated my mind; I was too upset and thrown too far 22 off balance by having one of the most important elements of *Hamlet* knocked straight out of the picture. Rather uncertainly I said that I thought they had the same mother, but I wasn't sure—the story didn't say. The old man told me severely that these genealogical details made all the difference and that when I got home I must ask the elders about it. He shouted out the door to one of this younger wives to bring his goatskin bag.

Determined to save what I could of the mother motif, I took a deep breath and 23 began again. "The son Hamlet was very sad because his mother had married again so quickly. There was no need for her to do so, and it is our custom for a widow not to go to her next husband until she has mourned for two years."

"Two years is too long," objected the wife, who had appeared with the old 24 man's battered goatskin bag. "Who will hoe your farms for you while you have no husband?"

"Hamlet," I retorted without thinking, "was old enough to hoe his mother's 25 farms himself. There was no need for her to remarry." No one looked convinced. I gave up. "His mother and the great chief told Hamlet not to be sad, for the great chief himself would be a father to Hamlet. Furthermore, Hamlet would be the next chief: therefore he must stay to learn the things of a chief. Hamlet agreed to remain, and all the rest went off to drink beer."

While I paused, perplexed at how to render Hamlet's disgusted soliloquy to an 26 audience convinced that Claudius and Gertrude had behaved in the best possible manner, one of the younger men asked me who had married the other wives of the dead chief.

"He had no other wives," I told him. 27

"But a chief must have many wives! How else can he brew beer and prepare 28 food for all his guests?"

I said firmly that in our country even chiefs had only one wife, that they had 29 servants to do their work, and that they paid them from tax money.

It was better, they returned, for a chief to have many wives and sons who 30 would help him hoe his farms and feed his people; then everyone loved the chief who gave much and took nothing—taxes were a bad thing.

I agreed with the last comment, but for the rest fell back on their favorite way 31 of fobbing off my questions: "That is the way it is done, so that is how we do it."

I decided to skip the soliloquy. Even if Claudius was here thought quite right 32 to marry his brother's widow, there remained the poison motif, and I knew they would disapprove of fratricide. More hopefully I resumed, "That night Hamlet kept watch with the three who had seen his dead father. The dead chief again appeared, and although the others were afraid, Hamlet followed his dead father off to one side. When they were alone, Hamlet's dead father spoke."

"Omens can't talk!" The old man was emphatic. 33

"Hamlet's dead father wasn't an omen. Seeing him might have been an omen, 34 but he was not." My audience looked as confused as I sounded. "It *was* Hamlet's dead father. It was a thing we call a 'ghost.'" I had to use the English word, for unlike many of the neighboring tribes, these people didn't believe in the survival after death of any individuating part of the personality.

"What is a 'ghost?' An omen?" 35

"No, a 'ghost' is someone who is dead but who walks around and can talk, 36
and people can hear him and see him but not touch him."

They objected. "One can touch zombis." 37

"No, no! It was not a dead body the witches had animated to sacrifice and eat. 38
No one else made Hamlet's dead father walk. He did it himself."

"Dead men can't walk," protested my audience as one man. 39

I was quite willing to compromise. "A 'ghost' is the dead man's shadow." 40

But again they objected. "Dead men cast no shadows." 41

"They do in my country," I snapped. 42

The old man quelled the babble of disbelief that arose immediately and told 43
me with that insincere, but courteous, agreement one extends to the fancies of the
young, ignorant, and superstitious, "No doubt in your country the dead can also
walk without being zombis." From the depths of his bag he produced a withered
fragment of kola nut, bit off one end to show it wasn't poisoned, and handed me the
rest as a peace offering.

"Anyhow," I resumed, "Hamlet's dead father said that his own brother, the 44
one who became chief, had poisoned him. He wanted Hamlet to avenge him.
Hamlet believed this in his heart, for he did not like his father's brother." I took
another swallow of beer. "In the country of the great chief, living in the same
homestead, for it was a very large one, was an important elder who was often with
the chief to advise and help him. His name was Polonius. Hamlet was courting his
daughter, but her father and her brother . . . [I cast hastily about for some tribal
analogy] warned her not to let Hamlet visit her when she was alone on her farm, for
he would be a great chief and so could not marry her."

"Why not?" asked the wife, who had settled down on the edge of the old 45
man's chair. He frowned at her for asking stupid questions and growled, "They
lived in the same homestead."

"That was not the reason," I informed them. "Polonius was a stranger who 46
lived in the homestead because he helped the chief, not because he was a relative."

"Then why couldn't Hamlet marry her?" 47

"He could have," I explained, "But Polonius didn't think he would. After all, 48
Hamlet was a man of great importance who ought to marry a chief's daughter, for
in his country a man could have only one wife. Polonius was afraid that if Hamlet
made love to his daughter, then no one else would give a high price for her."

"That might be true," remarked one of the shrewder elders, "but a chief's son 49
would give his mistress's father enough presents and patronage to more than make
up the difference. Polonius sounds like a fool to me."

"Many people think he was," I agreed. "Meanwhile Polonius sent his son 50
Laertes off to Paris to learn the things of that country, for it was the homestead of a
very great chief indeed. Because he was afraid that Laertes might waste a lot of
money on beer and women and gambling, or get into trouble by fighting, he sent
one of his servants to Paris secretly, to spy out what Laertes was doing. One day
Hamlet came upon Polonius's daughter Ophelia. He behaved so oddly he frightened her. Indeed"—I was fumbling for words to express the dubious quality of

Hamlet's madness—"the chief and many others had also noticed that when Hamlet talked one could understand the words but not what they meant. Many people thought that he had become mad." My audience suddenly became much more attentive. "The great chief wanted to know what was wrong with Hamlet, so he sent for two of Hamlets age mates [school friends would have taken long explanation] to talk to Hamlet and find out what troubled his heart. Hamlet, seeing that they had been bribed by the chief to betray him, told them nothing. Polonius, however, insisted that Hamlet was mad because he had been forbidden to see Ophelia, whom he loved."

"Why," inquired a bewildered voice, "should anyone bewitch Hamlet on that 51 account?"

"Bewitch him?" 52

"Yes, only witchcraft can make anyone mad, unless, of course, one sees the 53 beings that lurk in the forest."

I stopped being a storyteller, took out my notebook and demanded to be told 54 more about these two causes of madness. Even while they spoke and I jotted notes, I tried to calculate the effect of this new factor on the plot. Hamlet had not been exposed to the beings that lurked in the forests. Only his relatives in the male line could bewitch him. Barring relatives not mentioned by Shakespeare, it had to be Claudius who was attempting to harm him. And, of course, it was.

For the moment I staved off questions by saying that the great chief also 55 refused to believe that Hamlet was mad for the love of Ophelia and nothing else. "He was sure that something much more important was troubling Hamlet's heart."

"Now Hamlet's age mates," I continued, "had brought with them a famous 56 storyteller. Hamlet decided to have this man tell the chief and all his homestead a story about a man who had poisoned his brother because he desired his brother's wife and wished to be chief himself. Hamlet was sure the great chief could not hear the story without making a sign if he was indeed guilty, and then he would discover whether his dead father had told him the truth."

The old man interrupted, with deep cunning, "Why should a father lie to his 57 son?" he asked.

I hedged: "Hamlet wasn't sure that it really was his dead father." It was 58 impossible to say anything, in that language, about devil-inspired visions.

"You mean," he said, "it actually was an omen, and he knew witches some- 59 times send false ones. Hamlet was a fool not to go to one skilled in reading omens and divining truth in the first place. A man-who-sees-the-truth could have told him how his father died, if he really had been poisoned, and if there was witchcraft in it; then Hamlet could have called the elders to settle the matter."

The shrewd elder ventured to disagree. "Because his father's brother was a 60 great chief, one-who-sees-the-truth might therefore have been afraid to tell it. I think it was for that reason that a friend of Hamlet's father—a witch and an elder— sent an omen so his friend's son would know. Was the omen true?"

"Yes," I said, abandoning ghosts and the devil; a witch-sent omen it would 61 have to be. "It was true, for when the storyteller was telling his tale before all the homestead, the great chief rose in fear. Afraid that Hamlet knew his secret he planned to have him killed."

The stage set of the next bit presented some difficulties of translation. I began 62 cautiously. "The great chief told Hamlet's mother to find out from her son what he knew. But because a woman's children are always first in her heart, he had the important elder Polonius hide behind a cloth that hung against the wall of Hamlet's mother's sleeping hut. Hamlet started to scold his mother for what she had done."

There was a shocked murmur from everyone. A man should never scold his 63 mother.

"She called out in fear, and Polonius moved behind the cloth. Shouting 'A 64 rat!' Hamlet took his machete and slashed through the cloth." I paused for dramatic effect. "He had killed Polonius!"

The old men looked at each other in supreme disgust. "That Polonius truly 65 was a fool and a man who knew nothing! What child would not know enough to shout, 'It's me!'" With a pang, I remembered that these people are ardent hunters, always armed with bow, arrow, and machete; at the first rustle in the grass an arrow is aimed and ready, and the hunter shouts "Game!" If no human voice answers immediately, the arrow speeds on its way. Like a good hunter Hamlet had shouted, "A rat!"

I rushed in to save Polonius's reputation. "Polonius did speak. Hamlet heard 66 him. But he thought it was the chief and wished to kill him to avenge his father. He had meant to kill him earlier that evening. . . . " I broke down, unable to describe to these pagans, who had no belief in individual afterlife, the difference between dying at one's prayers and dying "unhousell'd, disappointed, unaneled."

This time I had shocked my audience seriously. "For a man to raise his hand 67 against his father's brother and the one who had become his father—that is a terrible thing. The elders ought to let such a man be bewitched."

I nibbled at my kola nut in some perplexity, then pointed out that after all the 68 man had killed Hamlet's father.

"No," pronounced the old man, speaking less to me than to the young men sit- 69 ting behind the elders. "If your father's brother has killed your father, you must appeal to your father's age mates; *they* may avenge him. No man may use violence against his senior relatives." Another thought struck him. "But if his father's brother had indeed been wicked enough to bewitch Hamlet and make him mad that would be a good story indeed, for it would be his fault that Hamlet, being mad, no longer had any sense and thus was ready to kill his father's brother."

There was a murmur of applause. *Hamlet* was again a good story to them, but 70 it no longer seemed quite the same story to me. As I thought over the coming complications of plot and motive, I lost courage and decided to skim over dangerous ground quickly.

"The great chief," I went on, "was not sorry that Hamlet had killed Polonius. 71 It gave him a reason to send Hamlet away, with his two treacherous age mates, with letters to a chief of a far country, saying that Hamlet should be killed. But Hamlet changed the writing on their papers, so that the chief killed his age mates instead." I encountered a reproachful glare from one of the men whom I had told undetectable forgery was not merely immoral but beyond human skill. I looked the other way.

"Before Hamlet could return, Laertes came back for his father's funeral. The 72 great chief told him Hamlet had killed Polonius. Laertes swore to kill Hamlet because of this, and because his sister Ophelia, hearing her father had been killed by the man she loved, went mad and drowned in the river."

"Have you already forgotten what we told you?" the old man was reproachful. 73 "One cannot take vengeance on a madman; Hamlet killed Polonius in his madness. As for the girl, she not only went mad, she was drowned. Only witches can make people drown. Water itself can't hurt anything. It is merely something one drinks and bathes in."

I began to get cross. "If you don't like the story, I'll stop." 74

The old man made soothing noises and himself poured me some more beer. 75 "You tell the story well, and we are listening. But it is clear that the elders of your country have never told you what the story really means. No, don't interrupt! We believe you when you say your marriage customs are different, or your clothes and weapons. But people are the same everywhere; therefore, there are always witches and it is we, the elders, who know how witches work. We told you it was the great chief who wished to kill Hamlet, and now your own words have proved us right. Who were Ophelia's male relatives?"

"There were only her father and her brother." Hamlet was clearly out of my 76 hands.

"There must have been many more; this also you must ask of your elders 77 when you get back to your country. From what you tell us, since Polonius was dead, it must have been Laertes who killed Ophelia, although I do not see the reason for it."

We had emptied one pot of beer, and the old men argued the point with slight- 78 ly tipsy interest. Finally one of them demanded of me, "What did the servant of Polonius say on his return?"

With difficulty I recollected Reynaldo and his mission. "I don't think he did 79 return before Polonius was killed."

"Listen," said the elder, "and I will tell you how it was and how your story 80 will go, then you may tell me if I am right. Polonius knew his son would get into trouble, and so he did. He had many fines to pay for fighting, and debts from gambling. But he had only two ways of getting money quickly. One was to marry off his sister at once, but it is difficult to find a man who will marry a woman desired by the son of a chief. For if the chief's heir commits adultery with your wife, what can you do? Only a fool calls a case against a man who will someday be his judge. Therefore Laertes had to take the second way: he killed his sister by witchcraft, drowning her so he could secretly sell her body to the witches."

I raised an objection. "They found her body and buried it. Indeed, Laertes 81 jumped into the grave to see his sister once more—so, you see, the body was truly there. Hamlet, who had just come back, jumped in after him."

"What did I tell you?" the elder appealed to the others. "Laertes was up to no 82 good with his sister's body. Hamlet prevented him, because the chief's heir, like a chief, does not wish any other man to grow rich and powerful. Laertes would be angry, because he would have killed his sister without benefit to himself. In our country he would try to kill Hamlet for that reason. Is this not what happened?"

"More or less," I admitted. "When the great chief found Hamlet was still 83 alive, he encouraged Laertes to try to kill Hamlet and arranged a fight with machetes between them. In the fight both the young men were wounded to death. Hamlet's mother drank the poisoned beer that the chief meant for Hamlet in case he won the fight. When he saw his mother die of poison, Hamlet, dying, managed to kill his father's brother with his machete."

"You see, I was right!" exclaimed the elder.   84

"That was a very good story," added the old man, "and you told it with very 85 few mistakes. There was just one more error, at the very end. The poison Hamlet's mother drank was obviously meant for the survivor of the fight, whichever it was. If Laertes had won, the great chief would have poisoned him, for no one would know that he arranged Hamlet's death. Then, too, he need not fear Laertes' witch-craft; it takes a strong heart to kill one's only sister by witchcraft.

"Sometime," concluded the old man, gathering his ragged toga about him, 86 "you must tell us some more stories of your country. We, who are elders, will instruct you in their true meaning, so that when you return to your own land your elders will see that you have not been sitting in the bush, but among those who know things and who have taught you wisdom."

■ *Questions for* . . . **Shakespeare in the Bush** by Laura Bohannan

Words to Note

misinterpret	universal	particular
tragedies	meditation	remote
homesteads	brewed	hillocks
ladle	genealogical	murmur
mourned	soliloquy	fobbing
animated	snapped	quelled
babble	withered	kola nut
tribal analogy	dubious	fumbling
bewitch	lurk	jotted
calculate	omen	scold
slashed	pagans	nibbled
elders	reproachful	cross
witchcraft	toga	

Language

1. Why can't Bohannan find equivalents in Tiv for *scholar, ghost, school friends,* and *wine?* What happens to her story as a result?
2. Towards the end of the essay, when Bohannan is trying to figure out how to explain why Hamlet doesn't kill Claudius at his prayers, she writes, "I broke down, unable to describe to these pagans, who had no belief in individual afterlife, the difference between dying at one's prayers and dying 'unhousell'd, disappointed, unaneled.'" Why did she choose *pagans* and not one of its synonyms? What is the word's tone in this context?

Style

1. What does the speaking style of the tribal elders tell us about them? Is their speaking style in keeping with how they conduct themselves and how they are dressed? What's a toga?
2. What is the essay's tone?

Development and Organization

1. How does Bohannan preface the story of trying to tell Hamlet's story to a group of Tiv tribal elders? Does she provide us with enough background to understand what happens?
2. How does Bohannan lose control of her story? Track the tribal takeover of *Hamlet.*
3. Who are the elders echoing when they say, "We believe you when you say your marriage customs are different, or your clothes and your weapons. But people are the same everywhere; therefore, there are always witches and it is we, the elders, who know how witches work"? What's the point of the echo?

Discussion and Journal Writing

1. How does Bohannan depict her audience? Is she implying that their interpretation of *Hamlet* is wrong?
2. If *Hamlet* isn't universal, what is? What would make a story universal?
3. What Tiv family beliefs, practices, and customs get in the way of their understanding *Hamlet?*

ooooo

Nisa: The Life and Words of a !Kung Woman

—Marjorie Shostak

Marjorie Shostak is an Associate of the Peabody Museum of Archaeology and Ethnology at Harvard University. An anthropologist and a feminist, she focused on the lives of women in the field work she did among the !Kung tribe of Africa's Kalahari Desert. The book that grew out of her research bears the name of the woman she spent the most time interviewing, *Nisa: The Life and Words of a !Kung Woman.* As you read and discuss the excerpt that follows, consider whether her approach clarifies or skews her account of the !Kung.

Young women are not considered truly adult or expected to assume full 1 responsibility for themselves or for others until they reach their late teens, have menstruated and married, and are likely soon to become mothers. Although in recent years girls have been marrying around the age of sixteen and a half—also the average age of first menstruation—previous generations sometimes married as early as ten or twelve years of age. Boys, in contrast, are usually not considered eligible for marriage until they are between twenty and thirty, and then only after they have demonstrated their ability to provide for a family by killing a large animal. Men, therefore, are often ten or more years older than their wives. No matter how early a girl marries, sexual relations are not expected to begin until she shows signs of sexual maturity—culturally recognized as the time around the first menstruation. These early marriages are unstable and often brief in duration, and a girl may enter several of them before she starts having children, usually with one life-long partner.

Parents and other close relatives arrange first marriages and, if the children are 2 still young, subsequent ones as well. Trips will be made to visit potential spouses residing within a wide geographical area, to ensure parents the broadest possible choice. But low population density often limits this number, and when rules of appropriateness and eligibility are applied, the choices are narrowed even further. The !Kung adhere to the nearly universal taboo of prohibiting marriage between closely related kin, but in contrast to many other gathering and hunting societies, they also forbid marriage between first cousins. In addition, they discourage marriage to anyone having the same name as one's father, one's mother, one's sibling, or, as might be the case in later marriages, one's child.

In choosing a son-in-law, parents consider age (the man should not be too 3 many years older than their daughter), marital status (an unmarried man is preferable to one already married and seeking a second wife), hunting ability, and willingness to accept the responsibilities of family life. A cooperative, generous, and unaggressive nature is looked for, as well. Or, an appropriate prospect might be the son of a close family friend or someone with access to an area covered with vegetable, game, or water resources. A first wife, meanwhile, should be young, industrious, agreeable, and capable of bearing children. I asked one man who was in his early forties and looking for a second wife, "Would you marry a woman smarter than you?" He answered without hesitation, "Of course. If I married her, she would teach me to be smart, too."

Once the two sets of parents agree, the marriage is likely to take place even if the girl has to be pressured into accepting it. Resistance to marriage is typical of young girls, and is usually interpreted as being directed at marriage itself, rather than at a specific man. After marriage, the husband usually joins his wife at her parents' village, because girls are not expected to leave their mothers while they are still young. Essentially informal, this "bride service" is one of the major inducements for marrying daughters off so young: the husband helps to provide meat for the girl and her family. Her parents can also watch how he behaves toward their daughter and themselves and can represent her interests in times of conflict. marriage also expands the parents' social world, giving them close ties to their son-in-law's family, as expressed through gift exchange, visiting, and the sharing of mutual concerns. It also ensures each family access to the resources and village life of the other in times of scarcity. Since the availability of edible plants can vary significantly from one area to another and rainfall often does the same, this access may be lifesaving, even if the two areas are only a few miles apart. 4

The girl's parents may encourage the couple to remain with them by making life as pleasant as possible for their son-in-law. Many men do take up long-term residence, staying from three to ten years, on average, or sometimes for life. This arrangement affords the girl's parents additional economic support, as well as the comfort of having their children and grandchildren around them. For these reasons, the husband's family may compete for the couple's attention, and many younger couples divide their time between the two families before settling in (more or less) with one. 5

If a girl is determined that she will never feel any affection for her husband she can insist on ending the marriage. She may try to elicit support from influential members of her family, or she may make life so unpleasant for her husband that he simply leaves. When she is older, she may decide for herself whom she wants to marry, and hope that the adults will accept her choice. If she becomes pregnant, she is likely to marry the father of the child, whatever objections are raised by others. (Such independently formed attachments usually involve men who are much younger than ones chosen by parents and much closer geographically.) 6

The early years of many marriages are stressful ones for both partners, especially when they differ widely in age. Although getting married does not suddenly fill a girl's life with responsibilities, she is expected to sleep in the same hut with a man ten years older than herself, a man she may not know very well. In addition, she is expected gradually to assume some of the burden of maintaining her household—while her unmarried peers are still essentially carefree. 7

The groom, meanwhile, is usually full grown and sexually mature. Marrying a   8
young girl means he has to wait, sometimes for as long as five years, while his wife
slowly develops. Living with her in her parents' village, he is expected to help her
father hunt and bring back food. He may also have to endure her indifference or
even rejection. Although these circumstances are far from ideal, many young men
are willing to accept them. Because some older men are married to two women,
young marriageable girls are at a premium. If a young man wants to be assured of
having a wife sooner rather than later, and a young woman rather than an older
widow or divorcee, he has little choice. The girl's parents can exercise a good deal
of control over him, but, to be sure, they do not want to drive him away. Despite his
willingness to cooperate and despite his patience, however, it is not likely that this
first marriage will last.

The marriage ceremony is quite modest, although negotiations and gift   9
exchange are typically begun long before the actual marriage takes place. A hut is
built for the couple by members of both families, and is set apart from the rest of
the village. As sunset approaches, friends bring the couple to the hut. The bride,
with head covered, is carried and laid down inside; the groom, walking, is led to the
hut and sits beside the door. Coals from the fires of both families are brought to
start the new fire in front of the marriage hut. Their friends stay with them, singing,
playing, and joking. The couple stay apart from each other, maintaining a respectful
reserve, and do not join in the festivities. After everyone leaves, they spend their
first night together in the hut. The next morning, oil is ceremonially rubbed on both
of them—each by the other's mother. Because sleeping next to a strange man can
be frightening for the girl, an older woman, usually a close relative, sometimes
accompanies the girl and sleeps beside her in the marriage hut until she begins to
adjust to her new status.

Most !Kung experience one long-term marriage, although most are also mar-   10
ried more than once. Dissolution of marriages by divorce is quite common. It usually occurs during the first few years of a marriage, before the couple has had children, and is usually initiated by the woman. No formalities or legal procedures are
necessary, but emotions often run high. Arguments for and against termination may
go on for days or even weeks, as everyone in the village expresses a point of view.
Eventually, a decision is made, and if the choice is separation, it ends there. Since
no dowry or bride-price is involved in getting married, there is nothing to be repaid
when getting divorced. (Gifts are exchanged during the marriage ceremony, but this
is primarily to celebrate the occasion.) Only a minimal investment in hut sites or
living compounds is made, so it is easy for one of the spouses simply to move
away. In addition, all goods are owned individually, not jointly, thus eliminating
possible disputes over the division of property. Whether the couple has ever
engaged in sexual relations does not become an issue. No premium is place on virginity—indeed, I could not find a word for virginity in the !Kung language. The
divorced girl or woman simply re-enters the category of highly desirable potential
wives, to be sought after by eligible men. Both divorced partners are likely to marry

again within a year. If children are involved they usually remain in the custody of the mother.

Women do not give up their friendships with other women when they marry. 11 Friendship is highly valued by the !Kung; their word ≠dara, meaning friend, age-mate, or peer, describes this relationship, which goes beyond kinship and name-relations. If girls who have grown up together remain in the same village after marriage, their relationships are not likely to change immediately, since little pressure is exerted on young brides to assume wifely roles. As they mature and have families, they will continue to cooperate in work and in leisure. An active exchange of gifts—typical of the network of exchange maintained by all !Kung adults with various others—will formalize and strengthen their ties. As their children grow older, they may even support each other's exploration of the spiritual realms of trancing and curing. Unless one of the women moves away, this friendship is likely to last throughout their lives. So, too, may the relationships between co-wives in successful polygynous marriage be sustained over the years. Although sexual jealousy and rivalry try these relationships, strong and loyal bonds of friendship between the women often form and last for many years.

When adults talked to me, I listened. When I was still a young girl 12 with no breasts, they told me that when a young woman grows up, her parents give her a husband and she continues to grow up next to him.

When they first talked to me about it, I said, "What kind of thing 13 am I that I should take a husband? When I grow up, I won't marry. I'll just lie by myself. If I married, what would I be doing it for?"

My father said, "You don't know what you're saying. I, I am your 14 father and am old; your mother is old, too. When you marry, you will gather food and give it to your husband to eat. He also will do things for you. If you refuse, who will give you food? Who will give you things to wear?"

I said, "There's no question about it, I won't take a husband. Why 15 should I? As I am now, I'm still a child and won't marry." I said to my mother, "You say you have a man for me to marry? Why don't you take him and set him beside Daddy? You marry him and let them be co-husbands. What have I done that you're telling me I should marry?"

My mother said, "Nonsense. When I tell you I'm going to give 16 you a husband, why do you say you want me to marry him? Why are you talking to me like this?"

I said, "Because I'm only a child. When I grow up and you tell me 17 to take a husband, I'll agree. But I haven't passed through my childhood yet and I won't marry!"

A long time passed before my mother talked about it again. "Nisa, 18 I want to give you a husband. Who shall it be?" I knew there was another man she wanted me to marry. I said, "I won't marry him." I almost added, "You marry him and set him beside Daddy," but I stopped. This time I was ashamed of myself and didn't say anything more. I thought, "Why am I not agreeing with her? When I speak like that, am I not shitting on her?"

We continued to live after that and just kept on living. It wasn't   19
until a very long time had passed that they talked about it again.

I've had many husbands—Bo, Tsaa, Tashay, Besa, and another   20
Bo. They all married me. Have men not liked me?

When I still had no breasts, when my genitals still weren't devel-   21
oped, when my chest was without anything on it, that was when a man named Bo came from a distant area and people started talking about marriage. Was I not almost a young woman?

One day, may parents and his parents began building our marriage   22
hut. The day we were married, they carried me to it and set me down inside. I cried and cried and cried. Later, I ran back to my parents' hut, lay down beside my little brother, and slept, a deep sleep like death.

The next night, Nukha, an older woman, took me into the hut and   23
stayed with me. She lay down between Bo and myself, because young girls who are still children are afraid of their husbands. So, it is our custom for an older woman to come into the young girl's hut to teach her not to be afraid. The woman is supposed to help the girl learn to like her husband. Once the couple is living nicely together and getting along, the older woman leaves them beside each other.

That's what Nukha was supposed to do. Even the people who saw   24
her come into the hut with me thought she would lay me down and that once I fell asleep, she would leave and go home to her husband.

But Nukha had within her clever deceit. My heart refused Bo   25
because I was a child, but Nukha, she liked him. That was why, when she laid me down in the hut with my husband, she was also laying me down with her lover. She put me in front and Bo was behind. We stayed like that for a very long time. As soon as I was asleep, they started to make love. But as Bo made love to Nukha, they knocked into me. I kept waking up as they bumped me, again and again.

I thought, "I'm just a child. I don't understand about such things.   26
What are people doing when they move around like that? How come Nukha took me into my marriage hut and laid me down beside my husband, but when I started to cry, she changed places with me and lay down next to him? Is he hers? How come he belongs to her yet Mommy and Daddy said I should marry him?"

I lay there, thinking my thoughts. Before dawn broke, Nukha got   27
up and went back to her husband. I lay there, sleeping, and when it started getting light, I went back to my mother's hut.

The next night, when darkness sat, Nukha came for me again. I   28 cried, "He's your man! Yesterday you took me and brought me inside the hut, but after we all lay there, he was with you! Why are you now bringing me to someone who is yours?" She said, "That's not true, he's not mine. He's *your* husband. Now, go to your hut and sit there. Later, we'll lie down."

She brought me to the hut, but once inside, I cried and cried and cried. I was still crying when Nukha lay down with us. After we had been lying there for a very long time, Bo started to make love to her again. I thought, "What is this? What am I? Am I supposed to watch this? Don't they see me? Do they think I'm only a baby?" Later, I got up and told them I had to urinate. I passed by them and went to lie down in mother's hut and stayed there until morning broke. 29

That day, I went gathering with my mother and father. As we were collecting mongongo nuts and klaru roots, my mother said, "Nisa, as you are, you're already a young woman. Yet, when you go into your marriage hut to lie down, you get up, come back, and lie down with me. Do you think I have married you? No, I'm the one who gave birth to you. Now, take this man as your husband, this strong man who will get food, for you and for me to eat. Is your father the only one who can find food? A husband kills things and gives them to you; a husband works on things that become your things; a husband gets meat that is food for you to eat. Now, you have a husband, Bo; he has married you." 30

I said, "Mommy, let me stay with you. When night sits, let me sleep next to you. What have you done to me that I'm only a child, yet the first husband you give me belongs to Nukha?" My mother said, "Why are you saying that? Nukha's husband is not your husband. Her husband sits elsewhere, in another hut." 31

I said, "Well . . . the other night when she took me and put me into the hut, she laid me down in front of her; Bo slept behind. But later, they woke me up, moving around the way they did. It was the same last night. Again, I slept in front and Bo behind and again, they kept bumping into me. I'm not sure exactly what they were doing, but that's why tonight, when night sits, I want to stay with you and sleep next to you. Don't take me over there again." 32

My mother said, "Yo! My daughter! They were moving about?" I said, "Mm. They woke me while I was sleeping. That's why I got up and came back to you." She said, "Yo! How horny that Bo is! He's screwing Nukha! You are going to leave that man, that's the only thing I will agree to now." 33

My father said, "I don't like what you've told us. You're only a child, Nisa, and adults are the ones responsible for arranging your marriage. But when an adult gives a husband and that husband makes love 34 to someone else, then that adult hasn't done well. I understand what you have told us and I say that Bo has deceived me. Therefore, when Nukha comes for you tonight, I will refuse to let you go. I will say, 'My daughter won't go into her marriage hut because you, Nukha, you have already taken him for husband.'"

We continued to talk on our way back. When we arrived at the   35
village, I sat down with my parents. Bo walked over to our marriage hut, then Nukha went over to him. I sat and watched as they talked. I thought, "Those two, they were screwing! That's why they kept bumping into me!"

I sat with Mother and Father while we ate. When evening came,   36
Nukha walked over to us. "Nisa, come, let me take you to your hut." I said, "I won't go." She said, "Get up. Let me take you over there. It's your hut. How come you're already married but today you won't make your hut your home?"

That's when my mother, drinking anger, went over to Nukha and   37
said, "As I'm standing here, I want you to tell me something. Nisa is a child who fears her husband. Yet, when you took her to her hut, you and her husband had sex together. Don't you know her husband should be trying to help bring her up? But that isn't something either of you are thinking about!"

Nukha didn't say anything, but the fire in my mother's words   38
burned. My mother began to yell, cursing her, "Horny, that's what you are! You're no longer going to take Nisa to her husband. And, if you ever have sex with him again, I'll crack your face open. You horny woman! You'd screw your own father!"

That's when my father said, "No, don't do all the talking. You're   39
a woman yet, how come you didn't ask me? I am a man and I will do the talking now. You, you just listen to what I say. Nisa is my child. I also gave birth to her. Now, you are a woman and will be quiet because I am a man."

Then he said, "Nukha, I'm going to tell you something. I am Gau   40
and today I'm going to pull my talk from inside myself and give it to you. We came together here for this marriage, but now something very bad has happened, something I do not agree to at all. Nisa is no longer going to go from here, where I am sitting, to that hut over there, that hut which you have already made your own. She is no longer going to look for anything for herself near that hut."

He continued, "Because, when I agree to give a man to my daugh-   41
ter, then he is only for my daughter. Nisa is a child and her husband isn't there for two to share. So go, take that man, he's already yours. Today my daughter will sit with me; she will sit here and sleep here. Tomorrow I will take her and we will move away. What you have

already done to this marriage is the way it will remain."

Nukha didn't say anything. She left and went to the hut without   42
me. Bo said, "Where's Nisa? Why are you empty, returning here
alone?" Nukha said, "Nisa's father refused to let her go. She told him
that you had made love to me and that's what he just now told me. I
don't know what to do about this, but I won't go back to their hut
again." Bo said, "I have no use for that kind of talk. Get the girl and
come back with her." She said, "I'm not going to Gau's hut. We're finished with that talk now. And when I say I'm finished, I'm saying I
won't go back there again."

She left and walked over to her own hut. When her husband saw   43
her, he said, "So, you and Bo are lovers! Nisa said that when you took
her to Bo, that the two of you . . . how exactly *did* Bo reward you for
your help?" But Nukha said, "No, I don't like Bo and he's not my
lover. Nisa is just a child and it is just a child's talk she is talking."

Bo walked over to us. He tried to talk but my father said, "You, be   44
quiet. I'm the one who's going to talk about this." So Bo didn't say
anything more, and my father talked until it was finished.

The next morning, very early, my father, mother, and aunt packed   45
our things and we all left. We slept in the mongongo groves that night
and traveled on until we reached another water hole where we continued to live.

We lived and lived and nothing more happened for a while. After   46
a long time had passed, Bo strung together some trade beads made of
wood, put them into a sack with food, and traveled the long distance to
the water hole where we were living.

It was late afternoon; the sun had almost left the sky. I had been   47
out gathering with my mother, and we were coming back from the
bush. We arrived in the village and my mother saw them, "Eh-hey,
Bo's over there. What's he doing here? I long ago refused him. I didn't
ask him to come back. I wonder what he thinks he's going to take away
from here?"

We put down our gatherings and sat. We greeted Bo and his rela-   48
tives—his mother, his aunt, Nukha, and Nukha's mother. Bo's mother
said, "We have come because we want to take Nisa back with us." Bo
said, "I'm again asking for your child. I want to take her back with
me."

My father said, "No, I only just took her from you. That was the   49
end. I won't take her and then give her again. Maybe you didn't hear
me the first time? I already told you that I refused. Bo is Nukha's husband and my daughter won't be with him again. An adult woman does
not make love to the man who marries Nisa."

Then he said, "Today, Nisa will just continue to live with us.   50
Some day, another man will come and marry her. If she stays healthy
and her eyes stand strong, if God doesn't kill her and she doesn't die, if
God stands beside her and helps, then we will find another man to give
to her."

That night, when darkness set, we all slept. I slept beside mother.   51
When morning broke, Bo took Nukha, her mother, and the others and
they left. I stayed behind. They were gone, finally gone.

We continued to stay at that water hole, eating things, doing   52
things, and just living. No one talked further about giving me another
husband, and we just lived and lived and lived.

I had refused Bo, but Tsaa, my next husband, I liked. When I mar-   53
ried him, my breasts were just beginning to develop.

A long time after Bo and I separated, after many seasons had   54
passed, my family and I moved to another water hole. One day, my
father left to visit people living at another water hole to exchange gifts
of hxaro with them. That's where he saw Tsaa.

When he came back, he said to my mother, "While I was away, I   55
saw a young man. I stood and watched him. Chuko, I'd like your
daughter to marry him." My mother asked, "Who is he?" My father
said, "Tsaa, the son my relative Bau gave birth to. Tsaa asked me if he
could marry Nisa." My mother said, "I've been refusing a second marriage for a long time. But now, I'll agree. We'll take her to him so he
can marry her. After he marries her we will see whether or not he takes
care of her well. After all, she is still a child."

The next morning we left for their village. That night we slept   56
along the way. The next morning we left again and walked, a very long
way, gathering and eating. We walked that day and slept that night. The
next morning we left and walked again, walked and walked and
walked. Finally, we arrived at their village. We slept there that night,
and the next morning when we woke we stayed there.

That morning, Tsaa's mother and father came to where my parents   57
were sitting. My father said, "Here I am, today, having brought you
your future daughter. We have journeyed far to come to you." His
father said, "You have done well. I'd like to take your daughter and
give her to my son. I haven't wanted to give any other girl to him. I
wanted to give him a girl who belongs to my own people, to the daughter of one of my relatives. Nisa is the one I want to give to my son."
Everyone agreed to the marriage, including me.

We slept that night, and the next morning they started to build the   58
marriage hut. That night they took me and put me inside the hut. Then
they took Tsaa and put him inside. We were in the hut, just the two of
us.

The next morning, they rubbed marriage oil first on me and then on Tsaa. I gave presents of beads to him and he gave other presents of beads to me.

We lived together a long time, and I began to like him. But then, he started to want me sexually. He didn't really bother me about it, not so that we argued, but I refused. I thought, "Oh, I'm still a child. Why do I have to have a husband?" And, "I have no breasts and my genitals haven't begun to develop. What does this person think my genitals can possibly have for him?"

I remember one night we were sitting around the fire, eating a large duiker he had caught in one of his traps. He had given it to my mother and father. They cooked it and we all ate. We lay down. Soon I got up and sat by the fire. I sat, looking at Tsaa's back, at scars he had from where he had been burned, years before. I thought, "This person, his back is ruined. Why was I given a man whose back has died?" Later, I got up, went into the hut again and lay down.

Another night, I left him in the hut by himself, and lay down beside my mother. The next night I went back to our hut. Some nights I would sleep in my mother's hut and others, in our hut. That's what finally ended the marriage.

One morning, when I woke in my mother's hut, I stayed there. Tsaa said, "This girl is already a young woman, so what is she doing? I've taken her as my wife, but she just leaves and sleeps with the adults. When, if ever, will the two of us really start living together? She doesn't like me. That's why I'm going to leave her." My father said, "Why are you going to leave her? Her thoughts are still those of a child."

But by then, my heart had changed and I no longer liked him. Once my breasts started to develop, I refused him completely.

One day, he left and went to a nearby village where an animal had been killed to ask his older brother for some meat. When he came back, he set the meat down. But after, he didn't sit; he just lay down.

I had been roasting some tsin beans. I peeled the skins, and when they were clean, I set them down beside him. He didn't want any. I thought, "Isn't it to your husband that you're supposed to give things? Isn't this the man I married? Why did he marry me if he refused to take food I prepare for him."

My father said, "Nisa, won't you give me some of the gemsbok meat Tsaa was carrying when he came back?" I asked Tsaa, "Give me some meat so I can roast it." But he refused. I asked him again and again he refused. Then my father asked, "Won't you give me some meat that I can cook for you and Nisa?" He refused my father, too.

Tsaa got up, took the meat from where he had set it down, and put it all up in a tree. Although there was a lot, he put it all in the tree.

59
60
61
62
63
64
65
66
67
68

My father watched. Then he said, "Eh! It really isn't important   69
that you refused to give meat to my daughter. You have married her
and she is your wife, so even if you refuse to give something to her, it
doesn't mean very much. But I, I am her father, and me you don't
refuse. Because when you do that, you make me feel very bad." He
continued, "Therefore, as you are now here, tonight you may lie here
and sleep in your hut. But tomorrow, when you wake, you will take all
your things—don't leave anything here—and you will go away. If you
ever come back, don't let me see you with my daughter!"

Then Tsaa said, "It doesn't matter, after all. Because me, I haven't   70
married. I have no wife. This girl has made me weary. I've given her
many beads and the meat I've brought back has been plentiful. But the
way she is with me defeats me. So, as I am now, I will sleep here
tonight, and tomorrow I will take my things and go back to my older
brother's village."

My father said, "Yes, that's the way it will be, so go along your   71
way." Tsaa said, "Eh, but if I go, I'm going to take every last one of my
things back from my wife." My father said, "Eh, very good. You take
your things. Even the presents we've given each other, I'll give those
back to you as well. Anything that is yours that any of us have taken . . .
take them all!"

I collected the things he had given me and gave them to him. My   72
father did the same. Tsaa lay down and slept, slept without giving any
meat to any of us, slept without even cooking it for himself. The next
morning, at dawn, he gathered his things, took others from my mother,
put them into a large bundle, and left.

When he arrived where his older brother was living, his brother   73
asked, "Where's your wife? Yesterday you were here alone. Today you
were going to come back with her. Will she join you another day?"
Tsaa said, "My wife . . . her parents spoke awful things to me. Her
father yelled at me about the meat. I told him I wanted to take his
daughter with me to come live here, but he refused."

They traveled the distance to their parents' village. When they   74
arrived, Tsaa told them, "My wife's father forced me to leave. He
chased me away." His parents said, "When he forced you to leave, what
was in his mind. What did he say?" Tsaa said, "Her father chased me
because . . . first my wife asked me for meat to roast and eat, but I
didn't give her any. I told her I wanted to wait until morning, that I
would cook it then. Her father also asked me for meat to cook for himself and for me. I told him I didn't want to cook the meat yet, that I
wanted to wait. When my father-in-law heard that, he told me that I
should keep the meat, just as it was, that I should sleep that night, but
that in the morning, I should pack my things and come back to you. I

stinged him, he said. That's why I took my things and am here, now. Is there anything more for you to ask?"

They slept that night. The next morning they packed the rest of the meat, left their village and traveled to us. **75**

The whole family arrived—Tsaa, his mother and father, his brother, even his older sister. His father said, "We have come to talk. We haven't come for any other purpose. I am Tsaa's father and have come here to talk to my in-laws. You, my son's father-in-law, are you going to take away your child after you yourself got up and gave her to him in marriage? What has my son done that today you have chased him away? What have you done that my son is no longer sitting beside your daughter?" **76**

My father said, "I am an old person and my heart is not strong. My heart is slight. If I have a son-in-law, when he has food, I expect him to set it beside me. I will prepare it because I know how. Then I will give it to him and to my daughter ant they will give me some so I can eat. I am an old person and my heart has little strength." **77**

Then he said, "Today, this marriage is dead. Once before Nisa married a man and he was a bad one. I dropped him. Now, today, another man has married her and he is also bad. So, get up, have your son get up and leave with you. Go back with the things you have brought. Find another woman for your son to marry. My daughter will just lie by herself and that is all there is to say. She is no longer married to your son." **78**

That was all. They stayed for a while longer, then they packed their things and left. I stayed behind with my family. My heart was happy. Was I not still a young girl? I didn't know much about things and was just happy. I'd sit by my hut and watch as the younger children played. My breasts were developing and I no longer played with them. I'd sit there and think about how adult I was, how I was almost a woman. **79**

■ *Questions for* . . . Nisa: The Life and Words of a !Kung Woman

Words to Note

eligibility	adhere	taboo
sibling	marital	status
prospect	bride service	elicit
stressful	burden	divorce
dowry,	bride price	virginity
≠dara	exchange	polygynous
custom		

Language

1. What does Shostak mean when she says there is no !Kung word for *virginity?*
2. Is there any other way to say *polygynous marriages?*

Style

1. What do we learn about Nisa's personality from the style of her speech?
2. Compare and contrast Shostak's and Nisa's styles. Why the difference?

Development and Organization

1. The first part of this piece is Shostak's anthropological overview of the !Kung custom of trial marriages, and the second part is a transcript of an interview Shostak conducted with a !Kung woman named Nisa on the subject of trial marriages. How do the two parts of the piece work together?
2. Do we need to know how many times Nukha went into the marriage hut with Bo and Nisa or what kind of meat Tsaa refuses to share with Nisa's father? In other words, should Shostak have edited and condensed Nisa's words?

Discussion and Journal Writing

1. How do !Kung parents select mates for their children? What do they look for? What roles do the parents of the bride and groom play in the marriage ceremony itself? Do parents play any role at all in the marriage customs of your culture or in any culture that you know?
2. Nisa is divorced twice in this piece on !Kung trial marriages. Why are those marriages ended? Who is involved in the proceedings?
3. Compare and contrast !Kung-style divorce with American-style divorce.

ooooo

Hopi Bride, American Bride

—Helen Sekaquaptewa, with Louise Udall

Helen Sekaquaptewa is a Hopi Indian who was born a couple of generations ago after U.S. expansion and wars consigned the Hopi and the other tribes of the Southwest to reservations. She was married twice: once the Hopi way and once the American way. Though Sekaquaptewa emphasizes the rituals of her Hopi wedding, there's a constant awareness of the rituals and laws that exist outside the reservation, raising painful questions of identity and legitimacy. The first wedding takes place in Oraibi, the village of her birth. This piece is taken from *Me and Mine* (1969), which Louise Udall, a journalist, wrote on the basis of a series of talks with Sekaquaptewa.

1   The home of the bridegroom is the center of activity in a Hopi wedding. When a couple decides to marry, the father of the groom takes over. He furnishes everything—cotton for the weaving and food to feed the workers during the time the weaving is in progress. Each household keeps a supply of cotton on hand against the time when a son may marry.

2   In Emory's case there was a problem. His parents had separated years before and his mother had remarried and lived in Oraibi. Emory lived with his mother during his childhood; Wickvaya, Emory's grandfather, also lived in the same household. This is why Wickvaya took his grandson to school at Keams Canyon and brought him back in the spring. Emory's father was among the men sent to the Indian School at Carlisle in Pennsylvania for five years, in 1906. When he returned he went to Hotevilla to live, and in due time remarried. Emory had never lived with his father.

3   Emory's mother wanted us to come to her home in Oraibi, but Emory had been away at school so many years that is wasn't really home to him. As he grew older he had lived in Bacabi, with his cousin Susie and her husband, who was his godfather, during the summers that he was home, helping in whatever way he could. Susie invited us to come to her home, and Emory's uncles and cousins all helped put in for the cotton and food and were the hosts for us.

4   After we decided to get married, I spent every minute that I could grinding in preparation for feeding the wedding guests. Women and girls of my relatives who wanted to help started grinding too. When my sister Verlie walked with me to Bacabi to Susie's house, I carried a big pan full of fine white cornmeal. I never left Susie's house for the entire period (about a month) and was under her watchful care, even slept with her the first three nights.

As a bride I was considered sacred the first few days, being in a room with the　5
shades on the windows, talking to no one. All this time I was steadily grinding corn
which was brought in by Emory's kinswomen. Each brought, say, a quart of corn in
a basket or on a plaque to be passed in to me to be ground, each lot separately.
After the first grinding I handed the corn out and waited while it was roasted and
passed back to me to be ground real fine. As each lot was finished, I put it back into
its own container, lining it up along the wall with others. When the aunts came
back in the evening to get their corn there was food on the table and they ate. White
corn was the grist the first day, blue corn the second and third days. At the end of
each day Susie gave me a relaxing rubdown.

Early each morning of the first three days, Cousin Susie went with me to the　6
east edge of the mesa, and there, facing the rising sun, we bowed our heads and
each offered a silent prayer for a happy married life. Our days began with the rising
of the sun and ended with its setting, because there was no artificial light for night
working.

The fourth day is the actual wedding day. Everyone of the relatives is up when　7
the cock crows, to participate in the marriage ritual, the hair washing. Suds are
made from the tuber of the yucca root, pounded into a pulp, put into two basins of
water, and worked with the hands until the pan is filled with foamy suds.

Two pans were place side by side on the floor, where Susie and my sister　8
Verlie prepared the suds. Usually the mothers of the bride and groom do this. Susie
and Verlie acted for our mothers. While Susie washed my hair, Verlie washed
Emory's. Then each took a strand of hair and twisted them together hard and tight
as a symbol of acceptance of the new in-law into the clan (family) and also to bind
the marriage contract, as they said, "Now you are united, never to go apart."

Next Emory was taken outside and stripped to the waist by women of my fam-　9
ily. Each had brought her small container of water which she poured over his shoulders as he knelt over a tub. They splashed the water over him with their hands. It
was still dark, so they could not see him; they put a blanket around him, and he
came back into the house to get warm from that icy bath.

Now, with out hair still wet and hanging loose, Emory and I walked together 10
to the eastern edge of the village and once more faced the rising sun, and with
bowed heads we prayed in silence for a long time; for a good life together, for children, and to be together all of our lives and never stray from each other.

After my hair was dry on this day, they combed it up like a married woman, 11
never to be worn in maiden style again. Married women parted their hair from the
center in the front to the nape of the neck. Each side was folded over the hand until
it reached nearly to the ear where it was bound with a cord made from hair and a
little yarn, leaving a soft puff at the ends. The hair in front of the ears was cut into
sideburns about two inches long.

The making of the robes begins on the morning of the nuptial hair washing. 12
The father or uncle of the groom (in our case Susie's father) took a bag of cotton

and, passing through the village, stopped at each house. He was expected, and each housewife opened her door and extended a plaque to receive some cotton (everyone was required to wash his hands before touching the cotton). Immediately all hands went to work cleaning the cotton of seeds, burrs, and little sticks. It was all cleaned that same day.

In the evening the uncles, godfather, and men who wished to help, gathered at 13 the groom's house to card the cotton. The cards were a pair of flat, wire-toothed brushes, four by twelve inches, with wooden handles at a slight angle, on the long side. They were bought from the trader and used for both wool and cotton. I watched my father and my grandfather us them in my time. A small handful of cotton was spread over all the teeth of one card; with the second card, the cotton was combed hack and forth until all the lumps were out and it became fluffy. Another motion made it into a strip as long as the card, which strip was put aside and another one started. The men worked late carding big piles of white cotton. Coal-oil lamps lighted their work. During this time the men told stories, with the bride sitting nearby, along with the kinswomen. From time to time the bride thanked the workers for their service. Everyone enjoyed the stories, and before they realized it, it was midnight and quitting time. The men were served refreshments and everyone went home to bed. It took several nights to do the carding.

All the men in the village worked to spin this cotton into thread in one day. 14 Food was obtained and prepared to feed the whole village. Ten of fifteen sheep were required. If the host didn't have sheep of his own, he bought them. One or two might be donated by someone. Wood had to be brought in for the cooking and to heat the kivas.

At sunrise on spinning day the custodian of each kiva went early to clean up 15 his kiva and start the fire and get it warm. The women were busy too, putting the big kettles on the fire and adding ingredients for the stew, making ready every plaque and basket.

After his breakfast, each man went to his kiva, taking his spindle (every adult 16 male owns one). Emory's uncle came around early to deliver to each kiva the carded cotton to be spun. In Bacabi there were three kivas. Soon all spindles were humming away. Emory's uncle checked the kivas from time to time to keep them supplied with carded cotton. Dinner should be late, so they were served a snack at noon in the kiva. The spun cotton was made into skeins; the warp thread was finer than the woof. The pile of light, fluffy hanks of warp and woof thread was beautiful.

In the meantime the women were getting the food and tables ready. My rela- 17 tives and myself were served earlier so we could be free to serve the community dinner. However, the bride did not serve but mingled with the other women. They teased me as all made merry and had a happy time. The men were served at the tables in Susie's house and neighboring houses as needed, and then the women and children of the village ate. Whatever food was left, especially the stew, was divided among the people.

The weaving took about two weeks, and it began a few days after the spinning   18
was finished. One sheep was butchered this time, and the other foods were made
ready for the first day of the weaving. At dawn and before breakfast the three special looms used in wedding weaving were brought out from their storage place to
the kiva (one kiva) where they were untied and spread out on the floor. Two or
three men at a time worked at the long and tedious job of stringing the loom, rolling
the warp back and forth to each other, over the notches close together on the two
end poles.

The bridal clothing consisted of a robe six by eight feet, a second one about   19
four by six feet to cover the shoulders, and a girdle about ten inches wide and eight
feet long, which is tied around the waist. The moccasins had leggings made of
white buckskin. Then there is the reed roll, which is a sort of suitcase in which to
wrap and carry extra gifts. Emory gathered the reed from the edge of the wash, cut
them into uniform lengths and tied them together with cord like a bamboo window
blind.

The threaded looms were hung from loops in the ceiling beams and fastened   20
to loops on the floor and stretched tight, and the weaving began, the best weavers
taking turns during the day. The belt is braided rather than woven.

At noon, food was brought to the kiva by relatives. After dinner a man took   21
his place at each loom and worked until evening. The host did not weave all the
time, but he stayed with them at all times. In the evening each man carried the loom
he had worked on to Susie's house, where I received them and put them away in a
back room for safekeeping. The men sat down to eat of piki and beans and leftover
food from dinner and somviki, which is tamales made from finely ground blue
corn, sweetened and wrapped in corn husks, and tied with yucca strips and then
boiled, and made by the bride every evening. As the weavers left after supper, I
gave each of them a few tamales on top of a folded piki. Each morning the weaving
continued. Only one man could work on each loom at a time, but the best weavers
came and took turns during the day. Other men came, bringing their spinning or
knitting, or just sat and visited and listened as the older men retold the traditional
stories. Sometimes they all sang together.

About halfway through the rites, our consciences troubled us, because we felt   22
the Hopi way was not quite right. We decided to get a license and be married legally. Emory told his folks what we wanted to do. He made application to the agency
at Keams Canyon, and a marriage license was obtained by mail from Holbrook, the
nearest county seat. It took about a week. In the afternoon that the license came, I
went to my father's house in Hotevilla; Emory went with me. I just walked in and
told my father that I was going to be married by license that night and had come to
get my clothes. I could feel the disapproval of my father and my sister as I gathered
the things I was going to wear. I just could not stay there and get dressed. I took my
clothes and went to one of the school teachers, and she let me dress in her house.

I was married in a white batiste dress, which was my pride and joy. I had   23
earned the money and bought the material and made the dress in domestic art class

in the Phoenix school. It had lace insertion set in bow knots around the gathered skirt, on the flared sleeves, and on the collar. My teacher had entered it in the State Fair, and I got second prize on it. I wore it once to a party and then decided it was too nice to wear and put it away in a box.

Later I made this dress into two little dresses for my first baby, our little girl 24 "Joy." About the second time that I hung these dresses out on the clothesline to dry, one of them disappeared. Two years later I was getting water at the spring one day, and there was a little two-year-old girl playing around, wearing that dress. I took her by the hand, led her to my house, and took off the dress (it was too little anyway). I put a nice colorful gingham dress on her, and gave her some bread and jam. She was pleased with it all, as I opened the door and sent her home. I heard no more on that. My babies wore out those dresses.

We were married in the evening on February 14, 1919, in the living room of 25 the home of Mr. Anderson, principal of the school in Hotevilla, by Reverend Dirkson of the Mennonite Mission. Emory's people, including some of his cousins, came to the ceremony. The teachers served some refreshments and gave us some little presents and a room where we could spend the night. In the morning they served a wedding breakfast, and then went back to finish the tribal wedding rites at Bacabi.

Emory was working at the school and had to be on the job, so he wasn't able 26 to participate in the weaving during the daytime. The activity died down after the first few days anyway, the weavers carrying on until everything was done. I helped with the grinding and cooking until the outfit was completed.

When the weaving was finished the men took the robes from the looms and 27 brought them into the house to be tried on. A border of sixteen running stitches in red was embroidered in the two corners, suggesting a limit of sixteen children, the most a person should have, and four stitches in each of the other two corners in orange, suggesting a minimum number of children. The white moccasins with leggings in one piece were finished just in time to be put on with the rest of the outfit. It was by then evening; food was placed before the guests and everyone ate again. (Hopis do not invite you to eat. They set the food before you, and the food invites.)

The next morning before sunup, Susie led the others in clothing me, first 28 washing my hair. Everyone admired the bride, and I was now ready to go back to my father's house. A line of white cornmeal was sprinkled on the ground, pointing the way. There was a lot of snow on the ground, so they wrapped rags over my white moccasins so I wouldn't get them wet or muddy. Emory's people went with me out of the village and over the little hill back to my home in Hotevilla. Emory did not go with me this time. How I wished that my own dear mother could be there to meet me. The sun was just coming up when we got to my father's house. Verlie opened the door, and my father thanked them for the beautiful bridal apparel that would make his daughter eligible to enter the world of the hereafter. Thus ends the wedding ritual.

I went inside and removed the wedding apparel and spread it out on the bed. 29
Then all the clan women came in and admired and tried on the robes. Then everything was rolled up and stored away. After a period of time these may be used
as needed, even cut into kilts for men to wear or to make bags to carry packs on
burros.

A bride of the village who has been married in the preceding year should dress 30
in her complete bridal attire and go into the plaza at the time of the Home Dance,
accompanied by her mother-in-law, and show herself to the kachinas during their
last round of the day, thus establishing her status as a married woman in their eyes.
We had gone to Idaho but were back by the Home Dance in July. My father had
shown his disapproval of me by cutting up my big robe and making little kilts out
of it. I had taken the small robe with me. I had my moccasins and did make this
appearance, accompanied by Susie.

Miss Abbott came to see me once during the thirty days of the tribal ceremo- 31
ny. She said she did not want to embarrass me, but she whispered in my ear, "You
have never looked better in your life. You look healthy and happy. You have rosy
cheeks. This has done you good."

The groom may follow the bride to her home as soon as he likes. Some go 32
right away, some wait a long time before claiming their brides. Emory came over
after a few days and stayed a couple of nights, but I could see that the tension and
hostility was hard on him; too many children, too little room, not even a room to
ourselves. After my going through all that ceremony just to please my family, my
sister was still so hostile that I felt neither wanted nor welcome.

One day, about a month after we were married, when no one was at home, I 33
felt that I could not stand it another minute. I gathered and packed my belongings,
as many as I could carry, returning later for the rest of them, and went to the house
where Emory lived near the school. He was at his work teaching shop when I got
there. I cleaned up the house and had a meal cooked when he came home, and we
were real happy. Soon afterward I got a job teaching beginners in the school. It was
hard to get teachers there because it was so isolated.

■ *Questions for* . . . **Hopi Bride, American Bride** by Helen Sekaquaptewa,
with Louise Udall

Words to Note

bridegroom	grinding	sacred
mesa	tuber	yucca root
symbol	bowed	stray
maiden	nape	cord
puff	kiva	spindles

warp	woof	hank
mingled	teased	loom
license	batiste	tribal wedding rites
kachinas	status	

Language

1. Sekaquaptewa doesn't name or describe most of the tribe who take part in her wedding rites. Instead, she refers to the men, the kinswomen, a man taking his place at the loom and so on. Why doesn't she name these people? What effect does it have on the piece that they remain nameless?
2. *Kachinas* is the only Hopi term she uses, but Hopi names and terms must exist for each part of the wedding ritual and for the apparel and items used. Why doesn't she use more Hopi language?

Style

1. How would you characterize Sekaquaptewa's style? Is it plain? Flat? Is it appropriate to the task of describing her weddings?
2. What kinds of transitional devices does she use to lead the reader through her weddings?

Development and Organization

1. Why does Sekaquaptewa spend more time describing the Hopi ceremony than the Christian, legal ceremony?
2. How does she organize the description of her two weddings?
3. Why does she dwell on the making of the bridal robe?

Discussion and Journal Writing

1. Why do Sekaquaptewa and Emory get married twice? What does it tell us about how Hopi culture was changing that the couple was troubled by their consciences halfway through the Hopi ritual and decided to marry legally?
2. Compare the two ceremonies. Where does the garment come from in the Hopi ceremony? In the ceremony performed in Mr. Anderson's living room? Who attends each ceremony? Why? Which one does Sekaquaptewa find most meaningful?
3. Compare her Hopi wedding to one that took place recently in your family.

ooooo

Black Kin Networks in Illinois: An Anthropological Approach

—Carol Stack

Carol Stack is a professor of anthropology at Boston University. She was born in New York City and educated at the University of California and the University of Illinois at Urbana. *All Our Kin,* the source of this selection, is a retort to Senator Daniel Patrick Moynihan's *The Negro Family: The Case for National Action* (1965), a government report. Moynihan went into the Black community looking for one type of family (the male-headed nuclear family) and consequently didn't see the type of family (female-headed kin networks) that was there.

Ruby Banks took a cab to visit Virginia Thomas, her baby's aunt, and they swapped some hot corn bread and greens for diapers and milk. In the cab going home Ruby said to me, "I don't believe in putting myself on nobody, but I know I need help every day. You can't get help just by sitting at home, laying around, house-nasty and everything. You got to get up and go out and meet people, because the very day you go out, that first person you meet may be the person that can help you get the things you want. I don't believe in begging, but I believe that people should help each other. I used to wish for lots of things like a living room suite, clothes, nice clothes, stylish clothes—I'm sick of wearing the same pieces. But I can't, I can't help myself because I have my children and I love them and I have my mother and all our kin. Sometimes I don't have a damn dime in my pocket, not a crying penny to get a box of paper diapers, milk, a loaf of bread. But you have to have help from everybody and anybody, so don't turn no one down when they come round for help." 1

Black families living in The Flats need a steady source of cooperative support to survive. They share with one another because of the urgency of their needs. Alliances between individuals are created around the clock as kin and friends exchange and give and obligate one another. They trade food stamps, rent money, a TV, hats, dice, a car, a nickel here, a cigarette there, food, milk, grits, and children. 2

Few if any black families living on welfare for the second generation are able to accumulate a surplus of the basic necessities to be able to remove themselves from poverty or from the collective demands of kin. Without the help of kin, fluctuations in the meager flow of available goods could easily destroy a family's ability to survive (Lombardi 1973). Kin and close friends who fall into similar economic crises know that they may share the food, dwelling, and even the few scarce luxuries of those individuals in their kin network. Despite the relatively high cost of rent and food in urban black communities, the collective power within kin-based exchange networks keeps people from going hungry. 3

As low-skilled workers, the urban poor in The Flats cannot earn sufficient 4 wages and cannot produce goods. Consequently, they cannot legitimately draw desired scarce goods into the community. Welfare benefits which barely provide the necessities of life—a bed, rent, and food—are allocated to households of women and children and are channeled into domestic networks of men, women, and children. All essential resources flow from families into kin networks.

Whether one's source of income is a welfare check or wages from labor, peo- 5 ple in The Flats borrow and trade with others in order to obtain daily necessities. The most important form of distribution and exchange of the limited resources available to the poor in The Flats is by means of trading, or what people usually call "swapping." As people swap, the limited supply of finished material goods in the community is perpetually redistributed among networks of kinsmen and throughout the community.

The resources, possessions, and services exchanged between individuals resid- 6 ing in The Flats are intricately interwoven. People exchange various objects gener-ously: new things, treasured items, furniture, cars, goods that are perishable, and services which are exchanged for child care, residence, or shared meals. Individuals enlarge their web of social relations through repetitive and seemingly habitual instances of swapping. Lily Jones, a resident in The Flats, had this to say about swapping, "That's just everyday life, swapping. You not really getting ahead of nobody, you just get better things as they go back and forth."

"Trading" in The Flats generally refers to any object or service offered with 7 the intent of obligating. An object given or traded represents a possession, a pledge, a loan, a trust, a bank account—given on the condition that something will be returned, that the giver can draw on the account, and that the initiator of the trade gains prerogatives in taking what he or she needs from the receiver.

Mauss's (1954) classic interpretation of gift exchange in primitive societies 8 stresses the essence of obligation in gift giving, receiving, and repaying. A gift received is not owned and sometimes can be reclaimed by the initiator of the swap. A person who gives something which the receiver needs or desires, gives under a voluntary guise. But the offering is essentially obligatory, and in The Flats, the obligation to repay carries kin and community sanctions.

An individual's reputation as a potential partner in exchange is created by the 9 opinions others have about him (Bailey 1971). Individuals who fail to reciprocate in swapping relationships are judged harshly. Julia Rose, a twenty-five-year-old mother of three, critically evaluated her cousin Mae's reputation, "If someone who takes things from me ain't giving me anything in return, she can't get nothing else. When someone like that, like my cousin Mae, comes to my house and says, 'Ooo, you should give me that chair, honey. I can use it in my living room, and my old man would just love to sit on it,' well, if she's like my cousin, you don't care what her old man wants, you satisfied with what yours wants. Some people like my cousin don't mind borrowing from anybody, but she don't loan you no money, her clothes, nothing. Well, she ain't shit. She don't believe in helping nobody and lots of folks gossip about her. I'll never give her nothing again. One time I went over there after I had given her all these things and I asked her, 'How about loaning me an outfit to wear?' She told me, 'Girl, I ain't got nothing, I ain't got nothing clean. I just put my clothes in the cleaners, and what I do have you can't wear 'cause it's too small for you.' Well, lots of people talks about someone who acts that way."

Degrees of entanglement among kinsmen and friends involved in networks of exchange differ in kind from casual swapping. Those actively involved in domestic networks swap goods and services on a daily, practically an hourly, basis. Ruby Banks, Magnolia Waters' twenty-three-year-old daughter, portrays her powerful sense of obligation to her mother in her words, "She's my mother and I don't want to turn her down." Ruby has a conflicting sense of obligation and of sacrifice toward her mother and her kinsmen. 10

"I swap back and forth with my mother's family. She wouldn't want nobody else to know how much I'm doing for her, but hell, that's money out of my pocket. We swap back and forth, food stamps, kids, clothes, money, and everything else. Last month the AFDC people had sent me forty dollars to get a couch. Instead of me getting a couch, I took my money over to Mama's and divided it with her. I gave her fifteen dollars of it and went on to wash because my kids didn't have a piece clean. I was washing with my hands and a bar of face soap before the money come. I took all the clothes I had, most of the dirty ones I could find, and washed them. It ran me up to six dollars and something with the cab that my sister took back home. I was sitting over at the laundry worrying that Mama didn't have nothing to eat. I took a cab over there and gave her ten more dollars. All I had left to my name was ten dollars to pay on my couch, get food, wash, and everything. But I ignored my problems and gave Mama the money I had. She didn't really have nothing after she paid some bills. She was over there black and blue from not eating—stomach growling. The craziest thing is that she wouldn't touch the rent money. I gave the last five dollars out of the rent money. She paid her sister her five and gave me five to get the kids something to eat. I said, 'What about my other ten?', but she put me off. She paid everybody else and I'm the one who's helping her the most. I could have most everything I needed if I didn't have to divide with my people. But they be just as poor as me, and I don't want to turn them down." 11

Close kin who have relied upon one another over the years often complain about the sacrifices they have made and the deprivation they have endured for one another. Statements similar to Ruby's were made by men and women describing the sense of obligation and sacrifice they feel toward female kin: their mothers, grandmothers, or "mamas." Commitment to mutual aid among close kin is sometimes characterized as if they were practically "possessed" or controlled by the relationship. Eloise, captured by the incessant demands of her mother, says, "A mother should realize that you have your own life to lead and your own family. You can't come when she calls all the time, although you might want to and feel bad if you can't. I'm all worn out from running from my house to her house like a pinball machine. That's the way I do. I'm doing it 'cause she's my mother and 'cause I don't want to hurt her. Yet, she's killing me." 12

When Magnolia and Kevin Waters inherited a sum of money, the information   13
spread quickly to every member of their domestic network. Within a month and a
half all of the money was absorbed by participants in their network whose demands
and needs could not be refused.

The ebb and flow of goods and services among kinsmen is illustrated in the   14
following example of economic and social transactions during one month in 1970
between participants in a kin-based cooperative network in The Flats. As I wrote in
my field notes:

> Cecil (35) lives in The Flats with his mother Willie Mae, his oldest sister and her
> two children, and his younger brother. Cecil's younger sister Lily lives with their
> mother's sister Bessie. Bessie has three children and Lily has two. Cecil and his
> mother have part-time jobs in a café and Lily's children are on aid. In July of
> 1970 Cecil and his mother had just put together enough money to cover their
> rent. Lily paid her utilities, but she did not have enough money to buy food
> stamps for herself and her children. Cecil and Willie Mae knew that after they
> paid their rent they would not have any money for food for the family. They
> helped out Lily by buying her food stamps, and then the two households shared
> meals together until Willie Mae was paid two weeks later. A week later Lily
> received her second ADC check and Bessie got some spending money from her
> boyfriend. They gave some of this money to Cecil and Willie Mae to pay their
> rent, and gave Willie Mae money to cover her insurance and pay a small sum on
> a living room suite at the local furniture store. Willie Mae reciprocated later on
> by buying dresses for Bessie and Lily's daughters and by caring for all the chil-
> dren when Bessie got a temporary job.

The people living in The Flats cannot keep their resources and their needs a   15
secret. Everyone knows who is working, when welfare checks arrive, and when
additional resources are available. Members of the middle class in America can
cherish privacy concerning their income and resources, but the daily intimacy created by exchange transactions in The Flats insures that any change in a poor family's
resources becomes "news." If a participant in an exchange network acquires a new
car, new clothes, or a sum of money, this information is immediately circulated
through gossip. People are able to calculate on a weekly basis the total sum of
money available to their kin network. This information is necessary to their own
solvency and stability.

Social relationships between kin who have consistently traded material and   16
cultural support over the years reveal feelings of both generosity and martyrdom.
Long-term social interactions, especially between female kin, sometimes become
highly competitive and aggressive. At family gatherings or at a family picnic it is
not unusual to see an exaggerated performance by someone, bragging about how
much he has done for a particular relative, or boasting that he provided all the food
and labor for the picnic himself. The performer often combines statements of his

parody

generosity with great claims of sacrifice. In the presence of other kin the performer displays loyalty and superiority to others. Even though these routines come to be expected from some individuals, they cause hurt feelings and prolonged arguments. Everyone wants to create the impression that he is generous and manipulative, but no one wants to admit how much he depends on others.

The trading of goods and services among the poor in complex industrial societies bears a striking resemblance to patterns of exchange organized around reciprocal gift giving in non-Western societies. The famous examples of reciprocal gift giving first described by Malinowski (1922), Mauss (1925), and Lévi-Strauss (1969) provided a basis for comparison. Patterns of exchange among people living in poverty and reciprocal exchanges in cultures lacking a political state are both embedded in well-defined kinship obligations. In each type of social system strategic resources are distributed from a family base to domestic groups, and exchange transactions pervade the whole social-economic life of participants. Neither industrial poor nor participants in nonindustrial economies have the opportunity to control their environment or to acquire a surplus of scarce goods (Dalton 1961; Harris 1971; Lee 1969; Sahlins 1965). In both of these systems a limited supply of goods is perpetually redistributed through the community. 17

The themes expressed by boasting female performers and gossiping kin and friends resemble themes which have emerged from black myth, fiction, and lore (Abrahams 1963; Dorson 1956, 1958). Conflicting values of trust and distrust, exploitation and friendship, the "trickster" and the "fool," have typically characterized patterns of social interaction between Blacks and Whites; notions of trust and distrust also suffuse interpersonal relations within the black community. These themes become daily utterances between cooperating kinsmen who find themselves trapped in a web of obligations. But the feelings of distrust are more conspicuous among friends than among kin. 18

Many students of social relations within the black community have concluded that friendships are embedded in an atmosphere of distrust. However, intense exchange behavior would not be possible if distrust predominated over all other attitudes toward personal relations. Distrust is offset by improvisation: an adaptive style of behavior acquired by persons using each situation to control, manipulate, and exploit others. Wherever there are friendships, exploitation possibilities exist (Abrahams 1970b, p. 125). Friends exploit one another in the game of swapping, and they expect to be exploited in return. There is a precarious line between acceptable and unacceptable returns on a swap. Individuals risk trusting others because they want to change their lives. Swapping offers a variety of goods and something to anticipate. Michael Lee, a twenty-eight-year-old Flats resident, talks about his need to trust others, "They say you shouldn't trust nobody, but that's wrong. You have to try to trust somebody, and somebody has to try to trust you, 'cause everybody need help in this world." 19

A person who gives and obligates a large number of individuals stands a better chance of receiving returns than a person who limits his circle of friends. In 20

IS GIFT GIVING IN MIDDLE-CLASS FAMILIES SIMILAR TO THIS? I THINK SO.

addition, repayments from a large number of individuals are returned intermittent-
ly: people can anticipate receiving a more-or-less continuous flow of goods. From
this perspective, swapping involves both calculation and planning.

Obtaining returns on a trade necessarily takes time. During this process, stable   21
friendships are formed. Individuals attempt to surpass one another's displays of
generosity; the extent to which these acts are mutually satisfying determines the
duration of friendship bonds. Non-kin who live up to one another's expectations
express elaborate vows of friendship and conduct their social relations within the
idiom of kinship. Exchange behavior between those friends "going for kin" is identical to exchange behavior between close kin.

"These days you ain't got nothing to be really giving, only to your true   22
friends, but most people trade," Ruby Banks told me. "Trading is a part of everybody's life. When I'm over at a girl friend's house, and I see something I want, I
say, 'You gotta give me this; you don't need it no way. I act the fool with them. If
they say no, I need that, then they keep it and give me something else. Whatever I
see that I want I usually get. If a friend lets me wear something of theirs, I let them
wear something of mine. I even let some of my new clothes out. If my friend has on
a new dress that I want, she might tell me to wait till she wear it first and then she'll
give it to me, or she might say, well take it on." Exchange transactions are easily
formed and create special bonds between friends. They initiate a social relationship
and agreed upon reciprocal obligations (Gouldner 1960; Foster 1963; Sahlins
1965).

Reciprocal obligations last as long as both participants are mutually satisfied.   23
Individuals remain involved in exchange relationships by adequately drawing upon
the credit they accumulate with others through swapping. Ruby Banks' description
of the swapping relationship that developed between us illustrates this notion.
"When I first met you, I didn't know you, did I? But I liked what you had on about
the second time you seen me, and you gave it to me. All right, that started us swapping back and forth. You ain't really giving nothing away because everything that
goes around comes around in my book. It's just like at stores where people give
you credit. They have to trust you to pay them back, and if you pay them you can
get more things.

Since an object is swapped with the intent of obligating the receiver over a   24
period of time, two individuals rarely simultaneously exchange things. Little or no
premium is placed upon immediate compensation; time has to pass before a
counter-gift or a series of gifts can be repaid. While waiting for repayments, participants in exchange are compelled to trust one another. As the need arises, reciprocity occurs. Opal Jones described the powerful obligation to give that pervades interpersonal relationships. "My girl friend Alice gave me a dress about a month ago,
and last time I went over to her house, she gave me sheets and towels for the kids,
'cause she knew I needed them. Every time I go over there, she always gives me
something. When she comes over to my house, I give her whatever she asks for.
We might not see each other in two or three months. But if she comes over after

that, and I got something, I give it to her if she want it. If I go over to her house and she got something, I take it—canned goods, food, milk—it don't make no difference.

"My TV's been over to my cousin's house for seven or eight months now. I 25
had a fine couch that she wanted and I gave it to her too. It don't make no difference with me what it is or what I have. I feel free knowing that I done my part in this world. I don't ever expect nothing back right away, but when I've given something to kin or friend, whenever they think about me they'll bring something on around. Even if we don't see each other for two or three months. Soon enough they'll come around and say, 'Come over my house, I got something to give you.?' When I get over there and they say, 'You want this?', even if I don't want it my kin will say, 'Well find something else you like and take it on.'"

When people in The Flats swap goods, a value is placed upon the goods given 26
away, but the value is not determined by the price or market value of the object. Some goods have been acquired through stealing rings, or previous trades, and they cost very little compared to their monetary value. The value of an object given away is based upon its retaining power over the receiver; that is, how much and over how long a time period the giver can expect returns of the gift. The value of commodities in systems of reciprocal gift giving is characterized by Lévi-Strauss (1969, p. 54), "Goods are not only economic commodities, but vehicles and instruments for realities of another order, such as power, influence, sympathy, status and emotion. . . ."

Gifts exchanged through swapping in The Flats are exchanged at irregular 27
intervals, although sometimes the gifts exchanged are of exactly the same kind. Despite the necessity to exchange, on the average no one is significantly better off. Ruby Banks captured the pendulous rhythm of exchange when she said, "You ain't really giving nothing away because everything that goes round comes round in my book."

These cooperating networks share many goals constituting a group identity— 28
goals so interrelated that the gains and losses of any of them are felt by all participants. The folk model of reciprocity is characterized by recognized and urgent reciprocal dependencies and mutual needs. These dependencies are recognized collectively and carry collective sanctions. Members of second-generation welfare families have calculated the risk of giving. As people say, "The poorer you are, the more likely you are to pay back." This criterion often determines which kin and friends are actively recruited into exchange networks.

Gift exchange is a style of interpersonal relationship by which local coalitions 29
of cooperating kinsmen distinguish themselves from other Blacks—those low-income or working-class Blacks who have access to steady employment. In contrast to the middle-class ethic of individualism and competition, the poor living in The Flats do not turn anyone down when they need help. The cooperative life style and the bonds created by the vast mass of moment-to-moment exchanges constitute an underlying element of black identity in The Flats. This powerful obligation to exchange is a profoundly creative adaptation to poverty.

■ *Questions for . . .* Black Kin Networks in Illinois: An Anthropological **Approach** by Carol Stack

Words to Note

kin	entwined	reciprocity
symbol	mutual	surplus
socially recognized	kin-based households	durable
parenthood	fluctuations	nuclear family
matrifocal family	swapping	house-nasty
interwoven	prerogatives	sanctions
degrees of	endured	mutual aid
entanglement	incessant	embedded
transactions	pervade	suffuse
improvisation	manipulate	exploit
precarious	bonds	profoundly creative
adaptation		

Language

1. Stack provides examples of what she means from her field notes, but generally her diction is somewhat abstract and Latinate. A glance at "Words to Note" makes the point: *migrated, fluctuations, suffuse,* and so on. Social scientists are often accused of being unnecessarily abstract. Is Stack guilty of that charge? Could she have written more plainly, or is the Latinate diction she uses essential to making her point?

Style

1. Why does Stack quote from her field notes about Willie Mae and Lily's family? Would it have been smoother to put that information into her own words?
2. Why does she interrupt herself from time to time with references to the works of other scholars?

Development and Organization

1. Map the piece. Is it smart or misleading of Stack to begin with Ruby Banks, in light of the general discussion of social patterns in The Flats that follows? How would a magazine writer approach the world of Ruby Banks?
2. Who is Stack writing for? How do you know?

Discussion and Journal Writing

1. According to Stack, why isn't a single household the significant unit in understanding family life in The Flats? Why does she prefer to note kin networks spread out over several households?
2. Define your family. Are its members and activities centered in one household, or are they spread out over several households?
3. Why does the shape family takes and the household or households it occupies vary from one economic cultural group to another?
4. It is said that in American society, only middle-class families have fairly independent and individual existences and that very rich and very poor families band together. Stack presents the reasons why the poor families she studied depend on one another. What about rich families? Why do they band together? Compare and contrast very rich and very poor families.

ooooo

The Life and Times of Don Taso,
Puerto Rican Sugar Cane Worker

—Sidney Mintz

Sidney Mintz is professor of anthropology at Johns Hopkins University and lives in Baltimore. He is author of *Worker in the Cane, Caribbean Transformations,* co-author of *The People of Puerto Rico,* and editor of *Slavery, Colonialism and Racism.* Don Taso, the man Mintz interviews and the key subject of his ethnography, lives in Barrio Jauca, a sugar town on the southwest coast of Puerto Rico. He is a worker in the cane, a former socialist and union activist, an evangelical Christian, and a family man.

From the air, the narrow coastal plain of southern Puerto Rico looks like an   1
irregular green ribbon. It contrasts sharply with the blues and azures of the sea to the south, and with the sere vegetation of the uplands to the north. The plain itself is covered with sugar cane. A road cuts through the cane, paralleling the sea, and linking towns along the coast. Most of the people live in rural areas rather than in the towns: in shacks that hug the shoulders of the road or stretch around the bays and inlets; in barracks and houses around the plazas of the old-time sugar hacien-

das; or in company towns built up near the monster cane-grinding mills. The mills are the most conspicuous landmarks from the air: their chimneys cast long shadows over the shacks and across the cane. From the air, the workers' shacks look regular and neat. There is a picturesqueness about the thatched roofs, the waving palms, and the nearness of the sea.

But walking through a village destroys such impressions. The ground is 2 pounded hard and dusty, littered with tin cans, paper, coconut husks, and cane trash. The houses are patched with old Coca Cola signs, boards torn from packing cases, and cardboard. Only a few are painted. The seeming order dissolves into disorder and crowding. Large families are packed into tight living places. The houses are variously divided into two, three, or more sections by partitions which never reach the ceiling. The cooking is done in ramshackle lean-tos behind the living quarters. And all around the houses grows the cane.

Such a village is Jauca. The barrio called Jauca contains clusters of houses, 3 some on the edge of the sea, some along the east-west highway, and others bunched around the centers of the *colonias*—the great farms of the corporations which control over 95 per cent of all the cultivated land in the municipality. In Barrio Jauca the largest aggregation of houses is along the highway; this village is called Poblado Jauca. The nearest large groupings are at the beach to the south and to the northwest near the plaza of the largest colonia in the barrio, Colonia Destino. There is a company store at Colonia Destino; 36 little two-room shacks provided rent free by the corporation to resident workers; a two-story house for the *mayordomo,* or overseer; two barracks left from slavery times and still occupied; and the ruined shell of the hacienda warehouse, now used to store machinery and fertilizer. The only trees in view are some palms growing near a point on the beach, the twin rows of tamarinds which line the approach to Colonia Destino, and a few scattered fruit trees among the houses of Poblado Jauca.

Poblado Jauca consists of a string of shacks lining the highway, and a substan- 4 tial cluster of additional houses—on an acre plot of land called Palmas Orillanas— which extend from the road southward toward the sea. There are fewer than a dozen small stores and bars, two school buildings, and, at one end of the village, the crumbling mill and chimney of an old sugar hacienda. The village has standpipes along the road to supply its water, many of the houses are electrified, and the road which connects the village to the towns of Santa Isabel to the west and Salinas to the east is well surfaced. In its outward appearance, Poblado Jauca does not differ significantly from hundreds of other such "line" villages in the sugar areas of Puerto Rico.

At five o'clock in the morning Poblado Jauca is still and deserted-looking. An 5 occasional touring car goes by on the coast road carrying passengers from Ponce to San Juan. The roosters crow and the dogs bark and the surf sounds softly. Every shack is shut tightly—the wooden shutters of the windows closed against the "night air," the doors barred. The cookhouses behind the shacks are cold; the sun is still low. An easterly breeze stirs the cane, rattles the Coca Cola signs, shakes loose a ripe nut in the palm grove near the water.

But by six o'clock the village comes to life. The first signs are the swinging 6
back of the shutters that give on the back yard and the tendrils of smoke curling out
of the stoves. The first need of the morning is food: the food, coffee. In the early
morning the air has a deceptive chilly freshness. Everything is coolly damp and
stimulating. In less than an hour the entire quality of the morning is transformed.
By the time the men have drunk their coffee, tied their cuffs to their ankles with
cords, and picked up machetes or hoes and the food for the midmorning breakfast,
the sun is high and glittering; it weighs on the skin like something tangible, burns
away the dampness from every surface, almost crackles as it grows hotter. The men
leave the houses, carrying their breakfasts and tools and dressed in rough work
clothes, wide-brimmed straw hats, and old shoes. They go to "defend themselves"
(*se defienden*) in the cane, which is their phrase for the struggle of making a living.
These men have lived with the cane, most of them, from the time they were born. It
grows up to the edges of the house plots. When it is in full glory it stands fifteen
feet high, and the villages are choked in it. It litters the roads; during harvest the
smell of it fills the air, the "hair" of its surface works into the skin like peach fuzz.
Men who work in the cane speak of "doing battle" (*bregando*) with it.

From the thatch shacks along the beach, from the wooden ones along the high- 7
way, the men move toward the plazas of the old haciendas to get their work orders
for the day. Some will form the cutting lines; others will lay rails for the wagons
that are loaded in the fields or will do the loading. There are cultivators and seed-
ers, seed cutters and winch operators, ditchers and gang bosses. Most of the jobs
can be done by nearly everyone, but individual workers have preferences and some
have special skills. Old Don Tómas, like many of the oldest Negro people in the
barrio, is a *palero*—a ditcher—the most skilled, the highest-paid, and the most
prestigeful "dirt" job in the fields. The cutters come mainly from the shacks at the
beach; they are white men, most of them named De Jesús, whose families migrated
to the coast from nearby highlands. The De Jesús are set somewhat apart by other
Jauqueños. Some of them take their Catholicism seriously and go to church; they
try to grow little vegetable gardens at the beach, and they fence their houses; they
"marry cousin with cousin"; and unlike the old coastal working families, they prefer cane cutting on a piecework basis to most other jobs. Aníbal and Fredo are truck
drivers; they were in the Army, and learned some skills there most Jauqueños, and
especially the older ones, could never acquire. Truck driving pays relatively well
and it is easy work compared to cutting or loading. Don Daniel likes to plant seed.
It is a curious choice, for Don Daniel is very tall and seeding requires that one bend
over continuously, setting and tapping the seed—which is not seed at all, but cut-
tings of cane stalk—into place.

By seven o'clock those who have work are out of the village. The children eat 8
and start for school, or begin their jobs at home—toting pails of water, mopping,
the floors, tending the baby, ironing—or play in the yards with toys made of old tin
cans and bits of wood. As the sun climbs, each woman begins to prepare the hot
lunch which must be carried out to her man in the fields, no matter how far away he

may be working. No Puerto Rican cane worker will settle for a cold midday meal. At nine o'clock he has his thermos of black coffee and a piece of bread smeared with margarine or topped with a slice of cheese or sausage—he feels it gives him the strength he needs to work till noon—but at noon someone must bring him a hot luncheon. Nests of pots hung on wire frames are the lunchboxes of the Puerto Rican countryside. Sometime the pots hold noodle soup, or a quantity of starches such as boiled green bananas, taro, yams, and Irish potatoes; fish broths, cornmeal cakes, and salads mixed with bits of boiled salt cod are common. But no matter what else, one tin container is always full of rice, another of red or white beans in a mild sauce. Rice and beans are the staple of the lower-class Puerto Rican.

After lunch the cane workers pick up their machetes once more. Back home   9 the wives are busy with the laundry. They scrub the clothes on washboards, remove stubborn dirt with scrapers fashioned from coconut shell, and hang the clean clothes on fences or stretch them over pieces of corrugated iron to dry. Then water is boiled for the afternoon coffee, and the youngest children must be bathed and dressed to await their fathers' return. By three or four o'clock the men have all returned, and the heat of the day has begun to abate slightly. The men bathe, crouching over the washtubs in the cookhouses or in showers fed from hand-filled tanks if they have them. It is in the late afternoon that the social life of the day begins. Men shave after their afternoon baths; young girls and boys put on their good clothes; the radios loudly announce the baseball scores, carry political discussions or Puerto Rican and other Latin American music.

Dinner is not eaten by the whole family seated at a table, but by each family   10 member independently, down to the littlest, during a two-hour period. The father sits at the table and is served by his wife, who hovers about him, often with her youngest child in her arms. Again rice and beans and black coffee are the core of the meal, but there may also be cornmeal slabs in fish broth; or stewed goat or beef; or boiled salt cod. Children eat standing in the kitchen, or sitting in the yard and feeding the chickens from their spoons. The dogs and the chickens scour the floors and yards and follow the housewife about with friendly but cautious importunacy.

After dinner the street becomes the setting for conversation and flirting.   11 Loafing groups gather in front of the small stores or in the yards of older men, where they squat and gossip; marriageable boys and girls promenade along the highway. Small groups form and dissolve in the bars. The women remain home; married couples rarely walk together, usually only on their way to revivalist prayer meetings. The more worldly young men—who have probably served in the Army and have a little money—may hail passing public cars and go to the movies in the nearby towns, or to see girls in neighboring villages. If it is a Tuesday or a Saturday night, illegal numbers-game sellers will be making their rounds, collecting bets placed on credit at an earlier time. The winning numbers (which are based on the winning numbers in the national *legal* lottery) will be announced the next morning over the radio, and nearly everyone in the village, knowing the favorite numbers of their fellows, will know who has won.

By nine o'clock—unless it is a Saturday—Jauca has grown quiet. Activity 12 continues within the houses, the stores, and the Pentecostal chapel. Youths may prepare to hunt octopus and lobster on the cays, while their younger brothers are catching crabs in the cane fields, along the irrigation ditches. Couples in love say their good nights in the shadows. By ten even the stores are closed; one bar or two may still be open. The Pentecostals come home from their services. Only if there is a wake, a local political meeting, or a fight will activity continue outside the houses. The surf, scarcely noticeable during the noise of the day, can be heard again after ten o'clock, and the dogs and roosters vie with the gentle little croaking frogs—the *coquí*—in breaking the night's stillness.

During the course of the week the character of a day's activity varies. 13 Saturdays are paydays, and Saturday nights are special. The nickelodeons play late into the night, and many people of all ages dance. Old Tomás Famanía, who has all his teeth and walks straight, though he carries a cane of *frescura* with a brass tip, and glories in his more than sixty years, comes up from his thatched shack at the beach to dance. He usually picks rumbas, and his partners will be Ceferino Hernández' daughters and granddaughters, none of them more than eight years old. The bachelors stand at the bar drinking their rum neat—each drink downed in a swallow from a tiny paper cup. The more affluent buy half pints of rum (called "Shirleys" after Shirley Temple) and finish them sitting at the tables. The teen-age males play pool on the much-ripped table in Cheo's bar and watch the girls walk by. Sometimes the barbecue pit at Cheo's will be going. A youth will crouch by the bed of hot charcoal, casually turning the long pole on which a whole pig is impaled.

On Saturday evenings during harvest the front doors of the houses are open. 14 One can peer in to see the dimly lighted "parlor," which is separated from the "dining room" by a low wooden partition. There is the mother with one child nursing, another sleeping in her lap, a third perhaps drowsing at her feet or pulling at her skirt. The grandmother may be visiting, rocking in a chair, sometimes smoking a cigar. Conversation is animated and humorous: Don Fonso had to chase his mare two miles tonight down the main road; Barbino has nearly worn out the record called *Vuelve* (Return) at the bar, because his girl friend Wilma is leaving for "El Norte": Don Fico hit on the *bolita* (numbers game) for $2,300 last Sunday; there is an elopement expected, or a revival meeting; how long will the *zafra* (harvest) last? The father returns from his visit to a *compadre* (godparent of one of his children) and greets his mother-in-law with respect and care. A man must maintain very good (but circumspect) relations with his mother-in-law. The children, those still awake, cling to him. He may put them to sleep by rocking and fondling them as the hours pass. When the front door is closed and the shutters are swung to, it is time for the parents to go to bed. One teen-age son may still be abroad; he will creep in after the house is dark, feast on the cold rice-and-bean leftovers from dinner, and crawl into bed, often alongside two or three brothers. And the bed may be a folding cot.

Sundays are quieter than weekdays, as Saturdays are noisier. The Pentecostal 15 church has its day and its night services. Older people dress up on Sunday, though very few ever go to church. In the summer townspeople come to swim at the Jauca beach, to sit under the palms and drink soda or coconut water. Passing cars may stop in Jauca—a merchant or salesman seeks to purchase a dozen succulent land crabs to take home to San Juan. Jauqueños wander down to the beach to watch the townsmen swim. These are a different sort of people. They are not explicit about how they regard each other, but town and country are not quite the same, and the townsmen who come to swim or to buy crabs are not merely cane cutters who may live in town but storekeepers, civil servants, and teachers. And, parenthetically, it is not their color that sets them apart but their class.

Just as Saturday and Sunday differ from weekdays, so the harvest time differs   16 from *el tiempo muerto*—dead time. From Christmas until early summer the cane is cut, and much cane is planted. The fields are alive with activity. Long lines of men stand before the cane like soldiers before an enemy. The machetes sweep down and across the stalks, cutting them close to the ground. The leaves are lopped off, the stalk cut in halves or thirds and dropped behind. It is a beautiful thing to watch from a hundred yards' distance. The men seem tiny but implacable, moving steadily against a green forest which recedes before them. When the cane has been piled and then scooped up, either by men who load it on carts brought into the fields on movable tracks, or by the new *arañas* (spiders), machines that load it on rubber-wheeled carts, the oxen may graze among the trash. And soon the field may be cleared for planting a new crop, which will be sprouting within weeks of the harvest.

From a distance, the scene is toylike and wholesome. Up close it is neither.   17 The men sweat freely; the cane chokes off the breeze, and the pace of cutting is awesome. The men's shirts hang loose and drip sweat continuously. The hair of the cane pierces the skin and works its way down the neck. The ground is furrowed and makes footing difficult, and the soil gives off heat like an oven. The mayordomo sits astride a roan mare and supervises the field operations. He wears khakis and cordovan riding accessories. To see him ride past a line of men bent over and dripping sweat, to hear the sounds of the oxen in the fields behind, the human and the animal grunting, and to feel the waves of heat billowing out of the ground and cane evoke images of other times. The men of Jauca grow drawn in the first two weeks of the harvest. This is the time to make the money to pay debts from the past dead time and to prepare for the next. It is a way of life that can make menial jobs in the continental United States seem like sinecures.

When the cane is entirely cut the intense activity ceases. The last trainload of   18 cane, from the westernmost plantations serviced by the Machete and Aguirre mills, is pulled through Jauca by the little engine to the accompaniment of an unceasing whistling. The train is crying; the next day the whistles of Machete and Aguirre will cry. And then, people joke sourly, the people will cry. The nickelodeons play less. The drinkers of bottled rum turn back to *cañita*— "the little cane," the illegal white rum. Don Tomás has no more dancing partners, because there are fewer nickels. The little account books each Puerto Rican family has for its food purchases begin to carry more unpaid entries. *Fia'o*—credit—gets extended two weeks instead of one, or four instead of two. Back before World War II, when Puerto Rico was much poorer, dead time was marked by a sharp increase in infant mortality, supposedly from a disease diagnosed as gastroenteritis; the correlation with the cessation of income does not seem to have been a coincidence.

In dead time one hears more reminiscence, there is more fishing, the ways to 19 turn an extra penny are given more thought. Around the houses one notices little treasures that were overlooked because they mean much less during the harvest: the bedraggled chickens, a melancholy goat, perhaps even a duck. There is a lime tree behind Don Cosme's house, and it will yield large quantities of lime drink. And if coffee is really short, one can brew *hedionda,* which grows all over. Headache powders may be better, but some headaches do pass if you crush a leaf of *naranja,* dip it in oil, and press it to the brow. Cheo has a hive of bees; and if one has a compadre who is a fisherman, he may make a present of the *carey* (turtle meat) that he could not sell or use this morning. A little cornmeal will make the land crabs fatter, and one's sons keep the crab traps going throughout the rainy season. The land is crowded with the growing cane and the yards are dry and sterile, but there is a tree here and a bush there, one hen still is laying, and octopuses live in the rocks of the cay. Everything belongs to Corporation Aguirre, it seems; but there is a little left that belongs to the people.

The feast day of the patron saint of Santa Isabel—who is not Saint Elizabeth, 20 despite the town's name, but Santiago Apóstol—comes in the summer, at a time when money is scarce. (Some wags have suggested that the town fathers should pick a new saint, preferably one whose birth may be commemorated during the harvest.) In October and November there is some work in the fields, for this is the planting period for the *gran cultura* (big growth) cane, which is allowed to stand fifteen or eighteen months before it is cut. Some Novembers there are three elections. The baseball season gets into swing. And when Christmas comes, the harvest is near once more. The year begins and ends with the swish of machetes.

The round of life varies also with exceptional happenings, natural and man- 21 made: elections, hurricanes, war. Yet the outside observer who will stay and watch long enough gets a strong feeling of continuity, stability, fulfilled expectation. A full year of watching reveals the circle of events. But it is only in looking at the history of a village like Jauca, and at the individual histories of its people, that one may see the tremendous changes in local life over the past half century. The lives of people and the life of the community unwind backward through time: the village gets a tarred road, its first car; standpipes replace the stagnant surface well. People are born, grow up, marry, have children. They learn to use a machete while they are still toddling, to pick medicinal plants and to catch land crabs in their early childhood, to cut the cane or to do the family cooking while in their teens. The village grows "modern": the people get electric lights and radios.

Taso's Written Autobiographical Statements

"In the year 1908, at the age of ten months, I was left fatherless with my 22 mother, one sister, and two brothers."

Thus begins the life history of Eustaquio Zayas Alvarado. When I started to 23 collect Taso's life history in the summer of 1953, I asked him first simply to tell me the story of his life as he remembered it. He asked for time to think about it, and I did not turn on the recording machine that first night. The following evening when we sat down together again, he produced from his pocket several sheets of lined paper, torn from a child's notebook, on which he had written down his story. Though few events in his written texts were dated, I could establish that it covered a period from his birth (1908) up to 1945. So the formal gathering of the data on Taso's life began with a written statement, and the life history begins with it here.

In 1956 when I returned to Jauca to check for inaccuracies in the information I 24 had already gathered, I asked Taso first of all if he would write down the remainder of his story, to cover the years of 1945–56. I wanted him to do this, if possible, before we discussed anything else, to permit him again to select in his own mind those events which ought to be mentioned for these later years. Again he asked for a day to think about it, and once more he produced a brief written statement.

The first statement runs to about 850 words; the second is about 780 words 25 long. I think they are probably the longest things Taso has ever written. Although the story is ragged, the emphases unexpected, and the continuity almost impercepti- ble at times to the reader, I have chosen to include the statements here as they stand. Granting all the limitations implicit in the task I posed for Taso, the texts are as purely expressive of the man and his retrospect as anything that came out of our work together. The events referred to take on meaning and continuity as the later interviews give depth and detail.

The reader may note that the second statement is more concerned with dating 26 events. I believe this was not only because the period covered was more easily recalled but also because of my insistence on chronology during our 1953 work. The second statement seems rather more self-conscious than the first. Though we had not worked together for nearly three full years, my constant probings during the summer of 1953 may have had their effect. Yet the second statement, almost as much as the first, is marked by a curious running-together of events, some of them deeply serious, others seemingly trivial. Occasionally, as later chapters reveal, life- and-death problems are ignored altogether or referred to in understatement.

These are documents written by a man unused to writing, and particularly 27 unused to writing of those events, sentiments, and emotions which are close to one's self. Taso, if the needs to express some fundamental or feeling, does so most spontaneously by acting; only rarely would he do it by speaking; and by writing, never. These are the words of the man himself, picking and choosing items out of more than half a lifetime of living that he regards as worthy of record. There is much more he will say before even this part of his story is told. These are its begin- nings.

In the year 1908, at the age of ten months, I was left fatherless with my moth- 28 er, one sister, and two brothers. Later on my older brother went to the town of Guayama. At that time my mother was working sewing clothes, washing, and ironing to make a living. At the age of about eight years I began working, earning thirty cents [a day]. Then my mother sent me to school, and in order to be able to get to the fourth grade I had to go to school for about five or six years. What would happen was, I used to have to quit school because of the economic situation. I would usually go to school half of the day and the other half of the day I'd be working. Yet I was never able to finish the fourth grade. Later, my sister married and my older brother left home, and we remained alone, Mama and I. Then my sister came back home; she separated from her husband. Right away she went and got married again; and again my mother and I were alone. Around 1920, my mother died. Then I went to live with my sister and my brother-in-law. By that time my sister had two children already, Rosaura [Rosa] the older and Eladio [Lalo] the younger. Then in about three or four years, more or less, my sister became pregnant again, and she died as a consequence of that birth. And there remained the two of us along with the three infants. At that time my brother-in-law was an irrigation foreman in the cane, and I was working with him. We took the smallest infant, the one to which Tomasa gave birth before she died, to a lady to take care of, and we used to pay for this. And we had to carry the other two to work and put them somewhere nearby until the afternoon, when we returned to the house. After, my brother-in-law began to board at someone's house; but not I. About two weeks later, we were coming home from a burial and he invited me to eat where he was eating and I went with him. Then the lady of the house and her husband told me that if I wanted, they would make meals [for me, too]. I accepted, and I began paying $1.50 [a week]. But when I saw how they treated me, I always paid more after. Soon they invited me to live in their house, and I went. Then I had great relief because they did everything for me in the house. And I was with them a long time, until I became a young man. Later on, though, I fell in love with the wife I have today, and I began another, different life. Then I went to live with my wife in her mother's house. At the time I was working in Colonia Cuatro Hermanos, about three kilometers from here. Then my wife's mother bought us a little house of the flat-roofed type, which was on the land of another person who was not the owner of the house. I improved the house; but later on I had to take it apart because they wanted me to pay an amount for [the use of] the lot which was more than the house was worth. So I returned again to the house of my wife's mother until I was able to get a lot where I could put up the house. And I had to wait a long time because no one wanted to rent lots. Then a boy who grew up with me told me I should speak with his mother to see if she might rent me a lot. I went, and after a great effort and with the help of my friend, I got the lot. Then my wife's father, who was a carpenter, began to build the house. It turned out that we needed [material for] a wall because we made the house bigger. Then I went to a friend of mine and borrowed $15, and I bought the lumber and finished the house. By that time my wife already had two children and was pregnant with another. When that one was born, my wife had a serious illness—for four days she knew no one, and we watched over her day and night. Dr. Vélez told me that she would not live. Yet after four days she recovered from that illness. At that time I was working on the railroad; I earned $5.10 weekly. By then, I had been given $43 credit in the store in which I traded, and I went along paying it off out of that same $5.10, and with [the sale of] some animals we were raising. At that time my brother-in-law, the father of Rosaura and Eladio, was located in Aguadilla, and I thought to go there to improve [my situation]. While I was there I received a letter from Guayama from my older brother, saying that his wife had died and that he was ill. Then I went to Guayama and took him [back with me] to Aguadilla. But there it was worse. At that time a man was earning only 50 cents [a day] in Aguadilla, and I decided to return to my house [i.e. to Barrio Jauca] again. My brother was already well and he went back to Guayama again. Then my wife got sick again and her mother told me to move my house to the lot where her house was, so that she would be able to attend to her. I would work during the day and when I came home I worked moving the house, until at last I finished.

The 1932 political campaign approached. Because I was a Socialist they left 29 me without work and at that time I suffered a lot. I had been working in the campaign but I did not get any protection from them [the Socialist party]. After, I returned to work at Colonia Destino. During all those times they were working by piecework on the colonias. If one agreed to a quantity of work for $1.50, and the work turned out so badly that you had to spend a whole week on it, then what you earned for the week was $1.50. Because of family differences I resolved to seek a place to which to move my house again. I went to the mayor and solicited a lot that the municipality had in the barrio. It was one single lot and there were two requests. Then we agreed to divide it between the two of us, and we did. And here I am, in the midst of so many inconveniences and fights, raising my family—my wife, and I, and our eight children.

Here is the second written statement.

Around 1945 they had already begun to eliminate the system of irrigation 30 which had been used before in Colonia Destino—that is, making *maclaines* [irrigation cross channels] and irrigation ditches [by hand]. It was changed for a system that they call "oil-line." They used machines for this new system; and so our work was finished, it was reduced to almost nothing. Then there arose certain differences in the CGT union [Confederación General de Trabajadores], and in 1946 they set up the independent union here, in which I worked as treasurer of the Barrio Jauca subcommittee. Later that [union] failed, too. On July 18, 1946, I began working [again] on the railway brigade. During the year 1945 I had had many difficulties with Carmen and Pablín [his oldest children] and their schooling, and they lost a whole year of school for lack of teachers. In the following year Pablín wanted to continue going to school but Carmen didn't. At that time one didn't have to worry about the money for trips to school because there was a bus that used to come to get the children. But later on they stopped the bus and then one had to pay travel costs so that the children would be able to go to school in town.

At that time we had seven men in the railway brigade. At the end of the har- 31
vest of 1947–48, they [the corporation] ordered that only five men be kept on the
brigade. At that time Elí was reaching the end of her pregnancy with Anastacia,
which was going to mean a pretty bad situation for me. They also ordered that the
men go to work only four days—that is, twenty day-salaries per week. Then I
claimed that they should give me [work] also out of those twenty day-salaries. And
they did it that way. When Elí began labor to bear Anastacia I had to get a public
car to go to look for the midwife whom they call Fermina, at the Quinta [quarters]
of Colonia Alomar. I did not find her there and I had to go to the beach of Santa
Isabel [to find her]. I brought her back with me, and Elí had a pretty good delivery.
Already at that time [1948] the political campaign was on, and certain differences
arose in the matter of the slate [of Popular party candidates] and they held some
meetings which were rather tumultuous. But everything came out all right. At that
time we had bought a little bicycle for Pablín, who was continuing with school in
town, from a cousin of Pablín's who had sent it from San Francisco.

Around the end of 1950 Elí decided to make a profession of faith [i.e. be con- 32
verted to the Pentecostal Church], and after, I [was converted] too. But Blanca had
done so before anyone else. Things went along, and in the year 1952 Pablín was
graduated [from high school]. At that point I had to get together the help of
Alejandro, my half brother by our father, and Cheo [Rosa's husband], and my own
efforts to buy a suit and the other things for the graduation. Then Pablín was at
home not doing anything. Later, there was an opportunity to work and he worked
about four and five weeks. With what he earned he bought Elí a stove and some
other things. Then once again he had nothing to do, and he secretly sent to ask travel money from Lalo to emigrate, and when Elí found out she had a nervous attack
such that he [decided he] did want to leave. He did not want to go on studying, but
it was impossible. I could not pay the costs. Then Cheo sent him to the Percy
[Secretarial] School [in Ponce] to take a course. Before he could finish, the Army
called him, May 13, 1953. At that time my niece Rosa had emigrated, and Cheo
had the bad luck of getting sick with the chicken pox and he was hospitalized at
San Lucas [Hospital, in Ponce]. Then I moved from my house to theirs to look after
the store and the house. Later Cheo came out and we moved back to the house
again. And in 1953 Noél was born. For that delivery a brother in the faith,
Benjamín, was the one who went to find the midwife. At that time there was none
in the barrio, and he brought her from Paso Seco. When Pablín set out for Korea,
afterward he sent Elí from there $65 a month with which we added two rooms to
the house, because we were already quite uncomfortable. But that was a sad period
in the house for the lack of him.

In this period of time, from the year 1945 till today, I have lived more tran- 33
quilly. Although during this time I suffered twice from a sickness which at the outset seemed dangerous, it was only a simple infection of a gland in the prostate. And
regarding my situation now, it is much better. For example, Carmen sews and from
what she earns she buys clothes for the [younger] children and at times she buys
them for Blanca, and even for us ourselves. Also Pablín at times helps out. In those

other [earlier] years they were not able to help me and I had to supply everything. And regarding the benefits of the church, I am very appreciative. For example, my girls are at home and even the littlest ones are being taught good precepts, to keep them far from juvenile delinquency, and to have respect for God. So that all this has come to be a great help to me. I feel more serene. I do not live a life as desperate as it was in the years before. And also, I earn a little more. In short any problem I have now I can resolve better.

These statements raise many questions. The individuals to whom Taso refers, 34 the half-explained events, the jobs held and lost, the place names, politics, union activities, religion, children—as Taso elaborates his story in later chapters these things become more significant and familiar. Many of the basic events are immediately understandable. But he refers only in passing to his conversion, and this event emerges as of profound importance in the later interviews. He says hardly anything of the children, except to mention their problems in school and the help they come to give him. Again, it turns out that the children—nine living, three dead—are of crucial emotional importance to him. And there is very little about his wife, with whom he has worked out a highly successful relationship at the cost of great suffering to them both. These are all things Taso deals with in later talks. They are highly personal matters, the stuff of one man's life. At this point, the lens through which they may be examined increases in magnification and narrows in scope.

■ *Questions for* . . . The Life and Times of Don Taso, Puerto Rico Sugar Cane Worker by Sidney Mintz

Words to Note

coastal	azures	sere vegetation
paralleling	linking	conspicuous
picturesqueness	thatched	littered
patched	dissolves	ramshackle lean-tos
clusters	*colonias*	municipality
aggregation	barracks	ruined shell
hacienda	warehouse	tamarinds
string	standpipes	electrified
shutters	tendrils	machetes
glittering	tangible	winch operators
ditchers	gang bosses	toting
corrugated	abate	toylike
wholesome	chokes off	billowing
menial	sinecures	sterile
stagnant	panorama	retrospect
chronology		

Language

1. Take a look at Mintz's language in the opening section. The coastal plain is an "irregular green ribbon." There are "coconut husks" on the ground, "ramshackle lean-tos" behind the houses, and so on. Mintz is an anthropologist, but his first five pages read like a passage from a novel. Shouldn't a social scientist show more reserve? Won't his objectivity be called into question if he doesn't?
2. How would you characterize Don Taso's vocabulary?

Style

1. Compare and contrast Mintz's style and Don Taso's style. Look at the words they choose, how they phrase their sentences, the tones they affect, and how they organize their thoughts. What do their styles reveal about them?
2. What is Don Taso's tone? Why?

Development and Organization

1. Mintz, like Shostak, provides a frame, then gives us a translated transcript of an interview. On the other hand, Stack works her interview material into her analysis of family life. Which approach do you prefer?
2. How does Mintz organize his opening description of Jauca? Why does he begin with a distant view of it from the air?
3. What has Don Taso left out of his life history?

Discussion and Journal Writing

1. How does Don Taso mark time? How do you mark time?
2. Mintz, Shostak, and Stack could have put the information they gathered in their interviews into their own words, which would have enabled them to edit, condense, and cover more ground more quickly. Instead, they prefer to give us the words of the people they interviewed. Why do anthropologists place such a premium on the literal transcripts of the interviews they conduct?
3. Is Mintz passing any judgments on Don Taso's way of life?

ooooo

Those Winter Sundays

—Robert Hayden

Robert Hayden, a Black Southerner who grew up during the reign of Jim Crow, published many volumes of poetry, became Poet Laureate at the Library of Congress, and taught English at the University of Michigan. "Those Winter Sundays," a brooding on his father's contribution to his family, is representative of his work.

Sundays too my father got up early   1
and put his clothes on in the blueblack cold,
then with cracked hands that ached
from labor in the weekday weather made
banked fires blaze. No one ever thanked him.

I'd wake and hear the cold splintering, breaking,   6
when the rooms were warm, he'd call,
and slowly I would rise and dress,
fearing the chronic angers of that house,

Speaking indifferently to him,   10
who had driven out the cold
and polished my good shoes as well.
What did I know, what did I know
of love's austere and lonely offices?

■ *Questions for* . . . **Those Winter Sundays** by Robert Hayden

Words to Note

blueblack cold	cracked hand	ached
banked	blaze	splintering
rise		chronic angers
love's austere and lonely offices		

Language

1. What's the difference between *cold* and *blueblack cold?*
2. In line 4, why doesn't Hayden use *work* instead of *labor?*

Style

1. How does Hayden vary sentence length for effect?
2. Why does Hayden repeat himself in line 13? Read the line as Hayden wrote it; then read it, eliminating the repetition. What's the difference?

Development and Organization

1. Who is speaking? When? About what? What does Hayden's handling of time add to the poem?
2. What does the speaker tell us about his father? In what order? Is it enough?

Discussion and Journal Writing

1. What are the chronic angers of the house? Do most houses have them?
2. What are love's austere and lonely offices?
3. How old is the speaker of the poem? How do we know? How does our knowledge of the speaker's age shade the poem?
4. Do we know the speaker's family by the end of the poem?

ooooo

Southern Princess

—Sallie Bingham

Sallie Bingham, of the Louisville, Kentucky Binghams, a family of media moguls, is a playwright, freelance writer and philanthropist. With her inherited wealth, she endowed a center for women's writing in Louisville, which publishes *The American Voice.* "Southern Princess," taken from her autobiography, *Passion and Prejudice,* is an account of the Bingham family's morning routines when she was a girl, including the movements and duties of the servants. There is a choreography of privilege implicit in this seemingly simple piece of writing.

On mornings when I did not get up before the other dozen or so people in the house, Lizzie Baker, the oldest of the four black servants, would come in to wake me. Rocking across my room on short, bent feet, she would go to the windows and crank open the wooden shutters.

In wintertime, Lizzie would strike a match to the coal fire in my grate. Then I would lie for a few more minutes, listening to the crackle of burning paper and kindling, the sharp burst as a lump of coal split and caught.

Breakfast was served to the three older children in what had once been the servants' dining room, a small room, tall as a well, next to the kitchen. On one wall hung a ghostly picture of a female figure, barefooted and draped in green, sitting astride what appeared to be the world. She sat in an attitude of mourning, her head bowed on a lyre. Years later, I learned to my surprise that the picture, by Elihu Vedder, was titled "Hope."

Breakfast was large and hot. Sometimes there were steaming griddle cakes, corn cakes, or large, doughy pancakes with syrup, sometimes stiffening scrambled eggs, broiled tomatoes and sausages, or the dreaded white calf's brains. When brains were served, my brother Worth refused to eat them, which meant he had to sit at the table while the brains congealed on his plate. I later learned, with considerable awe, that he had disposed of the problem by dumping the brains into the table drawer.

After breakfast, I would go up to my parents' bedroom, at the end of a long corridor on the second floor. Mother would be sitting up in the bed with the dipping-swan headposts, wearing a lace-bedecked bed jacket, often one made by her mother, whom we called Munda, in Richmond, Virginia. The snowy blanket cover with its satin binding and broad satin monogram lay evenly over her legs and feet; the breakfast tray, beside her on the cover, was set with flowered linen and china and what seemed to be an abstemious feast: a boiled egg, quite runny, and a bit of toast.

Across the room, Father, wearing his city trousers, shirt, and shoes and a sort of loose at-home jacket, was consuming more substantial fare.

Each parent had a complete morning newspaper. I could tell from the way the sections were separated and the pages folded back that these newspapers were to be read, cover to cover, as it were, not merely glanced at and tossed aside. Almost before I learned to speak, I understood that we, as a family, were responsible for every word in those newspapers, including the comics and the advertisements.

After 1950, Father also owned a television station, one of the first to receive a license in this country. From his father, the Judge, he had inherited a radio station and a printing company. But these other enterprises were seldom mentioned when I was a child. Instead, the newspapers, but especially the morning *Courier-Journal,* were the topic of much intense and mysterious conversation. I did not understand that there had been a time when the family had not owned the state's only newspapers, a time of smaller, more private concerns. It seemed to me that we *were* the newspapers, collectively, and that our kinship to their pages was so close it could not be questioned or discussed.

I seldom understood the conversations I heard between my parents about the   9
issues of the day; they seemed to speak in a foreign tongue, with shrugs and frowns
and telling pauses. I did not dare to ask questions which would reveal my ignorance. I remember my acute embarrassment when I asked, at ten or eleven, for the
meaning of "yellow-dog journalism"; no answer was forthcoming, only what I
interpreted as shocked silence. How could any member of the family know so little
about our parents' consuming passion?

For years, I associated the newspapers with those early-morning scenes in my   10
parents' bedroom rather than with the building, which took up a block in
Louisville, or with the staff or the readers, all of whom remained remote. People
spent their lives working "downtown" for "us," but what they actually *did* remained
elusive. The newspapers' readers were represented by the drunken Saturday-night
callers who raised hell with Father about editorials they considered liberal or even
radical—or about wedding announcements that omitted a crucial detail.

He never complained about these intrusions, always taking the calls himself   11
and listening resignedly. It seemed to me that he and all of us were supposed to be
teaching the people of our rural, impoverished state how they ought to think and be.
We were all meant to provide shining examples.

In elementary school I provided no example at all. I was a clown, and not a   12
very successful one. I was still trying to find my way between my parents' rules
about correct behavior and my classmates' leisurely pursuit of pleasure: candy, ice
cream, radio serials, ruffled dresses—all forbidden to me.

Coming home in the afternoon was coming back to silence and enchantment.   13
Sometimes Curtis Madison, our carpenter, handyman, and chauffeur, would drive
the station wagon full of little girls home. Once, we threw his black visored cap out
of the window. He stopped the car without a word and went back to get it.

If one of the mothers was driving the children home, I studied the back of her   14
neck, where pale or dark hair curled or twined. I did not understand why an adult
would permit herself to be enslaved by such a routine; I could not imagine, though,
what these women did with the rest of their time. Mother's life seemed far more
interesting, if equally mysterious.

She was usually at home or traveling somewhere with Father. He was usually   15
at work downtown at the newspapers or he was traveling, sometimes without
Mother. I did not question what Father did; he was gone, like all other fathers, from
early morning until evening. I wondered about Mother because she was present, yet
slightly withdrawn, like a figure in the brocade.

At times, she would appear, vigorously and suddenly, in the middle of our   16
lives; on our nurse's day off, she took over our routine until we were old enough to
manage on our own. Sometimes she would read "Peter Rabbit" or sing folk songs,
accompanying herself on the piano.

I see her now in several settings. One was her study at the top of the house,   17
where she often sat at a desk heaped with papers—letters, bills, speeches. She had a
filing system for her five children and could find report cards and test results quick-

ly. The rest of her paperwork, I assumed, concerned the outside world. She had many projects and served on committees, and all of this meant mail and time spent dealing with it.

Later I learned that she believed passionately in improving education, both 18 locally and nationally, and served on committees which strove to find ways to deal with the collapse of standards, the declining reading scores, the removal first of Latin and then of all foreign languages from our high school curriculum. She believed in reading as a moral force, a way to shape character, and felt that the world provided too many alternatives to good books, alternatives that came to include radio and television. Intent on getting books into the hands of the underprivileged, she organized Kentucky's first bookmobiles, which carried reading material into the remote Appalachian hollows. Later, she would turn her great energy to the cause of conservation, saving the beautiful green fields along the Ohio River from development. All of these concerns kept her desk piled high with mail, and the desk itself became, for me, one of her attributes—that and a spray of lilies.

In good weather, she spent the afternoon in a garden, a formal rectangle below 19 the tennis court. Here her battle was unending with weeds, pests, disappointing perennials, moles, dogs, and the unhandy help of Luebell, the black man who worked outside. The garden seemed pesky and demanding, and I resented its intrusions, yet I also knew that she was possessed by it, delighted by it, and that she rendered up its fruits—the splendid bouquets that adorned the Big House—as proof of her individuality, her talent, and her bone-breaking labor.

I did not see the results of Father's work, except as they were represented by 20 the newspapers. Nor did I expect to. Crises sometimes loomed behind the grownups' talk; sometimes Father would have to rush into town. But it was all, to me, insubstantial, imaginary. The real work of the world was done by Mother, in her garden, and by the five other people who tended our lives.

We called them the servants, yet they were never, by any stretch of the imagi- 21 nation, servants. They were sharply marked and to some extent unpredictable individuals who were spending their lives with us, for reasons that seemed to me to have more to do with companionship among themselves than with the fat envelopes of cash that were brought out of town every Friday. I was too young to be aware of their lack of choice. Instead, I noticed the dense, colorful fabric of their lives, which was only partly visible to me. They kept their secrets. In fact, they hoarded and delighted in them.

Cordie, in the kitchen, was taciturn about her special rituals. Her big black 22 stove was always covered with boiling pots and pans, the ovens going full blast to prepare a company dinner. Before those occasions I would see her going over an elaborate recipe, her finger underlining the words, her lips moving. Sometimes, in the afternoons, she could be found half dozing in her big wooden armchair; her feet rose out of her flat slippers like loaves. I knew she had a family up the road and had lost one son to the river.

Ollie Madison, rake thin in her candy-striped uniform, took care of the 23 upstairs. I would see her on her knees, scrubbing out one of the bathtubs, or jerking off sheets. Often I would hear her shouting for her husband, Curt, fighting the furnace in the bowels of the house.

Curt himself spent most of his time in the basement, where in winter he tend- 24
ed the enormous coal furnace; when he opened its door, a malevolent red eye of fire glared out. Near the furnace, he had set up a large, crowded workshop where he repaired broken furniture. He knew where each tool lay in the confusion. Once he copied an ornate French bureau for Mother, so perfectly no one could tell which was the original. I had heard that he had been a soldier in the First World War and had gone to France, but he never mentioned it.

The doyenne of the household was Lizzie Baker, who seemed unimaginably 25
old to me. She still wore the white turban of an earlier age, the white uniform and the long white apron. She had strong views on the family and now and then would let slip fascinating hints about our shared past. She had known Father as a child and claimed the special prerogative of that lost intimacy. She had known his older brother and sister, my Uncle Robert and Aunt Henrietta, too, and told stories about them with a submerged chuckle.

Our indoor life was organized and dominated by our nurse, who had been 26
hired just before I was born. Her name was Lucy Cummings, but we called her Nursie (spelled in various ways by various children) and loved her devotedly. She was a large, firm woman who meted out judgments and affection impartially. My two older brothers were already nearly beyond her when I was born, and so she focused her love on me.

Nursie had fallen into a fire as a small child, and the lower half of her face 27
was glazed with pinkish scars. A dent in her bottom lip was the result, she told me, of biting her mouth closed to keep out the flames. People stared at her, but we did not think she looked strange. Her square, strong hands, covered with freckles, could do everything. On one hand, she wore a braided gold friendship ring and a stout watch. She also proudly wore, when she dressed up, a small gold brooch from which hung a heart for each of us five children. Mother had given it to her.

Her sure sense of justice was the rock on which I leaned. There was a right 28
and a wrong in every situation, as she viewed it, and she could usually come up with a proverb to support her position: "A stitch in time saves nine"; "Take care of the pennies and the pounds will take care of themselves"; "Pretty is as pretty does." Her hand could smack hard on an offender's rear end, but she always offered a lap, an embrace, a quick kiss at the end of the day, expressions of an affection never lessened by our bad behavior. She knew how to dip fall leaves in paraffin to preserve their colors, how to soak pine cones in a chemical that caused them to burn green when used as kindling, how to mend and iron doll clothes, cut out valentines, and dye Easter eggs.

Our birthday parties were her greatest accomplishment. The table would be 29
decked with homemade baskets of candy, hats, and streamers; she even made costumes of crepe paper, covered with ruffles. One Halloween, she dressed up as a witch in Mother's old academic gown and allowed the little girls to be frightened of

her. She was always with us, except on Thursdays, her day off, when she would sometimes take one of us into town to visit her mother, a gaunt, terrifying old countrywoman whose failing health was a problem we all shared.

Sometimes Nursie fell asleep in the evening when I was sitting on her lap. I 30 had never before seen anyone exhausted from hard work. The black servants divided up their tasks among them and moved slowly, without urgency. But Nursie had no helper, unless she could dragoon one of us. I knew she was paid for her labor, but I also knew this was the least of it; she worked so hard because she loved us fiercely, yet with a sense, always, that we were not and would never be hers.

She taught us well, impressing on us the fact that life is hard, even for children 31 of privilege.

■ *Questions for . . .* **Southern Princess** by Sallie Bingham

Words to Note

crank	crackle	kindling
monogram	glanced	tossed
kinship	shrugs	frowns
acute	yellow-dog journalism	remote
intrusions	enchantment	visored
brocade	Appalachian hollows	spray of lilies
loomed	glared	ornate
doyenne	dragoon	children of privilege

Language

1. Bingham says Lizzie Baker was the "doyenne" of the household. What are *doyenne's* synonyms? Would any of them work better than *doyenne* in this sentence?
2. In the fifth paragraph, Bingham says her mother wore a "lace-bedecked bed jacket, often one made by her mother, whom we called Munda, in Richmond, Virginia." Why does she use *whom* instead of *who?* Would *who* be correct? According to whom?

Style

1. What do all the commas Bingham uses tell us about her sentence style?
2. In paragraph 24, she writes, "Curt himself spent most of his time in the basement, where in winter he tended the enormous coal furnace; when he opened its door, a malevolent red eye of fire glared out." Bingham is quite descriptive. Do you like the way she describes people, places, and things?

Development and Organization

1. Does this piece contain enough detail so that you could provide someone with a basic description of the Bingham mansion?
2. How does Bingham organize this description of her family? What ideas or themes does she use to knit her impressions together? Is it well organized?
3. We learn more about some of the servants than we do about Bingham's father. Do you think Bingham just forgot to say enough about him, or is the oversight intentional?

Discussion and Journal Writing

1. Is Lizzie Baker, the oldest of the four Black servants, part of the family? How about Lucy Cummings, also known as Nursie? Bingham writes of Nursie, "I knew she was paid for her labor, but I also knew this was the least of it; she worked so hard because she loved us fiercely, yet with a sense, always, that we were not and would never be hers." Should we take Bingham's words at face value?
2. Who makes breakfast? Where do the parents eat breakfast? The children? How is this scenario different from a typical breakfast in the life of a mid-dle-class family?
3. Often poor families in America are faulted for spending so little time with their children. In some cases, both parents work, and the children are called "latch-key" kids; in others, the fathers are absent. The Binghams don't seem to spend much time with their children, yet few would accuse them of neglect. Is it hypocritical to hold the families of one class to a standard and not the families of another class? Or, are there important differences, like the servants, that explain the different perceptions?

ooooo

*F*amily Document Three

Wedding Announcement

A.W. Stewart and M. L. Kaplan To Wed

Dr. and Mrs. Sheldon Kaplan of Boston have announced September wedding plans for their daughter, Martha Lee Kaplan, and Dr. Andrew Winslow Stewart, a son of Mr. and Mrs. Edward P. Stewart of Washington.

Ms. Kaplan graduated cum laude from Brown University and received a law degree from Columbia University. She is a lawyer at the Housing Litigation Bureau of the New York City Department of Housing Preservation and Development. Her father is a psychiatrist and a professor of psychiatry at Tufts University.

Dr. Stewart graduated summa cum laude from Amherst College, where he was elected to Phi Beta Kappa, and received an M.D. from Columbia University. He is a first-year resident in psychiatry at the New York Hospital–Cornell Medical Center. His father, who is retired, was one of the founding partners of Stewart and Burnham Associates, a lobbying concern in Washington.

■ *Questions for* . . . Wedding Announcement

Discussion and Journal Writing

1. Why are weddings announced at all? Why are they announced in newspapers like the *New York Times?*
2. Where and how else are weddings announced? What's emphasized in the other kinds of announcements you know? What's emphasized in this announcement?

*F*amily Album Three

Wedding Album

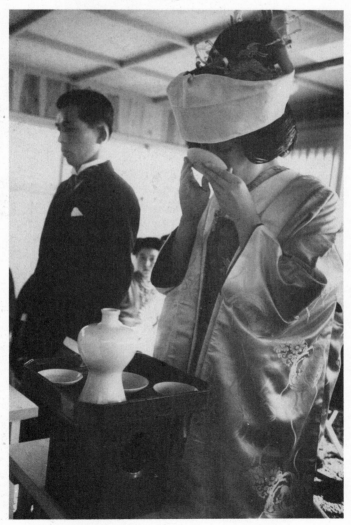

Japan *(Werner Bischof, Magnum Photos)*

Czechoslovakia *(Robert Capa, Magnum Photos)*

■ *Questions for* . . . Wedding Album

Discussion and Journal Writing

1. Compare and contrast these wedding photographs. How much culture can
   you see?

ooooo

✖ Expository Writing: Anthropology's Comparative Approach

The writers in this chapter are concerned with family customs, cultural values and ideas, and theories about them. They describe people, places, and things and use anecdotes, but these essays, with the exception of Bingham's "Southern Princess" and Robert Hayden's "Those Winter Sundays," are not fundamentally descriptive or narrative. They do not move from one detail or event to the next; they present a sequence of ideas that supports a central idea, proposition, or argument.

The contrast between the language of this chapter and that of the first two chapters makes the same point in a different way. The words cited in the "Words to Note" sections of the first two chapters are concrete, vivid, and evocative: *canopy, stairway to the plains, flinched,* and *skittering.* Here, diction is somewhat more abstract, analytical, and defining: *universal, matrifocal, aggregation, adaptive strategy,* and *children of privilege.* The language is different because the type of writing is different. These essays, as well as the essays in the next three chapters and most of the essays you will be asked to write in college, are *expository,* which comes from Latin words that mean "to set forth." In expository essays, writers set forth one point after another as they develop their main ideas, arguments, or theories.

Before continuing, it's important to dispel a few myths about the various types of writing. Expository writing is not superior to or harder than descriptive and narrative writing. Quite a bit of the most profound and moving writing is narrative and descriptive. The types of writing are simply different vehicles of expression: each is challenging, and each, in talented hands, is capable of sounding the depths and inspiring awe. Nor are the types distinct from one another: there are often patches of description in a piece of narrative or expository writing and so on.

You may be more familiar with description and narration because we share stories and descriptions of people and things every day. Arguments, issues, and theories are rarer fare for most mortals. However, familiarity with an approach doesn't automatically make one good at it. To get good at any type of writing, really good, takes study and practice, especially practice. End of sermon.

Description and narration are shot through with ideas, themes, points of view, and tones, but the primary purpose of expository writing is to put ideas on the page. Some expository writers are simply interested in explaining ideas; others want to persuade readers to believe in their ideas. Regardless of the writer's intent, expository writing, more than any other kind of writing, makes a point.

Kluckhohn's point, for instance, is that the concept of culture is crucial to understanding human behavior and has the explanatory importance of evolution in biology, gravity in physics, and disease in medicine. In "Shakespeare in the Bush," Bohannan proves that even a story as powerful and widely known as *Hamlet* is couched in particular customs and values that make it hard for those outside Hamlet's cultural circle to understand or even follow his story. Stack argues that the kin networks of poverty-stricken Black citizens of The Flats are a creative way of coping with poverty and racism.

Mintz is less contentious: though he criticizes the exploitative situation U.S.-owned sugar conglomerates impose on the work force of rural Puerto Rico, he is primarily concerned with explaining Don Taso's way of life. Bingham is less contentious still: she is simply interested in explaining the domestic arrangements of an upper-class Southern family.

All these writers use patches of narrative and descriptive writing to explain, illustrate, flesh out, and back up their ideas. Marjorie Shostak, in her explanation of !Kung marriage customs, describes the coals that are brought from the fires of the bride's and the groom's families to start a new fire in front of the marriage hut. To show how incest taboos vary from one culture to another, Clyde Kluckhohn tells about asking a non-Navaho teacher, who has been working at a Navaho school, how she would feel about getting into bed with her brother. She has just told him that she was impatient with two Navaho students who wouldn't dance with one another. She goes off in a huff, missing the point that dancing with a clan brother or sister is just as taboo for the Navaho as sleeping with a brother would be for her. Sidney Mintz describes the cane fields that surround Jauca to help us understand the difficulty of the work Don Taso does; and Carol Stack, quoting from her field notes, includes Ruby Banks's account of the goods, services, and money she shares with her mother, Magnolia Waters.

Mina Shaughnessy, probably the most perceptive critic to examine how writing is taught at American colleges, believes that writing in all academic fields boils down to seven basic patterns, which she poses as a series of propositions. The first two are narrative and descriptive; the last five are expository:

- This is what happened.
- This is the look (sound, smell, or feel) of something.
- This is like (or unlike) this.
- This (may have, probably, certainly) caused this.
- This is what ought to be done.
- This is what someone said.
- This is my opinion (or interpretation) of what someone said.

Everyone is familiar with these patterns. In everyday conversation, people compare musicians, commercial brands, movies, politicians, and plans; they tell others what someone said and what they think was meant by it; they argue about what should have been done or what ought to be done; and they explain what or who caused what.

In books, articles, and essays, Shaughnessy's propositions can be used to classify the different patterns of exposition; being aware of them can help a reader follow the thread of a writer's argument. More importantly, these propositions are writing strategies. Writers use them, sometimes consciously, sometimes subconsciously, to explore their topics, to brainstorm, research, organize, define, and present their ideas.

As I noted earlier, anthropology is comparative by nature, and anthropological writing demonstrates Shaughnessy's third proposition: This is like (or unlike) this. Anthropologists study the world's cultures and the subcultures of more complex societies. They expose us to other ways of life, which deepen our understanding of our own cultural values and patterns—if we read with an open mind. Because cultural studies are comparative by nature, this chapter's writing assignment is comparative.

✿ Writing Workshop

The Topic: Differences in marriage customs across cultures

The Assignment: Compare and contrast marriage among the !Kung with marriage as you know it in the United States.

Get out your journal or a few sheets of paper if you're not keeping a journal, and freewrite about the topic for approximately 15 minutes. Think on the page, let the pen follow your thoughts. Don't worry about writing something someone else will be able to understand. The purpose is to use the momentum of sentences and the associative power of words to call up other words for the purpose of getting as many ideas on the page as possible. Don't worry about word choice, paragraphing, spelling, sentence structure, or grammar. Remember, freewriting's one rule is that you keep writing, even if you have to repeat a phrase or a sentence from time to time. Keep the pen moving. Later, read what you've written, and underline the words, phrases, and sentences you might want to use.

For the next class, bring in some wedding photographs, preferably of a wedding you attended, and discuss them within a group of classmates. Take notes as you talk. How are people dressed? Why? What role did the bride's family play? The groom's? Did friends play a role? Where did it take place? Was there a reception? How did the bride and groom meet? Did both families approve? Why or why not? Was approval an issue? Is the couple from similar backgrounds? Where do they live? Do they both work? Doing what? Do they have children? Who is raising them? Are they regularly involved with their families?

If your classmates are from different backgrounds, you may find that you are having a difficult time agreeing about what constitutes marriage, American-style. American society is complex and marriage may differ from class to class, religion to religion, and ethnic group to ethnic group. You may want to write about a specific type of American marriage group. You may want to frame your points broadly enough so they apply to the entire society, if that's possible.

If you feel you still don't have enough material about American marriages, you may want to construct a questionnaire and interview a number of people. Take careful notes if you want to quote the people you interview. You may even want to use a tape recorder, but bear in mind that the more complicated the interviewing process becomes, the more time it will consume. The majority of your time should be spent writing and rewriting your essay.

Now, discuss the !Kung marriage customs; make sure that you touch on the same issues you discussed when considering American marriage. In a comparative paper, there must be a basis of comparison. Comparing the wedding rituals of the !Kung with childrearing practices in the United States would only produce confusion.

Study your notes and your freewriting, and try to decide which points you want to include. Don't overdo it; keep the length of the paper in mind. You may find it helpful to draw up two lists: one of the features the two cultures have in common, and one of the differences. In a sentence or two, try to jot down the point of the paper. If it hasn't come to you yet, it probably will as you go along. But remember, without some conclusion or observation, your paper will be nothing more than a confederation of loosely related paragraphs. Your main point is what gives the paper its sense of unity and direction.

Next, write the first draft. Some writers, after they have introduced their topic, cover the first subject (in this case, the marriage customs of one culture), then move on to the second (marriage customs of another culture). Others move back and forth from one subject to the other, covering the same aspect of each subject. Some mix the two approaches. Anything will work as long as you write about the same aspect of both subjects and guide the reader with transitional and connective words, phrases, and sentences.

As you are writing, try not to pause too long to fret about grammar, punctuation, spelling, and word choice. Mark words you're not sure of and look them up in a dictionary or a thesaurus after you have finished your draft. Read your draft aloud and rework any sentences that are difficult to follow or choppy. You may want to combine short sentences, divide long ones, or rephrase sentences that are indirect. Test whatever changes you make with your voice. Check the organization of your paragraphs, too. Perhaps rearranging them will make it easier for the reader to follow your thoughts.

Check grammar and punctuation. Writers tend to make the same kinds of mistakes until they get the error at the root. Look at your instructor's corrections on your previous papers, review the principles your errors involved, and proofread. If you have trouble with pronouns, check every pronoun for agreement; make sure its antecedent is clear. If you write run-ons, check the intersections of your sentences, and so on.

Now, exchange papers with a classmate, read, and discuss. You may want to read one another's drafts aloud or silently, making comments as you go. The advantage to reading aloud is that you can hear where your words, phrases, and sentences themselves don't provide the emphasis you intended. As you discuss one another's work, it's a good idea to have a handbook and a dictionary handy. If you read one another's papers in class, call your instructor over to referee when you're not sure or disagree about a point of grammar, punctuation, or phrasing. Pay especially close attention to any sentence or point that your classmate has a hard time understanding. If you agree with your classmate's judgment, try to come up with concrete ideas for revision while you're discussing your paper.

Rewrite by polishing, explaining, moving, rephrasing and tightening, correcting errors, and checking the spelling and definitions of words you're not sure of. Professional writers as a species would never think of submitting a first draft—only novices do that; professionals put their writing through several drafts, making substantial change with each draft because they have learned that insight and inspiration come on the installment plan. Some passages go, new passages come. Take chances when you revise.

Additional Writing Exercises

- Interview a classmate, friend, or acquaintance from a different cultural background about bringing up children. Compare your experience with hers or his.
- Read the rest of Shostak's book and compare and contrast divorce among the !Kung with divorce, American-style.
- Compare marriage as you know it with marriage as some other ethnic, racial, regional, religious, or economic group in America knows it. Despite the differences, is it possible to generalize about marriage in America?

Chapter 4

The Family, Past Tense

■

Family History

Antonio Gramsci, the Italian political theorist and historian who did most of his writing in Mussolini's jails, remarked in a famous essay called "Americanism and Fordism" that a new age requires a new man. I once observed in a lecture on the French Revolution's cultural program that a new man requires a new pair of pants (the *Sans Culottes* notwithstanding). In the present context, we can tame that wisecrack into a more serious observation: A new age requires a new family.

John Demos explains in "The American Family Then and Now," which is included in this chapter, that the families he studied in Plymouth Colony performed many functions that have been taken over by modern industry and corporations and the state. Families served as businesses, schools, vocational institutes, churches, houses of correction, welfare institutions, hospitals, orphanages, and poorhouses; these mid-seventeenth-century families were much more self-sufficient than today's families living in or near big cities around the world. Most of the Plymouth Colony families were farming families. Neither parent *went to work;* they worked at home—preparing food and making household necessities, such as candles and soap—and on the land around the home—hunting, farming, and gathering wood. Children worked alongside their parents from an early age, and parents were expected to instruct their children in the fundamentals of reading, writing, arithmetic, and religion.

The families of Plymouth Colony tended to have more children than their contemporary, urban counterparts; farming families worldwide, prior to the advent of tractors and other labor-saving machines, placed a premium on having enough "hands" to help with the work. However, Plymouth Colony families were essentially nuclear—parents and their children—although they expanded and contracted as circumstances required. For instance, colonists convicted of crimes were sentenced to live with and work for families in the community; orphans and infirm elderly were taken in by relatives or other families in the area. Emmanuel Le Roy Ladurie, the French historian who helped elevate the family as a subject of serious historical study to the level of the battlefield and the political arena, comes to a similar conclusion in his study of thirteenth-century farm families in southern France: families, which were typically nuclear, sometimes became *extended* (more than two generations living in the same house), and sometimes became *truncated* (two generations with only one parent). In Europe and America, with the important exception of certain Native American tribes, the extended family was never the norm; it is a myth we tell ourselves about the good old days. It is true that the postindustrial family has contracted, but chiefly that means urban families have fewer children, not fewer live-in grandparents and great-grandparents.

Incidentally, the postindustrial father's absence from the home is exactly what the poet Robert Bly has been lamenting on talk shows and in his book, *Iron John,* an excerpt of which appears in chapter 6. For Bly, the social institutions that have taken fathers out of the house to work, and hence away from their sons, have made it much harder for boys to become men. For Aldous Huxley, the British essayist and novelist, the institutionalization of family life, including the conception, gestation, birth, and automated nursing of babies in state-tooled squads, is a savage aspect of his futuristic nightmare, *Brave New World.*

Demos's overview applies to the other preindustrial families included in this chapter. Peter Laslett's English baker family in "The World We Have Lost"—father, mother, children, maidservants, apprentices, and journeymen (all thirteen or fourteen of them)—lived and worked together in a house that was also the bakery. The children learned their parents' trade, working alongside them at home, and the apprentices were answerable to their master as children in that society were answerable to their parents: they agreed to keep their master's secrets, obey his commands, and accept correction. In 1619, this family's finances appeared in a petition London bakers submitted to increase the bread prices: the cost of clothing and the children's education, in addition to the cost of flour, yeast, and coal, was factored into the cost of a loaf of bread; there was no line drawn between the finances of home and the finances of work.

At about the same time, the rural West Africans that Nathan Huggins writes about in "African Beginnings: The Seamless Web" were leading family-oriented lives. The polygynous family compounds of the Bambura, the Yoruba, the Ibo, and the Mandinka tribes were the centers of life. Children were born, raised, schooled, and apprenticed to their parents chiefly within the walls of the compound. Food was gathered, prepared, and eaten there; rituals were celebrated, palm wine poured, the ceremonial kola nut cracked. A family farmed and hunted the land around its compound; it settled its own disputes, sometimes enlisting the wisdom, authority, and assistance of the clan or tribe.

In the countryside of Puerto Rico a few hundred years later, Gerán Malánguez of Edward Rivera's "Antecedentes" supports his family with what he is able to grow on the miserable plot of land his mean-spirited father-in-law, Gigante Hernández, gives him for a wedding present. From time to time, Gigante tosses Gerán a handout from his *finca* (farm). It is more an act of hostility than charity, but the point is that the fictional Hernández and Malánguez families work the land that is outside their front doors.

Later on in *Family Installments,* the episodic novel the story is drawn from, the Malánguezes move to New York City, "the hot-dog, pizza capital of the world," and encounter most of the institutions that, according to Demos, have become involved in a family's affairs: welfare, wage labor (in a corrupt and prejudiced job market), and parochial and public education systems. They also experience the ideal (and a little bit of the reality) of generational mobility: the Malánguez boys do not work alongside their father Gerán on the family *finca* in Spanish Harlem. Of course, there are no *fincas* in Spanish Harlem. Instead, Mr. Malánguez takes the subway to Brooklyn each morning where he works at the American Carpet Company for starvation wages, which he supplements with welfare checks; and his sons walk down the block to Saint Miseria's, the Catholic school they attend.

This reorientation, or better still, disorientation of family life, plus the discrimination the Malánguezes encounter, is part of the culture shock they experience. Within the last one hundred years, most American families have undergone similar transitions, whether they migrated from America's farms and small towns to its big cities or emigrated from other countries. Barney Pace's essay "Grandpatrimony" is about the misunderstandings and tensions that run through immigrant family life. The larger, historical point, however, is that the family changes Demos records took place within the context of a demographic shift from the countryside to the world's cities, driven by the mechanization of farming and the rise of factories and office buildings. Talk to your *antecedentes,* your ancestors, or look into their lives. Go back a few generations, and you will find, with a few exceptions, that some of the same themes run through your family's history.

In the American popular imagination, the family stands for tradition: a conduit of values and customs, it is each American's personal connection to the past. Family can be those things, but it is not impervious to change. It's exciting, intriguing, and unsettling that so much of what we take for granted about family life is fairly new.

The family itself, as a central topic, is new to the field of history. During the past few hundred years in the West, the study of history has been accompanied by debate about method—what historians look at and how they look at it. During the past 50 years, the debate has escalated into a fight. Traditionalists have insisted that we look at great leaders and events: Julius Caesar, the Battle of Actium, Charlemagne, Columbus, Queen Elizabeth I, the Sun King (King Louis XIV of France), the French and American revolutions, Lincoln, World War I, Stalin, Gandhi, Mao, Churchill, and so on. They say that what we need to know are the deeds and contributions of the big people and the causes and consequences of the big events. Social historians have argued that this approach gives us a skewed and elitist view of history and that we need to know more: in addition to battlefields, courts, and halls of state, there are arenas of change such as communities, workplaces, families, and the streets. They add that there have been less well known actors on the historical stage whose lives can teach us quite a bit about the past, such as a miller named Menocchio in fifteenth-century Italy who was called before the Inquisition or a shoemaker named George Hewes in revolutionary Boston. The traditionalists retort that there's nothing the lives of ordinary people can teach us that we need to know, an argument that raises more questions than it answers. And so, the debate continues to rage on campus and in print. Constructive results of this debate include the emergence of social history as a distinct field and the increased stature of the family as a topic of serious study and as a social institution with enormous explanatory power. The key point that emerges is that *interpretation* is and always will be at history's heart.

🎖 Word Play: Heritage

Heritage is a fascinating word that makes most people's eyes glaze over. It's the sort of word that the clergy, teachers, and politicians inflict on us in speeches, sermons, and lectures that are always too long. It's faded around the edges. It could use a dose of Geritol. It's vaguely red, white, and blue when it's used in its broadest sense.

Heritage comes to us from the Old French verb *heriter,* meaning "to inherit." William the Conqueror, initially *Duc de Normandie* and ultimately *Roi d'Angleterre,* brought quite a bit of French language, tastes, and customs with him when he defeated the English in the Battle of Hastings, 1066. In fact, French became the language of the English court and was still the court's lingua franca nearly two centuries later when Chaucer was writing. During that period, quite a bit of English's Latinate vocabulary was transmitted indirectly through French, one of Latin's lineal descendants. *Heriter* is a case in point: it is a descendant of the Latin verb *hereditare,* which is in turn an offspring of the Latin noun *heriditas,* making *heritage* a cousin of *inheritance, heritable, hereditament, heredity,* and *hereditary.*

Inheritance is one of *heritage*'s synonyms, but it applies more strictly to property, a trait, or a characteristic that is passed on to an heir. *Heritage*'s meaning overlaps with *inheritance,* but it also means the traditions, practices, customs, values, and cultures passed on to a later generation. *Birthright,* another synonym, describes in its strictest sense the property rights of a first-born son, although throughout history other children and relatives have appropriated the word's meaning. *Patrimony* is also narrower in meaning than *heritage,* pertaining as it does to an estate inherited from one's father. Some writers are fast and loose with *patrimonies* and *birthrights* and use them as equivalents of *heritage* in its broadest sense.

In America, *heritage* is an especially complicated word because it has overtones of ethnic identity, which is the stuff thin skins, raw nerves, defensive pride, and ethnic slurs are made of; yet it also means the cultural legacy of past generations, which we are relatively oblivious of or indifferent to, compared to more traditional and homogenous societies. We Americans have long thought of ourselves as a society of new prospects, possibilities, progress, and change—America having some kind of corner on the future, being a place of new inventions, styles, attitudes, dances, music, and so on. (I wore a new shirt just last year.) America's reality is, of course, much more complicated, but fortunately for me, *heritage* is the topic of this word essay.

Heritage doesn't play well in such an atmosphere, except as an idea that we intone and forget. It is not a conscious preoccupation of most Americans. There are organizations for the preservation of specific cultural heritages, such as the Daughters of the American Revolution, the Jewish Historical Society of New York, and the Italian-American Foundation, and American subcultures periodically go through "roots" renaissances, during which the dress, dance, music, foods, and language of pre-American ancestors are celebrated. Those organizations and cultural renaissances, however, wouldn't be necessary in a society that valued heritage and tradition more than we do. Furthermore, ethnic fashion and identity statements, such as windshield decals of the Italian flag and African-style hats, say more about the present than they do about the past. They are not devoid of heritage, but heritage isn't the point.

Journal Entry

One of the secondary meanings of *roots* acquired popularity in the late 1960s. Research it. What does it mean? How do people use it? Write about *roots.*

$\mathcal{R}$eadings

Antecedentes

—Edward Rivera

Edward Rivera was born in Orocovis, Puerto Rico, and grew up in New York City. Educated at parochial and public schools in Spanish Harlem, the City College of New York, and Columbia University, he currently teaches English at the City College Center for Worker Education. Most of the episodes of Edward Rivera's life are evident in his autobiographical novel *Family Installments;* "Antecedentes," the first chapter, is a sketch of the fictional family and their village before they make their trek northward to New York, "the hot-dog, pizza capital of the world."

My paternal grandfather, Xavier F. Alegría, itinerant schoolteacher, part-time 1 painter, poetaster, guitar-picker, and Mariolater, jammed a small gun in his mouth and opened fire on his upper jaw. He died slowly, a lousy shot, or the hapless owner of a rusty second-rate *pistola.* The hole in his palate was pretty big; the bullet lodged somewhere in his brain. He should have died right away, but the All Powerful refused to take him then and there. Instead, He let Abuelo Xavier hold on for weeks, putting him in a coma before finally cutting him loose.

Xavier F. Alegría starved himself dead when my father, Gerán, his third child 2 and second son, was barely five. That was Papi's version, and my mother's. Papi said it had been a common occurrence all over Puerto Rico—all over the world, as a matter of fact. Mami, who claimed she knew little about the world, said sardonically that there had been nothing unusual in Abuelo Xavier's crash-diet death. She said that 1919, the year it happened, had been a good year for meeting the All Merciful, but not an exceptional one. "I could tell you stories, Santos," she told me, "that would make the little hairs on your *fundillo* stand straight out."

In 1919 she had been a little over three years old. Poverty, she said, *la* 3 *pobreza,* had done a lot of good people in, and some bad ones, too; and she would rattle off the names of people she'd known in Bautabarro, our home village, people whose names and lives, like the names and lives of their parents and grandparents, would disappear when Mami's generation died off. The hilly village of Bautabarro had no chroniclers; illiteracy was high in those days, headstones a luxury. Besides, who would have had time to record all the comings and goings, the births and deaths? Who would have bothered? The people of Bautabarro were peasants, not history-minded, culture-conscious scribes. You died, and a few years later people forgot where you'd been buried. Only the town church recorded the day God had cut you loose, but our town church burned down several times and its records were pretty meager.

Bautabarro was deep in the mountain range called Cordillera Central (the   4
Rockies of Puerto Rico), an area of lush green landscape, a tangle of tropical weeds, smooth and hilly, precipitous and sloped, the monotony of greens relieved only by bald patches of soft red clay called *barro,* which is also the name for mud. The Bauta River, a squiggle on the map, trickles down from somewhere in the Cordillera past Bautabarro and, after coupling with the Toro Negro, flows into the Mar Caribe.

They got Xavier to a hospital somewhere, or to a village clinic, where some   5
local G.P. probably stuffed his mouth with cotton or gauze sopping with anesthesia until a big-town surgeon arrived, took a look at his mouth, probably whispered a few prayers over him, and pronounced him technically dead. God had played a dirty joke on him; dead and alive, a breathing mummy. My grandmother's family took him home. He himself had no relatives in town; the nearest kin lived twenty-five miles away in Ponce, but they had lost track of his existence, and he of theirs. He'd been a loner, something of a snob because his parents, it was said, had been Spaniards, and because he'd received a university education. Besides, he had been too busy teaching and painting and caring for his wife and children to make close friends. They locked him up in a bedroom, though this was unnecessary, since almost no villagers came to see him. A small group of Xavier's pupils came by one day, bringing flowers and poems they had written and illustrated themselves, but his in-laws kept them out of the room. Xavier, they explained, was *"muy grave,"* too ill to receive visitors, and the children left their gifts behind and never saw him alive again.

His in-laws waited on him day and night, kept the flies off his face, lit candles,   6
recited rosaries and other rituals, moaned and belted their breasts, and watched him die. And God for his part let him suffer on and on with that hole in his palate. How long? Not even my aunt Celita, the family gossip, could remember for sure. "A very long time," she would say. "An eternity."

He received spiritual first aid in large doses. Padre Solimán, an Irish mission-   7
ary from Nueva Jersey, was there every day, bringing prayers, blessed candles, and holy water. Xavier was his Michelangelo, after all, and an educated man. A good father, too, and a missionary when you came down to it. For what else was a travel-ing schoolteacher in those days of unpaved roads, firetrap schoolhouses, and beg-gar's wages? Toward the end he got Extreme Unction, that last-ditch sacrament. If you believed in that stuff, and who in those days didn't (Xavier perhaps?), then Xavier was on his way to paradise.

As a schoolteacher Xavier couldn't have earned much, a couple of *dolares* a   8 day, five at most. But that was a good deal more than his neighbors, subsistence farmers, or their peons, made. Besides, he was also a painter—of canvases, not houses. But who needed art in those hills? Who could afford it? He painted portraits, tropical landscapes, birds, still lifes, anything, everything, even church altars. The portraits and landscapes he sold to bourgeois types form Mayagüez or Ponce for next to nothing. He was prolific, the village Velázquez, but very formal. And self-taught. What he didn't or couldn't sell, he gave away to his pupils, neighbors, and admiring strangers. His neat wooden house was full of those portraits and landscapes. As for the religious art, Abuelo had not only designed the altar of the church he, his wife, three sons, and daughter worshiped and confessed their sins in, but decorated it as well: a large mural depicting angels in multicolored flowing gowns, puffed cheeks blowing celestial notes from golden horns and trumpets, pliant fingers plucking harps, and bow-lipped mouths choiring hallelujahs; a score of well-known saints from the comely Virgen María to Santa Bárbara Bendita, patron saint of lightning; and the apostles, all twelve of them; Nuestro Señor Jesucristo, a portrait of Xavier himself, with beard and long black hair thrown in for authenticity, a handsome man; and a touch of evil, too—smirking Judas, that *maricón* traitor, son of the world's great whore, scowling off by himself, clutching soiled silver coins in one hand, the other propping up his pointed chin, two long-nailed, crooked fingers pointing straight down—a symbol of something or other.

The altar and the mural had been commissioned by Padre Soliván. Abuelo had 9 been paid something—not much, but something. He wasn't starving. His children were fed, were possibly plump. They wore starched clothes; the boys got haircuts once a month in the town barbershop, next to the Sundial store, the Thom McAn of Bautabarro, where they replaced their worn-out shoes with the latest styles: patent leather, usually, with brass buckles.

Only a few months before Xavier's death, a "rare disease" (my mother's mys- 10 terious phrase) had knocked off his wife, Sara. According to Papi's cloudy recollections, she had been the perfect wife and mother, the kind Puerto Ricans, men and women, like to call "saint," meaning a docile daughter, a submissive wife, and a totally devoted mother. And a saint she died, though a little young to be leaving her husband and four children for a better life. At her funeral Soliván probably pointed out her youth. "She was only thirty-five, my children. *Una muchachita.* We must be ready for God's call from the day we're born. . . ." It's nine to one that he compared her to the Virgin Mary, after whose perfect life she had modeled her own.

After Xavier's death, Sara's parents adopted my father and his two brothers. 11 Papá Santos Malánquez was a poor hillbilly, a *jíbaro desgraciado,* and, said my father, who was his favorite, the kindest man he ever knew. Papá Santos was so good that whenever there wasn't enough food for everyone—and that was often— he used to steal chickens and vegetables from his neighbors. He always paid them back by doing favors, without letting them know the reason. This chicken-thief Robin Hood of Bautabarro was likely to deny himself a pair of badly needed pants or a straw hat (he worked all day in the sun) so that his three grandsons wouldn't have to walk around those hills looking like orphans. Which they did just the same; but the point was that Papá Santos would do anything for those three orphans. He'd been, in short, a saint.

His wife, Josefa, added much misery to Papá Santos's hard-luck life. She was 12 a *loca,* and he had to look after her all the time. One time she tried to burn the house down. Another time she tried to kill Santos with his own machete. She put shit in the food, and sometimes, on a crazy whim, she would shit on the floor instead of using the chamber pot or making a trip to the outhouse. Nightmares haunted her. Seven times a week she woke up the house with her screams; she said her enemies—Papá Santos was one of them—were trying to kill her. Sometimes they tied her to a tree and tried to decapitate her with a machete, but just before the blade cut into her neck, she screamed and woke herself up. Some nights they tried to choke her by shoving human shit down her throat. To calm her down, Papá Santos would give her a concoction of boiled milk with ginger and some wild herb called "good grass," and soothe her with words while she drank it.

The worst thing about her, as far as the boys were concerned, was her violent 13 nature. She might sneak up on one of them and clobber him on the head with the broom or the chamber pot, or empty the chamber pot on their heads. My father blamed his poor eyesight on those regular beatings she gave him. She singled him out for extra torture because he couldn't help talking back to her. One day—he was ten—when he saw a pile of her shit in a corner of the kitchen, he threw up his food and called her a disgusting old *loca.* She came at him with a kitchen knife. He put the table between them. When she started to climb it, determined to get him, holding the knife up for a quick stab, he upended the table and knocked her over. She cut herself with the knife, in the groin, and began screaming: "*Asesino!* He's killing me!" Papi was sure she'd bleed to death. He panicked, ran away, and hid in the hilly woods, living on wild fruit and coffee berries. On the second day, an attack of diarrhea almost killed him.

A posse of village men headed by Papá Santos found him at sunset of the third 14 day. He was on his haunches, trying to move his empty bowels, when they caught up with him. He thought the men had come to hang him, but he was too proud to beg for his life. Instead, he confessed to having murdered Josefa. Accident or no accident, he had killed her, and for that he deserved to be killed in turn. At this point Papá Santos, already weeping, knelt and pulled up Papi's pants. But what difference did it make whether his pants were up or down? They were going to hang him that very day before the sun set. But the posse, all eight of them, were laughing at him.

He broke down, sat on the ground, and wept. Papá Santos took him in his 15 arms and they wept together. The posse of peons stopped laughing. Papá Santos explained that Josefa was still very much alive. The wound had been only a scratch. Papá Santos had somehow calmed her down, and had even gotten her to forgive Papi.

Back home they had a big reunion scene. Everybody wept, especially Papi, 16 when Josefa picked up her skirt and displayed her bandaged groin. Her hysteria when she saw her blood flowing—her nightmares come true—had worn off. She had calmed down while sipping a cupful of Papá Santos's "good grass" potion, and even recovered some semblance of sanity. The shock of seeing her blood may have done it. And for almost a week after the incident she behaved like the old Josefa, the sane and sound Josefa whom Papá Santos had eagerly married. God works in strange ways, he and his three adopted sons concluded. Instead of murdering her, as she had insisted, Papi had cured her with a knife wound. A novena was in order. They recited two of them on two successive nights; and for an entire week afterward they recited rosaries and lit votive candles in honor of Josefa's miraculous cure.

But her cure was much too good to last. Her wound had just begun to scab 17 when she relapsed. She got worse, in fact: screamed louder and longer at night, wet the bed and Papá Santos as well, and moved her bowels so often on the floor planks that the three brothers had to take turns cleaning it up; and once she cooked their *sancocho,* a vegetable and meat stew, in the chamber pot. For water she used her own piss. And as for violence, she began attacking the boys with a new passion, Papi especially, because he had tried to assassinate her. Friends of Papá Santos suggested that he have her put away; they were afraid she might attack their own children, or set fire to their firetrap *bohíos.* But he refused to part with her. He was too stuck on nostalgia and pity to abandon her just like that, as if she were some kind of rabid dog. He could still remember the sweet, hefty girl who'd been as good a wife and mother as any in Bautabarro. Also, crazy or not, she was his beloved wife; she was over sixty years old; they'd been married more than forty years. The mother of his poor dead *niños.* True, she'd become mysteriously barren after the birth of her second child, a boy who had died of some *enfermedad* (smallpox probably) at the age of five, but that cut no ice; she was his wife, a part of him, of his life. No, Papá Santos decided, if she goes, I go, and I'm not going anywhere yet.

So she stayed, for some four years, crazy and violent to the last. And when she 18 died, suddenly, of a heart failure, he went into mourning. He mourned for the rest of his life, the old-fashioned way: extra prayers at night for the repose of her soul (he figured she must be in purgatory, possibly heaven, but for sure not hell: the insane, like infants, cannot sin); downcast gloomy looks; a self-imposed silence, broken only when speech was absolutely necessary; no more fun, no more stealing, and no music. His old guitar, which he had enjoyed plucking at night after supper, he gave to the three boys, who taught themselves quickly. But they couldn't play it in the house when he was there.

He survived Josefa by four years, and when he died of old age, the three boys 19 and their neighbors buried him somewhere in the hills, alongside his crazy wife. No grave marker. The graves quickly disappeared into the wild vegetation, and even Papi, his favorite, lost sight of their graves.

The three brothers lived in Papá Santos's house for less than a year, planted 20 and picked their own subsistence crops, almost starved when the land, a few acres, overworked and barren to begin with, yielded less and less. The brothers took to blaming each other for its failure. The less it yielded, the more they quarreled, and more than once must have come close to machete blows. Elias, nineteen and the oldest, was also much taller than his brothers and began bossing them. Papi, seventeen, and Mito, sixteen, resented Elias's arrogance. They thought of themselves as equals in their work: no boss, no peons, no unequal distribution of the labor. If anything, Papi thought *he* should be the boss, because he was smarter when it came to farming. But he kept this to himself; Elias and Mito would have laughed in his face.

The quarrels increased and finally Papi and Mito agreed they'd had enough of   21 Elias. They told him off, called him a lazy bastard. Elias threw down his straw hat and challenged them to a fight—fists or machetes, Elias didn't give a damn. Mito backed down. Papi was mad enough to go for his machete, but chose his fists instead. He didn't want his brother's life on his hands. They would have bashed each other in if Mito hadn't stepped in and reminded them of Papá Santos: what would he think if he saw them fighting? Brothers, for God's sake. The old man would moan in his grave. The shame Mito poured on them was too much; they picked up their straw *pavas* and shook hands, and Mito the peacemaker had his way.

But the next day Elias quit on them. He'd had enough of that dirt farmer's life.   22 He said he was losing his mind in those hills, and his life was wasting away, just like Papá Santos's, or worse. If he stayed, he might even take Xavier's way out. He wanted to get married and settle down somewhere to raise a family. In the big city maybe. San Juan. Papi and Mito told him the big city would kill him faster than the farm. A hillbilly he was and would die one. It was in his blood. For *jíbaros* like them the city was a cemetery. But he insisted he could cope with city life and called them timid *peones.* They were going to rot in that poor excuse for a farm, he warned them; their brains would rot first, then their hearts, then their balls.

He hung his *pava* on a nail and left for the city. He gave them his share of the   23 farm. Some legacy, Papi said. Useless clay. Less than six months later he and Mito sold the farm for a few pesos to the family whose land adjoined theirs and hired themselves out as peons. They worked for anyone who'd hire them at something like fifty cents a day, average day's wages in those Depression years. But since they weren't always able to get work on the same *finca,* they gradually split up, found new friends and interests, different lodgings, and saw each other less and less.

Papi was almost eighteen now, thin, a little anemic, but not as fragile as he   24 looked. He was quite strong. His light skin was darkened from constant exposure to the burning sun. His face was smooth and sensitive; he had thin lips, hazel eyes, curly brown hair, and a thin nose that my mother was to call Spanish because it did not round off to a pimple-pocked dome like most of the snouts in her family.

He was nineteen when he hired himself out to Gigante Hernández as a full-   25 time field hand. The wages were grubby even for 1933. Gigante was a thrifty *patrón.* He underpaid and overworked his *peones,* who quit on him as soon as they could find better pay. But there were always enough half-starved men looking around for work—any work—to keep Gigante's fields tilled and his strongbox full, if not overflowing. Papi was one of those hard-up *jíbaros*. He looked five years younger than his actual age. An undernourished *niño* like him couldn't compete with the mobs of full-grown men who were willing to work sixteen-hour days all week to feed their large, sickly families. So he was bound to drift toward Gigante's *finca,* and there he stayed for over a year, on and off. When there were no crops to plant or pick, Gigante let all his hands go, empty-handed.

Gigante Hernández was a hard-working, puritanical dirt farmer who found 26 time to produce nine children. "Eight worthless daughters and one half-ass son" was how he used to put it. He could have passed for a Puerto Rican version of the hidalgo of La Mancha. At least in looks. He bore a strong resemblance to those crudely carved imported Quixotes that pass for art in the tourist shops of Old San Juan: wooden, lanky, mournful, the face sunburned and angular, the cheeks collapsed, and the eyes dark and brooding; the bony, lantern jaw extended out of proportion. There was something Taíno Indian about his face, enough to suggest that way back somewhere in the island's hills some ancestor got down off the family tree long enough to knock up an Indian maiden. Or the reverse: that some lickerish warrior from the tribe of Chief Orocovix or Guarionex scampered up the family tree and straddled a fertile virgin of the Hernández tribe. But if anyone had suggested this to Gigante Hernández, he would have reached for his machete and hacked the blasphemer's balls off in a single chop, like sugar cane.

This *puro-macho* old-time patriarch took no shit from either sex, in or out of 27 the family. He was proud, stern, and excessively strict, a boondocks tyrant who'd had the cunning to marry a submissive madonna. From his wicker rocking chair, *El Sillón,* he reared eight compliant daughters and one swaggering son. Hortensio more than any of his sisters, several of whom had the round pale face of their mother, was an A1 reproduction of his old man, except that he was not quite so sullen-looking; and he took after him. Whenever padrefamilias was sweating in the fields or in his paramour's bed after sunset, Hortensio was in the house keeping the girls in line.

Gigante's life must have been as bitter as the cheap, home-grown tobacco he 28 liked to chew and spit out at stinging flies and wasps. The farm he had bought as a young man—recently married and looking forward to siring five or six boys, and maybe a girl for the housework—had let him down. The land was too hilly, and too much of it was nothing but a dense mush that sucked you in up to the ankles, and during heavy rains poured downhill in red and yellow streams. What wasn't clay or hills was a jungle of choking undergrowth that grew back as fast as he and Hortensio and his *peones* could clear it away with their machetes. Some sixty acres he owned, but only a fraction of that was farmable. His dreams of owning a large hacienda someday and directing the labor from his horse came to *mierda.* God must have had it in for him. Gigante shat on Him seven times a day.

Even his offspring came out wrong: eight girls and one, just one, lousy son. 29 Eight useless daughters. No returns on that investment, just hard work to keep them fed, dressed, humble, and chaste. Hortensio was another losing proposition. He'd rather shoot craps with the village *peones* than squeeze the clay for whatever it still had. As for keeping an eye on his sisters, half the time the young lecher had it fixed on someone else's sister. And, as if God hadn't rubbed Gigante's life enough in shit, Hortensio, as soon as he turned twenty-one, went and signed up for Uncle Sam's army. With him gone, Gigante would have to play the master full-time once again. He cursed himself for having ever sent Hortensio and the eight girls to eight years of worthless school. He should have kept them all illiterate like himself.

Wifeless, too, he was. Abuela Socorro had died in childbirth, taking the last of her offspring, a boy, with her. Afraid he'd father still more girls, he refused to marry his *querida* Maritornes. What if he died first? Then she would become his legal heir and suck up a good hunk of his *finca*. Besides, the old Spanish customs of the countryside condemned remarriage. Not that Gigante couldn't have remarried and gotten away with it—who of those anemic neighbors of his would dare condemn him openly? But he liked to follow the old customs, the face-saving ones especially. So he stuck fast to the burdens of a *viudo*. Except for celibacy. That would have been too much for a *puro macho*.

Gigante's wife had passed away in labor pains. No photographs, no sketches of her exist. Even if Xavier had offered to paint her portrait gratis (for Gigante would never have wasted his money on *el arte*), she would not have consented. She was a self-effacing woman, and to pose her face for a painter, and then to have that image of herself in the house, even stashed away under the linen—that was vanity, a *pecado mayor*.

My mother said that Socorro had been a saint. A footstool, in other words, Gigante's footstool. But according to Mami, she had been a matchless wife and mother—a kitchen matyr and a bedroom madonna. The kitchen and the bedrooms, cubicles all, were her domain, and her husband was her overlord. He commanded, she obeyed, eyes to the ground. No questions asked and certainly no backtalk. All day she drudged away, fixing meals for the nine and the one (plus the field hands), with help from the older girls. She always ate last, almost never with her husband, who like to brood by himself while he chewed. She ate standing up, always on the go, piling up starchy stews, rice and beans, codfish, goat and chicken on wooden plates, and watchful as a finicky mother hen, double-checking to make sure they'd all had an equal share of food, urging more on them, when there was more. Several times a week she and two or three of the girls loaded dirty laundry on their backs, or set it firmly on their heads, and dragged themselves barefoot to the nearest stream, whre they squatted on a rock and scrubbed the wash clean with hard bars of Octagon soap. Socorro pounded away at her husband's underwear. She insisted on doing that herself.

At night, when Gigante was home, she bestowed herself on him, put his seed in private storage, and watched her belly swell right on time year after year. She was pregnant nine months out of twelve for ten years running, and on the tenth year her overworked womb quit on her. I think of her dying with a scream in her gaping mouth, or even a curse on her husband and that all-fours life she'd led. But my mother said she never cursed.

Gigante's neighbors envied him his success in rearing such close-to-perfect 34
daughters almost by himself. What hard workers they all were! What obedience
and loyalty! What humility! The Hernández girls were known as *las hermanas
humildes,* the humble sisters. And all eight of them, or at least seven, were proud of
it, to the point sometimes of committing the sin of *orgullo,* pride. But this the village cleric helped them overcome in the confessional. He reminded them of the
Mother of God and of their own mother, a favorite of his, whose humility they
could hardly hope to match. "But you can always try, Mija," he would tell each
one. And they did; they bent over backward for the Espíritu Santo, that taintless
dove who had somehow made María Inmaculada big with child.

Las hermanas humildes: too docile for their own good, a few misguided peo- 35
ple thought, too obedient, afraid of displeasing Papá Gigante and their brother
Hortensio. They never talked back to Papá Gigante, never even asked him for permission to smoke in his presence (he would have made them eat the cigarettes) or
to go out on dates. Gigante regulated everything, right down to sweeping the floor,
fetching water from the stream at the bottom of a steep hill, or feeding the pigs and
chickens. Anything that emphasized femininity—a blouse or dress that was too colorful or fit too snugly, a new hairdo—was sure to provoke Gigante's displeasure;
and displeasure led to chastisement; and God help the *hembra* who tried to defend
herself. Gigante would grab her by the hair, yank her head down close to his chest,
and let her have it with the flat of his horny right hand.

The head he yanked most was Celita's; she was the one he couldn't break. 36
The only one she bowed her head to, in self-defense, not humility, was Gigante.
Nobody messed with him. But behind his back she called him a putrid old pain in
the ass, something the other sisters considered blasphemous and cause for getting
one's tongue cut off with the machete.

Celita was not an attractive girl; she was short, but rough-hewn and hard- 37
faced like her father. Her sisters wore their dresses above the ankle; Celita wore
hers right down to her heels; when she walked, her heavy arms swung stiffly at her
side, as if she were clutching a pail of water in each hand. Her thick black hair was
done up in "rats." And her dark and sullen face was stippled with tiny pits, a combination of acne and smallpox scars, like the tiny craters raindrops make on dry dust.

When Papá Gigante wasn't around, Celita liked to sit on his old wicker rock- 38
ing chair in front of the house and keep an eye on things, the hills especially; she
liked to stare at the green, sunny mountains that surrounded the house. Perhaps she
daydreamed of *hombres* and of escape from *la finca;* or of the lonely life she would
probably have when Gigante died and the others married and left her in that dump
with only the wild chickens and pigs, the two horses and the half-dozen cows, and
la maleza, the forest that passed for a farm, and the bugs going at night all at once,
and especially the *coquí,* the little frog whose forlorn, ventriloquial mating call
could be heard all over those hills.

In Celita's outspoken opinion (for which her sisters avoided her as much as 39
possible) they were "a flock of timid chickens. Papá Gallo's chickens." When Papá
Rooster crowed the wrong way, displeased with his breakfast eggs or the taste of
his bean sauce, his *gallinitas* would duck their heads and scatter off to their cubi-

cles. Eventually Celita was bound to say something or do something that would make Papá Gallo crow the wrong way. And when that happened, there was no way she could make herself small enough and humble enough to escape his right hand.

One of Celita's daily chores was to carry the lunch to the *peones* in the fields. 40 Gigante had chosen wisely; her husky, peremptory voice was enough to scare away the most hard-up *jíbaro*. It grated like a millstone. And like her father, she took no shit from men.

She couldn't help talking back to Gigante whenever he ordered her to do 41 something she disliked, which was just about anything, from feeding the pigs and chickens to ironing his underwear. But of the eight sisters she was the only one he allowed to call him by his first name and to address him as *tú* instead of the formal, fearful *usted* that the others used. This indulgence of Gigante's probably came from her close resemblance to him and from her toughness that was not put-on like Hortensio's. In some subconscious way, Gigante must have seen himself as female in his third daughter. But this bond did not get Celita any special privileges. She often had to work harder than the others, almost as if Gigante were grooming her and not Hortensio to take over.

Gigante kept his daughters isolated. How many times had they attended a vil- 42 lage dance? No more than five or six. And who went with them? The sons of Bautabarro? God help them if the sisters so much as stared sideways at those lazy chicken and plantain thieves. Brother Hortensio had gone with them every time. Hortensio was a machete wielder from the womb, just about; and it was tough *tetas* for any *jíbaro* who even looked like he was tossing *florecitas* at one of the sisters.

Even at dances he wore his *pava,* with its long fringes and pointed peak, at a 43 sharp angle, and dusty baggy pants roped above the ankles with maguey. At his side, dangling from his maguey belt, the ends of which reached down to his *cojones* like a bull's pizzle, was a long, sharp, unsheathed machete. Hortensio, like his father, was all balls—in public at least, and around his eight sisters.

He'd never had to use his machete (which he took with him everywhere, as 44 well as a small switchblade in his back pocket, just in case); every Bautabarro *jíbaro* knew he was the son of Gigante and assumed he was a macho in his own right, and deferred to him. And stayed away from his *hermanas humildes.* Instead of asking one of them for a dance, a *jíbaro* would approach Hortensio first and ask his permission. "Hortensio, may I have the privilege of dancing with Iraida?" or "Hortensio, it would be a great honor for me if you would give me permission to dance with your sister Flavia." And Hortensio, who was destined to become a police sergeant in San Juan and after that the town marshal of Bautabarro, might or might not grant permission. Sometimes, for no clear reason, he would grant the privilege of dancing, not with the sister the *jíbaro* had asked for, but with another one. After a while the sly *jíbaros* learned to request the wrong sister and hope that Hortensio would give them the one they really wanted.

The only men he tolerated talking to his sisters, even on the dance floor, were 45 married, middle-aged *peones* and dried-up grandfathers; but even those had to meet certain qualifications: that he know them personally inside out, that they be responsible fathers, husbands, and hard workers, and that they not hang around too long with his sisters. He was following orders from his father, but the enthusiasm he brought to his task was all his own.

This custom, and others—Catholic and Spanish, with maybe a little Indio 46 thrown in—seven of the sisters never questioned. Every now and then one might be tempted by *el diablo* and his legions to live it up, break loose from the strong grip of their father and big brother; but that was a sinful thought, and never got beyond the temptation stage. Everyone took it for granted that they were all *vírgenes,* and that they would remain so until marriage. Dreams they couldn't help having; but even those, the sinful ones at least, they repented of and recited at confession. (Not Celita, though. When *she* went to confession, it was not to confess bad dreams, which she probably enjoyed too much to toss away on an old virgin priest, but to complain about her father's tyranny and her brother's meddling.) The village priest at the time, an elderly Polish one named Klimanskis (Soliván had died a few years before), also from the States, admonished them and gave them extra prayers to say whenever one of the *humilde* sisters, blushing, dropping sweat in the dark confessional, confessed that last night or the one before that—she couldn't be sure, so great was her desire to perish the sin from her mind—she had had a "bad dream."

Such a way of life Lilia had been born into and never once seriously thought 47 to question. Even when Papá Gigante or Hortensio said or did something displeasing to her sense of right and wrong, when some *diablito* somewhere in the back of her head told her she'd just been insulted, or when the blackbird Celita pointed out some injustice she'd been subjected to at the hands of her papá or big brother and tried to convert her to resentment, it was herself Lilia admonished, her own conscience she condemned for it: "Get behind me, Satanás." Because Mamá had taught her again and again, in her saintly fashion, that our earthly life is one trial after another and that "it's not for us to complain, Mija, but to endure. Endure and be humble, Lilia." And endure she did, with humility to spare.

She spent her days sloshing out slops for the pigs, casting dried corn at the 48 chickens, sweeping the dusty threshold, pulling grade-C eggs from beneath the undernourished hens, scooping out the ashes in the firewood stove, replacing the fast-diminishing supply of corn husks, abrasive leaves, and brown-bag paper in the outhouse. Whenever Celita was having her period, or when she couldn't stand the sight of those *peones,* who taunted her for her looks, Lilia exchanged tasks with her. She was happy to do it—she looked forward to breaking her daily routine, which was tedious and lonely, and she found the conversation of the field hands more interesting than the grunts and clucks of the barnyard.

Gerán, the youngest peon, was her favorite. She found him pleasant, delicate 49 though strong, serious but not lacking in humor, and sincere. They were of different stocks. She was a shade or two darker. Her hair, thick and long, was jet-black, like a Borinquen Indian girl's; she had high cheekbones, large limbs, and a strong constitution. She thought nothing of standing on her wide feet all day, from morning to bedtime, sometimes past midnight.

He was proud-looking and uncommonly courteous. From his weak hazel eyes 50 with the large lids she never got the sex-in-the-brain stares that the other men, eight or nine of them, gave her from the time she arrived with the gunny sack containing their lunch to the time, exactly forty-five minutes later, that she gathered all the forks, spoons, Thermos bottles, and leftovers and walked away with her eyes to the ground, taking quick, barefooted strides.

There, in those steep hills dotted with cows, goats, banana trees, and thatched 51 huts, Lilia and Gerán came to sit together while he ate his lunch of boiled green bananas, salty codfish, raw onion rings—the whole thing drenched in olive oil— fresh warm milk. He was nineteen; she was a year younger.

He told her about his father Xavier the schoolteacher and painter, and about 52 Papá Santos and Josefa and his two brothers. He told her he had no intention of staying in Bautabarro all his life; he wanted to be more than a peon in rags. He dreamed of having his own *finca* someday, a big one, flatland, not red clay hills and jungle; but for good land he needed a great deal of money. How could he possibly save up when he was just barely keeping his stomach fed on the wages Don Gigante paid him? Unless God worked a miracle on his behalf, he would either remain a hired slave all his life, or—something he'd been giving serious thought to lately—move north to Los Estados. In New York, he had heard from the friends and relatives of those who had gone there, to a place called El Barrio, a man could get a decent job and make enough money to put in the bank. Eventually, if you didn't waste your money on luxuries, you could save up enough to return to the island and buy a good *finca*. In New York you could find work that let you live decently. Not like here, in this vale of tears.

He was convinced, as she was, as most Bautabarreños were, that man is put on 53 this earth to suffer. But unlike her, he believed that man and woman are entitled to some felicity, that life doesn't have to be *totalmente un martirio*. She, instinctively, knew better. In addition to that, she was too attached to those hills, to her sisters, her brother, Papá Gigante, and to the memory of her mother, to contemplate leaving it just because life there was hard.

She could see his wanting to leave the village, moving to San Juan, Santurce, 54 Ponce, Mayagüez, or any other of the "big" cities and towns on the island where someone with ambition (and he seemed to have a good deal of that) could go into business for himself or find decent work. But Los Estados Unidos de América? No. She knew that other villagers had done what Gerán had in mind. It was nothing new. Those who could read and write sent long letters to their families telling them what a *ciudad magnífica* New York was. They had jobs and they were making, some of them, as much as twenty dollars a week in hotels and factories. That was a lot of money, twenty dollars. Too much. She was suspicious. They were padding their paychecks with lies to impress the *jíbaros* back home. Also, a few had come back after a year or so with different stories of Los Estados. Slums they talked about, rats and *cucarachas*, filth and degradation. And what had offended them most, they said, was that *los americanos* did not respect them, they treated our people with the kind of contempt and disgust a man feels when he sees one of his pigs wallowing in its own excrement.

And even if she was willing to go with Gerán to New York after they got mar- 55 ried (she assumed he wanted to marry her; otherwise why tell her all this?), did he think her father was going to bestow his blessing on them and wish them a *vaya con Dios? Con Satanás,* if anything. Papá Gigante had nothing but contempt for those who "abandoned" their families and their country and tried to make themselves into gringos. A man, he thought, should stick it out wherever God places him in life, not run away like panicked sow pursued by nipping dogs. And as for *las hembras,* their place was with their husbands. She would never have the nerve to tell Papá Gigante she was going to Los Estados with Gerán, married or not.

When word got to Gigante that Lilia had been seen talking to Gerán more than 56 once, he reacted as she'd known he would. He warned her against seeing that useless orphan. But she was in love and persisted. He beat her a couple of times and forbade her to go near Gerán.

The old man and his peon hadn't hit it off; necessity, cheap labor, was the 57 only thing that kept Gigante from throwing Gerán out. The *patrón* had a few other things against him, not the least of which was the strain of solitude, suicide, and madness in his family. Since it ran in both sides of the family, the children, all three of them, had to be screwed up. Gigante didn't want any lunatic grandchildren. Bad enough that eight-ninths of his own offspring were useless females.

It wasn't Lilia's well-being that concerned him. Females, *hembras,* as he 58 called them, were like *jobos,* a species of wild, fibrous mango that had no market value, were handicaps. Three of them at most were all he needed to keep house, feed the pigs, chickens, and cows, and help out in the fields during the busy season. The other five had been mistakes, cheap kindling, a pestilence on a man's life. Gigante would have willingly swapped them for a couple of fat pregnant sows, or a good milk cow. And now this Lilia has fallen for the first *vagabundo* that had sprinkled a few flowers in her path. But what rankled him most was the prospect of having grandchildren who would almost certainly carry that strain of madness in their blood. Never! he must have told himself during his pensive moments in the rocking chair.

Then there was the rumor among the field hands and other village men that 59 Gerán was a young stud, a skirt-lifting *desgraciado.* This was an unfounded rumor; in fact, it made Gigante laugh to himself that the anemic kid was capable of producing an erection, let alone laying one of those little battleaxes from Bautabarro. Even if it were true, Gigante had no objection to skirt-lifting. Hadn't he done it himself in his youth? In his childhood, for that matter. And still did when the lust came on him. But this was his daughter, now, not Fulano so-and-so's. Let Fulano worry about his own daughters. Gigante was looking out for *his* own.

A man with loose daughters was the victim of vicious rumors and ridicule. 60 Gigante was sure no one in that village would dare mock him to his face, not while he still had that machete arm of his intact. But behind a man's back things were said, evil things usually, that he had no means to prevent. Some men may not be hurt by what their eyes and ears miss, but Gigante was not one of them; he heard things in his sleep—buzzing voices mocking him and his kin. On his rocking chair, while his squinting eyes took in the sun setting, his large, leather-brown ears picked up his neighbors' gossip, the *bochincherías* of idle women and effeminate, hen-

pecked men and horny young *jíbaros*. Already he could hear them: "Gigante's oldest daughter, Lilia, the one with the thin strong legs, is carrying on with young
Gerán. He's giving her *las florecitas*. You just wait, in no time at all he'll make her
his *querida*."

His oldest daughter a skinny *peon*'s mistress? If he caught her, from this day   61
on, or even got a hint of a rumor that she was *cortejando* with that suicide's son—
ora pro nobis, as the town priest might put it, because who was going to stay his
strong right hand from violence? And who would condemn him for it? For sure not
God. Dios the Father always took the father's side.

Lilia found ways to steal out of the house and meet Gerán. When she took the   62
wash to the stream, he would sneak off from work and join her there. They considered themselves engaged, but who was going to break the bad news to her old man?
Gerán was all for it, but she wouldn't let him; she was afraid her father would hack
them both to pieces. In that case, Gerán told her, they should elope.

Elope? Only loose girls eloped. Besides, didn't he know Gigante would hunt   63
them down and kill them?

The plan was simple enough, and by no means original. Stealing a girl from   64
her father was common in a village whose marriage customs dated back to the
Spanish Catholic conquest. It was a solemn act, matrimony; even childbearing,
another blessing, was less important than taking a young bride's "flowers." Not that
Bautabarro girls were all that chaste; they were no more chaste nor yielding than
other girls in other villages. But, like their counterparts all over the island, they kept
up a virgin front. Had to: that was the point, a solid front, a look of vigilant virginity and cautious innocence.

Abducting a nubile girl, then, was a common custom, an old and practical one;   65
for it saved her menfolk's collective face, unburdened her father of an extra gut to
feed and her brothers of the strain of protecting her from the local Don Juans for
whom seducing unwatched girls was a principle. Still, no honor-conscious father
wanted his *hija* stolen from under his snoring nose on a moonless night if he could
give her hand away to any respectable, filial, up-and-coming young *jíbaro*. But
there weren't many of these young men around; they were the type who quit the
village as soon as they could cut themselves off from the family. So those fathers
who were tired of turning away unsuitable suitors for their virgin daughters often
had to settle for a face-saving abduction.

On a quiet summer night (no moon), Gerán met Lilia near the rock where she   66
scrubbed her father's underwear, and they spent the night, lying close but never
touching, beneath an old, dried-up lemon tree. The next morning, while Lilia hid in
his rented room, Gerán smeared her underwear with chicken blood and presented
Gigante with the "fact" of Lilia's womanhood. He waited until Gigante was
undressed and bathing in the stream, so that when he threw his fit and went for his
machete, he would have to wade to the shore and scramble up a slope, thick with
cattails and thorny weeds, to get to it. By that time, the nimble abductor would have
ample time to run for his life—time, if necessary, to race or the nearest bus, with
Lilia alongside him, and head for San Juan or Mayagüez.

But Gigante, without being at all conscious of it, sensed that the world was   67
changing, knew that this was only one telltale speck in the great pile to come—
women wearing pants and smoking in public, children refusing to be blessed by
parents, the loss of those venerable village customs, the end of *his* way. So he just
stood there in the stream, naked, the cold morning water lapping at his brown
behind, and said nothing, not even a curse for God.

For a wedding present Gigante gave them a part of his worst land, most of it   68
hilly and overgrown with weeds and thorny bushes. The shaky shack Gerán built
with the help of his brother Mito and some neighbors was situated on the only level
ground to be found in his two-acre wedding present, a convenient two or three up-
and-down miles from Gigante's house.

Gerán tried farming it, but that didn't work; somehow the clay wouldn't yield   69
to husbanding, at least not enough to support a family's needs. Only wild things
liked to grow on that *finca:* the prickly, starchy pear-shaped chayote; tiny, bitter
oranges so inaccessible you were better off buying them six for a cent in the town
market; yellow, buckshot-seeded guava; some small, sweet, slimy balls with a
tough green skin and a hard white seed called *quenepas;* bananas, plantains, and an
incredible abundance of starchy tubers whose Indian names they were seldom to
use after they came to the hot-dog, pizza capital of the world.

■ *Questions for* . . . Antecedentes by Edward Rivera

Words to Note

itinerant	Mariolater	*pistola*
fundillo lodged	chroniclers	scribes
piss	meager	squiggle
doses	still lifes	bourgeois types
mural	pliant	bow-lipped mouths
smirking	scowling	choiring hallelujahs
upended	balls	posse of peons
rot	*mierda*	celibacy
kitchen martyr and	squatted	putrid
bedroom madonna	blasphemous	peremptory
grated	bull's pizzle	machete
tyranny	meddling	padding
wallowing	virgin front	abducting
nubile	chayote	buckshot-seeded guava
tubers		

Language

1. Why does Rivera sprinkle the story with Spanish words and phrases? Are they hard to understand? Would it has a different feel or flavor if he had translated these words and phrases into English? Try out a few sentences and see.
2. Would it have been more literary of Rivera to write *urine* and *excrement,* rather than *piss* and *shit?* If it's a matter judgment, do the same rules apply to the essays you're writing for this English course?

Style

1. Santos Malánguez, grandson of Xavier F. Alegría, is the narrator. Study the first paragraph. How do people usually talk or write about their ancestors? How does Rivera undercut the reader's expectations to establish Santos's irreverent tone? Do the same techniques persist throughout the story?
2. In what sense can paychecks be padded with lies?

Development and Organization

1. How does Rivera used double-line breaks to structure and advance his story line?
2. Does the section about Santos and Josefa Malánguez add anything to Rivera's story? Is it a tangent that should have been cut?

Discussion and Journal Writing

1. What do we learn about the world of Bautabarro? Do these rural Puerto Rican families perform the same functions that John Demos attributes to Plymouth Colony families?
2. How does Rivera characterize Gerán Malánguez's and Lilia Hernandez's families?
3. What does Gigante Hernández stand for?

ooooo

The American Family Then and Now

—John Demos

John Demos is an American historian who teaches at Brandeis University in Massachusetts. His book *The Little Commonwealth: The Family in Puritan New England* (1970) is a path-blazing study of the domestic lives of Puritan colonists. "The American Family Then and Now," the book's final chapter, is Demos's attempt to put both seventeenth- and twentieth-century American families into perspective by comparing the way family work and responsibilities have been handled at those two points in time.

1   The relationship between the inner workings of the family and the larger historical process is extremely intricate. Few scholars have attempted to chart its course thorough time—to discover, that is, at what rate and for what reasons changes in the one sphere have significant effects in the other. Of course, no such effort is feasible here. Still it may be useful to attempt a brief comparative review of the family then and now, if only as a means of pulling together the various materials from Plymouth.

2   It seems, in the first place, that the whole area of membership and underlying structure presents some striking instances of continuity. From the very beginning of settlement at Plymouth the family was nuclear in its basic composition and it has not changed in this respect ever since. One adult couple and their own children formed the core of each household—with the addition in some cases of an aged grandparent or "servant." Only the latter term introduces a real element of difference from the pattern of our own day. Insofar as it designated children purposely "bound out" from some other family, it stands in some degree to confound us. Also (though less often) included among the servants were orphans and certain types of deviant or sick persons. But aside from this the typical domestic unit is easily recognized in our own terms. Moreover, the settlers' definition of kindred (beyond the immediate family), and the range of effective contacts between such people, seem equally similar.

3   Of course, families were considerably larger in the seventeenth century than they are today. And this difference is magnified by the further differences in typical house plans. Most Old Colony dwellings were extremely small by our own standards, and even so parts of them were not usable during the long winter months. Thus there was little privacy for the residents, and little chance to differentiate between various portions of living space. Life in these households was much less segmented, in a formal sense, than it usually is for us; individuals were more constantly together and their activities meshed and overlapped at many points.

Still, despite this rather different set of physical arrangements, the usual align-   4
ment of roles and responsibilities within the family was basically similar to the
modern American pattern. The husband was head of the household, and, at least in
theory, the final arbiter of its affairs. Yet the wife had her own sphere of competence and a corresponding measure of authority. In certain most important areas of
family life—the sale of real property or the disposition of children—the couple
would make decisions *together*.

Possibly the lines of authority between parent and child were much tighter and   5
more formal than in our own society; but the evidence on this point is not conclu-
sive. In any case, the experience of childhood and growth through time did follow a
course more distinctively its own. Childhood as we know it did not last much
beyond the age of six or seven years. After that, participation in adult activities
began in earnest. There was little schooling of the kind—the institutional kind—
which in our own day helps to set apart a very broad age group. Instead children
spent most of their time working (and relaxing) alongside older people, and were
generally perceived as "little adults." If six or seven marked a turning point of
greater import in the seventeenth than in the twentieth century, the opposite was
true of adolescence. At Plymouth the "teens" formed a period of relatively calm
and steady progress toward full maturity. Courtships began at this stage; and
though officially restricted by requirements of parental approval, they seem in
many respects to have followed the lines of personal inclination. Marriage came
somewhat later than it does now and needed at the outset substantial gifts of property from both sets of parents. But such gifts were never withheld, and were often
framed so as to establish the complete autonomy of the recipients. The later years
of life in Plymouth Colony brought, in most cases, no new departures of a major
kind. The process of managing a family, and tending an estate, provided an essential continuity. Positions of power and prestige came chiefly to those over forty,
and might indeed be retained to a very advanced age. Most men yielded reluctantly
to "old age" proper, "retiring" only when forced to do so by real infirmity.

The foregoing survey has focused chiefly on issues and trends internal to the   6
family. But it is also important to consider the whole field of relationships joining
the family with the community at large. And in doing so we reach at last an area
where the contrasts between the Plymouth pattern and our own are far more striking than the continuities.

Consider, for a start, the range of *functions*—material, psychological, social,   7
and otherwise—performed by the family then and now. Of course, there is an
underlying core common to both sides of the comparison, and indeed to virtually
all systems of family life. It comprises the fulfillment of certain basic and universal
needs—most obviously, those for shelter, food, and sexual release. But beyond this
lies a great variety of other possibilities—a vast territory of social purpose and
activity in which the family may or may not be involved. And, broadly speaking,
the history of the family in America has been a history of contraction and withdrawal; its central theme is the gradual surrender to other institutions of functions
that once lay very much within the realm of family responsibility. Plymouth

Colony, as much as any place, marks the beginning of this story. The point is implicit in much of our previous discussion, but it must now be brought directly to center stage.

The Old Colony family was, first of all, a "business"—an absolutely central   8
agency of economic production and exchange. Each household was more or less self-sufficient; and its various members were inextricably united in the work of providing for their fundamental material wants. Work, indeed, was a wholly natural extension of family life and merged imperceptibly with all of its other activities.

The family was also a "school." "Parents and masters" were charged by law to   9
attend to the education of all the children in their immediate care—"at least to be able duely to read the Scriptures." Most people had little chance for any other sort of education, though "common schools" were just beginning to appear by the end of the Old Colony period.

The family was a "vocational institute." However deficient it may have been   10
in transmitting the formal knowledge and skills associated with literacy, it clearly served to prepare its young for effective, independent performance in the larger economic system. For the great majority of persons—the majority who became farmers—the process was instinctive and almost unconscious. But it applied with equal force (and greater visibility) to the various trades and crafts of the time. The ordinary setting for an apprenticeship was, of course, a domestic one.

The family was a "church." To say this is not to slight the central importance   11
of churches in the usual sense. Here, indeed, the family's role was partial and subsidiary. Nonetheless the obligation of "family worship" seems to have been widely assumed. Daily prayers and personal meditation formed an indispensable adjunct to the more formal devotions of a whole community.

The family was a "house of correction." Idle and even criminal persons were   12
"sentenced" by the Court to live as servants in the families of more reputable citizens. The household seemed a natural setting both for imposing discipline and for encouraging some degree of character reformation.

The family was a "welfare institution"; in fact, it provided several different   13
kinds of welfare service. It was occasionally a "hospital"—at least insofar as certain men thought to have special medical knowledge would receive sick persons into their homes for day-to-day care and treatment. It was an "orphanage"—in that children whose parents had died were straightaway transferred into another household (often that of a relative). It was an "old people's home"—since the aged and infirm, no longer able to care for themselves, were usually incorporated into the households of their grown children. And it was a "poorhouse" too—for analogous, and obvious, reasons.

Since the entire community had an interest in the smooth performance of these   14
various tasks, it seemed only natural that there should be a certain amount of direct governmental supervision over the family. When a given family failed in some area, or experienced serious conflict among its individual members, the authorities might decide to intervene. The "harmony" of husband and wife, the subordination of children to parents—even such internal matters as these came, in theory, under

official scrutiny. The government was also empowered to determine *who* might head a household in the first place. Undesirables could, if necessary, be warned away. One quite early statute ordered that "no servant comeing out of England or elsewhere . . . be admitted his freedome or to be for himself untill he have served forth his tyme either with his master or some other although he shall buy out his tyme, except he have beene a housekeeper or master of a famyly or meete and fitt to bee so." A contract of servitude was not, in short, simply a business arrangement, in which the servant might substitute cash for labor in order to obtain immediate freedom. It was also a kind of apprenticeship in householding: a young man would learn how to head a family by living in one for a time. The sole exception to these provisions was—quite logically— the servant who had previously been a head-of-household ("or meete and fitt to bee so").

The very different situation of the modern family requires no such extended 15 review. But clearly most of the functions enumerated above have long since been transferred out of the family—transferred to other institutions specially contrived for the purpose. Once could say, therefore, that the family now occupies far less social "space," that profound environmental pressures have worked relentlessly to reduce its importance in the overall scheme of things.

And yet the situation has another side as well. For while the family is now less 16 important from a social standpoint, it may well be *more* important from a psychological one. The crucial factor here is a certain feeling of connectedness, or isolation, with regard to the community at large—the degree to which individual persons sense that their life in a family makes a natural whole with other aspects of their experience. At Plymouth, we have seen, the family was joined to other institutions and other purposes in an intricate web of interconnections. It did not stand out in any special way from adjacent parts of the social backdrop; it acquired no distinctive aura of emotional or ideological significance. Its importance, while impossible to doubt, was more assumed than understood—was, indeed, so basic and so automatic as to be almost invisible. Family and community, private and public life, formed part of the same moral equation. The one supported the other, and they became in a sense indistinguishable.

The point becomes clearer when set in contrast to the situation that obtains in 17 our own time. No longer can one feel such an essential continuity between the various spheres of experience; the central threads in the invisible web have been broken. Partial connections unquestionably remain, but they seem conspicuous on that very account. And in some overall reckoning elements of disjunction and even of opposition loom largest by far.

The family, in particular, stands quite apart from most other aspects of life. 18 We have come to assume that whenever a man leaves his home "to go out into the world" he crosses a very critical boundary. Different rules, different values, different feelings apply on either side, and any failure to appreciate this brings, inevitably, the most painful kind of personal distress. The contrast has, of course, a pejorative character. The family becomes a kind of shrine for upholding and exemplifying all of the softer virtues—love, generosity, tenderness, altruism, harmony, repose. The world at large presents a much more sinister aspect. Impersonal, chaotic, unpredictable, often characterized by strife and sometimes by outright malignity, it requires of a man that he be constantly "on his guard." It goads and challenges him at every point and occasionally provokes responses of a truly creative sort; but it also exhausts him. So it is that he must retreat periodically within the family circle, in order to rest and to marshal his energies for still another round. In this instance the family is important not so much as the foundation for an ideal social order, but as the foil to an actual state of social disorder. It forms a bulwark against the outside world—destroy it, and anarchy reigns everywhere. It forms, too, a bulwark against anxieties of the deepest and most personal kind. For we find in the family, as nowhere else in our "open society," an indispensable type of protection against the sense of utter isolation and helplessness. Given all these circumstances family life is bound to seem somewhat more intense, more contrived, and far more self-conscious.

The source of these changes between the seventeenth century and our own is 19 to some extent implicit in the foregoing discussion. The biggest single factor seems to have been the separation of work form the individual household, in connection with the growth of an urban, industrial system. This it was that gave profound meaning to the sense of an "outside" or "public" world. But in the American setting there was the added factor of mobility, geographical *and* social—all the competitive pressures generated by an expansive and democratic social order. Men had reason to feel somewhat anxious and insecure in the world of work: here, indeed, was the price they paid for the chance to better themselves—a whole darker side of "the American experiment." The family, meanwhile, was increasingly set off; and it was also invested with that special sort of moral halo which it still retains.

The crucial phase of this process lay within the nineteenth century and cannot 20 therefore have any substantial place in the current study. But were there no omens, no glimmerings of what lay ahead, in the experience of seventeenth-century families—and specifically, those of Plymouth Colony? Can we find in any of the material examined above a hint of the transformation the American family would later undergo? Or to put the question another way: can we discover any point of stress or conflict between the family system which the settlers brought with them from the Old World and the environment which they found in the New? The evidence is, as always, quite incomplete; but it does contain some tantalizing and provocative clues. These clues, when arranged together, serve to focus attention on one particular quadrant of Old Colony life: opportunity, mobility, expansion, and all the concomitant effects on the thought and actions of a great number of individual settlers.

There was, in the first place, the important factor of empty land—the appear- 21 ance, at least, of a whole continent awaiting settlement. We cannot recover all of the innermost feelings of the colonists as they faced this prospect, but it does seem likely that certain rather basic hopes and ambitions were powerfully stimulated. As noted earlier, there is much material from Plymouth suggesting a pervasive tendency to expand and to scatter—a tendency that the leaders of the Colony sought unsuccessfully to restrain. If the colonists' most deeply cherished ideals of community life yielded so readily to these expansive pressures, can the family have come through unscathed? Was there some analogous kind of "loosening" in this respect as well? Of course, in a broad sense dispersion attacked the notion of community head on—by definition, as it were; whereas families were transportable. And, in fact, the migration within the Colony was not the kind that split large numbers of families apart; in many cases complete nuclear units were centrally involved. Yet there was, most likely, a more subtle sort of corrosive effect. In the long run mobility was bound to weaken somewhat the lines authority around which the traditional family was structured.

Many individual pieces of evidence, cited in previous chapters, imply as much. Recall, for example, the testimony given in the case of the contested will of Samuel Ryder. Much of it concerned a time some years earlier when Ryder's son Joseph had proposed to "Goe away" if the father would not guarantee him title to a certain tract of land. The tension which suffused the whole episode was particularly apparent in the mother's intervention—her tearful plea to Joseph that "if hee went shee would Goe too." Who holds the powerful hand in this confrontation: the father with his control of the family land, or the son with his threat to move away? And should there have been any confrontation at all? Would such a thing have been as plausible in an Old World setting? Recall the *many* inheritances that were made conditional on the fulfillment by the recipient of some important filial obligations. Just how deeply did such conditions bite, in an environment which presented so many alternative (and perhaps more promising) opportunities? The Bradford metaphor of the "widow . . . grown old and forsaken of her children" gains additional meaning in this connection. And then, too, there is William Bonny telling the Court that he would rather "Renounce his legacy" than continue to live with his aged mistress, the widow Clark. [22]

There is more that can be said—but only in a speculative way, since the relevant evidence has not survived. Very likely, the advantages of young people in terms of adaptability, sturdiness, and resourcefulness were particularly important, and *visible,* in frontier circumstances; and perhaps for this reason it was unusually difficult to maintain the traditional subjection of youth to age. Possibly the high premium on labor—any labor—worked gradually to improve the position of both children and women. The failure to sustain a tight pattern of community organization may also have exerted some influence here. The community, after all, acting through its constituted authorities, was supposed to serve as a kind of overseer of family life; but what would happen when its own integrity began to be compromised? The Colony Records contain a variety of official complaints that parents were neglecting their duties to their children, or that "yeong men" were spending too much time in "Inns and Alehouses." It is hard to know exactly how to interpret these statements, but they do suggest at least some degree of worry about the quality of family life. [23]

Yet in the final analysis, we should beware of attributing too much importance to these hints of decline and decay. The family remained an absolutely central institution throughout the whole history of the Old Colony. Its power to withstand the challenge of a new physical setting and an increasingly fluid social structure is at [24] least as impressive as the concessions it made. There is no reason to think that a young man, undertaking a move to a new settlement, found it easy to break contact with his own family of origin. Moreover, it is striking that when such a man reached his destination he joined with others of a like mind to establish a community on the same demographic and emotional foundations which he had known in the place of his childhood. The basic arrangements of family life, and its importance as well, were little altered in the newer towns.

The situation is, then, best understood in terms of ambivalence and conflict 25 and a whole host of counter-tendencies that yielded no clear sense of direction, except perhaps in the very long run. In this sense, the story of the family forms only a part, albeit an important one, of the larger drama of early American history—the drama that lays bare the whole momentous process of interaction between the inherited traditions, values, and institutions which the first wave of settlers brought with them and the coercive pressures of a new and radically different environment.

■ *Questions for* . . . **The American Family Then and Now** by John Demos

Words to Note

chart	sphere	feasible
nuclear	core	deviant
segmented	meshed	overlapped
alignment	autonomy	courtships
yielded	trends	functions
contraction	withdrawal	surrender
realm	central agency	literacy
vocational institute	of economic	instinctive
partial and subsidiary	production and	adjunct
reputable	exchange	infirm
analogous	subordination	official scrutiny
undesirables	statute	substitute
apprenticeship	enumerated	intricate web of
distinctive aura	emotional or ideological	interconnections
pejorative	significance	altruism
repose	sinister	chaotic
strife	malignity	goads
bulwark	intense	contrived
self-conscious	urban	industrial system
moral halo	glimmerings	quadrant
mobility	concomitant	unscathed
pervasive	dispersion	corrosive
tension	suffused	overseer
integrity	coercive pressures	

Language

1. In what sense does Demos use *bulwark* in paragraph 17. Is the family a literal *bulwark?* What does the word mean in this context?
2. What does he mean when he says the Plymouth Colony family had "no distinctive aura of emotional or ideological significance"? Is there a simpler way to say the same thing?

Style

1. Why does Demos put *business, school, vocational institution, church, house of correction, welfare institution, hospital, orphanage,* and *poorhouse* in quotation marks?
2. How does he use questions? Why do most student writers avoid questions in their essays?

Development and Organization

1. What's the topic of paragraph 6? How does he develop that paragraph? The topic of paragraph 21? How does he back it up?
2. Demos writes four paragraphs about the contemporary middle-class family and ten paragraphs about the Plymouth Colony family. Why the difference? What's the point of the essay?

Discussion and Journal Writing

1. Can you think of any other ways that institutions have taken over functions formerly performed by families?
2. Is Demos's point about the institutionalization of American family functions more or less true for specific types of American families?
3. Demos studied the Pilgrim family of colonial Massachusetts, but most Americans are not descendants of Pilgrims and Puritans. Is his characterization of preindustrial family life generally valid for seventeenth- and eighteenth-century rural families in Poland, Ireland, Sicily, the Caribbean, and the part of contemporary Nigeria that was inhabited by the Ibo tribe? Are his observations limited?
4. Is the family changing for the better or the worse?

ooooo

African Beginnings: The Seamless Web

—Nathan Huggins

After completing his graduate work at Harvard University with the eminent American historian Oscar Handlin, Nathan Huggins taught at Columbia University until his death in 1989. The history of African Americans was his subject. *The Harlem Renaissance* is an illuminating study of the politics and culture of Harlem in the 1920s, when it became the home of the "New Negro" and the self-proclaimed capital of Black America. *Black Odyssey* is Huggins's account of the enslavement, transportation, and acculturation to slave labor and life in the New World. "African Beginnings: The Seamless Web," a selection from that book, is a vivid portrait of the tribal worlds enslaved Africans were torn from.

1   The Africans who were to become Americans came from a region of West Africa that fanned from its westernmost tip, around the Senegal River, south and east, along the Bight of Benin, and south again below the Congo River to include a region we now call Angola. Hardly a people living within this vast region, stretching inland for two to three hundred miles, was unrepresented in the creation of the Afro-American people. Bambura, Fulani, Mandinka, and Wolof from the Senegambia, the collection of peoples from Dahomey called Whydahs, the Ashanti, Coromantees, Fanti, Ga, Hausa, Ibo, Yoruba, Angola—they all came, like migrants from Europe and later from Asia, to mix their seed and substance in the making of the American and his civilization.

2   It was a treacherous and awful journey from whatever point they started, down the coast, through the unimaginably inhuman Atlantic crossing, into American slavery. Nor was that journey vast and torturous merely in physical distance and bodily pain. Those who were forced to make it traversed worlds of mind and spirit, leaving what they were and becoming the forebears of a people yet to be. Each man, woman, and child made that internal journey alone; but collectively, their odyssey is one of the great epics of modern times.

3   Some who started did not make it. Disease, frailty, brutality, and suicide took a heavy toll. But those whose way was stopped short for whatever reason will not hold us long, for ours is the story of those who endured, whether due to strength or chance or will to survive or abject surrender. They were the people who would become Afro-Americans.

4   Those whose origins were farthest inland came to the coast in coffles—caravans of fettered humanity—or by war canoe on the major rivers that cut deep into the African continent: the Senegal, Gambia, Niger, and the Congo—avenues over which slave raiders reached into the heartland among peoples who would never

otherwise have known either the grandeur of those rivers, coursing hundreds of miles and spilling into the ocean, or the ocean itself.

Others came from among peoples closer to the coast, where disorder and tribal weakness made them easy prey for neighbors looking for people to trade. 5

Brought together in the dungeons of the coastal slave castles—Gorée, Elmina, Cape Coast—or the corral-like barracoons of Bonny and Calabar, they were a mélange of peoples. They might seem to have little in common save color. Yet even that sameness—given the shades of blacks and browns—was remarkable only in that they shared in not being white. One who would search out one of his own would not attend to color. He would rather listen to language, the special inflections that were his and no other's, and he would look for those familiar tribal markings and mannerisms he knew as his own. There were countless distinctions that loomed large. Yet whatever their real and imagined differences, great or small, the progeny of these Africans were to lose all vestiges of tribal difference, making one people and giving ironic validity to a coming nation's slogan: *e pluribus unum.* 6

Whatever his people and from wherever he came, the African was first a part of a village. The village, a collection of family compounds organized around agriculture and trade, was the center of life and comprised his world. 7

Nature was the throb of the village's heart. Whether its people be simple farmers of rice, yams, or groundnuts; whether they cull the rivers and coastal waters for fish; whether they be herdsmen or artisans—makers and weavers of cloth, woodcarvers, or bronze-casters—the fundamental pulses of nature—the rains, the seasons, the tides—punctuated life. Thus, each place had a sameness, a common imperative pulling all together to an insistent command that was above and beyond the individual self, the family, or the clan. 8

The village was the expression of the need to hold together for existence. Isolation was unthinkable. Alone, awesome nature was a threat rather than a blessing. Alone, one was helpless before all that was unknown. The smallest thing could threaten the isolated person—the elements, inanimate objects, animals, and above all, other people. 9

Besides, alone, a person was nobody. The self was defined in relationship to others. One was a son, a daughter, a parent, or a grandparent, and had a place, large or small, in the village. What one was known to be rested on others. One shared the reputations of kin. A wastrel or cowardly brother was one's own shame; a relation who brought glory to himself was one's own pride. The kinsman whose name one bore shared force and qualities of character. Each was thus tied with others, past and present, and each was linked through family to others in the village. The bloodlines and associations that made up the village were a finely spun web, firmly and distinctly linking all together. The self, who one was, was of the village. What one was to become was of the village as well. 10

The families and clans that located themselves together, forming the village, gave over to those chosen or assumed wise the ultimate power for the maintenance of order. As elders, they were respected because they were the living repository for 11 community experience. Only those who lived long could contain within their memory precedents that would serve to unravel complicated knots of dispute.

Ideally, each family settled its problems within itself. When death set women 12 or children adrift, the family provided an anchor. When there was a confusion of rights and duties, the family was expected to find its own accord. When children or old people were without proper care, the family would seek a just solution. But sometimes such matters did not rest quietly within the family, or there were disputes that caused one family to confront another without agreement, or crises posed dangers to all; then it was the collective judgment and wisdom of the village, through its elders, its chief, or council, which provided the ultimate sanction and brought each person to know and to do what was expected.

While each served and in turn was served by the commonwealth of the village, there was no assumption of equality. Chiefs, elected or hereditary, leaders, 13 chosen or assumed, elders, patriarchs, matriarchs, commanded respect and gave respect in rightful order. One's age, experience, and resourcefulness could make one superior to others, obliging proper deference from them. One went on one's knees before father, mother, or elder. That being said, however, in the typical village there was little to distinguish one person or family from another in the way of material possessions and standard of living. The village did not support extremes of wealth and want.

The African was thus in a living web of interrelationships wherein personality 14 was defined, and the possibility of growth or change circumscribed. His character reflected his membership in an age group, clan, and family. He learned to understand and appreciate patterns that had endured for centuries and were but slightly changed over generations. The important relationships of life were controlled by a rigid etiquette learned through ritual, routine, and religion, occupying everyone and touching everything. Little of his thought was toward innovation. Age-old problems of farming, health, and warfare were solved by traditional means, or they persisted unsolved.

In the course of his life, he may have become especially honored by his people for some particular achievement or trait of character. But his real meaning lay 15 in the fact of his "being," that he existed and "fit" where he did in the network of tribal relationships. As the reason for village was not questioned and need not be explained, he, too, was justified by the simple fact that he *was*. Since his goals and those of the village were the same—to exist—"progress" was not something to be thought about.

One might say the village was the family writ large, so intimate and pervasive 16 were its influences. Indeed, given the intricacies of blood ties and kinship, it was difficult to be precise about the margins of family as the lines attenuated outward.

The inner regions of family were sharply enough defined. Were you born into 17 this world of relations, you would have found yourself centered in your mother's house with her other children, your brothers and sisters. But likely there would be near at hand other women, like your mother, the other wives of your father; their children, your half-brothers and half-sisters, like you, from the same father's seed. At the core of this universe would stand your father, whose greatness was in the produce of his land and his loins, whose greatest wealth was in his children. There would be a senior wife, who stood above the other women in authority. Then there would be the co-wives, with your mother and all the children ranging in age from infancy to adulthood. In such a compound, your network of relationships would begin, radiating outward to uncles and aunts, cousins, nieces and nephews. Beyond the compound and beyond the village would be others, tied to you by bloodlines, and others more remote but family nonetheless. Each such link had its discrete meaning, conferring upon the other person clear responsibilities to you and obliging you in turn.

Family compounds also housed persons who were neither of the father's nor 18 the mother's blood. They belonged to the father because they had been captured, given as an honor by a chief, or held as a pawn in place of debt. These "slaves," as they were called, sometimes represented several generations in that status, for the custom was that a female slave's children were slaves also. As slaves they might be servile or highly responsible persons, depending on their talents and character. They worked in the family's interest, were obedient to its authority, and might merge into the family through marriage. They were slaves only in the sense that they were held by the family. According to tradition, they could not be sold: they were not items of commerce.

The family was an economic unit, each member contributing to the whole. 19 There was room for the each to expend his energy and talent; no one was surplus. The rationale that underlay birth and nurture and training and succor was that the whole family would be harnessed to the tides of nature, that it might bring forth its fruits in abundance for the well-being of all.

Each wife had something that was hers—her land to cultivate, her chickens, 20 her goats—which came to her when she consented to be wife to her husband. While the single end of the family's efforts was to provide the means by which to live, there might well be more than a family could eat or use. That surplus, which came from the woman's land, was hers to trade for what she wanted but did not have.

The woman went to market in her village or in the principal village nearby. 21 Carrying her yams, peppers, groundnuts, or other produce, she would find a spot to await the right exchange. She might want poultry, hogs, goats, cloth, utensils, or whatever she could not raise or make herself. Since all the women at the market had much the same things to barter, it could be a long wait. But time was plentiful, and the market alive with news and tales from other villages. Sometimes, when nothing to exchange was found, she would take cowrie shells or other such money and await a better occasion when there would be goods to trade more to her liking.

Trading meant exchanging what one had for what one needed or desired, and 22 the skill was in knowing the true value of both. Ideally, an exchange was made when there was a matching of value for value. The woman could then return justly proud of a well-matched trade, but shame would be on her if she gave a great deal for little. There was much room for individual skills and shrewdness. Some women did better than others, and the rewards of their industry and cunning would be reflected in the well-being of their children.

In the economy of the village, the welfare of all was far too important to allow 23 crucial decisions to be made in personal and private ways. Thus, when to plant and harvest, when to cut and burn the fields, even what crops to plant were matters of consensus rather than individual judgment. Not that these questions were raised each year, or much at all. Rather, the logic and intelligence of experience had locked such matters into routine behavior, so that, except for crisis or disaster, questions of choice never rose to the level of conscious, deliberate decision making.

If disaster did strike—if nature, despite the combined knowledge of villagers 24 and elders, despite all the supplications and offerings, was too ungiving for too many seasons; if strange people moved too close, bringing violence and death—it was the unit of the family together with the unit of the village that decided what should be done.

As the welfare of each person was so intimately linked to that of the whole 25 family, the village, and the tribe, and all in turn rested on the person, no important decision was really personal. Surely, the matter of marriage and the augmentation of family could not be left to the judgment of young people. Kin and clan would assure that mating served both the young and all those who must, in time, depend upon the young. The young man acquired from his family (or, more likely, from the substance of his own labor) bridal dues, which he would give to the family of the woman to be his wife. The couple would then establish their household, according to custom, near the bride's or groom's family, keeping the growing unit a close-knit fabric.

For a person to be one of many was no strange thing, for from the time the 26 child left the back of his mother and started to walk on his own, he was among others and dependent on them. Older boys and girls cared for him and taught him the intricate social interplay of child society.

The child moved through stages of life together with others his age, all learn- 27 ing and experiencing the same quality of life. Before them were older children and adults in whose existence was clearly calibrated the stages of one's own development; behind were younger children, already one's charge and responsibility, whose almost every rough way one had already mastered. This made even children sense the rightness of the unalterable association between age and wisdom.

All that need be learned was, in time, before one's eyes—the mysteries of the 28 body, birth, life, death—all to be seen and explained. As a girl grew, she was pulled more closely into marriage, pregnancy, and the birth of others, until her own time came.

A boy could watch with silent awe as his elder brothers went through secret 29 rites from which they emerged with the marks of the tribe and a far-away look, as if they had seen into the most distant darkness. But it would be another year or two until his own time would come. Then he, too, would know the exquisite agony of the boy-man/man-child rite and confront enigmas that would stay with him forever. But he could look into the eyes of the others who had shared that moment, as they had shared all moments from leaving their mother's arms. They could look at each other and know their oneness.

It was a special way of life, being so intimately tied to others, being so defined 30 in terms of community. But the links that bound all together went beyond the compounds of the village and clan to the villages of the tribe. So, even when one went to neighboring villages, one was never a stranger. Through the kin of mother, father, uncles, and aunts, there was family and welcome. One was not likely to wander far from one's village, but wherever one went within the tribe, one was a person—the son or daughter of a person—related to someone known. The web of relationships extended far and gave one a sense of place and certainty. But it tied one to obligations and duties, and made the concept of individual freedom the fantasy of a lunatic.

It was right that one's destiny was of the group. For what one was, was of the 31 whole. Had it not been told and justified in the lives of those who had lived longer? Was not one tied to them in experience, just as they had been tied to their fathers before them, and their fathers to those who had sired them, right back to the fathers of the tribe? The present, where one stood in time, was a natural extension of all time and experience to that moment. One was a creature of a history that verified the rightness of things as they were; the lessons of human experience seemed so invariable, changing when they did by infinitesimal shifts of practice and habit.

Lest one lose sight of that experience or miscalculate its weight, it was wound 32 in an endless skein of history, told in stories hardly varying with each telling or in long narrative songs, which located each moment in its rightful place. Each person was made part of that historical strand and could find his way back to people and family no longer alive, to times and events before the actual recollection of even the oldest one present. One's family, details of personal character and achievement, lived in those songs and stories. Through them, one was lifted into the importance of one's birthright and made to share the greatness of his people and their past, beyond remembered times.

Such history, therefore, was tribal and familial, but it was also personal. Who 33 one was, where one came from, what one was expected to be, the heights of courage and character that were to be achieved, were woven into the fabric that linked one's self to all, touching, at last, the first father of the tribe, the one who, through superhuman power and character, had pulled together the people in the birth of the tribe itself.

When one imagined the first fathers of the tribe, one had gone beyond mere 34 history and touched upon the beginning of existence itself, for they were almost godlike. It was as if life itself had spun a web of infinite intricacy, beginning with the tribal fathers, tying all together and linking everything to the present self. Death mattered not. It was a mere punctuation. Life was of the person, and the person of life—all a continuum—so that the forces of life ebbed and flowed through him, making him a conduit of the life force. Dead or alive, he continued to impress on life the energy of his own spirit and character.

Was it not possible in time of need to call to those since departed the living, 35 who in their time had overcome such troubles? And was it not, in merely recollecting them, that one could feel the power of those who had overcome their trials? And was it not that inspiration that made one find, within himself, the resources to overcome one's own troubles.

Life was all there was; not good and evil alone, but good and evil bound 36 together in a mélange too complex to comprehend. When all one's easiest efforts came to fruition in bounty beyond expectations, that was the force of life working through the individual, multiplying the force of his own will and character. Doubtless, ancestors long since dead had brought their own force of character to his enterprise. But, on the other hand, when the best that one could do in mind, heart, and body led to meager and insubstantial results, that too was life's force in its diminished form. Chances were that people and spirits unfriendly to him had gained ascendance, and thus, for him, the tide was at ebb.

While a European might think of evil as an element of moral corruption, sin, 37 and personal culpability, the African was more likely to see evil as a natural part of the hand he was dealt. Evil came to him, as to all in their turn. One's best defense was respect for traditional obligation and the strength of personal character. Still, despite every plan and precaution, there was the unexpected—the joker in the deck. Thus the painful reminder that the life force, which had spun the web that made the person and all he knew, was at last an unfathomable mystery.

One could never forget one's helplessness before the great rush and surge of 38 life. Thus, as each morsel of food and drink one took was accepted, one's ancestors were remembered. One poured "libations" into the earth, thanking and invoking spirits and ancestors. One called them by name to share his substance so that they would be remembered and at home in his house, so that they would never leave him, especially in time of need.

The force of life that tied person to person and to all time past linked a person 39 as well to all things. The force that moved through him moved through plants of the field, trees, animals, and even stones. Spirits dwelt in each thing and imparted to it special character. Did not the fields throb with that spirit, sometimes flushing full and plentiful, sometimes waning meager, as that life force surged or slept within?

The spirit that dwelt within each thing had its own character, its own force to 40 be expressed. Out of the wood it came to command the wood-carver's hand to make itself manifest. The spirit of the wood, the stone, the clay, possessed the artisan to its own ends as much as the artisan expressed himself. One was fortunate and gifted if one could make oneself the instrument of those spirits that lurked within all things.

Ritual and ceremonial observation attended almost every event of the village 41 and family. The engagement of all in a vortex of music, dance, and celebration lifted the events of birth, marriage, and death to cosmic significance.

The whole of the community joined together to create that electric atmosphere 42
in which the world of palpable reality and the world of spirit would be as one: each
the instrument and the effect of the other—will beyond will, consciousness beyond
awareness, thought beyond mind. Each person within his place played a role but
understood himself only through the whole; like a member of a secret society, each
was linked to others by the mysteries that made them one. All moving, as would
sometimes appear, along no single thread or to no command. But the multiple
rhythms and apparent chaos of movement would, like life itself, come to focus in
the singularity of the most intense pulse of common ecstasy.

The drums sustained a relentless beat, flutes and voices spun an intricate pat- 43
tern of sound through the rhythms. The bodies of dancers turned and twisted and
spun within that music like tall blades of grass within the fingers of the wind.
Dancers' feet beat out the pulse of spirit against the earth; beads hissed, and bells
and metal rang with each movement of the body. Dancers and drums and flutes and
voices were all instruments of the same music and rhythms, playing against and
with one another to quicken the electric spark that moved them, until the atmosphere, too heavy to hold itself stable, would clap with the thunder and flash with
the glory of the spirits' presence among them.

Some special person—special because his nerves were attuned as no others 44
were—would be invaded and "possessed" by a spirit. An animal to be sacrificed—
goat or chicken—worked out the anguish of his pain and death through the surrogate human body. When the spirit of such an animal, or rain or wind or the genera-
tive force of the earth took possession of the body of doctor, priest, or priestess,
such a chosen one moved no longer to a rhythm and design of his own. Rather, like
a leaf in a high, turbulent wind he gyrated with dizzying convulsive starts, until
finally the spirit had departed, and he lay spent and empty.

The African's personal world, then, was both private and cosmic. Nothing he 45
was or did or that affected him was too small to be woven into the fabric of all
being. And, equally, nothing was so abstract, so divine, so sacred, as not to touch
him in an immediate and direct way. His was a self-contained world that would
account for all he would be expected to confront. His place in his world was
defined neatly and carefully through his relationships. His sense of person and purpose was sustained by the spiritual ambience that encapsulated his people. His
world had its comforts. While the room it left for mystery was infinite, there was
little, if any, place for doubt.

Yet, it was no Eden, no paradise, from which he was to be expelled. As much 46
as his world view took into account life as a dynamic and mysterious force, it could
not comprehend change coming from outside the framework it assumed. Status,
stability, and order were its values; change was unwanted and, thus, unprepared for.
So, the African's world was especially vulnerable to shocks and jolts from outside
an order whose principal strength was its parochial neatness.

At best, life was not unmitigated sweetness. The spirits of nature and life were 47
fickle partners and companions. Seldom did they behave as expected. They were

not to be taken for granted; they required constant attention and cajoling. And, sometimes, power fell into the wrong hands—those who would bend an individual to their will. Then he would have to bend lower under a burden that had once been light but now broke the back.

Rather than being an existence of pastoral simplicity, African life was charac- 48 terized by strong contrasts. Because the routines of daily living were flat and continuous, the special occurrence hit with more telling impact. One sensed in the purest form the extremes of suffering and joy, adversity and happiness. Lacking an array of instruments for planned dullness, the African's pleasure was ecstasy, but his pain was absolute agony. Except for plateaus of routine living, the African would experience both.

Without assumptions of change and plans for exigencies, calamities and affec- 49 tion fell harder on the African family and village than they would on people today. Droughts, floods, or raids that would claim a year's produce could mean total devastation, followed by starvation and death for nearly everyone. One was either in good health, and illness was the threshold of death.

The senses were honed to sharpness. The wetness of rain, the coldness of 50 night, the warmth of the sun, the hotness of fire, the blackness of the night's sky, the brilliance of stars and moon, were unmitigated sensations. We can have little sense of the keenness with which food, drink, and dance were enjoyed.

Where, as in some African societies, there was a regal and noble caste, one 51 could see it in the sparkle of gold and bronze ornaments, one could feel it in the difference between royal cloth and that worn by ordinary people. In such richness and power, rank and order were distinguished by pomp, which was heralded by proud or cruel publicity. The great chiefs never moved without glorious displays of arms and attendants, exciting fear and envy. Such richness and power were the more pronounced because of the plainness of everything else.

It is as one senses the emotive force of such contrasts, such purity of sensa- 52 tion, that one can comprehend the power of the chants, the music, the dance, the processions that attended funerals, births, marriages, executions, and all notable events. It was not merely these grand events that were raised by the sacredness of ceremony to the rank of mysteries, but incidents of less importance—a journey, a task, a visit—were equally attended by a thousand formalities, benedictions, and ceremonies. As one senses the explosive force of such contrasts, one can feel the impact of the start of rain after the dry months, a sudden fire in the darkness of the night, voices chanting in unison, the sharp report of drums splintering the air, the sudden violence of warriors sweeping down, shattering the calm of village life.

Whatever the neatness and completeness of the African's social fabric and 53 cosmology, there was a general feeling of insecurity because one was subject to the unknown, and swings of events provided vast contrasts, not finely calibrated shifts and changes. One could easily fall victim to the unknown or to the chronic form that wars might take. So one turned in everlasting fear to gods, doctors, and priests.

■ *Questions for* . . . African Beginnings: The Seamless Web
by Nathan Huggins

Words to Note

fanned	vast	traversed
abject	coffles	caravans
fettered	grandeur	coursing
spilling	corral-like	barracoons
loomed	progeny	vestiges
family compounds	wastrel	bloodlines
hereditary	patriarchs	matriarchs
living web of	margins	attenuated
interrelationships	senior wife	co-wives
radiating	discrete	conferring
slaves	kin and clan	bridal dues
calibrated	rites	enigmas
lunatic	verified	infinitesimal
an endless skein	mélange	fruition
of history	intense pulse of	hissed
spiritual ambience	common ecstasy	encapsulated
infinite	unmitigated	affliction

Language

1. In paragraph 18, why does Huggins put *slaves* in quotation marks? What issue lurks behind these punctuation marks?
2. Is Huggins's language objective?

Style

1. Huggins tells us that West Africans existed in a "living web of interrelationships," that "nature was the throb of the village's heart," and that tribal customs and habits were "wound in an endless skein of history." What tone does Huggins's phrasing and word choice help to establish?
2. Huggins uses quite a few semicolons. In paragraph 8, there are two. There's one in paragraphs 2, 10, 12, and so on. How does he use the semicolon? How do his semicolons affect the pace of his sentences?

Development and Organization

1. Is paragraph 17 too long? How does Huggins develop the paragraph's topic?

2. Map the piece. What general headings does Huggins's treatment of West African tribal life fall under? Did he overlook any important aspect of life? How would you know?
3. Would Huggins's essay benefit from the sort of specific instances and people that Demos and Laslett (author of the next selection) include in their pieces?

Discussion and Journal Writing

1. Has Huggins romanticized the West African family compounds, villages, and tribes he writes about? How would you go about making this judgment?
2. Compare and contrast Huggins's West African family compound with Demos's Plymouth Colony family. Do both families roughly perform the same functions?

ooooo

The World We Have Lost

—Peter Laslett

Peter Laslett, a Fellow of Trinity College, Cambridge University, is the author of books on political and social theory. Along with E. A. Wrigley, he founded and directs the Cambridge Group for the History of Population and Social Structure. In "The World We Have Lost," the beginning of a book by the same title, Laslett gives us a blueprint of a baker's family, household, and shop, and in the process provides a glimpse of everyday life in seventeenth-century London.

In the year 1619 the bakers of London applied to the authorities for an increase in the price of bread. They sent in support of their claim a complete description of a bakery and an account of its weekly costs. There were thirteen or fourteen people in such an undertaking: the baker and his wife, four paid employees who were called journeymen, two apprentices, two maidservants and the three or four children of the master baker himself. Six pounds ten shillings a week was reckoned to be the outgoings of this establishment of which only eleven shillings eightpence went for wages: half a crown a week for each of the journeymen and tenpence for each of the maids. Far and away the greatest expense was for food: two pounds nine shillings out of the six pounds ten shillings, at five shillings a head for the baker and his wife, four shillings a head for their helpers and two shillings for their children. It cost much more in food to keep a journeyman than it cost in money; four times as much to keep a maid. Clothing was charged up too, not only for the man, wife and children, but for the apprentices as well. Even school fees were claimed as a justifiable charge on the price of bread for sale, and sixpence a week was paid for the teaching and clothing of a baker's child.

A London bakery was undoubtedly what we should call a commercial or even   2
an industrial undertaking, turning out loaves by the thousand. Yet the business was carried on in the house of the baker himself. There was probably a *shop* as part of the house, *shop* as in *workshop* and not as meaning a retail establishment. Loaves were not ordinarily sold over the counter: they had to be carried to the open-air market and displayed on stalls. There was a garner behind the house, for which the baker paid two shillings a week in rent, and where he kept his wheat, his *sea-coal* for the fire and his store of salt. The house itself was one of those high, half-timbered overhanging structures on the narrow London street which we always think of when we remember the scene in which Shakespeare, Pepys or even Christopher Wren lived. Most of it was taken up with the living quarters of the dozen people who worked there.

It is obvious that all these people ate in the house since the cost of their food   3
helped to determine the production cost of the bread. Except for the journeymen they were all obliged to sleep in the house at night and live together as a family.   4

The only word used at that time to describe such a group of people was 'family'. The man at the head of the group, the entrepreneur, the employer, or the manager, was then known as the master or head of the family. He was father to some of its members and in place of father to the rest. There was no sharp distinction between his domestic and his economic functions. His wife was both his partner and his subordinate, a partner because she ran the family, took charge of the food and managed the women-servants, a subordinate because she was woman and wife, mother and in place of mother to the rest.

The paid servants of both sexes had their specified and familiar position in the   5
family, as much part of it as the children but not quite in the same position. At that time the family was not one society only but three societies fused together; the society of man and wife, of parents and children and of master and servant. But when they were young, and servants were, for the most part, young and unmarried people, they were very close to the children in their status and their function. Here is the agreement made between the parents of a boy about to become an apprentice and his future master. The boy covenants to dwell with his master for seven years, to keep his secrets and to obey his commandments.

Taverns and alehouses he shall not haunt, dice, cards or any other unlawful games he shall not use, fornication with any woman he shall not commit, matri-

mony with any woman he shall not commit, matrimony with any woman he shall
not contact. He shall not absent himself by night or by day without his master's
leave but be a true and faithful servant.

On his side, the master undertakes to teach his apprentice his *'art, science or occupation with moderate correction'*.

> Finding and allowing unto his said servant meat, drink, apparel, washing, lodging
> and all other things during the said term of seven years, and to give unto his said
> apprentice at the end of the said term double apparel, to wit, one suit for holy-
> days and one suit for worken days.

Apprentices, therefore, and many other servants, were workers who were also   6
children, extra sons or extra daughters (for girls could be apprenticed too), clothed
and educated as well as fed, obliged to obedience and forbidden to marry, often
unpaid and dependent until after the age of twenty-one. If such servants were workers in the position of sons and daughters, the sons and daughters of the house were
workers too. John Locke laid it down in 1697 that the children of the poor must
work for some part of the day when they reached the age of three. The children of a
London baker were not free to go to school for many years of their young lives, or
even to play as they wished when they came back home. Soon they would find
themselves doing what they could in *bolting,* that is sieving flour, or in helping the
maidservant with her panniers of loaves on the way to the market stall, or in playing their small parts in preparing the never-ending succession of meals for the
whole household.

We may see at once, therefore, that the world we have lost, as I have chosen   7
to call it, was no paradise or golden age of equality, tolerance or loving kindness. It
is so important that I should not be misunderstood on this point that I will say at
once that the coming of industry cannot be shown to have brought economic
oppression and exploitation along with it. It was there already. The patriarchal
arrangements which we have begun to explore were not new in the England of
Shakespeare and Elizabeth. They were as old as the Greeks, as old as European history, and not confined to Europe. And it may well be that they abused and enslaved
people quite as remorselessly as the economic arrangements which had replaced
them in the England of Blake and Victoria. When people could expect to live for so
short a time, how must a man have felt when he realized that so much of his adult
life must go in working for his keep and very little more in someone else's family?

But people very seldom recognize facts of this sort, and no one is content to   8
expect to live as long as the majority in fact will live. Every servant in the old
social world was probably quite confident that he or she would some day get married and be at the head of a new family, keeping others in subordination. If it is
legitimate to use the words exploitation and oppression in thinking of the economic
arrangement of the pre-industrial world, there were nonetheless differences in the
manner of oppressing and exploiting. The ancient order of society was felt to be

eternal and unchangeable by those who supported, enjoyed and endured it. There was no expectation of reform. How could there be when economic organization was domestic organization, and relationships were rigidly regulated by the social system, by the content of Christianity itself?

Here is a vivid contrast with social expectation in Victorian England, or in 9 industrial countries everywhere today. Every relationship in our world which can be seen to affect our economic life is open to change, is expected indeed to change of itself, or if it does not, to *be* changed, made better, by an omnicompetent authority. This makes for a less stable social world, though it is only one of the features of our society which impels us all in that direction. All industrial societies, we may suppose, are far less stable than their predecessors. They lack the extraordinarily cohesive influence which familial relationships carry with them, that power of reconciling the frustrated and the discontented by emotional means. Social revolution, meaning an irreversible changing of the pattern of social relationships, never happened in traditional, patriarchal, pre-industrial human society. It was almost impossible to contemplate.

Almost, but not quite. Sir Thomas More, in the reign of Henry VIII, could fol- 10 low Plato in imagining a life without privacy and money, even if he stopped short of imagining a life where children would not know their parents and where promiscuity could be a political institution. Sir William Petty, 150 years later, one of the very first of the political sociologists, could speculate about polygamy; and the England of the Tudors and the Stuarts already knew of social structures and sexual arrangements, existing in the newly discovered world, which were alarmingly different from their own. But is must have been an impossible effort of the imagination for them to suppose that they were anything like as satisfactory.

It will be noticed that the roles we have allotted to all the members of the 11 capacious family of the master-baker of London in the year 1619 are, emotionally, all highly symbolic and highly satisfying. We may feel that in a whole society organized like this, in spite of all the subordination, the exploitation and the obliteration of those who were young, or feminine, or in service, everyone belonged in a group, a family group. Everyone had his circle of affection: every relationship could be seen as a love-relationship.

Not so with us. Who could love the name of a limited company or of a gov- 12 ernment department as an apprentice could love his superbly satisfactory father-figure master, even if he were a bully and a beater, a usurer and a hypocrite? But if a family is a circle of affection, it can also be the scene of hatred. The worst tyrants among human beings, the murderers and the villains, are jealous husbands and resentful wives, possessive parents and deprived children. In the traditional, patriarchal society of Europe, where practically everyone lived out his whole life within the family, though not usually within one family, tension like this must have been incessant and unrelieved, incapable of release except in crisis. Men, women and children have to be very close together for a very long time to generate the emotional power which can give rise to a tragedy of Sophocles, or Shakespeare, or Racine. Conflict in such a society was between individual people, on the personal scale. Except when the Christians fought with the infidels, or Protestants fought with Catholics, clashes between masses of persons did not often arise. There could never be a situation such as that which makes our own time, as some men say, the scene of perpetual revolution.

All this is true to history only if the little knot of people making bread in 13 Stuart London was indeed the typical social unit of the old world in its size, composition and scale. There are reasons why a baker's household might have been a little out of the ordinary, for baking was a highly traditional occupation in a society increasingly subject to economic change. We shall see, in due course, that a family of thirteen people, which was also a unit of production of thirteen, less the children still incapable of work, was quite large for English society at that time. Only the families of the really important, the nobility and the gentry, the aldermen and the successful merchants, were ordinarily as large as this. In fact, we can take the bakery to represent the upper limit in size and scale of the group in which ordinary people lived and worked. Among the great mass of society which cultivated the land, and which will be the major preoccupation of this essay, the family group was smaller than a substantial London craftsman's entourage. There are other things we should observe about the industrial and commercial scene.

It is worth noticing to begin with, how prominently the town and the craft 14 appear in the folk-memory we still retain from the world we have lost. Agriculture and the countryside do not dominate our recollections to anything like the extent that they dominated that vanished world. We still talk to our children about the apprentices who married their master's daughter: these are the heroes. Or about the outsider who marries the widow left behind by the father/master when he comes to die: these unwelcome strangers to the family are villains. We refer to bakers as if they really baked in their homes; of spinsters who really sit by the fire and spin. A useful, if a rather arbitrary and romantic guide to the subject in hand, is the famous collection of Fairy Tales compiled by the brothers Grimm in Germany nearly 150 years ago, where the tales we tell to our children mostly have their source. Even in the form given to them by Walt Disney and the other makers of films and picture-books for the youngest members of our rich, leisurely, powerful, puzzled world of successful industrialization, stories like Cinderella are a sharp reminder of what life was once like for the apprentice, the journeyman, the master and all his family in the craftsman's household. Which means, in a sense, that we know it all already.

We know, or half-remember, that a journeyman might sometimes have to 15 spend a year or two on his journeys, serving out that difficult period after he was trained and capable of his craft, but before he had made, or inherited, or had the prospect of marrying, enough money to set up as master by himself. It takes a little reflection to recognize in this practice the reason why so many heroes of the nursery rhymes and stories are on the road, literally seeking their fortunes. We have to go even further to search here for the origin of the picaresque in literature, perhaps for the very germ of the novel. And conscious analysis, directed historical research of a kind only recently supposed to be possible and necessary, has had to be done before even a few fragmentary facts about the tendency of young people to move about could be recovered. It has been found that most young people in service, except, of course, the apprentices, seem to have looked upon a change of job bringing them into a new family as the normal thing every few years.

This feeling that it is all obvious is a curious and exasperating feature of the 16 whole issue, for it means that the historian has not hitherto felt a clear call to examine it as a subject. He has supposed that he knows it already, by rote if not by understanding. This means that the force of the contrast between our world and the world which the historian undertakes to describe has hitherto been somewhat indistinct. Without contrast there cannot be full comprehension. One reason for feeling puzzled by our own industrial society is because the historian has never set out to tell us what society was like before industry came and seems to assume that everyone knows.

We shall have much more to say about the movement of servants from farm- 17 house to farmhouse in the old world, and shall return to the problem of understanding ourselves in time, in contrast with our ancestors. Let us emphasize again the scale of life in the working family of the London baker. Few persons in the old world ever found themselves in groups larger than family groups, and there were few families of more than a dozen members. The largest household so far known to us, apart from the royal court and the establishments of the nobility, lay and spiritual, is that of Sir Richard Newdigate, Baronet, in his house of Arbury within his parish of Chilvers Coton in Warwickshire, in the year 1684. There were thirty-seven people in Sir Richard's family: himself; Lady Mary Newdigate his wife; seven daughters, all under the age of sixteen; and twenty-eight servants, seventeen men and boys and eleven women and girls. This was still a family, not an institution, a staff, an office or a firm.

Everything physical was on the human scale, for the commercial worker in 18 London, and the miner who lived and toiled in Newdigate's village of Chilvers Coton. No object in England was larger than London Bridge or St. Paul's Cathedral, no structure in the Western World to stand comparison with the Colosseum in Rome. Everything temporal was tied to the human life-span too. The death of the master baker, head of the family, ordinarily meant the end of the bakery. Of course there might be a son to succeed, but the master's surviving children would be young if he himself had lived only as long as most men. Or an apprentice might fulfil the final function of apprenticehood, substitute sonship, that is to say, and marry his master's daughter, or even his widow. Surprisingly often, the widow, if she could, would herself carry on the trade.

This, therefore, was not simply a world without factories, without firms, and 19 for the most part without economic continuity. Some partnerships between rich masters existed, especially in London, but since nearly every activity was limited to what could be organized within a family, and the lifetime of its head, there was an unending struggle to manufacture continuity and to provide an expectation of the future. 'One hundred and twenty family uprising and downlying, whereof you may take out six or seven and all the rest were servants and retainers': this was the household of the Herberts, Earls of Pembroke in the years before the Civil War, as it was remembered a generation later by the sentimental antiquarian of the West Country where the Herberts were seated, John Aubrey of the *Lives*. It is wise to be careful of what men liked to report about the size and splendour of the great families in days gone by: £16,000 a year was the Herbert revenue, so John Aubrey claimed, though 'with his offices, and all' the Earl 'had £30,000 per annum. And, as the revenue was great, so the greatness of his retinue and hospitality were answerable.' These are impossible figures, but we know that Lord William Howard kept between forty and fifty servants at Naworth Castle in Cumberland in the 1620's on a much smaller revenue. And as late as 1787, the Earl of Lonsdale, a very rich, mine-owning bachelor, lived in a household of fifty at Lowther in Westmorland, himself that is and forty-nine servants. All this illustrates the symbolic function of the aristocratic family in a society of families, which were generally surprisingly small as we shall see. They were there to defy the limitation on size, and to raise up a line which should remain for ever.

■ *Questions for* . . . **The World We Have Lost** by Peter Laslett

Words to Note

journeymen	justifiable	stalls
master or head of	economic oppression	garner
the household	and exploitation	patriarchal
frustrated	discontented	arrangements
contemplate	promiscuity	capacious
per annum		

Language

1. What does *world* mean in Laslett's title?

Style

1. Why are Laslett's sentences so easy to follow? What sorts of transitional devices does he use?

Development and Organization

1. Laslett doesn't get to the point of his essay until the fourth paragraph. Is that wise?
2. Why does he quote at such length from the apprentice's agreement? Wouldn't it have been quicker and easier to paraphrase the contents of this agreement?

Discussion and Journal Writing

1. Is the family still the chief organizing institution of society, or does it have competition?
2. Write a short story set in the baker's house.

ooooo

England's Slums

—Friedrich Engels

Friedrich Engels was a German socialist best known for coauthoring *The Communist Manifesto* with Karl Marx. Engels was involved in revolutionary agitation in Germany. When it failed in 1849, he fled to England, where he became a manufacturer in Manchester. During that time he supported Marx while Marx wrote *Das Kapital*. Manchester was the center of the industrial revolution and was a notorious example of the social order Engels was trying to overthrow. In this essay, Engels examines the miserable slums of London. Engels's politics gives these sketches their verve and direction.

Every great town has one or more slum areas into which the working classes   1
are packed. Sometimes, of course, poverty is to be found hidden away in alleys close to the stately homes of the wealthy. Generally, however, the workers are segregated in separate districts where they struggle through life as best they can out of sight of the more fortunate classes of society. The slums of the English towns have much in common—the worst houses in a town being found in the worst districts. They are generally unplanned wildernesses of one- or two-storied terrace houses built of brick. Wherever possible these have cellars which are also used as dwellings. These little houses of three or four rooms and a kitchen are called cottages, and throughout England, except for some parts of London, are where the working classes normally live. The streets themselves are usually unpaved and full of holes. They are filthy and strewn with animal and vegetable refuse. Since they have neither gutters nor drains the refuse accumulates in stagnant, stinking puddles. Ventilation in the slums is inadequate owing to the hopelessly unplanned nature of these areas. A great many people live huddled together in a very small area, and so it is easy to imagine the nature of the air in these workers' quarters. However, in fine weather the streets are used for the drying of washing and clothes lines are

stretched across the streets from house to house and wet garments are hung out on them.

We propose to describe some of these slums in detail. In London there is the well-known 'rookery' of St. Giles, which is to be demolished to make way for wide new thoroughfares. St. Giles is situated in the most densely-populated part of London and is surrounded by splendid wide streets which are used by the fashionable world. It is close to Oxford Street, Trafalgar Square and the Strand. It is a confused conglomeration of tall houses of three or four stories. The narrow, dirty streets are just as crowded as the main thoroughfares, but in St. Giles one sees only members of the working classes. The narrowness of the roads is accentuated by the presence of street-markets in which baskets of rotting and virtually uneatable vegetables and fruit are exposed for sale. The smell from these and from the butchers' stalls is appalling. The houses are packed from cellar to attic and they are as dirty inside as outside. No human being would willingly inhabit such dens. Yet even worse conditions are to be found in the houses which lie off the main road down narrow alleys leading to the courts. These dwellings are approached by covered passages between the houses. The extent to which these filthy passages are falling into decay beggars all description. There is hardly an unbroken windowpane to be seen, the walls are crumbling, the door posts and window frames are loose and rotten. The doors, where they exist, are made of old boards nailed together. Indeed in this nest of thieves doors are superfluous, because there is nothing worth stealing. Piles of refuse and ashes lie all over the place and the slops thrown out into the street collect in pools which emit a foul stench. Here live the poorest of the poor. Here the worst-paid workers rub shoulders with thieves, rogues and prostitutes. Most of them have come from Ireland or are of Irish extraction. Those who have not yet been entirely engulfed in the morass iniquity by which they are surrounded are daily losing the power to resist the demoralising influences of poverty, dirt and low environment.

St. Giles, however, is by no means the only London slum. In the vast mass of streets which make up the metropolis there are thousands of hidden alleys and passages where the houses are so bad that no one with an iota of self-respect would live in them unless forced to do so by dire poverty. Such dens of extreme poverty are often to be found close to the splendid mansions of the wealthy. Recently at a coroner's inquest an area near Portman Square—a very respectable part of London—was described as the abode of 'a large number of Irish demoralised by dirt and poverty'. In a street like Long Acre, which, although not fashionable, is still respectable, there are many cellar dwellings from which emerge into the light of day sickly children and half-starved, ragged women. In the immediate vicinity of the second most important theatre in London, that in Drury Lane, are to be found some of the worst streets in the metropolis. In Charles Street, King Street and Parker Street all the houses are crammed from cellar to roof with many poor families. In 1840, according to a report printed in the *Journal* of the Statistical Society of London, there were in the parishes of St. John and St. Margaret, Westminster, 5,366 working-class families living in 5,294 'dwellings' (if they deserve this appellation!). Altogether there were 16,176 men, women and children thrown together without distinction of age or sex. Three quarters of the families lived in a single room. It is stated in the same *Journal* that 1,465 working-class families totalling about 6,000 persons lived under similar condition in [the Inner Ward of] the aristocratic parish of St. George, Hanover Square. In two-thirds of the families investigated the members were packed into a single room. How shamefully do the wealthier classes exploit, under the protection of the law, these miserable slum-dwellers, who are so poor that no thief would think of trying to rob them. The following [weekly] rents are charged for accommodation in the revolting dwellings near Drury Lane which we have just described: 3s. for cellars, 4s. for a room on the ground floor, 4s. 6d. on the first floor, 4s. on the second floor, 3s. for an attic. The starving inhabitants of Charles Street pay their landlord an annual tribute of £2,000, while the 5,366 families in Westminster mentioned above together pay an annual rent of £40,000.

The largest working-class district lies in Whitechapel and Bethnal Green to the east of the Tower of London. Here live the great majority of London's workers. The Rev. G. Alston, incumbent of St. Philip's, Bethnal Green, has given the following account of conditions in his parish: 4

'It contains 1,400 houses, inhabited by 2,795 families, comprising a population of 12,000. The space within which this large amount of population are living is less than 400 yards square, and it is no uncommon thing for a man and his wife, with four or five children, and sometimes the grandfather and grandmother, to be found living in a room from ten to twelve feet square, and which serves them for eating and working in. I believe that till the Bishop of London called the attention of the public to the state of Bethnal-green, about as little was known at the West-end of the town of this most destitute parish as the wilds of Australia or the islands of the South Seas. If we really desire to find out the most destitute and deserving, we must lift the latch of their doors, and find them at their scanty meal; we must see them when suffering from sickness and want of work; and if we do this from day to day in such a neighbourhood as Bethnal-green, we shall become acquainted with a mass of wretchedness and misery such as a nation like our own ought to be ashamed to permit. I was Curate of a parish near Huddersfield during the three years of the greatest manufacturing distress; but I never witnessed such a thorough prostration of the poor as I have seen since I have been in Bethnal-green. There is not one father of a family in ten throughout the entire district that possesses any clothes but his working dress, and that too commonly in the worst tattered condition; and with many this wretched clothing form their only covering at night, with nothing better than a bag of straw or shavings to lie upon.'

This description enables us to appreciate the conditions inside these dwellings. We may add also some evidence given by public officials who sometimes have occasion to enter the homes of workers.   5

On November 16th, 1843, Mr. Carter, the coroner for Surrey, held an inquest   6
on the body of a certain Ann Galway, who died at the age of 45. We take the following account of her home from press reports. She lived in no. 3, White Lion
Court, Bermondsey Street, London, with her husband and nineteen-year-old son.
The family occupied a small room in which there were neither beds, bedding not
other furniture. She lay dead by the side of her son on a heap of feathers which
practically covered her naked body, for she had neither sheet nor blanket. The
feathers had stuck so fast to her that the doctor was unable to examine the body
until it had been washed. The doctor found that the body was emaciated and ver-
minous. Part of the floor in the room had been torn up and the hole used by the
family as a privy.

On Monday, January 15th, 1844, two boys appeared before the magistrate at   7
Worship Street police court, London, charged with stealing a half-cooked cow-heel
from a shop. They immediately devoured their spoils as they were ravenous. The
magistrate felt it necessary to enquire further into the circumstances and was given
the following information by the police. The boys were brothers and their mother
was a widow. Their father had served in the Army and had later been a policeman.
After the death of her husband, the widow was left to struggle along as best she
could with nine children. The family lived in dire poverty at no. 2 Pool's Place,
Quaker Court, Spitalfields. When visited by a policeman she was found with six of
her children.They were all huddled together and the only furniture consisted of two
rush-bottomed chairs with seats gone, a little table with two legs broken, one broken cup and one small dish. Hardly a spark of fire came from the hearth and in one
corner lay as many rags as would fill a woman's apron. It was on these rags that the
whole family slept at night. As they had no blankets they slept in the miserable tat-
ters worn during the daytime. The wretched woman told the policeman that she had
had to sell her bed during the previous year in order to buy food. She had pawned
her bedding with the grocer for food. Indeed everything had been sold to get bread.
The magistrate made her a generous grant from the poor-box.

In February 1844 an application for assistance was made to the Marlborough   8
Street magistrate on behalf of Theresa Bishop, a 60-year-old widow, and her 26-
year-old daughter who was ill. She lived at no. 5, Brown Street, Grosvenor Square,
in a little back room hardly bigger than a cupboard. The room contained no proper
furniture. A *chest* was used both as table and chair, while a heap of rags in a corner
served as a bed for both women. The mother earned a little money as a charwoman.
Her landlord stated that she and her daughter had lived in this condition since May
1843. Gradually all their remaining possessions had been sold or pawned, but even
so they had been unable to pay any rent. The magistrate allowed them 20s. out of
the poor-box.

It is not, of course, suggested that all London workers are so poverty-stricken   9
as these three families. There can be no doubt that for every worker who is rendered utterly destitute by society there are ten who are better off. On the other hand
it can be confidently asserted that thousands of decent and industrious families—far
more deserving of respect than all the rich people in London—live under truly

deplorable conditions which are an affront to human dignity. It is equally incontestable that every working man without exception may well suffer a similar fate through no fault of his own and despite all his efforts to keep his head above water.

However wretched may be the dwellings of some of the workers—who do at 10 least have a roof over their heads—the situation of the homeless is even more tragic. Every morning fifty thousand Londoners wake up not knowing where they are going to sleep at night. The most fortunate are those who have a few pence in their pocket in the evening and can afford to go to one of the many lodging houses which exist in all the big cities. But these establishments only provide the most miserable accommodation. They are crammed full of beds from top to bottom—four, five and even six beds in a room—until there is no room for more. Each bed is filled to capacity and may contain as many as four, five or even six lodgers. The lodging house keeper allocates his accommodation to all his customers in rotation as they arrive. No attempt is made to segregate the sick and the healthy, the old and the young, the men and the women, the drunk and the sober. If these ill-assorted bed-fellows do not agree there are quarrels and fights which often lead to injuries. But if they do agree among themselves, it is even worse, for they are either planning burglaries or are engaged in practices of so bestial a nature that no words exist in a modern civilised tongue to describe them. Those who cannot afford a bed in a lodging house sleep where they can, in passages, arcades or any corner where the police and the owners are unlikely to disturb their slumbers. A few find accommodation in the shelters provided by private charitable organizations. Others sleep on benches in the parks in full view of Queen Victoria's windows. An account of these conditions may be found in a leading article of the *Times* for October 12th, 1843:

> 'It appears from the report of the proceedings at Marlborough Street Police Office in our columns of yesterday, that there is an average number of 50 human beings, of all ages, who huddle together in the parks every night, having no other shelter than what is supplied by the trees and hollows of the embankment. Of these the majority are young girls, who have been seduced from the country by the soldiers, and turned loose on the world in all the destitution of friendless penury, and all the recklessness of early vice.
>
> 'This is truly horrible. Poor there must be everywhere. Indigence will find its way and set up its hideous state in the heart of a great and luxurious city. Amid the thousand narrow lanes and by-streets of a populous metropolis there must always, we fear, be much suffering—much that offends the eye—much that lurks unseen.
>
> 'But that within the precincts of wealth, gaiety, and fashion, nigh the regal grandeur of St. James's, close on the palatial splendour of Bayswater, on the confines of the old and new aristocratic quarters in a district where the cautious refinement of modern design has refrained from creating one single tenement for poverty; which seems, as it were, dedicated to the exclusive enjoyments of wealth—that *there* want, and famine, and disease, and vice should stalk in all their kindred horrors, consuming body by body, soul by soul!

'It is, indeed, a monstrous state of things! Enjoyment the most absolute, that bodily ease, intellectual excitement, or the more innocent pleasures of sense can supply to man's craving, brought in close contact with the most unmitigated misery! Wealth, from its bright saloons, laughing—an insolently heedless laugh—at the unknown wounds of want! Pleasure, cruelly but unconsciously mocking the pain that moans below! All contrary things mocking one another— all contrary, save the vice which tempts and the vice which is tempted! . . .

'But all men, whether of theory or of practice, remember this—that within the most courtly precincts of the richest city on GOD'S earth, there may be found, night after night, winter after winter, women—young in years—old in sin and suffering—outcasts from society—ROTTING FROM FAMINE, FILTH AND DISEASE. Let them remember this, and learn not to theorize but to act. God knows, there is much room from action now-a-days.'

Reference has already been made to the shelters for the destitute. Two exam- 11 ples may be given to illustrate the hopeless overcrowding in these establishments. In a new Refuge for the Houseless in Upper Ogle Street [Marylebone], which has accommodation for 300, no less than 2740 persons were given shelter for one or more nights between January 27th, and March 7th, 1844. Although it was mild winter the number of people seeking accommodation in the shelter in Upper Ogle Street—and also in the hostels in Whitecross Street and Wapping—increased rapidly, and every night many applicants had to be refused admission. In another shelter, the Central Asylum in Playhouse Yard, the average number of persons accommodated in the first three months of 1843 amounted to 460. The total number of persons sheltered was 6,681, while the number of portions of bread distributed amounted to 96,141. Yet the committee responsible for the administration of this institution reported that only after the opening of the new Eastern Asylum had they been able to afford adequate provision for the applicants.

■ *Questions for* . . . England's Slums by Friedrich Engels

Words to Note

slums	packed	struggle
fortunate	unplanned wildernesses	dwellings
cottages	strewn	gutters
stagnant	puddles	huddled
conglomeration	accentuated	appalling
nest of thieves	metropolis	dens
ragged	crammed	prostration
emaciated	verminous	privy
pawned	grant	torturous
deplorable		

Language

1. Engels writes, "Every great town has one or more slum areas into which the working classes are packed." Name some of the synonyms of *packed.* Would *crammed* or *crowded* be better?
2. Reread the first paragraph. Which words does Engels use to establish our sympathies for England's working class?

Style

1. The case Engels makes for England's working poor is beautifully developed and nicely written, but his prose feels a little old fashioned. Why?
2. How does Engels pace himself?

Development and Organization

1. Why does Engels quote at such length from the *Times* and from the Reverend G. Alston's account of his parish in Bethnal Green? Should he have paraphrased and condensed? What would he have lost? When should writers paraphrase? When should they quote?
2. What do the descriptions of hovels, destitution, and starvation add in paragraphs 6, 7, and 8? Should he have written more about these people?

Discussion and Journal Writing

1. How do the homes of London's working poor compare with the sharecropper's cabin in Agee's "The House of Gudger"? Mathabane's house in Alexandra?
2. How would you characterize Engels's perspective? Is his perspective on England's slums particularly Marxist or communist?
3. Compare the newspaper story about the homeless that Engels quotes from the *Times,* October 12, 1843, with newspaper coverage of homelessness today or with Jonathan Kozol's "The Complete Life Story of Benjamin Peters, Homeless Baby," which appears in chapter 6. Is the sentiment different? Similar?
4. Are Engels's observations still valid? If you're not sure, how would you find out? Is there anyone on campus you could interview? What would you read? How can you guard against bias?

ooooo

Grandpatrimony

—Barney Pace

After completing a Ph.D. in American Studies at the University of Michigan, Barney Pace moved to New York City to write and teach. He has taught writing, literature, and history at the City University of New York since 1983, and has published reviews, articles, and fiction in the *New York Times Book Review, Publishers Weekly,* the *New York Sunday Post,* the *Mississippi Review,* and other publications. He has also written two novels that are not yet published. Pace was born in Pittsburgh, Pennsylvania, in 1954, the child of the children of Irish and Italian immigrants. "Grandpatrimony" is a mediation on the Americanization of his Italian-immigrant grandfather, Agostino Pace, who was born in 1888 in Termine Imerese, Sicilia.

I didn't have much of a world view in the late 1950s, probably because I 1 didn't turn five until the very end of the decade. Names of places and things had just begun to stick—Egypt, bauxite, Bethlehem, coal, all the tea in China—and the faces of leaders, past and present, loomed like floats in the Thanksgiving Day Parade: President Eisenhower, Captain Hook, Dictator Khrushchev, Robin Hood, Christopher Columbus, George Washington, and my Italian grandfather. I had a sense even then that my grandfather didn't belong in such an august line-up. I had never seen his black-and-white face on TV, he had never crossed the Delaware and he was not leader of the free world. But he had crossed the Atlantic, he was leader of my family and he was the most charismatic person I had encountered in my wide travels of Pittsburgh's North Side—the piece of the New World on which he had planted his standard. I was fascinated with his story long before it matured into a parable, and then a riddle.

When my grandfather Agostino Pace (pronounced Pa´-chay) was twelve, he 2 left his home and parents in Termini Imerese to join his brother Ignatio in America. Like all good Sicilian boys, he had a trade—barbering—but in 1904 no one in Pittsburgh needed a thirteen-year-old assistant, so he sold carnations on the street, just three years after Andrew Carnegie sold U.S. Steel to J. P. Morgan for a billion dollars, another immigrant cashing in big on the American dream. My grandfather's English must have been bad; it was still broken when I met him fifty years later.

By the time August Pace (now pronounced Pace) was twenty-seven, he had a 3 corner store and his own barber shop, a two-seater where the barbers, who were recent immigrants, smoked Parodi cigars and would cut your hair in Italian for a nickel. He was one of the best pool players in Pittsburgh, and he had become a force in ward politics. He and Art Rooney, who owned the Pittsburgh Steelers until his death in 1989, were known as the little mayors of the North Side: Rooney swung the Irish vote; my grandfather, the Italian. Democratic votes, of course.

In other words, by the time my grandfather was twenty-seven, he was a small-   4
time success and an eligible bachelor. His family introduced him to the Ferraras, who had a sixteen-year-old daughter named Louisa. My grandfather had Sunday dinner with the Ferraras for half a year, arrangements were made, and my grandmother moved from her father's house to her husband's house before she turned seventeen. The poise my sixteen-year-old grandmother radiates in her wedding photos has always astonished me.

As their family grew, they moved from place to place, settling finally with   5
their eleven children in a big but modest house on Shadeland Avenue, a few miles from the corner where my grandfather had sold flowers. He planted a fig tree in the back yard and an engraving on the mantle of Dante first catching sight of Beatrice, his hand heavy on his heart (my grandfather swore that's how it was when he first saw Louisa Ferrara), but the rest of the decor was American. They gave their children American names—my father was named after the president who spoke softly but carried a big stick—and no Italian was spoken in the house. My grandfather believed in English, the Democratic Party, and the little enamel American flag he wore on his lapel.

August Pace did well enough for himself, but his moderate success did not   6
protect him from bigotry. There were neighborhoods where Italians were not welcome, businesses where Italians need not apply and bankers who wouldn't lend money to Italians who were trying to start their own businesses. "Dago" and "wop" were fighting words, usually the stuff of verbal skirmishes, sometimes worse. In 1891, for instance, a mob strung up eleven Italians from lampposts in New Orleans. My grandfather paid a price for the Italian on his tongue, and he made sure it never got onto the tongues of his children. He bought American and his children were fluent in it and in it only. Had his family become his country? Is that the key to the riddle? My grandfather was a family man in a way it is hard for Americans in the late twentieth century to comprehend.

He liked it when I went away to college. It proved the plan was working.   7
Whenever I came home for a visit, he would point to a chair, which was his invitation to sit and talk politics. He didn't read much beyond the front page of the Pittsburgh *Post Gazette,* but he watched the news twice a day and forgot nothing. He paraphrased speeches, quoted statistics, and invoked a wide range of laws and bills. Every now and then, I'd outflank him with a historical parallel or point he didn't know about, but he was unflappable. He would file the point and use it to his advantage the next time. He liked our bouts, especially when I started to get good. I can still remember the smile that stole across the old ward heeler's face when I brought home the word "ideology."

But he didn't like it when I stayed away and stayed on to study American lit-   8
erature and history—the plan was not working—and said so.

"Barney, what are you doing?" He had a small voice on the phone. It wasn't   9
his medium.

"Michigan has a good program, Grandpap. I like it here."   10

"Come home to Pittsburgh, Barney. We got lots of colleges here."   11

I didn't say anything.   12

"I was just talking to your dad. We'll put you through law school. The family   13
needs a lawyer. In this country, every family needs a lawyer. Besides, this is where
you belong. Your family's here."

Even though he lived to be ninety-three and to see a few great-great grandchil-   14
dren, he didn't live quite long enough to see the Ph.D. that went up on the wall
across from Dante and Beatrice. But my grandmother, who put it there, told me he
would have been proud.

"He wanted good things for his family," she said. "That's what he worked for,   15
good things for his family."

Perhaps the plan was working too well.   16

You see, I'm not sure what my grandfather left me: he was fiercely proud of   17
his language and culture, which he let fade bit by bit. He grew up with opera, loved
it and idolized the great Caruso above all others. When my grandfather was nineteen, Enrico Caruso came to Pittsburgh to sing, and somehow my grandfather fina-
gled the honor of cutting his idol's hair. He offered to travel with Caruso and cut
his hair for free. The great Caruso grimaced, rose from the chair, brushed the hair
from his lapels and asked in the voice of a god, "What do I need a *schicarello* (little
jackass) like you for?" My grandfather wore that insult like a medal.

About ten years ago, shortly after my grandfather died, I reverted to the origi-   18
nal pronunciation of my name out of disrespect for the disrespect that changed it.
The little Italian I speak, I learned in graduate school, which is where I picked up
most of what I know about Italian history and culture. But I'm not fooled: the tradition was tampered with. It was abbreviated, and what remains has been revised,
shaded and edited. My heritage, a hyphenated one, has taught me quite a bit about
America and almost nothing about Italy.

1986 was the year of the immigrant. The Lady was buffed up and equipped   19
with a new torch to shine o'er the golden doorway, and we endured gale-force
speeches about the melting pot and the contributions that immigrants from all over
the world have made to the nation's greatness.

But so much was left out. Historians who study immigration talk about hostile   20
receptions, acculturation and assimilation, which make up the gears of
Americanization. What they mean is that moving in and up meant moving away
from one's roots. People were persuaded to disesteem their cultures, and sacrifices
were made even if unconsciously and gradually. For immigrants, the American
dream meant and still means Americanization.

My grandfather would have watched all that coverage and liked it too, I think.   21
The fanfare and the fireworks would have mesmerized him, the speeches would
have pleased him, and the dance that Baryshnikov did for Lady Liberty—his first

dance as a naturalized citizen—would have amused him. "Ballet dancers gotta have a country too," he might have said. The show would have moved him to reminiscence and he probably would have retold me the story of his stay at Ellis Island. For a day and a half, they kept him in a room with high windows, from which he could only see the sky, and fed him baloney sandwiches. He clutched the sponsorship papers his older brother Ignatio had sent him like a ticket to a double feature and showed them to anyone who asked him a question. He was excited and confused but never afraid, he claimed. After all, what was there to be afraid of? The heavens over the New World were as blue as the Virgin's gown.

Then, we would have argued.   22

■ *Questions for* . . . **Grandpatrimony** by Barney Pace

Words to Note

world view	loomed	august
charismatic	standard	parable
riddle	poise	radiates
astonished	decor	fluent
comprehend	paraphrased	outflank
unflappable	bouts	ideology
medium	opera	idolized
finagled	grimaced	insult
medal	reverted	shaded
edited	buffed up	disesteem
Americanization	mesmerized	naturalized
sponsorship papers		

Language

1. In paragraph 19, Pace writes that the "Lady," that is, the Statue of Liberty, was "buffed up and equipped with a new torch" and that Americans "endured gale-force speeches about the melting pot." Is this language appropriate to a description of a national celebration? What tone do these words and phrases establish?
2. Pace says his grandfather was amused when he brought the word *ideology* home from graduate school. Why is the word in quotation marks? How can such a serious word be amusing?
3. Pace says the North Side of Pittsburgh was the piece of the New World his grandfather planted his *standard* on. Italian immigrants didn't have standards in the late nineteenth century. How is he using this word? Who is he alluding to?

Style

1. Toward the end of the third paragraph, Pace writes, "Rooney swung the Irish vote; my grandfather, the Italian. Democratic votes, of course." Why the sentence fragments?
2. Paragraph 20 has quite a bit of Latinate diction, and the points made there don't *directly* pertain to Pace's family. Is this paragraph a break in the essay's tone?

Development and Organization

1. Paragraphs 8–16 are short. A few of them are only a sentence, while other paragraphs throughout the essay are eight, ten, and twelve sentences. Should Pace have combined these short paragraphs into one or developed them more fully?
2. Is the anecdote about Caruso necessary?
3. Pace skims over his grandfather's life. Is that a flaw of the essay? Is there any principle to what he includes and excludes?

Discussion and Journal Writing

1. What would Pace and his grandfather have argued about?
2. Do you agree or disagree with Pace's assessment that Americanization is the price of success for immigrants and their families? Can you think of exceptions? Is Pace's characterization of Americanization accurate?

ooooo

*F*amily Documents Four

Passengers Bound for Virginia (1634)

Edward Towers	26	Gamaliel White	24
Henry Woodman	22	Richard Marks	19
Richard Seems	26	Tho. Clever	16
Vyncent Whatter	17	Jo. Kitchin	16
James Whithedd	14	Edmond Edwards	20
Jonas Watts	21	Lewes Miles	19
Peter Loe	22	Jo. Kennedy	20
Geo. Brocker	17	Sam Jackson	24
Henry Eeles	26	Allin King	19
Jo. Dennis	22	Rowland Sadler	19
Tho. Swayne	23	Jo. Phillips	28
Charles Rinsden	27	Daniel Endick	16
Jo. Exston	17	Jo. Chalk	25
Wm. Luck	14	Jo. Vynall	20
Jo. Thomas	19	Edward Smith	20
Jo. Archer	21	Jo. Rowlidge	19
Richard Williams	25	Wm. Westlie	40
Francis Hutton	20	Jo. Smith	18
Savill Gascoyne	29	Jo. Saunders	22
Rich. Bulfell	29	Tho. Bartcherd	16
Rich. Jones	26	Tho. Dodderidge	19
Tho. Wynes	30	Richard Williams	18
Humphrey Williams	22	Jo. Ballance	19
Edward Roberts	20	Wm. Baldin	21
Martin Atkinson	32	Wm. Pen	26
Edward Atkinson	28	Jo. Gerie	24
Wm. Edwards	30	Henry Baylie	18
Nathan Braddock	31	Rich. Anderson	50
Jeffrey Gurrish	23	Robert Kelum	51
Henry Carrell	16	Richard Fanshaw	22
Tho. Ryle	24	Tho. Bradford	40

Wm. Spencer	16		
Marmaduke Ella	22		

Women

Ann Swayne	22	Annis Hopkins	24
Eliz. Cote	22	Ann Mason	24
Ann Rice	23	Bridget Crompe	18
Kat. Wilson	23	Mary Hawkes	19
Maudlin Lloyd	24	Ellin Hawkes	18
Mabell Busher	14		

Source: The New England Historical and Genealogical Register, XV (1861), p. 142; XXV (1871), pp. 12–15.

Passengers Bound for New England (1634)

1. Joseph Hull, of Somerset, a minister, aged 40 years
2. Agnes Hull, his wife, aged 25 years
3. Joan Hull, his daughter, aged 15 years
4. Joseph Hull, his son, aged 13 years
5. Tristram, his son, aged 11 years
6. Elizabeth Hull, his daughter, aged 7 years
7. Temperance, his daughter, aged 9 years
8. Grissell Hull, his daughter, aged 5 years
9. Dorothy Hull, his daughter, aged 3 years
10. Judith French, his servant, aged 20 years
11. John Wood, his servant, aged 20 years
12. Robert Dabyn, his servant, aged 28 years
13. Musachiell Bernard, of Batcombe, clothier in the county of Somerset, 24 years
14. Mary Bernard, his wife, aged 28 years
15. John Bernard, his son, aged 3 years
16. Nathaniel, his son, aged 1 year
17. Rich. Persons, salter and his servant, 30 years
18. Francis Baber, chandler, aged 36 years
19. Jesope, joyner, aged 22 years
20. Walter Jesop, weaver, aged 21 years
21. Timothy Tabor, in Somerset of Batcombe, tailor, aged 35 years

22. Jane Tabor, his wife, aged 35 years
23. Jane Tabor, his daughter, aged 10 years
24. Anne Tabor, his daughter, aged 8 years
25. Sarah Tabor, his daughter, aged 5 years
26. William Fever, his servant, aged 20 years
27. John Whitmarke, aged 39 years
28. Alice Whitmarke, his wife, aged 35 years
29. James Whitmarke, his son, aged 11 years
30. Jane, his daughter, aged 7 years
31. Onseph Whitmarke, his son, aged 5 years
32. Rich. Whitmarke, his son, aged 2 years
33. William Read, of Batcombe, taylor in Somerset, aged 28 years
34. [name not entered]
35. Susan Read, his wife, aged 29 years
36. Hannah Read, his daughter, aged 3 years
37. Susan Read, his daughter, aged 1 year
38. Rich. Adams, his servant, 29 years
39. Mary, his wife, aged 26 years
40. Mary Cheame, his daughter, aged 1 year
41. Zachary Bickewell, aged 45 years
42. Agnes Bickewell, his wife, aged 27 years
43. John Bickewell, his son, aged 11 years
44. John Kitchin, his servant, 23 years
46. George Allin, aged 24 years
47. Katherine Allin, his wife, aged 30 years
48. George Allin, his son, aged 16 years
49. William Allin, his son, aged 8 years
50. Matthew Allin, his son, aged 6 years
51. Edward Poole, his servant, aged 26 years
52. Henry Kingman, aged 40 years
53. Joan, his wife, being aged 39
54. Edward Kingman, his son, aged 16 years
55. Joanne, his daughter, aged 11 years
56. Anne, his daughter, aged 9 years
57. Thomas Kingman, his son, aged 7 years
58. John Kingman, his son, aged 2 years
59. John Ford, his servant, aged 30 years
60. William King, aged 40 years
61. Dorothy, his wife, aged 34 years
62. Mary King, his daughter, aged 12 years

63. Katheryn, his daughter, aged 10 years
64. William King, his son, aged 8 years
65. Hannah King, his daughter, aged 6 years
66. Thomas Holbrooke, of Broadway, aged 34 years
67. Jane Holbrooke, his wife, aged 34 years
68. John Holbrooke, his son, aged 11 years
69. Thomas Holbrooke, his son, aged 10 years
70. Anne Holbrooke, his daughter, aged 5 years
71. Elizabeth, his daughter, aged 1 year
72. Thomas Dible, husbandman, aged 22 years
73. Francis Dible, sawyer, aged 24 years
74. Robert Lovell, husbandman, aged 40 years
75. Elizabeth Lovell, his wife, aged 35 years
76. Zacheus Lovell, his son, 15 years
77. Anne Lovell, his daughter, aged 16 years
78. John Lovell, his son, aged 8 years
79. Ellyn, his daughter, aged 1 year
80. James, his son, aged 1 year
81. Joseph Chickin, his servant, 16 years
82. Alice Kinham, aged 22 years
83. Angell Hollard, aged 21 years
84. Katheryn, his wife, 22 years
85. George Land, his servant, 22 years
86. Sarah Land, his kinswoman, 18 years
87. Richard Jones, of Dinder
88. Robert Martin, of Batcombe, husbandman, 44
89. Humphrey Shepard, husbandman, 32
90. John Upham, husbandman, 35
91. Joan Martin, 44
92. Elizabeth Upham, 32
93. John Upham, Junior, 7
94. Sarah Upham, 26
95. William Grane, 12
96. Nathaniel Upham, 5
97. Elizabeth Upham, 3
98. Dorset Richard Wade, of Simstyly, cooper, aged 60
99. Elizabeth Wade, his wife, 6[?]
100. Dinah, his daughter, 22
101. Henry Lush, his servant, aged 17
102. Andrew Hallett, his servant, 28

103. John Hoble, husbandman, 13
104. Robert Huste, husbandman, 40
105. John Woodcooke, 2[?]
106. Rich. Porter, husbandman, 3[?]

Source: The New England Historical and Genealogical Register, XV (1861), p. 142;
XXV (1871), pp. 12–15.

■ *Questions for* . . . Passengers Bound for Virginia and for New England
(1634)

Discussion and Journal Writing

1. What do these lists tell you about the passengers of each ship? What are the
   key differences? What can you conclude about the purpose and character of
   each colony?
2. What does the New England list tell you about the way of life, habits, patterns, and values of the people how settled there?
3. Did most of America's colonists, including enslaved Africans and indentured servants, come in families? Why? Why not? What about immigrants?
4. How do people come to America today? With their families? Alone? Can
   we generalize?

ooooo

Plymouth Colony Demographic Tables

Table I

SIZE OF FAMILIES IN PLYMOUTH COLONY

	Average Number of Children Born	Average Number Lived to Age 21	Size of Sample
First-Generation Families	7.8	7.2	16
Second-Generation Families	8.6	7.5	47
Third-Generation Families	9.3	7.9	33

Note: The ninety-six families in this sample were chosen for analysis because the evidence on their membership seemed especially complete and reliable. Also, in all these families both parents lived at least to age fifty, or else, if one parent died, the other quickly remarried. Thus in all cases there were parents who lived up to, and past, the prime years for childbearing.

Table II

LIFE EXPECTANCY IN PLYMOUTH COLONY

Age	Men	Women
21	69.2	62.4
30	70.0	64.7
40	71.2	69.7
50	73.7	73.4
60	76.3	76.8
70	79.9	80.7
80	85.1	86.7

Note: The figures in the left-hand column are the control points, that is, a twenty-one-year-old man might expect to live to age 69.2, a thirty-year-old to 70.0, and so forth. The sample on which this table is based comprises a total of 645 persons.

Table III

DEATHS ARRANGED ACCORDING TO AGE (PLYMOUTH COLONY)

Age Group	Men (percentages)	Women (percentages)
22–29	1.6	5.9
30–39	3.6	12.0
40–49	7.8	12.0
50–59	10.2	10.9
60–69	18.0	14.9
70–79	30.5	20.7
80–89	22.4	16.0
90 or over	5.9	7.6

Note: The figures in columns two and three represent the percentages of the men and women in the sample who died between the ages indicated in column one. The sample is the same as in Table II.

Table IV

FIRST MARRIAGES IN PLYMOUTH COLONY

	Born Before 1600	Born 1600–25	Born 1625–50	Born 1650–75	Born 1675–1700
Mean age of men at time of first marriage	27.0	27.0	26.1	25.4	24.6
Mean age of women at time of first marriage	—	20.6	20.2	21.3	22.3
Percentage of men married at age 23 or under	25	18	25	26	38
Percentage of men married at age 30 or over	44	23	27	18	14
Percentage of women married at age 25 or over	—	9	10	20	28

Note: The sample on which this table is based comprises a total of 650 persons. There is, however, insufficient data for women born before 1600.

Table V

RATES OF REMARRIAGE IN PLYMOUTH COLONY

Number of Marriages	Men (percentages)		Women (percentages)	
	Over 50	Over 70	Over 50	Over 70
1	60	55	74	69
2	34	36	25	30
3	6	8	1	1
4	*	.5	—	—
5	*	.5	—	—
Total married more than once	40	45	26	31

Note: The sample on which this table is based comprises 711 persons. The asterisks indicate a figure of less than one-half of one per cent.

Table VI

SIZE OF HOUSEHOLDS (BRISTOL CENSUS, 1689)

Number of Persons in Household	1	2	3	4	5	6	7	8	9	10	11	12	13	14	15
Number of Families	1	6	5	11	9	13	5	7	6	3	2	1	0	0	1

Table VII

CHILDREN PER FAMILY (BRISTOL CENSUS, 1689)

Number of Children in Family	0	1	2	3	4	5	6	7	8	9	10
Number of Families	7	10	11	12	9	8	6	4	1	0	1

Table VIII

SERVANTS PER FAMILY (BRISTOL CENSUS, 1689)

Number of Servants	0	1	2	3	4	8	11
Number of Families	48	8	8	3	1	1	1

Source: Reprinted with permission from John Demos, *A Little Commonwealth: Family Life in Plymouth Colony* (New York: Oxford University Press, 1970).

■ *Questions for* . . . **Plymouth Colony Demographic Tables**

Discussion and Journal Writing

1. What do these tables tell us about family practices, circumstances, and ideals in Plymouth Colony during the seventeenth century?
2. Where are the single people? The single-parent families? Why did women die on average at younger ages than men? The reverse is true in America today.
3. Do these numbers substantiate the claims Demos makes for Plymouth Colony families in "The American Family Then and Now?"

ooooo

Mothers' Day Proclamation

Congress and the President
Legalize and Immortalize
Mothers' Day
Second Sunday in May

A PROCLAMATION

"Whereas, by a joint resolution, approved May 8, 1914, designating the second Sunday in May as Mothers' Day, and for other purposes, the President is authorized and requested to issue a proclamation calling upon the government officials to display the United States flag on all government buildings, and the people of the United States to display the flag at their homes, or other suitable places on the second Sunday in May, as a public expression of our love and reverence for the mothers of our country:

"And. Whereas. by the said joint resolution it is made the duty of the President
to request the observance of the second
Sunday in May as provided for in the said
joint resolution:

"Now. therefore. I. Woodrow Wilson.
President of the United States of America, by virtue of the authority vested
in me by the said joint resolution, do
hereby direct the government officials
to display the United States flag on all
government buildings. and do invite the
people of the United States to display
the flag at their homes. or other suitable
places. on the second Sunday of May,
as a public expression of our love and
reverence for the mothers of our country. In witness whereof I have set my
hand and caused the seal of the United
States to be hereunto affixed.

"Done at the city of Washington this
9th day of May. in the year of our Lord.
one thousand nine hundred and fourteen
and of the independence of the United
States one hundred and thirty-eight. .
                          "WOODROW WILSON.
"By the President.
  "WILLIAM JENNINGS BRYAN.
                    "Secretary of State."

■ *Questions for* . . . Mothers' Day Proclamation

Discussion and Journal Writing

1. Is the language of this proclamation appropriate or exaggerated? Explain
   your answer.
2. Is there anything political about this proclamation?
3. Is flying the American flag a fitting tribute to America's mothers?
4. The second Sunday of May is designated in this proclamation as Mothers'
   Day. Is it a subtle slight that Mothers' Day isn't a national holiday, with a
   day off from work?
5. How is Mothers' Day celebrated? Does it tell us anything about mother-
   hood in our society that Mothers' Day is one of the busiest days of the year
   for America's restaurants?

ooooo

*F*amily Album Four

English Coal Heaver's Family

"A Flat in Poverty Gap, The Home of an English Coal Heaver and His Family." *(Jacob A. Riis. Courtesy, Museum of the City of New York)*

Black Migrant Workers

"A group of Florida migratory workers on their way to Cranberry, New Jersey, to pick potatoes. Sawboro, North Carolina. July, 1940." *(Jack Delano. Library of Congress)*

■ *Questions for* . . . English Coal Heaver's Family and Black Migrant Workers

Discussion and Journal Writing

1. What does the photograph of the English coal heaver's family reveal about this family's life?
2. Why did Jacob Riis take it?
3. Why is the boy at the center of the photograph of Black migrant workers?
4. What do the expressions and positions of the Black migrant workers tell us about the situation of the photograph?

ooooo

🍃 Expository Writing: Causes and Effects of History

History—its approach, not its contents—is one of the most basic ways humans have devised to make sense of the world. We understand a person, an event, a change, or the consequences of a change by looking at what happened before. We use chronological order to put something into perspective. Thinking historically is a way of thinking critically.

Nearly every culture and society does it or did it. Even preliterate cultures, those that have not yet developed reading and writing, encode their histories orally in sagas, songs, and ritualistic chants; for instance, scholars agree that the *Iliad* and the *Odyssey* were not written by an individual named Homer but instead were the work of a succession of oral poets who turned ancient Greek history—their sense of themselves, how they lived, the gods they worshiped—into poetry. Before these epics were written down, then, they were an oral poetic chronicle of the past. They formed an important part of the collective memory of preliterate Greece. The Norse sagas that form the backdrop of *Beowulf,* one of the first written narratives in English, are another instance. The forms of the world's histories—oral and written—differ, but every culture has a sense of what has been, what has persisted, and what has changed; every culture has ideas about the relationship between its past and its present.

Everyone reasons historically. Not that we spend a good deal of time wondering whether FDR meant to appease Stalin at Yalta but that we look at relationships from a chronological perspective when we're trying to make sense of them: we try to understand our parents historically when we remember that they are members of a different generation, and we make sense of conditions on the job or in our neighborhoods by thinking about what happened before. A historical approach is not the only one that can be taken, but it is a common one and an important one.

Historical writing has taken every form under the sun, especially if one includes all the kinds of writing and documents that historians look at: birth certificates, census data, death warrants, rent rolls, tax records, deeds, court transcripts and legal decisions, posters, pamphlets, telegrams, journals, and people's private letters—historians will look at anything, to their reader's advantage if they're any good. A good deal of the writing historians study wasn't written with historical intent but has acquired historical significance as time goes by.

A few historians, such as John Berger and Umberto Eco, have written fiction, but most of them write exposition of one sort or another. One can find all of Shaughnessy's patterns of academic reasoning in historical writing. Historians describe, narrate, compare, contrast, suggest or imply what should have been done, analyze causes and effects of events, changes, and people, and summarize what others have said and written, almost always scrutinizing, commenting on, or criticizing what was said.

At first glance, some historical writing seems to be simple narration or description, innocent of perspective and interpretation. But there is nothing innocent about historians: their stories and descriptions are loaded, like dice, with ideas, observations, and conclusions. Nathan Huggins's description of West African tribal life, for instance, is animated by the conviction that tribal life was rich, cultured, satisfying, and highly complex, despite the racist misunderstandings, distortions, and lies spread since the seventeenth century that Africans, prior to enslavement, were primitive and uncivilized. Laslett's description of a baker family is an argument for the centrality of family in seventeenth-century English life. Engels describes nineteenth-century London slums, but he does so to denounce the living conditions of the English working class and to attack capitalism, the economic system responsible for producing those living conditions.

Demos and others take a comparative approach. Demos compares seventeenth- and twentieth-century American families to identify distinctive features of the seventeenth-century colonial family. Joan Scott and Louise Tilley examine the lives of English and French working women in their book *Women, Work, and Family* to build a broad base for their generalizations. Crane Brinton studies the American, French, and Russian revolutions in his *Anatomy of Revolution,* and Harold Fredrickson compares the creation of two systems of European slavery, one in South Africa and one in England's North American colonies, in his book *White Supremacy.*

Causation, however, is the most important pattern in historical writing since historians are chiefly interested in change, persistence, and influence. They write about why event or changes occurred, the consequences of those events or changes, how individuals and groups gained or lost power, and the legacies they left.

As writers, historians use patterns of causation as a writing strategy to make sense of, organize, and present their materials and ideas; for instance, Philippe Ariès traces the evolution of childhood in France in *Centuries of Childhood: A Social History of Family Life,* E. P. Thompson chronicles the emergence of England's industrial working class in *The Making of the English Working Class,* and Bernard Bailyn explores the intellectual influences of American revolutionary thought in *The Ideological Origins of the American Revolution.*

Since the subjects of historians are not simple, a work of historical writing is never a matter of relating how one event, person, or idea produced another. In most cases, historians construct causal webs or causal chains. There is no single cause stated for the French Revolution, according to Charles Lefebvre's *The French Revolution* or Alain Soubol's *The French Revolution, 1789–1799,* two of the most respected books on the subject. Both scholars examine the complicated interaction of a wide array of political, economic, cultural, and intellectual factors, forces, and changes that brought about and shaped the French Revolution. Philippe Ariès, the historian of childhood in France, shows how factors close to home meshed with, were

fueled by, or clashed with larger societal forces and changes, altering concep-
tions of childhood and childrearing practices. The hallmark of good writing
that follows a pattern of causation is the care a writer takes in explaining the
connections between the causes and effects examined.

Historians who use a causation pattern are also interested in a comparative framework and vice versa. And, as in other types of writing, one often
finds a number of writing strategies—narration, description, and exposition—
in a single piece of writing. All historians do a certain amount of narrating
and describing, and most of them spend some time paraphrasing and commenting on the ideas of people they write about. The more aware you are of
the different patterns and strategies as readers, the more you will be able to
learn from these writers as writers.

There's good history and bad history; that's the case with scholarship in
every field. There are works of history that are rife with errors, muddy jargon,
logical inconsistencies, and wrong-headed or unsubstantiated claims, assertions, and conclusions. Historians are, after all, only human; some of them
are, in fact, quite a bit more human than others.

History at its best, however, is brilliant, offers profound insights into societies, events, people, and situations, and is powerfully and gracefully written.
For our purposes, the most exemplary aspect of historical writing is development, explanation, and evidence. Inexperienced writers often assume that the
reader understands what they say without explanation and evidence, the
result being undeveloped paragraphs and sketchy, gappy, unconvincing
essays. Historians, more than other social societies, know the burden of proof
is on them. The point is not simply to say what you think but to back your
views up with convincing, well-developed arguments that draw on pertinent
evidence.

Huggins, for instance, bases his generalizations about West African tribal
life on the experiences of 14 tribes. He delves into the seamless world
enslaved Africans were torn from, explaining familial, tribal, and spiritual
aspects of the lives they led. He describes the family compounds in detail,
discussing family patterns, family economy, and the socialization of children.
He tells us about the crops they raised and the animals they kept. He gives us
a full picture of African tribal life. Laslett constructs a detailed blueprint of the
economic and domestic life of a London baking family. Demos could have
listed the functions of a Plymouth Colony family in a sentence, which would
not have been nearly as informative or convincing. Instead, he explains each
function and gives examples that illustrate them. Engels describes England's
slums. He paints a picture of specific houses, streets, and neighborhoods. He
gives individual examples of the harsh living conditions the nineteenth-century working class endured. He goes into the histories of several older neighborhoods and the building plans of the newer neighborhoods in an effort to
describe and denounce the economic and political forces that produced so
much misery.

Keep their high standards of development and explanation in mind as you write this chapter's essay.

✺ Writing Workshop

The Topic: Changing attitudes toward dating/courtship and marriage, raising children, education, and work

The Assignment: Compare and contrast how attitudes and practices involving one particular aspect of family life have changed across generations. What has changed? What has stayed the same? Are the changes for the best or the worst? Make sure to include your thoughts and feelings about the subject: your interpretation of family changes and your feelings about those changes will be the heart of your essay. Write as if your essay will appear in a local magazine or newspaper. If possible, interview a grandparent or someone from that generation. You are more likely to find pronounced differences if you go back two generations. Even if you can't interview someone from that generation, you may be able to piece together enough information from what you know and what you can find out. Perhaps you can interview someone about one of your grandparents. Before and after you conduct your interview, ask yourself the same questions to clarify your ideas. The tips for interviewing and the checklist that follows should help you to collect, organize, and think about your material.

Tips for Interviewing

Since people are curious, it's a good idea to explain your assignment to the person you are interviewing before you get started. Also, knowing your purpose might help your interviewee to decide how to put things.

A mix of specific and general questions works best. Specific questions refresh the memory; general questions prompt a person to reflect and comment on the specifics. You might, for example, ask what your interviewee's first job was and then ask why he or she chose that kind of job. After you finish the interview, you might want to share your answers to the same questions and invite your interviewee to say why things have changed.

What follows is a short list of suggested questions for each area of change:

Dating/Courtship and Marriage: How did you meet your spouse? How old were you? How old was your spouse? What sort of person were you looking for? Why? Where did you see one another before you married? Did your families play a role in the meetings, courtship, or dating? When and where did you get married? Who planned the wedding ceremony and celebration? Who came to the celebration? Just family? Just friends? Both? Where did you live after marrying? Why?

Raising Children: How many children did you have? What are their names and ages? Where did you raise them? When and how did you discipline them? What kind of guidance and supervision do children need? How do you give it? Should they do chores? How should children treat adults? Why? What's the key to raising children?

Education: Where and when did you go to school? Was it segregated? How many years did you attend? Did you like the school? Was it a good school? How do you know? Describe some of the teachers and/or professors. What was emphasized at your school? Why? Did you get more schooling than others in your family or neighborhood? Why did you leave school? Did school prepare you well?

Work: How old were you when you took your first job or began to do substantial work at home? What was your first job? Why that job? Did you take your first job to help support yourself and your family or to earn spending money? Both? Did you like your first job? Was anyone else in your family or community working there? If so, did that have anything to do with how you got the job or how you got along on the job? What was the best thing about the job? The worst? What qualifications did a person need to get and hold the job? Was there room for advancement? What was the job's status?

Checklist

Complete this after you do the interview; it should help you identify the main points you'll make in your essay. Bring it to class with your first draft. Your instructor and your peer editor may want to see it.

1. Name one difference of viewpoint between you and the person you interviewed. Explain and give examples.

   a) Your view:

   Examples:

b) Interviewee's view:

Examples:

2. Name a second difference.
   a) Your view:

Examples:

b) Interviewee's view:

Examples:

3. Name a similarity of viewpoint between you and the person you interviewed, if there is one.
   a) Your view:

Examples:

b) Interviewee's view:

Examples:

4. Explain the first difference. Has the person you interviewed moved since he or she was young? Do social movements, such as the Civil Rights Movement or the Women's Movement, help explain the differences? Other large social changes? How important is personality in explaining the differences?

5. Explain the second difference.

6. Explain the similarity.

Study your notes and the checklist. If the changes you have turned up clearly are the result of a social movement, you may want to go to the library and do a little reading. Even an encyclopedia article would refresh your memory or inform you of key dates, people, places, objectives, and obstacles of such movements. Limit your reading time to an hour or so. Don't turn the paper into a research project.

Next, write a draft and let it sit. Then, revise by explaining yourself more fully. Finally, polish by correcting and tightening sentences. Use your voice and your ear to tune your sentences. If a sentence doesn't sound right, rephrase it until it does.

Exchange drafts and checklists with a classmate. Check to see that your classmate has developed each point. If you find yourself wanting to know more, jot down a question asking for more. The more specific you can be about what the paragraph needs, the more helpful your classmate will find it. Is there material in the checklist that would do the job? Is the paper well organized? Is the point of the paper—the writer's explanation of the changes he or she recorded—clear? Do you have any suggestions to make about word choice? Grammar? Punctuation? Phrasing? Write notes, questions, and suggestions in the margin; then, discuss.

Now, rewrite the essay. Remember, it's fine to come up with new ideas, sentences, and paragraphs when you rewrite. Edit, polish, and proofread; and type the final draft even if your instructor doesn't require it: writers tend to polish one last time when they type, and the final product is more satisfying.

After giving the essay a title that expresses your key point and your tone, hand it in.

Additional Writing Exercises

- Write about an aspect of the family you grew up in that you are not perpetuating or do not intend to perpetuate. Why? How will you eliminate it? What will take its place?
- Write about an aspect you intend to perpetuate. Will it be harder for you than it was for your parents? Why or why not?
- Focus on some aspect of family life that has, in your opinion, changed for the better or the worse. Why did the change occur?

Chapter 5

Today's Families

■

How's the Family?

It would be fascinating to take a global approach to the contemporary family, if only for the sheer variety of family trends, situations, and predicaments. The government of the People's Republic of China, for instance, has imposed a one-child-per-family cap to counter the population explosion; families that fail to comply are economically penalized. Is it working? And if it's working and the family is shrinking, are norms and attitudes changing? Understanding how people are responding to this policy would teach us quite a bit about Chinese politics, culture, and society.

Across the Pacific, the Native American families of Colombia's highlands have been exposed as never before to outside forces, ways, and products because of their widespread cultivation of coca, which is used to make cocaine. Many have been killed for refusing to cooperate with the drug lords, but most find themselves with more money than they ever dreamed of. The kids all have Walkmans. Are they essentially the same people, with Walkmans? Or is $C_{17}H_{21}NO_4$ changing their communities, their families, their lives?

In the Middle East, Islamic fundamentalism is on the rise. What is this movement's family plan and how does it mesh with the movement's cultural and political objectives.

It would also be revealing to compare the predicaments and changes that America's families are facing with those of families around the world. How, for instance, are mothers in Italy, Cuba, and Germany who work full time outside the home coping with the demands of their jobs and families? Do cultural and social differences make it easier or harder for them than for super moms in America? Do Brazilian underclass families wrestle with the same sort of family-destroying government policies that their American counterparts face? Is parenting fundamentally the same or different for the !Kung, who have no generation gap?

However, there isn't world enough, and time in a single chapter, to chase the contemporary family around the globe. We can, however, raise some questions about the state of American families.

There is only one point that experts, practitioners, and bystanders, innocent and not-so-innocent, can agree on: The family is changing. Beyond that one still point, people's assumptions, perspectives, and agendas vary, producing a babel of overlapping debates and arguments about how and why the family is changing, whether it is changing at an unprecedented rate and is out of control, whether the changes are for better or worse, what it needs to cope and thrive as it changes, and who should provide for its needs. There is little agreement about whether the family is falling apart or evolving.

The divorce rate, for instance, is high—one in two marriages today will end in divorce—and it has been that high for over 20 years. But why and to what end? Are Americans divorcing because expectations have increased? If so, is that good or bad? Are we divorcing because women are changing and men are not? Because we are less religious? Because spouses have trouble sustaining their commitment to one another in a permissive environment? Will AIDS bring the divorce rate down?

Though a substantial number of Americans become disenchanted with one another, they do not become disenchanted with the institution of marriage. Most of them remarry, which leaves us where? Among other things, the high rate of remarriage means that children whose parents divorce tend to find themselves in reconstituted families, not "broken" ones. But is that good or bad? Diane Medved, who speaks for herself later in the chapter, believes that divorce is worse than the situation it remedies because the pain and trauma of divorce persist long after the divorce is granted, for children as well as parents. Others argue that keeping a bad marriage together for the sake of the children can be harmful to all concerned and that divorce is a realistic and constructive solution to the situations that people sometimes find themselves in because they are not perfect and make mistakes.

Are America's children whose parents have divorced growing up in happier or sadder homes? It's hard to say, but family-court judges in several states are making sure that divorcing parents think about it in the divorce classes they must take before the divorce is granted.

More children than ever before are growing up in single-parent homes because more children than ever before are being born to parents who do not marry. In fact, one in every five White children and two in every three Black children are born to unmarried mothers. Why? What does it tell us that most of these single-parent families are poor? Right-wing commentators, such as Charles Murray of the American Heritage Institute, suggest that government assistance has made this trend possible and that it won't stop until we turn off the tap. Left-wing reformers argue that opportunities of every sort have decreased, undermining the confidence and resources a person needs to set up a new household. The disincentives to family unity that are written into government assistance programs increase the severity of the situation; for instance, a mother receiving Aid to Families with Dependent Children (AFDC) receives less if a husband is present. See Jonathan Kozol's book *Rachel and Her Children: Homeless Families in America* for a critique of these disincentives.

Regardless of the shape America's families are in, there's a general concern in the air about how families spend their time—together and apart. It's a concern one can hear in the recently coined expression "quality time." It's voiced in countless articles and books and on countless talk shows. Television is, for example, one of the villains of the piece. In *Television: The Plug-in Drug,* Marie Winn argues that watching TV isolates family members from one another in multiple-set America, that family schedules revolve around network schedules, and that, most importantly, TV-watching consumes time that family members would have spent together, diminishing the daily rituals that are the glue of family. Many families watch TV right through dinner, even though it's thought to be bad manners (or at least not very good manners), so when do they talk?

During commercials?

As you consider Winn's argument later in the chapter, bear in mind that TV is a given of American life, but a new one. The majority of American households did not have TVs until the mid-1960s, and it wasn't until the mid-1970s that most households had more than one set. The cheaper, better, and more portable sets, brought to us by transistor technology, made it possible for individual family members or little groups of them to watch separate programs in separate rooms. Is this an instance of technology filling or creating a need?

Sidney Mintz, who introduced you to the Puerto Rican sugarcane worker Don Taso in chapter 3, wonders in his book *Sweetness and Power: A History of Sugar* if the family meal is an endangered species. Increasingly, he observes, the schedules of family members are not in sync; and there are more and more foods in America's supermarkets that don't have to be prepared or cooked, especially since the advent of microwaves and microwaveable food. All you have to do is change the temperature of the food and eat. Throw in the TV and it's easy to imagine Sister and Brother eating frozen lasagna in front of "The Cosby Show" in one room while Mom, or Mom and Dad, or Dad and Stepmom, or Mom and Boyfriend sit down to microwaved pepper steak and calorie-counter stuffed peppers in front of the evening news in another room.

So when do they talk?

There is reason to worry that homes are becoming way stations. During the day, there's work for Mom and Dad, school for the kids, and preschool or day-care for the "prekids"; in the late afternoon and evenings, there are after-school play groups, band or athletics practice, trips to the mall or the library, cooking, cleaning, business dinners, union or parents meetings, adult education classes, sessions at the gym or the therapist's, and so on; and on weekends, there are friends, workouts, laundry, lawn work, grocery shopping, part-time jobs, parties, movies, more mall, mildly illicit behavior, relaxation, and so on.

Is the American home becoming a shell, or is that the point of view of people who are wedded to the past and can't adjust to new rhythms, patterns, and pursuits? Has the American family always been this busy? Remember that barely 70 years ago (that is, in the good old days), the average American work week was 60 hours, and the average American woman has always worked for wages, doing piece work at home or leaving the home for a job.

And is time spent together the only factor? What about love and understanding? But can love and understanding of one's spouse, one's children, or one's parents be sustained if the family spends next-to-no time together?

These problems, questions, and worries—the ones fairly typical families wrestle with—are harrowing enough, but the contemporary family portrait is much darker for dysfunctional families and families in crisis. Spouse abuse, which in most cases means wife abuse, is rampant. According to an *NBC News* report on domestic violence, which aired on July 28, 1992, 50 percent of American women find themselves in an abusive relationship or marriage at some point in their lives and one-third of all emergency room cases are battered women: every 15 seconds a woman is battered in America by a husband or boyfriend. In too many instances, battered women become dead women, because the courts fail to provide women with the protection they need and because, as neighbors and relatives, we tend to look the other way. In the Boston area alone, 50 women were killed in 1991 by their husbands or boyfriends.

The welfare of children is even more precarious. Lisa Steinberg is dead, killed by her adoptive father. Yaakov Riegler is dead, battered to death by his mother; and as horrific as these murders are, it is even more chilling to realize that they are the media tips of the iceberg. How many children are killed each year in America by their parents? Babies, dead and alive, are found abandoned in dumpsters, trash cans, and toilet tanks. Drug-addicted mothers give birth to premature infants who weigh a couple of pounds, must be kept alive on painful life-sustaining equipment, and can expect lives hampered by physical and neurological problems; children fall out of unprotected windows, regardless of race, creed, sex, or class; teenage alcoholism, drug addiction, and suicide are up; and the list goes on. Children have been neglected, malnourished, injured, molested, and even killed by their parents—the people who are legally entrusted with their welfare. Children are especially vulnerable to violence and sexual abuse. Who can protect them from their own guardians? We are aghast each time another instance of abuse hits the papers, and family-court judges find themselves in Solomon's unenviable shoes.

There are also instances in which the guilt is not so easily assigned. When children suffer from lead poisoning because they have eaten lead paint from the walls of shelters that should have been condemned, can we blame the parents alone? When children on their way to the store to buy groceries are caught in the drug trade's crossfire, can we say the parents should have been more vigilant and let it rest there? Our laws, policies, and spending priorities sometimes have a direct and harmful impact on the welfare of thousands of children. Thousands and thousands.

The media gives the impression that we are experiencing an unprecedented epidemic of domestic violence. Are we? How would you find out? And if violence in America's homes is up, what's causing it to go up? Even if it's not, what are the causes of domestic violence?

Some types of domestic violence are new, but most of them, such as incest and child and wife abuse, have been with us for a long time. It is hard to say whether the increase in reportage reflects an actual increase in domestic violence, because we don't have reliable figures. People looked the other way in the past even more than they do today and the legal system did not encourage families to resolve their internecine conflicts through the law. Furthermore, what was regarded as good discipline in the past might be regarded today as child abuse, a punishable criminal offense. The point is to solve these problems now, but we make our task harder if we romanticize the past, which was not, in fact, an idyllic time for how many children we will never know.

Many family advocates say part of the problem is that we have practiced a domestic Monroe Doctrine of nonintervention, which must be repealed. As neighbors, friends, and relatives, we must stop looking the other way when we see domestic violence or its signs. How many people saw Lisa Steinberg's bruises? And the legal system, these advocates argue, must adopt a more aggressive stance because too many people cannot treat their family members decently. Acts of domestic violence are not little slips, indiscretions, or eccentricities that should be tolerated; they are crimes.

It's no wonder nostalgia for a simpler past is in the air. In the 1992 elections, politicians, who have expensive antennae, sensed it and played on it each time they intoned the phrase that became the talisman of the presidential race: "family values."

What ever happened to Dick and Jane? Quite a few Americans miss them, even though their single-family dwelling, white picket, Mom-at-home, Dad-at-work nuclear family corresponds less and less to the reality of America's families. Extreme nostalgists hold Dick and Jane in their heart of hearts as guide and measure, hiding their heads in the sands of a mythic past, assuring themselves that nothing has changed, or needed to change, and that they are just like Grandma and Grandpa, more or less, in new clothes. It's a seductive vision, but so much has changed since Grandma was young, including Grandma.

Others are hopeful about the family's future in a guarded way. The bright side of the family's dark side is that domestic violence—which used to be one of our society's dirty little secrets—is out in the open, where it is more likely to be addressed. The legal system, in some states at least, is intervening more swiftly and constructively in family crises. Women aren't as constrained in limiting roles as they used to be. The social atmosphere is more supportive of women who work outside the home in addition to their roles as wives and mothers. And the spread of day-care centers and preschools has helped, too. Fathers, in some sectors of the population, are becoming more involved in raising their children. Some of them are changing diapers, giving bottles, and walking kids to school; the ones who are not know the expectations now exist.

But even the hopeful are anxious about their families and the family in general. Change will do that to people, even if it's what they want.

🦝 Word Play: *Quality Time* (QT)

Words and expressions are usually coined to describe new things or new ways of looking at old things. Nuclear physicists learned how to smash atoms earlier this century using an atom-smashing machine. Someone devised a name for that machine: *cyclotron. Skyscrapers* and *gridlock* are also fairly new words.

As for expressions, writers are often responsible for them, especially the good ones. Freud gave us *the Oedipal complex,* Darwin gave us *survival of the fittest,* and Adam Smith gave us *the invisible hand* in 1776, which Marx's *class struggle* tried to shake over 70 years later. More recently, Tom Wolfe gave us *radical chic* and *the right stuff,* and some lesser mortal gave us *quality time.* I have no idea who coined it, which is often the case with less distinguished expressions. It is much easier to track a word down, because our dictionaries are predominantly word books. Dictionaries do contain some expressions; however, *quality time* is not in any of the dictionaries I have checked (and if the language is lucky, it never will be). *Quality control,* yes, but not *quality time.* To my knowledge, it hasn't spread to other English-speaking countries, with the possible exception of Canada, making it considerably less mobile and virulent than the Asian Flu. Crocodile Dundee has never uttered it, and I haven't heard or read it in recent trips to England and Ireland.

I don't like the expression because I think it's vague, dishonest, smug, and superior, and I hope it withers on the vine. But it is a bellwether of upper middle-class attitudes toward family during the last decade because, despite its vagueness, it comes equipped with a theory of child development and a program of parenting that is a reaction against the parenting style of the 1950s.

In the early to mid-1980s, *quality time* came into vogue on the talk shows (another new coinage) and in the advice columns and then proceeded to make unscheduled appearances in the mouths of countless Americans. These days, people use the expression in reference to romantic relationships. In the personals, singles say that quality time with that certain someone is what they want, and I don't doubt it; but *QT* came into being as a pseudo-psychological instrument of childrearing, implying a developmental need that only it can fill. *Quality time* is time spent with your child or children that matters, that makes a difference. Time spent in the same apartment, house, or room doesn't necessarily count. The idea is that children thrive on the active attention of their parents and require large amounts of it. Quality time stimulates them—and more importantly, it cultivates them. Changing diapers doesn't count, because it doesn't contribute to a future beyond diaper rash in any significant way that we can measure. A new diaper does not make an infant or toddler a better person. Nor does nagging them to eat their peas. Even taking children to the playground to play with their friends doesn't count with strict adherents because QT is not a spectator sport. It's a one-on-one phenomenon, and active interaction is its hallmark. Developmental bang for the buck—that's the point and the charge.

Quality time is often seen in the company of other newcomers to the language of parenting. Parents are often referred to as *caregivers;* the most active one is the *primary caregiver.* Caregivers should strive to be nurturing, which means lots of QT. Furthermore, activities the caregivers choreograph for their offspring should be *child-centered,* which means time on your hands and knees, which means QT. Quality time is today's parental code.

And, QT is not just for moms. It is also an appeal for dads to come out from behind the paper and the backward socialization they underwent in the 1950s and 1960s, Iron John or no Iron John, to change some diapers and generally to get their hands dirty with the joys of parenthood.

No one would argue that parents shouldn't spend time doing things with their children: it's a wonderful thing—when both the parents and the children are in the mood for it. The point is that *quality time* is a term of invidious comparison, and there's a charge to log as many QT hours with your children as possible on the pain of being thought or thinking yourself an irresponsible parent. It's whiny, it's guilty, and it's guilt-producing.

In fact, I believe the gospel of quality time contains an accusation that is being transmitted across generational lines by today's parents to yesterday's parents: You were too remote, you were preoccupied with your adult lives, you didn't pay enough attention to us, you didn't listen to us, and you didn't take us seriously until we made you take us seriously. *Quality time* is an expression with an attitude.

Not that the charge isn't at all justified. In so many cases, it is. But a generational complaint isn't necessarily the best starting point for reforming something as complicated as parenting. As a generation of parents, we may be giving our kids what we wanted or needed as kids in the 1950s and 1960s; it may or may not be what our children want or need.

When my first child, Sonia, was born in 1988 I remember thinking as I ran up the subway steps on my way to see her at the hospital that I would never hold her responsible for how I was brought up. I can't count how many times I've laughed at my own naiveté since then. It is impossible to keep one's upbringing out of something as involving as parenting; however, that doesn't mean it's wise to make a reaction to one's upbringing the central tenet of parenting.

If *QT* never makes it to the dictionaries, it will disappear. Though language is first and foremost a spoken thing, makers of dictionaries (lexicographers) tend to rely on the written word, despite the slang, colloquialisms, and dialect dictionaries contain; *quality time* has enjoyed greater currency as a spoken expression. Do dictionaries give a skewed version of the English language? Is that necessarily a bad thing? What kinds of writers cast a broader net than lexicographers?

Journal Entry

If you disagree with Pace's dyspeptic assessment of the expression *quality time,* especially if you are a parent, say so. What does the expression mean to you? How have you heard it used or have you used it yourself?

Or, write about another family word or term that's current these days. Some candidates are *child-centered, the zero-parent family, nurturing, acting out, dysfunctional families, the child within,* and *family values.*

━━━━━━━━━━━━━━ $\mathcal{R}$eadings ━━━━━━━━━━━━━━

At Yankee Stadium

—Don DeLillo

Don DeLillo was born, raised, and educated in New York City and currently lives to the north of it, in Westchester. He is one of the most innovative and powerful writers of fiction in America today. His novels, a number of which are set in New York, work the crease between reportage and fiction and are simultaneously solid and surreal. His novel, *Mao II,* opens with the following scene that ordinarily would be a proud moment for a parent, the marriage of a child, but this wedding is set in Yankee Stadium and the parents of the bride are in the stands.

Here they come, marching into American sunlight. They are grouped in twos, eternal boy-girl, stepping out of the runway beyond the fence in left-center field. The music draws them across the grass, dozens, hundreds, already too many to count. They assemble themselves so tightly, crossing the vast arc of the outfield, that the effect is one of transformation. From a series of linked couples they become one continuous wave, larger all the time, covering the open spaces in navy and white.

Karen's daddy, watching from the grandstand, can't help thinking this is the point. They're one body now, an undifferentiated mass, and this makes him uneasy. He focuses his binoculars on a young woman, another, still another. So many columns set so closely. He has never seen anything like this or ever imagined it could happen. He hasn't come here for the spectacle but it is starting to astonish him. They're in the thousands now, approaching division strength, and the old seemly tear-jerk music begins to sound sardonic. Wife Maureen is sitting next to him. She is bold and bright today, wearing candy colors to offset the damp she feels in her heart. Rodge understands completely. They had almost no warning. Grabbed a flight, got a hotel, took the subway, passed through the metal detector and here they are, trying to comprehend. Rodge is not unequipped for the rude turns of normal fraught experience. He's got a degree and a business and a tax attorney and a cardiologist and a mutual fund and whole life and major medical. But do the assurances always apply? There is a strangeness down there that he never thought he'd see in a ballpark. They take a time-honored event and repeat it, repeat it, repeat it until something new enters the world.

Look at the girl in the front row, about twenty couples in from the left. He 3 adjusts the eyepiece lever and zooms to max power, hoping to see her features through the bridal veil.

There are still more couples coming out of the runway and folding into the 4 crowd, although "crowd" is not the right word. He doesn't know what to call them. He imagines they are uniformly smiling, showing the face they squeeze out with the toothpaste every morning. The bridegrooms in identical blue suits, the brides in lace-and-satin gowns. Maureen looks around at the people in the stands. Parents are easy enough to spot and there are curiosity seekers scattered about, ordinary slouchers and loiterers, others deeper in the mystery, dark-eyed and separate, secretly alert, people who seem to be wearing everything they own, layered and mounded in garments with missing parts, city nomads more strange to her than herdsmen in the Sahel, who at least turn up on the documentary channel. There is no admission fee and gangs of boys roam the far reaches, setting off firecrackers that carry a robust acoustical wallop, barrel bombs and ash cans booming along the concrete ramps and sending people into self-protective spasms. Maureen concentrates on the parents and other relatives, some of the women done up touchingly in best dress and white corsage, staring dead-eyed out of tinted faces. She reports to Rodge that there's a lot of looking back and forth. Nobody knows how to feel and they're checking around for hints. Rodge stays fixed to his binoculars. Six thousand five hundred couples and their daughter is down there somewhere about to marry a man she met two days ago. He's either Japanese or Korean. Rodge didn't get it straight. And he knows about eight words of English. He and Karen spoke through an interpreter, who taught them how to say Hello, it is Tuesday, here is my passport. Fifteen minutes in a bare room and they're chain-linked for life.

He works his glasses across the mass, the crowd, the movement, the member- 5 ship, the flock, the following. It would make him feel a little better if he could find her.

"You know what it's as though?" Maureen says. 6

"Let me concentrate." 7

"It's as though they designed this to the maximum degree of let the relatives 8 squirm."

"We can do our moaning at the hotel." 9

"I'm simply stating." 10

"I did suggest, did I not, that you stay at home." 11

"How could I not come? What's my excuse?" 12

"I see a lot of faces that don't look American. They send them out in mission- 13 ary teams. Maybe they think we've sunk to the status of less developed country. They're here to show us the way and the light."

"And make sharp investments. After, can we take in a play?" 14

"Let me look, okay. I want to find her." 15

"We're here. We may as well avail ourselves."   16
"It's hard for the mind to conceive. Thirteen thousand people."   17
"What are you going to do when you find her?"   18
"Who the hell thought it up? What does it mean?"   19
"What are you going to do when you find her? Wave goodbye?"   20
"I just need to know she's here," Rodge says. "I want to document it, okay."   21
"Because that's what it is. If it hasn't been goodbye up to this point, it certain- 22
ly is now."

"Hey, Maureen? Shut up."   23

From the bandstand at home plate the Mendelssohn march carries a stadium 24
echo, with lost notes drifting back from recesses between tiers. Flags and bunting
everywhere. The blessed couples face the infield, where their true father, Master
Moon, stands in three dimensions. He looks down at them from a railed pulpit that
rides above a platform of silver and crimson. He wears a white silk robe and a high
crown figured with stylized irises. They know him at a molecular level. He lives in
them like chains of matter that determine who they are. This is a man of chunky
build who saw Jesus on a mountainside. He spent nine years praying and wept so
long and hard his tears formed puddles and soaked through the floor and dripped
into the room below and filtered through the foundation of the house into the earth.
The couples know there are things he must leave unsaid, words whose planetary
impact no one could bear. He is the messianic secret, ordinary-looking, his skin a
weathered bronze. When the communists sent him to a labor camp the other
inmates knew who he was because they'd dreamed about him before he got there.
He gave away half his food but never grew weak. He worked seventeen hours a day
in the mines but always found time to pray, to keep his body clean and tuck in his
shirt. The blessed couples eat kiddie food and use baby names because they feel so
small in his presence. This is a man who lived in a hut made of U.S. Army ration
tins and now he is here, in American light, come to lead them to the end of human
history.

The brides and grooms exchange rings and vows and many people in the 25
grandstand are taking pictures, standing in the aisles and crowding the rails, whole
families snapping anxiously, trying to shape a response or organize a memory, trying to neutralize the event, drain it of eeriness and power. Master chants the ritual
in Korean. The couples file past the platform and he sprinkles water on their heads.
Rodge sees the brides lift their veils and he zooms in urgently, feeling at the same
moment a growing distance from events, a sorriness of spirit. But he watches and
muses. When the Old God leaves the world, what happens to all the unexpended
faith? He looks at each sweet face, round face, long, wrong, darkish, plain. They
are a nation, he supposes, founded on the principle of easy belief. A unit fueled by
credulousness. They speak a half language, a set of ready-made terms and empty
repetitions. All things, the sum of the knowable, everything true, it all comes down
to a few simple formulas copied and memorized and passed on. And here is the
drama of mechanical routine played out with living figures. It knocks him back in
awe, the loss of scale and intimacy, the way love and sex are multiplied out, the

numbers and shaped crowd. This really scares him, a mass of people turned into a sculptured object. It is like a toy with thirteen thousand parts, just tootling along, an innocent and menacing thing. He keeps the glasses trained, feeling a slight desperation now, a need to find her and remind himself who she is. Healthy, intelligent, twenty-one, serious-sided, possessed of a selfness, a teeming soul, nuance and shadow, grids of pinpoint singularities they will never drill out of her. Or so he hopes and prays, wondering about the power of their own massed prayer. When the Old God goes, they pray to flies and bottletops. The terrible thing is they follow the man because he gives them what they need. He answers their yearning, unburdens them of free will and independent thought. See how happy they look.

Around the great stadium the tenement barrens stretch, miles of delirium, men 26 sitting in tipped-back chairs against the walls of hollow buildings, sofas burning in the lots, and there is a sense these chanting thousands have, wincing in the sun, that the future is pressing in, collapsing toward them, that they are everywhere surrounded by signs of the fated landscape and human struggle of the Last Days, and here in the middle of their columned body, lank-haired and up-close, stands Karen Janney, holding a cluster of starry jasmine and thinking of the bloodstorm to come. She is waiting to file past Master and sees him with the single floating eye of the crowd, inseparable from her own apparatus of vision but sharper-sighted, able to perceive more deeply. She feels intact, rayed with well-being. They all feel the same, young people from fifty countries, immunized against the language of self. They're forgetting who they are under their clothes, leaving behind all the small banes and body woes, the daylong list of sore gums and sweaty nape and need to pee, ancient rumbles in the gut, momentary chills and tics, the fungoid dampness between the toes, the deep spasm near the shoulder blade that's charged with mortal reckoning. All gone now. They stand and chant, fortified by the blood of numbers.

Karen glances over at Kim Jo Pak, soft-eyed and plump in his nice new suit 27 and boxy shoes, husband-for-eternity.

She knows her flesh parents are in the stands somewhere. Knows what they're 28 saying, sees the gestures and expressions. Dad trying to use the old college logic to make sense of it all. Mom wearing the haunted stare that means she was put on earth strictly to suffer. They're all around us, parents in the thousands, afraid of our intensity. This is what frightens them. We really believe. They bring us up to believe but when we show them true belief they call out psychiatrists and police. We know who God is. This makes us crazy in the world.

Karen's mindstream sometimes slows down, veering into sets of whole words. 29 They take a funny snub-nosed form, the rudimentary English spoken by some of Master's chief assistants.

They have God once-week. Do not understand. Must sacrifice together. Build 30 with hands God's home on earth.

Karen says to Kim, "This is where the Yankees play." 31

He nods and smiles, blankly. Nothing about him strikes her so forcefully as 32 his hair, which is shiny and fine and ink-black, with a Sunday-comics look. It is the thing that makes him real to her.

"Baseball," she says, using the word to sum up a hundred happy abstractions, 33
themes that flare to life in the crowd shout and diamond symmetry, in the details of
a dusty slide. The word has resonance if you're American, a sense of shared heart
and untranslatable lore. But she only means to suggest the democratic clamor, a
history of sweat and play on sun-dazed afternoons, an openness of form that makes
the game a kind of welcome to my country.

The other word is "cult." How they love to use it against us. Gives them the 34
false term they need to define us as eerie-eyed children. And how they hate our
willingness to work and struggle. They want to snatch us back to the land of lawns.
That we are willing to live on the road, sleep on the floor, crowd into vans and
drive all night, fund-raising, serving Master. That our true father is a foreigner and
nonwhite. How they silently despise. They keep our rooms ready. They have our
names on their lips. But we're a lifetime away, weeping through hours of fist-
pounding prayer.

World in pieces. It is shock of shocks. But there is plan. Pali-pali. Bring hurry- 35
up time to all man.

She does not dream anymore, except about Master. They all dream about him. 36
They see him in visions. He stands in the room with them when his three-dimen-
sional body is thousands of miles away. They talk about him and weep. The tears
roll down their faces and form puddles on the floor and drip into the room below.
He is part of the structure of their protein. He lifts them out of ordinary strips of
space and time and then shows them the blessedness of lives devoted to the ordinary, to work, prayer, and obedience.

Rodge offers the binoculars to Maureen. She shakes her head firmly. It is like 37
looking for the body of a loved one after a typhoon.

Balloons in clusters rise by the thousands, sailing past the rim of the upper 38
deck. Karen lifts her veil and passes below the pulpit, which is rimmed on three
sides by bulletproof panels. She feels the blast of Master's being, the solar force of
a charismatic soul. Never so close before. He sprinkles mist from a holy bottle in
her face. She sees Kim move his lips, following Master's chant word for word.
She's close enough to the grandstand to see people crowding the rails, standing
everywhere to take pictures. Did she ever think she'd find herself in a stadium in
New York, photographed by thousands of people? There may be as many people
taking pictures as there are brides and grooms. One of them for every one of us.
Clickety-click. The thought makes the couples a little giddy. They feel that space is
contagious. They're here but also there, already in the albums and slide projectors,
filling picture frames with their microcosmic bodies, the minikin selves they are
trying to become.

They veer back to the outfield grass to resume formation. There are folk 39
troupes near both dugouts dancing to gongs and drums. Karen fades into the thousands, the columned mass. She feels the meter of their breathing. They're a world
family now, each marriage a channel to salvation. Master chooses every mate, seeing in a vision how backgrounds and characters match. It is a mandate from heaven,
preordained, each person put here to meet the perfect other. Forty days of separa-

tion before they're alone in a room, allowed to touch and love. Or longer. Or years if Master sees the need. Take cold showers. It is this rigor that draws the strong. Their self-control cuts deep against the age, against the private ciphers, the systems of isolated craving. Husband and wife agree to live in different countries, doing missionary work, extending the breadth of the body common. Satan hates cold showers.

The crowd-eye hangs brightly above them like the triangle eye on a dollar bill.   40

A firecracker goes off, another M-80 banging out of an exit ramp with a hard   41 flat impact that drives people's heads into their torsos. Maureen looks battle-stunned. There are lines of boys wending through empty rows high in the upper deck, some of them only ten or twelve years old, moving with the princely swagger of famous street-felons. She decides she doesn't see them.

"I'll tell you this," Rodge says. "I fully intend to examine this organization.   42 Hit the libraries, get on the phone, contact parents, truly delve. You hear about support groups that people call for all kinds of things."

"We need support. I grant you that. But you're light-years too late."   43

"I think we ought to change our flight as soon as we get back to the hotel and   44 then check out and get going."

"They'll charge us for the room for tonight anyway. We may as well get tick-   45 ets to something."

"The sooner we get started on this."   46

"Raring to go. Oh boy. What fun."   47

"I want to read everything I can get my hands on. Only did some skimming   48 but that's because I didn't know she was involved in something so grandiose. We ought to get some hotline numbers and see who's out there that we can talk to."

"You sound like one of those people, you know, when they get struck down   49 by some rare disease they learn every inch of material they can find in the medical books and phone up doctors on three continents and hunt day and night for people with the same awful thing."

"Makes good sense, Maureen."   50

"They fly to Houston to see the top man. The top man is always in Houston."   51

"What's wrong with learning everything you can?"   52

"You don't have to *enjoy* it."   53

"It's not a question of enjoy it. It's our responsibility to Karen."   54

"Where is she, by the way?"   55

"I fully intend."   56

"You were scanning so duteously. What, bored already?"   57

A wind springs up, causing veils to rustle and lift. Couples cry out, surprised,   58 caught in a sudden lightsome glide, a buoyancy. They remember they are kids, mostly, and not altogether done with infections of glee. They have a shared past after all. Karen thinks of all those nights she slept in a van or crowded room, rising at five for prayer condition, then into the streets with her flower team. There was a girl named June who felt she was shrinking, falling back to child size. They called her Junette. Her hands could not grip the midget bars of soap in the motel toilets of

America. This did not seem unreasonable to the rest of the team. She was only seeing what was really there, the slinking shape of eternity beneath the paint layers and
glutamates of physical earth.

All those lost landscapes. Nights downtown, live nude shows in cinder-block 59
bunkers, slums with their dumpster garbage. All those depopulated streets in subdivisions at the edge of Metroplex, waist-high trees and fresh tar smoking in the dri-
veways and nice-size rattlers that cozy out of the rocks behind the last split-level.
Karen worked to make the four-hundred-dollar-a-day standard, peddling mainly
bud roses and sweet williams. Just dream-walking into places and dashing out.
Rows of neat homes in crashing rain. People drooped over tables at five a.m. at
casinos in the desert. Progressive Slot Jackpots. Welcome Teamsters. She fasted on
liquids for a week, then fell upon a stack of Big Macs. Through revolving doors
into hotel lobbies and department stores until security came scurrying with their
walkie-talkies and beepers and combat magnums.

They prayed kneeling with hands crossed at forehead, bowed deep, folded like 60
unborn young.

In the van everything mattered, every word counted, sometimes fifteen, six- 61
teen sisters packed in tight, singing you are my sunshine, row row row, chanting
their monetary goal. Satan owns the fallen world.

She stacked bundles of baby yellows in groups of seven, the number-symbol 62
of perfection. There were times when she not only thought in broken English but
spoke aloud in the voices of the workshops and training sessions, lecturing the sisters in the van, pressing them to sell, make the goal, grab the cash, and they didn't
know whether to be inspired by the uncanny mimicry or report her for disrespect.

Junette was a whirlwind of awe. Everything was too much for her, too large 63
and living. The sisters prayed with her and wept. Water rocked in the flower buck-
ets. They had twenty-one-day selling contests, three hours' sleep. When a sister ran
off, they holy-salted the clothes she'd left behind. They chanted, We're the greatest,
there's no doubt, heavenly father, we'll sell out.

After midnight in some bar in that winter stillness called the inner city. God's 64
own lonely call. Buy a carnation, sir. Karen welcomed the chance to walk among
the lower-downs, the sort of legions of the night. She slipped into semi-trance,
detached and martyrish, passing through those bare-looking storefronts, the air jan-
gly with other-mindedness. A number of dug-in drinkers bought a flower or two,
men with long flat fingers and pearly nails, awake to the novelty, or hat-wearing
men with looks of high scruple, staring hard at the rain-slickered girl. What new
harassment they pushing in off the street? An old hoocher told her funny things, a
line of sweat sitting on his upper lip. She got the bum's rush fairly often. Don't be
so subjective, sir. Then scanned the street for another weary saloon.

Team leader said, Gotta get goin', kids. Pali-pali.   65

In the van every truth was magnified, everything they said and did separated 66
them from the misery jig going on out there. They looked through the windows and
saw the faces of fallen-world people. It totalized their attachment to true father.
Pray all night at times, all of them, chanting, shouting out, leaping up from prayer

stance, lovely moaning prayers to Master, oh *please,* oh *yes,* huddled in motel room in nowhere part of Denver.

Karen said to them, Which you like to sleep, five hour or four? 67

FOUR. 68

She said, Which you like to sleep, four hour or three? 69

THREE. 70

She said, Which you like to sleep, three hour or none? 71

NONE. 72

In the van every rule counted double, every sister was subject to routine 73 scrutiny in the way she dressed, prayed, brushed her hair, brushed her teeth. They knew there was only one way to leave the van without risking the horror of lifetime drift and guilt. Follow the wrist-slashing fad. Or walk out a high-rise window. It's better to enter gray space than disappoint Master.

Team leader said, Prethink your total day. Then jump it, jump it, jump it. 74

Oatmeal and water. Bread and jelly. Row row row your boat. Karen said to 75 them, Lose sleep, it is for sins. Lose weight, it is for sins. Lose hair, lose nail off finger, lose whole hand, whole arm, it go on scale to stand against sins.

The man in Indiana who ate the rose she sold him. 76

Racing through malls at sundown to reach the daily goal. Blitzing the coin 77 laundries and bus terminals. Door to door in police-dog projects, saying the money's for drug centers ma'am. Junette kidnapped by her parents in Skokie, Illinois. Scotch-taping limp flowers to make them halfway salable. Crazy weather on the plains. Falling asleep at meals, heavy-eyed, dozing on the toilet, sneaking some Z's, catching forty winks, nodding off, hitting the hay, crashing where you can, flaked out, dead to the world, sleep like a top, like a log, desperate for some shut-eye, some sack time, anything for beddy-bye, a cat nap, a snooze, a minute with the sandman. Prayer condition helped them jump it to the limit, got the sorry blood pounding. Aware of all the nego media, which multiplied a ton of doubt for less committed sisters. Doing the hokey-pokey. Coldest winter in these parts since they started keeping records. Chanting the monetary goal.

Team leader said, Gotta hurry hurry hurry. Pali-pali, kids. 78

Rodge sits there in his rumpled sport coat, pockets crammed with traveler's 79 checks, credit cards and subway maps, and he looks through the precision glasses, and looks and looks, and all he sees is repetition and despair. They are chanting again, one word this time, over and over, and he can't tell if it is English or some other known language or some football holler from heaven. No sign of Karen. He puts down the binoculars. People are still taking pictures. He half expects the chanting mass of bodies to rise in the air, all thirteen thousand ascending slowly to the height of the stadium roof, lifted by the picture-taking, the forming of aura, radiant brides clutching their bouquets, grooms showing sunny teeth. A smoke bomb sails out of the bleachers, releasing a trail of Day-Glo fog.

Master leads the chant, *Mansei,* ten thousand years of victory. The blessed 80 couples move their lips in unison, matching the echo of his amplified voice. There is stark awareness in their faces, a near pain of rapt adoration. He is Lord of the

Second Advent, the unriddling of many ills. His voice leads them out past love and joy, past the beauty of their mission, out past miracles and surrendered self. There is something in the chant, the fact of chanting, the being-one, that transports them with its power. Their voices grow in intensity. They are carried on the sound, the soar and fall. The chant becomes the boundaries of the world. They see their Master frozen in his whiteness against the patches and shadows, the towering sweep of the stadium. He raises his arms and the chant grows louder and the young arms rise. He leads them out past religion and history, thousands weeping now, all arms high. They are gripped by the force of a longing. They know at once, they feel it, all of them together, a longing deep in time, running in the earthly blood. This is what people have wanted since consciousness became corrupt. The chant brings the End Time closer. The chant is the End Time. They feel the power of the human voice, the power of a single word repeated as it moves them deeper into oneness. They chant for world-shattering rapture, for the truth of prophecies and astonishments. They chant for new life, peace eternal, the end of soul-lonely pain. Someone on the bandstand beats a massive drum. They chant for one language, one word, for the time when names are lost.

Karen, strangely, is daydreaming. It will take some getting used to, a husband 81 named Kim. She has known girls named Kim since she was a squirt in a sunsuit. Quite a few really. Kimberleys and plain Kims. Look at his hair gleaming in the sun. My husband, weird as it sounds. They will pray together, whole-skinned, and memorize every word of Master's teaching.

The thousands stand and chant. Around them in the world, people ride escala- 82 tors going up and sneak secret glances at the faces coming down. People dangle teabags over hot water in white cups. Cars run silently on the autobahns, streaks of painted light. People sit at desks and stare at office walls. They smell their shirts and drop them in the hamper. People bind themselves into numbered seats and fly across time zones and high cirrus and deep night, knowing there is something they've forgotten to do.

The future belongs to crowds.   83

■ *Questions for* . . . At Yankee Stadium by Don DeLillo

Words to Note

eternal	runway	draws
assemble	arc	an undifferentiated mass
uneasy	spectacle	comprehend
fraught	scattered	ordinary slouchers and
city nomads	a robust acoustical	loiterers
ramps	wallop	spasms
chain-linked	document	planetary impact
messianic	hut	unburdens

tenement barrens

mindstream

flesh parents

cult

bulletproof panels

the solar force of a
 charismatic soul

world family

preordained

dumpster

autobahns

wincing

immunized

flare

a sense of shared heart
 and untranslatable
 lore

contagious

channel to salvation

glide

cinder-block bunkers

cirrus

apparatus

chant

democratic clamor

rimmed

blast

sprinkles

veer

mandate

Metroplex

world-shattering rapture

Language

1. In paragraph 20, DeLillo coins the word *Metroplex*. What does it mean? What is its connotation? How can you tell? What words did he derive it from?
2. What is a *world family? Flesh parents?* A *true father?*
3. DeLillo tells us Karen's *mindstream* slows down sometimes. Why doesn't he just say *thoughts?*

Style

1. In paragraph 2, DeLillo writes, "Grabbed a flight, got a hotel, took the subway, passed through the metal detector and here they are, trying to comprehend." Insert the subjects and compare it with the original. What's the point of DeLillo's phrasing?
2. Again and again, DeLillo resorts to spates of quick, short sentences. How do these passages affect the pace and tone?
3. How does the *rudimentary English* of some of Master's chief assistants read? For instance, DeLillo writes, "World in pieces. It is shock of shocks. But there is plan. Pali-pali. Bring hurry-up time to all man."

Development and Organization

1. What would be lost if Karen's parents sitting in the bleachers were omitted from this selection? Is there a pattern to the way DeLillo moves back and forth from Rodge and Maureen Janney, Karen's parents, to the mass wedding on the field?
2. What is the topic of the paragraph that begins with the following sentence: "From the bandstand at home plate the Mendelssohn march carries a stadium echo, with lost notes drifting back from the recesses between tiers"? How does he develop it? In your opinion, are there any irrelevant details here that could have been cut?

Discussion and Journal Writing

1. Compare this spectacle with a normal wedding.
2. What does DeLillo mean when he says that Master Moon is the true father of the 7500 couples that are being simultaneously married and that they know him at a molecular level? "He lives in them like chains of matter that determine who they are. . . . He is part of the structure of their protein." Are Master Moon and his 7500 happy couples a colossal nuclear family?
3. According to DeLillo, why are all the *flesh parents* there? Is it symbolic that they are in the bleachers?

ooooo

What Happened to the Family?

—Jerrold Footlick, with Elizabeth Leonard

Jerrold Footlick is a senior editor at *Newsweek,* whose writing on legal matters and his work as editor of *Newsweek on Campus* have won him journalism honors. The following piece, which he wrote with Elizabeth Leonard, was the head article in *Newsweek's* special edition *The Twenty-First Century Family* (Winter/Spring 1990) and attempts to plot the bearings of the contemporary American family.

The American family does not exist. Rather, we are creating many American   1
families of diverse styles and shapes. In unprecedented numbers, our families are unalike: We have fathers working while mothers keep house; fathers and mothers both working away from home; single parents; second marriages bringing children together from unrelated backgrounds; childless couples; unmarried couples, with and without children; gay and lesbian parents. We are living through a period of historic change in American family life.

The upheaval is evident everywhere in our culture. Babies have babies, kids   2
refuse to grow up and leave home, affluent Yuppies prize their BMWs more than children, rich and poor children alike blot their minds with drugs, people casually move in with each other and out again. The divorce rate has doubled since 1965, and demographers project that half of all first marriages made today will end in divorce. Six out of 10 second marriages will probably collapse. One third of all children born in the past decade will probably live in a stepfamily before they are 18. One out of every four children today is being raised by a single parent. About

22 percent of children today were born out of wedlock; of those, about a third were born to a teenage mother. One out of every five children lives in poverty; the rate is twice as high among blacks and Hispanics.

Most of us are still reeling from the shock of such turmoil. Americans—in their living rooms, in their boardrooms and in the halls of Congress—are struggling to understand what has gone wrong. We find family life worse than it was a decade ago, according to a NEWSWEEK Poll, and we are not sanguine about the next decade. For instance, two thirds of those polled think a family should be prepared to make "financial sacrifices so that one parent can stay home to raise the children." But that isn't likely to happen. An astonishing two thirds of all mothers are in the labor force, roughly double the rate in 1955, and more than half of all mothers of infants are in the work force. 3

Parents feel torn between work and family obligations. Marriage is a fragile institution—not something anyone can count on. Children seem to be paying the price for their elders' confusion. "There is an increasing understanding of the emotional cost of having children," says Larry L. Bumpass, a University of Wisconsin demographer. "People once thought parenting ended when their children were 18. Now they know it stretches into the 20s and beyond." Divorce has left a devastated generation in its wake, and for many youngsters, the pain is compounded by poverty and neglect. While politicians and psychologists debate cause and solution, everyone suffers. Even the most traditional of families feel an uneasy sense of emotional dislocation. Three decades ago the mother who kept the house spotless and cooked dinner for her husband and children each evening could be confident and secure in her role. Today, although her numbers are still strong—a third of mothers whose children are under 18 stay home—the woman who opts out of a paycheck may well feel defensive, undervalued, as though she were too incompetent to get "a real job." And yet the traditional family retains a profound hold on the American imagination. 4

The historical irony here is that the traditional family is something of an anomaly. From Colonial days to the mid-19th century, most fathers and mothers worked side by side, in or near their homes, farming or plying trades. Each contributed to family income, and—within carefully delineated roles—they shared the responsibility of child rearing. Only with the advent of the Industrial Revolution did men go off to work in a distant place like a factory or an office. Men alone began producing the family income; by being away from home much of the time, however, they also surrendered much of their influence on their children. Mothers, who by social custom weren't supposed to work for pay outside the home, minded the hearth, nurtured the children and placed their economic well-being totally in the hands of their husbands. 5

Most scholars now consider the "bread-winner-homemaker" model unusual, applicable in limited circumstances for a limited time. It was a distinctly white middle-class phenomenon, for example; it never applied widely among blacks or new immigrants, who could rarely afford to have only a single earner in the family. This model thrived roughly from 1860 to 1920, peaking, as far as demographers can 6 measure, about 1890. Demographers and historians see no dramatic turning point just then, but rather a confluence of social and economic circumstances. Husbands' absolute control of family finances and their independent lives away from home shook the family structure. A long recession beginning in 1893 strained family finances. At the same time, new attention was being paid to women's education. Around this period, the Census Bureau captured a slow, steady, parallel climb in the rates of working women and divorce—a climb that has shown few signs of slowing down throughout this century.

The years immediately after World War II, however, seemed to mark a reaffir- 7 mation of the traditional family. The return of the soldiers led directly to high fertility rates and the famous baby boom. The median age of first marriage, which had been climbing for decades, fell in 1956 to a historic low, 22.5 years for men and 20.1 for women. The divorce rate slumped slightly. Women, suddenly more likely to be married and to have children, were also satisfied to give up the paid jobs they had held in record numbers during the war. A general prosperity made it possible for men alone to support their families. Then, by the early '60s, all those developments, caused by aberrational postwar conditions, reverted to the patterns they had followed throughout the century. The fertility rate went down, and the age of first marriage went back up. Prosperity cycled to recession, and the divorce rate again rose and women plunged back heartily into the job market. In 1960, 19 percent of mothers with children under 6 were in the work force, along with 39 percent of those with children between 6 and 17. Thus, while the Cleaver family and Ozzie and Harriet were still planting the idealized family deeper into the national subconscious, it was struggling.

Now the tradition survives, in a way, precisely because of Ozzie and Harriet. 8 The television programs of the '50s and '60s validated a family style during a period in which today's leaders—congressmen, corporate executives, university professors, magazine editors—were growing up or beginning to establish their own families. (The impact of the idealized family was further magnified by the very size of the postwar generation.) "The traditional model reaches back as far as personal memory goes for most of those who [currently] teach and write and philosophize," says Yale University historian John Demos. "And in a time when parents seem to feel a great deal of change in family experience, that image is comfortingly solid and secure, a counterpoint to what we think is threatening for the future."

We *do* feel uneasy about the future. We have just begun to admit that 9 exchanging old-fashioned family values for independence and self-expression may exact a price. "This is an incendiary issue," says Arlie Hochschild, a sociologist at the University of California, Berkeley, and author of the controversial book "The Second Shift." "Husbands, wives, children are not getting enough family life. Nobody is. People are hurting." A mother may go to work because her family needs the money, or to afford luxuries, or because she is educated for a career or because she wants to; she will be more independent but she will probably see less of her children. And her husband, if she has a husband, is not likely to make up the difference with the children. We want it both ways. We're glad we live in a society that is more comfortable living with gay couples, working women, divorced men and stepparents and single mothers—people who are reaching in some fashion for self-fulfillment. But we also understand the value of a family life that will provide a stable and nurturing environment in which to raise children—in other words, an environment in which personal goals have to be sacrificed. How do we reconcile the two?

The answer lies in some hard thinking about what a family is for. What do we 10 talk about when we talk about family? Many of us have an emotional reaction to that question. Thinking about family reminds us of the way we were, and the way we dreamed we might be. We remember trips in the car, eager to find out whose side of the road would have more cows and horses to count. We remember raking leaves and the sound of a marching band at the high-school football game. We remember doing homework and wondering what college might be like. It was not all fun and games, of course. There were angry words spoken, and parents and grandparents who somehow were no longer around, and for some of us not enough to eat or clothes not warm enough or nice enough. Then we grow up and marvel at what we can accomplish, and the human beings we can produce, and we sometimes doubt our ability to do the things we want to do—have to do—for our children. And live our own lives besides.

Practical considerations require us to pin down what the family is all about. 11 Tax bills, welfare and insurance payments, adoption rights and other real-life events can turn on what constitutes a family. Our expectations of what a family ought to be will also shape the kinds of social policies we want. Webster's offers 22 definitions. The Census Bureau has settled on "two or more persons related by birth, marriage or adoption who reside in the same household." New York state's highest court stretched the definition last summer: it held that the survivor of a gay couple retained the legal rights to an apartment they had long shared, just as a surviving husband or wife could. Looking to the "totality of the relationship," the court set four standards for a family: (1) the "exclusivity and longevity of a relationship"; (2) the "level of emotional and financial commitment"; (3) how the couple "conducted their everyday lives and held themselves out to society"; (4) the "reliance placed upon one another for daily services." That approach incenses social critic Midge Decter. "You can call homosexual households 'families,' and you can define 'family' any way you want to, but you can't fool Mother Nature," says Decter. "A family is a mommy and a daddy and their children."

A State of California task force on the future of the family came up with still 12 another conclusion. It decided a family could be measured by the things it should do for its members, which it called "functions": maintain the physical health and safety of its members; help shape a belief system of goals and values; teach social skills, and create a place for recuperation from external stresses. In a recent "family values" survey conducted for the Massachusetts Mutual Insurance Co., respondents were given several choices of family definitions; three quarters of them chose "a group who love and care for each other." Ultimately, to appropriate U.S. Supreme Court Justice Potter Stewart's memorable dictum, we may not be able to define a family, but we know one when we see it.

We enter the 21st century with a heightened sensitivity to family issues. 13 Helping parents and children is a bottom-line concern, no longer a matter of debate. Economists say the smaller labor force of the future means that every skilled employee will be an increasingly valuable asset; we won't be able to afford to waste human resources. Even now companies cannot ignore the needs of working parents. Support systems like day care are becoming a necessity. High rates of child poverty and child abuse are everybody's problem, as is declining school perfor-mance and anything else that threatens our global competitiveness. "By the end of the century," says Columbia University sociologist Sheila B. Kamerman, "it will be conventional wisdom to invest in our children."

Those are the familiar demographic forces. But there are other potential 14 tremors just below the surface. By 2020, one in three children will come from a minority group—Hispanic-Americans, African-Americans, Asian-Americans and others. Their parents will command unprecedented political clout. Minorities and women together will make up the majority of new entrants into the work force. Minority children are usually the neediest among us, and they will want govern-ment support, especially in the schools. At about the same time, many baby boomers will be retired, and they will want help from Washington as well. Billions of dollars are at stake, and the country's priorities in handing out those dollars are not yet clear. After all, children and the elderly are both part of our families. How should the government spend taxpayers' dollars—on long-term nursing care or bet-ter day care?

So far, the political debate on family issues has split largely along predictable 15 ideological lines. Conservatives want to preserve the family of the '50s; they say there has been too much governmental intrusion already, with disastrous results. Their evidence: the underclass, a veritable caste of untouchables in the inner cities where the cycle of welfare dependency and teenage pregnancy thwarts attempts at reform. Liberals say government can and should help. We can measure which pro-grams work, they say; we just don't put our money and support in the right places. Enrichment programs like Head Start, better prenatal care, quality day care—no one questions the effectiveness of these efforts. And liberals see even more to be done. "We have a rare opportunity to make changes now that could be meaningful into the next century," says Marian Wright Edelman, president of the Children's Defense Fund. But many elements that liberals would like to see on a children's agenda are certain to generate bitter political controversy. Among some of the things that could be included in a national family policy:

- Child and family allowances with payments scaled to the number of chil-dren in each family;
- Guarantees to mothers of full job protection, seniority and benefits upon their return to work after maternity leave;

- Pay equity for working women;
- Cash payments to mothers for wages lost during maternity leave;
- Full health-care programs for all children;
- National standards for day-care.

Our legacy to the future must be a program of action that transcends ideology. 16
And there are indications that we are watching the birth of a liberal/conservative
coalition on family issues. "Family issues ring true for people across the political
spectrum," says David Blankenhorn, president of the Institute for American Values,
a New York think tank on family policy issues. "The well-being of families is both
politically and culturally resonant; it is something that touches people's everyday
lives." The government is already responding to the challenge in some ways. For
example, President George Bush agreed at the recent Education Summit to support
increased funding for Head Start, which is by common consent the most successful
federal program for preschoolers, yet now reaches only 18 percent of the eligible
children.

These issues will occupy us on a national level well into the next century. Yet 17
in our everyday lives, we have begun to find solutions. Some mothers, torn
between a desire to stay home with their children and to move ahead in their
careers, are adopting a style known as sequencing. After establishing themselves in
their career or earning an advanced degree, they step off the career ladder for a few
years to focus on children and home. When children reach school age, they return
to full-time jobs. Others take a less drastic approach, temporarily switching to part-
time work or lower-pressure jobs to carve out more time with their young children.
But renewing careers that have been on hiatus is not easy, and women will always
suffer vocationally if it is they who must take off to nurture children. There is,
obviously, another way: fathers can accept more home and family responsibilities,
even to the point of interrupting their own careers. "I expect a significant change by
2020," says sociologist Hochschild. "A majority of men married to working wives
will share equally in the responsibilities of home." Perhaps tradition will keep us
from ever truly equalizing either child rearing or ironing—in fact, surveys on chore
sharing don't hold much promise for the harried working mother. But we have
moved a long way since the 1950s. And just because we haven't tried family equality yet doesn't mean we won't ever try it.

That's the magic for American families in the 21st century: we can try many 18
things. As certainly as anything can be estimated, women are not going to turn their
backs on education and careers, are not going to leave the work force for adult lives
as full-time homemakers and mothers. And the nation's businesses will encourage
their efforts, if only because they will need the skilled labor. Yet Americans will
not turn their backs completely on the idealized family we remember fondly. Thus,
we must create accommodations that are new, but reflect our heritage. Our families
will continue to be different in the 21st century except in one way. They will give
us sustenance and love as they always have.

■ *Questions for* . . . **What Happened to the Family?** by Jerrold Footlick, with Elizabeth Leonard

Words to Note

diverse	unprecedented	upheaval
blot	demographers	reeling
sanguine	devastated	wake
compounded	defensive	undervalued
incompetent	anomaly	delineated
advent	surrendered	confluence
shook	parallel	reaffirmation
slumped	aberrational	reverted
cycled	plunged	national subconscious
validated	counterpoint	incendiary
marvel	pin	incenses
recuperation	memorable dictum	human resources
clout	governmental intrusion	legacy
transcends	resonant	sequencing
harried	the idealized family	sustenance
love		

Language

1. At the beginning of the third paragraph, Footlick says we are "reeling" from the shock of family changes. Are we? Is *reeling* too strong a word? Just right? What other words could he have used?
2. Look at how Footlick uses the word *sequencing* in the next to the last paragraph? Is it a helpful term? Is it jargon? Is it a euphemism that masks unfairness and inequality? In the legal profession, sequencing is known as the *mommy track*. Compare the tones of the two terms.

Style

1. Journalists like to begin their articles with sentences, called *leads,* that catch and hold the reader's attention. Footlick begins, "The American family does not exist." Is his opening sentence an effective lead? Why or why not? Can you use the same technique for college papers?
2. Footlick uses bullets and a list format to present proposals that might be included in a national family policy. Would numbers or just plain sentences have been more effective? Why do writing instructors discourage students from making lists in their papers?

Development and Organization

1. Footlick quotes demographers, sociologists, and historians. Why does he quote so many academics? What kind of expertise do they have? What do their names, titles, statistics, and opinions add to the article?
2. Why doesn't he quote politicians, ministers, pediatricians, family therapists, or simply people who are or have been members of families?
3. Paragraphs 5, 6, and 7 are about the family's history in America. Are these paragraphs a digression, or do they contribute something important to the article?

Discussion and Journal Writing

1. Conservative ideologue Midge Decter criticized the New York State Supreme Court's definition of family because it included gay couples: "You can call homosexual households 'families,' and you can define 'family' any way you want to, but you can't fool Mother Nature. A family is a mommy and a daddy and their children." Do you agree with her definition? There are three other definitions of family in paragraphs 11 and 12. In your opinion, which definition is the most valid?
2. Why do people argue about how family is defined? What's at stake?
3. How is your family different from the families of your grandparents? Based on your experience, do you agree with Footlick's observations about the direction the family is taking? Or do you think it's heading in another direction? Explain, illustrate.
4. Does America currently have a national family policy? How about England, Brazil, South Africa, and the People's Republic of China?

ooooo

Rich Kids and Their Families

—John Sedgwick

John Sedgwick was born in Dedham, Massachusetts, in 1954. He attended Groton, one of America's most exclusive prep schools, and Harvard. He is a freelance writer whose articles have appeared in *Esquire, Connoisseur,* and other magazines. He lives in Boston with his wife and their daughter. This selection appears in his book *Rich Kids.*

The money stuffing rich kids' Gucci billfolds is different from the regular   1
kind lining the skinny wallets of the average citizen. The bills of the rich kids are
not adorned with the usual engravings of Washington, Jackson, and Grant. No,
their cash has Daddy's picture on it, or their great-uncle's, or their great-great-
grandfather's—whoever it was back there who made the money and then passed it
down.

In rich kids' lives, the founder of the family fortune looms as a far greater fig-   2
ure than any mere president. Large as such billionaires as J. P. Morgan, John D.
Rockefeller, Joseph Pulitzer, and Eugene Meyer stand in history, they bestride
these little rich kids like so many colossuses. Even though the family founder may
be long dead, he exerts an influence these kids feel every day of their lives. He
made the kids rich, for one thing. Often, he made the kids famous, too. Oil portraits
of the great man burden the walls where the rich kids grew up; visions of him
pester their dreams. Sometimes they live in his house. And they dutifully gather
biographies and leatherbound editions of collected letters on their shelves in a kind
of shrine.

The rich kids' money inevitably leads them back to their family. In one case,   3
it used to do so literally. Helen Strauss's family company so dominated her home-
town's economy in the nineteenth century that the family minted its own bills and
coins. Usually the intermingling of family and money in family money is only figurative, but it is still compelling.

The rich kids' peers in the workaday world have to leave home to seek their   4
fortunes, trotting off to take jobs in business or law. But for the rich kids to seek
their fortune, they look back up to the august family founder. Among the recipients
of Great-Granddad's largesse within the family, this shared financial heritage reinforces the natural ties of blood. In the immediate family, it turns brothers and sisters, economically speaking, into identical twins. But it also tightens the bonds with
distant cousins, great-aunts, half-brothers, thereby transforming the greater family
of descendants into something that more closely resembles a tribe or, even, an ethnicity. Rich kids are Rockefellers or Mellons or Pulitzers the way the common-born
Americans are Irish or Greek or Lithuanian: they have a shared heritage that goes
beyond their individual identities to unite them.

When a rich kid thinks of his family, he doesn't think of Mom and Pop and   5
Bub and Sis. His family reaches back generations to Great-Great-Great-Grandfather
and spans outward to fourth cousins. He sees his family as a long and ever-widen-
ing line of nobility, of which his immediate family is just one speck. In family
genealogies, the whole business is usually pictured as a tree, with the founding
ancestor as the sturdy trunk at the bottom and the descendants branching out above.
But the rich kid himself views it the other way up—with the illustrious ancestor far
above him, huge and imposing, like a Greek god, forever out of reach, and the kid
himself down on the bottom.

And, in keeping with this view of himself as having come from a royal lin-   6
eage, the rich kid always knows from what "house" he issues. The Rockefeller

descendant I've called Terry, the one who is still waiting for his full inheritance to rain down upon him, has gone through life explaining that he isn't a John D. Rockefeller but a William, as though that settled something important about his character. In his case, the "house" is manifested quite literally as the fenced-in family compound in Greenwich, Connecticut. He grew up there with his extended family, all of the members linked by their descent from their Founder, William Rockefeller. Terry counted twenty-five cousins in his age group in the neighborhood; five of them ended up in his elementary-school class.

In the case of brand-name heirs, their "house" is more metaphorical—it is a 7 matter for them of whether they are one of *the* Fords, *the* du Ponts, or *the* Pillsburys. George Pillsbury reported that he was plagued by the question when he was growing up in Minneapolis. "But when I told them I was," he said, "they never had much of a response. They seemed to wonder why they had asked the question."

The money reinforces the familial line, partly by drawing attention to it. The 8 family money is like the wire connecting the Christmas tree lights: it makes all the bulbs light up. That can even catch some of the family members by surprise, as it did the Paine Webber heir Roger Elkin. Amazed as he was to discover his own fortune at twenty-one, he was even more taken aback a year or so into his daughter's life when he tried to establish a trust fund for her; he found out that his dead grandfather had already beaten him to it, endowing her handsomely from the moment of her birth by a provision of his will. She was a Paine as soon as she was an Elkin.

There are other ancestral links in a family, but the money line is the one that 9 counts. Often, the wealthy families themselves believe that a special nobility has been conferred upon that particular strain of the family lineage that bears the money, and arrange their genealogies with that in mind. Michael Pratt was disturbed enough when he saw what effect the monied Pratts had on Amherst College; he was appalled when he saw their effect on the family tree. "The guy who made the money in our family is my great-great-great-grandfather Charles Bradley Pratt," he said. "He was a senior partner at Standard Oil, and he made his money running the country for a few years with Rockefeller. He is called the Founder. Of course, his father Ezra Pratt was a very good carpenter in Watertown, Massachusetts. Why shouldn't he be the Founder? Well, he's not. Charles Bradley is the Founder."

And the Pratts gather regularly to pay homage. When they assemble they all 10 wear coded badges to show how they are related to the Founder. Michael found it amusing. "I was C1 something," he said, "but I can't remember exactly how it goes. I went with my girl friend, and they gave her my number with a plus sign beside it to designate 'paramour.' I asked what would happen if someone showed up with a gay lover. Would they get a minus? No one was amused by that."

Other families have better senses of humor. Roger Elkin says that at one 11 recent reunion, hundreds of descendants of William A. Paine, one of the original partners of Paine Webber, stood up and raised a glass to themselves as *"real Paines."*

In the extended Wynne family of Texas, including Jimmy and Shannon, the 12 gang has split into rival factions called the Snakes and the Mongooses depending on whether or not they are in direct line of the money. The Snakes are all descended from the wealthy lawyer Buck Wynne and are so named because of those Tiffany-designed gold rings of bejeweled serpents of the Nile that Jimmy and Shannon wear so proudly. They are copies of one awarded to Buck by a client grateful for the way he disposed of a major lawsuit. The Mongooses were formed by a cousin who married into the family and are so named because, of course, mongooses eat snakes—and gobble up their inheritances in this case. But instead of going at it like natural enemies, the Snakes and Mongooses gather peaceably every year at one of the Six Flags parks built by Shannon Wynne's father Angus, where they have a kind of hootenanny, including a fashion show for the Snakes and initiation rites for that year's crop of Mongooses.

It's natural that rich kids should attend a lot of reunions of the whole clan, for 13 the money has a way of reaching out beyond the nuclear family to pull distant relatives into the family fold. The true father here is the Family Founder, and all his descendants are his children. Consequently, in these rich families, cousins often feel as close as siblings. Charlie Chiara, the grandson of financier John Loeb, grew up with his cousins, the Bronfmans of Seagram's Liquors; their houses stood side by side on common property in Westchester County, New York. Charlie's mother's sister had married Edgar Bronfman but had obviously been unwilling to leave her Loeb family too far behind. "There were ten of us children as you drove up the property," said Charlie. "Our house was first and theirs second. It was a big party all the time." Although the Bronfmans eventually divorced, severing lucrative business ties between Seagram's and what was then Shearson Loeb Rhoades, the family bonds remained intact. One of the cousins remains Charlie's best friend. Charlie was best man at his wedding, and his picture hangs over Charlie's desk at his little production company in Hollywood.

With their control of the family purse strings, the grandparents act more like 14 Mom and Dad. That can get a little strange. Barbara Behn, now in her thirties, recalled that when she was a small child, her grandfather Sosthenes Behn, the "Prince of Telephones" and founder of ITT, absolutely doted on her, carrying on as if he had sired her himself. Accustomed to material pleasures himself—for an office, he occupied a salon done in the style of Louis XIV—he would take her to F.A.O. Schwartz and, she said, "nearly buy out the store," then round out the occasion by asking her, although she was only four or five, to have luncheon (no mere lunch, of course) with him every Saturday at his corner table at La Côte Basque. And every year until he died when she was six, he celebrated her birthday in the penthouse suite of the corporation's thirty-three-story Gothic skyscraper on Manhattan's Broad Street. There he would summon the directors to a long boardroom table, pull Barbara's chair—bolstered by the Manhattan phone book—in the place of honor, and, as the company's French chef wheeled out a huge birthday cake, lead all the executives in singing Happy Birthday.

And that wasn't all. There were other distinguished relatives on her well- 15 fertilized family tree. Barbara used to pass her summers in Newport in a modest place, by local standards, called Stonybrook. But her great-uncle was Edward Julius Berwind, the coal king, who built for himself a château to rival the Vanderbilts' monument to conspicuous consumption, The Breakers. His was the Elms, inspired by France's Château Daniel; and Barbara's great-aunt, then in her nineties and confined to a wheelchair, used to invite Barbara and her sister to come over to play there every Sunday as children. They had a wonderful time climbing on the statues in the garden. "We were so small," said Barbara, "we'd ride them like horses." They'd visit the extensive greenhouses with the gardener. And they would watch delightedly as their great-aunt summoned the butler, Benson, to feed their dog. "Benson was more of a snob than my great-aunt was," said Barbara. With great ceremony, Benson would serve the animal roast beef off a silver platter. On rainy days Mrs. Berwind would invite them to bring their games inside. "The house had a huge ballroom," said Barbara, "and my aunt would take us kids into the ballroom and get a ball and say, 'Come on, let's play. That's what ballrooms are for.' So we'd go inside, her in her wheelchair, my sister and me, and we'd play catch."

Few rich kids grew up in close contact with their parents; instead they had 16 maids to bring them up. In more high-toned families she was called the nanny or governess; in the less, the baby-sitter. Either way, these women ended up mothering these rich kids well into adolescence, when the kids went off to boarding school.

Heartless as this arrangement may seem, the children almost universally liked 17 it. As Cary Ridder, a cheery heiress to the Knight-Ridder newspaper fortune, blurted out: "I wasn't raised by my parents—thank God!" She explained that her mother was far too busy with her political career and her packed social schedule to keep track of such petty details as picking her children up from school.

While a certain coldness creeps into most of the rich kids' recollections of life 18 with Father and Mother, their hearts leap up as they recall their nannies. Sometimes the objects of their adoration are so unlikely, it seems that some primitive psychological force must be at work akin to the imprinting that allows baby ducklings to fall in love with cardboard boxes. Terry Hunt, an heir to the Alcoa aluminum fortune now working as a psychologist in Boston, has spent many an hour contemplating the rapture he felt for a deaf, arthritic eighty-five-year-old Czechoslovakian woman named Apola. Strictly speaking, she was the family cook, but she ended up giving so much quality time to Terry she might as well have been his nanny. Terry had, in fact, developed strong feelings for the woman who really was his nanny, but he was squeezed out of her affections when his younger sister came along. So he turned with love in his heart to Apola. "I had a very intimate relationship with her," he told me. "It was very intimate, very secret, and very special. She was a woman who could hardly walk, but she and I together were like a pair of teenagers in love. I'd say things like, 'I can't wait for my parents to leave so Apola and I can be together.'" Unfortunately, Terry's mother found such sentiments alarming and sent

Apola packing. "Ostensibly that was because Apola couldn't get along with the rest of the help, and she would turn off her hearing aid when she wanted to tune people out," Terry explained. "But I knew the real reason." Terry was crushed, and, like a tiny Romeo, he pursued his love to her new place of employment, where, with tears streaming down his cheeks, he pleaded with her to come back. Unfortunately, Apola's new mistress wouldn't let her go. So his first great love passed out of his life. Terry was all of five years old.

These maids were all strange objects of affection, coming from backgrounds 19 so different from the rich kids' own. They were poor, for one thing, and they were usually foreign, frequently French or German. Michael Pratt's family went for a series of Nordic blondes. Now, he said, "portions of my childhood are scattered all through Scandinavia." And there were, as with Annie Owen's beloved Goldie, a good number of southern black women as well.

But in the very difference lay these women's strength. They supplied some 20 basic human values, a kind of reality principle, to lives that might otherwise have floated away entirely in the ether of financial freedom.

Elizabeth Meyer, the self-professed "porpoise in the sea," believed she might 21 have gone under if it hadn't been for her Lil. She was a savvy black woman who, even if she had herself grown up as one of eighteen children in a sharecropper's family, had a special insight into how to handle her princely charges. She paid them to be good, laying out cash for making their beds and taking baths.

In middle-class families, the time of greatest closeness between parents and 22 children and between brothers and sisters comes when the kids are still young. The family still lives together in the same house, some of the siblings possibly sharing the same room. The children wear hand-me-downs from their elders, attend the same local schools, go to the same hangouts, perhaps share the same friends. How different this is from the childhoods of the rich kids, so isolated from their parents and from their brothers and sisters inside their vast houses. But they do catch up eventually. For them, the time of greatest family feeling comes after they have grown up and left home.

Their inheritances, surprisingly, bring them together. The money pays for 23 long-distance calls and regular visits, of course. But more importantly, it provides a shared and extremely private bond. When a rich kid finds out about his own trust fund, he also finds out about the holdings of his brothers and sisters, and, often, gets a pretty good idea about those of his parents' as well. In uncovering something so intimate, it is as if he had seen their private diaries. On becoming adults, all the members of the family learn something about each other that no one else will possibly ever know. By sharing such a secret, the family members develop a rare and solid form of trust that is not so different from love. All rich kids feel that, deep down, only their families really understand.

Sometimes the siblings act on their money identically, in the way that Sarah 24 Pillsbury founded Liberty Hill shortly after her brother George founded Haymarket.

And in those families where the children all go off in separate directions, as is more often the case, the money in some way keeps them connected. While Ando Hixon, for example, is a professional investor, his brother is a spiritual talk-show host; while the woman I've called Marie, who lost much of her money through improvident investments, is in a seminary, her brother is a rancher; Elizabeth Meyer is a real-estate developer and yachting enthusiast, her sister a Jehovah's Witness. But running through these different personalities is the same money, and it unites them. In Elizabeth's case, and in others, there is a practical aspect to the shared wealth, since she has to join her siblings on a regular basis in a conference call to decide how to manage their joint holdings. As she says, "We're all caught up together in the spiderweb of *Washington Post* stock."

And this unifying principle applies between children and parents as well. 25 When rich kids come into their money, they see life from their parents' perspective in ways that the non-wealthy will probably never manage. When the middle-class kid turns twenty-one, his father has finally become well established in his profession and in his life. That's not necessarily true for the fathers of the rich kids, for, at least in the old-money families, they are living off their own inheritances from *their* fathers, so they are rich kids, too, just older ones. In these wealthy families, there is only one true father, the Family Founder who made all the money. All his heirs are his children, regardless of their age. That awareness, while it can upset the power balance, can also breed a special intimacy between parents and children. Sonia Belahovski confided that she likes to sleep with her mother in her double bed when she goes home to visit. Other relationships are nearly as close.

■ *Questions for* . . . **Rich Kids and Their Families** by John Sedgwick

Words to Note

stuffing	adorned	founder
looms	bestride	colossuses
exerts	burden	shrine
intermingling	largesse	spans
nobility	illustrious	imposing
trust fund	money line	genealogies
appalled		

Language

1. In paragraph 9, Sedgwick writes, "There are other ancestral links in a family, but the money line is the one that counts." What does *money line* mean? Where does the expression come from?

2. He says that most of the rich kids he interviewed had little contact with their parents and were brought up by nannies; then, he calls this arrangement "heartless." Would most people agree with this assessment? What's the source of this value judgment?

3. Sedgwick contrasts rich kids with "common-born Americans." What is a *common-born American?* Would most common-born Americans describe themselves as *common born?* What is the expression's connotation? What does it reveal about Sedgwick's background?

Style

1. Why does Sedgwick capitalize *Family Founder?*

2. In the fourth paragraph, Sedgwick writes, "Rich kids are Rockefellers or Mellons or Pulitzers the way the common-born Americans are Irish or Greek or Lithuanian: they have a shared heritage that goes beyond their individual identities to unite them." What effect does the colon have on the pacing and meaning of this sentence?

Development and Organization

1. Why does Sedgwick include a description of the Pratt family coded badges?

2. How does he develop the point about nannies raising rich kids?

3. Why does he repeatedly contrast upper-class families with middle-class families?

Discussion and Journal Writing

1. Sedgwick contrasts the family form of the wealthy with the middle-class nuclear family. If the upper-class family isn't nuclear, what is it?

2. What role does the *Family Founder* play in the upper-class family?

3. According to Sedgwick's portrait, are American upper-class families less happy, as happy, or happier than middle-class and lower-class families?

ooooo

The Case Against Divorce

—Diane Medved

Diane Medved, Ph.D. is a clinical psychologist specializing in short-term therapy with couples and individuals making life choices and transitions. She is author of *Children: To Have or Have Not?* and *First Comes Love: Deciding Whether or Not To Get Married,* and has written feature articles for *Ladies Home Journal, McCall's, Glamour, Mademoiselle,* and other periodicals. She lives in Santa Monica with her husband, film critic Michael Medved, and their children.

I have to start with a confession: This isn't the book I set out to write. 1

I planned to write something consistent with my previous professional experi- 2 ence—helping people with decision making. In ten years as a psychologist, I've run scores of workshops that specialized in weighing the pros and cons of major life choices. I've even published books on two of life's major turning points: whether or not to have a child and whether or not to get married. When I conceptualized this book on divorce, it was in that mold—a guide to help people decide if separation is appropriate.

I based this concept on some firmly held assumptions and beliefs. For exam- 3 ple, I started this project believing that people who suffer over an extended period in unhappy marriages ought to get out. In my private practice, I'd seen plenty of struggling couples, and in every case, I anguished along with them when they described manipulation, lack of attention, or emotional dissatisfaction. I knew from their stories, as well as from my own experience, the heart-wrenching desperation that precedes separating and the liberation that leaving represents. I originally thought that staying together in turmoil was ultimately more traumatic than simply making the break.

I was convinced that recent no-fault divorce laws were a praiseworthy step 4 toward simplifying a legally, psychologically, and emotionally punishing process. I thought that striking down taboos about divorce was another part of the ongoing enlightenment of the women's, civil rights, and human potential movements of the last twenty-five years. I had learned early in my graduate school training that crisis fosters growth, and therefore I assumed that the jolt of divorce almost always brings beneficial psychological change.

To my utter befuddlement, the extensive research I conducted for this book 5 brought me to one inescapable and irrefutable conclusion: I had been wrong. The statistics and anecdotes I gathered forced me to scuttle my well-prepared plans. I had to face the fact that writing a "morally neutral" book showing divorce to be just another option—a life choice no better or worse than staying married—would be irreparably damaging to the audience I wanted to help.

The change came as I shifted my focus from still-married couples in conflict, 6 who made up the bulk of my practice, to now-single individuals who had already received their decrees.

I asked questions—and got some predictable answers: Are you glad you 7 divorced? Yes. Do you regret getting your divorce? No. I was pleased that the responses to these two questions confirmed my original thinking.

But then I plumbed beneath the surface: What kind of contact do you have 8 with your ex-spouse? How has the divorce affected your children? What kinds of experiences have you had in the dating world since your divorce? How has your style of living changed?

"Oh, everything's fine, fine," the respondents at first insisted. Everyone was 9 without a doubt stronger and more hearty than ever.

But my questions kept coming. And the truth was difficult to avoid. Often in a 10 rush of tears, they described the suffering and anguish they had endured—nights of fantasies about the husband or wife who left them; days of guilt after abandoning a once-devoted mate. They talked about the nuts-and-bolts of daily life, of uprooting, of shifting to an apartment and splitting possessions, of balancing parental duties with now-pressing work demands. They spoke of changing relationships with their children, who moved from innocent babes to confidants to arbitrators and sometimes to scapegoats.

And they mourned a part of themselves never to be recaptured. The part they 11 had once invested in a marital or family unit was now destroyed. Wearily, they told of the transformation of the optimism and enthusiasm they had devoted to the now-crushed marriage to bitterness, skepticism, and self-preservation. "Never again," echoed my respondents. "Never again will I combine my income with another's." "Never again will I trust my spouse away overnight." "Never again will I believe someone when he says 'I'll take care of you.'"

I didn't want to hear it. I wanted to hear that they got past their divorces and 12 emerged better for it. And while the women and men I spoke to were more sure of themselves and capable of living independently, I also heard that they had gained this self-reliance out of painful necessity, not out of free choice.

For given a choice, they preferred to be married. Everyone said he or she 13 wanted to find somebody new. Many women were panic-stricken, afraid they would not find the "right" man before their childbearing years were lost. Others had become so jaded that they lamented the sobering truth that they were unlikely to find another mate at all. With their newfound strength, they all said they would survive; all said they were perfectly content with themselves and the lives they'd recently reconstructed. Still, there was regret. "Looking back now, do you think that you could have made it work with your first husband?" I asked.

"Well, he was crazy," they'd begin. "He was a slob. He was unromantic. He 14 only thought of himself and his career. But knowing what I know now . . . yes, I probably could have made it work."

I was aghast. But the more I heard these or similar words, and the more I read 15 from the library, the more I was forced to concede that the ruinous stories of my divorced clients and interviewees were true. Divorce was catastrophic—but not in the commonly acceptable terms of a simple year or two thrown away. I found that the mere contemplation of divorce—the acceptance of it as an imminent option (rather than dedication to working on a wounded marriage) is debilitating. The process of evaluating the injuries—of cajoling and pleading and threatening—is emotionally exhausting. The physical act of packing a bag and moving out is traumatic. And from there the trauma escalates.

Quite simply, I discovered in my research that the process and aftermath of 16 divorce is so pervasively disastrous—to body, mind, and spirit—that in an overwhelming number of cases, the "cure" that it brings is surely worse than marriage's "disease."

Of course, there are exceptions. There are times when divorce is clearly the 17 only recourse. When physical or mental abuse exists. When emotional cruelty or neglect becomes intolerable. When one partner adamantly refuses to stay in the marriage or withdraws to the point where in reality you're alone.

I used to think that the range of situations when divorce is appropriate encom- 18 passed quite a bit more than that. But when I look at the balance of the bad and the good that divorced individuals endure, my only possible conclusion is that people could be spared enormous suffering if they scotched their permissive acceptance of divorce and viewed marriage as a serious, lifelong commitment, a bond not to be entered into—or wriggled out of—lightly.

The old wedding vows read "for better or for worse . . . until death do us 19 part." They now commonly intone, "through good times and bad . . . as long as our love shall last." Until recently, I nodded at the "improvement"; now I soberly acknowledge the wisdom in the message of the past.

Too Late for Marleen

The grim stories of crippled couples whom I interviewed for this book got me 20 thinking about the permanent distrust, anguish, and bitterness divorce brings. But the catalyst coalescing these thoughts was a simple workaday lunch with a friend I've known for about eight years. Marleen Gaines, a school district administrator, is a handsome woman of forty who wears sophisticated silks, renews season tickets to the symphony, and stays sharp on the decisions of the courts, cabinet, and city council. When a mutual friend originally introduced us, I instantly clicked into Marleen's quick wit, upbeat attitude, and direct, self-confident zest. But as we sat down to salads at a café near my office, her usual sunny veneer gave way to a depressing monotone of desolation.

Three years ago, Marleen startled her friends by suddenly walking out of her 21 nine-year marriage. At the time she left him, her husband Bob, now forty-two, seemed unbearably boring, uneducated, and unmotivated to achieve. Marleen wanted more of a dynamo, a brilliant intellectual she could admire, successful in his career. She met lots of these stimulating men at the office, and casual flirtations suggested to her that once she was free to pursue them, she would have plenty of opportunities for a more satisfying marriage.

But after three years single, she has found only frustration—and the humiliat-   22 ing realization that at her age, she is considered witty and glib but not especially desirable. There were a couple of flings with married men and an unrequited crush on her self-absorbed boss, who encouraged her attention merely to further inflate his swollen ego. She fell in love with a coworker, who treasured her company so much he told her every excruciating detail of his romantic exploits and eventual engagement. Meanwhile, her three closest friends remarried one by one and had stylishly late-in-life babies.

Now alone in a rambling house in San Bernardino with only her three dogs for   23 companionship, she yearns for the simple warmth of Bob's presence. Though he was a college dropout and works now as a supermarket manager, Bob had his virtues. Always gentle and good-natured, he doted on Marleen and provided consistent encouragement. He may not have been the go-getter she desired, but he had an intuitive intelligence and a good, steady income to maintain their comfortable lifestyle.

It took all this time for Marleen to realize her mistake. At first, Bob had   24 begged her to return; rebuked, he rebounded into one, then another serious relationship. He now lives with a woman who's pushing for marriage, and he's grown quite fond of her two teenage sons. When they speak every few weeks, Bob confesses to Marleen that his current companion "can be a pain" and swears that Marleen is the only woman he's ever "really" loved. Now Marleen has asked for a reconciliation, but weak-willed Bob is too dominated in his new world to leave, and Marleen, realizing that "possession is nine-tenths of the law," has resigned herself to the fact that he's not coming back.

Divorces Are Forever

Sitting in the restaurant trying to console my friend, I was struck by the fre-   25 quency with which I've heard stories similar to hers—not only in my workshops and clinical psychology practice, but increasingly in everyday social chatter. It's a well-known U.S. Census Bureau statistic that half of all marriages fail; equally well-publicized is how both men and women suffer financially as a result. Sociologist Leonore Weitzman found that women's standard of living declines by a whopping 73 percent in the first year after divorce, and those who are mothers are further saddled with additional child care and logistics chores.

While everyone laments the immediate trauma of "going through a divorce,"   26 more discomfiting is the alarming news of its lingering emotional and psychological effects. Research by the California Children of Divorce Project headed by Judith Wallerstein, for example, shows an especially dismal future for women forty and over—even ten years after the divorce. Half of the women studied at that distant point could be diagnosed as "clinically depressed," and all were moderately or severely lonely, despite the fact that 50 percent of them had initiated the divorce themselves. Exacerbating their malaise might be alarming new statistics on their chances of finding another husband—chances *Newsweek* magazine (June 1986) claims are so low that these women face a greater likelihood of being struck by a terrorist!

Uncovering these facts during the preparation of this book only made me 27 determined to probe reactions to divorce further. I jotted down some ideas and then developed an informal questionnaire that I distributed to an unscientific but diverse sample of two hundred people who had been separated or divorced. The results brought home undeniably that the effects of divorce last a lifetime. And they are in actuality far worse than we care to confront.

Everyone has some understanding of the pain of divorce. And yet, in these 28 days of disposable marriage, at one time or another every married person contemplates separation. It may be in the heat of an argument, or during a fantasy about a more perfect mate. It may appear amid recurrent minor irritations, or it may come as the cumulative result of larger problems stored away for years. Everyone in the throes of a flirtation or affair considers the possibility of chucking the safe and boring for the exciting and glamorous. And people on the cusp of new success are tempted to leave reminders of the less glorious past and begin anew.

Clashing with this casual attitude toward divorce is America's reclaiming of 29 traditional values. Religion has gained renewed respectability. Women who cried "career first" are now honoring their maternal instincts and realizing they may not be able to "have it all." Conservative politics have recently attracted many of yesterday's liberals. And college students, once esoterically majoring in philosophy and sociology, are taking the most direct routes to their MBAs.

Personal lives are more conservative as well, due to the sheer terror provoked 30 by the specter of AIDS. People are practicing "safe sex" not only with frank conversation prior to intimacy and with the use of condoms, but through definite changes in outlook toward recreational sex. A 1987 bestseller, taken seriously enough to be the subject of a day's discussion on the Oprah Winfrey television talk show and a return appearance by the author, advocated sexual abstinence before marriage. In addition, a representative national survey of twelve hundred college students undertaken by *Glamour* magazine revealed that "the AIDS epidemic is a serious damper on sexual activity: about half of all college students say the threat of AIDS has caused them to change their sexual habits."

The AIDS scare and the broader shift toward conservative attitudes, however, 31 seem distant to couples in the throes of conjugal combat. In the midst of a shouting match, a gloriously portrayed single life and freedom from the oppression of a particular spouse call much more loudly. Unfortunately, veterans of divorce like my friend Marleen, who yearn for families and secure, permanent relationships, now see that they have been sadly duped by those compelling myths, which suggest that divorce "can open up new horizons," that the dating scene is exciting, and that bright, attractive people will always find new partners with whom to share their lives.

It's finally time to renounce—openly and clearly—these self-serving plati- 32 tudes about independence and fulfillment and look at the reality of divorce. We act too frequently as if every infirm marriage deserves to die, based simply upon the emotional report of one distressed partner. Rather than viewing a separation first with alarm, we're full of sympathy for a divorcing friend, and we offer understanding of the temporary insanity involved in severing old ties.

Still influenced by the "do your own thing" era, we don't act constructively. 33 We don't take the husband (or wife) by the shoulders and shake him. We don't shout in his ear that he might be making a disastrous mistake. Even if we care immensely about him, we feel it's too intrusively "judgmental" to do more than step back and say, "Okay, if that's what you want," and close our eyes to the consequences. My research suggests that this is more cruelty than friendship.

Even Winners Pay the Price

Some people who know me well ask how I could take this position, having 34 been divorced and then happily remarried myself. It is partially because I have faced divorce that I can speak with some authority. It is true that I am one of the very lucky few who entered the chancy world of potential happiness or permanent pain and was ultimately given a break. But there are so many others—just as bright, just as desirable or more so—who bitterly ask why their "best years" must be spent alone. Even though I found a satisfying relationship, I am still paying the price of my divorce.

It is difficult for me to discuss something as personal as my own divorce, par- 35 tially because I now invest so much in the new life I have created. I also don't like writing about my divorce because I am embarrassed and ashamed, and those feelings are painful to express.

Though my ex-husband and I were constitutionally quite different, we were 36 nevertheless also the same in many ways, or at least had grown that way over the years. And because we shared our adolescence and formative adult period, we had a bond I found excruciating to discard. Unfortunately, like almost all of the divorced couples I have seen and researched, we cannot manage that ridiculous myth of being "just friends." So in becoming divorced, I severed an important extension of myself, negating a crucial and memorable chunk of my history and development. It is an enormous loss.

I am humiliated and mortified at failing in a relationship others at one time 37 held exemplary. My divorce clashes with the self-image I work earnestly to cultivate: that I am triumphant in my endeavors, that the things I attempt are not only worthwhile but likely to succeed. By divorcing, I have proven myself inept—at least once—in perhaps the most crucial arena, one which by profession is my stock-in-trade—the ability to analyze choices and proceed wisely.

My divorce would have been bad enough were I able to keep my downfall a 38 secret, like the dieter who sneaks a bag of cookies while driving on the anonymous freeway. But I am embarrassed further because of the public discredit and the possibility that former admirers now view me as diminished. Whether or not my associates really do see my character as smirched, or whether they are truly forgiving, is not as relevant as the fact that I *feel* I am now less worthy of their regard.

For those who do go on to build a second life, the future, built more on hope 39 than confidence, may falter. Only about half of those I interviewed who remarried stayed with the second spouse or reported conjugal satisfaction; many found themselves reeling from their first marriages years later and admitted repeating the same mistakes.

The book *Crazy Time* by Abigail Trafford describes the weeks and months 40 after separation, when typically people replay those crushing moments over and over in their minds. The one who is rejected remembers the years together in measured fragments, dissecting every retort, every misplaced movement, for signs of failure or symbols of flawed passion.

The one who leaves in search of something better is so wracked by guilt and 41 remorse that he can do nothing more than look ahead, shielding himself from the overwhelming self-loathing and embarrassment of looking at his past. Like Pharaoh, who refused the Jews' pleas for freedom even when confronted by the convincing pressure of the ten plagues, a spouse who negates his marriage must harden his heart against it. He must bury all the love that still exists for his partner, even if he realizes that it is love shaped by gratitude rather than attraction. The safe and cozy, welcoming home that the estranged partner once provided must be temporarily barred from consciousness. Years of striving together for the success of the other, for the enhancement of the unit, must be eliminated from the mind.

No one ever emerges from a divorce unscathed—he or she is inevitably per- 42 manently harmed.

That the divorced end up even more unhappy is not their fault. They're told by 43 innumerable subtle and direct messages that they ought to be "mad as hell and unwilling to take it anymore," to paraphrase the inciteful slogan of the movie *Network*. They're encouraged by magazines sold at checkout stands to dissect their relationships. They're led by business-seeking shrinks to believe they can't possibly be fulfilled unless they're undergoing turmoil and instigating change.

I've read more than fifty books off my local public library shelves that com- 44 fort and cheer on those involved in divorce. These volumes take you step-by-step through the court procedure and tell you what stages of distress your "normal" child will endure. These books ease you like silk into the singles game and tout your "new freedom" as if it, rather than marriage, is the ultimate means toward fulfillment.

I write this book as a counterbalance, to shake a few shoulders, with hopes 45 that I might spare some children helplessness and some partners pain. I want to expose the forces that strive to hide the damage of divorce. Too many people think "If only I could be out of this marriage . . . " and conclude that sentence with their own private miracles. To repeat: It's not their fault; they're victims of propaganda. But the lure lets them down, for after they buy it they inevitably remain the same people, with the same problem-solving skills, values, and styles of relating to another. And so they can't help but choose and shape new relationships into duplications of their spoiled romance. How can they be expected to see that divorce is, with very few exceptions, the wrong way to improve their lives?

And so this book is for everyone who is now focusing on some infuriating 46 characteristic of their mate and thinking, "I can't take this much longer." It is for those who have already packed and moved out, either physically or emotionally, who look ahead and therefore can't see that their brightest path lies behind them. It is for those who have been hurt, whose wounds are so painful that they simply want to run away, and for others who see signs and want to prevent a breakup before the repairs become too overwhelming.

Perhaps you or someone you know has uttered something similar to one or 47 more of these lines:

> "Our fights are getting so fierce, the good times don't seem worth the arguments anymore."
>
> "Sure I love him. But I know I could do better."
>
> "I've found the love of my life—I have to get out of my marriage because I just can't end this affair and give up such a good thing."
>
> "I've been smothered in this marriage too long—I need to go off on my own and prove myself."
>
> "I don't respect or admire her anymore."
>
> "He's been bugging me for a long time. I've just stuck it out for the sake of the children."

When any of these statements are used long after the fact—years beyond a 48 final decree—there's nothing to be done. But in many other cases, it may not be too late. I've found that none of these sentiments automatically signals an irreparable tear in the basic fiber of a marriage. If you hear someone for whom you have any feeling at all hinting at separation, instead of tacitly endorsing the move, instantly protest. Nearly every marriage has something worth preserving, something that can be restored. Revitalizing a relationship brings triumph and ongoing reward; and as you'll see, avoiding divorce spares those concerned from the greatest trauma of their lives.

The Case Against Divorce

Of course, nobody *wants* to get divorced. Or does he? Joseph Epstein, in 49 *Divorced in America,* recognizes the respectability of divorce: "In some circles, not to have gone through a divorce seems more exceptional than having gone through one; here living out one's days within the confines of a single marriage might even be thought to show an insufficiency of imagination, evidence that one is possibly a bit callow emotionally."

God forbid we appear emotionally callow! How dare we assume that those in 50 the same dreary marriage they claim to have treasured for years could have gotten a lot out of it! The unspoken popular wisdom declares that only by undergoing this rite of psychological passage can anyone mature. I've heard the tales of postdivorce development: people who finally find themselves; who finally learn to be self-sufficient; who finally achieve independence. It is true that after divorce women especially, and men to some extent, report emotional growth. But they won't admit that they might have blossomed even more had they gathered the gumption to stick with and heal the marriage.

Of course, it's useless to speculate about what might have been accomplished 51 in any particular relationship. But some things we *do* know—and these comprise the major arguments in the case against divorce:

1. *Divorce hurts you.* Divorce brings out selfishness, hostility, and vindictiveness. It ruins your idealism about marriage. It leaves emotional scars from which you can never be free. It costs a bunch of money—and significantly reduces your standard of living.
2. *Divorce hurts those around you.* It devastates your children for at least two years and probably for life. It hurts your family by splitting it in two; both family and friends are compelled to take sides. It forces you to be hardened against people you once loved. It rips the fabric of our society, each divorce providing another example of marriage devalued.
3. *The single life isn't what it's cracked up to be.* Ask anyone—the "swinging singles" life is full of frustration, rejection, and disappointment. The Mr. and Ms. Right you assume waits for you may be only a futile fantasy. Even a successful affair that bridges you from one marriage to another often becomes merely a second failure.
4. *Staying married is better for you.* You don't have to disrupt your life for two to seven years; instead, solving marital problems provides a sense of teamwork and stands as a concrete accomplishment that enhances problem-solving skills in the larger world. Marriage is statistically proven to be the best status for your health, divorce the worst. Marriage gives you something to show for your time on earth—children (usually) and a bond built on continuity and history.

I don't expect that everyone will agree with what I've found. It's largely a matter of values and also one of semantics. For example, I write that a family is 52 worth preserving, and therefore it is worth compromising your goals or habits to save your marriage. Others holding different values might say that no marriage is worth burying your "true self" by dashing the goals you truly desire or stifling your personal inclinations. Obviously, it's not so easy to make a marriage work. But few achievements are as major or lasting.

■ *Questions for* . . . **The Case Against Divorce** by Diane Medved

Words to Note

conceptualized	mold	suffer
extended	anguished	manipulation
emotional	heart-wrenching	crisis
dissatisfaction	desperation	fosters
befuddlement	irrefutable	scuttle
confidants	mourned	bitterness

skepticism	jaded	catastrophic
debilitating	wriggled	catalyst
coalescing	dynamo	yearns
go-getter	intuitive	rebuked
rebounded	reconciliation	saddled
these days of	throes	maternal instincts
disposable marriage	unscathed	inclinations

Language

1. In paragraph 20, Medved writes, "The grim stories of crippled couples whom I interviewed for this book got me thinking about the permanent distrust, anguish, and bitterness divorce brings." Which words stand out? Is the sentence overwritten? How can you tell if something is overwritten?
2. She begins the fifth paragraph with the phrase "to my utter befuddlement." What does *befuddlement* mean? Could she have chosen a more effective word?
3. Medved writes, "Women who cried 'career first' are now honoring their maternal instincts and realizing they may not be able to 'have it all.'" What are *maternal instincts?* Would everyone agree about what they are? Are they the same in all cultures? Have they been a constant throughout history?

Style

1. Compare Medved's lead with Footlick's. Which do you like better? Why?
2. Look at Medved's subtitles. Are they effective? Do they make her thoughts easier to follow, or are they excessive verbiage?

Development and Organization

1. In the section called "Even Winners Pay the Price," Medved includes five paragraphs about her own divorce. Is this an indulgent digression or do these paragraphs contribute to the essay's ideas?
2. Would it have been more effective to begin with "The Case Against Divorce," the final section in which she spells out her opposition to divorce? Why? Why not?
3. What do all the examples and quotations contribute to the themes, tone, and feel of the essay?

Discussion and Journal Writing

1. Consider a divorce or some divorces that you know about to appraise Medved's ideas.

2. Medved cites many instances of unhappy divorcees she talked to when researching her book, but how can we be sure her conclusions are accurate? She says she distributed informal questionnaires to a diverse but unscientific sample of 200 people who had been divorced or separated. Did she interview enough people to be able to generalize? Was the group she interviewed diverse enough so that her conclusions apply across class, ethnic, and racial lines, or did she just interview friends and patients, making her conclusions potentially valid only for the well-to-do and for professionals in Santa Barbara, California? Were her questions neutral, or were they leading? How would you find all this out? Is it possible to come to a final judgment of Medved's ideas without knowing about her research methods?
3. Why have divorce rates in America escalated since the 1950s? Have they increased at the same rate in all the world's cultures and societies? Why or why not?

ooooo

Television: The Plug-in Drug

—Marie Winn

Marie Winn was born in Hungary but educated in America, which gives her the run of the culture and the sharp eye of an outsider. Here she tackles the nemesis of social critics, educators, and family therapists: TV. In just a few deft strokes Winn characterizes the ways in which television-watching undermines the family.

A quarter of a century after the introduction of television into American society, a period that has seen the medium become so deeply ingrained in American life that in at least one state the television set has attained the rank of a legal necessity, safe from repossession in case of debt along with clothes, cooking utensils, and the like, television viewing has become an inevitable and ordinary part of daily life. Only in the early years of television did writers and commentators have sufficient perspective to separate the activity of watching television from the actual content it offers the viewer. In those early days writers frequently discussed the effects of television on family life. However, a curious myopia afflicted those early observers: almost without exception they regarded television as a favorable, beneficial, indeed, wondrous influence upon the family.

"Television is going to be a real asset in every home where there are chil- 2 dren," predicts a writer in 1949.

"Television will take over your way of living and change your children's 3 habits, but this change can be a wonderful improvement," claims another commentator.

"No survey's needed, of course, to establish that television has brought the 4 family together in one room," writes *The New York Times* television critic in 1949.

Each of the early articles about television is invariably accompanied by a 5 photograph or illustration showing a family cozily sitting together before the television set, Sis on Mom's lap, Buddy perched on the arm of Dad's chair, Dad with his arm around Mom's shoulder. Who could have guessed that twenty or so years later Mom would be watching drama in the kitchen, the kids would be looking at cartoons in their room, while Dad would be taking in the ball game in the living room?

Of course television sets were enormously expensive in those early days. The 6 idea that by 1975 more than 60 percent of American families would own two or more sets was preposterous. The splintering of the multiple-set family was something the early writers could not foresee. Nor did anyone imagine the numbers of hours children would eventually devote to television, the common use of television by parents as a child pacifier, the changes television would effect upon child-rearing methods, the increasing domination of family schedules by children's viewing requirements—in short, the *power* of the new medium to dominate family life.

After the first years, as children's consumption of the new medium increased, 7 together with parental concern about the possible effects of so much television viewing, a steady refrain helped to soothe and reassure anxious parents. "Television always enters a pattern of influences that already exist: the home, the peer group, the school, the church and culture generally," write the authors of an early and influential study of television's effects on children. In other words, if the child's home life is all right, parents need not worry about the effects of all that television watching.

But television does not merely influence the child; it deeply influences that 8 "pattern of influences" that is meant to ameliorate its effects. Home and family life has changed in important ways since the advent of television. The peer group has become television-oriented, and much of the time children spend together is occupied by television viewing. Culture generally has been transformed by television. Therefore it is improper to assign to television the subsidiary role its many apologists (too often members of the television industry) insist it plays. Television is not merely one of a number of important influences upon today's child. Through the changes it has made in family life, television emerges as *the* important influence in children's lives today.

Television's contribution to family life has been an equivocal one. For while it 9 has, indeed, kept the members of the family from dispersing, it has not served to bring them *together*. By its domination of the time families spend together, it destroys the special quality that distinguishes one family from another, a quality that depends to a great extent on what a family *does,* what special rituals, games, recurrent jokes, familiar songs, and shared activities it accumulates.

"Like the sorcerer of old," writes Urie Bronfenbrenner, "the television set 10 casts its magic spell, freezing speech and action, turning the living into silent statues so long as the enchantment lasts. The primary danger of the television screen lies not so much in the behavior it produces—although there is danger there—as in the behavior it prevents: the talks, the games, the family festivities and arguments through which much of the child's learning takes place and through which his character is formed. Turning on the television set can turn off the process that transforms children into people."

Yet parents have accepted a television-dominated family life so completely 11 that they cannot see how the medium is involved in whatever problems they might be having. A first-grade teacher reports:

"I have one child in the group who's an only child. I wanted to find out more 12 about her family life because this little girl was quite isolated from the group, didn't make friends, so I talked to her mother. Well, they don't have time to do anything in the evening, the mother said. The parents come home after picking up the child at the baby-sitter's. Then the mother fixes dinner while the child watches TV. Then they have dinner and the child goes to bed. I said to this mother, 'Well, couldn't she help you fix dinner? That would be a nice time for the two of you to talk,' and the mother said, 'Oh, but I'd hate to have her miss "Zoom." It's such a good program!'"

Even when families make efforts to control television, too often its very pres- 13 ence counterbalances the positive features of family life. A writer and mother of two boys aged 3 and 7 described her family's television schedule in an article for *The New York Times:*

> We were in the midst of a full-scale War. Every day was a new battle and every program was a major skirmish. We agreed it was a bad scene all around and were ready to enter diplomatic negotiations. . . . In principle we have agreed on 2 ¹/₂ hours of TV a day, "Sesame Street," "Electric Company" (with dinner gobbled up in between) and two half-hour shows between 7 and 8:30 which enables the grown-ups to eat in peace and prevents the two boys from destroying one another. Their pre-bedtime choice is dreadful, because, as Josh recently admitted, "There's nothing much on I really like." So . . . it's "What's My Line" or "To Tell the Truth . . . Clearly there is a need for first-rate children's shows at this time. . . .

Consider the "family life" described here: Presumably the father comes home 14 from work during the "Sesame Street"–"Electric Company" stint. The children are either watching television, gobbling their dinner, or both. While the parents eat their dinner in peaceful privacy, the children watch another hour of television. Then there is only a half-hour left before bedtime, just enough time for baths, getting pajamas on, brushing teeth, and so on. The children's evening is regimented with an almost military precision. They watch their favorite programs, and when there is "nothing much on I really like," they watch whatever else is on—because *watching* is the important thing. Their mother does not see anything amiss with watching programs just for the sake of watching; she only wishes there were some first-rate children's shows on at those times.

Without conjuring up memories of the Victorian era with family games and 15 long, leisurely meals, and large families, the question arises: isn't there a better family life available than this dismal, mechanized arrangement of children watching television for however long is allowed them, evening after evening?

Of course, families today still do *special* things together at times: go camping 16 in the summer, go to the zoo on a nice Saturday, take various trips and expeditions. But their *ordinary* daily life together is diminished—that sitting around the dinner table, that spontaneous taking up of an activity, those little games invented by children on the spur of the moment when there is nothing else to do, the scribbling, the chatting, and even the quarreling, all the things that form the fabric of a family, that define a childhood. Instead, the children have their regular schedule of television programs and bedtime, and the parents have their peaceful dinner together.

The author of the article in the *Times* notes that "keeping a family sane means 17 mediating between the needs of both children and adults." But surely the needs of adults are being better met than the needs of the children, who are effectively shunted away and rendered untroublesome, while their parents enjoy a life as undemanding as that of any childless couple. In reality, it is those very demands that young children make upon a family that lead to growth, and it is the way parents accede to those demands that builds the relationships upon which the future of the family depends. If the family does not accumulate its backlog of shared experiences, shared everyday experiences that occur and recur and change and develop, then it is not likely to survive as anything other than a caretaking institution.

Family Rituals

Ritual is defined by sociologists as "that part of family life that the family 18 likes about itself, is proud of and wants formally to continue." Another text notes that "the development of a ritual by a family is an index of the common interest of its members in the family as a group."

What has happened to family rituals, those regular, dependable, recurrent hap- 19 penings that gave members of a family a feeling of *belonging* to a home rather than living in it merely for the sake of convenience, those experiences that act as the adhesive of family unity far more than any material advantages?

Mealtime rituals, going-to-bed rituals, illness rituals, holiday rituals, how 20 many of these have survived the inroads of the television set?

A young woman who grew up near Chicago reminisces about her childhood 21 and gives an idea of the effects of television upon family rituals:

"As a child I had millions of relatives around—my parents both come from 22 relatively large families. My father had nine brothers and sisters. And so every holiday there was this great swoop-down of aunts, uncles, and millions of cousins. I just remember how wonderful it used to be. These thousands of cousins would come and everyone would play and ultimately, after dinner, all the women would be in the front of the house, drinking coffee and talking, all the men would be in the back of the house, drinking and smoking, and all the kids would be all over the place, playing hide and seek. Christmas time was particularly nice because everyone always brought all their toys and games. Our house had a couple of rooms with go-through closets, so there were always kids running in a great circle route. I remember it was just wonderful.

"And then all of a sudden one year I remember becoming suddenly aware of   23 how different everything had become. The kids were no longer playing Monopoly or Clue or the other games we used to play together. It was because we had a television set which had been turned on for a football game. All of that socializing that had gone on previously had ended. Now everyone was sitting in front of the television set, on a holiday, at a family party! I remember being stunned by how awful that was. Somehow the television had become more attractive."

As families have come to spend more and more of their time together engaged   24 in the single activity of television watching, those rituals and pastimes that once gave family life its special quality have become more and more uncommon. Not since prehistoric times when cave families hunted, gathered, ate, and slept, with little time remaining to accumulate a culture of any significance, have families been reduced to such a sameness.

Real People

It is not only the activities that a family might engage in together that are   25 diminished by the powerful presence of television in the home. The relationships of the family members to each other are also affected, in both obvious and subtle ways. The hours that the young child spends in a one-way relationship with television people, an involvement that allows for no communication or interaction, surely affect his relationships with real-life people.

Studies show the importance of eye-to-eye contact, for instance, in real-life   26 relationships, and indicate that the nature of a person's eye-contact patterns, whether he looks another squarely in the eye or looks to the side or shifts his gaze from side to side, may play a significant role in his success or failure in human relationships. But no eye contact is possible in the child-television relationship, although in certain children's programs people purport to speak directly to the child and the camera fosters this illusion by focusing directly upon the person being filmed. (Mr. Rogers is an example, telling the child "I like you, you're special," etc.) How might such a distortion of real-life relationships affect a child's development of trust, of openness, of an ability to relate well to other *real* people?

Bruno Bettelheim writes: 27

Children who have been taught, or conditioned to listen passively most of the day to the warm verbal communications coming from the TV screen, to the deep emotional appeal of the so-called TV personality, are often unable to respond to real persons because they arouse so much less feeling than the skilled actor.

Worse, they lose the ability to learn from reality because life experiences are much more complicated than the ones they see on the screen. . . .

A teacher makes a similar observation about her personal viewing experi- 28
ences:

"I have trouble mobilizing myself and dealing with real people after watching 29
a few hours of television. It's just hard to make that transition from watching television to a real relationship. I suppose it's because there was no effort necessary
while I was watching, and dealing with real people always requires a bit of effort.
Imagine, then, how much harder it might be to do the same thing for a small child,
particularly one who watches a lot of television every day."

But more obviously damaging to family relationships is the elimination of 30
opportunities to talk, and perhaps more important, to argue, to air grievances,
between parents and children and brothers and sisters. Families frequently use television to avoid confronting their problems, problems that will not go away if they
are ignored but will only fester and become less easily resolvable as time goes on.

A mother reports: 31

"I find myself, with three children, wanting to turn on the TV set when they're 32
fighting. I really have to struggle not to do it because I feel that's telling them this
is the solution to the quarrel—but it's so tempting that I often do it."

A family therapist discusses the use of television as an avoidance mechanism: 33

"In a family I know the father comes home from work and turns on the televi- 34
sion set. The children come and watch with him and the wife serves them their
meal in front of the set. He then goes and takes a shower, or works on the car or
something. She then goes and has her own dinner in front of the television set. It's
a symptom of a deeper-rooted problem, sure. But it would help them all to get rid
of the set. It would be far easier to work on what the symptom really means without
the television. The television simply encourages a double avoidance of each other.
They'd find out more quickly what was going on if they weren't able to hide
behind the TV. Things wouldn't necessarily be better, of course, but they wouldn't
be anesthetized."

The decreased opportunities for simple conversation between parents and chil- 35
dren in the television-centered home may help explain an observation made by an
emergency room nurse at a Boston hospital. She reports that parents just seem to sit
there these days when they come in with a sick or seriously injured child, although
talking to the child would distract and comfort him. "They don't seem to know *how*
to talk to their own children at any length," the nurse observes. Similarly, a television critic writes in *The New York Times:* "I had just a day ago taken my son to the
emergency ward of a hospital for stitches above his left eye, and the occasion
seemed no more real to me than Maalot or 54th Street, south-central Los Angeles.
There was distance and numbness and an inability to turn off the total institution. I
didn't behave at all; I just watched. . . . "

A number of research studies substantiate the assumption that television inter- 36
feres with family activities and the formation of family relationships. One survey
shows that 78 percent of the respondents indicated no conversation taking place

during viewing except at specified times such as commercials. The study notes: "The television atmosphere in most households is one of quiet absorption on the part of family members who are present. The nature of the family social life during a program could be described as 'parallel' rather than interactive, and the set does seem to dominate family life when it is on." Thirty-six percent of the respondents in another study indicated that television viewing was the only family activity participated in during the week.

In a summary of research findings on television's effect on family interactions 37 James Gabardino states: "The early findings suggest that television had a disruptive effect upon interaction and thus presumably human development. . . . It is not unreasonable to ask: 'Is the fact that the average American family during the 1950s came to include two parents, two children and a television set somehow related to the psychosocial characteristics of the young adults of the 1970s?'"

Undermining the Family

In its effect on family relationships, in its facilitation of parental withdrawal 38 from an active roles in the socialization of their children, and in its replacement of family rituals and special events, television has played an important role in the disintegration of the American family. But of course it has not been the only contributing factor, perhaps not even the most important one. The steadily rising divorce rate, the increase in the number of working mothers, the decline of the extended family, the breakdown of neighborhoods and communities, the growing isolation of the nuclear family—all have seriously affected the family.

As Urie Bronfenbrenner suggests, the sources of family breakdown do not 39 come from the family itself, but from the circumstances in which the family finds itself and the way of life imposed upon it by those circumstances. "When those circumstances and the way of life they generate undermine relationships of trust and emotional security between family members, when they make it difficult for parents to care for, educate and enjoy their children, when there is no support or recognition from the outside world for one's role as a parent and when time spent with one's family means frustration of career, personal fulfillment and peace of mind, then the development of the child is adversely affected," he writes.

But while the roots of alienation go deep into the fabric of American social 40 history, television's presence in the home fertilizes them, encourages their wild and unchecked growth. Perhaps it is true that America's commitment to the television experience masks a spiritual vacuum, an empty and barren way of life, a desert of materialism. But it is television's dominant role in the family that anesthetizes the family into accepting its unhappy state and prevents it from struggling to better its condition, to improve its relationships, and to regain some of the richness it once possessed.

Others have noted the role of mass media in perpetuating an unsatisfactory 41 *status quo*. Leisure-time activity, writes Irving Howe, "must provide relief from work monotony without making the return to work too unbearable; it must provide amusement without insight and pleasure without disturbance—as distinct from art which gives pleasure through disturbance. Mass culture is thus oriented towards a central aspect of industrial society: the depersonalization of the individual." Similarly, Jacques Ellul rejects the idea that television is a legitimate means of educating the citizen: "Education . . . takes place only incidentally. The clouding of his consciousness is paramount. . . ."

And so the American family muddles on, dimly aware that something is amiss 42 but distracted from an understanding of its plight by an endless stream of television images. As family ties grow weaker and vaguer, as children's lives become more separate from their parents', as parents' educational role in their children's lives is taken over by television and schools, family life becomes increasingly more unsatisfying for both parents and children. All that seems to be left is Love, an abstraction that family members *know* is necessary but find great difficulty giving each other because the traditional opportunities for expressing love within the family have been reduced or destroyed.

For contemporary parents, love toward each other has increasingly come to 43 mean successful sexual relations, as witnessed by the proliferation of sex manuals and sex therapists. The opportunities for manifesting other forms of love through mutual support, understanding, nurturing, even, to use an unpopular word, *serving* each other, are less and less available as mothers and fathers seek their independent destinies outside the family.

As for love of children, this love is increasingly expressed through supplying 44 material comforts, amusements, and educational opportunities. Parents show their love for their children by sending them to good schools and camps, by providing them with good food and good doctors, by buying them toys, books, games, and a television set of their very own. Parents will even go further and express their love by attending PTA meetings to improve their children's schools, or by joining groups that are acting to improve the quality of their children's television programs.

But this is love at a remove, and is rarely understood by children. The more 45 direct forms of parental love require time and patience, steady, dependable, ungrudgingly given time actually spent *with* a child, reading to him, comforting him, playing, joking, and working with him. But even if a parent were eager and willing to demonstrate that sort of direct love to his children today, the opportunities are diminished. What with school and Little League and piano lessons and, of course, the inevitable television programs, a day seems to offer just enough time for a good-night kiss.

■ *Questions for* . . . **Television: The Plug-in Drug** by Marie Winn

Words to Note

ingrained	rank	myopia
afflicted	wondrous	asset
predicts	preposterous	subsidiary
ameliorate	equivocal	stint

regimented	precision	dismal
mechanized	diminished	spur of the moment
arrangement	the fabric of a family	shunted
avoidance mechanism	psychosocial	anesthetizes
depersonalization of	the clouding of his	muddles
the individual	consciousness	

Language

1. How does Winn use *ritual?*
2. Is the distinction made in paragraph 36 between parallel and interactive family social life clear?
3. What is a *television-centered home?* Is it a good phrase?

Style

1. Why does Winn repeat *ritual* so many times in paragraph 20? Why is the paragraph just one sentence long?
2. In every paragraph, there is an *of course,* a *but,* a *however,* or a *therefore.* Does she use too many transitional words and phrases?

Development and Organization

1. What does the subtitle "Real People" mean? Could Winn have come up with a better subtitle?
2. She quotes Bruno Bettleheim in paragraph 27. Who is he? Was it an oversight on Winn's part not to tell the reader who he is? Did she assume all her readers would recognize his name? Do his words have more force once a reader finds out who he is?
3. The first sentence of paragraph 38 is a transitional sentence that contains the essay's key points. Should she have saved it for the last paragraph? Is it repetitious?
4. How does she organize her assessment of television's impact? Are her categories helpful? Are they meaningful?
5. Should she have included more quotations, examples, and case studies? More experts? Should she have given more time to authorities who believe television has not had such a negative influence, if only to poke holes in their arguments? What is the value of taking time to refute the opposition?

Discussion and Journal Writing

1. Compile a record of your family's TV-watching. Who watches what, when, and with whom? How many sets are in the house or apartment? Is there any conversation while the TV is on? Does your family watch TV during

meals? Do Winn's conclusions apply to your family? Are there other conclusions you would draw about the impact of TV on your family?

2. Winn writes, "Television is not merely one of a number of important influences upon today's child. Through the changes it has made in family life, television emerges as *the* important influence in children's lives today." Is she overestimating the influence of television? Explain yourself. What other forces, factors, and developments rival television as important influences on children's lives? Look at paragraph 38. Are the important influences the same for all classes of our society?

3. Winn wrote about television before the advent of VCRs and cable. Have VCRs and cable changed or will they change how American families watch television?

4. Analyze the role television plays in your family. Is it all positive? All negative?

ooooo

Collapse of Inner-City Families Creates America's New Orphans

—Jane Gross

Jane Gross is a reporter for the *New York Times,* whose beat is national social trends. Here, she chronicles the hardships of the zero-parent family, the consequence of over a decade of drugs, violence, and disease in America's cities.

OAKLAND, Calif., March 28—Marianne Nolte avoids saying "mom" or "dad"   1
in her ninth-grade math class, referring instead to "family" in deference to the many shamefaced children who have been abandoned to other relatives, foster homes or institutions.

Slyvia Parker knows she will dial multiple wrong numbers when she tries to   2
call a student's home, spending hours if not days retracing the zigzag path these children travel from parent to grandparent to foster home and sometimes back again.

And Carolyn Ayana has written a song called "Gimme Back My Mama" for   3
her seventh-grade music class, hoping it will open discussion among students who avert their eyes and whisper that everything is fine at home long after their parents are lost to crack or locked in jail, and they are living with grandma, auntie or a stranger.

These teachers and their students are struggling with a profound social prob- 4
lem, the disintegration of the inner city family, which has taken a terrible toll at
Frick Junior High School here. The principal and a school social worker estimate
that more than half the 750 youngsters at Frick live with neither a mother nor a
father.

Frick is rare among schools in trying to count how many of its children are 5
without either parent. But experts say high concentrations of these children,
America's new orphans, are common in schools in the inner city, where father have
long been absent and mothers have more recently disappeared into the nether world
of crack.

In Every City

"You could use expressions like, 'It's mushrooming' or 'growing exponential- 6
ly,' but these words aren't strong enough," said Lois G. Forer, a retired judge in
Philadelphia and the author of a provocative 1988 article in The Washington
Monthly calling for the return of orphanages to help with the problem. "It's everywhere—New York, Los Angeles, Chicago, Detroit, you name it."

The phenomenon of children with no parents is prompting educators to 7
rethink how to run schools that were meant to serve nuclear families. Even more
tellingly, it is creating growing support for the idea of bringing back the orphanages
of the 19th and early 20th centuries.

"This is still a high voltage subject," said Senator Daniel Patrick Moynihan, 8
the New York Democrat, who in 1989 wrote a paper forecasting the explosion of
zero-parent families. "You get an awful shock if you go near it, so people avoid it.
But custodial institutions are clearly on their way."

Senator Moynihan added that crack is creating not only orphans but a need for 9
orphanages, in the same way that epidemics of diphtheria, influenza and tuberculo-
sis did.

There is some dispute about how best to count these children, who over- 10
whelmingly live in neighborhoods where drugs, AIDS and guns are rampant and
the zero-parent family is replacing the single-parent family as the emblem of social
distress. Their situations vary, but in all categories the numbers of these new
orphans are increasing.

Some are true zero-parent children, living permanently with relatives, in foster 11
homes or institutions because their parents are dead, incarcerated or have disappeared. Many more are youngsters who are shuttled from pillar to post, farmed out
to a shifting cast of relatives while a drug-abusing or vagabond parent is unable or
unwilling to care for them.

According to the Federal Bureau of the Census, 2.8 million children, or 4.5 12
percent of America's 63.8 million children were true zero-parent children in 1980,
up from 3.5 percent 10 years before. And the numbers are far worse among black
children: In 1980, 10.6 percent of them lived in parentless households, up from 9.4
percent in 1970. The 1990 census data on these children is not yet available.

Measuring the Problem

But some demographers are looking for a more inclusive description for the 13
messy way that families fall apart, a better statistical measure for this new social
problem.

According to the Kids Count Data Book, an annual profile of American chil- 14
dren by the Annie E. Casey Foundation and the Center for the Study of Social
Policy, nearly 1 of every 10 American children lived in household headed by someone other than a parent in 1990, up from 6.7 percent in 1970.

A mother is sometimes present in these homes, but she is often a drug addict 15
or a teen-ager who comes and goes while someone else cares for her children. At a
recent conference at the American Enterprise Institute these households were
described as "family radicals," using the scientific jargon for unbalanced atoms.

At Frick Junior High and similar schools in inner-city neighborhoods, the sta- 16
tistics are even more extreme. At least two-thirds of the school's 750 pupils are
new orphans.

Forty percent live in county foster homes. At least half that many are living 17
with grandmothers or aunts. Many more live with a drug-abusing mother one week
and a weary relative the next. The principal, Murphy Taylor, said virtually all these
children are black. The Hispanic families, he said, almost always remain intact.

Mr. Taylor, a first-year principal who is black and a longtime foster parent, 18
decided to learn where his students were living after he found that many of them
were routinely out of control: fighting with classmates and shoving or cursing
teachers. This behavior, he knew, matched what child development experts see in
abandoned youngsters.

Scarred by years of abuse and neglect, many of these children are angry and 19
disruptive, even after they settle in loving foster homes or with doting grandmothers. They are distrustful of adults, greedy for attention and convinced that they
must be worthless or their parents would not have left them. They are unresponsive
to threats that their misbehavior will land them in trouble, because things already
seem as bad as they can get.

"People look at these kids and think they're crazy," said Nanette Sanders, the 20
mother of a ninth grader and president of the Parent Teachers Association at Frick,
where an average meeting draws a half-dozen parents. "Well, society hasn't dealt
them a fair hand. The person who's supposed to have taken care of them didn't. So
they develop an attitude. They get hard."

The teachers at Frick are scornful of foster homes and say that most of them 21
are economic arrangements that do not nurture children. The children with relatives
are loved, the teachers say, but often poorly supervised because the grandmothers
and aunts are exhausted, afraid to come out at night to attend school events and
unwilling to hear bad news about the youngsters. The children who move from
house to house have no stability and bear the wounds of repeated rejection.

The new orphans, particularly those in foster homes, are ashamed and secre- 22
tive, never volunteering information about who they live with, refusing rides home
and not inviting friends to visit.

"They have a keen awareness of what a family should be like," said Cheryl 23

Vawter, a history teacher. "And they desperately want that."

Teachers usually have no idea who students live with because the children do   24
not tell, different last names are the norm, and such information is not routinely
available or changes so often that school records cannot be kept up to date.

Ms. Ayana, the music teacher, said she learned that one of her favorite stu-   25
dents was living in a foster home only after the girl arrived at school with black-
and-blue marks suffered from a beating. The police were then summoned. Mrs.
Vawter said she had a similar surprise after a student disappeared from the school.
The girl, despite frequent references to her mother and father, had been living in a
group foster home and had run away.

Disciplining these children is tricky. Miss Ayana showed why by citing a typi-   26
cal exchange.

TEACHER: "All right, Charles, I'm going to call your mother."
STUDENT: "Go on ahead. I don't have no mother no way."

When the children are moving from relative to relative, or their telephone has   27
been disconnected, they act up with impunity. "They know you can't get in touch,"
said Bob Kenney, a social studies teacher.

The 'Concentration Effect'

Schools like Frick have disproportionate numbers of orphans, just as certain   28
neighborhoods wind up overwhelmed by the most disadvantaged people after the
others flee. And the results are much the same, said William Julius Wilson, a professor of sociology at the University of Chicago, who coined the phrase "concentration effect" to describe the corrosion of a community when only the most impoverished people remain.

At Frick, many of the more organized families have fled the chaos by   29
enrolling their children in magnet or parochial schools. "This further isolates and
stigmatizes these youngsters," said Toni Cook, a member of the Oakland Board of
Education. "They don't get to mix and mingle with other youngsters for whom the
ball has bounced right. They don't get to see how the grass can be greener."

Mr. Taylor, the principal at Frick, is trying to lure the stable families back. He   30
took the 20 most disruptive children from all three grades and moved them to a
satellite classroom in a nearby church. The children seem to be doing better with
one teacher responsible for them all day. And the main school building is a less
threatening place with these disruptive students gone.

Mr. Taylor has also encouraged more appealing activities for families, includ-   31
ing weekly math nights in the computer laboratory so that the adults can learn
along with the children. He also hopes to open the gymnasium on nights and weekends so that children from other schools will play alongside Frick's youngsters.

Across the country, inner-city schools are tentatively making changes because   32
of the proliferation of new orphans.

In some districts health services have relocated to school buildings so that   33
needy children will not have to depend on absent or inattentive parents to take them

to a clinic. In many junior high schools, including Frick, students are moving from subject to subject in intact classes to create a sense of family.

In New York City, the Parents Association handbook is being revised to   34 explain that the term "parent" includes "guardians and persons in parental relationships to children." And in the District of Columbia, the school board is considering residential schools.

"These kids can't fit into the boxes we've created," Mr. Taylor said. "And it's   35 not their fault. Very dysfunctional children need something significantly different, and it's up to us to figure out what that is."

■ *Questions for . . .* **Collapse of Inner-City Families Creates America's New Orphans** by Jane Gross

Words to Note

deference	shamefaced	retracing
zigzag	avert	the nether world of crack
emblem of	zero-parent families	vagabond parent
social distress		dysfunctional

Language

1. What are the *wounds of repeated rejection?*
2. What other words or terms could be used to describe what Senator Daniel Patrick Moynihan and others are calling *zero-parent families?* Do you like the term? What are its connotations?
3. How and why is the word *parent* being redefined in the Parents Association handbook in New York City?

Style

1. What is Gross's tone? How do you know?

Development and Organization

1. Why didn't Gross begin with paragraph 4?
2. Categorize the different kinds of evidence and testimony Gross uses to explain, illustrate, and back up her ideas.
3. Read the last paragraph. Why did she choose to conclude with the principal's words?

Discussion and Journal Writing

1. You're a city council member representing an inner-city district like the one in Oakland, California that contains Frick Junior High School. What can you do to help these kids?
2. Compare this article with Marie Winn's piece on television. Do they complement or contradict one another?
3. Can or should the schools do anything to make up for the pain and chaos of the home lives of zero-parent students?
4. Write a letter to the editor of the *New York Times* calling for funds to support special programs for these students. What sorts of programs do they need? Why should the public fund them?

ooooo

LaJoe Anderson of the Governor Henry Horner Homes, Chicago, Illinois

—Alex Kotlowitz

Alex Kotlowitz lives in Chicago and writes for the *Wall Street Journal* about urban affairs and social issues. The following selection is an excerpt from *There Are No Children Here,* a book that grew out of articles he wrote about raising children in Chicago's Horner Projects. The articles won him the Robert F. Kennedy Journalism Award.

A shy, soft-spoken woman, LaJoe was known for her warmth and generosity, not only to her own children but to her children's friends. Though she received Aid to Families with Dependent Children, neighbors frequently knocked on her door to borrow a can of soup or a cup of flour. She always obliged. LaJoe had often mothered children who needed advice or comforting. Many young men and women still called her "Mom." She let so many people through her apartment, sometimes just to use the bathroom, that she hid the toilet paper in the kitchen because it had often been stolen. 1

But the neighborhood, which hungrily devoured its children, had taken its toll 2 of LaJoe as well. In recent years, she had become more tired as she questioned her ability to raise her children here. She no longer fixed her kids' breakfasts every day—and there were times when the children had to wash their own clothes in the bathtub. Many of the adults had aged with the neighborhood, looking as worn and empty as the abandoned stores that lined the once-thriving Madison Street. By their mid-thirties, many women had become grandmothers; by their mid-forties, great-grandmothers. They nurtured and cared for their boyfriends and former boyfriends and sons and grandsons and great-grandsons.

LaJoe, in her youth, had been stunning, her smooth, light brown complexion   3
highlighted by an open smile. When she pulled her hair back in a ponytail, she appeared almost Asian, her almond-shaped eyes gazing out from a heart-shaped face. She had been so pretty in her mid-twenties that she briefly tried a modeling career. Now she was thirty-five, and men still whistled and smiled at her on the street. Unlike many other women her age, she hadn't put on much weight, and her high-cheekboned face still had a sculptured look. But the confidence of her youth had left her. Her shoulders were often hunched. She occasionally awoke with dark circles under her eyes. And her smile was less frequent now.

LaJoe had watched and held on as the neighborhood slowly decayed, as had   4
many urban communities like Horner over the past two decades. First, the middle-class whites fled to the suburbs. Then the middle-class blacks left for safer neighborhoods. Then businesses moved, some to the suburbs, others to the South. Over the past ten years, the city had lost a third of its manufacturing jobs, and there were few jobs left for those who lived in Henry Horner. Unemployment was officially estimated at 19 percent; unofficially, it was probably much higher. There were neighborhoods in Chicago worse off than Horner, but the demise of this particular community was often noted because it had once been among the city's wealthiest areas.

Though only four years old at the time, LaJoe forever remembered the day she   5
and her family moved into the Henry Horner Homes. It was October 15, 1956, a Monday.

The complex was so new that some of the buildings had yet to be completed.   6
Thick paths of mud ran where the sidewalks should have been. A thin, warped plank of wood substituted for the unbuilt steps.

But to LaJoe and her brothers and sisters, it all looked dazzling. The build-   7
ing's brand-new bricks were a deep and luscious red, and they were smooth and solid to the touch. The clean windows reflected the day's movements with a shimmering clarity that gave the building an almost magical quality. Even the two unfinished buildings, one to the west and one to the south, their concrete frames still exposed, appeared stately.

It was quiet and peaceful; there were not even any passersby. On this unusual-   8
ly warm fall day—the temperature topped 70 degrees by noon—LaJoe could even hear the shrill songs of the sparrows. The building, 1920 West Washington, stood empty. They were to be the first family to occupy one of its sixty-five apartments.

LaJoe's father, Roy Anderson, pulled the car and its trailer up to the build-   9
ing's back entrance. He was a ruggedly handsome man whose steely stare belied his affable nature and his affection for children. He and his wife, Lelia Mae, had been eagerly awaiting this move. They and their thirteen children, including three sets of twins, had been living in a spacious five-bedroom apartment, but the coal-heated flat got so cold in the winter that the pipes frequently froze. On those days

they fetched their water from a fire hydrant. The apartment was above a Baptist church, and there were times when the rooms overflowed with the wailings of funerals or the joyful songs accompanying baptisms. And the building canted to the east, so whenever a truck passed, the floors and walls shook vigorously, sometimes scaring the children into thinking the entire structure might collapse.

For Lelia Mae and Roy their south side apartment seemed adequate enough. 10 Both had come from the shacks and the shanties of the South. Lelia Mae had left Charleston, West Virginia, at the age of twenty in 1937. Her father had been a coal miner and a part-time preacher for the Ebenezer Baptist Church. She headed for Chicago, where she'd been told she could make good money. Her older sister, who had moved to Chicago a few years earlier, promised Lelia Mae to get her a job in the laundry where she worked. Once in Chicago, Lelia Mae, already divorced and with one child, met her second husband, Roy, who worked in one of the city's numerous steel mills. Roy hailed from Camden, Arkansas, where his father had been the deacon of a Baptist church. Roy was a spiffy dresser whose trademark was a small Stetson; it balanced with astounding ease on his large, dignified head.

The two had raised their family in the second-floor Chicago apartment above 11 the church, but their home was to be demolished to make way for a university building, part of the new Illinois Institute of Technology, and they had to move. They were given the opportunity to move into public housing, the grand castles being built for the nation's urban poor.

In the middle and late 1950s, publicly financed high-rise complexes sprang up 12 across the country like dandelions in a rainy spring. In 1949, Congress, in addressing a postwar housing crisis, had authorized loans and subsidies to construct 810,000 units of low-rent housing units nationwide. At the time, it was viewed as an impressive effort to provide shelter for the less fortunate.

But the program's controversial beginnings were an ominous sign of what lay 13 ahead. White politicians wanted neither poor nor black families in their communities, and they resisted the publically financed housing. In over seventy communities, public housing opponents brought the issue before the electorate in referenda. In California, voters amended the state constitution so that all public housing projects required their approval. In Detroit, a 14,350-unit public housing program was reduced when a public housing opponent was elected mayor. In Chicago, the opposition was fierce. The city's aldermen first bullied the state legislature into giving them the power of selecting public housing sites, a prerogative that had previously belonged to the local housing authority.

Then a group of leading aldermen, who were not above petty vindictiveness, 14 chartered a bus to tour the city in search of potential sites. On the bus ride, they told reporters that they were out to seek vengeance against the Chicago Housing Authority and the seven aldermen who supported public housing, and they chose sites in neighborhoods represented by these aldermen. Like prankish teenagers, they selected the most outrageous of possibilities, including the tennis courts at the University of Chicago and a parcel of land that sat smack in the middle of a major local highway. The message was clear: the CHA and its liberal backers could build public housing but not in their back yards.

The complexes were not, in the end, built at these sites. Instead, they were 15 constructed on the edges of the city's black ghettoes. Rather than providing alternatives to what had become decrepit living conditions, public housing became anchors for existing slums. And because there were few sites available, the housing authority had no alternative but to build up rather than out. So the ghettoes grew toward the heavens, and public housing became a bulwark of urban segregation.

On the city's near west side, on the periphery of one of the city's black ghettoes, was built the Henry Horner Homes. The complex of sixteen high-rises bore 16 the name of an Illinois governor best known for his obsession with Abraham Lincoln and his penchant for bucking the Chicago Democratic machine.

The buildings were constructed on the cheap. There were no lobbies to speak 17 of, only the open breezeways. There was no communication system from the breezeways to the tenants. During the city's harsh winters, elevator cables froze; in one year alone the housing authority of Chicago needed to make over fifteen-hundred elevator repairs. And that was in just one development.

The trash chutes within each building were too narrow to handle the garbage 18 of all its tenants. The boiler systems continually broke down. There were insufficient overhead lighting installations and wall outlets in each unit. And the medicine cabinet in each apartment's bathroom was not only easily removed, but connected to the medicine chest in the adjoining apartment. Over the years, residents had been robbed, assaulted, and even murdered by people crawling through their medicine cabinet.

When a group of Soviet housing officials visited Henry Horner in October of 19 1955, while it was still under construction, they were appalled that the walls in the apartments were of cinder block. Why not build plastered walls, they suggested. "We would be thrown off our jobs in Moscow if we left unfinished walls like this," I. K. Kozvilia, minister of city and urban construction in the Soviet Union, told local reporters.

"In the American way of doing things," huffed *The Chicago Daily News* in an 20 editorial the next day, "there is little use for luxury in building subsidized low-cost housing." It was no surprise, then, that thirteen years later a federal report on public housing would describe Henry Horner and the city's other developments as "remindful of gigantic filing cabinets with separate cubicles for each human household."

But on this day, LaJoe and her siblings were bubbling over with joy at the 21 sight of their new home. It was, after all, considerably prettier and sturdier and warmer than the flat they'd left behind. Before their father could unload the rented trailer and hand his children the picnic table, which he planned to use in the kitchen, and the cots, which he hoped to replace soon with bunk beds, they ran into the newly finished building. He and his wife could only smile at the children's excitement.

LaJoe's older sister, LaGreta, then seven, urged the others into the apartment. 22 As LaJoe scurried through the open doorway, they counted off the five bedrooms in delighted giggles. They were struck by the apartment's immensity; the hallway seemed to go on forever, one room following another and another and another. What's more, the freshly painted walls shone a glistening white; even the brown linoleum floors had a luster to them. The youngest children found the coziness of the doorless closets inviting; LaJoe's infant twin brothers spent much of the first day playing in one. And because of the apartment's first-floor location, the older children quickly learned, they could exit through the windows, a route they would use in their teens when they wanted to leave unseen by their mother.

In those early years, the children of Horner thrived. LaJoe and LaGreta joined 23 the Girl Scouts. They attended dances and roller-skating parties in their building's basement. They delighted in the new playground, which boasted swings, sliding boards, and a jungle gym. Their brothers frequented the project's grass baseball diamond, which was regularly mowed.

All of them spent time at the spanking new Boys Club, which had a gym and 24 in later years an indoor Olympic-size swimming pool. On Friday nights, the family attended fish fries. LaJoe joined the 250-member Drum and Bugle Corps, a group so popular among the area's youth that some came from two miles away to partici-pate. The marching teenagers, attired in white shirts, thin black ties, and black jack-ets, were a common sight in city parades.

The Anderson children were exposed to politics as well. Their mother was 25 active in the local Democratic Party, and politicians, from aldermen to United States senators, would visit the complex and on occasion stop by the Anderson's home. Elected officials paid attention to the people's concerns. They had to. People were well organized. In the 1960s, area residents formed the Miles Square Federation, which vigorously fought for better schools and health clinics. The Black Panthers' city headquarters was only a few blocks from Horner. Martin Luther King, Jr., on his visits to the city would preach at the First Congregational Baptist Church.

Nurtured by a strong sense of community as well as the programs at the Boys 26 Club and other social agencies, Henry Horner boasted numerous success stories: an executive at a *Fortune 500* company, a principal of one of the city's top parochial schools, the medical director of a nearby hospital, and a professor at a local univer-sity.

On that first day at Horner, the Anderson family knew only hope and pride. 27 The future seemed bright. The moment, particularly for the children, was nearly blissful. Lelia Mae made doughnuts to celebrate and played Sam Cooke and Nat King Cole albums on her hi-fi through the evening. That night, in one of the back bedrooms, the sisters lay on their narrow cots and stared out the windows. Because there was no one yet living in the building and few streetlights, they could clearly see the moon and the stars. They had their very own window on the universe.

LaJoe held on tightly to those early memories because so much had since 28 gone sour. By the 1970s, the housing authority ran out of money to paint the apart-ments. The cinder-block walls became permanently smudged and dirty. The build-ing's bricks faded. The windows had collected too heavy a coat of grime to reflect much of anything. In 1975, someone, to this day unknown, strangled one of

LaJoe's grown sisters in her bathtub. The oldest brother, home on leave from the Marines, died of a heart attack on that day on hearing the news. LaJoe's parents moved out of Horner because of the murder. Roy died of bone cancer in 1982.

LaJoe hadn't moved far since that fall day in 1956; she was just down the hall, 29 where she now lived with Lafeyette, Pharoah, her two oldest sons, Paul and Terence, and the triplets.

"When I got my apartment I thought this is what it was meant to be," she said 30 thirty-one years later. "I never looked any further than here. It wasn't like it is now. The grass was greener. We had light poles on the front of the building. We had little yellow flowers. We had it all. I really thought this was it. And I never knew, until I lost it all, that it wasn't."

■ *Questions for* . . . **LaJoe Anderson of the Governor Henry Horner Homes, Chicago, Illinois** by Alex Kotlowitz

Words to Note

devoured	toll	abandoned
nurtured	stunning	sculptured
decayed	demise	warped
plank	dazzling	luscious
shimmering	exposed	stately
shrill	wailings	fetched
collapse	spiffy	astounding
dignified	demolished	subsidies
ominous	referenda	aldermen
vindictiveness	decrepit	bulwark
breezeways	scurried	luster
blissful	smudged	

Language

1. In paragraph 11, Kotlowitz calls public housing "the grand castles being built for the nation's urban poor." Why does he call these buildings *castles?* What is the tone of the word?
2. Henry Horner and the city's other projects were referred to in a federal report on public housing as "gigantic filing cabinets with separate cubicles for each human household." Why did the writers of this report choose these precise words? Please translate.

Style

1. Study paragraphs 17 and 18. What is the pace of these paragraphs? How does Kotlowitz set it? Why doesn't he comment on the problems he enumerates in these paragraphs?
2. Look at how he uses the colon in paragraph 25. Do you think he should have phrased this one-sentence paragraph differently? Do you think he should have said more about each of the successes he mentions?

Development and Organization

1. Why does Kotlowitz describe the Anderson's apartment above the church in such detail?
2. Why does he spend so much time dramatizing the Anderson family's first day at Horner? Why does he return to it again in paragraph 26? What do the details he has included in that paragraph say?
3. Why does he include the detail about criminals breaking into Henry Horner apartments through medicine cabinets?
4. Do you think the critical remarks of the Soviet housing officials and the retort of *The Chicago Daily News* should have been omitted?

Discussion and Journal Writing

1. What does Kotlowitz's description of LaJoe's apartments tell us about her? Does he tell us too much about the politics, history, and look of LaJoe's apartments and neighborhood and not enough about LaJoe herself?
2. According to Kotlowitz, why and how was the original plan for the Governor Henry Horner Homes and similar projects flawed?
3. How did Horner affect LaJoe's family life when she was young? Now that she's an adult and mother? How does Kotlowitz explain the difference? Do you agree?

ooooo

$\mathcal{F}$amily Documents Five

Working Mothers

Responses from a Gallup Poll conducted Dec. 9, 1992, of 506 women in the Northeast 20 to 55 years old with children under 18 years old living at home. Margin of sampling error is four percentage points. The Northeast region includes Connecticut, Delaware, Maryland, Maine, New Hampshire, New Jersey, New York, Pennsylvania, Rhode Island, Vermont and Virginia.

Source: Gallup Poll

1 Do you work outside the home?

No 33%
Yes 67%

---

2 Would you say that most women who work outside the home generally seem to make better or worse mothers than women who do not work outside the home or is there no difference?

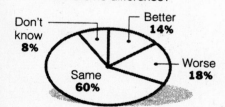

Don't know 8%
Better 14%
Worse 18%
Same 60%

3 Do you feel that conditions for working mothers would improve if more women were elected to prominent Federal government positions?

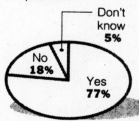

Don't know 5%
No 18%
Yes 77%

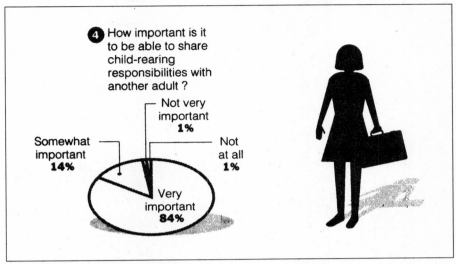

How important is it to be able to share child-rearing responsibilities with another adult ?

Not very important **1%**

Somewhat important **14%**

Not at all **1%**

Very important **84%**

Reprinted with permission from the *New York Times.*

■ *Questions for* . . . Working Mothers

Discussion and Journal Writing

1. Study the responses to questions 2, 3, and 4 in the poll. Why do you think these women responded the way they did?
2. Discuss the questions and responses. Poll one another. Are there related questions that need to be answered?
3. Why isn't this poll about working fathers too? Why did Gallup conduct this poll at this time in this way?
4　Write about the picture or point that emerges from this poll.

ooooo

─── $\mathcal{F}$amily Album Five ───

Couples Attending Divorce Class

(Alan S. Weiner for the New York Times*)*

■ *Questions for* . . . Couples Attending Divorce Class

Discussion and Journal Writing

1. This photo shows couples who are seeking a divorce attending a seminar that stresses the impact of divorce on children. Some states require divorcing couples to take divorce classes. Is that a good idea or a violation of individual rights?
2. Look at the faces of the parents. What attitudes do you read?
3. If you think divorce class should be required, what should parents be taught?

ooooo

❊ Expository Writing: Journalistic and Sociological Analysis

Fiction writers, social scientists, and journalists are all trying to get the contemporary family down on paper. They draw portraits, real or imagined; they sift through data and incidents; and they zoom in on particular aspects of family life, especially ones that are new, different, or in trouble. There's nothing particularly neutral about most of the writing the contemporary family evokes, which is no surprise. People have powerful family feelings and convictions, and words have consequences. Problems can be exposed and people can be persuaded.

There's certainly nothing neutral about any of the pieces included in this chapter. DeLillo's "At Yankee Stadium" is disturbing: Marge and Rodge Janney, the "flesh parents," sit and watch their daughter, along with thousands of other daughters and sons, join the spiritual family of the Reverend Sun Myung Moon. And the other pieces, which are nonfiction, are critical. Some of these writers, such as Sedgwick and Gross, simply point out the problems of the people they are writing about (rich kids and zero-parent kids), but the rest of them are openly argumentative. They word, phrase, develop, and organize their thoughts to criticize and persuade.

Marie Winn marshals ideas and evidence from psychologists, journalists, and the annals of TV history to prove that TV has had a powerfully negative influence on America's families. She splices anecdotal testimony into each section of the essay to back up her ideas and to give a human face to each part of her argument. The words she uses are simple and lucid; her sentences are direct and emphatic. Her style amplifies her reasons.

Some of these writers are accomplished stylists, and all of them work with complicated material and ideas. They can be intimidating if you let them. But they share a common and simple purpose: They want us to consider things as they see them. Everything else follows from that purpose, and if you keep it in mind, you will find their arguments and techniques easier to understand and absorb, which will make it easier to profit from their example as you write this chapter's essay. You will find yourself especially open to the techniques they use if you take a second look at some of the essays after you have completed a first draft. By that point, most writers have a good idea where they need help. If, for example, you are having trouble working examples or quotations into your paper (perhaps your connecting sentences feel choppy or awkward), take a second look at how Gross does it. She is a master splicer.

🎴 Writing Workshop

The Topics:
- In your opinion, what should a good family do for and provide for a child?
- Is the role of wife and mother changing in America today? Husband and father? How? Why?
- What role do grandparents play in nomadic, nursing-home America? What about grandparents in the inner cities?
- What are the causes of domestic violence?
- What can we do to curb domestic violence?
- Compare and contrast what well-off families and poor families can offer their children. You may want to create composite families for this paper.
- Is home becoming a way station, a depot?
- Write about a specific change the family is undergoing or a challenge or problem it is facing. What's causing it? What are its consequences likely to be? There's no need to choose *the* most crucial change, challenge, or problem. Choose one that you care about, one that you have something to say about.
- In your opinion, why is divorce so prevalent today?
- Compare and contrast the different ways families cope with divorce.
- It is said that families teach and socialize their children more powerfully than any other institution or force in society. What are families b teaching their children today? How?
- Is television the destructive force Winn makes it out to be?
- Study an American family income chart, which you can find in the library. How many families are poor? In America, given the high cost of living and the materialism that pervades our cultures, can a poor parent be a good parent? In whose eyes?

The Assignment: Take out your journal or some paper and write a brief response to each topic, as if it were a simple question. Try for a paragraph per topic.

Next, read the paragraphs you wrote, and choose the one you like the best. Get together with a group of your classmates who chose the same topic and read your paragraphs aloud to one another. Form a second group if there are more than four or five people interested in the same topic. Take notes, talk, and ask questions. Use one another as sounding boards and sources of opinions, experience, and ideas.

Take another look at the topic, your paragraph, and your notes, then freewrite for 20 minutes. Try to fill about three pages.

Before you study what you wrote or try to write any more, talk to some people—classmates, neighbors, friends, relatives, or people you work with. Try to choose two or three people who will tell you what they think and who don't necessarily look at the world the same way you do. Try your ideas out on them. Simply explaining your ideas should strengthen your hold on them; anything else is a bonus. Listen to their responses, argue with them, and jot down anything you think might help when it's time to write a first draft.

You might also want to read a recent article or two on your topic just to test and flesh out your thoughts by looking at someone else's. The most recent annual volume of *The Reader's Guide to Periodical Literature* should turn up more articles than you would ever want to read on every topic in this chapter. There are also computerized indexes you can consult. Then, just read. Take a few notes if you can't help yourself. The purpose isn't to do research but to think through your own thoughts.

Now it's time to write a first draft. Study the freewriting you did. Underline or circle phrases and sentences that seem promising and review your notes. Make a list of the points you think you want to pursue and try mapping them. Put the main point in the middle of the page and put the supporting points in orbit around the main one. Circle them. Jot down details and facts that flesh out or back up each supporting point next to the point they support. Your page should resemble Jupiter and its twelve moons, give or take a few moons. Study your supporting points; number them in the order in which you think you want to approach them. You may change your mind as you write, but it's a good idea to think about order throughout the writing process. Just try not to become obsessed with it.

Next, write a first draft. Remember, it's best to set aside enough time to write an entire draft. And again, don't worry about word choice, spelling, grammar, and phrasing at this point. Check words, phrases, and sentences you want to come back to, but for now, follow your train of thought.

Let the paper sit for a day before coming back to it. Read it out loud to yourself, making notes in the margins or on another piece of paper as you go, and rewrite. Compare the introduction with the conclusion. Does the introduction need to be expanded so that it covers more of what follows? Does the lead-in need work? Would the paper benefit from a reordering of the middle paragraphs? Are the transitional sentences helpful? Clear? Tight? Are any of the paragraphs unnecessary? Are there points that occur to you now that you need to include? Remember that the first draft is the writer's scaffolding; don't be afraid to make major deletions or additions. Is each point clearly explained? Do any of them need to be backed up more fully with examples, facts, and so on? Does the conclusion pull your thoughts and sentiments together? Does it give the reader something to take away? Something to think about?

Now, zoom in on phrasing, word choice, grammar, and punctuation. Do your sentences read well? If not, try rephrasing them, which means combining them, breaking them up, or reordering them. Replace words you're not happy with and check for errors. Remain diligent about your common mistakes until you get them out by the root; if you have trouble with common splices, check all of your commas. If you're not clear on the rules of punctuation, review your problem points in a handbook or talk to your instructor or a tutor. If you're thorough about checking for errors, you will find yourself, bit by bit, making fewer of them. Check spelling, too. Recall that the best way to proofread for spelling errors is to read your paper backwards. It doesn't take long with a short paper.

Exchange your draft with a classmate, read, and discuss. Take notes as you read and talk. The advantage to doing this during class time is that your instructor can answer questions and mediate differences of opinion and taste. The point is to see how your paper reads and to rewrite it with that awareness in mind.

Read it aloud to yourself and rewrite a second time. Again, don't be afraid to make major changes. If you write any new passages or paragraphs, take a close look at phrasing, sentence order, progression, and grammar. Now, polish and proofread the entire paper. Before you type or print out a final copy, make sure you are clear on requirements for margins, spacing, and title pages.

If you typed the first draft on a word processor—which is a good idea—type in your revisions, print out a copy, and proofread it carefully for typos and minor slips. If you have been working in longhand—which isn't a bad idea—type the final draft, if possible. Remember, you will probably polish your paper one last time when you type it, and a typed final draft is more satisfying to the eye—to yours and to your instructor's.

 Chapter 6

The Family and Politics

■

A Political Football

Most Americans have a hard time thinking about family and politics in the same breath because family is supposed to be a haven from the outside world of government, society, economics, and political forces. It isn't, and it never has been. Political winds rustle the curtains of every home, regardless of income, race, or region; sometimes, those winds blow the doors wide open.

When the Congress and president approve a new tax code, politics comes right in the front door. Families have more or less money to spend, depending on the specifics of the code and their income brackets. Belts are tightened; belts are loosened; real, live children and parents feel the differences. There is more or less money in the public coffers; and there is more or less housing available, more or less funding for Head Start and nutrition programs. . . .

Judges make decisions that establish new precedents in matters of divorce, custody, child abuse, and other family matters—and thousands of families, this year and in years to come, will be reformed.

Popular culture unleashes new heroes and new music: the generation gap widens, so do the breakfast and dinner tables.

When family issues and problems dominate the news or when a protest movement broadcasts its message, there will be people in homes across the country who will reassess their daily routines and their long-term goals; they will rethink themselves. And changes, some big, some small, will be made.

No family is an island, rich or poor. That's the point. Debates, struggles, and changes constantly occur in the overlapping arenas of work, culture, and social policy that directly or indirectly influence how and why families lead the lives they do.

For that matter, families are repositories of cultural and political values. There are many places and players in the socialization of an American child, but there is no place as important as the home and no individual as influential as a parent. The politics of gender are especially prominent in the home: to this day, I believe, despite the growing number of women with jobs and professional careers, in most American homes little girls are taught to be less ambitious in their aspirations and to identify with the work of the home; little boys, generally given freer reign, are encouraged to take the support a home provides for granted and to dream big. The family is a formidable institution in its own right, despite the cues and directives it receives from other sectors of our society; the lessons the family teaches and the patterns it models make an indelible print on our culture and society.

Work and the Economy.   Kenneth Keniston, writing for the Carnegie Council on Children, calls attention to the relationship between work and home in "Family Work and Wage Work," which appears later in the chapter. As he sees it, the relationship isn't a happy one because the family usually suffers when conflicting demands are placed on the parent/worker. The particular way this tension plays itself out varies from job to job and field to field, but as long as the economic interests of employers are paramount, workers who are parents will have to cope with it; we rationalize the cost, even though we pride ourselves in being family-oriented people, by saying that's the way it is.

Keniston goes on to explore alternatives to current arrangements that would not diminish productivity but would diminish the stress working parents experience. Most of the alternatives they mention, such as *flextime* (a system in which workers choose their working hours within a broad range), originated in Western Europe. There, parents generally receive more financial assistance and services, such as childcare, that make it easier to juggle the demands of home and work. In America, Phyllis Schlafly and other critics on the far Right warn that government assistance to working parents will "sovietize" the American family. Sovietization doesn't appear to be a concern in Germany, France, and Holland. Perhaps it's a distinctly American, distinctly Cold War fear.

Larger economic shifts, which are driven by political forces, can change the situation of millions of families. From the late 1970s through the present, well-paying jobs for blue-collar Americans, especially unionized jobs, have been disappearing. There have been successive lay-offs (despite, or perhaps because of the great pie-eating contest Wall Street staged all 1980s long), families have modified their plans, more wives and mothers have gone to work outside the home, and babysitters and grandparents have been deployed in caregiver legions as the daily rhythms of many homes have changed.

To cite another instance, this one from the 1940s, women were needed in the nation's defense plants to take the places of the men who had enlisted or been drafted to fight the Second World War. These women drilled, welded, and riveted—hence, the hit song "Rosie the Riveter." Rosie was treated to two distinct, politicized gospels of the family. When she was being lured into the plants, primarily by wages that were much higher than traditional "woman's work" paid, the federal government broadcast an image of the industrial, patriotic woman. In documentaries, newsreels at movie theaters, and radio announcements, Rosie was told she could be the best mom and wife by helping make planes, guns, and bombs for her husband or son overseas. Day-care centers were organized; recipes for quick suppers were popular. When the men returned from the war, Rosie was told her family needed her at home: your man needs some home cooking after four years of k-rations, you will demoralize him if you compete with him as breadwinner, and your children will become delinquents without proper supervision. Twice within four years, Rosie found herself on the receiving end of a major shift in the work force and a public relations program meant to grease the gears of that shift, which brings us to the part culture plays in the politics of the family.

The Politics of Culture.   The role models we encounter at close quarters within our families, immediate and extended, are tremendously influential in ways many of us spend most of our lives realizing. But we also encounter cultural role models in books, on stage and screen, and in temples and churches. Self-images and family roles are shored-up; sometimes, they are challenged, because culture, no matter how it is defined, is not static. Old styles of parenting are reaffirmed, new styles get loose. On talk shows and in magazines, family problems that never had a name are named, old problems are renamed and we talk, think, and sometimes reconsider.

In short, there is an ongoing, somewhat unconscious, but highly politicized struggle to define family norms—in words, in pictures, in songs. Norman Rockwell exalted the nuclear family, and it would seem that TV directors in the 1950s couldn't have agreed more. They gave us "The Donna Reed Show," "Ozzie and Harriet," "Father Knows Best," and the roster goes on and on. Of course, there were writers, like John Cheever and Flannery O'Connor, who were presenting more troubled portraits of the nuclear family at the same time, but it wasn't until the 1970s that Rockwell's vision of the family was challenged in the mass media. Since then, many photographers, illustrators, cartoonists, films, and TV shows, even "Sesame Street," have tried to put the nuclear family into perspective. Teachers, clergy, television commentators, syndicated columnists, and textbook writers regularly join the effort because norms are powerful, even in a society that is diverse by class, region, ethnicity, and religion. Family norms and popular images of family stick, like gum to people's shoes. They influence the way we see things and get into our plans and dreams.

Ironically, norms also seed reform and reactionary movements, which blow through our culture regularly, like political thunderstorms. The Moral Majority, for instance, which made its debut as a political force during Reagan's presidential candidacy in 1980, was stirred to action as a reaction against the ascendancy of a new set of liberal norms. The Reverend Jerry Falwell, one of the movement's leaders, called for a return to traditional American values in his bestseller *Listen, America*. The Moral Majority called dissenters from their orthodoxy sinners, deviants, and enemies of the American family. One can hear echoes of their program in former Vice-President Quayle's Murphy Brown speech, one of this chapter's family documents.

These political movements register dissatisfaction with the status quo from the Left and the Right. Some of them place their hopes in an imagined, somewhat utopian future; others, in the revival of a mythically tinted past. Two of this chapter's writers, Robert Bly and Letty Cottin Pogrebin, were inspired, respectively, by the Men's Movement and the Women's Movement. Their radically different critiques of fatherhood are informed by ideas and insights from the movements they have come to represent.

Family Social Policy.   Family social policy is a complicated topic that deserves more time than I can give it here; however, it is possible to draw a few broad brush strokes that may help you write your own paper and appreciate the essays that follow. Social policy encompasses the elected and appointed officials and judges who make family laws, policies, and decisions, as well as the officials, agencies, and institutions that enforce them: city councils, state legislatures, the Congress, the president, mayors, governors, judges, police forces, probation officers, welfare case workers, and so on. Family activists of every political stripe, private foundations, and not-for-profit organizations, such as Marian Wright Edelman's Children's Defense Fund, regularly try to influence how family policies are written and carried out. One can see every aspect of this complex world in motion in Jonathan Kozol's and Celia W. Dugger's muckraking accounts of the tragic deaths of two innocent children, which are included later in the chapter. Kozol tells us how Benjamin Peters's medical problems worsened because of hazardous and illegal accommodations New York City's Housing Resource Administration offered his homeless mother Holly and because of bureaucratic tangles that deprived Benjamin of timely medical care. Yaakov Riegler's story is simpler.

His mother beat and cut him, broke his bones, and finally killed him; this escalating cycle of abuse was detected by many—social workers, teachers, judges, a therapist, and counselors—but stopped by no one.

The issues currently before our family social policy community are whether or not we will do something about child abuse and wife abuse; whether we will continue to cut funding to public health care and education; whether we will subsidize the education and health care of the well-to-do more than we do at present by passing tax cuts, credits, and vouchers like those former President Bush, among others, has advocated; and whether we will continue to abandon the families of the poor, especially the inner-city poor, as we did during the Reagan and Bush administrations, not that we did so well by them before that. Jane Gross's article in the last chapter on America's new orphans, the inner city's zero-parent kids, gives a sense of the harvest of abandonment.

In my opinion, the key principle of American family social policy was written by blues singer Billie Holiday: "God bless the child that's got his own." Despite notable exceptions, the tax codes, zoning laws, private health care and education, radically unequal public education—from kindergarten to graduate school—and wide disparities in income and wealth have long worked together to benefit the advantaged child at the expense of the disadvantaged child. Money *is* spent to help those who need it, but generally it is a matter of too little too late; the lion's share of that money goes to top-heavy bureaucracies (their salaries and supplies) before a single individual is touched. Politicians with good hearts and good ideas come along, but few of them have the political will, imagination, and backing to spend the money needed to offset the inequities and repair the damage that our economy and society are ceaselessly in the process of creating. The bottom of the sea is littered with the hulls of their abandoned programs and policies, and the rule remains, "God bless the child that's got his own, that's got his own."

The disparities in quality of life between rich and poor in America are incredible; in the eyes of some, they are obscene. Think of the prospects of a child whose parents are well-off. Now think of the prospects of a child born to impoverished parents. Of course, we will always have our Cornelius Vanderbilts and our Famous Amoses who rise from rags to riches, but they are the exceptions that prove the rule. Some defenders of the status quo are quick to point out that the miserable in America are not as miserable as the miserable in other countries, but that's not a very compelling argument in such a rich nation. Who are we as a society to reward or punish children on the basis of what their parents inherited, earned, or did not earn?

Think about Benjamin Peters. Did he slip through a crack that is an unavoidable imperfection of any human system, or did he fall into a man-made pit? How many Benjamins do we bury a year?

It's in the vast arena of social policy that the loudest and fiercest battles over family affairs are fought, and in light of what's at stake, it's surprising the battles aren't fiercer. People fight for what they believe in, they fight for the welfare and, ultimately, the future of their children and the children of others.

There are other places where the future is made, but none more important than the family.

✺ Word Play: *Parenting*

Parent, like *family,* is another common word that is uncommonly loaded. It comes from the Latin *parens,* which means "giving birth to, begetting, producing." *Fathering* and the archaic word *siring* come close to the emphasis of *parens* on conceiving and giving birth to. There is also the word *mothering,* which can mean giving birth, but the word's primary meaning is nurturing and taking care of children. It's telling that there are no exact female equivalents of *fathering* and *siring* in a society in which names, property, and even legitimacy tend to pass along paternal lines.

Parent exists in contemporary American English as a verb, meaning "the process of raising a child," but it is much more common as a noun. *Parent* the noun describes a biological relationship that is invested with social, moral, and legal significance and power, the specifics of which are not universal or timeless (as quite a few of the essays in this book demonstrate). Parenting entails rights and responsibilities: parents are expected to protect, provide for, and guide their children morally, emotionally, and psychologically.

Parenting styles vary by culture, class, and region in the United States, but there are norms or limits which are clearly demonstrated by parents who fail to measure up in the eyes of relatives, neighbors, social workers, or judges and are shunned or deemed to be unfit. In the courts, in particular, parents encounter a distinct and different language of parenting and family: *custody* or *joint-custody* is awarded or denied, *visitation rights* are assigned, stepparents or adoptive parents become legal *guardians* of children, and so on. What is noteworthy about the law's language, whether it describes a desired or punitive outcome, is that it seems chilly and abstract because it lacks the emotional connotations of ordinary family language. Not that it's inappropriate; it's just different from many of the ways in which we talk and write about family.

The normative force of *parent* is clearest when we contrast it with our modified and hyphenated *parents,* which revolve in orbit like planets around the sun. There's *stepparent* and its subdivisions, *stepfather* and *stepmother;* there's *social parent,* a term that the anthropologist Carol Stack and other social scientists use to describe an adult who helps raise a child who is not the biological or "natural" child of the adult; and there's *foster parent. Stepmother,* which has a menacing undertone because of the cultural archetype of the wicked stepmother, as in Cinderella's stepmother, is the exception that proves the rule. These terms aren't negative; they're just not as positive and substantial as *parent.* They don't have the full legitimacy of the title *parent;* put more broadly, the hierarchy of our vocabulary of parenting expresses our normative hierarchy of values and preferences.

There are also *single parent* and *single mother,* both recent coinages, which demonstrate that these hierarchies are not static, nor do they enjoy unanimous support. *Single parent* and *single mother* are the work of people who were unhappy with how society penalized and verbally stigmatized women who had children without husbands. They are the work of liberal and feminist reformers who believe it is not constructive or fair to blame women for situations that also involve men and to stigmatize children who had nothing to do with anything. Even as recently as the 1970s, one frequently ran across the term *unwed mothers* in the paper and in conversation. It is significant that *unwed mothers* appears in the title of the piece written by conservative ideologue Charles Murray, which is included in this chapter. The children of *unwed mothers* were *illegitimate* in polite company and *bastards* after the company went home. They were *fatherless,* which takes us back to the paternalistic framework of the language of parenting.

Partisans use language to describe, define, and judge a situation. The side whose words and terms prevail enjoys a home-court advantage. In this case, the asymmetry exists on the male side: the term *single father* is rarely encountered. And even though one runs into *single parent* and *single mother* in magazines, newspapers, and books all the time, these terms have not yet made it into most commonly used dictionaries.

Caretaker has been around for centuries, but until recently it meant someone, usually a man, who took care of an estate, a lavish home, or a church. Eighteenth- and nineteenth-century British novels abound with *caretakers,* and I believe the word was used more frequently on the other side of the Atlantic. Recently, social scientists paired it with the word *primary,* creating the term primary caretaker, and used it as a verbal tool to distinguish the parent or adult in a household who takes care of the children from the other parent, adult, or adults. It has been a useful term in sociological discussions of domesticity, but the term can seem unintentionally comic because of the original sense of *caretaker.* Even though the denotation is right, the word's connotation is not in tune with the attitudes and emotions that parenting evokes. *Primary caretaker* sounds heavy and awkward but it is probably attractive to writers who like new terminology and tend to use jargon.

Surrogate mother is another relatively new term, brought to us by technological advances in artificial insemination. It's important, however, to bear in mind that the wording of the term was not inevitable. The term is a tonal oxymoron: *mother,* a respected title, is tinged with sentiment; *surrogate* is abstract and contractual. The term expresses our ambivalence about a contractual situation in which, for a fee, a woman conceives through scientifically administered sperm, then gestates the baby for the sperm source and the sperm source's wife. *Surrogate mother* has also increased the incidence of the odd-sounding terms *biological parent, biological father,* and *biological mother,* which are odd. Say them out loud a few times, and you will see what I mean.

Flesh parents establishes the outer limits of parental language. As you may recall, the novelist Don DeLillo coins this surreal term in "At Yankee Stadium," which appears in the previous chapter. Roger and Maureen, Karen's *flesh parents,* sit in the stands of Yankee Stadium to watch their daughter get married simultaneously with 6499 other couples, the Reverend Sun Myung Moon, the spiritual father, presiding. Roger and Maureen represent the typical white, middle-class family. Nothing in their experience prepares them for this event, which dashes all their expectations for their daughter and threatens their way of life. They are at the edge of some sort of weird precipice, a future they hadn't anticipated; Karen has been pried loose from them and their way of life by cultural forces so incomprehensible to them that they seem mystical. In the stands of Yankee Stadium, searching for their daughter's face through binoculars, they are demoted to *flesh parents.*

Two key points emerge from this excursion through the language of parenting. First, challenging prevalent attitudes and practices frequently entails picking a fight with the language. Our dictionaries are teeming with the victors and the vanquished of countless political debates and struggles. Second, there are webs of words throughout our language: the words in each web situate and resonate with one another, even when they are in opposition to one another.

Journal Entry

Can you think of situations—from experience or the nightly news—that strain the language of parenting? How? Why?

———————————— ℛeadings ————————————

If the Child Is Safe: A Struggle for America's Conscience and Future

—Marian Wright Edelman

Marian Wright Edelman is founder and head of the Children's Defense Fund, an advocacy organization that has enjoyed the participation and insights of Hillary Clinton and Donna Shalala, President Clinton's Secretary of Health and Human Services. She and her husband live in Washington, D.C.; their children are grown and at school and work. In fact, the book the following excerpt was taken from, *The Measure of Our Success: A Letter to My Children and Yours,* was conceived of as a series of letters to her children, in which Wright Edelman tries to distill the lessons of decades of family life and years of hard work at the Children's Defense Fund.

> *If the child is safe everyone is safe.*
> —G. Campbell Morgan, "The Children's
> Playground in the City of God," The Westminster
> Pulpit (circa 1908)

> *There is no finer investment for any country than*
> *putting milk into babies.*
> —Winston Churchill

The most important work to help our children is done quietly—in our homes and neighborhoods, our parishes and community organizations. No government can love a child and no policy can substitute for a family's care, but clearly families can be helped or hurt in their irreplaceable roles. Government can either support or undermine families as they cope with the moral, social, and economic stresses of caring for children.

There has been an unfortunate, unnecessary, and unreal polarization in discussions of how best to help families. Some

emphasize the primary role of moral values and personal responsibility, the sacrifices to be made and the personal behaviors to be
avoided, but often ignore or deemphasize the broader forces
which hurt families, e.g. the impact of economics, discrimination,
and anti-family policies. Others emphasize the social and economic forces that undermine families and the responsibility of
government to meet human needs, but they often neglect the
importance of basic values and personal responsibility.

The undeniable fact is that our children's future is shaped by
both the values of their parents and the policies of our nation.

—Putting Children and Families First:
A Challenge for our Church, Nation, and World,
National Conference of Catholic Bishops—Pastoral
Letter, November 1991

The 1990s' struggle is for America's conscience and future—a future that is   1
being determined right now in the bodies and minds and spirits of *every* American
child—white, African American, Latino, Asian American, Native American, rich,
middle class, and poor. Many of the battles for this future will not be as dramatic as
Gettysburg or Vietnam or Desert Storm, but they will shape our place in the twenty-first century no less.

Ironically, as Communism is collapsing all around the world, the American   2
Dream is collapsing all around America for millions of children, youths, and families in all racial and income groups. American is pitted against American as economic uncertainty and downturn increase our fears, our business failures, our
poverty rates, our racial divisions, and the dangers of political demagoguery.

Family and community values and supports are disintegrating among all races   3
and income groups, reflecting the spiritual as well as economic poverty of our
nation. All our children are growing up in an ethically polluted nation where instant
sex without responsibility, instant gratification without effort, instant solutions
without sacrifice, getting rather than giving, and hoarding rather than sharing are
the too-frequent signals of our mass media, business, and political life.

All our children are threatened by pesticides and toxic wastes and chemicals   4
polluting the air, water, and earth. No parent can shut out completely the pollution
of our airwaves and popular culture, which glorify excessive violence, profligate
consumption, easy sex and greed, and depict deadly alcohol and tobacco products
as fun, glamorous, and macho.

All our children are affected by the absence of enough heroines and heroes in   5
public and daily life, as the standard for success for too many Americans has
become personal greed rather than common good, and as it has become enough to
just get by rather than do one's best.

All our children are affected by escalating violence fueled by unbridled traf-   6 ficking in guns and in the drugs that are pervasive in suburb, rural area and inner city alike.

Young families of all races, on whom we count to raise healthy children for 7 America's future, are in extraordinary trouble. They have suffered since the early 1970s a frightening cycle of plummeting earnings, a near doubling of birth rates among unmarried women, increasing numbers of single-parent families, falling income—the median income of young families with children fell by 26 percent between 1973 and 1989—and skyrocketing poverty rates. Forty percent of all children in families with a household head under thirty are poor. While many middle-class youths and young families see the future as a choice between a house and a child, many undereducated, jobless, poor youths and young adults trapped in inner-city war zones see the future as a choice between prison or death at the hands of gangs and drug dealers.

More and more Americans feel their children are being left behind. But poor 8 children suffer most, and their numbers are growing—841,000 in 1990 alone. They are the small, faceless victims who have no one to speak and fight for them. We were mesmerized by the 1987 death of Lisa Steinberg, a child whose adoption was never completed or abuse detected by our overburdened, inadequate child welfare system. We cheered when Jessica McClure was rescued from an open well shaft in the yard of an unregulated family day care center run by a relative, a danger she should not have come close to in the first place. But when eight-month-old Shamal Jackson died in New York City from low birth-weight, poor nutrition, and viral infection—from poverty and homelessness we didn't hear much about him. During his short life, he slept in shelters with strangers, in hospitals, in welfare hotels, in the welfare office, and in the subways he and his mother rode late at night when there was no place else to go. In the richest nation on earth, he never slept in an apartment or house. Nor have we heard about two-pound "Jason" fighting for his life at Children's Hospital in Washington, D.C., or about thousands of other babies in similar neonatal intensive care wards all over America. At birth—three months before he was due—Jason weighed just over one pound. He lives because tubes connect his lungs and every available vein to the many machines that are needed to feed him and keep him warm and enable him to take his next breath. He has a heart problem and has already suffered seizures because of damage to his nervous system caused by bleeding into his head—damage that, if he lives, will probably be permanent.

What exactly led to Jason's premature birth will never be known. We do 9 know, however, that unless a mother receives early and ongoing prenatal care, conditions that lead to prematurity cannot be detected or treated. A third of our mothers do not receive the care they need because our health care system, unlike that of every other major industrialized nation, does not provide universal basic coverage for mothers and children.

Remember these children behind the statistics. All over America, they are the 10 small human tragedies who will determine the quality and safety and economic security of America's future as much as your and my children will. The decision you and I and our leaders must make is whether we are going to invest in every American child or continue to produce thousands of school dropouts, teen parents, welfare recipients, criminals—many of whom are alienated from a society that turns a deaf ear to the basic human needs and longings of every child.

If recent trends continue, by the end of the century poverty will overtake one 11 in every four children, and the share of children living with single parents will also rise. One in every five births and more than one in three black births in the year 2000 will be to a mother who did not receive cost-effective early prenatal care. One of every five twenty-year-old women will be a mother, and more than four out of five of those young mothers will not be married. And the social security system that all of us count on to support us in our old age will depend on the contributions of fewer children—children we are failing today.

If we do not act immediately to protect America's children and change the 12 misguided national choices that leave too many of them unhealthy, unhoused, ill-fed, and undereducated, during the next four years

1,080,000 American babies will be born at low birth-weight, multiplying their risk of death or disability,

143,619 babies will die before their first birthday,

4,400,000 babies will be born to unmarried women,

2,000,000 babies will be born to teen mothers,

15,856 children 19 or younger will die by firearms,

2,784 children younger than 5 will die by homicide,

9,208 children 19 or younger will commit suicide,

1,620,000 young people ages 16 to 24 will fail to complete high school,

3,780,000 young people will finish high school but not enroll in college,

599,076 children younger than 18 will be arrested for alcohol-related offenses, 359,600 for drug offenses, and 338,292 for violent crimes,

7,911,532 public school students will be suspended, and

3,600,000 infants will be born into poverty.

It is a spiritually impoverished nation that permits infants and children to be 13 the poorest Americans. Over 13 million children in our rich land go without the basic amenities of life—more than the total population of Illinois, Pennsylvania, or Florida. If every citizen in the state of Florida became poor, the president would declare a national disaster. Yet he and Congress have yet to recognize child and family poverty and financial insecurity as the national disaster it is and attack it with a fraction of the zeal and shared commitment we now apply to digging out after a devastating hurricane or earthquake or fire. We moved more than 1.7 million elderly persons out of poverty in the three years following the 1972 revisions to the Social Security Act that indexed senior citizens' benefits to inflation. Surely we can provide families with children equitable treatment.

It is a morally lost nation that is unable and unwilling to disarm our children 14
and those who kill our children in their school buses, strollers, yards, and schools,
in movie theaters, and in McDonald's. Death stalks America's playgrounds and
streets without a declaration of war—or even a sustained declaration of concern by
our president, Congress, governors, state and local elected officials, and citizens.

Every day, 135,000 children bring a gun to school. In 1987, 415,000 violent 15
crimes occurred in and around schools. Some inner-city children are exposed to
violence so routinely that they exhibit post-traumatic stress symptoms similar to
those that plague many Vietnam combat veterans. Still, our country is unwilling to
take semiautomatic machine guns out of the hands of its citizens. Where are the
moral guerrillas and protesters crying out that life at home is as precious as life
abroad? Isn't it time for a critical mass of Americans to join our law enforcement
agencies and force our political leaders to halt the proliferation of guns? Every day
twenty-three teens and young adults are killed by firearms in America.

In response to a distant tyrant, we sent hundreds of thousands of American 16
mothers and fathers, sons and daughters, husbands and wives, sisters and brothers
to the Persian Gulf. According to Secretary of State James Baker, the Gulf War was
fought to protect our "life style" and standard of living and the rights of the Kuwaiti
people. No deficit of recession was allowed to stand in the way. How, then, can we
reconcile our failure to engage equally the enemies of poverty and violence and
family disintegration within our own nation? When are we going to mobilize and
send troops to fight for the "life style" of the 100,000 American children who are
homeless each night, to fight for the standard of living of thousands of young families whose earning capacity is eroding and who are struggling to buy homes, pay
off college loans, and find and afford child care? Where are the leaders coming to
the rescue of millions of poor working- and middle-class families fighting to hold
together their fragile households on declining wages and jobs? Why are they not
acting to help the one in six families with children headed by a working single
mother—29 percent of whom are poor? Isn't it time to tell our leaders to bail out
our young families with the same zeal as they bailed out failed thrift and banking
institutions to the tune of an estimated $115 billion by 1992?

What do we *really* value as Americans when the president's 1992 budget pro- 17
posed only $100 million to increase Head Start for *one year* and no addition for
child care for working families, but $500 million *each day* for Desert Storm, $90
million *each day* to bail out profligate savings and loan institutions, and hundreds
of millions more to give capital gains tax breaks to the rich? Between 1979 and
1989, the average income (adjusted for inflation) of the bottom fifth of families
dropped by 6 percent while that of the top fifth surged upward by 17 percent. The
poorest fifth of American families with children lost 21 percent of their income.

Why were we able to put hundreds of thousands of troops and support person- 18
nel in Saudi Arabia within a few months to fight Saddam Hussein when we are
unable to mobilize hundreds of teachers or doctors and nurses and social workers
for desperately underserved inner cities and rural areas to fight the tyranny of
poverty and ignorance and child neglect and abuse?

Isn't it time for the president and Congress and all of us to redefine our 19
national security and invest as much time and leadership and energy to solving our
problems at home as we do to our problems abroad?

It is an ethically confused nation that has allowed truth-telling and moral 20
example to become devalued commodities. Too many of us hold to the philosophy
that "government is not the solution to our problems, government is the problem."
If government is seen as an illegitimate enterprise, if the public purposes of one's
job are not considered a high calling, and if government has no purpose other than
its own destruction, the restraints against unethical behavior in both the public and
private sectors quickly erode. As a result, for every Michael Deaver and for every
Elliot Abrams, from the public sector, there is an Ivan Boesky or a Reverend Jim
Bakker in the private sector. If the only principle our society adheres to is economist Adam Smith's "Invisible Hand," it leaves little or no room for the human
hand, or the hand of God, whom the prophet Micah said enjoined us "to be fair and
just and merciful." There is a hollowness at the core of a society if its members
share no common purpose, no mutual goals, no joint vision—nothing to believe in
except self-aggrandizement.

Isn't it time for us to hold our political leaders to their professed beliefs and 21
promises about getting children ready for school and providing them health care
and education?

It is a dangerously short-sighted nation that fantasizes absolute self-sufficien- 22
cy as the only correct way of life. Throughout our history, we have given government help to our people and then have forgotten that fact when it came time to celebrate our people's achievements. Two hundred years ago, Congress granted federal
lands to the states to help maintain public schools. In 1862, President Lincoln
signed the Morrill Land-Grant Act, granting land for colleges. The first food vouch-
er and energy assistance programs came, not during the New Deal or the War on
Poverty, but at the end of the Civil War, when Congress and President Lincoln created the Freedman's Bureau. Federal help for vaccinations, vocational education,
and maternal health began, not with Kennedy, Johnson, and Carter, but under
Madison, Wilson, and Harding, respectively.

Our parents, grandparents, and great-grandparents benefited from this govern- 23
ment help just as we all do today. Only the most blind of economists could doubt
that American prosperity, like Japan's, is built on the synergistic relations between
government and private initiative. But it is some of the most blind economists,
political scientists, and "moral philosophers" who have the ear of many of our leaders or are themselves political leaders. Too many of them suffer from the peculiarly
American amnesia or hypocrisy that wants us to think that poor and middle-class
families must fend entirely for themselves; that makes us forget how government
helps us all, regardless of class; and that makes us believe that the government is
simply wasting its billions supporting a wholly dependent, self-perpetuating class
of poor people, while doing nothing but taxing the rest of us.

Chrysler and Lee Iacocca didn't do it alone. Defense contractors don't do it 24
alone. Welfare queens can't hold a candle to corporate kings in raiding the public

purse. Most wealthy and middle-class families don't do it alone. Yet some begrudge the same security for low- and moderate-income families with children who must grow up healthy, educated, and productive to support our aging population.

The president and Congress and public must take the time and have the 25 courage to make specific choices and not wield an indiscriminate budget ax or hide behind uniform but unjust freezes of current inequalities. They must also take time to distinguish between programs that work (like immunization, preventive health care, and Head Start) and programs that don't (like the B2 stealth bomber). They must apply the same standards of accountability for programs benefiting the rich and poor and middle class alike. They must hold the Pentagon to the same standards of efficiency as social programs. And isn't it time for the president and Congress to invest more in preventing rather than trying to mop up problems after the fact? Isn't it time to reassess national investment priorities in light of changing national and world needs? Does it make sense for our federal government to spend each hour this fiscal year $33.7 million on national defense, $23.6 million on the national debt, $8.7 million on the savings and loan bailout, $2.9 million on education, and $1.8 million on children's health?

Making hard choices and investing in our own people may help restore the 26 confidence of citizens in government. The overarching task of leadership today in every segment of American society is to give our youths, and all Americans, a sense that we can be engaged in enterprises that lend meaning to life, that we can regain control over our families and our national destiny, and that we can make a positive difference individually and collectively in building a decent, safe nation and world.

America cannot afford to waste resources by failing to prevent and curb the 27 national human deficit, which cripples our children's welfare today and costs billions in later remedial and custodial dollars. Every dollar we invest in preventive health care for mothers and children saves more than $3 later. Every dollar put into quality preschool education like Head Start saves $4.75 later. It costs more than twice as much to place a child in foster care as to provide family preservation services. The question is not whether we can afford to invest in every child; it is whether we can afford not to. At a time when future demographic trends guarantee a shortage of young adults who will be workers, soldiers, leaders, and parents, America cannot to waste a single child. With unprecedented economic competition from abroad and changing patterns of production at home that demand higher basic educational skills, America cannot wait another minute to do whatever is needed to ensure that today's and tomorrow's workers are well prepared rather than useless and alienated—whatever their color.

We cannot go back and change the last decade's birth rates. But we can pre- 28 vent and reduce the damages to our children and families and ensure every child a healthy start, a head start, and a fair start right now. In the waning years of the twentieth century, doing what is right for children and doing what is necessary to save our national economic skin have converged.

When the new century dawns with new global economic and military chal- 29
lenges, America will be ready to compete economically and lead morally only if we

1. stop cheating and neglecting our children for selfish, short-sighted, personal, and political gain;
2. stop clinging to our racial past and recognize that America's ideals, future,
   and fate are as inextricably intertwined with the fate of its poor and nonwhite children as with its privileged and white ones;
3. love our children more than we fear each other and our perceived or real
   external enemies;
4. acquire the discipline to invest preventively and systematically in all of our
   children *now* in order to reap a better trained work force and more stable
   future *tomorrow;*
5. curb the desires of the overprivileged so that the survival needs of the less
   privileged may be met, and spend less on weapons of death and more on
   lifelines of constructive development for our citizens;
6. set clear, national, state, city, community, and personal goals for child survival and development, and invest whatever leadership, commitment, time,
   money, and sustained effort are needed to achieve them;
7. struggle to begin to live our lives in less selfish and more purposeful ways,
   redefining success by national and individual character and service rather
   than by national consumption and the superficial barriers of race and class.

The mounting crisis of our children and families is a rebuke to everything 30
America professes to be. While the cost of repairing our crumbling national foundation will be expensive in more ways than one, the cost of not repairing it, or of
patching cosmetically, may be fatal.

The place to begin is with ourselves. Care. As you read about or meet some of 31
the children and families in this country who need your help, put yourself in their
places as fellow Americans. Imagine you or your spouse being pregnant, and not
being able to get enough to eat or see a doctor or know that you have a hospital for
delivery. Imagine your child hungry or injured, and you cannot pay for food or find
health care. Imagine losing your job and having no income, having your unemployment compensation run out, not being able to pay your note or rent, having no place
to sleep with your children, having nothing. Imagine having to stand in a soup line
at a church or Salvation Army station after you've worked all your life, or having to
sleep in a shelter with strangers and get up and out early each morning, find some
place to go with your children, and not know if you can sleep there again that night.
If you take the time to imagine this, perhaps you can also take the time to do for
them what you would want a fellow citizen to do for you. Volunteer in a homeless
shelter or soup kitchen or an afterschool tutoring or mentoring program. Vote. Help
to organize your community to speak out for the children who need you. Visit a
hospital neonatal intensive care nursery or AIDS and boarder baby ward and spend
time rocking and caring for an individual child. Adopt as a pen pal a lonely child
who never gets a letter from anyone. Give a youth a summer job. Teach your child
tolerance and empathy by your example.

Essential individual service and private charity are not substitutes for public 32
justice, or enough alone to right what's wrong in America. Collective mobilization
and political action are also necessary to move our nation forward in the quest for
fairness and opportunity for every American.

So pledge to take responsibility not only for your child but for all children or 33
at least for one child who may not be your own. Finally, as you read the prayer
below by Ina J. Hughs, include with every "we pray" the promise "I take responsibility for":

We pray for children
 who sneak popsicles before supper,
 who erase holes in math workbooks,
 who can never find their shoes.
And we pray for those
 who stare at photographers from behind barbed wire,
 who can't bound down the street in a new pair of sneakers,
  who never "counted potatoes,"
 who are born in places we wouldn't be caught dead,
 who never go to the circus,
 who live in an X-rated world.
We pray for children
 who bring us sticky kisses and fistfuls of dandelions,
 who hug us in a hurry and forget their lunch money.
And we pray for those
 who never get dessert,
 who have no safe blanket to drag behind them,
 who watch their parents watch them die,
 who can't find any bread to steal,
 who don't have any rooms to clean up,
 whose pictures aren't on anybody's dresser,
 whose monsters are real.
We pray for children
 who spend all their allowance before Tuesday,
 who throw tantrums in the grocery store and pick at their food,
 who like ghost stories,
 who shove dirty clothes under the bed, and never rinse out the tub,
 who get visits from the tooth fairy,
 who don't like to be kissed in front of the carpool,
 who squirm in church or temple and scream in the phone,
  whose tears we sometimes laugh at and whose smiles can make us cry.
And we pray for those
 whose nightmares come in the daytime,
 who will eat anything,
 who have never seen a dentist,
 who aren't spoiled by anybody,

who go to bed hungry and cry themselves to sleep,
who live and move, but have no being.
We pray for children who want to be carried
and for those who must,
for those we never give up on and for those
who don't get a second chance.
For those we smother. . . and those who will grab
the hand of anybody kind enough to offer it.

Please offer your hands to them so that no child is left behind because we did not act.

■ *Questions for* . . . **If the Child Is Safe: A Struggle for America's Conscience and Future** by Marian Wright Edelman

Words to Note

shape	collapsing	pitted
downturn	an ethically polluted	hoarding
escalating	nation	unbridled trafficking
plummeting earnings	mesmerized	neonatal
stalks	desperately underserved	synergistic relations
fend	inner cities and	welfare queens
corporate kings	rural areas	raiding the public purse
curb	the national human	boarder baby ward
quest	deficit	

Language

1. In paragraph 27, Wright Edelman rebukes America for "failing to prevent and curb the national human deficit." How is *deficit* usually used? Does it work with *human?*
2. President Ronald Reagan popularized the expression *welfare queen* in his acceptance speech at the 1980 Republican National Convention in Detroit. How does she play on it in paragraph 24? In your opinion, is her word play successful?

Style

1. What do the four italicized phrases do for Wright Edelman's essay? Is the nearly identical phrasing important?
2. A rhetorical question, as you may know, is not really a question because its answer is implicit and obvious. Wright Edelman uses them throughout her essay. Paragraph 25 ends with three rhetorical questions, and paragraph 21

is a single rhetorical question: "Isn't it time for us to hold our political leaders to their professed beliefs and promises about getting children ready for school and providing them health care and education?" What do the rhetorical questions contribute to the essay's tone?

Development and Organization

1. What's Wright Edelman's key point? How does she advance it?
2. Do all the numbers she cites help, or are they unfathomable because they're so big?
3. Why does she take more time in paragraph 8 with Shamal Jackson and Jason than she does with Lisa Steinberg and Jessica McClure?

Discussion and Journal Writing

1. Toward the end of the essay, Wright Edelman asks us to put ourselves in the shoes of America's most desperate parents. Give it a try in your journal.
2. Why does she believe it is more cost effective, not just more moral, to provide amply for America's children? Do you find her argument convincing?

ooooo

Family Work and Wage Work

—Kenneth Keniston

Kenneth Keniston is an American sociologist who headed the Carnegie Council on Children. The Council, which was established in 1972, numbered in its ranks two other writers who appear in this book: the historian John Demos and the child welfare advocate Marian Wright Edelman. Keniston has made a career of analyzing people's feelings about and relationships to America's dominant social structure. He was chief author of *All Our Children, The American Family Under Pressure,* a 1978 book-length report by the Council, from which this selection is excerpted. In the report, he turns his gaze on the contemporary family.

"The timing of work" and "the organization of work" sound like terms that   1
belong in corporate planning offices, but the meaning of the two phrases comes in the door of most American households five days a week. Families are connected to

the work their members do in ways far beyond income alone. If a middle-management father's job moves from Detroit to Baltimore, so does his family. If a mother has to meet a crisis deadline at the office, she will probably have to miss the school play. If a pregnant woman works at a job where the strain or the environment can damage the fetus, her child may feel the effects for a lifetime. Yet the work world itself, and national policies affecting work, take almost no account of family needs.

A child's fear of going to the dentist is not written into employment contracts   2
as a valid reason for the parent to take the morning off. The intangible benefits that might come to a four-year-old girl from spending a few unhurried hours at midday with her father, however important he may feel it to be, may seem almost frivolous, dangerously self-indulgent, and unbusinesslike to his supervisors. Who can weigh the balance between the family's needs for a parent's wages and the children's need to have more of that parent's warmth, attention, and energy than they may get? Why should women have to lose pay and benefits (not to mention promotions) when they take time out to bear and begin raising children? Why should fathers who wish to help raise their children be denied a significant part in the process because of too heavy a work load?

Parents in their new role as family coordinators may have little power in the   3
face of professionals they have to deal with regarding their children; ironically, they may have even less power in the very place where they themselves are professionals: that is, trying to hold out for family interests in the face of their paid work. The inevitable conflicts that arise between the demands of a job and the needs of a family are almost always settled in favor of the job .

Is there no other way for that job to be designed? In a conflict, does the family   4
always have to be the one that gives? We do not believe so. It should no longer be assumed that families are not the business of employers or public officials. Corporate and government policies that influence work structure already have a deep influence on the supposedly self-reliant, self-sufficient, independent family unit.*

Our society can and should move toward balancing the competing demands of   5
wage work and child rearing so that children's needs are taken more seriously. There are many ways to give both parents more satisfactory choices: through flexible work hours or carefully arranged part-time work, through improved ways of arranging time off for pregnancy and childhood emergencies, and through new ways to encourage several years' time out for child rearing.

In recommending changes in work practices, we do not suggest that they are a   6
panacea for the problems of balancing work and family life. In fact, to have any impact, all of our work-practices recommendations depend on progress toward full employment, fairer treatment of women in the labor market, an income-support

---

*There has been very little serious research done on critical details of this link between the customs and policies of work and what goes on in the home. See *Growing Up American,* a report of the Carnegie Council on Children by Joan Costello and Phyllis LaFarge. New York: Harcourt Brace Jovanovich, 1978.

policy, and child-care and other supportive services for families with working parents.

In the short run, the greatest urgency must be given to providing all heads of 7 households that contain children with full-year, full-time jobs. But it is also important to accomodate the desire of many parents, especially mothers, for flexible hours in full-time jobs, for part-time jobs, and even for "part-career" employment* so that they are not forced to leave their children in the care of others when they would rather not, and so that men, too, can genuinely share the work of child rearing.

Our proposals for full employment coupled with income support would 8 restore some measure of choice to low-income parents with primary child-rearing responsibility who are now either forced into the labor market by the pressure of desperate economic need, or forced to stay at home because they cannot get a job. A credit tax or any other basic income-support system would somewhat reduce one of the most disastrous consequences of the separation of work and family: the financial pressure to work outside the home when the parent feels that staying with the children, especially preschool children, is far more important.

But even with modest income support available for the parent with primary 9 responsibilities for small children, one or both parents in almost all two-parent households and many single parents as well will still need or want to work. Apart from the income work is bound to bring, work has its own intrinsic pleasures and rewards. Even if all our proposals were implemented tomorrow, we would not expect—or wish—to see a dramatic reversal of the steady growth in the proportion of mothers who work. And so the problem of juggling the responsibilities of parenthood and jobs will remain, and changes in the timing and structure of work are essential to reduce the conflicts.

Flexible Scheduling

The typical American work week has shrunk considerably without losses in 10 pay since the time when six days on the job was considered normal and seven not unusual in many industries. In all likelihood the working hours needed to earn a full salary will go on shrinking. For the time being, however, for most families shorter hours are impractical because they mean less income. In addition, many adults enjoy work that requires long hours or intense commitment. While flexibility is no substitute for shorter hours, it does help parents balance the competing demands of home and work responsibilities. To be sure, some of the self-employed—independent craftsmen, for example—can set their own work hours. But barring a dramatic reversal in the trend that decreased the proportion of self-employed workers in the labor force from 20 percent in 1940 to about 8 percent in 1970, changes in the

---

*It is possible that eventually greater flexibility in the allocation of work time will involve not only the reorganization of daily, weekly, and annual work schedules but more widespread use of work patterns now used by only a few: life-cycle patterns that permit years of time taken out without great damage to a career.

working conditions of the 92 percent who work for others will have the greatest impact.

A form of scheduling with special advantages for family life is "flexible 11 hours" or "flexitime," in which employees decide a great deal about their own working hours. The term "flexible hours" is sometimes misleadingly used for other unconventional work arrangements, such as "4/40" (in which employees work four ten-hour days and get three-day weekends) and staggered hours (in which employees arrive and leave at different set times on overlapping schedules). Under truly flexible hours, employees can determine the number of hours they will work on any given day so long as the weekly hours add up to a required total in any given one- or two-week period. In some firms, this flexibility is modified by requiring all workers to be present during a core period but permitting them to arrive and leave at will before and after that. The Metropolitan Life Insurance Company in New York, for example, gives employees the choice of coming in to work any time between 7:30 A.M. and 10 A.M., requiring only that they work a full eight-hour day once they have arrived. Such schedules allow parents to organize their work days to coincide more nearly with their children's schedules—to care for sick children, avoid the rush hour, run errands, or take a child to the doctor. Furthermore, the worker who can make adjustments in work schedules if the need arises has the psychological satisfaction of being able to control her or his own time.

The idea of flexible hours was first promoted by a German economist and 12 management consultant, Christel Kaemmerev, in 1956. Put into operation on a large scale in West Germany in 1967, the idea has since spread throughout Europe, Japan, and Canada. Today in West Germany over 3,000 companies use some form of flexible hours, directly involving over one million employees; in Great Britain, eighty companies and 500,000 civil servants are on flexible hours. In the United States, by 1973 twenty-four firms had converted to flexitime, including Hewlett-Packard, Scott Paper, Sun Oil, Nestle's division in White Plains, New York, and Lufthansa German Airlines.

Early evaluation has shown that when flexible working hours are adopted with 13 genuine management support, productivity and morale improve and turnover, absenteeism, and overtime decline. Obviously, this kind of plan can be as beneficial for employers as for employees. Flexible hours eliminate time lost through lateness and early departure, or through time taken off during the day, or sick leaves used for needs unconnected with illness. Although there are some problems for employers—most notably, added costs of administration, and perhaps keeping plants open longer hours—many employers find these costs are outweighed by the benefits to management. Some problems can occur for employees, too: voluntary flexibility can become forced, and pay for voluntary overtime can be jeopardized. In all the schemes where there has been careful planning with good employee participation, these problems have been avoided. The applicability of flexible hours varies with the type of work and whether a firm faces regular hours of peak demand. Flexitime clearly is more possible in banks and insurance offices, less possible on assembly lines where work cannot go on unless workers are all on hand at once to perform each specialized function, but even in industrial situations some experiments are now under way.

One "flexible" innovation that does *not* seem promising to us involves the var-   14
ious kinds of "compressed" work weeks currently operating in the United States.
The most common of these is "4/40," an arrangement that began primarily as a
management idea for achieving high utilization of equipment, not as the employee's answer to the strains of combining home and family life. In fact, problems
faced by working mothers are a disadvantage mentioned frequently by management. Ten-hour working days tend to heighten rather than alleviate conflicts
between family responsibilities and work demands. Time off during a work day is
all but unattainable under 4/40, and fatigue is a significant problem. Children's
needs are immediate; they cannot wait until Friday. This is not the kind of flexibility families need.

What interests us in the structuring of work time is not only that employers be   15
convinced of added benefits to management in giving their employees more freedom to schedule their hours, but also that employers and employees begin to recognize more fully what a tremendous impact work patterns have on children. Some
are beginning to. One vice president of Data Control Corporation, asked about his
firm's new flexible program. said, "Flexible hours make better mothers and fathers
of our employees."

Part-Time Jobs

Parents' needs for more flexible schedules can also be met through the estab-   16
lishment of permanent part-time jobs.

At present, part-time jobs are rarely a satisfactory alternative for most   17
Americans. Part-time work is usually found in the least skilled and lowest paying
occupations, and it tends to be temporary and highly precarious. Most part-time
employees are not unionized; many are excluded from health insurance and other
benefits. In return for flexibility, many people who want part-time work have to
take a job far below their skill levels and accept the fact that they may be out of
even that job in a few months.*

Part-time workers, moreover, may get pushed around and have less control   18
over their jobs than full-time workers. According to a survey at the University of
Michigan Hospital, part-time nurses felt that they were less valued than full-time
nurses; they also felt that their positions were less stable. Most employers assume
that since part-time workers are not present the whole time, they cannot be entrusted with supervisory functions. In firms where promotion means a management post
with responsibility or supervisory functions, part-time workers are automatically
excluded from moving up. The fact that in so many ways part-time work usually
does not "pay" helps explain why so many parents who are primarily responsible
for raising children also work on a full-time job.

The life of many families would improve with the restructuring of part-time   19

---

*In this discussion of part-time work, we are referring exclusively to "sunlighters"—
that is, people whose part-time jobs are their only paid work—not "moonlighters," who are
doing a second job for extra money.

jobs as full-time jobs in miniature. Part-time employees need the same rights on the job as their full-time counterparts. They need guarantees of job security and weekly hours, equal wages for equal work, and benefits such as paid vacations, holidays, paid leave for jury duty, and sick leave computed on a prorated basis according to the number of hours worked. For other benefits, both full- and part-time employees would profit from being offered the chance to choose a prorated benefit package they themselves selected from such offerings as health insurance, additional vacation time, life insurance, and so on.

To minimize costs to employers innovations in management and scheduling are important. For example, to overcome problems when one employee takes over from another, some firms have tried split-level arrangements, where part-time employees of different levels, such as secretaries and executives, are paired together half-time and work the same hours. 20

The government can help to upgrade part-time jobs by including them under workmen's compensation and minimum wage laws. Although the National Labor Relations Board covers part-time workers, in most factories and offices there is a presumption that they do not have to be included in regular bargaining units. Also, a number of laws specifically bar part-time workers from unionization in certain job sectors, such as state and municipal employment. 21

One way of creating part-time work is job sharing or splitting, whereby two people share one job, each working half time. This approach has been tried in the New York school system, in the Roxbury Welfare Department, and on the production line at the Volvo plant in Sweden. 22

Work sharing by married couples was tried experimentally in Norway in 1971, with job schedules arranged so that each parent worked between sixteen and twenty-eight hours per week. The decision about how to split their time was worked out by each couple according to their particular needs. Some couples split the day evenly, with one parent working in the morning and one in the afternoon; others chose to work the same half-day hours while their children attended a day-care center. Most parents involved expressed satisfaction with the work-sharing plan, particularly because of the greater time they were able to spend with their children.* 23

We support legislative proposals to require federal and state governments in the United States to set an example by creating more part-time jobs. 24

None of these strategies to upgrade and expand part-time work has much chance of succeeding unless we have full employment. In periods of economic recession, part-time workers can be among the first to go. Full employment is essential to forestall such layoffs; a high general demand for workers would also increase the demand for more part-time employees and help overcome the fear some unions have expressed that part-time jobs will be created at the expense of full-time jobs. 25

*It should be noted that part-time work for two parents is only feasible in families earning gross salaries over $8,000 a year. Below this level, two combined part-time salaries would not be adequate to support a family.

Time Out for Children

The one flexibility for families that has existed in American work schedules 26 for some time is maternity leave for pregnancy and childbirth. This immensely important principle has historically been put into effect, however, at the expense of women's status on the job. Leave may have been available or even compulsory, but along with it came a loss in seniority and in promotion possibilities, and sometimes loss of all pay for the entire period of absence.

In the United States, paid maternity leave, for those few women who receive 27 it, has been financed through disability insurance. Under its provisions, women have been eligible for paid compensation only as long as they were technically "disabled," usually two to four weeks. This approach does not begin to meet their needs or those of their children. In particular, current practice rarely takes into account the need for time off before the baby's birth.

Other nations provide greater support and protection for pregnant women and 28 women with newborn children. In 1952, the International Labor Organization fixed minimal standards governing maternity benefits, which included six weeks' compulsory leave after childbirth, six weeks' optional leave before the expected date of birth, security of tenure for pregnant women, and payment of allowances during their leave. In France, women are entitled to six weeks' prenatal leave, eight weeks' postnatal leave, and an allowance of 50 percent of earnings plus continuing employer contributions to social insurance programs. Likewise, in Western Germany women are entitled to six weeks' leave before and six weeks after childbirth and to partial social security benefits.

We believe American employers should be required to support future children 29 by granting their mothers a twelve-week leave of absence to be used before and after the birth of the baby in any proportion the mother chooses. The leave should not cause her to lose seniority, advancement privileges, or job security. To pay for these leaves, the disability system is workable, given an expanded definition of "disability" which would include psychological needs as well as physical incapacity and, to some extent, babies' needs for a mother's time. Clearly there is a need for longer leaves of absence in particular situations. Here, other funding mechanisms deserve further study, including employee compensation by employers for more prolonged childbearing leaves, perhaps at a reduced percentage of normal earnings, or an extension of unemployment compensation to cover maternity leaves financed through matching contributions by all workers, the employers, and the government. As an employer, the government could lead the way by establishing this kind of maternity leave in all its departments and services. Furthermore, we believe that one option the government and later all other employers should explore is combining such maternity leave with leave for the father from his job to care for the new child.*

Another area related to childbirth is protection of the health and safety of the 30 unborn child while the mother is still on the job. If the woman is in a dangerous

---

*Sweden recently adopted measures that give a couple seven months of paid leave for a new child. The man and woman are free to split this time according to their needs.

job, we support the right to change to a safer, less tiring job with the same employer during pregnancy without loss of pay or seniority, the right to rest breaks and reasonable working hours, and the right to a healthful and supportive environment with a minimum of tension and stress, as well as the right to stop working several months before childbirth without loss of pay.

Many mothers do not return to work immediately after the birth of a child but 31 quit their jobs in order to stay home for a few years. That decision has always been a career liability: their seniority rights are lost and their skills can become rusty. The potential risks of child rearing to a career discourage many parents—and we explicitly include fathers—from taking time off when their children could benefit from it. If we believe that parents should be able to take time out that they need for child care, we must enable them to get decent jobs when they choose to return to work.

Existing policies that enable parents to take time out for childbirth should be 32 expanded to let them take more time off—as much as several years—and then return to work without having lost their former status. One model is wartime policy which required employers to hold a position open, including seniority rights, for workers drafted into the armed services. Perhaps it is unrealistic to expect a guarantee of the same job after an interval of many years, since the worker may have forgotten as much as the job has changed, but in that case at the very least industries and government should have programs to facilitate return to work.

Such policies could have a strong effect on the work patterns of both fathers 33 and mothers, with tremendous benefits to their children. It could encourage women and men to approach their education and early jobs with a firm conviction that they would be free to return to interesting work after an interval away. We would like to see a broad effort to improve counseling and information that would encourage young men and women to consider the possibility that they may wish to intersperse wage work and family work throughout their lives. We also support services that encourage and assist mature women who want to return to work. For parents reentering the job market with rusty skills or obsolete credentials, schools and colleges fortunately are beginning to accommodate adults at night or at odd hours.

Part-time education for those who still have active home responsibilities 34 should receive more scholarships and other support, such as child care for parents attending. More schools should offer refresher and updating courses, and more adult classes should be scheduled at times when young children are in school.

Making "reentry" easier may seem to have little to do with children, but our 35 proposals are based on our belief that parents will feel freer to take time off to raise their children when they know that decent jobs will open to them afterward. Needless to say, a national policy of full employment is once again the prerequisite to making this possible. As with counseling and training programs for teenagers, all the reentry programs in the world will be pointless if jobs are not waiting at the end of the line.

There are many rearrangements and precautions that would tangibly reduce 36 the present conflict between being a good parent and being a productive worker.

The essential first step toward bringing work practices into line with families' and children's needs is a commitment to do so on the part of policy makers in business, labor, and private groups, including families themselves. A task force report on work in the United States has illustrated how great a part of our nation's crime and delinquency, mental and physical health problems, and manpower and welfare dilemmas have their genesis in the world of work.

■ *Questions for* . . . Family Work and Wage Work by Kenneth Keniston

Words to Note

crisis	frivolous	family coordinators
panacea	supportive	two-parent households
juggling	intrinsic	restore
low-income parents	flexible hours or	alleviate
structuring	flexitime	tremendous impact
career liability	status	interval
facilitate	dilemmas	

Language

1. What does it say about managerial attitudes that a maternity leave is technically a *disability* leave?
2. What does Keniston mean when he refers to parents as "family coordinators"? Do you like the phrase? Is it an accurate assessment of one of the roles a modern parent must perform? How do you feel about that?
3. Why, in the ninth paragraph, does he refer to "two-parent households"? Why not just households or typical households?

Style

1. There are hypothetical situations, but there are actual situations, families, and people, and the language is a bit abstract and colorless. Is the style appropriate to the purpose of the writer, or should the words and situations have been more tangible and vivid, the way they would be if Keniston had written for a Sunday paper's magazine section?

Development and Organization

1. Are there too many examples and too much explanation? Would it have been more effective if Keniston left all that out and just got to the point?
2. Are the subtitles crucial?

Discussion and Journal Writing

1. Should paid maternity leaves of three months be mandated by law?
2. Are Keniston's proposals realistic? Can the private sector be competitive and can public agencies perform their duties without running over budget while offering benefits like flextime and paid maternity leaves?
3. Are we a work- or family-oriented society? What would Keniston say?

ooooo

Stop Favoring Unwed Mothers

—Charles Murray

Charles Murray, a social scientist and writer, is a Senior Research Fellow at the Manhattan Institute for Policy Research. Murray's *Losing Ground,* an account of how government aid to the poor backfired and created dependence and resentment, is one of the major works of Reagan-era conservatism. This essay, which appeared in the Op-ed pages of the *New York Times,* is politically consistent with *Losing Ground;* as you read it, try to keep track of all the reasons Murray thinks government assistance to families is counter-productive.

The New Jersey Legislature took the plunge this week and passed a welfare 1
package that, if signed by Gov. Jim Florio, would limit the benefits for women on
welfare if they have additional children. Opponents and advocates alike have called
the plan revolutionary. It is not.

We have been this way before. The seemingly small exceptions to the stern 2
new requirements would turn out to be gaping loopholes. Giving a single mother
incentive to marry by permitting her to keep her welfare benefits would have unin-
tended consequences. Reducing benefits for additional children sounds like a major
step, but few welfare mothers have more than two children.

The New Jersey plan would neither help nor hurt. It just won't make much 3
difference.

The New Jersey plan, like similar carrot-and-stick packages proposed in 4
California and other states that offer incentives for job training and education, does
not go far enough or address the right problems. Our social tragedy has nothing to

do with the money we spend on welfare and little to do with "welfare dependency." The problem is not that single mothers are on welfare, but that there are so many single mothers concentrated in poor communities.

The single-parent family does not work very well, even under the best of circumstances: when the mother is divorced and the father remains involved with the children. When the woman is unmarried and immature and the father of her children is as poorly equipped to be a parent as she is, the single-parent family tends to be a disaster. 5

Even the earliest childhood and prenatal programs barely improve the situation and then only under conditions that cannot work nationwide. We do not know how—*no matter how much money we spend*—to substitute social programs for competent parents. 6

The clichés about role models are true. Children learn to be responsible adults by watching what responsible adults do. The absence of such examples for young men is especially dangerous. The violence and social chaos in the inner cities show us what happens when about half a generation of males is born to single women. In most of these areas today, the figure is about 80 percent. When predicting the future of the inner city, pessimism is realism. 7

The solution lies neither in social programs nor in making women on welfare go to work. It lies in restoring a situation in which almost all women either get pregnant after they get married or get married after they get pregnant, or failing that, in which a single mother who cannot support a child—and has no other adults who will take responsibility—is motivated to give her child up for adoption. 8

Communities did not need lessons in how to bring these things about until welfare took over. But to revitalize the natural mechanisms that used to work so effectively we have to come to terms with a fact that is unfashionable to acknowledge and palpably inequitable. For whatever complicated reasons—not least, because women bear children—communities have much more leverage over the woman's behavior than the man's. 9

The evil of the modern welfare system is not that it bribes women to have babies—wanting to have babies is natural—but that it enables women to bear children without the natural social restraints and without bringing pressure on the fathers to behave responsibly. 10

The welfare system bypasses the process that limits the babies born to single women. No incremental reform—including the New Jersey plan—will change this fundamental defect. The only long-term solution is to get rid of the welfare system. 11

Instead, government policy must be founded on the premise that to bring a baby into the world when one is not emotionally or economically equipped to be a parent is not just ill-advised. It is profoundly wrong. 12

Government cannot interfere with individual decisions to bear children without destroying the most basic restraints on state power. But it can properly refuse to be a party to wrong behavior. It will keep the Faustian bargain it has made with women already on the rolls. But, starting now, it should make single mothers eligi- 13 ble for the same unemployment benefits and social programs as everyone else. Let government try, with the mother's cooperation, to make the father bear financial responsibility.

Because the children themselves remain innocent victims, let government do   14
what it can to improve their prospects, spending as lavishly as need be on adoption services and, yes, on orphanages. But let us demand that government no longer try to help the innocent children by subsidizing the parents who made them victims.

■ *Questions for* . . . Stop Favoring **Unwed Mothers** by Charles Murray

Words to Note

plunge	welfare package	advocates
stern	gaping loopholes	incentive
carrot-and-stick	competent	motivated
packages	revitalize	natural mechanisms
unfashionable	palpably inequitable	bribes
leverage	natural social restraints	ill-advised
victims	prospects	lavishly

Language

1. What is a *natural mechanism?* Look at how Murray uses the expression in the ninth paragraph. What about *natural social restraints* in the next paragraph?
2. What is a *Faustian bargain?*

Style

1. Charles Murray is a skilled writer. His writing is easy to read, lucid, and effective. Is his secret the way he phrases his sentences? His word choice?

Development and Organization

1. In the sixth paragraph, Murray writes, "Even the earliest childhood and prenatal programs barely improve the situation." Where is his proof? Marian Wright Edelman ("If the Child Is Safe: A Struggle for America's Conscience and Future") argues that these programs are terrific investments, especially prenatal care, because problems are detected early when they can be solved with the least amount of damage and money. Who is right?

Discussion and Journal Writing

1. At the end of the sixth paragraph, Murray says we don't know how "to substitute social programs for competent parents." Look carefully at his words.
   Is that the issue—substituting social programs for competent parents?

2. In what ways do parents at all income levels depend on others to help them
   raise their families?

3. Do Murray's conclusions—ending welfare "to revitalize the 'natural mechanisms'" that keep single women from having babies and to allow government to spend "lavishly" on adoption services and orphanages—follow
   from his argument?

4. Compare former Vice-President Quayle's speech, which appears later in
   this chapter, with Murray's editorial. Is Murray's influence on Quayle very
   apparent?

5. Does his conclusion—"the only long-term solution is to get rid of the welfare system"—follow from his argument?

ooooo

The Child Care Crisis Provokes a Response

—Ellen Goodman

Ellen Goodman is a syndicated columnist. Her editorials,
which won her a Pulitzer Prize, appear in the *Boston Globe*, New
York *Newsday* and many other papers. This editorial appeared in
Newsday in March 1988. Goodman usually comments on politics
and contemporary trends and problems from a feminist perspective.
Though many views have gathered under the big top of the
Women's Movement and many, many writers have sounded feminist themes, especially over the past 20 years, Goodman's is the
daily voice of liberal feminism, just as Gloria Steinem has been its
titular head for a few decades.

For those who were still in bell-bottoms at the time, a small historic note from   1
the Nixon era: In 1971, Richard Milhous Nixon vetoed the last comprehensive
child-care bill to come out of Congress. It would, he insisted, "commit the vast
moral authority of the national government to the side of communal approaches to
child-rearing over the family-centered approach."

From then on "the vast moral authority" of the government was committed to 2
neglect. Child care all but disappeared from the federal agenda. Kids were private
property. Working parents had to find places for them the way they might find a
parking space in a downtown crossing.

But now the times they are a-changing. This year even Orrin Hatch has intro- 3
duced a child-bill. Only Phyllis Schlafly still writes what sound like parodies about
attempts to "sovietize the American family by warehousing babies in government-
licensed institutions . . . where they would be subjected to secular, unisex custodial
care . . ." There are now 10.5 million children under six being cared for by people
other than their parents. By 1995, two-thirds of all preschool children and four out
of five school children will have both parents in the work force. We have drifted
our way into a national child-care crisis. And finally we're paying attention.

"We have a clipping file that would warm your heart," says Helen Blank, who 4
has been a child-care stalwart through the lean years at the Children's Defense
Fund. In these files are dozens of freshly minted pieces on "The Child Care Crisis."
Stuffed between them are the reports of myriad polls showing that some two-thirds
of Americans believe the government should do some undesignated "more" about
child care.

"We've turned the corner in recognizing that society has responsibility for 5
child care," says Blank. But out of long experience she adds: "I'm still worried that
all this attention won't ultimately mean much for children."

The desire to turn a problem into a policy has energized the huge coalition 6
behind the ABC bill, the Act for Better Child Care. Last week, at a packed Senate
hearing, people representing vastly different worlds and worries—from an
American Express employer to the parents of a murdered child—came forward to
testify in favor of it.

For a price of $2,5 billion, the ABC bill would start up a national infrastruc- 7
ture for day care based on what the states are already doing. It's a package proposal
that would begin to deal with the quality as well as the quantity of care.

Of the money, 75 percent would be targeted to help moderate- and low- 8
income families pay for child care. Another 15 percent would go to training
providers, setting up standards and trying to keep people in the profession. The
final 10 percent would go to administrative costs.

If $2.5 billion sounds like a hefty new burden in a deficit-conscious era, Ellen 9
Galinsky of the Bank Street College, a coalition leader, says: "There are also costs
when children don't get cared for." Helen Blank puts the money in another context:
"The Congress spends money for emergencies all the time. When we need tankers
in the Gulf. When Len Bias dies. Well, child care is an emergency."

The bill's sponsors—37 in the Senate and 160 in the House—are counting on 10
a sense of emergency coming from many directions. All the talk about welfare
reform, after all, leads inexorably back to child care. The talk about educational
excellence flows directly down to the early years.

There are horror stories one day about an abusive day-care center, the next 11
day about children who played with matches or driers while their parents were at

work. Parents are worried about children, and employers are worried about workers, present and future. As one person summed it up at the hearings: "The future is in very small hands."

■ *Questions for . . .* The Child Care Crisis Provokes a Response by Ellen Goodman

Words to Note

comprehensive	the vast moral authority of the government
communal	neglect
private property	parodies
drifted	sovietize the American family
warehousing babies	child-care stalwart
lean	national infrastructure
hefty	

Language

1. Take a close look at Phyllis Schafly's words in the third paragraph. Which ones stand out? What does she mean by *sovietize* and *secular?* Does her word choice explain why she is so opposed to day care subsidized and operated by the government?
2. Can you spell out what President Nixon meant by "the vast moral authority" of the government?
3. At the end of the third paragraph, Goodman says we have drifted into a "national child-care crisis.? Take a look at her numbers. Do they bear out the word *crisis?* Or is it inflammatory word choice?

Style

1. What's Goodman's tone? Where does it come from?
2. Does she use too many transitional words and phrases? Do they clog and slow her sentences down?

Development and Organization

1. In how many different ways does Goodman use the words of others?
2. Has she told us enough about the ABC bill, so that we understand what the Senate and House voted on?

Discussion and Journal Writing

1. Why do so many Americans find the prospect of federally run child care threatening?
2. The Act for Better Child Care, the ABC bill, was defeated; we still have no national child-care act. Write for or against it.
3. If you are a parent and have used or decided not to use a day-care center, write about your decision and experience. Or interview a parent about the use of day care and write about what you find out.

ooooo

The Complete Life Story of Benjamin Peters, Homeless Baby

—Jonathan Kozol

Jonathan Kozol began his career as a teacher in Boston's inner city and has gone on to become an American muckraking journalist, a venerable American tradition. *The Night is Dark and I Am Far From Home* and *Savage Inequalities* are heartfelt and critical treatments of his first field, education, but Kozol has also written about American illiteracy and homelessness. This section is excerpted from Kozol's *Rachel and Her Children: Homeless Families in America*, which won the Robert F. Kennedy Journalism Award. This is the most nightmarish episode of that study. What does Kozol's account of Holly's story say about how homeless families are viewed and treated in America?

Holly Peters lives in the Henry Street Settlement House for now—a homeless   1
shelter, but a better one than she has ever known since she was pregnant in the
Martinique Hotel. She introduces me to her two children and husband, David, and
invites me to sit down. She's thin and small and rather nervous at the start. While
we talk she braids her hair.

I've already been informed that she is twenty-four and that she was taken   2
from her mother as a child and put into foster care. She tells me that she spent most
of her childhood in state-run institutions and in several foster homes throughout
New York. Despite the many interruptions in her education caused by frequent
transfers from one home or institution to another, she stayed in school until twelfth
grade. She became pregnant that year and quit school.

By this time, she had been reunited with her mother and was living with her.   3
After her child was born she entered a program of job training. It appears she had a

good employment record for the next few years. "I worked for Stouffer's. Now that was an interesting job. You got these carts: sandwiches and coffee, even a cash register, it's right here on this wagon. You're in an office building. So you go to every floor. You got a little bell. You ring your bell. If anybody on the floor wants something, they come to the wagon. Order a chef's salad, that's $2.60. Add the coffee, fifty cents. So that's $3.10. Give you five, you give them back their change. That's how it was."

Early on, however, she encountered a problem faced by many young and pret- 4 ty women with their male employers. "One job I had—you got to wonder if it's you or if it's just the way some people are. I had been there as a waitress for some time. The owner told me that he had an opening for a cashier. He had restaurants all over. Every borough of New York. He said he was goin' to take me to the one in Queens so the girl could show me how to do it. Maybe I'd start workin' there. I said okay.

"It was in the summertime. I wanted to go dressed appropriate. He told me: 5 'You can wear your regular clothes.' So he come there in the van and we go drivin' out to Queens. All of a sudden he pull up in front of this hotel. He offered me a hundred dollars if I go inside. I told him no. I wasn't goin' for it.

"Ever since that day he had me workin' like a slave. Never once in this here 6 job did I receive more than a hundred dollars. He was gonna pay me that much just to go inside of the hotel."

Her daughter was nearly two by now. Another child was born one year later. 7 She says she had returned to school to get her G.E.D. (high school equivalency), but that she was forced to interrupt her studies when her mother was evicted. Holly was obliged to turn to welfare for emergency assistance. She lived for eight months in two homeless shelters in Manhattan, only to be transferred to the Holland— viewed by many people as the worst of all hotels for homeless families in New York. While living there, she learned that she was pregnant for a third time.

It was winter. The hotel was poorly heated and, as she reports, the place was 8 rat infested. "Just about this hour—you see how it is outside?—they startin' to come out. Evening sun be goin' down, they playin' on the floor. We sit on the bed. We didn't move. They right there on the floor. Go [stamp!] like this! They race around. They right there on the floor."

After the Holland, Holly's wanderings become unclear. At various points in 9 the subsequent year she lived in at least seven hotels and, for certain nights at least, she slept in EAUs. "They tried to send me once to the Clemente shelter, but they wouldn't take me in. I got as far as the front door. They told me: 'Go back to the EAU and tell them not to send you here.'"

Holly moved into the Martinique in early 1984 and was living there until the 10 day that her third child, Benjamin, was born in late September. Mothers at the Martinique had no refrigerators at that time. Information given me by other women living there indicates that conditions in the Martinique were even worse than at the time of my first visit.

"Yes, I believe that it affected him," she says without assertiveness but with a 11 quiet note of acquiescence in accomplished fact. "How do I know? You do *not* know. I only know that life in that hotel was hell. I can't say that living in the

Martinique Hotel is why this happened. But I do believe a woman ought to have a better place to stay when she is carrying a child. If I would have had a little more, the proper medical care, the proper housing—if I had a place like this, I believe he would have had a better chance than what he did."

She finds a cigarette, talks to her children in the bedroom, says something to   12
her husband in the kitchen, and returns to find a match to light the cigarette.

"He was born on Saturday. He weighed four pounds, eight ounces. When I   13
came downstairs to see him Sunday, he was in the incubator. When I came on Monday, they was giving him I.V. When I came the next day, he had oxygen. Then they had to start giving him blood. I had to go around to people getting blood . . .

"Then from there he stayed, you know, inside the incubator. I used to cry.   14
Sometimes I'd pray. Something I've always done is pray. If I meet somebody— they start talkin' that there ain't no God, you know, I don't be bothered. Anyway, I used to go to see him and he laid there for three months. He didn't move."

Why was she forced to leave the Martinique? Holly says at first that she was   15
robbed repeatedly while she was there. From her later conversation it appears that the real reason had to do with David. She was afraid to be alone, especially while Benjamin's condition remained so uncertain. David was also scared to be without her. I believe it was his presence in her room that finally led to her eviction or departure.

"So I was in the Hotel Mayfair, near Times Square." She tells me of walking   16
from Forty-ninth Street to Beth Israel, standing by the baby's bed for hours. "I would stand there by his bed and pray. I have a Bible but I didn't need it. I prayed from my own.

"I had him baptized in the hospital. They asked me would I like a priest to   17
bless him. I said yes 'cause he was critical. The doctor said: 'Point-blank, I'm gonna tell you. I'll be honest with you—.'" She said Benjamin was not s'posed to live.

"I was not on WIC. Each time for my appointment, each time I got ready, he   18
was in the hospital. Medicaid, he wasn't on my card. I don't know why. Maybe, if a baby's in the hospital, they believe that he's provided for. He wasn't on my budget."

Some of her suppositions seem at first to be implausible. It does not make   19
sense to me that Benjamin was not on Medicaid and not on Holly's budget. When she tells me this, I mark her statement in my notes with a large question mark. An HRA report later confirms her words: "Infant not on IM [welfare] budget or Medicaid. . . . Social worker working on this."

The facts, as best I understand, are these: Some days after Benjamin was born   20
he contracted a viral infection. The virus left him partially blind, brain-damaged, deaf, hydrocephalic. He is also said to have developed a "seizure disorder." Three months after birth he was released by hospital officials and was taken to the Mayfair. Holly says that he was having seizures at the time. She had been told to give him phenobarbital, but she says she had to pay for it out of her other children's food allowance since he wasn't yet included on her budget. His weight was seven pounds.

I ask her if they had refrigerators at the Mayfair. 21

"Not in the Martinique. Not in the Mayfair. Nope." 22

She was evicted from the Mayfair five weeks later. The reason again, she 23 says, was her request that David stay with her and the refusal of the hotel to permit this. So it was winter, four months since the child's birth, a year since his conception. They were homeless.

"After that, they couldn't find no place for me to live. I was a little every- 24 where." She lists a number of hotels: the Madison, the Prospect, and (again) the Holland. "So we have been all over. I would carry all his things—disposable bottles, Pampers and his clothes, his phenobarbital, his toys, pregested milk. I carried it in bags each place we went. By that time he was completely blind."

The city reports that Benjamin did not have phenobarbital from January 4 to 25 January 8 and that he had twenty seizures in those days. On January 15, Benjamin had not been given Medicaid. A temporary card was issued on that date.

"All this time I had been looking for apartments. I saw lots of places that I 26 didn't have the money for. Two hundred seventy dollars was my budget limit. I used to tell them: 'All the money you will pay for me to stay in a hotel? You can't give me half that money *once* to pay the rent and rent deposit? I could get me an apartment. You won't ever see me anymore!'

"Even at the project the committee turned me down. They asked me if I ever 27 been evicted. If you ever been evicted they hold that against you. I said no. I have never been evicted 'cause I never had my own. I had only had my mother's home. Then because I had the kids, they say: 'We don't want them writin' on the walls.' I said: 'Look. My daughter's five. My son is three. Benjamin is four months old. Do you think this baby will be writin' on your walls?' They turned me down."

Benjamin was readmitted to Beth Israel twice during this time. Four nights 28 before his second admission, the HRA reports: "Baby stays overnight at EAU." On his release from the hospital on March 13, Holly was at the Holland Hotel for a second time. On March 20 she was told she had to leave the Holland, according to the HRA, "because of a City policy that allows families to stay 28 days." Two days later, after she had left the Holland, the HRA temporarily lost track of her: "case to be closed due to circumstances." Five days later, Benjamin was readmitted to Beth Israel.

Holly: "It was near the end of March. The baby had to go back to the hospital 29 again. His skull was widening. The fluid, I believe, was putting pressure on his brain. I stayed there with him in the hospital. EAU can't find me nothin' so I slept there with him in his room. David came to visit but he stayed out with his mother and the other children on Long Island. David's mother has a heart condition. She can't do but so much—I mean, takin' care of children, puttin' up with noise and the confusion. But this was a crisis so we had no choice. She done the best she can . . .

"So I was alone now with my baby. Apart from having no place else to stay, I 30 wanted to be with him at this time. I would get up each mornin' and I'd bathe him. I would wash his clothes. I preferred to care for him myself than anybody else. The people in the hospital can care for him but just so much. I wanted to be *with* him. Period!

"Even though I was afraid, it is the truth to say that I was happy. I was happy 31 to be with him in a place where he was safe and where we could not be evicted. Only place he had a home in all those months was in the hospital. That be one place where they don't evict you.

"David came to be with me while Benjamin was in the surgery. We waited for 32 him to come out—in recovery. They brought him up. They said: 'Well, we will see how he will be.' They wouldn't know if it was a success until a couple days."

Medical records indicate the hospital had put a "shunt" into the baby's skull 33 on April 22 to drain off fluid. Holly describes it to me vividly: "The shunt is a tube that goes into the brain. It goes under the skin, under one layer of the skin, and it goes down to the stomach. It was like a plastic tube, a fat tube, you could see under the skin. Goes to the stomach. You could see it, you could see the print of it under the skin."

On May 1, the hospital told her they were going to release him. This informa- 34 tion startled her and it would later startle many people in the press. A spokesperson for Beth Israel Hospital later said the hospital would never have released the baby had it known he had no proper shelter. The hospital, however, had provided Holly with a note to be submitted to her welfare worker. The letter asked that she be given shelter.

Holly tells me: "I was worried if it was too soon. 'Well, Mrs. Peters, he will 35 be all right.' But I was feelin' scared. First, because the shunt was in his head. Second, even with him bein' like he was, they couldn't find no place for me to be."

Because of the controversial nature of this story, I will add one observation 36 here. I do not believe the probity of health officials should be called into question. Holly speaks with obvious affection of her doctor. It is unimaginable that any of those who came in contact with the child wished him ill or that officials conscious-ly released him to the street. Hospitals all over the Unites States, faced with hun-dreds of thousands of unsheltered people and with millions of the very, very poor, do the best they can, and sometimes do so quite heroically. The issue is not medical or bureaucratic mishap in Manhattan. It is destitution.

"I told my social worker: 'I don't have no place to take him.' So she said that, 37 if I had no home, then I could leave him and they'd put him in an institution. I said: 'You are tellin' me that you can't help me in no kind of way? You know that I have no place to stay. Are you tellin' me ain't nobody can help me? I been tellin' you for weeks that I don't have no place to take him. Now you say that you are takin' him away? I am leavin' with my baby and you *know* that I ain't got no place to live.'

"So there was the two of us, Benjamin and me, we was discharged, and it was 38 evenin', like about four-thirty, five o'clock, and we was walkin' in the street.

"It was rainin', as a matter of fact. Not a warm night, kind of cool. I had to go 39 straight to the EAU. When I got there I went in and I explained: 'My son has had an operation.' I had brought the letter from the doctor. I had had that letter from day one. It didn't help me. I was on the street. For seven days, a whole week, I was on the street. That was in May. He come out from havin' surgery, shunt was in him, I was pretty weak. The EAU, to me, is in the street.

"I would sit from nine to five, the welfare center. They'd come out and give 40 me a referral: 'Here, go to the EAU. We couldn't find no place for you tonight.' Benjamin was in his carriage and I had the letter with me and we sat from nine to five there in the center and from five to eight o'clock at EAU. I lay him down. I was sleepin' in the chair. He was in his carriage. They say in the paper that he died there on the floor. That isn't true. I lay him in his carriage.

"All the time that we was on the street we carried all his things. Carryin' 41 everything, his milk, his phenobarbital. In the mornin' I would wake up in the chair. By that time I had the other children. David's mother couldn't keep them anymore. She was a sick woman. So David was with me—and the children. We were at the EAU. Get up in the mornin', wash 'em in the bathroom, comb their hair . . . I be scared he have another seizure.

"Only time they placed us was for two nights at a nice hotel in Queens. This 42 hotel is not for welfare and they let you know that right away. Tell you that you're there one night and you cannot come back. We stayed for two . . .

"You can say we got two nights, but it is not like *nights* because we didn't get 43 there until 3:00 A.M. How much sleep, then, is a child gettin'? Two children and a baby that has had an operation? Is that gettin' any sleep? So we get up and get the train. The rest of the time we stayed there in the center."

The city reports that, on the day of Benjamin's release after his surgery, Holly 44 brought him to the EAU in early evening. She was sent to the Turf, a Queens hotel, at one-thirty in the morning. Two nights later she was sent back to the Martinique but was turned away, she said, because there was no vacancy. She returned to the EAU at four-thirty in the afternoon on May 4 and waited there with Benjamin for *about ten hours*. At two-forty-five in the morning, they were assigned to a hotel. Benjamin and Holly spent the entire next night at the EAU.

"So he was goin' in the cold and rain. I was givin' him all that I could. They 45 wasn't givin' me a stable place for him to be. The place the shunt went in, his wound had gotten bad. It was sunk in and you could see his skull. His eyes was sinkin' too. And I said: 'David, look at him.' He looked at him. His father looked. And there was dark around his eyes. His eyes was dark and sinkin' in.

"Nothin' that I tell you, when it comes down to that baby, is untrue. You 46 could look at him and tell. One lady at the welfare that I didn't know her name, when I said that he was sick would she come over she would not come there to look. She would *not* come over there to see my son was sick. So I begged her: 'Please, my baby's dyin'.' I had brought the letter I was s'posed to. I said: 'David, look at Benjamin's eyes is sinkin' in.' 'Cause you could look at him and tell.

"That was the seventh of May. Then the lady in the welfare said: 'The baby 47 looks like it is dyin'.' So we raised him up. We lifted him again and looked and you could see it. You could *see*. He had these scars from the I.V. He had a scar up here. There was a hole like where the needle was put in. We was sittin' in the EAU, in Brooklyn, on the right-hand side.

"I said: 'David, take him to the hospital. I'll sit here and wait and see in case 48 they find a place for us to stay.' He asked someone if they have the money for a cab. Takin' the train meant switchin' trains. I didn't think we had the time. But they said no. They did not pay money for no cab. They did offer us to call an ambulance. That was no good. The ambulance would take you to the nearest hospital. Brooklyn Hospital's the nearest hospital to EAU. We had to get him to Beth Israel. That's where all his records was. If we took him to another hospital, by the time they find out what is wrong he would be dead. I said we was gonna to take him to the hospital that know him from the day that he was born. The hospital that *knows* his situation."

David, who has interrupted only once or twice up to this point, fills in the rest: 49 "I got ten dollars from a friend who knows me and I took a taxi to Beth Israel. I brought him in. As soon as I come in they ask me what had happened, where he was? I said: 'We've been out there at the welfare.' The doctor said: 'Are there sick children there?' And I said yes. At welfare there is nothin' but sick children. Little kids with coughs and runnin' noses runnin' up and down. They're runnin' everywhere. You know? So he said: 'The baby caught a stomach virus.' That explains why he had diarrhea. He was sick to start with. When you add the stomach virus . . . He had been dehydrated so bad. The skin on him was dry, like this. That was seven days since he come home. So he was in the hospital again. He stayed there after that."

After a silence, he goes on: "I came back to Brooklyn, to the EAU. Holly 50 says: 'They found a place for me to stay.' I was thinkin' they have pity for her now—and ever since. She don't need no sympathy no more. She needed it back then. Now he dyin', now you offer her a place to live."

After Benjamin's death, the city seemed to place much of the blame upon his 51 parents. Holly, said the city, had been beaten by the father of her other children. As a consequence, the *New York Times* reported, "the baby was not fed for several hours." Holly denies both accusations. But, assuming that these things are true, it remains incomprehensible that a disaster fostered, countenanced, ignored for over half a year should retroactively be blamed upon parental failure—an alleged delay of "several hours" in the feeding of a child—at a point at which his health had been already damaged past repair.

The city also maintained it gave the family shelter, transportation, food. In 52 fact, according to the Legal Aid Society, the city galvanized itself to action only on the night before her baby was brought back into the hospital to die and only after Legal Aid, having been alerted to the child's plight, had telephoned the HRA, demanding that the child be afforded suitable shelter.

HRA officials placed a special emphasis upon the fact that Holly was repeat- 53 edly evicted from hotels because of David's presence or that she rejected placements in hotels where he would not have been allowed to stay. Holly places far more emphasis upon the dangerous conditions in the various hotels and on the fact that she was forced to sit and wait so many hours on so many evenings at the EAU while Benjamin was gravely ill. But, granting that the statements of the HRA are true, we may wonder at an agency of government that, even unwittingly, punishes a mother in a time of crisis for her desperation to remain close to the one adult in the entire world who seems to love her. Why would a society alarmed by the decline in family values try to separate a mother from her child's father at the time she needs him most and when he displays that willingness to share responsibility whose absence we repeatedly deplore?

This, then, is a case not of the breakdown of a family but of a bureaucratic 54 mechanism that *disintegrates* the family, tearing apart a mother and father in a time of shared ordeal. Sharing pain does not merely bring relief to people under siege; it often forms a bond that gives them stronger reason to remain together later. So the efforts of the city, as belated as they were, to offer Holly shelter if she would agree to shed her child's father, like its offer to remove her as a parent altogether and to place the child in an institution—not because the child *needed* institutional care but because the city could not give her a safe home—represent destructive social policy on several levels.

I have deleted some of the words that David spoke while Holly told me of the 55 months after her baby's birth. He is recounting the events of early January 1985 after Benjamin was discharged from Beth Israel. They were living in a hotel near Times Square. It appears, from what he says, that Benjamin may not yet have been entirely blind.

"Nighttime he'd be with us in our bed. I'd be here. Holly be there. He be in 56 the middle. Plenty of nights I'd jump because I had forgot that he was there. He would work his way down in the bed. Sometimes he would get under my arm and go to sleep.

"He used to smile—sit and smile. He would gurgle and make sounds like he 57 was tryin' to speak. He'd go [sings a long contented baby's sigh] and then he'd go to sleep. Go *right* to sleep. He never cried but once.

"When she would go out I'd stay with him, give him his bath. Feedin' him, I'd 58 sit him on my lap. I would talk to him. He would make sounds like he was talkin' back. Once I had him in the bathtub with me, washin' him, and he start slidin' down. I pick him up, he slide back down. I let the water hit 'bout to his neck. He sit there in the water and he move his head and look at me like 'What you doin' to me?' So I fed him and I got him dressed to take him for a walk. Go in the stroller. Go around the block. I have some friends. I liked to show him off.

"So I was goin' to take him out. He fell asleep on me! I put him in the bed. I 59 watch him. This is how he moves: He use his head.

"That mornin', like I say: A split-second reaction. I turned around and he was 60 slidin' off. I could see his little feet just danglin' in the air. I reached down. I picked him up. That was the first time that he ever cried! I just looked at him. I was amazed. I was shakin'. Four months old and he had never made a cry till then. I just sat there lookin' at him, hopin' that he'd cry again.

"So I set him back in bed and I laid down tryin' to sleep. I pat him softly on 61 his back to make him go to sleep. Soon as I close my eyes I'd open them and he is starin' at my eyes. Then he'd close his eyes, I'd open mine, then he'll close his, and every time I open mine he close his eyes. I just had fun with him, that's all. I had a lot of hope during that time."

■ *Questions for . . .* The Complete Life Story of Benjamin Peters, Homeless Baby by Jonathan Kozol

Words to Note

state-run institutions	foster homes	obliged
rat infested	acquiescence	incubator
WIC	HRA	EAU
viral	hydrocephalic	evicted
shunt	destitution	incomprehensible
galvanized	deplore	belated
destructive social policy		

Language

1. How do the institutional acronyms that pepper the piece flavor it?
2. Compare and contrast the language of Kozol and Peters? Should Kozol have corrected her speech? His own?

Style

1. What gives the following sentence its tone: "But, assuming that these things are true, it remains incomprehensible that a disaster fostered, countenanced, ignored for over half a year should retroactively be blamed upon parental failure—an alleged delay of 'several hours' in the feeding of a child—at a point at which his health had been already damaged past repair."
2. Do the two voices that run through this account create dissonance or strength?

Development and Organization

1. How does Kozol move in and out of Holly Peters's account of her son Benjamin's death?
2. Does Kozol tell us enough about Holly, her background, her experiences with Beth Israel Hospital, the EAU, and the HRA to understand the role she played in her son's death?

Discussion and Journal Writing

1. Who killed Benjamin Peters?
2. Is Kozol too easy on Holly Peters? Do you believe his account of her son's death?

ooooo

The Teflon Father

—Letty Cottin Pogrebin

Letty Cottin Pogrebin, a founding editor of *Ms* magazine, has been writing and speaking about feminist issues for a few decades now. In her own essays, she tends to highlight the political in the personal, which has been one of the most popular and successful writing strategies of late twentieth-century feminism. According to Sara Evans, in her book on the rise of the Women's Movement, *Personal Politics,* it is a habit of mind feminists acquired while serving a political apprenticeship in the Civil Rights Movement.

1   I used to complain about my stepmother monopolizing my father's time, always dragging him to *her* relatives, buying my kids such tacky birthday presents—until one day my husband said, "Stop letting your father off the hook."

2   "Huh?" I responded, sublimely obtuse.

3   "He does what he pleases most of the time," said Bert. "And if he cared more, he'd visit more and buy the presents himself." The idea that my father was responsible for all that inattentiveness struck me with the force of a fist. It was much easier to blame my wicked stepmother than to see my father for what he was and had always been—inconsiderate, self-centered, and largely absent from my life.

4   He was out every night of my childhood; not gambling, whoring, or drinking—but presiding over meetings. My father was a big shot in so many civic and religious organizations there were not enough nights for all the meetings that fed his ego. But I was able to ignore his absences because of how deftly my mother compensated. Like millions of women, she both mothered me and magnified his fathering for my sake. Whenever he graced us with his time she embellished each experience—a trip to the zoo, a Sunday of horseback riding—until those rare outings slid into my memory as family traditions. She provided simultaneous translation of his behavior, filling his silences, protecting me from the truth of his neglect; she reinterpreted his absences as measures of his importance, thus helping me to substitute my daughter-pride for his father-love.

5   I was 15 when she died. Now there was no one to cover for him, but she had trained me well in the art of paternal invention—a survival technique for the women men leave behind. I went off to college at 16 with a mythology constructed to fit my circumstances: I was a motherless child with a very important father who respected me as an equal, who gave me my independence. That's why he rarely called or visited. He knew I could make it on my own.

6   When I was 17, without a word of warning, he sold my childhood home and all its furnishings. I forgave him because he was a man and couldn't be expected to know that those objects might contain memories of my mother or understand how a

teenage girl might be attached to her "things." A few months later, he remarried without preparing me for the news. They moved to a one-bedroom apartment with a daybed for me in the vestibule. I forgave him because his actions fit my mythology: we were both adults living our own lives. I decided this was his way of setting me free.

For years, I kept decoding him in a positive light. It took me a long time to blame *him*—and all the fathers who have been inadequate, neglectful, cold, silent, unavailable, insensitive, absent or abusive to their children. Rethinking my own experience, which was hardly the worst of the genre, has led me to ask that fathers be held accountable and fatherhood be "deconstructed"—its distortions named and acknowledged—and then reconstructed to suit the needs of children, not the pathologies of men. Father failure is a continuum of sins, the worst of which can be found in child abuse data: nationally, 90 percent of sexual abuse is committed by men; a study of children in battered women's shelters found that, in 70 percent of the cases, men were the victimizers. Why mask these facts by talking about "family" violence? Other failures are discoverable in statistics quantifying men's abandonment, neglect, delinquency in child support; still more surfaces in social science research, friends' reminiscences, confessional literature, newspaper stories of ordinary folks, and books by the rich and famous. Bill Cosby, the guru of male parenting, writes jokingly, "My own father used me for batting practice," but otherwise barely mentions him. Bette Davis' father left his family when the actress was seven. Actor Gene Hackman's father walked in and out of his life. Walter Sisulu, respected strategist of the African National Congress, was abandoned by his father in early childhood; so was Joyce Carol Oates. 7

Millions of men are little more than sperm donors in their children's lives. They leave their children with mothers who are trapped in poverty and despair and cannot possibly provide for them adequately. These men are deserters. When a man deserts the army, he is court-martialed, stigmatized, despised. When a father deserts his own flesh and blood, all we do is (sometimes) track him down to get him to pay the freight, but otherwise he's off the hook. 8

The deserting father is to the abusive father as disappearing ink is to the indelible pen. I'm not sure which is worse: to have a blank where the male parent should be or to suffer a lifelong stain. But in both cases, and in the case of the most common father failure—father silence—children seem able to grow and forgive the man. 9

In her book *Like Father, Like Daughter,* Suzanne Fields determined after hundreds of interviews that "Daddy hides and we forever seek him, only occasionally flushing him out of his hiding places . . . behind his newspaper . . . behind his wife . . . behind his authority. Most of all, he hides behind his fear of intimacy." Fields forgives fathers because it is "the nature of the beast." 10

"Some silences are maintained to enable the nonspeaker to listen to the world," writes Harry Brod in the introduction to *A Mensch Among Men.* "Others are maintained to compel the world to listen to the nonspeaker. Such is the male silence of which my father and I and our fathers before us partook. Relieving our- 11 selves of the obligation to communicate and disclose our feelings and desires, others are forced to be inordinately attentive to us so that they can decode our muted messages, or simply not learn what we choose to keep hidden. The silence of my father's pain was also the silence of his power."

Like my mother, Harry Brod's mother covered for her husband. I'm con- 12 vinced mothers must let fathers sink or swim. Otherwise, children are the ones who drown.

While both women and men experience inadequate fathering, men cope by 13 shutting down their needs while women are more likely to excuse, explain, and forgive. Thus fathers benefit twice from the healing impulses of female acculturation. First, men benefit from wives who run interference for them—including the feminist version of all this: compensatory nonsexist chid-rearing. That's where a mother teaches ideal male behavior the children are not actually witnessing in their fathers.

Second, fathers reap the undeserved benefits of the daughters' mother-mediat- 14 ed view and culturally trained empathy. Those girls whose mothers choose to bad-mouth rather than mediate or enhance the father often imagine themselves to have a "special" understanding of Daddy. Feminist-minded daughters may apply a deeper critique, but ironically, our command of the power complexities is frequently reconstituted as a bemused "there he goes again" tolerance, or an activist-style one-on-one rescue operation. Add these female-specific impulses to the desire of all children to think well of their parents and you have a powerful incentive for father forgiveness.

Many of us do not hold our father accountable for behavior we would find 15 unforgivable in our mothers. It is as if mothers were coated with Velcro and fathers with Teflon, not just at home but in the world. A mother who beats her kids is a monster, a violent father has to be Joel Steinberg before *he* is called a monster.

Remember the roommate test? We used to ask ourselves whether we were tol- 16 erating behavior from our male partners—sloppiness, task evasion, and so on—that we would not accept from a female roommate. A similar test of our relationships with our parents might inspire us to add some Teflon to Mom and Velcro to Dad. I'm not arguing against forgiveness as a moral choice, nor suggesting that direct negotiation of improved father-daughter relations is "politically correct." But father failure must be confronted as a *systemic* problem. While it's obvious that some individuals need help healing the wounds inflicted by inadequate or abusive father-ing, the total picture must not be privatized, viewed merely as an interpersonal difficulty to be repaired in the courtroom or therapist's office. Nor must it be compart-mentalized, as if the problem of fathers who don't pay child support is disconnected from the problems of fathers who disappear, or batter, or coerce their daughters into sex.

Put together, the multiple shortcomings of fathers add up to a social calamity 17 of major proportions: an epidemic of role dysfunction whose deleterious impact on children is as serious as malnutrition, illiteracy, the drug scourge, or anything else that wins headlines. The trouble lies in the parental double standard and the whole institution of fatherhood. The solution can only be a radical one, that is, one that goes to its root: to the way we raise boys to be men but not fathers, and the way we raise girls to let men get away with it.

■ *Questions for . . .* The Teflon Father by Letty Cottin Pogrebin

Words to Note

monopolizing	dragging	tacky
sublimely obtuse	magnified	graced
embellished	slid	vestibule
decoded	pathologies of men	sperm donors
deserters	stigmatized	female-specific
a systemic problem	social calamity	impulses
role dysfunction	deleterious	scourge
parental double standard		

Language

1. Why does Cottin Pogrebin take issue with the expression *family violence?*
2. Is she counter-productively provocative when she calls millions of men little more than "sperm donors" in the lives of their children?
3. She refers to "the healing impulses of female acculturation." Translate. What does she mean? Do you agree with her assumptions?

Style

1. Could Cottin Pogrebin have used simpler English and more direct phrasing when she wrote, "Second, fathers reap the undeserved benefits of the daughters' mother-mediated view and culturally trained empathy"? Or has she said exactly what she means, word for word?
2. Does her Teflon metaphor work for fathers? Her Velcro metaphor for mothers? Why or why not?
3. Why did she put *systemic* in italics?

Development and Organization

1. Cottin Pogrebin uses her experience with her father as a way into a culture-wide critique of the institution of fatherhood. Is that the best approach, or would it have been more effective to begin with the generalizations as a frame for her experience?
2. Do her discussions of Fields's and Brod's books add any ideas that are indispensable to her argument, or could those paragraphs have been cut?

3. Does she provide enough evidence to support her claim that "the multiple shortcomings of fathers add up to a social calamity of major proportions"?

Discussion and Journal Writing

1. What are the practical implications of what Cottin Pogrebin says? Are there laws we should pass? Judicial procedures that should be changed? What are the personal implications?
2. Cottin Pogrebin claims that a mother who beats her kids is a monster but a father has to be a Joel Steinberg before he is a monster. Do you agree? Would most people you know agree with that assessment?
3. Do you agree that there is a parental double standard in American culture? Would you define it the same way Cottin Pogrebin does?
4. How would Pogrebin respond to Bly's ideas in the next selection? Bly to Pogrebin?

ooooo

Father Hunger

—Robert Bly

Robert Bly is a poet, storyteller, translator, and worldwide lecturer. His poetry has won many awards, including the National Book Award. *Iron John,* the book from which this selection was excerpted, was his first full-length book of prose. It was preceded by a PBS special on Bly with Bill Moyers—"A Gathering of Men." Bly lives on a lake in Minnesota with his wife Ruth.

Disturbances in Sonhood

As I've participated in men's gatherings since the early 1980s, I've heard one 1 statement over and over from American males, which has been phrased in a hundred different ways: "There is not enough father." The sentence implies that father is a substance like salt, which in earlier times was occasionally in short supply, or like groundwater, which in some areas now has simply disappeared.

Geoffrey Gorer remarked in his book *The American People* that for a boy to 2 become a man in the United States in 1940 only one thing was required: namely, that he reject his father. He noticed, moreover, that American fathers expected to be rejected. Young men in Europe, by contrast, have traditionally imagined the father to be a demonic being whom they must wrestle with (and the son in Kafka's "The Judgment" does wrestle his father to the death and loses). Many sons in the United States, however, visualize the father as a simple object of ridicule to be made fun of, as, in fact, he is so often in comic strips and television commercials. One young man summed it up: "A father is a person who rustles newspapers in the living room."

Clearly, "father water" in the home has sunk below the reach of most wells.   3

Too Little Father

When the father-table, the groundwater, drops, so to speak, and there is too lit-   4
tle father, instead of too much father, the sons find themselves in a new situation. What do they do: drill for new father water, ration the father water, hoard it, distill mother water into father water?

Traditional cultures still in existence seem to have plenty of father. In so-   5
called traditional cultures, many substitute fathers work with the young man. Uncles loosen the son up, or tell him about women. Grandfathers give him stories. Warrior types teach weaponry and discipline, old men teach ritual and soul—all of them honorary fathers.

Bruno Bettelheim noticed, too, that in most traditional cultures Freud's ver-   6
sion of father-son hatred doesn't hold. The wordless tension between fathers and sons in Vienna, which he assumed to be universal and based on sexual jealousy, was, in Bettelheim's opinion, true mostly in Vienna in the late nineteenth century.

Fathers and sons in most tribal cultures live in an amused tolerance of each   7
other. The son has a lot to learn, and so the father and son spend hours trying and failing together to make arrowheads or to repair a spear or track a clever animal. When a father and son do spend long hours together, which some fathers and sons still do, we could say that a substance almost like food passes from the older body to the younger.

The contemporary mind might want to describe the exchange between father   8
and son as a likening of attitude, a miming, but I think a physical exchange takes place, as if some substance was passing directly to the cells. The son's body—not his mind—receives and the father gives this food at a level far below conscious-ness. The son does not receive a hands-on healing, but a body-on healing. His cells receive some knowledge of what an adult masculine body is. The younger body learns at what frequency the masculine body vibrates. It begins to grasp the song that the adult male cells sing, and how the charming, elegant, lonely, courageous, half-shamed male molecules dance.

During the long months the son spent in the mother's body, his body got well   9
tuned to female frequencies: it learned how a woman's cells broadcast, who bows to whom in that resonant field, what animals run across the grassy clearing, what the body listens for at night, what the upper and lower fears are. How firmly the son's body becomes, before birth and after, a good receiver for the upper and lower frequencies of the mother's voice! The son either tunes to that frequency or he dies.

Now, standing next to the father, as they repair arrowheads, or repair plows, 10
or wash pistons in gasoline, or care for birthing animals, the son's body has the
chance to retune. Slowly, over months or years, that son's body-strings begin to
resonate to the harsh, sometimes demanding, testily humorous, irreverent, impatient, opinionated, forward-driving, silence-loving older masculine body. Both male
and female cells carry marvelous music, but the son needs to resonate to the masculine frequency as well as to the female frequency.

Sons who have not received this retuning will have father-hunger all their 11
lives. I think calling the longing "hunger" is accurate: the young man's body lacks
salt, water, or protein, just as a starving person's body and lower digestive tract
lack protein. If it finds none, the stomach will eventually eat up the muscles themselves. Such hungry sons hang around older men like the homeless do around a
soup kitchen. Like the homeless, they feel shame over their condition, and it is
nameless, bitter, unexpungeable shame.

Women cannot, no matter how much they sympathize with their starving sons, 12
replace that particular missing substance. The son later may try to get it from a
woman his own age, but that doesn't work either.

Distrust of Older Men

Only one hundred and forty years have passed since factory work began in 13
earnest in the West, and we see in each generation poorer bonding between father
and son, with catastrophic results. A close study of the Enclosure Act of England
shows that the English government, toward the end of that long legislative process,
denied the landless father access to free pasture and common land with the precise
aim of forcing him, with or without his family, to travel to the factory. The South
Africans still do that to black fathers today.

By the middle of the twentieth century in Europe and North America a mas- 14
sive change had taken place: the father was working, but the son could not see him
working.

Throughout the ancient hunter societies, which apparently lasted thousands of 15
years—perhaps hundreds of thousands—and throughout the hunter-gatherer societies that followed them, and the subsequent agricultural and craft societies, fathers
and sons worked and lived together. As late as 1900 in the United States about
ninety percent of fathers were engaged in agriculture. In all these societies the son
characteristically saw his father working at all times of the day and all seasons of
the year.

When the son no longer sees that, what happens? After thirty years of working 16
with young German men, as fatherless in their industrial society as young
American men today, Alexander Mitscherlich, whom we spoke of in the first chapter, developed a metaphor: a hole appears in the son's psyche. When the son does
not see his father's workplace, or what he produces, does he imagine his father to
be a hero, a fighter for good, a saint, or a white knight? Mitscherlich's answer is
sad: demons move into that empty place—demons of suspicion.

The demons, invisible but talkative, encourage suspicion of all older men. 17

Such suspicion effects a breaking of the community of old and young men. One could feel this distrust deepen in the sixties: "Never trust anyone over thirty."

The older men in the American military establishment and government did 18 betray the younger men in Vietnam, lying about the nature of the war, remaining in safe places themselves, after having asked the young men to be warriors and then in effect sending them out to be ordinary murderers. And so the demons have had a lot to work with in recent American history. The demons urge all young men to see *Lawrence of Arabia* and *Dead Poets Society* because they remind us how corrupt all men in authority are and how thoroughly they betray the young male idealist. Mentorship becomes difficult to sustain; initiation is rejected.

Anthropologists affected by those demons suggest that elders in primitive cul- 19 tures always perform sadistic and humiliating acts on young men under cover of initiatory ritual. A young architect controlled by the demons secretly rejoices when a Louis Sullivan building gets knocked down; and the rock musician plays with a touch of malice the music that his grandfather could never understand.

This distrust is not good for the son's stability either. The son, having used up 20 much of his critical, cynical energy suspecting old men, may compensate by being naive about women—or men—his own age. A contemporary man often assumes that a woman knows more about a relationship than he does, allows a woman's moods to run the house, assumes that when she attacks him, she is doing it "for his own good." Many marriages are lost that way. He may be unsuspecting in business also: he may allow a man his own age to steal all his money, or he may accept humiliation from another man under cover of friendship or teaching. Having all the suspicion in one place—toward older men—often leads to disaster in relationships and great isolation in spirit and soul.

In the next decade we can expect these demons of suspicion to cause more and 21 more damage to men's vision of what a man is, or what the masculine is. Between twenty and thirty percent of American boys now live in a house with no father present, and the demons there have full permission to rage.

It seems possible, too, that as more and more mothers work out of the house, 22 and cannot show their daughters what they produce, similar emotions may develop in the daughter's psyche, with a consequent suspicion of grown women. But that remains to be seen.

Temperament Without Teaching

When a father, absent during the day, returns home at six, his children receive 23 only his temperament, and not his teaching. If the father is working for a corporation, what is there to teach? He is reluctant to tell his son what is really going on. The fragmentation of decision making in corporate life, the massive effort that produces the corporate willingness to destroy the environment for the sake of profit, the prudence, even cowardice, that one learns in bureaucracy—who wants to teach that?

We know of rare cases in which the father takes sons or daughters into his fac- 24 tory, judge's chambers, used-car lot, or insurance building, and those efforts at teaching do reap some of the rewards of teaching craft cultures. But in most families today, the sons and daughters receive, when the father returns home at six, only his disposition, or his temperament, which is usually irritable and remote.

What the father brings home today is usually a touchy mood, springing from 25 powerlessness and despair mingled with longstanding shame and the numbness peculiar to those who hate their jobs. Fathers in earlier times could often break through their own humanly inadequate temperaments by teaching rope-making, fishing, posthole digging, grain cutting, drumming, harness making, animal care, even singing and storytelling. That teaching sweetened the effect of the temperament.

The longing for the father's blessing through teaching is still present, if a little 26 fossilized; but the children do not receive that blessing. The son particularly receives instead the nonblesser, the threatened, jealous "Nobodaddy," as Blake calls him: "No One's Father"—the male principle that lives in the Kingdom of Jealousy.

A father's remoteness may severely damage the daughter's ability to partici- 27 pate good-heartedly in later relationships with men. Much of the rage that some women direct to the patriarchy stems from a vast disappointment over this lack of teaching from their own fathers.

We have said that the father as a living force in the home disappeared when 28 those forces demanding industry sent him on various railroads out of his various villages.

No historical models prepare us for the contemporary son's psychic condition. 29 To understand the son's psyche we have to imagine new furniture, new psychic figures, new demon possessions, new terrors, new incapacities, new flights.

Enormous changes have appeared at the last minute; few of us—fathers or 30 sons—are prepared for such vast changes. I have mentioned so far the young men's father-hunger and the starving bodies of the sons; also the demons of suspicion who have invaded the psyches of young men; and the son's dissatisfaction when he receives only temperament and no teaching.

■ *Questions for* . . . Father Hunger by Robert Bly

Words to Note

implies	demonic	wrestle
visualize	ridicule	rustles
father water	father-table	mother water
distill	loosen	wordless tension
amused tolerance	tuned	between fathers
female frequencies	retune	and sons
father-hunger	nameless	bitter
unexpungeable shame	psyche	demons

sadistic	humiliating	numbness
fragmentation	disposition	temperament
irritable	remote	touchy
mingled		

Language

1. Interpret Bly's language and his metaphors in the following sentence: "It [the son's body] begins to grasp the song that adult male cells sing, and how the charming, elegant, lonely, courageous, half-shamed male molecules dance."
2. What or who are the demons he talks about? Is *demons* the right word?

Style

1. Bly writes of father water, half-shamed male molecules dancing, and the frequencies of female cells that children learn in the womb. His style is metaphoric, which is not surprising when one learns poetry is Bly's day job. But do his metaphors work? Do they deepen your understanding of his message, or do they obscure it?
2. In paragraphs 8 and 10, there are traffic jams of modifiers in front of the words *molecule* and *body*. Can he do that? How are we supposed to read such extravagantly phrased sentences?

Development and Organization

1. How much time does Bly cover? Is his movement through history easy or difficult to follow?
2. Bly does explain some of his ideas; he even backs some of them up with the authority of experts—Freud and Bettelheim are two of the authorities he refers to. But he is also given to making pronouncements and assertions, in the manner of a tribal elder or a priest, that stand or fall on the light they shed. His pronouncements, like his metaphors, are another rhetorical habit he brings with him from his poetry, but do they work in the wide-open spaces of prose? He tells us that in traditional cultures, when a son works alongside his father, "a substance almost like food passes from the older body to the younger." He tells us fetuses in the womb become attuned to the frequencies of a woman's cells, that demons appear when a son does not see his father's workplace, and that some of the anger women vent at the patriarchy stems from the absence of father-teaching. What do you make of these pronouncements? Should he have explained himself more fully?

Discussion and Journal Writing

1. In Bly's opinion, what impact did the advent of factory work have on bonding between fathers and sons? Why? What do you think of this theory?
2. What is Bly's attitude towards women, generally, and mothers, specifically? Is there enough to go on in this piece?
3. Is Bly right? Is Cottin Pogrebin right? Can they both be right?

ooooo

As Mother Killed Her Son, Protectors Observed Privacy

—Celia W. Dugger

Celia W. Dugger is a reporter for the *New York Times*. She specializes in family problems and issues. In the following article, she skillfully moves back and forth from Yaakov Riegler's death to the system that allowed his mother to beat and maim him and his siblings again and again until she finally killed Yaakov.

In 1986, Shulamis Riegler beat her 8-year-old son Israel so badly that he was   1
hospitalized in a coma. Doctors noticed human bite marks on his shoulder.

When the boy recovered, he and his two little brothers spent several years in   2
foster care before going home in 1988 and 1989.

Then, barely a year later, Mrs. Riegler beat another son, Yaakov. She twisted   3
his leg so viciously that she heard his thigh bone crack. The retarded boy, 8 years
old, 3-feet-8 and 48 pounds, was taken to the hospital in a coma and never woke up.

Known as Abusive

Yaakov was one of seven children who died in 1990 after repeated beatings   4
and whose families were known to New York City's child welfare system as abusive or neglectful, a recent city report found.

In the report, the only public accounting of how the city's Human Resources   5
Administration handled such cases, Yaakov was an anonymous statistic, unnamed
because of strict state confidentiality laws that protect the privacy of informants and
families, even, as in Yaakov's case, when the mother has pleaded guilty to killing
her child. Mrs. Riegler is to be sentenced today to 71/2 to 15 years in prison.

Yaakov's story, pieced together through interviews and medical, school and   6
court records, is about an affectionate if sometimes demanding boy, who could
speak only in monosyllables, but whose bruises and broken bones would later tell
of his pain. It is about a mother who married at 19, had children quickly and was
overwhelmed by the unending tasks of homemaking.

Agency's Scattered Work

And it is about a child welfare system that was unable, despite repeated warn-   7
ings, to help the child. The work the agency did was so scattered and uncoordinated
that at one point a city worker was ending the supervision of Mrs. Riegler—
because she had supposedly learned to be a nonviolent parent—on the same day
that another worker was investigating a new report that Yaakov was being abused.
And confidentiality laws also played a part, preventing Mrs. Riegler's probation
officer from finding out about new reports of abuse in her home.

Lastly, it is a story about a pediatrician who, though he knew of Mrs.   8
Riegler's abusive history and was called on several times to treat Yaakov's
wounds, said he recognized in the Riegler household only a harried mother, not a
battered child.

When Mrs. Riegler pleaded guilty in State Supreme Court last month, Judge   9
Francis X. Egitto condemned the city's child protection system—a system whose
goal is to reunite children with their natural parents whenever possible—and the
boy's doctor for not saving Yaakov's life.

"It's not just Mrs. Riegler who is guilty of the death of Yaakov," the judge   10
said.

BIRTH

'Confidentiality' for the Mother

Yaakov Riegler was born on July 1, 1982, the third son of Moses and   11
Shulamis Riegler. The family lived in the insular Orthodox Jewish world of
Borough Park, Brooklyn.

Mrs. Riegler had trouble coping with the demands of raising and disciplining   12
her boys, she later told a psychiatrist. Sometimes she lost her temper and struck
them.

Yaakov was almost 4 when she beat her eldest son, Israel, so harshly that he   13
arrived at Maimonides Medical Center unconscious. Medical records show that his
body was covered with bruises and that he had burns in various stages of healing on
his face, back and arms.

"The child is not so good on his feet and he falls a lot and could have hit his   14
head," Mrs. Riegler told the hospital social worker at the time.

But later that year, Mrs. Riegler pleaded guilty to attempted assault and was   15
placed on five years probation, with a requirement that she receive psychiatric
treatment. Her children were sent into foster care. The two oldest, Israel and Zelig,
6, were sent to live with an uncle by the Ohel Children's Home and Family

Services, a private foster care agency under contract with the city. Yaakov was sent to a home that cared for retarded children.

Mrs. Riegler regularly attended appointments with a Manhattan psychiatrist, 16 Arthur Cronen, and began visiting her children in late 1987.

Dr. Cronen said Mrs. Riegler had very little self-confidence and a troubled 17 marriage. "She had no pressure valve, no place to ventilate," he said. She told the doctor she felt that her husband undermined her when she disciplined the children: when she tried to get the boys to bed, her husband would say, "Oh, don't listen to her."

Dr. Cronen tried to get Mr. Riegler to come for counseling, too, but after the 18 first few sessions he quit, saying his back hurt. So Dr. Cronen concentrated on teaching Mrs. Riegler how to control her temper. She seemed to be improving, he said, and did well on extended visits with her children.

Between September 1988 and September 1989 Mrs. Riegler got her children 19 back one at a time, Yaakov last. She also gave birth to a boy, Ben-Zion. And she stopped seeing her psychiatrist. Her last face-to-face session with Dr. Cronen was in March 1989. After that, they only chatted occasionally on the phone. "It seemed O.K.," Dr. Cronen recalled. "She said things were fine."

SCHOOL

Beloved Aide Grows Suspicious

When Yaakov came home, he was enrolled at Public School 205. He was 20 happy with simple things: playing with construction paper, saying his colors out loud. He doted on Jo Anne Pesce, a teacher's helper in his class.

"He always wanted to hold my hand," Ms. Pesce said.   21

But just a month after school began, Ms. Pesce began to notice that Yaakov 22 was bruised. One day, he pointed to his chest and said, "Boo-boo." She lifted his shirt and saw bruises on his chest and back. Later, she said, she saw an impression of fingernails on his cheek. Another time, the skin above his right ear was bruised and cut.

Worried, Ms. Pesce went to the school guidance counselor, Elizabeth 23 Lantiere. Mrs. Riegler's explanation was that Yaakov had fallen down on the kitchen floor.

Mrs. Lantiere, unaware of Mrs. Riegler's history of abusiveness, was uncer- 24 tain what to do. The boy was difficult to understand. He had brothers at home. Maybe they fought, Mrs. Lantiere told herself.

'I Didn't Think of This'

"Jo Anne was most worried," Mrs. Lantiere said. "She kept pestering me. But 25 I didn't think of this kind of abuse from the mother."

Nonetheless, on Nov. 27, 1989, Mrs. Lantiere called the state child abuse line. 26 Her report stated only that there were marks on Yaakov's face, ear, and back.

The case was assigned to a city child abuse investigator, David Schwartz, who 27 had been hired eight months earlier—one of hundreds of caseworkers hired to handle an exploding number of abuse reports.

Mr. Schwartz went to the school the day after Mrs. Lantiere called. Ms. Pesce 28 said she lifted Yaakov's shirt to show Mr. Schwartz the marks on the boy's back. "He was shocked," she said.

But that same day in Family Court, the Human Resources Administration, 29 apparently unaware of the new investigation by one of its own workers, asked a judge to approve a final return home for the Riegler children and end its supervision of the family.

Judge Did Not See Yaakov

Ohel, the agency that the city had assigned the case, recommended that the 30 family be reunited. Yaakov was not present in court where the judge could have seen his bruised face. School officials said no one from Ohel ever contacted them to ask how Yaakov was doing. Lester Kaufman, Ohel's executive director, said he could not comment because of confidentiality.

Days after the abuse report was filed, Yaakov disappeared from school for vir- 31 tually the entire month of December and much of January. On Feb. 7, 1990, the school attendance officer called the boy's home. Mrs. Riegler told her that Yaakov "is sick til further notice," a school log shows.

Mrs. Riegler's peremptory tone aroused the school's suspicions. A week later, 32 Mrs. Lantiere's records show, she called Mr. Schwartz and left a message that Yaakov had been absent too much. The school's truant officer went to Yaakov's home. Mrs. Riegler told him over the intercom that Yaakov had an ear infection. The records have no further details on the incident, and it is unclear whether the truant officer insisted on seeing the boy.

During this time Mrs. Riegler was also on probation for Israel's beating. But 33 in March 1990, a year and a half before her five years probation were up, the city's Probation Department moved to end its supervision. Such early releases are not unusual when the person on probation keeps appointments and the department learns of no new problems. Twice, her probation officer had asked Human Resources for any reports that the mother had again abused her children, and was told the information was confidential.

Trouble Throwing a Ball

On March 5, Yaakov briefly returned to school and his teacher noticed he was 34 having trouble throwing a ball in gym. His right elbow was swollen and bruised. School records show that the teacher called Mrs. Riegler, who said she hadn't noticed anything, but would take Yaakov to a doctor.

An autopsy after his death found signs of a partly healed broken right elbow, 35 which may never have been treated.

On March 15, 10 days after the school noticed the swollen elbow, Mrs. 36

Riegler took Yaakov to the family pediatrician, Max Bulmash. The doctor said he noticed nothing wrong with the boy's elbow. "Unless I'd put him through the maneuvers of ball throwing," the doctor said recently, "I would not have noticed that."

Yaakov did have a scrape on his forehead. Dr. Bulmash said Mrs. Riegler told 37 him that Yaakov had walked into a wall—an explanation that the doctor said he found plausible. Yaakov was a clumsy child who bumped into things, the doctor said—a description of the boy that school officials dispute.

A Reminder to Call Welfare

A handwritten note at the bottom of Yaakov's chart that day includes a 38 reminder the doctor wrote himself to call city child welfare workers. Dr. Bulmash said he did not suspect abuse, but did think Mrs. Riegler was having trouble coping with Yaakov and needed homemaker services.

"He was a lovable child, no question," the doctor said. "He was responsive to 39 human touch, but he needed care like an infant. He frequently soiled himself and got into things."

Dr. Bulmash said that some time before Yaakov's death, he had heard that 40 Mrs. Riegler had beaten one of her other sons. He had also talked with the city investigator, Mr. Schwartz. At one point, Mrs. Riegler called him while Mr. Schwartz was at her home, complaining that the investigator was snooping around. Mr. Schwartz told the doctor over the phone that he had found no problems, Dr. Bulmash said. 41

Mr. Schwartz declined to speak about the case. 42

The doctor said he never saw any signs of abuse on Yaakov, nor did he ever call the state child abuse number.

CRISIS

Putting Off Frantic Teachers

Yaakov's absences from school began again, starting two days before he went 43 to see Dr. Bulmash and lasting for two solid months, until May 15. During that time, the school again called the child abuse line to report the absences.

On May 21, 1990, just a week after Yaakov finally returned to school, Ms. 44 Pesce noticed that his right cheek was bruised. Again, she took him to Mrs. Lantiere's office. The counselor took out dolls. When she asked who had hurt him, the boy picked up the female doll and said, "Mommy boo-boo."

Two days later, Mrs. Lantiere got in touch with Mr. Schwartz, the investiga- 45 tor, to let him know Yaakov was back in school and still bruised.

'Used to Make Me Crazy'

"Mr. Schwartz used to make me crazy," Mrs. Lantiere said. "The teachers 46 were begging me every day to call and find out. He never said anything concrete.

He would say, 'We're looking into it. We're aware of it.'"

The next day, Mrs. Riegler again took Yaakov to see Dr. Bulmash. The doctor 47 said he saw no suspicious bruises. "I always undressed him entirely," he said. "I never noticed anything."

That day, Dr. Bulmash gave Yaakov stitches for a cut near his eye. The moth- 48 er told him her son had cut herself with scissors at school. "The explanation was plausible and didn't seem suspicious," the doctor said. "But I thought a child like that shouldn't be handling scissors."

He said Yaakov's eye might have been bruised, though he made no note of it. 49 "A cut near the eye will settle blood around the soft tissue of the eye," he said.

Oozing Gash on Head

A month later, on June 20, Yaakov's teacher noticed an oozing gash on top of 50 his head, which was "severely bruised." Mrs. Lantiere called Mr. Schwartz's super-visor, Harold Damas. He promised to look into it, she said.

That same day, Mrs. Riegler took Yaakov to see Dr. Bulmash. The doctor's 51 chart notes "a wound on back of head." The mother "denied knowing how it hap-pened," he wrote. "I elected to treat with Bactoban."

A week later, Mrs. Lantiere called Mr. Schwartz again. School was almost out 52 for summer, and she wanted to be sure Yaakov was safe. He assured her that the city was referring the family to the Ohel agency.

She sighed in relief, only to learn later that the children remained in the home 53 without Ohel's supervision.

DEATH

A Month of Signs and Excuses

The next school year began almost ominously. On Sept. 13, Yaakov's teacher 54 noticed a burn under his right eye. The next day, Mrs. Lantiere was on the phone to Mr. Schwartz, asking him to find a home for Yaakov "where he will not be getting hurt all the time," her notes say.

Sept. 18: Yaakov is black and blue on his chest, his hip, along his spine and 55 close to his collarbone.

Sept. 19: "Yaakov is walking strangely. His left knee gave way while walking 56 up the stairs." At lunch time, he was "extremely frightened of water," school records say. "He screamed and his whole body was trembling."

Sept. 24: He had scratches on the left side of his neck and a bruise on his 57 cheek and forehead. He had fingerprints on his neck.

"I was frantic," Mrs. Lantiere said.   58

Sept. 25: Mrs. Lantiere called Mr. Schwartz again.   59

Sept. 26: She went over the investigator's head and called the state child abuse 60 line, the third such report made by the school.

Appeared to Be Burn Marks

The next day, another H.R.A. investigator, Keith Glascoe, visited the Riegler 61
home. He later told a hospital social worker that he had seen what appeared to be
burn marks on the boy. Yaakov told him that both his mother and father had hurt
him, but that his mother hurt him more. Mrs. Riegler's explanation was that
Yaakov always fell and hurt himself.

Mr. Glascoe visited the school and told the principal, Philip Tritt, that he was 62
having trouble finding an Orthodox Jewish foster home for Yaakov.

Sept. 29 was Yom Kippur, the holiest day of the Jewish year, a day of atone- 63
ment. Yaakov stayed home with his mother while his father and older brothers went
to temple.

Mrs. Riegler was pregnant with her fifth child, and felt sick. Yaakov had diar- 64
rhea and soiled himself several times. Mrs. Riegler had to clean up after him repeatedly. She later confessed in court that she "lost control" and beat Yaakov. His head
hit hard against the wall.

The comatose boy was taken to Maimonides, where his brother had been 65
treated four years earlier. Mrs. Riegler blamed Yaakov's injuries on his clumsiness,
just as she had with Israel. She told a hospital administrator that she was praying in
the dining room when Yaakov fell.

The mother, dressed in a nightgown, sat talking with Dr. Bulmash, who had 66
come into the emergency room looking "white" and very upset, the hospital social
work report stated.

"I did not push him!" hospital workers heard her shout. 67

On Oct. 14, 1990, Yaakov died. 68

In a subsequent trial of the parents in Family Court, it took a medical examin- 69
er almost an hour just to describe the bruises on Yaakov's arms.

Epitaph

Mild Punishment, Much Secrecy

Postscript: Yaakov's death led to new calls by the city's Probation 70
Commissioner, Catherine M. Abate, to ease confidentiality laws. New legislation is
pending.

Dr. Bulmash is under investigation by the Brooklyn District Attorney's office, 71
which is trying to determine whether he violated laws that require doctors to report
signs of child abuse to the state phone line.

H.R.A.'s child fatality review panel recommended that the agency report Dr. 72
Bulmash to the state Office of Professional Medical Conduct, but was prevented
from doing so by the agency's lawyers, who said confidentiality laws forbade it.

Mrs. Riegler's probation officer, Yvonne Hernandez, who was carrying about 73
160 cases at the time Mrs. Riegler's probation ended, was mildly disciplined for
sloppy record keeping. Her supervisor agreed to early retirement after an internal

investigation of the case, probation officials said.

The abuse investigators, Mr. Schwartz and Mr. Glascoe, as well as their super- 74
visor, are still working in the same Brooklyn office. H.R.A. would not say whether
they were disciplined, citing confidentiality.

Mr. Riegler pleaded guilty to failing to stop Yaakov's abuse and is on proba- 75
tion. Yaakov's brothers are living with an uncle.

■ *Questions for* . . . As Mother Killed Her Son, Protectors Observed Privacy
by Celia W. Dugger

Words to Note

abusive	neglectful	anonymous statistic
overwhelmed	tasks	scattered
uncoordinated	harried mother	battered child
peremptory tone	confidential	plausible
dispute	wound	elected

Language

1. Is "Epitaph" a fitting title for the article's conclusion? Is it too heavy handed? What's the point of this section? Is it an appropriate conclusion?
2. Take a look at the language of the welfare system's case workers. What do
   you see?

Style

1. Why does Dugger use a calendar format towards the end of her account of
   Yaakov's death? Sept. 18, Sept. 19: what tone do these dateline entries give
   that part of the piece?
2. Is Dugger too restrained for your taste? What tones are appropriate? Why?

Development and Organization

1. Do we learn anything indispensable in Dugger's long and thorough account
   of all the instances of child abuse in the Riegler family? Should it have
   been condensed?
2. Why does Dugger end her account by noting "it took a medical examiner
   almost an hour just to describe the bruises on Yaakov's arms"?

3. Why does she take the trouble to describe the religious significance of Yom Kippur, the day that Shulamis Riegler killed her son Yaakov?

Discussion and Journal Writing

1. How can we protect the Yaakov Rieglers and Lisa Steinbergs of our society without violating the constitutional rights of citizens and undermining the authority of parents?
2. Judge Francis X. Egitto of the New York State Supreme Court said it's not just Yaakov's mother who is guilty of his death. As you read this account, who must share the blame?
3. Try rewriting part of Yaakov's story in an outraged tone. Compare it with Dugger's account. What do you think?
4. Why do Dugger, Kotlowitz, and Kozol—this book's three muckraking journalists—prefer to write in an understated tone?

ooooo

Requiring Classes in Divorce

—Carol Lawson

Carol Lawson writes for the *New York Times* about new wrinkles in the fabric of American society. In the piece that follows, she examines a newcomer to the American scene: classes that divorce-court judges in certain states and cities require couples seeking a divorce to take. The classes stress the impact of divorce on children.

MARIETTA, Ga.   Before a very still and somber-looking audience of 80 parents, a social worker portrayed a slice of contemporary American life. 1

"I am a 6-year-old boy, and I live with Dad," said Aubrey Lee, the social worker, in his southern drawl. "One hour before I am supposed to visit Mom, Dad says, 'You can't see Mom. The check didn't come.'" 2

Mr. Lee looked hard at his audience, all mothers and fathers with pending divorce cases in this Atlanta suburb, and asked, "How do I feel?" 3

How a child feels in the turmoil of divorce—before, during and after the breakup of the family—was the subject of a four-hour seminar that brought these 4 parents one morning last week to the Cobb County Juvenile Court. They were not there voluntarily: They were ordered by the court to attend.

"If you don't go, you don't get a divorce," said Judge Watson L. White, chief 5 judge of the Cobb County Superior Court.

Here and in some other parts of the country, judges in divorce proceedings are 6 sending warring parents to court-required seminars to open their eyes to the trauma of divorce for children. Their aim, they say, is to force parents to cease battle long enough to consider the repercussions for the innocent victims caught in their cross-fire.

"The purpose," Judge White said, "is to make parents listen to experts who 7 say, 'This is what is happening to your children, this is what they are feeling, and here are some things you can do to lessen the trauma.'

"Parents are so involved in hating each other. They tell a child the other is no 8 good. Children don't want to take sides, but they are pushed and pulled and torn. We want to lessen the bitterness and help parents communicate with each other for the benefit of their children."

Judge White said he believed the program was having an effect. "Some cou- 9 ples are compromising and are settling their cases without a bitter court fight because they realize it would hurt their child and isn't worth it," he said. "We don't have statistics to back this up, but we know it's happening."

Cobb County's program, which is called "Children Cope With Divorce: 10 Seminar for Divorcing Parents," began in October 1988 and has served as the model for similar programs that began recently in Atlanta, Savannah and Decatur, Ga. It has also been duplicated in Marion, Ohio, St. Petersburg, Fla., and Indianapolis.

"This is the wave of the future," said Judge Cynthia J. Ayers of the Family 11 Law Division of the Marion County Superior Court in Indianapolis, where the pro-gram began last July. "Fifty percent of all marriages end in divorce, and 70 percent of those families have children. Many people never consider the impact of divorce on their children."

The fast-paced curriculum touches on emotional, psychological, social and 12 economic implications for children in a divorce. It also deals with how and what parents should tell children about a divorce, and how they can help them deal with separation and visitation.

The program addresses the needs of children according to their age and devel- 13 opmental level. It is a mixture of lectures, films and role-playing by a pair of semi-nar leaders, who dramatize common conflicts that arise in families as a result of divorce. The audience is encouraged to comment on the behavior of parents and children in those scenarios, and how they affect and often manipulate each other.

"Parents see themselves in our role-playing, and they begin to recognize 14 things they typically do out of anger toward each other," said Bev Bradburn-Stern, the social worker who designed the seminar for Families First, an Atlanta social service and counseling agency that runs the program.

Supporters of the program concede that in four hours it can barely skim the 15 surface of a difficult and complex subject. "Instead of four hours, it ought to be 40 hours," Judge White said. "I hope it will be expanded."

Nancy J. Parkhouse, a deputy court administrator for the Cobb Superior Court 16 who is coordinator of the seminar, said: "It is an overview, but the main thing is awareness. It makes some very strong points, and hopefully they will stick in people's minds."

It was Ms. Parkhouse who brought the program to the attention of judges here. 17 She said the concept for the seminar began several years ago in Wichita, Kan., where it is also court-mandated, but that a new curriculum was developed here.

The growing interest in this type of program is buttressed by research suggest- 18 ing that divorce can have deep and long-lasting consequences for children. Some researchers have found that emotional scars can remain well beyond childhood, into adult life, resulting in anger, depression and fears of betrayal and abandonment.

Dr. Judith S. Wallerstein, a psychologist who has studied long-term effects of 19 divorce, said that while the four-hour seminar was useful, she would prefer a more ambitious series of required seminars that wove together the needs of parents with those of children.

"You have to recognize how much parents are hurting," Dr. Wallerstein said. 20 "You have to help them to feel less bewildered and to make informed decisions about custody and visitation. Still, the four-hour course sends a morally important message to parents: your children are of concern to society, and divorce has consequences for them. Not everybody knows that."

Judges say there have been complaints from lawyers about the program, espe- 21 cially at the beginning. "Lawyers thought we were intervening with their clients and were creating another bureaucratic step in the divorce process," said Judge Ayers of Indianapolis.

Judge White of Marietta added: "There was a lot of grumbling from lawyers 22 at first—they do not like new procedures—but there was no organized resistance."

About 7,000 parents have attended the seminar here since it began. The pro- 23 gram is largely supported by a $30 fee, which parents pay. The fee is waived for the 6 percent of parents who the court determines cannot afford it.

At the session last week, which was led by Ms. Bradburn-Stern and Mr. 24 Aubrey, parents heard some basic facts about divorce in America, including these:

- More than one million children are affected by divorce every year.
- Half of those children will grow up in families where parents stay angry.
- Sixty percent of them will feel rejected by at least one parent.

"For children in a divorce, the family as they know it is no longer," Ms. 25 Bradburn-Stern said. "That stability is now gone. Divorce is a process of loss. Children are scared.

"The family goes on after divorce, but it is restructured. How can you make it 26 work, and make children feel loved and secure? Children need both parents. It is not easy to work that out. It takes time."

A few people in the audience dabbed at their eyes. Ms. Bradburn-Stern sug- 27
gested that divorced parents create a business-style relationship with each other for
matters concerning the children.

"Has anyone had the experience of doing business with someone you didn't 28
like?" she asked. There was immediate laughter. "That is what this is like. You
have to deal with the widget seller because you need a widget."

After the seminar, many parents said they had not wanted to attend, and in 29
some cases were angry about being forced to do so. But they also said that in the
end, they had found the morning useful.

"I thought, 'I don't need it, they won't tell me anything,'" said Patrick 30
Brownlee, a restaurant manager who has two sons, 4 years and 19 months old. "But
I learned I need to listen more to my kids, and not be so strict when they first come
back after visiting their mother."

Jim Brown, a drafting engineer who has a 3-year-old son, said: "I don't advo- 31
cate mandated programs, but this has a lot of value. I was aware that my son needs
to be comforted by both his parents, but now I will make an extra effort."

Carla Kirby, a Juvenile Court clerical worker who has two sons, 1 and 2, said 32
she had not looked forward to the program.

"I was apprehensive and didn't know what to expect," she recalled. "I did get 33
something out of it. There is so much uncertainty when you get a divorce. This
helps you know what to expect."

■ *Questions for* . . . Requiring Classes in Divorce by Carol Lawson

Words to Note

a very still and somber-looking audience	pending	turmoil
	warring	seminar
	voluntarily	trauma
repercussions	crossfire	torn
visitation	manipulate	skim
court-mandated	buttressed	betrayal
abandonment	wove	intervening
dabbed	resistance	restructured

Language

1. Dr. Judith Wallerstein, a national expert on divorce, would prefer a series
   of seminars that "wove together the needs of parents with those of children." *Wove* is used as part of a metaphor. What does it mean in this context? Is it effective?

2. Lawson uses the word *warring* to describe divorcing parents. Is it accurate?
3. Lawson reports that a few parents in the audience "dabbed" at their eyes. Can you think of a better word?

Style

1. Does Lawson's style tell you how she feels about these classes? Is she too easy on them? Too uncritical?
2. How does Lawson steer the reader through the article?

Development and Organization

1. Would Lawson's article have been more effective if she had begun with the fifth paragraph? What does that paragraph do that the first four paragraphs don't do and vice versa?
2. There are no statistics about the consequences of these classes. Is the article incomplete without them? What sort of statistics would help the reader judge the effectiveness of these classes?
3. Lawson concludes with testimony from parents who have taken these classes. Is that the best place for their experiences? Do they make a good conclusion? Why or why not? Would a summary be more effective?

Discussion and Journal Writing

1. Do you think it's a good idea for couples who have applied for a divorce to take a class on the consequences of divorce? Why? Why not?
2. Do you think it's fair to make parents pay for a class the court requires?
3. Do you think these classes are making a genuine contribution to family happiness, or are they just providing work and revenues for the social workers who created them? What evidence does the article provide?

○○○○○

A Modest Proposal

For Preventing the Children of Poor People in Ireland from Being a Burden to Their Parents or Country, and for Making Them Beneficial to the Public

—Jonathan Swift

Jonathan Swift is the most famous satirist to have plied the English language. Though he died in 1745, his ire makes him seem far more contemporary than that. He was born to English parents in Dublin, Ireland, in 1667 and was educated at the Kilkenny School and Trinity College. He lived in London for a while, making himself and his pen useful to the Tory government while becoming one of the literary lights of the era. Deciding reluctantly on a career in the Anglican Church, he took orders and in 1713 was given the Deanship of St. Patrick's Cathedral in Dublin. He became involved in politics and wrote a number of straightforward essays proposing various ways of remedying Ireland's poverty and suffering. Enraged that these essays were ignored, he then wrote the infamous and abominable "A Modest Proposal." His masterpiece, a novel called *Gulliver's Travels,* satirizes mankind.

1   It is a melancholy object to those who walk through this great town or travel in the country, when they see the streets, the roads, and cabin doors, crowded with beggars of the female sex, followed by three, four, or six children, all in rags and importuning every passenger for an alms. These mothers, instead of being able to work for their honest livelihood, are forced to employ all their time in strolling to beg sustenance for their helpless infants, who, as they grow up, either turn thieves for want of work, or leave their dear native country to fight for the Pretender in Spain, or sell themselves to the Barbadoes.

2   I think it is agreed by all parties that this prodigious number of children in the arms, or on the backs, or at the heels of their mothers, and frequently of their fathers, is in the present deplorable state of the kingdom a very great additional grievance; and therefore whoever could find out a fair, cheap, and easy method of making these children sound, useful members of the commonwealth would deserve so well of the public as to have his statue set up for a preserver of the nation.

3   But my intention is very far from being confined to provide only for the children of professed beggars; it is of much greater extent, and shall take in the whole number of infants at a certain age who are born of parents in effect as little able to support them as those who demand our charity in the streets.

As to my own part, having turned my thoughts for many years upon this 4
important subject, and maturely weighed the several schemes of other projectors, I
have always found them grossly mistaken in their computation. It is true, a child
just dropped from its dam may be supported by her milk for a solar year, with little
other nourishment; at most not above the value of two shillings, which the mother
may certainly get, or the value in scraps, by her lawful occupation of begging; and
it is exactly at one year old that I propose to provide for them in such a manner as
instead of being a charge upon their parents or the parish, or wanting food and raiment for the rest of their lives, they shall on the contrary contribute to the feeding,
and partly to the clothing, of many thousands.

There is likewise another great advantage in my scheme, that it will prevent 5
those voluntary abortions, and that horrid practice of women murdering their bastard children, alas, too frequent among us, sacrificing the poor innocent babes, I
doubt, more to avoid the expense than the shame, which would move tears and pity
in the most savage and inhuman breast.

The number of souls in this kingdom being usually reckoned one million and 6
a half, of these I calculate there may be about two hundred thousand couples whose
wives are breeders; from which number I subtract thirty thousand couples who are
able to maintain their own children, although I apprehend there cannot be so many
under the present distress of the kingdom; but this being granted, there will remain
an hundred and seventy thousand breeders. I again subtract fifty thousand for those
women who miscarry, or whose children die by accident or disease within the year.
There only remain an hundred and twenty thousand children of poor parents annually born. The question therefore is, how this number shall be reared and provided
for, which, as I have already said, under the present situation of affairs, is utterly
impossible by all the methods hitherto proposed. For we can neither employ them
in handicraft nor agriculture; we neither build houses (I mean in the country) nor
cultivate land. They can very seldom pick up a livelihood by stealing till they arrive
at six years old, except where they are of towardly parts; although I confess they
learn the rudiments much earlier, during which time they can however be looked
upon only as probationers, as I have been informed by a principal gentleman in the
country of Cavan, who protested to me that he never knew above one or two
instances under the age of six, even in a part of the kingdom so renowned for the
quickest proficiency in that art.

I am assured by our merchants that a boy or a girl before twelve years old is 7
no salable commodity; and even when they come to this age, they will not yield
above three pounds, or three pounds and half a crown at most on the Exchange;
which cannot turn to account either to the parents or the kingdom, the charge of
nutriment and rags having been at least four times that value.

I shall now therefore propose my own thoughts, which I hope will not be 8
liable to the least objection.

I have been assured by a very knowing American of my acquaintance in 9
London, that a young healthy child well nursed is at a year old a most delicious,
nourishing, and wholesome food, whether stewed, roasted, baked, or boiled; and I

make no doubt that it will equally serve in a fricassee or a ragout.

I do therefore humbly offer it to public consideration that of the hundred and 10 twenty thousand children, already computed, twenty thousand may be reserved for breed, whereof only one fourth part to be males, which is more than we allow to sheep, black cattle, or swine; and my reason is that these children are seldom the fruits of marriage, a circumstance not much regarded by our savages, therefore one male will be sufficient to serve four females. That the remaining hundred thousand may at a year old be offered in sale to the persons of quality and fortune through the kingdom, always advising the mother to let them suck plentifully in the last month, so as to render them plumb and fat for a good table. A child will make two dishes at an entertainment for friends; and when the family dines alone, the fore or hind quarter will make a reasonable dish, and seasoned with a little pepper or salt will be very good boiled on the fourth day, especially in winter.

I have reckoned upon a medium that a child just born will weigh twelve 11 pounds, and in a solar year if tolerably nursed increaseth to twenty-eight pounds.

I grant this food will be somewhat dear, and therefore very proper for land- 12 lords, who, as they have already devoured most of the parents, seem to have the best title to the children.

Infant's flesh will be in season throughout the year, but more plentiful in 13 March, and a little before and after. For we are told by a grave author, an eminent French physician, that fish being a prolific diet, there are more children born in Roman Catholic countries about nine months after Lent, than at any other season; therefore, reckoning a year after Lent, the markets will be more glutted than usual, because the number of popish infants is at least three to one in this kingdom; and therefore it will have one other collateral advantage, by lessening the number of Papists among us.

I have already computed the charge of nursing a beggar's child (in which list I 14 reckon all cottagers, laborers, and four fifths of the farmers) to be about two shillings per annum, rags included; and I believe no gentleman would repine to give ten shillings for the carcass of a good fat child, which, as I have said, will make four dishes of excellent nutritive meat, when he hath only some particular friend or his own family to dine with him. Thus the squire will learn to be a good landlord, and grow popular among the tenants; the mother will have eight shillings net profit, and be fit for work till she produces another child.

Those who are more thrifty (as I must confess the times require) may flay the 15 carcass; the skin of which artificially dressed will make admirable gloves for ladies, and summer boots for fine gentlemen.

As to our city of Dublin, shambles may be appointed for this purpose in the 16 most convenient parts of it, and butchers we may be assured will not be wanting; although I rather recommend buying the children alive, and dressing them hot from the knife as we do roasting pigs.

A very worthy person, a true lover of his country, and whose virtues I highly 17 esteem, was lately pleased in discoursing on this matter to offer a refinement upon my scheme. He said that many gentlemen of his kingdom, having of late destroyed their deer, he conceived that the want of venison might be well supplied by the bodies of young lads and maidens, not exceeding fourteen years of age nor under twelve, so great a number of both sexes in every country being now ready to starve for want of work and service; and these to be disposed of by their parents, if alive, or otherwise by their nearest relations. But with due deference to so excellent a friend and so deserving a patriot, I cannot be altogether in his sentiments; for as to the males, my American acquaintance assured me from frequent experience that their flesh was generally tough and lean, like that of our schoolboys, by continual exercise, and their taste disagreeable; and to fatten them would not answer the charge. Then as to the females, it would, I think with humble submission, be a loss to the public, because they soon would become breeders themselves; and besides, it is not improbable that some scrupulous people might be apt to censure such a practice (although indeed very unjustly) as a little bordering upon cruelty; which, I confess, hath always been with me the strongest objection against any project, how well soever intended.

18 But in order to justify my friend, he confessed that this expedient was put into his head by the famous Psalmanazar, a native of the island Formosa, who came from thence to London above twenty years ago, and in conversation told my friend that in his country when any young person happened to be put to death, the executioner sold the carcass to the persons of quality as a prime dainty; and that in his time the body of a plump girl of fifteen, who was crucified for an attempt to poison the emperor, was sold to his Imperial Majesty's prime minister of state, and other great mandarins of the court, in joints from the gibbet, at four hundred crowns. Neither indeed can I deny that if the same use were made of several plump young girls in this town, who without one single groat to their fortunes cannot stir abroad without a chair, and appear at the playhouse and assemblies in foreign fineries which they never will pay for, the kingdom would not be the worse.

19 Some persons of a desponding spirit are in great concern about that vast number of poor people who are aged, diseased, or maimed, and I have been desired to employ my thoughts what course may be taken to ease the nation of so grievous an encumbrance. But I am not in the least pain upon that matter, because it is very well known that they are every day dying and rotting by cold and famine, and filth and vermin, as fast as can be reasonably expected. And as to the younger laborers, they are now in almost as hopeful a condition. They cannot get work, and consequently pine away for want of nourishment to a degree that if any time they are accidentally hired to common labor, they have not strength to perform it; and thus the country and themselves are happily delivered from the evils to come.

20 I have too long digressed, and therefore shall return to my subject. I think the advantages by the proposal which I have made are obvious and many, as well as of the highest importance.

21 For first, as I have already observed, it would greatly lessen the number of Papists, with whom we are yearly overrun, being the principal breeders of the nation as well as our most dangerous enemies; and who stay at home on purpose to deliver the kingdom to the Pretender, hoping to take their advantage by the absence

of so many good Protestants, who have chosen rather to leave their country than to stay at home and pay tithes against their conscience to an Episcopal curate.

Secondly, the poorer tenants will have something valuable of their own, which 22 by law may be liable to distress, and help to pay their landlord's rent, their corn and cattle being already seized and money a thing unknown.

Thirdly, whereas the maintenance of an hundred thousand children, from two 23 years old and upwards, cannot be computed at less than ten shillings a piece per annum, the nation's stock will be thereby increased fifty thousand pounds per annum, besides the profit of a new dish introduced to the tables of all gentlemen of fortune in the kingdom who have any refinement in taste. And the money will circulate among ourselves, the goods being entirely of our own growth and manufacture.

Fourthly, the constant breeders, besides the gain of eight shillings sterling per 24 annum by the sale of their children, will be rid of the charge for maintaining them after the first year.

Fifthly, this food would likewise bring great custom to taverns, where the 25 vintners will certainly be so prudent as to procure the best receipts for dressing it to perfection, and consequently have their houses frequented by all the fine gentlemen, who justly value themselves upon their knowledge in good eating; and a skillful cook, who understands how to oblige his guests, will contrive to make it as expensive as they please.

Sixthly, this would be a great inducement to marriage, which all wise nations 26 have either encouraged by rewards or enforced by laws and penalties. It would increase the care and tenderness of mothers toward their children, when they were sure of a settlement for life to the poor babes, provided in some sort by the public, to their annual profit instead of expense. We should see an honest emulation among the married women, which of them could bring the fattest child to the market. Men would become as fond of their wives during the time of their pregnancy as they are now of their mares in foal, their cows in calf, or sows when they are ready to farrow; nor offer to beat or kick them (as is too frequent a practice) for fear of a miscarriage.

Many other advantages might be enumerated. For instance, the addition of 27 some thousand carcasses in our exportation of barreled beef, the propagation of swine's flesh, and improvements in the art of making good bacon, so much wanted among us by the great destruction of pigs, too frequent at our tables, which are no way comparable in taste or magnificence to a well-grown, fat, yearling child, which roasted whole will make a considerable figure at a lord mayor's feast or any other public entertainment. But this and many others I omit, being studious of brevity.

Supposing that one thousand families in this city would be constant customers 28 for infants' flesh, besides others who might have it at merry meetings, particularly weddings and christenings, I compute that Dublin would take off annually about twenty thousand carcasses, and the rest of the kingdom (where probably they will be sold somewhat cheaper) the remaining eighty thousand.

I can think of no one objection that will possibly be raised against this propos- 29 al, unless it should be urged that the number of people will be thereby much less-ened in the kingdom. This I freely own, and it was indeed one principal design in offering it to the world. I desire the reader will observe, that I calculate my remedy for this one individual kingdom of Ireland and for no other that ever was, is, or I think ever can be upon earth. Therefore, let no man talk to me of other expedients: of taxing our absentees at five shillings a pound: of using neither clothes nor house-hold furniture except what is of our own growth and manufacture: of utterly reject-ing the materials and instruments that promote foreign luxury: of curing the expen-siveness of pride, vanity, idleness, and gaming in our women: of introducing a vein of parsimony, prudence, and temperance: of learning to love our country, in the want of which we differ even from Laplanders and the inhabitants of Topinamboo: of quitting our animosities and factions, nor acting any longer like the Jews, who were murdering one another at the very moment their city was taken: of being a lit-tle cautious not to sell our country and conscience for nothing: of teaching land-lords to have at least one degree of mercy toward their tenants: lastly, of putting a spirit of honesty, industry, and skill into our shopkeepers; who, if a resolution could now be taken to buy only our native goods, would immediately unite to cheat and exact upon us in the price, the measure, and the goodness, nor could ever yet be brought to make one fair proposal of just dealing, though often and earnestly invit-ed to it.

Therefore, I repeat, let no man talk to me of these and the like expedients, till 30 he hath at least some glimpse of hope that there will ever be some hearty and sin-cere attempt to put them in practice.

But as to myself, having been wearied out for many years with offering vain, 31 idle, visionary thoughts, and at length utterly despairing of success, I fortunately fell upon this proposal, which, as it is wholly new, so it hath something solid and real, of no expense and little trouble, full in our own power, and whereby we can incur no danger in disobliging England. For this kind of commodity will not bear exportation, the flesh being of too tender a consistence to admit a long continuance in salt, although perhaps I could name a country which would be glad to eat up our whole nation without it.

After all, I am not so violently bent upon my own opinion as to reject any 32 offer proposed by wise men, which shall be found equally innocent, cheap, easy, and effectual. But before something of that kind shall be advanced in contradiction to my scheme, and offering a better, I desire the author or authors will be pleased maturely to consider two points. First, as things now stand, how they will be able to find food and raiment for an hundred thousand useless mouths and backs. And sec-ondly, there being a round million of creatures in human figure throughout this kingdom, whose sole subsistence put into a common stock would leave them in debt two millions of pounds sterling, adding those who are beggars by profession to the bulk of farmers, cottagers, and laborers, with their wives and children who are beggars in effect; I desire those politicians who dislike my overture, and may per-haps be so bold to attempt an answer, that they will first ask the parents of these mortals whether they would not at this day think it a great happiness to have been sold for food at a year old in this manner I prescribe, and thereby have avoided such a perpetual scene of misfortunes as they have since gone through by the oppression of landlords, the impossibility of paying rent without money or trade, the want of common sustenance, with neither house nor clothes to cover them from the inclemencies of the weather, and the most inevitable prospect of entailing the like or greater miseries upon their breed forever.

I profess, in the sincerity of my heart, that I have not the least personal interest 33 in endeavoring to promote this necessary work, having no other motive than the public good of my country, by advancing our trade, providing for infants, relieving the poor, and giving some pleasure to the rich. I have no children by which I can propose to get a single penny; the youngest being nine years old, and my wife past childbearing.

■ *Questions for* . . . A **Modest Proposal** by Jonathan Swift

Words to Note

melancholy	beggars	importuning
deplorable	a very great additional grievance	
computation	dropped from its dam	
raiment	that horrid practice of women murdering their	
apprehend	bastard children	
rudiments	the most savage and inhuman breast	
proficiency	salable commodity	
glutted	popish infants	Papists
repine	carcass	shambles
breeders	expedients	

Language

1. The speaker of Swift's essay uses the language of animal husbandry and accounting: mothers are *breeders* and *dams,* and he spends whole paragraphs *calculating* and *computing* the size of the herd. What do these motifs reveal about the speaker's outlook?
2. How many times does the meaning of Swift's title change throughout the essay?
3. Characterize the voice the speaker's abstract and Latinate diction projects.

Style

1. The average sentence in this essay is long and is interrupted by a number of interjections. The first few sentences are good examples of this. Why did a

writer as skilled as Swift write so many indirect, roundabout sentences?
2. Swift comes close to letting his mask slip in paragraph 12 when he says the landlords have the best title to the children "as they have already devoured most of the parents." What does he mean by this statement?

Development and Organization

1. The speaker doesn't get to his humble or modest proposal until the tenth paragraph. Why the rambling start?
2. What effect do all the lists and computations have?

Discussion and Journal Writing

1. Countless writers have adapted Swift's "A Modest Proposal" to their own causes and purposes. Give it a try. Write a modest proposal for solving the homeless problem in America today. You might want to review Kozol's piece for details.
2. Swift was misunderstood by some in Dublin, where the essay first appeared. Some mothers were seen hurrying their children across the street when they saw Swift coming. What are the risks and advantages of satire?

ooooo

———————— *F*amily Documents Six ————————

The Speech of Polly Baker

—Benjamin Franklin

The Speech of Miss Polly Baker before a Court of Judicature, at Connecticut near Boston in New England; where she was prosecuted the fifth time, for having a Bastard Child: Which influenced the Court to dispense with her Punishment, and which induced one of her Judges to marry her the next Day—by whom she had fifteen children.

"May it please the honorable bench to indulge me in a few words: I am a poor, unhappy woman, who have no money to fee lawyers to plead for me, being hard put to it to get a living. I shall not trouble your honors with long speeches; for I have not the presumption to expect that you may, by any means, be prevailed on to deviate in your Sentence from the law, in my favor. All I humbly hope is, that your honors would charitably move the governor's goodness on my behalf, that my fine may be remitted. This is the fifth time, gentlemen, that I have been dragg'd before your court on the same account; twice I have paid heavy fines, and twice have been brought to publick punishment, for want of money to pay those fines. This may have been agreeable to the laws, and I don't dispute it; but since laws are sometimes unreasonable in themselves, and therefore repealed; and others bear too hard on the subject in particular circumstances, and therefore there is left a power somewhere to dispense with the execution of them; I take the liberty to say, that I think this law, by which I am punished, both unreasonable in itself, and particularly severe with regard to me, who have always lived an inoffensive life in the neighborhood where I was born, and defy my enemies (if I have any) to say I ever wrong'd any man, woman, or child. Abstracted from the law, I cannot conceive (may it please your honors) what the nature of my offense is. I have brought five fine children into the world, at the risque of my life; I have maintain'd them well by my own industry, without burthening the township, and would have done better, if it had not been for the heavy charges and fines I have paid. Can it be a crime (in the nature of things, I mean) to add to the king's subjects, in a new country, that really wants people? I own it, I should think it rather a praiseworthy than a punishable action. I have debauched no other woman's husband, nor enticed any other youth; these things I never was charg'd with; nor has any one the least cause of complaint against me, unless, perhaps, the ministers of justice, because I have had children without being married, by which they have missed a wedding fee. But can this be a fault of mine? I appeal to your honors. You are pleased to allow I don't want sense; but I must be stupefied to the last degree, not to prefer the honorable state of wedlock to the condition I have lived in. I always was, and still am willing to enter into it; and doubt not my behaving well in it, having all the industry, frugality, fertility, and skill in economy appertaining to a good wife's character. I defy any one to say I ever refused an offer of that sort: on the contrary, I readily consented to the only proposal of marriage that ever was made me, which was when I was a virgin, but too easily confiding in the person's sincerity that made it, I unhappily lost my honor by trusting to his; for he got me with child, and then forsook me.

"That very person, you all know, he is now become a magistrate of this country; and I had hopes he would have appeared this day on the bench, and have endeavored to moderate the Court in my favor; then I should have scorn'd to have mentioned it; but I must now complain of it, as unjust and unequal, that my betrayer and undoer, the first cause of all my faults and miscarriages (if they must be deemed such), should be advanced to honor and power in this government that punishes my misfortune with stripes and infamy. I should be told, 'tis like, that were there no act of Assembly in the case, the precepts of religion are violated by my transgressions. If mine is a religious offense, leave it to religious punishments. You have already excluded me from the comforts of your church communion. Is not that sufficient? You believe I have offended heaven, and must suffer eternal fire: Will not that be sufficient? What need is there then of your additional fines and whipping? I own I do not think as you do, for, if I thought what you call a sin was really such, I could not presumptuously commit it. But, how can it be believed that heaven is angry at my having children, when to the little done by me towards it, God has been pleased to add his divine skill and admirable workmanship in the formation of their bodies, and crowned the whole by furnishing them with rational and immortal souls?

"Forgive me, gentlemen, if I talk a little extravagantly on these matters; I am no divine, but if you, gentlemen, must be making laws, do not turn natural and useful actions into crimes by your prohibitions. But take into your wise consideration the great and growing number of bachelors in the country, many of whom, from the mean fear of the expenses of a family, have never sincerely and honorably courted a woman in their lives; and by their manner of living leave unproduced (which is little better than murder) hundreds of their posterity to the thousandth generation. Is not this a greater offense against the publick good than mine? Compel them, then, by law, either to marriage, or to pay double the fine of fornication every year. What must poor

women do, whom customs and nature forbid to solicit the men, and who cannot force themselves upon husbands, when the laws take no care to provide
them any, and yet severely punish them if they do their duty without them;
the duty of the first and great command of nature and nature's God, *encrease
and multiply;* a duty, from the steady performance of which nothing has been
able to deter me, but for its sake I have hazarded the loss of the publick
esteem, and have frequently endured publick disgrace and punishment; and
therefore ought, in my humble opinion, instead of a whipping, to have a statue erected to my memory."

Excerpts From Vice President's Speech on Cities and Poverty

*Washington, May 19 [1992] (Rueters)—Following are excerpts from remarks pre-
pared for delivery by Vice President Dan Quayle before the Commonwealth Club of
California, as transcribed by News Transcripts Inc.*

I believe the lawless social anarchy which we saw is directly related to
the breakdown of family structure, personal responsibility and social order in
too many areas of our society. For the poor the situation is compounded by a
welfare ethos that impedes individual efforts to move ahead in society, and
hampers their ability to take advantage of the opportunities America offers.

There is no question that this country has had a terrible problem with
race and racism. The evil of slavery has left a long legacy. But we have faced
racism squarely, and we have made progress in the past quarter century. The
landmark civil rights bills of the 1960's removed legal barriers to allow full
participation by blacks in the economic, social and political life of the nation.
By any measure the America of 1992 is more egalitarian, more integrated, and
offers more opportunities to black Americans and all other minority group
members than the America of 1964. There is more to be done. But I think all
of us can be proud of our progress.

I was born in 1947; so I'm considered one of those "baby boomers" we
keep reading about. But let's look at one unfortunate legacy of the boomer
generation. When we were young, it was fashionable to declare war against
traditional values. Indulgence and self-gratification seemed to have no consequences. Many of our generation glamorized casual sex and drug use, evaded
responsibility and trashed authority.

Today the boomers are middle-aged and middle class. The responsibility of having families has helped many recover traditional values. And, of course, the great majority of those in the middle class survived the turbulent legacy of the 60's and 70's. But many of the poor, with less to fall back on, did not.

The intergenerational poverty that troubles us so much today is predominantly a poverty of values. Our inner cities are filled with children having children, with people who have not been able to take advantage of educational opportunities, with people who are dependent on drugs or the narcotic of welfare.

We are for law and order. If a single mother raising her children in the ghetto has to worry about drive-by shootings, drug deals, or whether her children will join gangs and die violently, her difficult task becomes impossible. We're for law and order because we can't expect children to learn in dangerous schools. We're for law and order because if property isn't protected, who will build businesses?

Right now the failure of our families is hurting America deeply. When families fail, society fails. The anarchy and lack of structure are testament to how quickly civilization falls apart when the family foundation cracks.

Children need love and discipline. They need mothers and fathers. A welfare check is not a husband. The state is not a father. It is from parents that children learn how to behave in society; it is from parents above all that children come to understand values and themselves as men and women, mothers and fathers.

And for those concerned about children growing up in poverty, we should know this: Marriage is probably the best anti-poverty program of all. Among families headed by married couples today, there is a poverty rate of 5.7 percent. But 33.4 percent of families headed by a single mother are in poverty today.

Nature abhors a vacuum. When there are no mature, responsible men around to teach boys to be good men, gangs serve in their place.

Answers to our problems won't be easy. We can start by dismantling a welfare system that encourages dependency and subsidizes broken families. We can attach conditions such as school attendance or work to welfare. We can limit the time a recipient gets benefits. We can stop penalizing marriage for welfare mothers. We can enforce child support payments.

Ultimately, however, marriage is a moral issue that requires cultural consensus, and the use of social sanctions. Bearing babies irresponsibly is, simply, wrong. Failing to support children one has fathered is wrong.

We must be unequivocal about this. It doesn't help matters when prime time TV has Murphy Brown—a character who epitomizes today's intelligent, highly paid, professional woman—mocking the importance of fathers by bearing a child alone and calling it just another "life style choice."

I know it is not fashionable to talk about moral values, but we need to do it. Even though our cultural leaders in Hollywood, network TV, the national newspapers routinely jeer at them, I think that most of us in this room know that some things are good, and other things are wrong.

Now it's time to make the discussion public. It's time to talk again about family, hard work, integrity, and personal responsibility. We cannot be embarrassed out of our belief that two parents, married to each other, are better in most cases for children than one.

■ *Questions for* . . . **The Speech of Polly Baker** and **Excerpts From Vice President's Speech on Cities and Poverty**

Discussion and Journal Writing

1. Compare and contrast Quayle's and Franklin's thoughts about single-parent families.

ooooo

$\mathcal{F}$amily Album Six

Shulamis Riegler, in Custody After Killing Her Son Yaakov (*Ruby Washington for the* New York Times*)*

■ *Questions for* . . . Shulamis Riegler, in Custody After Killing Her
Son Yaakov

Discussion and Journal Writing

1. Was it responsible of the *New York Times* to print this photograph of
   Shulamis Riegler after she was arrested for murdering her son Yaakov?
   Study the photograph. What does it reveal? Does it or the article it accompanied, Celia W. Dugger's "As Mother Killed Her Son, Protectors
   Observed Privacy," tell us why parents and guardians abuse and sometimes
   even kill their children? Are we doing enough as a society to prevent such
   family tragedies?

ooooo

🎟 Expository Writing: Political Arguments, Proposals, and Diatribes

This chapter's writers have ideas to grind: they write to dislodge, over-
turn, propose, sway, persuade, or convince. By example, they continue the
lessons in argumentative and persuasive writing that last chapter's writers
began. With the exception of Jonathan Swift, who throws a stylistic curve ball
in "A Modest Proposal," their word choice is lucid, effective, and often quite
powerful. Their prose is taut even when it is understated (as in the newspaper
articles by Dugger and Lawson). The instances and details they choose, which
are apt and substantial, are evocatively worded and strategically deployed.
Their ideas, which are felt as well as thought, add up; there is a strong sense
of direction and progression, often accompanied by mounting intellectual and
emotional tension; and the unity of each piece is emphatically apparent in the
argument the writer makes. Their arguments are also adroitly positioned: each
writer has a sense of what most readers know about his or her issue and what
the prevailing political and emotional winds are.

Charles Murray, for instance, argues that government assistance undermines the social mores and constraints that, before the welfare state came
into existence, discouraged women from having babies if they had no means
of supporting children. The solution is implicit in his analysis of the problem:
dismantle the welfare state. He knows many people believe the welfare state
is part of the problem, not part of the solution; he encouraged this belief. His
book *Losing Ground* (1982) was one of the touchstones of the Reagan/Bush
revolution; conservatives, such as former Vice-President Quayle, still rely on
it for ammo. But wisely, Murray does not assume that all his readers agree
with his proposition about the welfare state; instead, he takes the opportunity

to explain and convince. The New Jersey Legislature's attempt to tune-up and fix welfare is doomed, he argues, because it is out of sync with reality, because it comes equipped with loopholes, and because welfare itself is the problem. He skillfully uses the piece of legislature that is the occasion for this editorial as a starting point for a discussion of what he believes are the underlying issues. Paragraph by paragraph, he broadens his essay until the reader is staring down the barrel of his argument: Repeal welfare, period. Each paragraph is sharply focused and is well explained and substantiated. His language is precise and sometimes metaphoric. The New Jersey Legislature "took the plunge," "incremental" reform will solve nothing, communities have "leverage," and the welfare system "bypasses" important "natural mechanisms." "Pessimism is realism," he writes, which is artful, arresting phrasing. He also uses sophisticated rhetorical devices that amplify his meaning; in the final paragraph, for instance, he uses "victims" twice to remind us that the children, not the "unwed mothers," deserve our concern and assistance. Murray's ideas are current, influential, and disputable; in fact, his assumptions are elitist and invalid, and hence, his conclusions are badly flawed and do real damage to real people. The craft of his writing, however, is indisputably sound and exemplary.

There are writing lessons in every piece in the chapter, whether or not we agree with the ideas of the writers. Marian Wright Edelman opens with a catalogue of abuse and neglect meant to secure our attention and sympathies before she launches a diatribe against America's misspent dollars, energy, and priorities that have put so many children in jeopardy. Kozol begins Holly Peters's story in what seems to be a dispassionate, neutral tone and reserves his indignation for the end. But if you examine his word choice and phrasing, you can see he styles her story so that it anticipates and resonates with the conclusions he deduces.

Take a second look at these pieces after you have written a first draft of this chapter's paper; at that point, your eyes will be wide open to the techniques these writers use to make their cases.

✖ Writing Workshop

The Topics:
- Is the family dying?
- Draft a proposal for curbing domestic violence.
- What can government do to make it easier for more families to provide more for their children?
- Argue for or against government-funded child care for preschoolers.
- In your opinion, who or what is to blame for the hardships poor children suffer in America? Their parents? Racism? Inequality? Politicians? Who? What?

- Predict the future of the American family.
- Write your own "modest proposal" for America's poor families today.
- Redesign the family so that it works. Who stays home? Who works? Who takes care of the kids? How? Does society help in any way?
- What are the chief family problems going to be in the next century? Why?
- Write an introduction to a family textbook, 2025.

The Assignment: Choose a topic, pair up with a classmate, and interview one another. The interviewer should take careful, legible notes, which will become the property of the interviewee after the interview is over. It doesn't matter if you're working on the same topic. As you interview, try to keep your questions simple, straightforward, and on the topic. If you hear anything you don't understand, make a note; and when your classmate finishes her or his response, ask follow-up questions. The point of the interview is to provide your classmate with an opportunity to brainstorm.

As you are interviewed, try to be as clear and complete as possible. Explain your ideas and feelings; give examples, hypothetical or actual, especially when you feel an example would help to clarify your point.

Study the interview notes, then move 180 degrees away from your perspective and argue against yourself. In other words, brainstorm the opposing or an opposing point of view—using only words and phrases. A tactic many writers use to make their readers more receptive to their arguments is to refute a key point or two of the opposition. Kozol, for instance, refutes the accusations New York City officials made against Holly Peters in the death of her son Benjamin, Murray takes on a few of the slogans of liberalism, and Jonathan Swift, in a satiric and convoluted way, refutes serious proposals to help the poor of Ireland he had made in previous essays. Even if you don't come up with any points to debate in your paper, you should find that thinking about your topic from an opposing point of view strengthens and deepens your view. Sussing out the opposition, something of a mental calisthenic, takes a little bit of time and effort if it is to pay off. Practice also helps. Try it each time you write about a controversial topic.

Go to the library and read for an hour or so only if you feel the urge. Research isn't necessary for any of these topics. But again, other people's ideas and experiences can help you to sharpen your own, and you may be able to incorporate some of the material you encounter into your paper.

Next, prepare yourself to make a presentation to a few classmates. Study your notes, and draw up a list of the ideas or points, pro and con, you think you will make. Identify the key point if you can, and begin with it. Take notes while your classmates make their presentations, and ask questions after they finish. The point of the questions is to coax your classmates to spell out the ideas that exist in their minds as mental shorthand and to think about the connections between those ideas, specifically how they work together and add up to an argument. After you make your presentation, take notes so that you will be sure to remember the ideas, points, and details that came up.

Now, study your notes again and write an entire first draft in one sitting, if possible. Setting aside enough uninterrupted time makes it more likely that you will succeed. If you get stuck, take a break, but try your best to come back to the paper later that same day.

Let the draft sit for a day. Then, rewrite, working through every aspect of development, organization, phrasing, grammar, and punctuation detailed in previous chapters. Reread the section on rewriting in the Introduction if you haven't looked at it for a while.

Exchange drafts with a classmate and mark them up. Write questions and suggestions about meaning and development in the margins, circle words that aren't right, put question marks next to sentences that need to be rephrased. Discuss your classmate's comments with her or him, and rewrite another time.

Now, write or type the final draft, observing format requirements. If a title is required and you haven't come up with one yet, now is the time. Finally, hand your paper in. Save your notes and drafts, and review them one last time when your instructor returns your paper.

Chapter 7

Fiction's Families

■

Short Stories: Windows on the World

Novelists and short story writers do not spot and analyze demographic trends. They don't diagnose family ills on the strength of interviews, questionnaires, or census data and propose solutions—clinical, political, or otherwise. Even when their stories bank on or incorporate researched material, they don't comb archives to reconstruct a person, an event, an era, or a dynasty, record by record, detail by detail.

Fiction writers are answerable to reality, but in a much less direct way than the social scientists, journalists, and autobiographers we have read. In realist fiction, writers use a recognizable world as both a point of departure and a point of return for the characters, settings, and situations in the stories they create. All writers reinvent and comment on the world, in addition to whatever other aims they might have. Writers establish and then rely on expectations about the extent to which their stories resemble or do not resemble recognizable situations—in their language, settings, characters, and plots.

Writers are the antennae of their cultures; their pens register tremors and shock waves. Readers often use the themes, plots, or characters created by writers to make sense of life. Shortly after Joseph Heller's *Catch 22* was published in the early 1960s, it became a lens through which many of its readers scrutinized America's violence and contradictions. Heller's title passed into the language, made the dictionaries, and is still used more than 30 years later to describe illogical situations, especially institutional ones, in which one is a victim of inscrutable, irrational, or unjust forces. In the 1980s, cynics who couldn't or wouldn't look beyond their fellow man's sneakers or Gucci loafers nodded their heads in recognition at Tom Wolfe's bonfire of the stereotypes (a.k.a., *Bonfire of the Vanities*), a book the fifteenth-century moral reformer Savanarola would have saved from the fire.

Ernest Hemingway's and John Steinbeck's characters became reference points for journalists in the 1930s and 1940s, and feminist critics have long regarded Charlotte Perkins Gilman's "The Yellow Wall-Paper" (included in this chapter) as an allegory that criticizes the inequality and suffering women experience in domestic life. Some writers, through an accident of fate, timing, or genius, give their names to an era or a milieu: there's Shakespeare's England, Baudelaire's Paris, and Dickens's London. American historians call the period following the Civil War, The Gilded Age, from a novel of the same name by Mark Twain and Charles Dudley Warner; situations that are modern, surreal, and degrading are called Kafkaesque, after the works of the writer Franz Kafka; and F. Scott Fitzgerald's Gatsby (from his novel *The Great Gatsby*) lingers in the wings of any discussion of the Jazz Age, or the Roaring Twenties. Gatsby's name also turns up on the labels of shirts and on the menus of restaurants that try to evoke the era.

We will, therefore, regard the short story writers here as social critics and their stories as windows on the world. It's one of the many valid approaches a writer can take to literature, and it's one that's most consistent with a book that is essentially an interdisciplinary meditation on the family.

The most famous line about family belongs to Leo Tolstoy: "Happy families are all alike; every unhappy family is unhappy in its own way." It is the first sentence of his novel *Anna Karenina,* and it is arguably a one-line prologue to the 900 pages that follow. Certainly the Oblonskys and the Karenins are unhappy in their own ways. The larger point is that fiction contains some of the most memorable and profound family portraits there are and some of the most illuminating insights into family. None of the other types of writing we have read can match fiction's vision and its power to involve the reader.

If fiction is indispensable to our understanding of family, family is also indispensable to fiction; it is hard to think of many great novels and short stories in which family does not figure in a vital way. Novelists, short story writers, and playwrights imply through the central place they give family in their stories that there is no group, organization, institution, or idea more important to human identity and drama than the family. Family is one of fiction's moorings.

This chapter's writers span a century of modern life. Gilman's "The Yellow Wall-Paper," which was published in 1893, is the story of an upper middle-class woman—a wife, mother, and writer—who struggles for her sanity in the face of the "rest cure" that her domineering physician husband prescribes for her. Krebs, the main character in Hemingway's "Soldier's Home," returns home from the First World War and recoils from the way of life he fought for. Joyce Carol Oates's Sissie is a blue-collar kid in the Detroit area at the beginning of "Four Summers," circa 1950. Sissie tries unsuccessfully to conceal from herself and the reader the pain she experiences as she grows up into the teenager, then the young wife and mother she is supposed to be. Gabriel García Márquez's narrator chronicles the death of Big Mama, the character who gives the story its name. The reading of her will and her funeral mark the end of a family, a colonial dynasty, and an era. Raymond Carver's "Boxes" was published in 1986. Family is a guilty memory for the story's three, late twentieth-century, superhighway nomads. Paulette Childress White's "Getting the Facts of Life," written in 1989 but set in Detroit, 1961, is a coming-of-age story; its narrator, a Black girl on the verge of becoming a teenager, accompanies her mother to the welfare office and realizes more than she can say about her mother and herself. The world is wider than she ever imagined, and more perilous.

Each story is complete in and of itself, but as a group, these writers cast a wide net. They write in different voices from different places, different perspectives, and different times; however, their characters are all caught in webs of family duty and feeling, and collectively, these writers give us a sense of the commonality as well as the variety of family life, which is an essential part of the human experience.

🔊 The Art of Short Fiction: Reading to Write

Students come to college with varying degrees of experience with literature. Everyone has read some, some have read quite a bit. Some, beyond quizzes and exams, have never written about it, while others have already logged a number of papers; thus, the following brief discussion of the elements of short fiction will be a review for some and an introduction for others. Your instructor will add to the overview in this class discussion of the stories.

The tools fiction writers use are simple; the ways in which they use them are not. Virginia Woolf observed in an essay called "Mr. Bennet and Mrs. Brown" that when we think of the great novels, we think first of the characters of those works; then, through them, we think of what they do—the plot—and why they do it—the themes. Of course, characterization, plot, and theme are inseparable: we come to know a story's characters, in part, through what they do and why, the story's plot springs from the temperaments and psyches of its characters and finds its rationale in the story's themes, and a story's themes are the product of plot and character. It's not just what happens, it's why it happens and who it happens to that make a story compelling and meaningful.

Character, plot, and theme are fiction's principal elements; point of view, setting, and language inform and color how we see and experience these elements.

As you probably know, *point of view* means who is telling the story. A first-person narrator is the "I" who tells the story. "The Yellow Wall-Paper," "Four Summers," "Boxes," and "Getting the Facts of Life" are first-person narratives. These narrators play parts in the stories they tell and, more important, filter the stories they tell through themselves. Their responses, thoughts, feelings, and impressions are woven into the narrative fabric. In fact, the consciousness of the first-person narrator is the skein of the story; even when the story seems to be about another character, as is the case in Herman Melville's "Bartleby the Scrivener" or Fitzgerald's *The Great Gatsby,* the first-person narrator is the main character.

Hemingway's "Soldier's Home" and García Márquez's "Big Mama's Funeral" are third-person narratives. These narrators play no part in the stories they tell. It's important not to confuse the third-person narrator with the author. Often, the way the third-person narrator sees things and tells the story is part of what the writer wants us to react to. As Wayne Booth argues in *The Rhetoric of Fiction,* there is an implied authorial intelligence behind the narrator's voice that puts that voice into perspective, that inflects it.

Hemingway and García Márquezgive their narrators unlimited access to the thoughts and actions of their characters. These narrators are called third-person omniscient narrators. They are all-knowing. García Márquez's narrator, in particular, traverses whole continents, centuries, and concepts.

It is arguable that a third-person narrator, even though he or she has no face, name, or address, is also the main character, but that's a technical squabble. The main point is that in a third-person narrative, we see the actions and learn the thoughts of the story's chief actor through another intelligence or perspective—that of the narrator.

The setting in a good piece of short fiction is alive. The narrator presents the setting, giving it a sound and a voice and connecting it through the narrator's perspective to the story's fabric. Writers use the setting to establish or develop a story's atmosphere or feel and to put the characters and their actions in relief. In Hemingway's story, for instance, the claustrophobic home Krebs returns to from the war helps us to understand and feel his plight. The mother of Carver's narrator lives with a kitchen full of boxes that convey her unhappiness and hopelessness; they are also a hostile gesture aimed at her son. In other words, the setting can resonate with the story's themes in a symbolic way. The narrator of Gilman's "The Yellow Wall-Paper" sees herself in the wallpaper of the room. Is she hallucinating? That's beside the point. It is hard to say where the setting ends and the characters begin. Setting is continuous with characterization. It penetrates the characters' skins and reflects or resonates with their psyches.

Language is a peculiar category because a short story is nothing but words; however, short story writers use language in special, poetic ways. The connotations, sounds, and feel of words contribute to a story's tone and atmosphere; and we come to know a writer's characters not only through what they do and what others say about them but also through the words the writer puts into each character's mouth. Each time characters speak, regardless of the subject, they reveal something about themselves. At the end of "Boxes," Carver's narrator is on the phone with his mother, who, as usual, is complaining about her life. He doesn't know what to say, and he goes silent. As the awkwardness builds, second by second, he snatches a word out of the air, out of the past, a word his dad used when the narrator was a kid and his father wasn't drunk and was being nice to his wife. "Dear, try not to be afraid," the narrator tells his mother, breaking the silence. The roots of the word *dear* go deep into the narrator's family past. The word, like the narrator, is well intentioned but ineffectual. *Dear*: He feels better for an instant, perhaps she does too, and nothing changes.

Short story writers, who in this century have emulated the compression of poetry, often use metaphoric and symbolic language to develop a theme or a character—to put spin on the ball. At the end of "Getting the Facts of Life," Minerva and her mother walk past the poolroom and a hotel called "Moonflower." They felt a sense of dread when they walked past it earlier on their way to the welfare office. A drunk had heckled Minerva with a half-hearted, "hey, baby." That block is where the bad boys hang out; there's an occasional stabbing in the poolroom. When Minerva and her mother pass a second time, the men are out in groups, and they're "standing in the shadows of the poolroom and the Moonflower Hotel." No one heckles them this time because, Minerva guesses, the men can see they're not afraid. Minerva and her mother had been to welfare, and the facts of life, which were "no burning mysteries," were fixed in their minds "like the sun in the sky." Through a few deftly placed metaphoric words—*shadows* and *sun,* in particular—White elevates a mundane moment to the status of a turning point in Minerva's life. This twelve-year-old girl/woman sees and understands more of the world than she ever has before, especially the man/woman thing. Her name shimmers with the mythic significance of her namesake, Minerva, Roman goddess of wisdom.

Gilman applies so many metaphoric strokes to her wallpaper that by the end of the story it is an overarching symbol of the oppression of women. And in García Márquez's story, the narrator's litany of Big Mama's immaterial possessions stands for all the lies, deceptions, and ideological swindles the ruling class has perpetrated on workers, peasants, and ordinary citizens to maintain an imbalance of power.

Finally, phrasing and the rhythm of phrases is an important resource. Gilman conveys the anxiety and nervousness of her narrator through short, choppy sentences and paragraphs. Reading the story makes most readers nervous. The narrator's eye and tongue dart around, resting nowhere and with no one for long. In "Soldier's Home," Krebs's effort to block out life's complications comes through in the simple, repetitious sentences the narrator uses to convey Krebs's thoughts, especially while he watches from his front porch as the town's girls walk by.

In short, it's not just what the characters say or what happens; it's the precise words characters use and how those words are phrased that make a story's meaning. Read closely. Read aloud passages you find moving; the ear can help the eye to see. It's best to save the reading questions until you finish each story, but if a story puzzles you, looking ahead to the questions may help you to follow it.

—————————————— $\mathcal{R}$eadings ——————————————

The Yellow Wall-Paper

—Charlotte Perkins Gilman

Charlotte Perkins Gilman was born in 1860 to an illustrious New England family: her father was the grandson of the theologian Lyman Beecher and the nephew of the abolitionist preacher Henry Ward Beecher and the abolitionist writer Harriet Beecher Stowe and her mother was a Fitch, a family that had been prominent in Rhode Island since the middle of the seventeenth century. She had a hard life as a child, however, because her father deserted the family. And she had an emotionally turbulent time as wife to Charles Stetson, her first husband, and as mother to their daughter Katherine. Suffering depression after giving birth to Katherine, she was urged, pushed by her husband to undergo Dr. S. Weir Mitchell's "rest cure." Dr. Mitchell sent her home "to live as domestic a life as possible . . . to have but two hours intellectual life a day . . . never to touch a pen or brush again" (*Why I Wrote "The Yellow Wall-Paper,"* 1913). Mitchell's cure almost drove Gilman over the edge; we can feel the force of her revulsion in "The Yellow Wall-Paper," the story that came out of the experience. She discontinued the "rest cure" and her marriage to Stetson and, after the divorce, agreed to let Katherine live with her father and his new wife, Grace Ellery Channing,—a decision that drew an enormous amount of criticism. She bore the criticism and went on to forge a new life and persona for herself, writing and speaking against male dominance, oppression, and irrationality. She published *Women and Economics* in 1898 and *Herland,* a feminist utopian novel, in 1915, just to name a few of her works; she continued to be a force in modern American feminism until her death in 1935. As you read the story, consider in what sense "The Yellow Wall-Paper" is a feminist manifesto.

It is very seldom that mere ordinary people like John and myself secure ances- 1
tral halls for the summer.

A colonial mansion, a hereditary estate, I would say a haunted house, and
reach the height of romantic felicity—but that would be asking too much of fate!

Still I will proudly declare that there is something queer about it.

Else, why should it be let so cheaply? And why have stood so long untenanted?

John laughs at me, of course, but one expects that in marriage. 5

John is practical in the extreme. He has no patience with faith, an intense horror of superstition, and he scoffs at any talk of things not to be felt and seen and put
down in figures.

John is a physician, and *perhaps*—(I would not say it to a living soul, of
course, but this is dead paper and a great relief to my mind—) *perhaps* that is one
reason I do not get well faster.

You see he does not believe I am sick!

And what can one do?

If a physician of high standing, and one's own husband, assures friends and 10
relatives that there is really nothing the matter with one but temporary nervous
depression—a slight hysterical tendency—what is one to do?

My brother is also a physician, and also of high standing, and he says the
same thing.

So I take phosphates or phosphites—whichever it is, and tonics, and journeys,
and air, and exercise, and am absolutely forbidden to "work" until I am well again.

Personally, I disagree with their ideas.

Personally, I believe that congenial work, with excitement and change, would
do me good.

But what is one to do? 15

I did write for a while in spite of them; but it *does* exhaust me a good deal—
having to be so sly about it, or else meet with heavy opposition.

I sometimes fancy that in my condition if I had less opposition and more society and stimulus—but John says the very worst thing I can do is to think about my
condition, and I confess it always makes me feel bad.

So I will let it alone and talk about the house.

The most beautiful place! It is quite alone, standing well back from the road,
quite three miles from the village. It makes me think of English places that you read
about, for there are hedges and walls and gates that lock, and lots of separate little
houses for the gardeners and people.

There is a *delicious* garden! I never saw such a garden—large and shady, full 20
of box-bordered paths, and lined with long grape-covered arbors with seats under
them.

There were greenhouses, too, but they are all broken now.

There was some legal trouble, I believe, something about the heirs and
coheirs; anyhow, the place has been empty for years.

That spoils my ghostliness, I am afraid, but I don't care—there is something
strange about the house—I can feel it.

I even said so to John one moonlight evening, abut he said what I felt was a *draught*, and shut the window.

I get unreasonably angry with John sometimes. I'm sure I never used to be so 25 sensitive. I think it is due to this nervous condition.

But John says if I feel so, I shall neglect proper self-control; so I take pains to control myself—before him, at least, and that makes me very tired.

I don't like our room a bit. I wanted one downstairs that opened on the piazza and had roses all over the window, and such pretty old-fashioned chintz hangings! but John would not hear of it.

He said there was only one window and not room for two beds, and no near room for him if he took another.

He is very careful and loving, and hardly lets me stir without special direction.

I have a schedule prescription for each hour in the day; he takes all care from 30 me, and so I feel basely ungrateful not to value it more.

He said we came here solely on my account, that I was to have perfect rest and all the air I could get. "Your exercise depends on your strength, my dear," said he, "and your food somewhat on your appetite; but air you can absorb all the time." So we took the nursery at the top of the house.

It is a big, airy room, the whole floor nearly, with windows that look all ways and air and sunshine galore. It was nursery first and then playroom and gymnasium, I should judge; for the windows are barred for little children, and there are rings and things in the walls.

The paint and paper look as if a boys' school had used it. It is stripped off— the paper—in great patches all around the head of my bed, about as far as I can reach, and in a great place on the other side of the room low down. I never saw a worse paper in my life.

One of those sprawling flamboyant patterns committing every artistic sin.

It is dull enough to confuse the eye in following, pronounced enough to con- 35 stantly irritate and provoke study, and when you follow the lame uncertain curves for a little distance they suddenly commit suicide—plunge off at outrageous angles, destroy themselves in unheard of contradictions.

The color is repellent, almost revolting; a smouldering unclean yellow, strangely faded by the slow-turning sunlight.

It is a dull yet lurid orange in some places, a sickly sulphur tint in others.

No wonder the children hated it! I should hate it myself if I had to live in this room long.

There comes John, and I must put this away,—he hates to have me write a word.

I

We have been here two weeks, and I haven't felt like writing before, since that 40 first day.

I am sitting by the window now, up in this atrocious nursery, and there is nothing to hinder my writing as much as I please, save lack of strength.

John is away all day, and even some nights when his cases are serious.

I am glad my case is not serious!

But these nervous troubles are dreadfully depressing.

John does not know how much I really suffer. He knows there is no *reason* to 45 suffer, and that satisfies him.

Of course it is only nervousness. It does weigh on me so not to do my duty in any way!

I meant to be such a help to John, such a real rest and comfort, and here I am a comparative burden already!

Nobody would believe what an effort it is to do what little I am able,—to dress and entertain, and order things.

It is fortunate Mary is so good with the baby. Such a dear baby!

And yet I *cannot* be with him, it makes me so nervous. 50

I suppose John never was nervous in his life. He laughs at me so about this wall-paper!

At first he meant to repaper the room, but afterwards he said that I was letting it get the better of me, and that nothing was worse for a nervous patient than to give way to such fancies.

He said that after the wall-paper was changed it would be the heavy bedstead, and then the barred windows, and then that gate at the head of the stairs, and so on.

"You know the place is doing you good," he said, "and really, dear, I don't care to renovate the house just for a three months' rental."

"Then do let us go downstairs," I said, "there are such pretty rooms there." 55

Then he took me in his arms and called me a blessed little goose, and said he would go down cellar, if I wished, and have it whitewashed into the bargain.

But he is right enough about the beds and windows and things.

It is an airy and comfortable room as any one need wish, and, of course, I would not be so silly as to make him uncomfortable just for a whim.

I'm really getting quite fond of the big room, all but that horrid paper.

Out of one window I can see the garden, those mysterious deep-shaded arbors, 60 the riotous old-fashioned flowers, and bushes and gnarly trees.

Out of another I get a lovely view of the bay and a little private wharf belonging to the estate. There is a beautiful shaded lane that runs down there from the house. I always fancy I see people walking in these numerous paths and arbors, but John has cautioned me not to give way to fancy in the least. He says that with my imaginative power and habit of story-making, a nervous weakness like mine is sure to lead to all manner of excited fancies, and that I ought to use my will and good sense to check the tendency. So I try.

I think sometimes that if I were only well enough to write a little it would relieve the press of ideas and rest me.

But I find I get pretty tired when I try.

It is so discouraging not to have any advice and companionship about my work. When I get really well, John says we will ask Cousin Henry and Julia down for a long visit; but he says he would as soon put fireworks in my pillow-case as to let me have those stimulating people about now.

I wish I could get well faster.   65

But I must not think about that. This paper looks to me as if it *knew* what a vicious influence it had!

There is a recurrent spot where the pattern lolls like a broken neck and two bulbous eyes stare at you upside down.

I get positively angry with the impertinence of it and the everlastingness. Up and down and sideways they crawl, and those absurd, unblinking eyes are everywhere. There is one place where two breadths didn't match, and the eyes go all up and down the line, one a little higher than the other.

I never saw so much expression in an inanimate thing before, and we all know how much expression they have! I used to lie awake as a child and get more entertainment and terror out of blank walls and plain furniture than most children could find in a toy-store.

I remember what a kindly wink the knobs of our big, old bureau used to have, 70 and there was one chair that always seemed like a strong friend.

I used to feel that if any of the other things looked too fierce I could always hop into that chair and be safe.

The furniture in this room is no worse than inharmonious, however, for we had to bring it all from downstairs. I suppose when this was used as a playroom they had to take the nursery things out, and no wonder! I never saw such ravages as the children have made here.

The wall-paper, as I said before, is torn off in spots, and it sticketh closer than a brother—they must have had perseverance as well as hatred.

Then the floor is scratched and gouged and splintered, the plaster itself is dug out here and there, and this great heavy bed which is all we found in the room, looks as if it had been through the wars.

But I don't mind it a bit—only the paper.   75

There comes John's sister. Such a dear girl as she is, and so careful of me! I must not let her find me writing.

She is a perfect and enthusiastic housekeeper, and hopes for no better profession. I verily believe she thinks it is the writing which made me sick!

But I can write when she is out, and see her a long way off from these windows.

There is one that commands the road, a lovely shaded winding road, and one that just looks off over the country. A lovely country, too, full of great elms and velvet meadows.

The wall-paper has a kind of subpattern in a different shade, a particularly irri- 80 tating one, for you can only see it in certain lights, and not clearly then.

But in the places where it isn't faded and where the sun is just so—I can see a strange, provoking, formless sort of figure, that seems to skulk about behind that sill and conspicuous front design.

There's sister on the stairs!

II

Well, the Fourth of July is over! The people are all gone and I am tired out. John thought it might do me good to see a little company, so we just had mother and Nellie and the children down for a week.

Of course I didn't do a thing. Jennie see to everything now.

But it tires me all the same.   85

John says if I don't pick up faster he shall send me to Weir Mitchell[1] in the fall.

But I don't want to go there at all. I had a friend who was in his hands once, and she says he is just like John and my brother, only more so!

Besides, it is such an undertaking to go so far.

I don't feel as if it was worth while to turn my hand over for anything, and I'm getting dreadfully fretful and querulous.

I cry at nothing, and cry most of the time.   90

Of course I don't when John is here, or anybody else, but when I am alone.

And I am alone a good deal just now. John is kept in town very often by serious cases, and Jennie is good and lets me alone when I want her to.

So I walk a little in the garden or down that lovely lane, sit on the porch under the roses, and lie down up here a good deal.

I'm getting really fond of the room in spite of the wall-paper. Perhaps *because* of the wall-paper.

It dwells in my mind so!   95

I lie here on this great immovable bed—it is nailed down, I believe—and follow that pattern about by the hour. It is as good as gymnastics, I assure you. I start, we'll say, at the bottom, down in the corner over there where it has not been touched, and I determine for the thousandth time that I will follow that pointless pattern to some sort of a conclusion.

I know a little of the principle of design, and I know this thing was not arranged on any laws of radiation, or alternation, or repetition, or symmetry, or anything else that I ever heard of.

It is repeated, of course, by the breadths, but not otherwise.

Looked at in one way each breadth stands alone, the bloated curves and flourishes—a kind of "debased Romanesque" with delirium tremens go waddling up and down in isolated columns of fatuity.

But, on the other hand, they connect diagonally, and the sprawling outlines 100 run off in great slanting waves of optic horror, like a lot of wallowing seaweeds in full chase.

The whole thing goes horizontally, too, at least it seems so, and I exhaust myself in trying to distinguish the order of its going in that direction.

---

[1]Silas Weir Mitchell (1829–1914) was the Philadelphia neurologist-psychologist who introduced "rest cure" for nervous diseases. His medical books include *Diseases of the Nervous System, Especially of Women* (1887).

They have used a horizontal breadth for a frieze, and that adds wonderfully to the confusion.

There is one end of the room where it is almost intact, and there, when the crosslights fade and the low sun shines directly upon it, I can almost fancy radiation after all,—the interminable grotesques seem to form around a common centre and rush off in headlong plunges of equal distraction.

It makes me tired to follow it. I will take a nap I guess.

III

I don't know why I should write this.   105

I don't want to.

I don't feel able.

And I know John would think it absurd. But I *must* say what I feel and think in some way—it is such a relief!

But the effort is getting to be greater than the relief.

Half the time now I am awfully lazy, and lie down ever so much.   110

John says I mustn't lose my strength, and has me take cod liver oil and lots of tonics and things, to say nothing of ale and wine and rare meat.

Dear John! He loves me very dearly, and hates to have me sick. I tried to have a real earnest reasonable talk with him the other day, and tell him how I wish he would let me go and make a visit to Cousin Henry and Julia.

But he said I wasn't able to go, nor able to stand it after I got there; and I did not make out a very good case for myself, for I was crying before I had finished.

It is getting to be a great effort for me to think straight. Just this nervous weakness I suppose.

And dear John gathered me up in his arms, and just carried me upstairs and 115 laid me on the bed, and sat by me and read to me till it tired my head.

He said I was his darling and his comfort and all he had, and that I must take care of myself for his sake, and keep well.

He says no one but myself can help me out of it, that I must use my will and self-control and not let any silly fancies run away with me.

There's one comfort, the baby is well and happy, and does not have to occupy this nursery with the horrid wall-paper.

If we had not used it, that blessed child would have! What a fortunate escape! Why, I wouldn't have a child of mine, an impressionable little thing, live in such a room for worlds.

I never thought of it before, but it is lucky that John kept me here after all, I 120 can stand it so much easier than a baby, you see.

Of course I never mention it to them any more—I am too wise,—but I keep watch of it all the same.

There are things in that paper that nobody knows but me, or ever will.

Behind that outside pattern the dim shapes get clearer every day.

It is always the same shape, only very numerous.

And it is like a woman stooping down and creeping about behind that pattern. 125

I don't like it a bit. I wonder—I begin to think—I wish John would take me away from here!

IV

It is so hard to talk with John about my case, because he is so wise, and because he loves me so.

But I tried it last night.

It was moonlight. The moon shines in all around just as the sun does.

I hate to see it sometimes, it creeps so slowly, and always comes in by one window or another.

John was asleep and I hated to waken him, so I kept still and watched the moonlight on that undulating wall-paper till I felt creepy.

The faint figure behind seemed to shake the pattern, just as if she wanted to get out.

I got up softly and went to feel and see if the paper *did* move, and when I came back John was awake.

"What is it, little girl?" he said. "Don't go walking about like that—you'll get cold."

I thought it was a good time to talk, so I told him that I really was not gaining here, and that I wished he would take me away.

"Why, darling!" said he, "our lease will be up in three weeks, and I can't see how to leave before.

"The repairs are not done at home, and I cannot possibly leave town just now. Of course if you were in any danger, I could and would, but you really are better, dear, whether you can see it or not. I am a doctor, dear, and I know. You are gaining flesh and color, your appetite is better, I feel really much easier about you."

"I don't weigh a bit more," said I, "nor as much; and my appetite may be better in the evening when you are here, but it is worse in the morning when you are away!"

"Bless her little heart!" said he with a big hug, "she shall be as sick as she pleases! But now let's improve the shining hours by going to sleep, and talk about it in the morning!"

"And you won't go away?" I asked gloomily.

"Why, how can I, dear? It is only three weeks more and then we will take a nice little trip of a few days while Jennie is getting the house ready. Really dear you are better!"

"Better in body perhaps—" I began, and stopped short, for he sat up straight and looked at me with such a stern, reproachful look that I could not say another word.

"My darling," said he, "I beg of you, for my sake and for our child's sake, as well as for your own, that you will never for one instant let that idea enter your mind! There is nothing so dangerous, so fascinating, to a temperament like yours. It is a false and foolish fancy. Can you not trust me as a physician when I tell you so?"

So of course I said no more on that score, and we went to sleep before long. He thought I was asleep first, but I wasn't, and lay there for hours trying to decide whether that front pattern and the back pattern really did move together or separately.

V

On a pattern like this, by daylight, there is a lack of sequence, a defiance of law, that is a constant irritant to a normal mind.

The color is hideous enough, and reliable enough, and infuriating enough, but 145 the pattern is torturing.

You think you have mastered it, but just as you get well underway in following, it turns a back-somersault and there you are. It slaps you in the face, knocks you down, and tramples upon you. It is like a bad dream.

The outside pattern is a florid arabesque, reminding one of a fungus. If you can imagine a toadstool in joints, an interminable string of toadstools, budding and sprouting in endless convolutions—why, that is something like it.

That is, sometimes!

There is one marked peculiarity about this paper, a thing nobody seems to notice but myself, and that is that it changes as the light changes.

When the sun shoots in through the east window—I always watch for that first 150 long, straight ray—it changes so quickly that I never can quite believe it.

That is why I watch it always.

By moonlight—the moon shines in all night when there is a moon—I wouldn't know it was the same paper.

At night in any kind of light, in twilight, candlelight, lamplight, and worst of all by moonlight, it becomes bars! The outside pattern I mean, and the woman behind it is as plain as can be.

I didn't realize for a long time what the thing was that showed behind, that dim sub-pattern, but now I am quite sure it is a woman.

By daylight she is subdued, quiet. I fancy it is the pattern that keeps her so 155 still. It is so puzzling. It keeps me quiet by the hour.

I lie down ever so much now. John says it is good for me, and to sleep all I can.

Indeed he started the habit by making me lie down for an hour after each meal.

It is a very bad habit I am convinced, for you see I don't sleep.

And that cultivates deceit, for I don't tell them I'm awake—O no!

The fact is I am getting a little afraid of John.   160

He seems very queer sometimes, and even Jennie has an inexplicable look.

It strikes me occasionally, just as a scientific hypothesis,—that perhaps it is the paper!

I have watched John when he did not know I was looking, and come into the room suddenly on the most innocent excuses, and I've caught him several times *looking at the paper!* And Jennie, too. I caught Jennie with her hand on it once.

She didn't know I was in the room, and when I asked her in a quiet, a very quiet voice, with the most restrained manner possible, what she was doing with the paper—she turned around as if she had been caught stealing, and looked quite angry—asked me why I should frighten her so!

Then she said that the paper stained everything it touched, that she had found 165 yellow smooches on all my clothes and John's, and she wished we would be more careful!

Did not that sound innocent? But I know she was studying that pattern, and I am determined that nobody shall find it out but myself!

VI

Life is very much more exciting now than it used to be. You see I have something more to expect, to look forward to, to watch. I really do eat better, and am more quiet than I was.

John is so pleased to see me improve! He laughed a little the other day, and said I seemed to be flourishing in spite of my wall-paper.

I turned it off with a laugh. I had no intention of telling him it was *because* of the wall-paper—he would make fun of me. He might even want to take me away.

I don't want to leave now until I have found it out. There is a week more, and 170 I think that will be enough.

VII

I'm feeling ever so much better! I don't sleep much at night, for it is so interesting to watch developments; but I sleep a good deal in the daytime.

In the daytime it is tiresome and perplexing.

There are always new shoots on the fungus, and new shades of yellow all over it. I cannot keep count of them, though I have tried conscientiously.

It is the strangest yellow, that wall-paper! It makes me think of all the yellow things I ever saw—not beautiful ones like buttercups, but old foul, bad yellow things.

But there is something else about that paper—the smell! I noticed it the 175 moment we came into the room, but with so much air and sun it was not bad. Now we have had a week of fog and rain, and whether the windows are open or not, the smell is here.

It creeps all over the house.

I find it hovering in the dining-room, skulking in the parlor, hiding in the hall, lying in wait for me on the stairs.

It gets into my hair.

Even when I go to ride, if I turn my head suddenly and surprise it—there is that smell!

Such a peculiar odor, too! I have spent hours in trying to analyze it, to find 180 what it smelled like.

It is not bad—at first, and very gentle, but quite the subtlest, most enduring odor I ever met.

In this damp weather it is awful, I wake up in the night and find it hanging over me.

It used to disturb me at first. I thought seriously of burning the house—to reach the smell.

But now I am used to it. The only thing I can think of that it is like is the *color* of the paper! A yellow smell.

There is a very funny mark on this wall, low down, near the mopboard. A 185 streak that runs round the room. It goes behind every piece of furniture, except the bed, a long, straight, even *smooch,* as if it had been rubbed over and over.

I wonder how it was done and who did it, and what they did it for. Round and round and round—round and round and round!—it makes me dizzy!

VIII

I really have discovered something at last.

Through watching so much at night, when it changes so, I have finally found out.

The front pattern *does* move—and no wonder! The woman behind shakes it!

Sometimes I think there are a great many women behind, and sometimes only 190 one, and she crawls around fast, and her crawling shakes it all over.

Then in the very bright spots she keeps still, and in the very shady spots she just takes hold of the bars and shakes them hard.

And she is all the time trying to climb through. But nobody could climb through that pattern—it strangles so; I think that is why it has so many heads.

They get through, and then the pattern strangles them off and turns them upside down, and makes their eyes white!

If those heads were covered or taken off it would not be half so bad.

IX

I think that woman gets out in the daytime!   195

And I'll tell you why—privately—I've seen her!

I can see her out of every one of my windows!

It is the same woman, I know, for she is always creeping, and most women do not creep by daylight.

I see her in that long shaded lane, creeping up and down. I see her in those dark grape arbors, creeping all around the garden.

I see her on that long road under the trees, creeping along, and when a car- 200 riage comes she hides under the blackberry vines.

I don't blame her a bit. It must be very humiliating to be caught creeping by daylight!

I always lock the door when I creep by daylight. I can't do it at night, for I know John would suspect something at once.

And John is so queer now, that I don't want to irritate him. I wish he would take another room! Besides, I don't want anybody to get that woman out at night but myself.

I often wonder if I could see her out of all the windows at once.

But, turn as fast as I can, I can only see out of one at one time. 205

And though I always see her, she *may* be able to creep faster than I can turn!

I have watched her sometimes away off in the open country, creeping as fast as a cloud shadow in a high wind.

X

If only that top pattern could be gotten off from the under one! I mean to try it, little by little.

I have found out another funny thing, but I shan't tell it this time! It does not do to trust people too much.

There are only two more days to get this paper off, and I believe John is 210 beginning to notice. I don't like the look in his eyes.

And I heard him ask Jennie a lot of professional questions about me. She had a very good report to give.

She said I slept a good deal in the daytime.

John knows I don't sleep very well at night, for all I'm so quiet!

He asked me all sorts of questions, too, and pretended to be very loving and kind.

As if I couldn't see through him! 215

Still, I don't wonder he acts so, sleeping under this paper for three months.

It only interests me, but I feel sure John and Jennie are secretly affected by it.

XI

Hurrah! This is the last day, but it is enough. John is to stay in town over night, and won't be out until this evening.

Jennie wanted to sleep with me—the sly thing! but I told her I should undoubtedly rest better for a night all alone.

That was clever, for really I wasn't alone a bit! As soon as it was moonlight 220 and that poor thing began to crawl and shake the pattern, I got up and ran to help her.

I pulled and she shook, I shook and she pulled, and before morning we had peeled off yards of that paper.

A strip about as high as my head and half around the room.

And then when the sun came and that awful pattern began to laugh at me, I declared I would finish it to-day!

We go away to-morrow, and they are moving all my furniture down again to leave things as they were before.

Jennie looked at the wall in amazement, but I told her merrily that I did it out 225 of pure spite at the vicious thing.

She laughed and said she wouldn't mind doing it herself, but I must not get tired.

How she betrayed herself that time!

But I am here, and no person touches this paper but me,—not *alive!*

She tried to get me out of the room—it was too patent! But I said it was so quiet and empty and clean now that I believed I would lie down again and sleep all I could; and not to wake me even for dinner—I would call when I woke.

So now she is gone, and the servants are gone, and the things are gone, and 230 there is nothing left but that great bedstead nailed down, with the canvas mattress we found on it.

We shall sleep downstairs to-night, and take the boat home to-morrow.

I quite enjoy the room, now it is bare again.

How those children did tear about here!

This bedstead is fairly gnawed!

But I must get to work.   235

I have locked the door and thrown the key down into the front path.

I don't want to go out, and I don't want to have anybody come in, till John comes.

I want to astonish him.

I've got a rope up here that even Jennie did not find. If that woman does get out, and tries to get away, I can tie her!

But I forgot I could not reach far without anything to stand on!   240

The bed will *not* move!

I tried to lift and push it until I was lame, and then I got so angry I bit off a little piece at one corner—but it hurt my teeth.

Then I peeled off all the paper I could reach standing on the floor. It sticks horribly and the pattern just enjoys it! All those strangled heads and bulbous eyes and waddling fungus growths just shriek with derision!

I am getting angry enough to do something desperate. To jump out of the window would be admirable exercise, but the bars are too strong even to try.

Besides I wouldn't do it. Of course not. I know well enough that a step like 245 that is improper and might be misconstrued.

I don't like to *look* out of the windows even—there are so many of those creeping women, and they creep so fast.

I wonder if they all come out of that wall-paper as I did?

But I am securely fastened now by my well-hidden rope—you don't get *me* out in the road there!

I suppose I shall have to get back behind the pattern when it comes night, and that is hard!

It is so pleasant to be out in this great room and creep around as I please!   250

I don't want to go outside. I won't, even if Jennie asks me to.

For outside you have to creep on the ground, and everything is green instead of yellow.

But here I can creep smoothly on the floor, and my shoulder just fits in that long smooch around the wall, so I cannot lose my way.

Why there's John at the door!

It is no use, young man, you can't open it!   255

How he does call and pound!

Now he's crying for an axe.

It would be a shame to break down that beautiful door!

"John, dear!" said I in the gentlest voice, "the key is down by the front steps, under a plantain leaf!"

That silenced him for a few moments.   260

Then he said—very quietly indeed, "Open the door, my darling!"

"I can't," said I. "The key is down by the front door under a plantain leaf!"

And then I said it again, several times, very gently and slowly, and said it so often that he had to go and see, and he got it of course, and came in. He stopped short by the door.

"What is the matter?" he cried. "For God's sake, what are you doing!"

I kept on creeping just the same, but I looked at him over my shoulder.   265

"I've got out at last," said I, "in spite of you and Jane! And I've pulled off most of the paper, so you can't put me back!"

Now why should that man have fainted? But he did, and right across my path by the wall, so that I had to creep over him every time!

■ *Questions for* . . . The Yellow Wall-Paper by Charlotte Perkins Gilman

Discussion and Journal Writing

1. Why has the narrator and her family rented these ancestral halls for the summer?

2. How have they arranged their living quarters? Who sleeps where and how are the family's domestic arrangements organized? Why?

3. What does the narrator mean when she says her husband John is a physician, which is one of the reasons she doesn't get well faster?

4. Why are the narrator's sentences and paragraphs so short? What do they add to her character?

5. What does the yellow wallpaper symbolize?

6. Does Gilman expect us to believe the narrator when she says that her bedroom, to which she is confined, used to be a nursery?

7. At the end of the story, the narrator mentions someone named Jane. Who is she? How does the ending resolve the story?

8. Gilman's story is often read as a critique of the relations between the sexes and the institution of marriage, circa 1893. Do Gilman's themes have the same bite today?

ooooo

Soldier's Home

—Ernest Hemingway

Ernest Hemingway won a Pulitzer Prize in 1953 for his novella *The Old Man and the Sea,* and a Nobel Prize the next year; many writers, critics, and scholars believe the set of spare stories he published in 1925, entitled *In Our Time,* altered the tone, tenor, and shape of the short story in America. "Soldier's Home" is one of those stories, and the best, in my opinion. Hemingway served as an ambulance driver in the First World War and was badly wounded after three weeks. He went home to Oak Park, Illinois, to convalesce but couldn't adjust to the stultifying atmosphere of his parents' middle-class, late-Victorian household. He felt especially estranged from his mother. Krebs, Hemingway's protagonist in "Soldier's Home," also has a hard time coming home from the war.

Krebs went to the war from a Methodist college in Kansas. There is a picture which shows him among his fraternity brothers, all of them wearing exactly the same height and style collar. He enlisted in the Marines in 1917 and did not return to the United States until the second division returned from the Rhine in the summer of 1919.

There is a picture which shows him on the Rhine with two German girls and another corporal. Krebs and the corporal look too big for their uniforms. The German girls are not beautiful. The Rhine does not show in the picture.

By the time Krebs returned to his home town in Oklahoma the greeting of heroes was over. He came back much too late. the men from the town who had been drafted had all been welcomed elaborately on their return. There had been a great deal of hysteria. Now the reaction had set in. People seemed to think it was rather ridiculous for Krebs to be getting back so late, years after the war was over.

At first Krebs, who had been at Belleau Wood, Soissons, the Champagne, St. Mihiel, and in the Argonne[1] did not want to talk about the war at all. Later he felt the need to talk but no one wanted to hear about it. His town had heard too many atrocity stories to be thrilled by actualities. Krebs found that to be listened to at all he had to lie, and after he had done this twice he, too, had a reaction against the war and against talking about it. A distaste for everything that had happened to him in the war set in because of the lies he had told. All of the times that had been able to make him feel cool and clear inside himself when he thought of them; the times

---

[1]*Belleau Wood* . . . : Sites of battles in World War I in which American troops were instrumental in pushing back the Germans.

so long back when he had done the one thing, the only thing for a man to do, easily and naturally, when he might have done something else, now lost their cool, valuable quality and then were lost themselves.

His lies were quite unimportant lies and consisted in attributing to himself things other men had seen, done, or heard of, and stating as facts certain apocryphal incidents familiar to all soldiers. Even his lies were not sensational at the pool room. His acquaintances, who had heard detailed accounts of German women found chained to machine guns in the Argonne forest and who could not comprehend, or were barred by their patriotism from interest in, any German machine gunners who were not chained, were not thrilled by his stories.

Krebs acquired the nausea in regard to experience that is the result of untruth or exaggeration, and when he occasionally met another man who had really been a soldier and they talked a few minutes in the dressing room at a dance he fell into the easy pose of the old soldier among other soldiers: that he had been badly, sickeningly frightened all the time. In this way he lost everything.

During this time, it was late summer, he was sleeping late in bed, getting up to walk down town to the library to get a book, eating lunch at home, reading on the front porch until he became bored, and then walking down through the town to spend the hottest hours of the day in the cool dark of the pool room. He loved to play pool.

In the evening he practiced on his clarinet, strolled down town, read, and went to bed. He was still a hero to his two young sisters. His mother would have given him breakfast in bed if he had wanted it. She often came in when he was in bed and asked him to tell her about the war, but her attention always wandered. His father was noncommittal.

Before Krebs went away to the war he had never been allowed to drive the family motor car. His father was in the real estate business and always wanted the car to be at his command when he required it to take clients out into the country to show them a piece of farm property. The car always stood outside the First National Bank building where his father had an office on the second floor. Now, after the war, it was still the same car.

Nothing was changed in the town except that the young girls had grown up. But they lived in such a complicated world of already defined alliances and shifting feuds that Krebs did not feel the energy or the courage to break into it. He liked to look at them, though. There were so many good-looking young girls. Most of them had their hair cut short. When he went away only little girls wore their hair like that or girls who were fast. They all wore sweaters and shirt waists with round Dutch collars. It was a pattern. He liked to look at them from the front porch as they walked on the other side of the street. He liked to watch them walking under the shade of the trees. He liked the round Dutch collars above their sweaters. He liked their silk stockings and flat shoes. He liked their bobbed hair and the way they walked.

When he was in town their appeal to him was not very strong. He did not like them when he saw them in the Greek's ice cream parlor. He did not want them themselves really. They were too complicated. There was something else. Vaguely he wanted a girl but he did not want to have to work to get her. He would have liked to have girl but he did not want to have to spend a long time getting her. He did not want to get into the intrigue and the politics. He did not want to have to do any courting. He did not want to tell any more lies. It wasn't worth it.

He did not want any consequences. He did not want any consequences ever again. He wanted to live along without consequences. Besides he did not really need a girl. The army had taught him that. It was all right to pose as though you had to have a girl. Nearly everybody did that. But it wasn't true. You did not need a girl. That was the funny thing. First a fellow boasted how girls mean nothing to him, that he never thought of them, that they could not touch him. Then a fellow boasted that he could not get along without girls, that he had to have them all the time, that he could not go to sleep without them.

That was all a lie. It was all a lie both ways. You did not need a girl unless you thought about them. He learned that in the army. Then sooner or later you always got one. When you were really ripe for a girl you always got one. You did not have to think about it. Sooner or later it would come. He had learned that in the army.

Now he would have liked a girl if she had come to him and not wanted to talk. But here at home it was all too complicated. He knew he could never get through it all again. It was not worth the trouble. That was the thing about French girls and German girls. There was not all this talking. You couldn't talk much and you did not need to talk. It was simple and you were friends. He thought about France and then he began to think about Germany. On the whole he had liked Germany better. He did not want to leave Germany. He did not want to come home. Still, he had come home. He sat on the front porch.

He liked the girls that were walking along the other side of the street. He liked   15
the look of them much better than the French girls or the German girls. But the world they were in was not the world he was in. He would like to have one of them. But it was not worth it. They were such a nice pattern. He liked the pattern. It was exciting. But he would not go through all the talking. He did not want one badly enough. He liked to look at them all, though. It was not worth it. Not now when things were getting good again.

He sat there on the porch reading a book on the war. It was a history and he was reading about all the engagements he had been in. It was the most interesting reading he had ever done. He wished there were more maps. He looked forward with a good feeling to reading all the really good histories when they would come out with good detail maps. Now he was really learning about the war. He had been a good soldier. That made a difference.

One morning after he had been home about a month his mother came into his bedroom and sat on the bed. She smoothed her apron.

"I had a talk with your father last night, Harold," she said, "and he is willing for you to take the car out in the evenings."

"Yeah?" said Krebs, who was not fully awake. "Take the car out? Yeah?"

"Yes. Your father has felt for some time that you should be able to take the   20 car out in the evenings whenever you wished but we only talked it over last night."

"I'll bet you made him," Krebs said.

"No. It was your father's suggestion that we talk the matter over."

"Yeah. I'll bet you made him," Krebs sat up in bed.

"Will you come down to breakfast, Harold?" his mother said.

"As soon as I get my clothes on," Krebs said.   25

His mother went out of the room and he could hear her frying something downstairs while he washed, shaved, and dressed to go down into the dining-room for breakfast. While he was eating breakfast his sister brought in the mail.

"Well, Hare," she said. "You old sleepyhead. What do you ever get up for?"

Krebs looked at her. He liked her. She was his best sister.

"Have you got the paper?" he asked.

She handed him the Kansas City *Star* and he shucked off its brown wrapper 30
and opened it to the sporting page. He folded the *Star* open and propped it against the water pitcher with his cereal dish to steady it, so he could read while he ate.

"Harold," his mother stood in the kitchen doorway, "Harold, please don't muss up the paper. Your father can't read his *Star* if it's been mussed."

"I won't muss it," Krebs said.

His sister sat down at the table and watched him while he read.

"We're playing indoor over at school this afternoon," she said. "I'm going to pitch."

"Good," said Krebs. "How's the old wing?"   35

"I can pitch better than lots of the boys. I tell them all you taught me. The other girls aren't much good."

"Yeah?" said Krebs.

"I tell them all you're my beau. Aren't you my beau, Hare?"

"You bet."

"Couldn't your brother really be your beau just because he's your brother?"   40

"I don't know."

"Sure you know. Couldn't you be my beau, Hare, if I was old enough and if you wanted to?"

"Sure. You're my girl now."

"Am I really your girl?"

"Sure."   45

"Do you love me?"

"Uh, huh."

"Will you love me always?"

"Sure."

"Will you come over and watch me play indoor?"   50

"Maybe."

"Aw, Hare, you don't love me. If you loved me, you'd want to come over and watch me play indoor."

Krebs's mother came into the dining-room from the kitchen. She carried a plate with two fried eggs and some crisp bacon on it and a plate of buckwheat cakes.

"You run along, Helen," she said. "I want to talk to Harold."

She put the eggs and bacon down in front of him and brought in a jug of 55
maple syrup for the buckwheat cakes. Then she sat down across the table from
Krebs.

"I wish you'd put down the paper a minute, Harold," she said.

Krebs took down the paper and folded it.

"Have you decided what you are going to do yet, Harold?" his mother said,
taking off her glasses.

"No," said Krebs.

"Don't you think it's about time?" His mother did not say this in a mean way. 60
She seemed worried.

"I hadn't thought about it," Krebs said.

"God has some work for everyone to do," his mother said. "There can be no
idle hands in His Kingdom."

"I'm not in His Kingdom," Krebs said.

"We are all of us in His Kingdom."

Krebs felt embarrassed and resentful as always.   65

"I've worried about you so much, Harold," his mother went on. "I know the
temptations you must have been exposed to. I know how weak men are. I know
what your own dear grandfather, my own father, told us about the Civil War and I
have prayed for you. I pray for you all day long, Harold."

Krebs looked at the bacon fat hardening on his plate.

"Your father is worried, too," his mother went on. "He thinks you have lost
your ambition, that you haven't got a definite aim in life. Charley Simmons, who is
just your age, has a good job and is going to be married. The boys are all settling
down; they're all determined to get somewhere; you can see that boys like Charley
Simmons are on their way to being really a credit to the community."

Krebs said nothing.

"Don't look that way, Harold," his mother said. "You know we love you and I 70
want to tell you for your own good how matters stand. Your father does not want to
hamper your freedom. He thinks you should be allowed to drive the car. If you
want to take some of the nice girls out riding with you, we are only too pleased. We
want you to enjoy yourself. But you are going to have to settle down to work,
Harold. Your father doesn't care what you start in at. All work is honorable as he
says. But you've got to make a start at something. He asked me to speak to you this
morning and then you can stop in and see him at his office."

"Is that all?" Krebs said.

"Yes. Don't you love your mother, dear boy?"

"No," Krebs said.

His mother looked at him across the table. Her eyes were shiny. She started
crying.

"I don't love anybody," Krebs said.   75

It wasn't any good. He couldn't tell her, he couldn't make her see it. It was
silly to have said it. He had only hurt her. He went over and took hold of her arm.
She was crying with her head in her hands.

"I didn't mean it," he said. "I was just angry at something. I didn't mean I didn't love you."

His mother went on crying. Krebs put his arm on her shoulder.

"Can't you believe me, mother?"

His mother shook her head.   80

"Please, please, mother. Please believe me."

"All right," his mother said chokily. She looked up at him. "I believe you, Harold."

Krebs kissed her hair. She put her face up to him.

"I'm your mother," she said. "I held you next to my heart when you were a tiny baby."

Krebs felt sick and slightly nauseated.   85

"I know, Mummy," he said. "I'll try to be a good boy for you."

"Would you kneel and pray with me, Harold?" his mother asked.

They knelt down beside the dining-room table and Krebs's mother prayed.

"Now, you pray, Harold," she said.

"I can't."   90

"Try, Harold."

"I can't."

"Do you want me to pray for you?"

"Yes."

So his mother prayed for him and then they stood up and Krebs kissed his 95 mother and went out of the house. He had tried so to keep his life from being complicated. Still, none of it had touched him. He had felt sorry for his mother and she had made him lie. He would go to Kansas City and get a job and she would feel all right about it. There would be one more scene maybe before he got away. He would not go down to his father's office. He would miss that one. He wanted his life to go smoothly. It had just gotten going that way. Well, that was all over now, anyway. He would go over to the schoolyard and watch Helen play indoor baseball.

■ *Questions for . . .* Soldier's Home by Ernest Hemingway

Discussion and Journal Writing

1. Is the *'s* in the title a contraction or an indication of a possessive?

2. Hemingway covers Krebs's military career in just two paragraphs, the first two. What's the effect of this abbreviated coverage? Look at the details he uses—the pictures, for instance. Note his word choice and the rhythm of his short sentences. What tone does he establish by the end of the second paragraph?

3. Read paragraph 10 aloud, paying close attention to detail, sentence pattern, rhythm, and repetition. What does this paragraph tell us about the town? The girls? Krebs? The narrator?

4. Put the story's plot into your own words. How important is it to the story's significance and power?

5. What does the narrator mean when he tells us Krebs "did not want any consequences ever again"? Why does Krebs avoid situations that are "complicated"?
6. What does it tell us about Krebs's mother and father and the family dynamic that his mother tells him not to "muss up" the paper because his father can't read it if it's been mussed? What effect does it have on the story that his father's wishes come through his mother?
7. Why does Krebs tell his mother he doesn't love her? Why does he refuse to pray with her? Why does he decide at the end of the story to move to Kansas City, get a job, and live by himself?

∞∞∞∞∞

Four Summers

—Joyce Carol Oates

Joyce Carol Oates was born in Lockport, New York in 1938 and currently lives in Princeton, New Jersey where she writes, edits the *Ontario Review* with her husband, and teaches creative writing at Princeton University. She is the most prolific writer of serious fiction in America; some of her novels, like *Them,* which won the National Book Award in 1969, have enjoyed critical acclaim and commercial success—a rare combination. Oates has also embraced and been embraced by feminism, which in her fiction means that authentic female voices tell and dominate her stories. "Four Summers" clearly marks Oates as an artistic heir of Charlotte Perkins Gilman, one of the first American writers to create a powerful feminist consciousness in a work of fiction.

I

It is some kind of special day. "Where's Sissie?" Ma says. Her face gets sharp, she is frightened. When I run around her chair she laughs and hugs me. She is pretty when she laughs. Her hair is long and pretty.

We are sitting at the best table of all, out near the water. The sun is warm and the air smells nice. Daddy is coming back from the building with some glasses of beer, held in his arms. He makes a grunting noise when he sits down.

"Is the lake deep?" I ask them.

They don't hear me, they're talking. A woman and a man are sitting with us. The man marched in the parade we saw just awhile ago; he is a volunteer fireman and is wearing a uniform. Now his shirt is pulled open because it is hot. I can see the dark curly hair way up by his throat; it looks hot and prickly.

A man in a soldier's uniform comes over to us. They are all friends, but I can't   5 remember him. We used to live around here, Ma told me, and then we moved away. The men are laughing. The man in the uniform leans back against the railing, laughing, and I am afraid it will break and he will fall into the water.

"Can we go out in a boat, Dad?" says Jerry.

He and Frank keep running back and forth. I don't want to go with them. I want to stay by Ma. She smells nice. Frank's face is dirty with sweat. "Dad," he says, whining, "can't we go out in a boat? Them kids are going out."

A big lake is behind the building and the open part where we are sitting. Some people are rowing on it. This tavern is noisy and everyone is laughing; it is too noisy for Dad to think about what Frank said.

"Harry," says Ma, "the kids want a boat ride. Why don't you leave off drinking and take them?"

"What?" says Dad.   10

He looks up from laughing with the men. His face is damp with sweat and he is happy. "Yeah, sure, in a few minutes. Go over there and play and I'll take you out in a few minutes."

The boys run out back by the rowboats, and I run after them. I have a bag of potato chips.

An old man with a white hat pulled down over his forehead is sitting by the boats, smoking. "You kids be careful," he says.

Frank is leaning over and looking at one of the boats. "This here is the best one," he says.

"Why's this one got water in it?" says Jerry.   15

"You kids watch out. Where's your father?" the man says.

"He's gonna take us for a ride," says Frank.

"Where is he?"

The boys run along, looking at the boats that are tied up. They don't bother with me. The boats are all painted dark green, but the paint is peeling off some of them in little pieces. There is water inside some of them. We watch two people come in, a man and a woman. The woman is giggling. She has on a pink dress and she leans over to trail one finger in the water. "What's all this filthy stuff by the shore?" she says. There is some scum in the water. It is colored a light brown, and there are little seeds and twigs and leaves in it.

The man helps the woman out of the boat. They laugh together. Around their   20 rowboat little waves are still moving; they make a churning noise that I like.

"Where's Dad?" Frank says.

"He ain't coming," says Jerry.

They are tossing pebbles out into the water. Frank throws his sideways, twisting his body. He is ten and very big. "I bet he ain't coming," Jerry says, wiping his nose with the back of his hand.

After awhile we go back to the table. Behind the table is the white railing, and

then the water, and then the bank curves out so that the weeping willow trees droop
over the water. More men in uniforms, from the parade, are walking by.

"Dad," says Frank, "can't we go out? Can't we? There's a real nice boat 25
there—"

"For Christ's sake, get them off me," Dad says. He is angry with Ma. "Why
don't you take them out?"

"Honey, I can't row."

"Should we take out a boat, us two?" the other woman says. She has very
short, wet-looking hair. It is curled in tiny little curls close to her head and is very
bright. "We'll show them, Lenore. Come on, let's give your kids a ride. Show these
guys how strong we are."

"That's all you need, to sink a boat," her husband says.

They all laugh.   30

The table is filled with brown beer bottles and wrappers of things. I can feel
how happy they all are together, drawn together by the round table. I lean against
Ma's warm leg and she pats me without looking down. She lunges forward and I
can tell even before she says something that she is going to be loud.

"You guys're just jealous! Afraid we'll meet some soldiers!" she says.

"Can't we go out, Dad? Please?" Frank says. "We won't fight. . . ."

"Go and play over there. What're those kids doing—over there?" Dad says,
frowning. His face is damp and loose, the way it is sometimes when he drinks. "In
a little while, okay? Ask your mother."

"She can't do it," Frank says.   35

"They're just jealous," Ma says to the other woman, giggling. "They're afraid
we might meet somebody somewhere."

"Just who's gonna meet this one here?" the other man says, nodding with his
head at his wife.

Frank and Jerry walk away. I stay by Ma. My eyes burn and I want to sleep,
but they won't be leaving for a long time. It is still daylight. When we go home
from places like this it is always dark and getting chilly and the grass by our house
is wet.

"Duane Dorsey's in jail," Dad says. "You guys heard about that?"

"Duane? Yeah, really?"   40

"It was in the newspaper. His mother-in-law or somebody called the police, he
was breaking windows in her house."

"That Duane was always a nut!"

"Is he out now, or what?"

"I don't know, I don't see him these days. We had a fight," Dad says.

The woman with the short hair looks at me. "She's a real cute little thing," she 45
says, stretching her mouth. "She drink beer, Lenore?"

"I don't know."

"Want some of mine?"

She leans toward me and holds the glass by my mouth. I can smell the beer
and the warm stale smell of perfume. There are pink lipstick smudges on the glass.

"Hey, what the hell are you doing?" her husband says.

When he talks rough like that I remember him: we were with him once before. 50

"Are you swearing at me?" the woman says.

"Leave off the kid, you want to make her a drunk like yourself?"

"It don't hurt, one little sip. . . ."

"It's okay," Ma says. She puts her arm around my shoulders and pulls me closer to the table.

"Let's play cards. Who wants to?" Dad says. 55

"Sissie wants a little sip, don't you?" the woman says. She is smiling at me and I can see that her teeth are darkish, not nice like Ma's.

"Sure, go ahead," says Ma.

"I said leave off that, Sue, for Christ's sake," the man says. He jerks the table. He is a big man with a thick neck; he is bigger than Dad. His eyebrows are blond, lighter than his hair, and are thick and tufted. Dad is staring at something out on the lake without seeing it. "Harry, look, my goddamn wife is trying to make your kid drink beer."

"Who's getting hurt?" Ma says angrily.

Pa looks at me all at once and smiles. "Do you want it, baby?" 60

I have to say yes. The woman grins and holds the glass down to me, and it clicks against my teeth. They laugh. I stop swallowing right away because it is ugly, and some of the beer drips down on me. "Honey, you're so clumsy," Ma says, wiping me with a napkin.

"She's a real cute girl," the woman says, sitting back in her chair. "I wish I had a nice little girl like that."

"Lay off that," says her husband.

"Hey, did you bring any cards?" Dad says to the soldier.

"They got some inside." 65

"Look, I'm sick of cards," Ma says.

"Yeah, why don't we all go for a boat ride?" says the woman. "Be real nice, something new. Every time we get together we play cards. How's about a boat ride?"

"It'd better be a big boat, with you in it," her husband says. He is pleased when everyone laughs, even the woman. The soldier lights a cigarette and laughs. "How come your cousin here's so skinny and you're so fat?"

"She isn't fat," says Ma. "What the hell do you want? Look at yourself."

"Yes, the best days of my life are behind me," the man says. He wipes his face 70 and then presses a beer bottle against it. "Harry, you're lucky you moved out. It's all going downhill, back in the neighborhood."

"You should talk, you let our house look like hell," the woman says. Her face is blotched now, some parts pale and some red. "Harry don't sit out in his back yard all weekend drinking. He gets something done."

"Harry's younger than me."

Ma reaches over and touches Dad's arm. "Harry, why don't you take the kids out? Before it gets dark."

Dad lifts his glass and finishes his beer. "Who else wants more?" he says.

"I'll get them, you went last time," the soldier says.   75

"Get a chair for yourself," says Dad. "We can play poker."

"I don't want to play poker, I want to play rummy," the woman says.

"At church this morning Father Reilly was real mad," says Ma. "He said some kids or somebody was out in the cemetery and left some beer bottles. Isn't that awful?"

"Duane Dorsey used to do worse than that," the man says, winking.

"Hey, who's that over there?"   80

"You mean that fat guy?"

"Isn't that the guy at the lumberyard that owes all that money?"

Dad turns around. His chair wobbles and he almost falls; he is angry.

"This goddamn place is too crowded," he says.

"This is a real nice place," the woman says. She is taking something our of her   85
purse. "I always liked it, didn't you, Lenore?"

"Sue and me used to come here a lot," says Ma. "And not just with you two either."

"Yeah, we're real jealous," the man says.

"You should be," says the woman.

The soldier comes back. Now I can see that he is really a boy. He runs to the table with the beer before he drops anything. He laughs.

"Jimmy, your ma wouldn't like to see you drinking!" the woman says happily.   90

"Well, she ain't here."

"Are they still living out in the country?" Ma says to the woman.

"Sure. No electricity, no running water, no bathroom—same old thing. What can you do with people like that?"

"She always talks about going back to the Old Country," the soldier says. "Thinks she can save up money and go back."

"Poor old bastards don't know there was a war," Dad says. He looks as if   95
something tasted bad in his mouth. "My old man died thinking he could go back in a year or two. Stupid old bastards!"

"Your father was real nice. . . ." Ma says.

"Yeah, real nice," says Dad. "Better off dead."

Everybody is quiet.

"June Dieter's mother's got the same thing," the woman says in a low voice to Ma. "She's had it a year now and don't weigh a hundred pounds—you remember how big she used to be."

"She was big, all right," Ma says.   100

"Remember how she ran after June and slapped her? We were there—some guys were driving us home."

"Yeah. So she's got it too."

"Hey," says Dad, "why don't you get a chair, Jimmy? Sit down here."

The soldier looks around. His face is raw in spots, broken out. But his eyes are nice. He never looks at me.

"Get a chair from that table," Dad says.   105

"Those people might want it."

"Hell, just take it. Nobody's sitting on it."

"They might—"

Dad reaches around and yanks the chair over. The people look at him but don't say anything. Dad is breathing hard. "Here, sit here," he says. The soldier sits down.

Frank and Jerry come back. They stand by Dad, watching him. "Can we go 110 out now?" Frank says.

"What?"

"Out for a boat ride."

"What? No, next week. Do it next week. We're going to play cards."

"You said—"

"Shut up, we'll do it next week." Dad looks up and shades his eyes. "The lake 115 don't look right anyway."

"Lots of people are out there—"

"I said shut up."

"Honey," Ma whispers, "let him alone. Go and play by yourselves."

"Can we sit in the car?"

"Okay, but don't honk the horn."   120

"Ma, can't we go for a ride?"

"Go and play by yourselves, stop bothering us," she says. "Hey, will you take Sissie?"

They look at me. They don't like me, I can see it, but they take me with them. We run through the crowd and somebody spills a drink—he yells at us. "Oops, got to watch it!" Frank giggles.

We run along the walk by the boat. A woman in a yellow dress is carrying a baby. She looks at us like she doesn't like us.

Down at the far end some kids are standing together.   125

"Hey, lookit that," Frank says.

A blackbird is caught in the scum, by one of the boats. It can't fly up. One of the kids, a long-legged girl in a dirty dress, is poking at it with a stick.

The bird's wings keep fluttering but it can't get out. If it could get free it would fly and be safe, but the scum holds it down.

One of the kids throws a stone at it. "Stupid old goddamn bird," somebody says. Frank throws a stone. They are all throwing stones. The bird doesn't know enough to turn away. Its feathers are all wet and dirty. One of the stones hits the bird's head.

"Take that!" Frank says, throwing a rock. The water splashes up and some of 130 the girls scream.

I watch them throwing stones. I am standing at the side. If the bird dies, then everything can die, I think. Inside the tavern there is music from the jukebox.

II

We are at the boathouse tavern again. It is a mild day, a Sunday afternoon. Dad is talking with some men; Jerry and I are waiting by the boats. Mommy is at home with the new baby. Frank has gone off with some friends of his, to a stock-car race. There are some people here, sitting out at the tables, but they don't notice us.

"Why doesn't he hurry up?" Jerry says.

Jerry is twelve now. He has pimples on his forehead and chin.

He pushes one of the rowboats with his foot. He is wearing sneakers that are 135 dirty. I wish I could get in that boat and sit down, but I am afraid. A boy not much older than Jerry is squatting on the boardwalk, smoking. You can tell he is in charge of the boats.

"Daddy, come on. Come on," Jerry says, whining. Daddy can't hear him.

I have mosquito bites on my arms and legs. There are mosquitos and flies around here; the flies crawl around the sticky mess left on tables. A car over in the parking lot has its radio on loud. You can hear the music all this way. "He's coming," I tell Jerry so he won't be mad. Jerry is like Dad, the way his eyes look.

"Oh, that fat guy keeps talking to him," Jerry says.

The fat man is one of the bartenders; he has on a dirty white apron. All these men are familiar. We have been seeing them for years. He punches Dad's arm, up by the shoulder, and Dad pushes him. They are laughing, though. Nobody is mad.

"I'd sooner let a nigger—" the bartender says. We can't hear anything more, 140 but the men laugh again.

"All he does is drink," Jerry says. "I hate him."

At school, up on the sixth-grade floor, Jerry got in trouble last month. The principal slapped him. I am afraid to look at Jerry when he's mad.

"I hate him, I wish he'd die," Jerry says.

Dad is trying to come to us, but every time he takes a step backward and gets ready to turn, one of the men says something. There are three men beside him. Their stomachs are big, but Dad's isn't. He is wearing dark pants and a white shirt; his tie is in the car. He wears a tie to church, then takes it off. He has his shirt sleeves rolled up and you can see how strong his arms must be.

Two women cross over from the parking lot. They are wearing high-heeled 145 shoes and hats and bright dresses—orange and yellow—and when they walk past the men look at them. They go into the tavern. The men laugh about something. The way they laugh makes my eyes focus on something away from them—a bird flying in the sky—and it is hard for me to look anywhere else. I feel as if I am falling asleep.

"Here he comes!" Jerry says.

Dad walks over to us, with his big steps. He is smiling and carrying a bottle of beer. "Hey, kid," he says to the boy squatting on the walk, "how's about a boat?"

"This one is the best," Jerry says.

"The best, huh? Great." Dad grins at us. "Okay, Sissie, let's get you in. Be careful now." He picks me up even though I am too heavy for it, and sets me in the boat. It hurts a little where he held me, under the arms, but I don't care.

Jerry climbs in. Dad steps and something happens—he almost slips, but he 150 catches himself. With the wet oar he pushes us off from the boardwalk.

Dad can row fast. The sunlight is gleaming on the water. I sit very still, facing him, afraid to move. The boat goes fast, and Dad is leaning back and forth and pulling on the oars, breathing hard, doing everything fast like he always does. He is always in a hurry to get things done. He has set the bottle of beer down by his leg, pressed against the side of the boat so it won't fall.

"There's the guys we saw go out before," Jerry says. Coming around the island is a boat with three boys in it, older than Jerry. "They went on the island. Can we go there too?"

"Sure," says Dad. His eyes squint in the sun. He is suntanned, and there are freckles on his forehead. I am sitting close to him, facing him, and it surprises me what he looks like—he is a stranger, with his eyes narrowed. The water beneath the boat makes me feel funny. It keeps us up now, but if I fell over the side I would sink and drown.

"Nice out here, huh?" Dad says. His is breathing hard.

"We should go over that way to get on the island," Jerry says.   155

"This goddamn oar has splinters in it," Dad says. He hooks the oar up and lets us glide. He reaches down to get the bottle of beer. Though the lake and some trees and the buildings back on shore are in front of me, what makes me look at it is my father's throat, the way it bobs when he swallows. He wipes his forehead. "Want to row, Sissie?" he says.

"Can I?"

"Let me do it," says Jerry.

"Naw, I was just kidding," Dad says.

"I can do it. It ain't hard."   160

"Stay where you are," Dad says.

He starts rowing again, faster. Why does he go so fast? His face is getting red, the way it does at home when he has trouble with Frank. He clears his throat and spits over the side; I don't like to see that but I can't help but watch. The other boat glides past us, heading for shore. The boys don't look over at us.

Jerry and I look to see if anyone else is on the island, but no one is. The island is very small. You can see around it.

"Are you going to land on it, Dad?" Jerry says.

"Sure, okay." Dad's face is flushed and looks angry.   165

The boat scrapes bottom and bumps. "Jump out and pull it in," Dad says. Jerry jumps out. His shoes and socks are wet now, but Dad doesn't notice. The boat bumps; it hurts me. I am afraid. But then we're up on the land and Dad is out and lifting me. "Nice ride, sugar?" he says.

Jerry and I run around the island. It is different from what we thought, but we don't know why. There are some trees on it, some wild grass, and then bare caked mud that goes down to the water. The water looks dark and deep on the other side, but when we get there it's shallow. Lily pads grow there; everything is thick and tangled. Jerry wades in the water and gets his pants legs wet. "There might be money in the water," he says.

Some napkins and beer cans are nearby. There is part of a hotdog bun, with flies buzzing around it.

When we go back to Dad, we see him squatting over the water doing something. His back jerks. Then I see that he is being sick. He is throwing up in the
water and making a noise like coughing.

Jerry turns around right away and runs back. I follow him, afraid. On the other 170
side we can look back at the boathouse and wish we were there.

III

Marian and Betty went to the show, but I couldn't. She made me come along
here with them. "And cut out that snippy face," Ma said, to let me know she's
watching. I have to help her take care of Linda—poor fat Linda, with her runny
nose! So here we are inside the tavern. There's too much smoke, I hate smoke. Dad
is smoking a cigar. I won't drink any more root beer, it's flat, and I'm sick of potato
chips. Inside me there is something that wants to run away, that hates them. How
loud they are, my parents! My mother spilled something on the front of her dress,
but does she notice? And my aunt Lucy and uncle Joe, they're here. Try to avoid
them. Lucy has false teeth that make everyone stare at her. I know that everyone is
staring at us. I could hide my head in my arms and turn away, I'm so tired and my
legs hurt from sunburn and I can't stand them any more.

"So did you ever hear from them? That letter you wrote?" Ma says to Lucy.

"I'm still waiting. Somebody said you got to have connections to get on the
show. But I don't believe it. That Howie Masterson that's the emcee, he's a real
nice guy. I can tell."

"It's all crap," Dad says. "You women believe anything."

"I don't believe it," I say.   175

"Phony as hell," says my uncle.

"You do too believe it, Sissie," says my mother. "Sissie thinks he's cute. I
know she does."

"I hate that guy!" I tell her, but she and my aunt are laughing. "I said I hate
him! He's greasy."

"All that stuff is phony as hell," says my Uncle Joe. He is tired all the time,
and right now he sits with head bowed. I hate his bald head with the little fringe of
gray hair on it. At least my father is still handsome. His jaws sag and there are lines
in his neck—edged with dirt, I can see, embarrassed—and his stomach is bulging a
little against the table, but still he is a handsome man. In a place like this women
look at him. What's he see in *her?* they think. My mother had her hair cut too short
last time; she looks queer. There is a photograph taken of her when she was young,
standing by someone's motorcycle, with her hair long. In the photograph she was
pretty, almost beautiful, but I don't believe it. Not really. I can't believe it, and I
hate her. Her forehead gathers itself up in little wrinkles whenever she glances
down at Linda, as if she can't remember who Linda is.

"Well, nobody wanted you, kid," she once said to Linda. Linda was a baby 180
then, one year old. Ma was furious, standing in the kitchen where she was washing
the floor, screaming: "Nobody wanted you, it was a goddamn accident! An acci-

dent!" That surprised me so I didn't know what to think, and I didn't know if I hated Ma or not; but I kept it all a secret . . . only my girl friends know, and I won't tell the priest either. Nobody can make me tell. I narrow my eyes and watch my mother leaning forward to say something—it's like she's going to toss something out on the table—and think that maybe she isn't my mother after all, and she isn't that pretty girl in the photograph, but someone else.

"A woman was on the show last night that lost two kids in a fire. Her house burned down," my aunt says loudly. "And she answered the questions right off and got a lot of money and the audience went wild. You could see she was a real lady. I love that guy, Howie Masterson. He's real sweet."

"He's a bastard," Dad says.

"Harry, what the hell? You never even seen him," Ma says.

"I sure as hell never did. Got better things to do at night." Dad turns to my uncle and his voice changes. "I'm on the night shift, now."

"Yeah, I hate that, I—"   185

"I can sleep during the day. What's the difference?"

"I hate those night shifts."

"What's there to do during the day?" Dad says flatly. His eyes scan us at the table as if he doesn't see anything, then they seem to fall off me and go behind me, looking at nothing.

"Not much," says my uncle, and I can see his white scalp beneath his hair. Both men are silent.

Dad pours beer into his glass and spills some of it. I wish I could look away. I 190 love him, I think, but I hate to be here. Where would I rather be? With Marian and Betty at the movies, or in my room, lying on the bed and staring at the photographs of movie stars on my walls—those beautiful people that never say anything—while out in the kitchen my mother is waiting for my father to come home so they can continue their quarrel. It never stops, that quarrel. Sometimes they laugh together, kid around, they kiss. Then the quarrel starts up again in a few minutes.

"Ma, can I go outside and wait in the car?" I say. "Linda's asleep."

"What's so hot about the car?" she says, looking at me.

"I'm tired. My sunburn hurts."

Linda is sleeping in Ma's lap, with her mouth open and drooling on the front of her dress. "Okay, go on," Ma says. "But we're not going to hurry just for you." When she has drunk too much there is a struggle in her between being angry and being affectionate; she fights both of them, as if standing with her legs apart and her hands on her hips, bracing a strong wind.

When I cross through the crowded tavern I'm conscious of people looking at 195 me. My hair lost its curl because it was so humid today, my legs are too thin, my figure is flat and not nice like Marian's—I want to hide somewhere, hide my face from them. I hate this noisy place and these people. Even the music is ugly because it belongs to them. Then, when I'm outside, the music gets faint right away and it doesn't sound so bad. It's cooler out here. No one is around. Out back, the old row-boats are tied up. Nobody's on the lake. There's no moon, the sky is overcast, it was raining earlier.

When I turn around, a man is standing by the door watching me.

"What're you doing?" he says.

"Nothing."

He has dark hair and a tanned face, I think, but everything is confused because the light from the door is pinkish—there's a neon sign there. My heart starts to pound. The man leans forward to stare at me. "Oh, I thought you were somebody else," he says.

I want to show him I'm not afraid. "Yeah, really? Who did you think I was?" 200 When we ride on the school bus we smile out the windows at strange men, just for fun. We do that all the time. I'm not afraid of any of them.

"You're not her," he says.

Some people come out the door and he has to step out of their way. I say to him, "Maybe you seen me around here before. We come here pretty often."

"Who do you come with?" He is smiling as if he thinks I'm funny. "Anybody I know?"

"That's my business."

It's a game. I'm not afraid. When I think of my mother and father inside, 205 something makes me want to step closer to this man—why should I be afraid? I could be wild like some of the other girls. Nothing surprises me.

We keep on talking. At first I can tell he wants me to come inside the tavern with him, but then he forgets about it; he keeps talking. I don't know what we say, but we talk in drawling voices, smiling at each other but in a secret, knowing way, as if each one of us knew more than the other. My cheeks start to burn. I could be wild like Betty is sometimes—like some of the other girls. Why not? Once before I talked with a man like this, on the bus. We were both sitting in the back. I wasn't afraid. This man and I keep talking and we talk about nothing, he wants to know how old I am, but it makes my heart pound so hard that I want to touch my chest to calm it. We are walking along the old boardwalk and I say: "Somebody took me out rowing once here."

"Is that so?" he says. "You want me to take you out?"

He has a hard, handsome face. I like that face. Why is he alone? When he smiles I know he's laughing at me, and this makes me stand taller, walk with my shoulders raised.

"Hey, are you with somebody inside there?" he says.

"I left them."

"Have a fight?"   210

"A fight, yes."

He looks at me quickly. "How old are you anyway?"

"That's none of your business."

"Girls your age are all alike."   215

"We're not all alike!" I arch my back and look at him in a way I must have learned somewhere—where?—with my lips not smiling but ready to smile, and my eyes narrowed. One leg is turned as if I'm ready to jump from him. He sees all this. He smiles.

"Say, you're real cute."

We're walking over by the parking lot now. He touches my arm. Right away my heart trips, but I say nothing, I keep walking. High above us the tree branches are moving in the wind. It's cold for June. It's late—after eleven. The man is wearing a jacket, but I have on a sleeveless dress and there are goose-pimples on my arms.

"Cold, huh?" he says.

He takes hold of my shoulders and leans toward me. This is to show me he's 220 no kid, he's grown-up, this is how they do things; when he kisses me his grip on my shoulders gets tighter. "I better go back," I say to him. My voice is queer.

"What?" he says.

I am wearing a face like one of those faces pinned up in my room, and what if I lose it? This is not my face. I try to turn away from him.

He kisses me again. His breath smells like beer, maybe, it's like my father's breath, and my mind is empty; I can't think what to do. Why am I here? My legs feel numb, my fingers are cold. The man rubs my arms and says, "You should have a sweater or something. . . ."

He is waiting for me to say something, to keep on the way I was before. But I have forgotten how to do it. Before, I was Marian or one of the older girls; now I am just myself. I am fourteen. I think of Linda sleeping in my mother's lap, and something frightens me.

"Hey, what's wrong?" the man says. 225

He sees I'm afraid but pretends he doesn't. He comes to me again and embraces me, his mouth presses against my neck and shoulder, I feel as if I'm suffocating. "My car's over here," he says, trying to catch his breath. I can't move. Something dazzling and icy rises up in me, an awful fear, but I can't move and can't say anything. He is touching me with his hands. His mouth is soft but wants too much from me. I think, What is he doing? Do they all do this? Do I have to have it done to me too?

"You cut that out," I tell him.

He steps away. His chest is heaving and his eyes look like a dog's eyes, surprised and betrayed. The last thing I see of him is those eyes, before I turn and run back to the tavern.

IV

Jesse says, "Let's stop at this place. I been here a few times before."

It's the Lakeside Bar. That big old building with the grubby siding, and a big 230 pink neon sign in front, and the cinder driveway that's so bumpy. Yes, everything the same. But different too—smaller, dirtier. There is a custard stand nearby with a glaring orange roof, and people crowded around it. That's new. I haven't been here for years.

"I feel like a beer," he says.

He smiles at me and caresses my arm. He treats me as if I were something that might break; in my cheap linen maternity dress I feel ugly and heavy. My flesh is so soft and thick that nothing could hurt it.

"Sure, honey. Pa used to stop in here too."

We cross through the parking lot to the tavern. Wild grass grows along the sidewalk and in the cracks of the sidewalk. Why is this place so ugly to me? I feel as if a hand were pressing against my chest, shutting off my breath. Is there some secret here? Why am I afraid?

I catch sight of myself in a dusty window as we pass. My hair is long, down to 235 my shoulders. I am pretty, but my secret is that I am pretty like everyone is. My husband loves me for this but doesn't know it. I have a pink mouth and plucked darkened eyebrows and soft bangs over my forehead; I know everything, I have no need to learn from anyone else now. I am one of those girls younger girls study closely, to learn from. On buses, in five-and-tens, thirteen-year-old girls must look at me solemnly, learning, memorizing.

"Pretty Sissie!" my mother likes to say when we visit, though I told her how I hate that name. She is proud of me for being pretty, but thinks I'm too thin. "You'll fill out nice, after the baby," she says. Herself, she is fat and veins have begun to darken on her legs; she scuffs around the house in bedroom slippers. Who is my mother? When I think of her I can't think of anything—do I love her or hate her, or is there nothing there?

Jesse forgets and walks ahead of me, I have to walk fast to catch up. I'm wearing pastel-blue high heels—that must be because I am proud of my legs. I have little else. Then he remembers and turns to put out his hand for me, smiling to show he is sorry. Jesse is the kind of young man thirteen-year-old girls stare at secretly; he is not a man, not old enough, but not a boy either. He is a year older than I am, twenty. When I met him he was wearing a navy uniform and he was with a girl friend of mine.

Just a few people sitting outside at the tables. They're afraid of rain—the sky doesn't look good. And how bumpy the ground is here, bare spots and little holes and patches of crab grass, and everywhere napkins and junk. Too many flies outside. Has this place changed hands? The screens at the window don't fit right; you can see why flies get inside. Jesse opens the door for me and I go in. All bars smell alike. There is a damp, dark odor of beer and something indefinable—spilled soft drinks, pretzels getting stale? This bar is just like any other. Before we were married we went to places like this, Jesse and me and other couples. We had to spend a certain amount of time doing things like that—and going to movies, playing miniature golf, bowling, dancing, swimming—then we got married, now we're going to have a baby. I think of the baby all the time, because my life will be changed then; everything will be different. Four months from now. I should be frightened, but a calm laziness has come over me. It was so easy for my mother. . . . But it will be different with me because my life will be changed by it, and nothing ever changed my mother. You couldn't change her! Why should I think? Why should I be afraid? My body is filled with love for this baby, and I will never be the same again.

We sit down at a table near the bar. Jesse is in a good mood. My father would have liked him, I think; when he laughs Jesse reminds me of him. Why is a certain kind of simple, healthy, honest man always destined to lose everything? Their souls are as clean and smooth as the muscular line of their arms. At night, I hold Jesse, thinking of my father and what happened to him—all that drinking, then the accident at the factory—and I pray that Jesse will be different. I hope that his quick, open, loud way of talking is just a disguise, that he really is someone else—slower and calculating. That kind of man grows old without jerks and spasms. Why did I marry Jesse?

Someone at the bar turns around, and it's a man I think I know—I have known. Yes. That man outside, the man I met outside. I stare at him, my heart pounding, and he doesn't see me. He is dark, his hair is neatly combed but is thinner than before; he is wearing a cheap gray suit. But is it the same man? He is standing with a friend and looking around, as if he doesn't like what he sees. He is tired too. He has grown years older.

Our eyes meet. He glances away. He doesn't remember—that frightened girl he held in his arms.

I am tempted to put my hand on Jesse's arm and tell him about that man, but how can I? Jesse is talking about trading in our car for a new one. . . . I can't move, my mind seems to be coming to a stop. Is that the man I kissed, or someone else? A feeling of angry loss comes over me. Why should I lose everything? Everything? Is it the same man, and would he remember? My heart bothers me, it's stupid to be like this: here I sit, powdered and sweet, a girl safely married, pregnant and secured to the earth, with my husband beside me. He still loves me. Our love keeps on. Like my parents' love, it will subside someday, but nothing surprises me because I have learned everything.

The man turns away, talking to his friend. They are weary, tired of something. He isn't married yet, I think, and that pleases me. Good. But why are these men always tired? Is it the jobs they hold, the kind of men who stop in at this tavern? Why do they flash their teeth when they smile, but stop smiling so quickly? Why do their children cringe from them sometimes—an innocent upraised arm a frightening thing? Why do they grow old so quickly, sitting at kitchen tables with bottles of beer? They are everywhere, in every house. All the houses in this neighborhood and all neighborhoods around here. Jesse is young, but the outline of what he will be is already in his face; do you think I can't see it? Their lives are like hands dealt out to them in their innumerable card games. You pick up the sticky cards, and there it is: there it is. Can't change anything, all you can do is switch some cards around, stick one in here, one over there . . . pretend there is some sense, a secret scheme.

The man at the bar tosses some coins down and turns to go. I want to cry out to him, "Wait, wait!" But I cannot. I sit helplessly and watch him leave. Is it the same man? If he leaves I will be caught here, what can I do? I can almost hear my mother's shrill laughter coming in from the outside, and some drawling remark of my father's—lifting for a moment above the music. Those little explosions of laughter, the slap of someone's hand on the damp table in anger, the clink of bottles accidentally touching—and there, there, my drunken aunt's voice, what is she saying? I am terrified at being left with them. I watch the man at the door and think that I could have loved him. I know it.

He has left, he and his friend. He is nothing to me, but suddenly I feel tears in 245 my eyes. What's wrong with me? I hate everything that springs upon me and seems to draw itself down and oppress me in a way I could never explain to anyone. . . . I am crying because I am pregnant, but not with that man's child. It could have been his child, I could have gone with him to his car; but I did nothing, I ran away, I was afraid, and now I'm sitting here with Jesse, who is picking the label off his beer bottle with his thick squarish fingernails. I did nothing. I was afraid. Now he has left me here and what can I do?

I let my hand fall onto my stomach to remind myself that I am in love: with this baby, with Jesse, with everything. I am in love with our house and our life and the future and even this moment—right now—that I am struggling to live through.

■ *Questions for* . . . Four Summers by Joyce Carol Oates

Discussion and Journal Writing

1. Why doesn't Oates tell the first three installments of her story in the past tense?
2. How does Sissie feel about her father and the other men in the first part of the story? How does her attitude change as the story progresses?
3. In the first part of the story, how does Harry respond to his wife's requests that he take the kids for a rowboat ride? What do her requests and his responses tell us about their marriage?
4. How does Sissie feel about the blackbird the kids stone?
5. How would you characterize Harry's relationships with his sons? What evidence do you have to go on?
6. How does the texture of Sissie's narration change as she grows up?
7. As Sissie grows up, she tells us, "Nothing surprises me." She says, "I know everything, I have no need to learn from anyone else now." Does Oates expect us to believe her?
8. What is Oates's vision of family in this story? What does it hold for girls and women?

ooooo

Big Mama's Funeral

—Gabriel García Márquez

In the world of literature, García Márquez's name is synony-
mous with "magical realism," a term used to describe fiction in
which realistic and fantastic characters, events, and items coexist. In
García Márquez's *One Hundred Years of Solitude,* probably his
best-known novel, generations of ancestors, though long dead,
share a house with the novel's main family, and characters with
magical powers blow through a plot that otherwise conforms to the
history of García Márquez's native Columbia. "Big Mama's
Funeral," (translated by J. S. Bernstein) was published in 1962 and
was his first foray into this new kind of fiction. Big Mama is gargan-
tuan in many ways. She is so much more then fat. She is enormous
and she presides over the fictional Latin American kingdom of
Macondo. Legitimate and illegitimate branches of her family fan out
into a country that seems to be without boundaries, like the power
she exercises; and the inheritance her heirs carve up is huge, both
the visible, and invisible portions of it.

This is, for all the world's unbelievers, the true account of Big Mama, 1
absolute sovereign of the Kingdom of Macondo, who lived for ninety-two years,
and died in the odor of sanctity one Tuesday last September, and whose funeral was
attended by the Pope.

Now that the nation, which was shaken to its vitals, has recovered its balance; 2
now that the bagpipers of San Jacinto, the smugglers of Guajira, the rice planters of
Sinú, the prostitutes of Caucamayal, the wizards of Sierpe, and the banana workers
of Aracataca have folded up their tents to recover from the exhausting vigil and
have regained their serenity, and the President of the Republic and his Ministers
and all those who represented the public and supernatural powers on the most magnificent funeral occasion recorded in the annals of history have regained control of
their estates; now that the Holy Pontiff has risen up to Heaven in body and soul;
and now that it is impossible to walk around in Macondo because of the empty bottles, the cigarette butts, and gnawed bones, the cans and rags and excrement that the
crowd which came to the burial left behind; now is the time to lean a stool against
the front door and relate from the beginning the details of this national commotion,
before the historians have a chance to get at it.

Fourteen weeks ago, after endless nights of poultices, mustard plasters, and 3
leeches, and weak with the delirium of her death agony, Big Mama ordered them to
seat her in her old rattan rocker so she could express her last wishes. It was the only
thing she needed to do before she died. That morning, with the intervention of

Father Anthony Isabel, she had put the affairs of her soul in order, and now she needed only to put her worldly affairs in order with her nine nieces and nephews, her sole heirs, who were standing around her bed. The priest, talking to himself and on the verge of his hundredth birthday, stayed in the room. Ten men had been needed to take him up to Big Mama's bedroom, and it was decided that he should stay there so they should not have to take him down and then take him up again at the last minute.

Nicanor, the eldest nephew, gigantic and savage, dressed in khaki and spurred 4 boots, with a .38-caliber long-barreled revolver holstered under his shirt, went to look for the notary. The enormous two-story mansion, fragrant from molasses and oregano, with its dark apartments crammed with chests and the odds and ends of four generations turned to dust, had become paralyzed since the week before, in expectation of that moment. In the long central hall, with hooks on the walls where in another time butchered pigs had been hung and deer were slaughtered on sleepy August Sundays, the peons were sleeping on farm equipment and bags of salt, awaiting the order to saddle the mules to spread the bad news to the four corners of the huge hacienda. The rest of the family was in the living room. The women were limp, exhausted by the inheritance proceedings and lack of sleep; they kept a strict mourning which was the culmination of countless accumulated mournings. Big Mama's matriarchal rigidity had surrounded her fortune and her name with a sacramental fence, within which uncles married the daughters of their nieces, and the cousins married their aunts, and brothers their sisters-in-law, until an intricate mesh of consanguinity was formed, which turned procreation into a vicious circle. Only Magdalena, the youngest of the nieces, managed to escape it. Terrified by hallucinations, she made Father Anthony Isabel exorcise her, shaved her head, and renounced the glories and vanities of the world in the novitiate of the Mission District.

On the margin of the official family, and in exercise of the *jus primae noctis,* 5 the males had fertilized ranches, byways, and settlements with an entire bastard line, which circulated among the servants without surnames, as godchildren, employees, favorites, and protégés of Big Mama.

The imminence of her death stirred the exhausting expectation. The dying 6 woman's voice, accustomed to homage and obedience, was no louder than a bass organ pipe in the closed room, but it echoed in the most far-flung corners of the hacienda. No one was indifferent to this death. During this century, Big Mama had been Macondo's center of gravity, as had her brothers, her parents, and the parents of her parents in the past, in a dominance which covered two centuries. The town was founded on her surname. No one knew the origin, or the limits or the real value of her estate, but everyone was used to believing that Big Mama was owner of the waters, running and still, of rain and drought, and of the district's roads, telegraph poles, leap years, and heat waves, and that she had furthermore a hereditary right over life and property. When she sat on her balcony in the cool afternoon air, with all the weight of her belly and authority squeezed into her old rattan rocker, she seemed, in truth, infinitely rich and powerful, the richest and most powerful matron in the world.

It had not occurred to anyone to think that Big Mama was mortal, except the members of her tribe, and Big Mama herself, prodded by the senile premonitions of Father Anthony Isabel. But she believed that she would live more than a hundred years, as did her maternal grandmother, who in the War of 1885, confronted a patrol of Colonel Aureliano Buendía's, barricaded in the kitchen of the hacienda. Only in April of this year did Big Mama realize that God would not grant her the privilege of personally liquidating, in an open skirmish, a horde of Federalist Masons. 7

During the first week of pain, the family doctor maintained her with mustard plasters and woolen stockings. He was a hereditary doctor, a graduate of Montpellier, hostile by philosophical conviction to the progress of his science, whom Big Mama had accorded the lifetime privilege of preventing the establishment in Macondo of any other doctors. At one time he covered the town on horseback, visiting the doleful, sick people at dusk, and Nature had accorded him the privilege of being the father of many another's children. But arthritis kept him stiff-jointed in bed, and he ended up attending to his patients without calling on them, by means of suppositions, messengers, and errands. Summoned by Big Mama, he crossed the plaza in his pajamas, leaning on two canes, and he installed himself in the sick woman's bedroom. Only when he realized that Big Mama was dying did he order a chest with porcelain jars labeled in Latin brought, and for three weeks he besmeared the dying woman inside and out with all sorts of academic salves, magnificent stimulants, and masterful suppositories. Then he applied bloated toads to the site of her pain, and leeches to her kidneys, until the early morning of that day when he had to face the dilemma of either having her bled by the barber of exorcised by Father Anthony Isabel. 8

Nicanor sent for the priest. His ten best men carried him from the parish house to Big Mama's bedroom, seated on a creaking willow rocker, under the mildewed canopy reserved for great occasions. The little bell of the Viaticum in the warm September dawn was the first notification to the inhabitants of Macondo. When the sun rose, the little plaza in front of Big Mama's house looked like a country fair. 9

It was like a memory of another era. Until she was seventy, Big Mama used to celebrate her birthday with the most prolonged and tumultuous carnivals within memory. Demijohns of rum were placed at the townspeople's disposal, cattle were sacrificed in the public plaza, and a band installed on top of a table played for three days without stopping. Under the dusty almond trees, where, in the first week of the century, Colonel Aureliano Buendía's troops had camped, stalls were set up which sold banana liquor, rolls, blood puddings, chopped fried meat, meat pies, sausage, yucca breads, crullers, buns, corn breads, puff paste, *longanizas,* tripes, coconut nougats, rum toddies, along with all sorts of trifles, gewgaws, trinkets, and knick-nacks, and cockfights and lottery tickets. In the midst of the confusion of the agitated mob, prints and scapularies with Big Mama's likeness were sold. 10

The festivities used to begin two days before and end on the day of her birth- 11
day, with the thunder of fireworks and a family dance at Big Mama's house. The
carefully chosen guests and the legitimate members of the family, generously
attended by the bastard line, danced to the beat of the old pianola which was
equipped with the rolls most in style. Big Mama presided over the party from the
rear of the hall in an easy chair with linen pillows, imparting discreet instructions
with her right hand, adorned with rings on all her fingers. On that night the coming
year's marriages were arranged, at times in complicity with the lovers, but almost
always counseled by her own inspiration. To finish off the jubilation, Big Mama
went out to the balcony, which was decorated with diadems and Japanese lanterns,
and threw coins to the crowd.

That tradition had been interrupted, in part because of the successive mourn- 12
ings of the family and in part because of the political instability of the last few
years. The new generations only heard stories of those splendid celebrations. They
never managed to see Big Mama at High Mass, fanned by some functionary of the
Civil Authority, enjoying the privilege of not kneeling, even at the moment of ele-
vation, so as not to ruin her Dutch-flounced skirt and her starched cambric petti-
coats. The old people remembered, like a hallucination out of their youth, the two
hundred yards of matting which were laid down from the manorial house to the
main altar the afternoon on which Maria del Rosario Castañeda y Montero attended
her father's funeral and returned along the matted street endowed with a new and
radiant dignity, turned into Big Mama at the age of twenty-two. That medieval
vision belonged then not only to the family's past but also to the nation's past. Ever
more indistinct and remote, hardly visible on her balcony, stifled by the geraniums
on hot afternoons, Big Mama was melting into her own legend. Her authority was
exercised through Nicanor. The tacit promise existed, formulated by tradition, that
the day Big Mama sealed her will the heirs would declare three nights of public
merrymaking. But at the same time it was known that she had decided not to
express her last wishes until a few hours before dying, and no one thought seriously
about the possibility that Big Mama was mortal. Only this morning, awakened by
the tinkling of the Viaticum, did the inhabitants of Macondo become convinced not
only that Big Mama was mortal but also that she was dying.

Her hour had come. Seeing her in her linen bed, bedaubed with aloes up to her 13
ears, under the dust-laden canopy of Oriental crêpe, one could hardly make out any
life in the thin respiration of her matriarchal breasts. Big Mama, who until she was
fifty rejected the most passionate suitors, and who was well enough endowed by
Nature to suckle her whole issue all by herself, was dying a virgin and childless. At
the moment of extreme unction, Father Anthony Isabel had to ask for help in order
to apply the oils to the palms of her hands, for since the beginning of her death
throes Big Mama had had her fists closed. The attendance of the nieces was useless.
In the struggle, for the first time in a week, the dying woman pressed against her
chest the hand bejeweled with precious stones and fixed her colorless look on the
nieces, saying, "Highway robbers." Then she saw Father Anthony Isabel in his
liturgical habit and the acolyte with the sacramental implements, and with calm

conviction she murmured, "I am dying." Then she took off the ring with the great diamond and gave it to Magdalena, the novice, to whom it belonged since she was the youngest heir. That was the end of a tradition: Magdalena had renounced her inheritance in favor of the Church.

At dawn Big Mama asked to be left alone with Nicanor to impart her last 14 instructions. For half an hour, in perfect command of her faculties, she asked about the conduct of her affairs. She gave special instructions about the disposition of her body, and finally concerned herself with the wake. "You have to keep your eyes open," she said. "Keep everything of value under lock and key, because many people come to wakes only to steal." A moment later, alone with the priest, she made an extravagant confession, sincere and detailed, and later on took Communion in the presence of her nieces and nephews. It was then that she asked them to seat her in her rattan rocker so that she could express her last wishes.

Nicanor had prepared, on twenty-four folios written in a very clear hand, a 15 scrupulous account of her possessions. Breathing calmly, with the doctor and Father Anthony Isabel as witnesses, Big Mama dictated to the notary the list of her property, the supreme and unique source of her grandeur and authority. Reduced to its true proportions, the real estate was limited to three districts, awarded by Royal Decree at the founding of the Colony; with the passage of time, by dint of intricate marriages of convenience, they had accumulated under the control of Big Mama. In that unworked territory, without definite borders, which comprised five townships and in which not one single grain had ever been sown at the expense of the proprietors, three hundred and fifty-two families lived as tenant farmers. Every year, on the eve of her name day, Big Mama exercised the only act of control which prevented the lands from reverting to the state: the collection of rent. Seated on the back porch of her house, she personally received the payment for the right to live on her lands, as for more than a century her ancestors had received it from the ancestors of the tenants. When the three-day collection was over, the patio was crammed with pigs, turkeys, and chickens, and with the tithes and first fruits of the land which were deposited there as gifts. In reality, that was the only harvest the family ever collected from a territory which had been dead since its beginnings, and which was calculated on first examination at a hundred thousand hectares. But historical circumstances had brought it about that within those boundaries the six towns of Macondo district should grow and prosper, even the county seat, so that no person who lived in a house had any property rights other than those which pertained to the house itself, since the land belonged to Big Mama, and the rent was paid to her, just as the government had to pay her for the use the citizens made of the streets.

On the outskirts of the settlements, a number of animals, never counted and 16 even less looked after, roamed, branded on the hindquarters with the shape of a padlock. This hereditary brand, which more out of disorder than out of quantity had become familiar in distant districts where the scattered cattle, dying of thirst, strayed in summer, was one of the most solid supports of the legend. For reasons which no one had bothered to explain, the extensive stables of the house had progressively emptied since the last civil war, and lately sugarcane presses, milking parlors, and a rice mill had been installed in them.

Aside from the items enumerated, she mentioned in her will the existence of 17 three containers of gold coins buried somewhere in the house during the War of Independence, which had not been found after periodic and laborious excavations. Along with the right to continue the exploitation of the rented land, and to receive tithes and first fruits and all sorts of extraordinary donations, the heirs received a chart kept up from generation to generation, and perfected by each generation, which facilitated the finding of the buried treasure.

Big Mama needed three hours to enumerate her earthly possessions. In the sti- 18 fling bedroom, the voice of the dying woman seemed to dignify in its place each thing named. When she affixed her trembling signature, and the witnesses affixed theirs below, a secret tremor shook the hearts of the crowds which were beginning to gather in front of the house, in the shade of the dusty almond trees of the plaza.

The only thing lacking then was the detailed listing of her immaterial posses- 19 sions. Making a supreme effort—the same kind that her forebears made before they died to assure the dominance of their line—Big Mama raised herself up on her monumental buttocks, and in a domineering and sincere voice, lost in her memories, dictated to the notary this list of her invisible estate:

The wealth of the subsoil, the territorial waters, the colors of the flag, national 20 sovereignty, the traditional parties, the rights of man, civil rights, the nation's leadership, the right of appeal, Congressional hearings, letters of recommendation, historical records, free elections, beauty queens, transcendental speeches, huge demonstrations, distinguished young ladies, proper gentlemen, punctilious military men, His Illustrious Eminence, the Supreme Court, goods whose importation was forbidden, liberal ladies, the meat problem, the purity of the language, setting a good example, the free but responsible press, the Athens of South America, public opinion, the lessons of democracy, Christian morality, the shortage of foreign exchange, the right of asylum, the Communist menace, the ship of state, the high cost of living, republican traditions, the underprivileged classes, statements of political support.

She didn't manage to finish. The laborious enumeration cut off her last breath. 21 Drowning in the pandemonium of abstract formulas which for two centuries had constituted the moral justification of the family's power, Big Mama emitted a loud belch and expired.

That afternoon the inhabitants of the distant and somber capital saw the pic- 22 ture of a twenty-year-old woman on the first page of the extra editions, and thought that it was a new beauty queen. Big Mama lived again in the momentary youth of her photograph, enlarged to four columns and with needed retouching, her abundant hair caught up atop her skull with an ivory comb and a diadem on her lace collar. That image, captured by a street photographer who passed through Macondo at the beginning of the century, and kept in the newspaper's morgue for many years in the section of unidentified persons, was destined to endure in the memory of future generations. In the dilapidated buses, in the elevators at the Ministries, and in the dismal tearooms hung with pale decorations, people whispered with veneration and respect about the dead personage in her sultry, malarial region, whose name was unknown in the rest of the country a few hours before—before it had been sanctified by the printed word. A fine drizzle covered the passers-by with misgiving and mist. All the church bells tolled for the dead. The President of the Republic, taken by surprise by the news when on his way to the commencement exercises for the new cadets, suggested to the War Minister, in a note in his own hand on the back of the telegram, that he conclude his speech with a minute of silent homage to Big Mama.

The social order had been brushed by death. The President of the Republic 23 himself, who was affected by urban feelings as if they reached him through a purifying filter, managed to perceive from his car in a momentary but to a certain extent brutal vision the silent consternation of the city. Only a few low cafés remained open; the Metropolitan Cathedral was readied for nine days of funeral rites. At the National Capitol, where the beggars wrapped in newspapers slept in the shelter of the Doric columns and the silent statues of dead Presidents, the lights of Congress were lit. When the President entered his office, moved by the vision of the capital in mourning, his Ministers were waiting for him dressed in funereal garb, standing, paler and more solemn than usual.

The events of that night and the following ones would later be identified as a 24 historic lesson. Not only because of the Christian spirit which inspired the most lofty personages of public power, but also because of the abnegation with which dissimilar interests and conflicting judgments were conciliated in the common goal of burying the illustrious body. For many years Big Mama had guaranteed the social peace and political harmony of her empire, by virtue of the three trunks full of forged electoral certificates which formed part of her secret estate. The men in her service, her protégés and tenants, elder and younger, exercised not only their own rights of suffrage but also those of electors dead for a century. She exercised the priority of traditional power over transitory authority, the predominance of class over the common people, the transcendence of divine wisdom over human improvisation. In times of peace, her dominant will approved and disapproved canonries, benefices, and sinecures, and watched over the welfare of her associates, even if she had to resort to clandestine maneuvers or election fraud in order to obtain it. In troubled times, Big Mama contributed secretly for weapons for her partisans, but came to the aid of her victims in public. That patriotic zeal guaranteed the highest honors for her.

The President of the Republic had not needed to consult with his advisers in 25 order to weigh the gravity of his responsibility. Between the Palace reception hall and the little paved patio which had served the viceroys as a *cochére,* there was an interior garden of dark cypresses where a Portuguese monk had hanged himself out of love in the last days of the Colony. Despite his noisy coterie of bemedaled officials, the President could not suppress a slight tremor of uncertainty when he passed that spot after dusk. But that night his trembling had the strength of a premonition. Then the full awareness of his historical destiny dawned on him, and he decreed nine days of national mourning, and posthumous honors for Big Mama at the rank befitting a heroine who had died for the fatherland on the field of battle. As he expressed it in the dramatic address wihch he delivered that morning to his compatriots over the national radio and television network, the Nation's Leader trusted that the funeral rites for Big Mama would set a new example for the world.

Such a noble aim was to collide nevertheless with certain grave inconve- 26 niences. The judicial structure of the country, built by remote ancestors of Big Mama, was not prepared for events such as those which began to occur. Wise Doctors of Law, certified alchemists of the statutes, plunged into hermeneutics and syllogisms in search of the formula which would permit the President of the Republic to attend the funeral. The upper strata of politics, the clergy, the financiers lived through entire days of alarm. In the vast semicircle of Congress, rarefied by a century of abstract legislation, amid oil paintings of National Heroes and busts of Greek thinkers, the vocation of Big Mama reached unheard-of proportions, while her body filled with bubbles in the harsh Macondo September. For the first time, people spoke of her and conceived of her without her rattan rocker, her afternoon stupors, and her mustard plasters, and they saw her ageless and pure, distilled by legend.

Interminable hours were filled with words, words, words, which resounded 27 throughout the Republic, made prestigious by the spokesmen of the printed word. Until, endowed with a sense of reality in that assembly of aseptic lawgivers, the historic blahblahblah was interrupted by the reminder that Big Mama's corpse awaited their decision at 104° in the shade. No one batted an eye in the face of that eruption of common sense in the pure atmosphere of the written law. Orders were issued to embalm the cadaver, while formulas were adduced, viewpoints were reconciled, or constitutional amendments were made to permit the President to attend the burial.

So much had been said that the discussions crossed the borders, traversed the 28 ocean, and blew like an omen through the pontifical apartments at Castel Gandolfo. Recovered from the drowsiness of the torpid days of August, the Supreme Pontiff was at the window watching the lake where the divers were searching for the head of a decapitated young girl. For the last few weeks, the evening newspapers had been concerned with nothing else, and the Supreme Pontiff could not be indifferent to an enigma located such a short distance from his summer residence. But that evening, in an unforeseen substitution, the newspaper changed the photographs of the possible victims for that of one single twenty-year-old woman, marked off with black margins. "Big Mama," exclaimed the Supreme Pontiff, recognizing instantly the hazy daguerreotype which many years before had been offered to him on the occasion of his ascent to the Throne of Saint Peter. "Big Mama," exclaimed in chorus the members of the College of Cardinals in their private apartments, and for the third time in twenty centuries there was an hour of confusion, chagrin, and bustle in the limitless empire of Christendom, until the Supreme Pontiff was installed in his long black limousine en route to Big Mama's fantastic and far-off funeral.

The shining peach orchards were left behind, the Via Appia Antica with warm 29 movie stars tanning on terraces without as yet having heard any news of the commotion, and then the somber promontory of Castel Sant' Angelo on the edge of the Tiber. At dusk the resonant pealing of St. Peter's Basilica mingled with the cracked tinklings of Macondo. Inside his stifling tent across the tangled reeds and the silent bogs which marked the boundary between the Roman Empire and the ranches of Big Mama, the Supreme Pontiff heard the uproar of the monkeys agitated all night long by the passing of the crowds. On his nocturnal itinerary, the canoe had been filled with bags of yucca, stalks of green bananas, and crates of chickens, and with men and women who abandoned their customary pursuits to try their luck at selling things at Big Mama's funeral. His Holiness suffered that night, for the first time in the history of the Church, from the fever of insomnia and the torment of the mosquitoes. But the marvelous dawn over the Great Old Woman's domains, the primeval vision of the balsam apple and the iguana, erased from his memory the suffering of his trip and compensated him for his sacrifice.

Nicanor had been awakened by three knocks at the door which announced the 30 imminent arrival of His Holiness. Death had taken possession of the house. Inspired by successive and urgent Presidential addresses, by the feverish controversies which has been silenced but continued to be heard by means of conventional symbols, men and congregations the world over dropped everything and with their presence filled the dark hallways, the jammed passageways, the stifling attics; and those who arrived later climbed up on the low walls around the church, the palisades, vantage points, timberwork, and parapets, where they accommodated themselves as best they could. In the central hall, Big Mama's cadaver lay mummifying while it waited for the momentous decisions contained in a quivering mound of telegrams. Weakened by their weeping, the nine nephews sat the wake beside the body in an ecstasy of reciprocal surveillance.

And still the universe was to prolong the waiting for many more days. In the 31 city-council hall, fitted out with four leather stools, a jug of purified water, and a burdock hammock, the Supreme Pontiff suffered from a perspiring insomnia, diverting himself by reading memorials and administrative orders in the lengthy, stifling nights. During the day, he distributed Italian candy to the children who approached to see him through the window, and lunched beneath the hibiscus arbor with Father Anthony Isabel, and occasionally with Nicanor. Thus he lived for interminable weeks and months which were protracted by the waiting and the heat, until the day Father Pastrana appeared with his drummer in the middle of the plaza and read the proclamation of the decision. It was declared that Public Order was disturbed, ratatatat, and that the President of the Republic, ratatatat, had in his power the extraordinary prerogatives, ratatatat, which permitted him to attend Big Mama's funeral, ratatatat, tatatat, tatat, tatat.

The great day had arrived. In the streets crowded with carts, hawkers of fried 32 foods, and lottery stalls, and men with snakes wrapped around their necks who peddled a balm which would definitively cure erysipelas and guarantee eternal life; in the mottled little plaza where the crowds had set up their tents and unrolled their sleeping mats, dapper archers cleared the Authorities' way. There they were, awaiting the supreme moment: the washerwomen of San Jorge, the pearl fishers from Cabo de la Vela, the fishermen from Ciénaga, the shrimp fishermen from Tasajera, the sorcerers from Mojajana, the salt miners from Manaure, the accordionists from Valledupar, the fine horsemen of Ayapel, the ragtag musicians from San Pelayo, the cock breeders from La Cueva, the improvisers from Sábanas de Bolívar, the dandies from Rebolo, the oarsmen of the Magdalena, the shysters from Monpox, in addition to those enumerated at the beginning of this chronicle, and many others. Even the veterans of Colonel Aureliano Buendía's camp—the duke of Marlborough at their head, with the pomp of his furs and tiger's claws and teeth—overcame their centenarian hatred of Big Mama and those of her line and came to the funeral to ask the President of the Republic for the payment of their veterans' pensions which they had been waiting for for sixty years.

A little before eleven the delirious crowd which was sweltering in the sun, 33 held back by an imperturbable élite force of warriors decked out in embellished jackets and filigreed morions, emitted a powerful roar of jubilation. Dignified, solemn in their cutaways and top hats, the President of the Republic and his Ministers, the delegations from Parliament, the Supreme Court, the Council of State, the traditional parties and the clergy, and representatives of Banking, Commerce, and Industry made their appearance around the corner of the telegraph office. Bald and chubby, the old and ailing President of the Republic paraded before the astonished eyes of the crowds who had seen him inaugurated without knowing who he was and who only now could give a true account of his existence. Among the archbishops enfeebled by the gravity of their ministry, and the military men with robust chests armored with medals, the Leader of the Nation exuded the unmistakable air of power.

In the second rank, in a serene array of mourning crêpe, paraded the national 34 queens of all things that have been or ever will be. Stripped of their earthly splendor for the first time, they marched by, preceded by the universal queen: the soybean queen, the green-squash queen, the banana queen, the meal yucca queen, the guava queen, the coconut queen, the kidney-bean queen, the 255-mile-long-string-of-iguana-eggs queen, and all the others who are omitted so as not to make this account interminable.

In her coffin draped in purple, separated from reality by eight copper turn- 35 buckles, Big Mama was at that moment too absorbed in her formaldehyde eternity to realize the magnitude of her grandeur. All the splendor which she had dreamed of on the balcony of her house during her heat-induced insomnia was fulfilled by those forty-eight glorious hours during which all the symbols of the age paid homage to her memory. The Supreme Pontiff himself, whom she in her delirium imagined floating above the gardens of the Vatican in a resplendent carriage, conquered the heat with a plaited palm fan, and honored with his Supreme Dignity the greatest funeral in the world.

Dazzled by the show of power, the common people did not discern the cov- 36 etous bustling which occurred on the rooftree of the house when agreement was imposed on the town grandees' wrangling and catafalque was taken into the street on the shoulders of the grandest of them all. No one saw the vigilant shadow of the buzzards which followed the cortege through the sweltering little streets of Macondo, nor did they notice that as the grandees passed they left a pestilential train of garbage in the street. No one noticed that the nephews, godchildren, servants, and protégés of Big Mama closed the doors as soon as the body was taken out, and dismantled the doors, pulled the nails out of the planks, and dug up the foundations to divide up the house. The only thing which was not missed by anyone amid the noise of that funeral was the thunderous sigh of relief which the crowd let loose when fourteen days of supplications, exaltations, and dithyrambs were over, and the tomb was sealed with a lead plinth. Some of those present were sufficiently aware as to understand that they were witnessing the birth of a new era. Now the Supreme Pontiff could ascend to Heaven in body and soul, his mission on earth fulfilled, and the President of the Republic could sit down and govern according to his good judgment, and the queens of all things that have been or ever will be could marry and be happy and conceive and give birth to many sons, and the common people could set up their tents where they damn well pleased in the limitless domains of Big Mama, because the only one who could oppose them and had sufficient power to do so had begun to rot beneath a lead plinth. The only thing left then was for someone to lean a stool against the doorway to tell this story, lesson and example for future generations, so that not one of the world's disbelievers would be left who did not know the story of Big Mama, because tomorrow, Wednesday, the garbage men will come and will sweep up the garbage from her funeral, forever and ever.

■ *Questions for* . . . **Big Mama's Funeral** by Gabriel García Márquez

Discussion and Journal Writing

1. How does García Márquez characterize Maria del Rosario Castañeda y Montero, alias Big Mama? What does she represent?
2. What is the narrator's tone? What's the effect of his exaggerations?
3. What's the difference between a normal family and a *dynasty?* Can a family be both? Is the Castañeda family a *dynasty?*
4. How much does García Márquez tell us about Big Mama's family history? What does the family history add to the family portrait?
5. The narrator informs us, "Big Mama's matriarchal rigidity had surrounded her fortune and her name with a sacramental fence, within which uncles married the daughters of their nieces, and the cousins married their aunts, and brothers their sisters-in-law, until an intricate mesh of consanguinity was formed, which turned procreation into a vicious circle." What is *consanguinity* and why is it important? What is this family's reason for being?
6. Draw a family tree of the family's legitimate and bastard lines. Where does the fictional country of Macondo begin and the Castañeda family end? Study Big Mama's earthly and immaterial possessions. Who are these people?

ooooo

Boxes

—Raymond Carver

Raymond Carver is the most famous writer the Oregon town of Clatskanie has yet produced. His career got off to a slow start: he worked a string of day jobs at gas stations and sawmills while his distinctive brand of minimalist realism took shape. In the 1970s and 1980s, however, he made up for lost time, winning many of the awards and fellowships available to an American short story writer and publishing in the most prestigious magazines and journals. If imitation is the highest form of flattery, students in America's graduate writing programs have been flattering Carver for the past ten years more frequently than any other writer. "Boxes" is typical of Carver's fiction and one of the best stories he wrote. The setting is evocative despite its plainness, and the narrator, his mother, and his girlfriend are powerfully drawn. Not much happens in "Boxes," but as the story progresses, the narrator becomes aware of how impossible and unending his predicament is.

My mother is packed and ready to move. But Sunday afternoon, at the last minute, she calls and says for us to come eat with her. "My icebox is defrosting," she tells me. "I have to fry up this chicken before it rots." She says we should bring our own plates and some knives and forks. She's packed most of her dishes and kitchen things. "Come on and eat with me one last time," she says. "You and Jill."

I hang up the phone and stand at the window for a minute longer, wishing I could figure this thing out. But I can't. So finally I turn to Jill and say, "Let's go to my mother's for a goodbye meal."

Jill is at the table with a Sears catalog in front of her, trying to find us some curtains. But she's been listening. She makes a face. "Do we have to?" she says. She bends down the corner of a page and closes the catalog. She sighs, "God, we been over there to eat two or three times in this last month alone. Is she ever actually going to leave?"

Jill always says what's on her mind. She's thirty-five years old, wears her hair short, and grooms dogs for a living. Before she became a groomer, something she likes, she used to be a housewife and mother. Then all hell broke loose. Her two children were kidnapped by her first husband and taken to live in Australia. Her second husband, who drank, left her with a broken eardrum before he drove their car through a bridge into the Elwha River. He didn't have life insurance, not to mention property-damage insurance. Jill had to borrow money to bury him, and then—can you beat it?—she was presented with a bill for the bridge repair. Plus, she had her own medical bills. She can tell this story now. She's bounced back. But she has run out of patience with my mother. I've run out of patience, too. But I don't see any options.

"She's leaving day after tomorrow," I say. "Hey, Jill, don't do any favors. Do you want to come with me or not?" I tell her it doesn't matter to me one way or the other. I'll say she has a migraine. It's not like I've never told a lie before.

"I'm coming," she says. And like that she gets up and goes into the bathroom, where she likes to pout.

We've been together since last August, about the time my mother picked to move up here to Longview from California. Jill tried to make the best of it. But my mother pulling into town just when we were trying to get our act together was nothing either of us had bargained for. Jill said it reminded her of the situation with her first husband's mother. "She's a clinger," Jill said. "You know what I mean? I thought I was going to suffocate."

It's fair to say that my mother sees Jill as an intruder. As far as she's concerned, Jill is just another girl in a series of girls who have appeared in my life since my wife left me. Someone, to her mind, likely to take away affection, attention, maybe even some money that might otherwise come to her. But someone deserving of respect? No way. I remember—how can I forget it?—she called my wife a whore before we were married, and then called her a whore fifteen years later, after she left me for someone else.

Jill and my mother act friendly enough when they find themselves together. They hug each other when they say hello or goodbye. They talk about shopping specials. But Jill dreads the time she has to spend in my mother's company. She claims my mother bums her out. She says my mother is negative about everything and everybody and ought to find an outlet, like other people in her age bracket. Crocheting, maybe, or card games at the Senior Citizens Center, or else going to church. Something, anyway, so that she'll leave us in peace. But my mother had her own way of solving things. She announced she was moving back to California. The hell with everything and everybody in this town. What a place to live! She wouldn't continue to live in this town if they gave her the place and six more like it.

Within a day or two of deciding to move, she'd packed her things into boxes. That was last January. Or maybe it was February. Anyway, last winter sometime. Now it's the end of June. Boxes have been sitting around inside her house for months. You have to walk around them or step over them to get from one room to another. This is no way for anyone's mother to live.

After a while, ten minutes or so, Jill comes out of the bathroom. I've found a roach and am trying to smoke that and drink a bottle of ginger ale while I watch one of the neighbors change the oil in his car. Jill doesn't look at me. Instead, she goes into the kitchen and puts some plates and utensils into a paper sack. But when she comes back through the living room I stand up, and we hug each other. Jill says, "It's okay." What's okay, I wonder. As far as I can see, nothing's okay. But she holds me and keeps patting my shoulder. I can smell the pet shampoo on her. She comes home from work wearing the stuff. It's everywhere. Even when we're in bed together. She gives me a final pat. Then we go out to the car and drive across town to my mother's.

I like where I live. I didn't when I first moved here. There was nothing to do at night, and I was lonely. Then I met Jill. Pretty soon, after a few weeks, she brought her things over and started living with me. We didn't set any long-term goals. We were happy and we had a life together. We told each other we'd finally got lucky. But my mother didn't have anything going in her life. So she wrote me and said she'd decided on moving here. I wrote her back and said I didn't think it was such a good idea. The weather's terrible in the winter, I said. They're building a prison a few miles from town, I told her. The place is bumper-to-bumper tourists all summer, I said. But she acted as if she never got my letters, and came anyway. Then, after she'd been in town a little less than a month, she told me she hated the place. She acted as if it were my fault she'd moved here and my fault she found everything so disagreeable. She started calling me up and telling me how crummy the place was. "Laying guilt trips," Jill called it. She told me the bus service was terrible and the drivers unfriendly. As for the people at the Senior Citizens—well, she didn't want to play casino. "They can go to hell," she said, "and take their card games with them." The clerks at the supermarket were surly, the guys in the service station didn't give a damn about her or her car. And she'd made up her mind about the man she rented from, Larry Hadlock. King Larry, she called him. "He thinks he's *superior* to everyone because he has some shacks for rent and a few dollars. I wish to God I'd never laid eyes on him."

It was too hot for her when she arrived in August, and in September it started to rain. It rained almost every day for weeks. In October it turned cold. There was snow in November and December. But long before that she began to put the bad mouth on the place and the people to the extent that I didn't want to hear about it anymore, and I told her so finally. She cried, and I hugged her and thought that was the end of it. But a few days later she started in again, same stuff. Just before Christmas she called to see when I was coming by with her presents. She hadn't put up a tree and didn't intend to, she said. Then she said something else. She said if this weather didn't improve she was going to kill herself.

"Don't talk crazy," I said.

She said, "I mean it, honey. I don't want to see this place again except from my coffin. I hate this g.d. place. I don't know why I moved here. I wish I could just die and get it over with."

I remember hanging on to the phone and watching a man high up on a pole doing something to a power line. Snow whirled around his head. As I watched, he leaned out from the pole, supported only by his safety belt. Suppose he falls, I thought. I didn't have any idea what I was going to say next. I had to say something. But I was filled with unworthy feelings, thoughts no son should admit to. "You're my mother," I said finally. "What can I do to help?"

"Honey, you can't do anything," she said. "The time for doing anything has come and gone. It's too late to do anything. I wanted to like it here. I thought we'd go on picnics and take drives together. But none of that happened. You're always busy. You're off working, you and Jill. You're never at home. Or else if you are at home you have the phone off the hook all day. Anyway, I never see you," she said.

"That's not true," I said. And it wasn't. But she went on as if she hadn't heard me. Maybe she hadn't.

"Besides," she said, "this weather is killing me. It's too damned cold here. Why didn't you tell me this was the North Pole? If you had, I'd never have come. I want to go back to California, honey. I can get out and go places there. I don't know anywhere to go here. There are people back in California. I've got friends there who care what happens to me. Nobody gives a damn here. Well, I just pray I can get through to June. If I can make it that long, if I can last to June, I'm leaving this place forever. This is the worst place I've ever lived in."

What could I say? I didn't know what to say. I couldn't even say anything 20 about the weather. Weather was a real sore point. We said goodbye and hung up.

Other people take vacations in the summer, but my mother moves. She started moving years ago, after my dad lost his job. When that happened, when he was laid off, they sold their home, as if this were what they should do, and went to where they thought things would be better. But things weren't any better there, either. They moved again. They kept on moving. They lived in rented houses, apartments, mobile homes, and motel units even. They kept moving, lightening their load with each move they made. A couple of times they landed in a town where I lived. They'd move in with my wife and me for a while and then they'd move on again. They were like migrating animals in this regard, except there was no pattern to their movement. They moved around for years, sometimes even leaving the state for what they thought would be greener pastures. But mostly they stayed in Northern California and did their moving there. Then my dad died, and I thought my mother would stop moving and stay in one place for a while. But she didn't. She kept moving. I suggested once that she go to a psychiatrist. I even said I'd pay for it. But she wouldn't hear of it. She packed and moved out of town instead. I was desperate about things or I wouldn't had said that about the psychiatrist.

She was always in the process of packing or else unpacking. Sometimes she'd move two or three times in the same year. She talked bitterly about the place she was leaving and optimistically about the place she was going to. Her mail got fouled up, her benefit checks went off somewhere else, and she spent hours writing letters, trying to get it all straightened out. Sometimes she'd move out of an apartment house, move to another one a few blocks away, and then, a month later, move back to the place she'd left, only to a different floor or a different side of the building. That's why when she moved here I rented a house for her and saw to it that it was furnished to her liking. "Moving around keeps her alive," Jill said. "It gives her something to do. She must get some kind of weird enjoyment out of it, I guess." But enjoyment or not, Jill thinks my mother must be losing her mind. I think so, too. But how do you tell your mother this? How do your deal with her if this is the case? Crazy doesn't stop her from planning and getting on with her next move.

She is waiting at the back door for us when we pull in. She's seventy years old, has gray hair, wears glasses with rhinestone frames, and has never been sick a day in her life. She hugs Jill, and then she hugs me. Her eyes are bright, as if she's been drinking. But she doesn't drink. She quit years ago, after my dad went on the wagon. We finish hugging and go inside. It's around five in the afternoon. I smell whatever it is drifting out of her kitchen and remember I haven't eaten since breakfast. My buzz has worn off.

"I'm starved," I say.

"Something smells good," Jill says.   25

"I hope it tastes good," my mother says. "I hope this chicken's done." She raises the lid on a fry pan and pushes a fork into a chicken breast. "If there's anything I can't stand, it's raw chicken. I think it's done. Why don't you sit down? Sit anyplace. I still can't regulate my stove. The burners heat up too fast. I don't like electric stoves and never have. Move that junk off the chair, Jill. I'm living here like a damned gypsy. But not for much longer, I hope." She sees me looking around for the ashtray. "Behind you," she says. "On the windowsill, honey. Before you sit down, why don't you pour us some of that Pepsi? You'll have to use these paper cups. I should have told you to bring some glasses. Is the Pepsi cold? I don't have any ice. This icebox won't keep anything cold. It isn't worth a damn. My ice cream turns to soup. It's the worst icebox I've ever had."

She forks the chicken onto a plate and puts the plate on the table along with beans and coleslaw and white bread. Then she looks to see if there is anything she's forgetting. Salt and pepper! "Sit down," she says.

We draw our chairs up to the table, and Jill takes the plates out of the sack and hands them around the table to us. "Where are you going to live when you go back?" she says. "Do you have a place lined up?"

My mother passes the chicken to Jill and says, "I wrote that lady rented from before. She wrote back and said she had a nice first-floor place I could have. It's close to the bus stop and there's lots of stores in the area. There's a bank and a Safeway. It's the nicest place. I don't know why I left there." She says that and helps herself to some coleslaw.

"Why'd you leave then?" Jill says. "If it was so nice and all." She picks up her   30 drumstick, looks at it, and takes a bite of the meat.

"I'll tell you why. There was an old alcoholic woman who lived next door to me. She drank from morning to night. The walls were so thin I could hear her munching ice cubes all day. She had to use a walker to get around, but that still didn't stop her. I'd hear that walker *scrape, scrape* against the floor from morning to night. That and her icebox door closing." She shakes her head at all she had to put up with. "I had to get out of there. *Scrape, scrape* all day. I couldn't stand it. I just couldn't live like that. This time I told the manager I didn't want to be next to any alcoholics. And I didn't want anything on the second floor. The second floor looks out on the parking lot. Nothing to see from there." She waits for Jill to say something more. But Jill doesn't comment. My mother looks over at me.

I'm eating like a wolf and don't say anything, either. In any case, there's nothing more to say on the subject. I keep chewing and look over at the boxes stacked against the fridge. Then I help myself to more coleslaw.

Pretty soon I finish and push my chair back. Larry Hadlock pulls up in back of the house, next to my car, and takes a lawnmower out of his pickup. I watch him through the window behind the table. He doesn't look in our direction.

"What's he want?" my mother says and stops eating.

"He's going to cut your grass, it looks like," I say.   35

"It doesn't need cutting," she says. "He cut it last week. What's there for him to cut?"

"It's for the new tenant," Jill says. "Whoever that turns out to be."

My mother takes this in and then goes back to eating.

Larry Hadlock starts his mower and begins to cut the grass. I know him a little. He lowered the rent twenty-five a month when I told him it was my mother. He is a widower—a big fellow, mid-sixties. An unhappy man with a good sense of humor. His arms are covered with white hair, and white hair stands out from under his cap. He looks like a magazine illustration of a farmer. But he isn't a farmer. He is a retired construction worker who's saved a little money. For a while, in the beginning, I let myself imagine that he and my mother might take some meals together and become friends.

"There's the king," my mother says. "King Larry. Not everyone has as much 40 money as he does and can live in a big house and charge other people high rents. Well, I hope I never see his cheap old face again once I leave here. Eat the rest of this chicken," she says to me. But I shake my head and light a cigarette. Larry pushes his mower past the window.

"You won't have to look at it much longer," Jill says.

"I'm sure glad of that, Jill. But I know he won't give me my deposit back."

"How do you know that?" I say.

"I just know," she says. "I've had dealings with his kind before. They're out for all they can get."

Jill says, "It won't be long now and you won't have to have anything more to 45 do with him."

"I'll be so glad."

"But it'll be somebody just like him," Jill says.

"I don't want to think that, Jill," my mother says.

She makes coffee while Jill clears the table. I rinse the cups. Then I pour coffee, and we step around a box marked "Knick-knacks" and take our cups into the living room.

Larry Hadlock is at the side of the house. Traffic moves slowly on the street 50 out in front, and the sun has started down over the trees. I can hear the commotion the mower makes. Some crows leave the phone line and settle onto the newly cut grass in the front yard.

"I'm going to miss you, honey," my mother says. Then she says, "I'll miss you, too, Jill. I'm going to miss both of you."

Jill sips her coffee and nods. Then she says, "I hope you have a safe trip back and find the place you're looking for at the end of the road."

"When I get settled—and this is my last move, so help me—I hope you'll come and visit," my mother says. She looks at me and waits to be reassured.

"We will," I say. But even as I say it I know it isn't true. My life caved in on me down there, and I won't be going back.

"I wish you could have been happier here," Jill says. "I wish you'd been able 55 to stick it out or something. You know what? Your son is worried sick about you."

"Jill," I say.

But she gives her head a little shake and goes on. "Sometimes he can't sleep over it. He wakes up sometimes in the night and says, 'I can't sleep. I'm thinking about my mother.' There," she looks at me. "I've said it. But it was on my mind."

"How do you think I must feel?" my mother says. Then she says, "Other women my age can be happy. Why can't I be like other women? All I want is a house and a town to live in that will make me happy. That isn't a crime, is it? I hope not. I hope I'm not asking too much out of life." She puts her cup on the floor next to her chair and waits for Jill to tell her she isn't asking too much. But Jill doesn't say anything, and in a minute my mother begins to outline her plans to be happy.

After a time Jill lowers her eyes to her cup and has some more coffee. I can tell she's stopped listening. But my mother keeps talking anyway. The crows work their way through the grass in the front yard. I hear the mower howl and then thud as it picks up a clump of grass in the blade and comes to a stop. In a minute, after several tries, Larry gets it going again. The crows fly off, back to their wire. Jill picks at a fingernail. My mother is saying that the secondhand-furniture dealer is coming around the next morning to collect the things she isn't going to send on the bus or carry with her in the car. The table and chairs, TV, sofa, and bed are going with the dealer. But he's told her he doesn't have any use for the card table, so my mother is going to throw it out unless we want it.

"We'll take it," I say. Jill looks over. She starts to say something but changes 60 her mind.

I will drive the boxes to the Greyhound station the next afternoon and start them on the way to California. My mother will spend the last night with us, as arranged. And then, early the next morning, two days from now, she'll be on her way.

She continues to talk. She talks on and on as she describes the trip she is about to make. She'll drive until four o'clock in the afternoon and then take a motel room for the night. She figures to make Eugene by dark. Eugene is a nice town—she stayed there once before, on the way up here. When she leaves the motel, she'll leave at sunrise and should, if God is looking out for her, be in California that afternoon. And God *is* looking out for her, she knows he is. How else explain her being kept around on the face of the earth? He has a plan for her. She's been praying a lot lately. She's been praying for me, too.

"Why are you praying for him?" Jill wants to know.

"Because I feel like it. Because he's my son," my mother says. "Is there anything the matter with that? Don't we all need praying for sometimes? Maybe some people don't. I don't know. What do I know anymore?" She brings a hand to her forehead and arranges some hair that's come loose from a pin.

The mower sputters off, and pretty soon we see Larry go around the house 65 pulling the hose. He sets the hose out and then goes slowly back around the house to turn the water on. The sprinkler begins to turn.

My mother starts listing the ways she imagines Larry has wronged her since she's been in the house. But now I'm not listening, either. I am thinking how she is about to go down the highway again, and nobody can reason with her or do anything to stop her. What can I do? I can't tie her up, or commit her, though it may come to that eventually. I worry for her, and she is a heartache to me. She is all the family I have left. I'm sorry she didn't like it here and wants to leave. But I'm never going back to California. And when that's clear to me I understand something else, too. I understand that after she leaves I'm probably never going to see her again.

I look over at my mother. She stops talking. Jill raises her eyes. Both of them look at me.

"What is it, honey?" my mother says.

"What's wrong?" Jill says.

I lean forward in the chair and cover my face with my hands. I sit like that for 70 a minute, feeling bad and stupid for doing it. But I can't help it. And the woman who brought me into this life, and this other woman I picked up with less than a year ago, they exclaim together and rise and come over to where I sit with my head in my hands like a fool. I don't open my eyes. I listen to the sprinkler whipping the grass.

"What's wrong? What's the matter?" they say.

"It's okay," I say. And in a minute it is. I open my eyes and bring my head up. I reach for a cigarette.

"See what I mean?" Jill says. "You're driving him crazy. He's going crazy with worry over you." She is on one side of my chair, and my mother is on the other side. They could tear me apart in no time at all.

"I wish I could die and get out of everyone's way," my mother says quietly. "So help me Hannah, I can't take much more of this."

"How about some more coffee?" I say. "Maybe we ought to catch the news," I 75 say. "Then I guess Jill and I better head for home."

Two days later, early in the morning, I say goodbye to my mother for what may be the last time. I've let Jill sleep. It won't hurt if she's late to work for a change. The dogs can wait for their baths and trimmings and such. My mother holds my arm as I walk her down the steps to the driveway and open the car door for her. She is wearing white slacks and a white blouse and white sandals. Her hair is pulled back and tied with a scarf. That's white, too. It's going to be a nice day, and the sky is clear and already blue.

On the front seat of the car I see maps and a thermos of coffee. My mother looks at these things as if she can't recall having come outside with them just a few minutes ago. She turns to me then and says, "Let me hug you once more. Let me love your neck. I know I won't see you for a long time." She puts an arm around my neck, draws me to her, and then begins to cry. But she stops almost at once and steps back, pushing the heel of her hand against her eyes. "I said I wouldn't do that, and I won't. But let me get a last look at you anyway. I'll miss you, honey," she says. "I'm just going to have to live through this. I've already lived through things I didn't think were possible. But I'll live through this too, I guess." She gets into the car, starts it, and runs the engine for a minute. She rolls her window down.

"I'm going to miss you," I say. And I *am* going to miss her. She's my mother, after all, and why shouldn't I miss her? But, God forgive me, I'm glad, too, that it's finally time and that she is leaving.

"Goodbye," she says. "Tell Jill thanks for supper last night. Tell her I said goodbye."

"I will," I say. I stand there wanting to say something else. But I don't know 80 what. We keep looking at each other, trying to smile and reassure each other. Then something comes into her eyes, and I believe she is thinking about the highway and how far she is going to have to drive that day. She takes her eyes off me and looks down the road. Then she rolls her window up, puts the car into gear, and drives to the intersection, where she has to wait for the light to change. When I see she's made it into traffic and headed toward the highway, I go back in the house and drink some coffee. I feel sad for a while, and then the sadness goes away and I start thinking about other things.

A few nights later my mother calls to say she is in her new place. She is busy fixing it up, the way she does when she has a new place. She tells me I'll be happy to know she likes it just fine to be back in sunny California. But she says there's something in the air where she is living, maybe it's pollen, that is causing her to sneeze a lot. And the traffic is heavier than she remembers from before. She doesn't recall there being so much traffic in her neighborhood. Naturally, everyone still drives like crazy down there. "California drivers," she says. "What can you expect?" She says it's hot for this time of the year. She doesn't think the air-conditioning unit in her apartment is working right. I tell her she should talk to the manager. "She's never around when you need her," my mother says. She hopes she hasn't made a mistake in moving back to California. She waits before she says anything else.

I'm standing at the window with the phone pressed to my ear, looking out at the lights from town and at the lighted houses closer by. Jill is at the table with the catalog, listening.

"Are you still there?" my mother asks. "I wish you'd say something."

I don't know why, but it's then I recall the affectionate name my dad used sometimes when he was talking nice to my mother—those times, that is, when he wasn't drunk. It was a long time ago, and I was a kid, but always, hearing it, I felt better, less afraid, more hopeful about the future. *"Dear,"* he'd say. He called her "dear" sometimes—a sweet name. "Dear," he'd say, "if you're going to the store, will you bring me some cigarettes?" Or, "Dear, is your cold any better?" "Dear, where is my coffee cup?"

The word issues from my lips before I can think what else I want to say to go along with it. "Dear." I say it again. I call her "dear." "Dear, try not to be afraid," I say. I tell my mother I love her and I'll write to her, yes. Then I say goodbye, and I hang up. 85

For a while I don't move from the window. I keep standing there, looking out at the lighted houses in our neighborhood. As I watch, a car turns off the road and pulls into a driveway. The porch light goes on. The door to the house opens and someone comes out on the porch and stands there waiting.

Jill turns the pages of her catalog, and then she stops turning them. "This is what we want," she says. "This is more like what I had in mind. Look at this, will you." But I don't look. I don't care five cents for curtains. "What is it you see out there, honey?" Jill says. "Tell me."

What's there to tell? The people over there embrace for a minute, and then they go inside the house together. They leave the light burning. Then they remember, and it goes out.

■ *Questions for . . .* Boxes by Raymond Carver

Discussion and Journal Writing

1. How much do we know about the story's three main characters by the end of the fourth paragraph and how do we know it?
2. What are the family histories of each of the story's main characters? What light do these histories shed on their present predicament?
3. Why does Carver put so many clichés into the mouth of the narrator? Do they add to or detract from the quality of the story? Why?
4. What do the mother's boxes symbolize to her? To her son? To Jill? To the reader?
5. How do you think Carver wants us to feel about the mother? What elements of fiction does he use to establish those feelings?
6. How does Carver do the family meal?
7. Why do you think Carver put most of the story in the present tense? How does Carver use verb tense to organize his story? Do the four panels he divides the story into help the reader follow the story?

ooooo

Getting the Facts of Life

—Paulette Childress White

Paulette Childress White grew up in Detroit in the 1950s and 1960s, during the time when the city and its environs were transformed by White flight—the exodus of White people from the inner city to the suburbs. White's story is shot through with racial division and hostility, despite the fact that Minerva, the story's Black protagonist, is the daughter of a White mother; and there's a sense that Minerva's neighborhood has seen better days. The hotel and pool parlor that Minerva and her mother pass on the way to the welfare office are especially down at the heels. It's also noteworthy that White's story, unlike the stories of many American women writers, doesn't take place at home. It's a family story that takes place in the open air of the neighborhood and the stale air of an institution that has recently become central to this family's livelihood, the welfare office.

The August morning was ripening into a day that promised to be a burner. By the time we'd walked three blocks, dark patches were showing beneath Momma's arms, and inside tennis shoes thick with white polish, my feet were wet against the cushions. I was beginning to regret how quickly I'd volunteered to go.

"Dog. My feet are getting mushy," I complained.

"You should've wore socks," Momma said, without looking my way or slowing down.

I frowned. In 1961, nobody wore socks with tennis shoes. It was bare legs, Bermuda shorts and a sleeveless blouse. Period.

Momma was chubby but she could really walk. She walked the same way she   5 washed clothes—up-and-down, up-and-down until she was done. She didn't believe in taking breaks.

This was my first time going to the welfare office with Momma. After breakfast, before we'd had time to scatter, she corralled everyone old enough to consider and announced in her serious-business voice that someone was going to the welfare office with her this morning. Cries went up.

Junior had his papers to do. Stella was going swimming at the high school. Dennis was already pulling the *Free Press* wagon across town every first Wednesday to get the surplus food—like that.

"You want clothes for school, don't you?" That landed. School opened in two weeks.

"I'll go," I said.

"Who's going to baby-sit if Minerva goes?" Momma asked.   10

Stella smiled and lifted her small golden nose. "I will," she said. "I'd rather baby-sit than do *that*."

That should have warned me. Anything that would make Stella offer to baby-sit had to be bad.

A small cheer probably went up among my younger brothers in the back rooms where I was not too secretly known as "The Witch" because of the criminal licks I'd learned to give on my rise to power. I was twelve, third oldest under Junior and Stella, but I had long established myself as first in command among the kids. I was chief baby-sitter, biscuit-maker and broom-wielder. Unlike Stella, who'd begun her development at ten, I still had my girl's body and wasn't anxious to have that changed. What would it mean but a loss of power? I liked things just the way they were. My interest in bras was even less than my interest in boys, and that was limited to keeping my brothers—who seemed destined for wildness—from taking over completely.

Even before we left, Stella had Little Stevie Wonder turned up on the radio in the living room, and suspicious jumping-bumping sounds were beginning in the back. They'll tear the house down, I thought, following Momma out the door.

We turned at Salliotte, the street that would take us straight up to Jefferson 15
Avenue where the welfare office was. Momma's face was pinking in the heat, and I was huffing to keep up. From here, it was seven more blocks on the colored side, the railroad tracks, five blocks on the white side and there you were. We'd be cooked.

"Is the welfare office near the Harbor Show?" I asked. I knew the answer. I just wanted some talk.

"Across the street."

"Umm. Glad it's not way down Jefferson somewhere."

Nothing. Momma didn't talk much when she was outside. I knew that the reason she wanted one of us along when she had far to go was not for company but so she wouldn't have to walk by herself. I could understand that. To me, walking alone was like being naked or deformed—everyone seemed to look at you harder and longer. With Momma, the feeling was probably worse because you knew people were wondering if she were white, Indian maybe or really colored. Having one of us along, brown and clearly hers, probably helped define that. Still, it was like being a little parade, with Momma's pale skin and straight brown hair turning heads like the clang of cymbals. Especially on the colored side.

"Well," I said, "here we come to the bad part."   20

Momma gave a tiny laugh.

Most of Salliotte was a business street, with Old West-looking storefronts and some office places that never seemed to open. Ecorse, hinged onto southwest Detroit like a clothes closet, didn't seem to take itself seriously. There were lots of empty fields, some of which folks down the residential streets turned into vegetable gardens every summer. And there was this block where the Moonflower Hotel raised itself to three stories over the poolroom and Beaman's drugstore. Here, bad boys and drunks made their noise and did an occasional stabbing. Except for the cars that lined both sides of the block, only one side was busy—the other bordered a field of weeds. We walked on the safe side.

If you were a woman or a girl over twelve, walking this block—even on the safe side—could be painful. They usually hollered at you and never mind what they said. Today, because it was hot and early, we made it by with only one weak *Hey baby* from a drunk sitting in the poolroom door.

"Hey baby yourself," I said but not too loudly, pushing my flat chest out and stabbing my eyes in his direction.

"Minerva girl, you better watch your mouth with grown men like that," 25 Momma said, her eyes catching me up in real warning though I could see that she was holding down a smile.

"Well, he can't do nothing to me when I'm with you, can he?" I asked, striving to match the rise and fall of her black pumps.

She said nothing. She just walked on, churning away under a sun that clearly meant to melt us. From here to the tracks it was mostly gardens. It felt like the Dixie Peach I'd used to help water-wave my hair was sliding down with the sweat on my face, and my throat was tight with thirst. Boy, did I want a pop. I looked at the last little store before we crossed the tracks without bothering to ask.

Across the tracks, there were no stores and no gardens. It was shady, and the grass was June green. Perfect-looking houses sat in unfenced spaces far back from the street. We walked these five blocks without a word. We just looked and hurried to get through it. I was beginning to worry about the welfare office in earnest. A fool could see that in this part of Ecorse, things got serious.

We had been on welfare for almost a year. I didn't have any strong feelings about it—my life went on pretty much the same. It just meant watching the mail for a check instead of Daddy getting paid, and occasional visits from a social worker that I'd always managed to miss. For Momma and whoever went with her, it meant this walk to the office and whatever went on there that made everyone hate to go. For Daddy, it seemed to bring the most change. For him, it meant staying away from home more than when he was working and a reason not to answer the phone.

At Jefferson, we turned left and there it was, halfway down the block. The 30 Department of Social Services. I discovered some strong feelings. That fine name meant nothing. This was the welfare. The place for poor people. People who couldn't or wouldn't take care of themselves. Now I was going to face it, and suddenly I thought what I knew the others had thought, *What if I see someone I know?* I wanted to run back all those blocks to home.

I looked at Momma for comfort, but her face was closed and her mouth looked locked.

Inside, the place was gray. There were rows of long benches like church pews facing each other across a middle aisle that led to a central desk. Beyond the benches and the desk, four hallways led off to a maze of partitioned offices. In opposite corners, huge fans hung from the ceiling, humming from side to side, blowing the heavy air for a breeze.

Momma walked to the desk, answered some questions, was given a number and told to take a seat. I followed her through, trying not to see the waiting people—as though that would keep them from seeing me.

Gradually, as we waited, I took them all in. There was no one there that I knew, but somehow they all looked familiar. Or maybe I only thought they did, because when your eyes connected with someone's, they didn't quickly look away and they usually smiled. They were mostly women and children, and a few low-looking men. Some of them were white, which surprised me. I hadn't expected to see them in there.

Directly in front of the bench where we sat, a little girl with blond curls was 35 trying to handle a bottle of coke. Now and then, she'd manage to turn herself and the bottle around and watch me with big gray eyes that seemed to know quite well how badly I wanted a pop. I thought of asking Momma for fifteen cents so I could get one from the machine in the back but I was afraid she'd still say no so I just kept planning more and more convincing ways to ask. Besides, there was a water fountain near the door if I could make myself rise and walk to it.

We waited three hours. White ladies dressed like secretaries kept coming out to call numbers, and people on the benches would get up and follow down a hall. Then more people came in to replace them. I drank water from the fountain three times and was ready to put my feet up on the bench before us—the little girl with the Coke and her momma got called—by the time we heard Momma's number.

"You wait here," Momma said as I rose with her.

I sat down with a plop.

The lady with the number looked at me. Her face reminded me of the librarian's at Bunch school. Looked like she never cracked a smile. "Let her come," she said.

"She can wait here," Momma repeated, weakly.   40

"It's OK. She can come in. Come on," the lady insisted at me.

I hesitated, knowing that Momma's face was telling me to sit.

"Come on," the woman said.

Momma said nothing.

I got up and followed them into the maze. We came to a small room where 45 there was a desk and three chairs. The woman sat behind the desk and we before it.

For a while, no one spoke. The woman studied a folder open before her, brows drawn together. On the wall behind her there was a calendar with one heavy black line drawn slantwise through each day of August, up to the twenty-first. That was today.

"Mrs. Blue, I have a notation here that Mr. Blue has not reported to the department on his efforts to obtain employment since the sixteenth of June. Before that, it was the tenth of April. You understand that department regulations require that he report monthly to this office, do you not?" Eyes brown as a wren's belly came up at Momma.

"Yes," Momma answered, sounding as small as I felt.

"Can you explain his failure to do so?"

Pause. "He's been looking. He says he's been looking."   50

"That may be. However, his failure to report those efforts here is my only concern."

Silence.

"We cannot continue with your case as it now stands if Mr. Blue refuses to comply with departmental regulations. He is still residing with the family, is he not?"

"Yes, he is. I've been reminding him to come in . . . he said he would."

"Well, he hasn't. Regulations are that any able-bodied man, head-of-house- 55 hold and receiving assistance who neglects to report to this office any effort to obtain work for a period of sixty days or more is to be cut off for a minimum of three months, at which time he may reapply. As of this date, Mr. Blue is over sixty days delinquent, and officially, I am obliged to close the case and direct you to other sources of aid."

"What is that?"

"Aid to Dependent Children would be the only source available to you. Then, of course, you would not be eligible unless it was verified that Mr. Blue was no longer residing with the family."

Another silence. I stared into the gray steel front of the desk, everything stopped but my heart.

"Well, can you keep the case open until Monday? If he comes in by Monday?"

"According to my records, Mr. Blue failed to come in May and such an agree- 60 ment was made then. In all, we allowed him a period of seventy days. You must understand that what happens in such cases as this is not wholly my decision." She sighed and watched Momma with hopeless eyes, tapping the soft end of her pencil on the papers before her. "Mrs. Blue, I will speak to my superiors on your behalf. I can allow you until Monday next . . . that's the"—she swung around to the calen-dar—"twenty-sixth of August, to get him in here."

"Thank you. He'll be in," Momma breathed. "Will I be able to get the clothing order today?"

Hands and eyes searched the folder for an answer before she cleared her throat and tilted her face at Momma. "We'll see what we can do," she said, finally.

My back touched the chair. Without turning my head, I moved my eyes down to Momma's dusty feet and wondered it she could still feel them; my own were numb. I felt bodyless—there was only my face, which wouldn't disappear, and behind it, one word pinging against another in a buzz that made no sense. At home, we'd have the house cleaned by now, and I'd be waiting for the daily appearance of my best friend, Bernadine, so we could comb each other's hair or talk about stuck-up Evelyn and Brenda. Maybe Bernadine was already there, and Stella was teach-ing her to dance the bop.

Then I heard our names and ages—all eight of them—being called off like items in a grocery list.

"Clifford, Junior, age fourteen." She waited. 65

"Yes."

"Born? Give me the month and year."

"October 1946," Momma answered, and I could hear in her voice that she'd been through these questions before.

"Stella, age thirteen."

"Yes."   70

"Born?"

"November 1947."

"Minerva, age twelve." She looked at me. "This is Minerva?"

"Yes."

No. I thought, no, this is not Minerva. You can write it down if you want to, 75
but Minerva is not here.

"Born?"

"December 1948"

The woman went on down the list, sounding more and more like Momma should be sorry or ashamed, and Momma's answers grew fainter and fainter. So this was welfare. I wondered how many times Momma had had to do this. Once before? Three times? Every time?

More questions? How many in school? Six. Who needs shoes? Everybody.

"Everybody needs shoes? The youngest two?"   80

"Well, they don't go to school . . . but they walk."

My head came up to look at Momma and the woman. The woman's mouth was left open. Momma didn't blink.

The brown eyes went down. "Our allowances are based on the median cost for moderately priced clothing at Sears, Roebuck." She figured on paper as she spoke. "That will mean thirty-four dollars for children over ten . . . thirty dollars for children under ten. It comes to one hundred ninety-eight dollars. I can allow eight dollars for two additional pairs of shoes."

"Thank-you."

"You will present your clothing order to a salesperson at the store, who will 85
be happy to assist you in your selections. Please be practical as further clothing requests will not be considered for a period of six months. In cases of necessity, however, requests for winter outerwear will be considered beginning November first.

Momma said nothing.

The woman rose and left the room.

For the first time, I shifted in the chair. Momma was looking into the calendar as though she could see through the pages to November first. Everybody needed a coat.

I'm never coming here again, I thought. If I do, I'll stay out front. Not coming back in here. Ever again.

She came back and sat behind here desk. "Mrs. Blue, I must make it clear that, 90
regardless of my feelings, I will be forced to close your case if your husband does not report to this office by Monday, the twenty-sixth. Do you understand?"

"Yes. Thank you. He'll come. I'll see to it."

"Very well." She held a paper out to Momma.

We stood. Momma reached over and took the slip of paper. I moved toward the door.

"Excuse me, Mrs. Blue, but are you pregnant?"

"What?"

"I asked if you were expecting another child."

"Oh. No, I'm not," Momma answered, biting down on her lips.

"Well, I'm sure you'll want to be careful about a thing like that in your present situation."

"Yes."

I looked quickly to Momma's loose white blouse. We'd never known when another baby was coming until it was almost there.

"I suppose that eight children are enough for anyone," the woman said, and for the first time her face broke into a smile.

Momma didn't answer that. Somehow, we left the room and found our way out onto the street. We stood for a moment as though lost. My eyes followed Momma's up to where the sun was burning high. It was still there, blazing white against a cloudless blue. Slowly, Momma put the clothing order into her purse and snapped it shut. She looked around as if uncertain which way to go. I led the way to the corner. We turned. We walked the first five blocks.

I was thinking about how stupid I'd been a year ago, when Daddy lost his job. I'd been happy.

"You-all better be thinking about moving to Indianapolis," he announced one day after work, looking like he didn't think much of it himself. He was a welder with the railroad company. He'd worked there for eleven years. But now, "Company's moving to Indianapolis," he said. "Gonna be gone by November. If I want to keep my job, we've got to move with it."

We didn't. Nobody wanted to move to Indianapolis—not even Daddy. Here, we had uncles, aunts and cousins on both sides. Friends. Everybody and everything we knew. Daddy could get another job. First came unemployment compensation. Then came welfare. Thank goodness for welfare, we said, while we waited and waited for the job that hadn't yet come.

The problem was that Daddy couldn't take it. If something got repossessed or somebody took sick or something was broken or another kid was coming, he'd carry on terribly until things got better—by which time things were always worse. He'd always been that way. So when the railroad left, he began to do everything wrong. Stayed out all hours. Drank and drank some more. When he was home, he was so grouchy we were afraid to squeak. Now when we saw him coming, we got lost. Even our friends ran for cover.

At the railroad tracks, we sped up. The tracks were as far across as a block was long. Silently, I counted the rails by the heat of the steel bars through my thin soles. On the other side, I felt something heavy rise up in my chest and I knew that I wanted to cry. I wanted to cry or run or kiss the dusty ground. The little houses with their sun-scorched lawns and backyard gardens were mansions in my eyes.

"Ohh, Ma . . . look at those collards!"

"Umm-humm," she agreed, and I knew that she saw it too.

"Wonder how they grew so big?"

"Cow dung, probably. Big Poppa used to put cow dung out to fertilize the 110 vegetable plots, and everything just grew like crazy. We used to get tomatoes this big"—she circled with her hands—"and don't talk about squash or melons."

"I bet y'all ate like rich people. Bet y'all had everything you could want."

"We sure did," she said. "We never wanted for anything when it came to food. And when the cash crops were sold, we could get whatever else that was needed. We never wanted for a thing."

"What about the time you and cousin Emma threw out the supper peas?"

"Oh! Did I tell you about that?" she asked. Then she told it all over again. I didn't listen. I watched her face and guarded her smile with a smile of my own.

We walked together, step for step. The sun was still burning, but we forgot to 115 mind it. We talked about an Alabama girlhood in a time and place I'd never know. We talked about the wringer washer and how it could be fixed, because washing every day on a scrub-board was something Alabama could keep. We talked about how to get Daddy to the Department of Social Services.

Then we talked about having babies. She began to tell me things I'd never known, and the idea of womanhood blossomed in my mind like some kind of suffocating rose.

"Momma," I said, "I don't think I can be a woman."

"You can," she laughed, "and if you live, you will be. You gotta be some kind of woman."

"But it's hard," I said, "sometimes it must be hard."

"Umm-humm," she said, "sometimes it is hard."   120

When we got to the bad block, we crossed to Beaman's drugstore for two orange crushes. Then we walked right through the groups of men standing in the shadows of the poolroom and the Moonflower Hotel. Not one of them said a word to us. I supposed they could see in the way we walked that we weren't afraid. We'd been to the welfare office and back again. And the facts of life, fixed in our minds like the sun in the sky, were no burning mysteries.

■ *Questions for* . . . Getting the Facts of Life by Paulette Childress White

Discussion and Journal Writing

1. Is it selfish of Mrs. Blue to take Minerva, the story's narrator, along with her to the welfare office? Is Mrs. Blue a responsible mother?
2. What are the facts of life?
3. How does White describe the welfare office?
4. The story is set in Ecorse, a little suburb, "hinged onto southwest Detroit like a clothes closet," and White expends quite a few words mapping the

neighborhood. What does the geography of the neighborhood contribute to the story?

5. Look at the way the welfare caseworker speaks. Look at the way Mrs. Blue, Minerva, and her siblings speak. What's the feeling and point of the contrast?

6. Where's Mr. Blue? What impact does going on relief have on the Blues?

7. Characterize Momma and Minerva's relationship.

8. In terms of White's story, what are the facts of life? By the end of the story, what has Minerva learned?

ooooo

🎭 Writing Workshop

When people, amateurs as well as professionals, write about literature, they tend to focus on one of the elements we have discussed or on the links between two or three of them. The point, especially in a short paper or article, is to interpret a manageable and important aspect of a story, one that takes you to the heart of things.

Complete the following assignment or one of the writing exercises at the end of the chapter. Or, you may also choose to write about one of the topics raised by the questions following the stories, or about a topic of your own creation. It is always a good idea to discuss topics you create with your instructor before going to work. The writing process mapped out below will work, regardless of the topic you choose.

The Topic: The portrayal of home or of family in short fiction.

The Assignment: Compare the homes or the families in two of this chapter's short stories. Any two will work, but certain combinations suggest themselves. There are, for instance, mothers and sons in Hemingway's and Carver's stories. Oates, Gilman, and White have quite a bit to say about women's family roles. Oates and White, in particular, dramatize mother/daughter relationships. There are proper, affluent, and troubled homes in the stories by Gilman and Hemingway.

The best place to start is with your impressions. Please take out a pen and some paper, and jot down all the words and phrases that come to mind as you think of home and family in all of this chapter's stories. Perhaps you would like to organize your impressions into columns; perhaps not. The point is to choose the two stories you want to write about; if you come up with a few points or observations for the paper, so much the better.

Your choice will probably make itself as you brainstorm. If not, study your words and phrases and choose. Don't worry, you can change your mind later.

Now, freewrite for about 20 minutes. Don't worry about finding a basis of comparison or coverage at this stage. Just explore the stories you have chosen. Try to get down as many impressions, questions, and responses as possible.

Then, let your freewriting sit for a few hours so that you can come back to it and the assignment fresh. Reread what you have written. Note any ideas that come to you, especially ideas about what the point of the paper might be. Study the questions following the stories, and reread the stories you have chosen, taking careful notes this time. The point of rereading is to test and develop your insights; the point of taking notes is to gather material and evidence for your paper. Pay especially close attention to wording. It is important in all types of writing to note how writers phrase their ideas, but it is crucial with short fiction, which is compact and condensed by nature. A short story's larger themes emerge in part from the nuances of a writer's words and the rhythms of a writer's phrases.

Study your notes and brainstorm again. Try to focus on the topic this time since the point is to clarify the approach you are taking and to begin to develop your ideas. Map the results of your brainstorming. Circle and connect ideas, points, and observations that you want to group together. And, in a sentence, write down your key point. Look your ideas over and write a first draft. Again, try to set aside enough time to write an entire draft. Don't worry about grammar and punctuation at this stage, and don't pause to fret over word choice. Keep your eyes on the thread of your argument. Follow it word by word, idea by idea. Concentrate on your ideas.

The rules for quoting are in any writing handbook. Review them, if necessary. Generally, you should quote only when a writer's words are crucial to your meaning. Otherwise, put the aspect of the story you are discussing into your own words. Besides, it is easier to make a paraphrased passage mesh with the flow of your paper.

Exchange photocopies of the first draft with a classmate. First, read his or her paper silently, jotting down any questions or comments you have about the paper's substance. Next, read the drafts out loud to one another, paying close attention to grammar, punctuation, word choice, and phrasing. Consult a dictionary, handbook, or an instructor when you need a second opinion. Take notes as you discuss your papers. Then, rewrite: reorganize, develop ideas, write additional paragraphs to incorporate new ideas, and work hard on word choice and phrasing. Read your second draft aloud. Rephrase sentences that don't sound right. Try combining short sentences to work any choppiness out of your writing, and simplify tangled or winding sentences. Again, don't be afraid to tamper with your preliminary drafts. Try to make this the most polished paper of the semester.

Additional Writing Exercises

- Use Tolstoy's first sentence from *Anna Karenina* as a starting point for a comparative essay. Can one generalize about the happy and unhappy families? How are they happy? Unhappy? What about the families in this chapter's short stories? Is Tolstoy essentially right?
- Write a short story based on something that happened to your family or a family you know well.
- Compose fictitious diary entries of someone experiencing family difficulties.
- Write a long autobiographical or fictional letter from one family member to another about a third.

$\mathcal{A}$cknowledgments and Credits

Nathan Huggins, "African Beginnings: The Seamless Web," from *Black Odyssey* by Nathan Irvin Huggins. Copyright © 1988 by Nathan Irvin Huggins. Reprinted by permission of Pantheon Books, a division of Random House, Inc.

Alfred Kazin, "The Kitchen: The Great Machine That Set Our Lives Running," excerpt from "The Kitchen" in *A Walker in the City,* copyright 1951 and renewed 1978 by Alfred Kazin. Reprinted by Harcourt Brace & Company.

Kenneth Keniston, "Family Work and Wage Work," from *All Our Children, The American Family Under Pressure,* copyright © 1978 by Kenneth Keniston, Carnegie Corporation of New York. Reprinted by permission of Harcourt Brace & Company.

Maxine Hong Kingston, "Photographs of My Parents," from *The Woman Warrior* by Maxine Hong Kingston. Copyright © 1975, 1976 by Maxine Hong Kingston. Reprinted by permission of Alfred A. Knopf, Inc.

Clyde Kluckhohn, "The Concept of Culture," from *Mirror for Man* by Clyde Kluckhohn. Copyright © 1949 by Clyde Kluckhohn. Reprinted by permission of George Taylor.

Alex Kotlowitz, "LaJoe Anderson of the Governor Henry Horner Homes, Chicago, Illinois," from *There Are No Children Here* by Alex Kotlowitz. Copyright © 1991 by Alex Kotlowitz. Used by permission of Doubleday, a division of Bantam Doubleday Dell Publishing Group, Inc.

Jonathan Kozol, "The Complete Life Story of Benjamin Peters, Homeless Baby," from *Rachel and Her Children* by Jonathan Kozol. Copyright © 1988 by Jonathan Kozol. Reprinted by permission of Crown Publishers, Inc.

Peter Laslett, "The World We Have Lost." Reprinted with the permission of Macmillan Publishing Company from *The World We Have Lost,* Third Edition by Peter Laslett. Copyright © 1965, 1971, 1984 by Peter Laslett. (Originally published by Charles Scribner's Sons.)

Carol Lawson, "Requiring Classes in Divorce," from the *New York Times,* January 23, 1992. Copyright © 1992 by The New York Times Company. Reprinted with permission.

Gabriel García Márquez, "Big Mama's Funeral," selected excerpt "Big Mama's Funeral" from *Collected Stories* (pp. 184–200) by Gabriel García Márquez. Copyright © 1968 in the English translation by Harper & Row, Inc. Reprinted by permission of HarperCollins, Publishers, Inc.

Index

■